Handbook of Research on Ubiquitous Computing Technology for Real Time Enterprises

Max Mühlhäuser
Technische Universität Darmstadt, Germany

Iryna Gurevych
Technische Universität Darmstadt, Germany

 **INFORMATION SCIENCE REFERENCE**

Hershey · New York

Acquisitions Editor:	Kristin Klinger
Development Editor:	Kristin Roth
Editorial Assistants:	Ross Miller, Deborah Yahnke
Senior Managing Editor:	Jennifer Neidig
Managing Editor:	Sara Reed
Copy Editors:	Alana Bubnis, Erin Meyer
Typesetter:	Michael Brehm
Cover Design:	Lisa Tosheff
Printed at:	Yurchak Printing Inc.

Published in the United States of America by
Information Science Reference (an imprint of IGI Global)
701 E. Chocolate Avenue, Suite 200
Hershey PA 17033
Tel: 717-533-8845
Fax: 717-533-8661
E-mail: cust@igi-global.com
Web site: http://www.igi-global.com

and in the United Kingdom by
Information Science Reference (an imprint of IGI Global)
3 Henrietta Street
Covent Garden
London WC2E 8LU
Tel: 44 20 7240 0856
Fax: 44 20 7379 0609
Web site: http://www.eurospanonline.com

Library of Congress Cataloging-in-Publication Data

Handbook of research on ubiquitous computing technology for real time enterprises / Max Muhlhauser and Iryna Gurevych, editors.
     p. cm.
  Summary: "This book combines the fundamental methods, algorithms, and concepts of pervasive computing with current innovations and solutions to emerging challenges. It systemically covers such topics as network and application scalability, wireless network connectivity, adaptability and "context-aware" computing, information technology security and liability, and human-computer interaction"--Provided by publisher.
  Includes bibliographical references and index.
  ISBN-13: 978-1-59904-832-1 (hardcover)
  ISBN-13: 978-1-59904-835-2 (ebook)
  1. Ubiquitous computing--Handbooks, manuals, etc. 2. Real-time data processing--Handbooks, manuals, etc. I. Mühlhäuser, Max. II. Gurevych, Iryna.
  QA76.5915.H35 2007
  004--dc22
                          2007032050

British Cataloguing in Publication Data
A Cataloguing in Publication record for this book is available from the British Library.

Editorial Advisory Board

Table of Contents

Section V
Ease-of-Use: Natural and Multimodal Interaction

Section VI
Pilots and Trends at SAP Research

Detailed Table of Contents

Chapter I

The authors briefly describe the history of ubiquitous computing. Some terms and a few important standards are subsequently introduced. In the last part, two kinds of reference architectures for ubiquitous computing systems are discussed by way of example.

Section I
Scalability: Two Issues of Global Scale

Chapter II

The chapter focuses on distributed approaches to address the scalability challenges in ubiquitous computing by means of bio-analog algorithms, which draw upon the realm of biology. The author describes the algorithms based on the phenomena found on the organism level of biological systems and examines the algorithms imitating procedures both on the cell and the molecular levels. Bio-analog approaches are finally extrapolated to data management as a novel field.

Chapter III

The author describes service-oriented architecture (SOA) based on Web services interfaces and messaging, and service composition through single-party process orchestration and multi-party choreography languages. For the latter, concrete patterns are used to describe the capabilities of prospective standards. Ways in which SOA needs to be extended to allow wider and more flexible service trading, typified in current developments through service marketplaces, are then discussed. Such extensions converge with directions in ubiquitous computing through so-called ubiquitous service networks and service ecosystems.

Chapter IV

Ontologies for Scalable Services-Based Ubiquitous Computing / *Daniel Oberle,*

Ontologies are proposed to address the scalability problems in ubiquitous computing, such as: (i) identifying relevant services for deployment, (ii) verifying a composition by a logical rule framework, and (iii) enabling the mapping of required services to the "best" available device. The authors focus on the ontology languages emerging from the corresponding W3C Semantic Web Activity. The pros and cons of ontologies are contrasted at a general level and the benefits and challenges in concrete smart items middleware are demonstrated.

Chapter V

The chapter briefly discusses the attributes that define SOA and the roles of the participants in a service oriented environment. In essence, SOA permits clients in open systems to use services offered by a service provider in the context of a workflow or complex task. Services are offered with a description at well-known "places" (also called registries, repositories), where clients choose services according to their needs. The chapter discusses several approaches to describing services and to searching for them. Moreover, some well-known systems and current related research are discussed.

Section II
Connectivity: Tapping into Humans and items

Chapter VI

The chapter focuses on different wireless and mobile communication systems that form the technological basis for ubiquitous computing applications. Depending on many parameters, such as transmission range, desired data rates, cost, mobility, power consumption, scalability in the number of users, and so forth, different communication systems have been developed. They are surveyed and compared and future directions are highlighted.

Chapter VII

The chapter introduces a taxonomy of communication models and emphasizes the event-based model and publish-subscribe paradigm that will supersede the client-server paradigm in the ubiquitous computing era. The relevant aspects of the publish-subscribe paradigm are introduced along with known approaches. The inner working of distributed event-based systems is thoroughly treated.

Wide-spread and novel application domains for peer-to-peer technology are described; challenges for appropriate support of the latter are pointed out. Unstructured peer-to-peer networks and their variants are contrasted with structured ones. The suitability and open issues in the context of ubiquitous computing are highlighted.

Opportunistic networks support an increasingly interesting class of ubiquitous computing applications, which deliberately limit connectivity to physical proximity of users. This application class and its variants are described and contrasted with wireless ad hoc networks and mobile peer-to-peer systems. Important human factors are treated, in particular privacy conservation and incentive schemes. Pertinent approaches are introduced by way of examples.

This chapter deals with the idea of how smart items, that is, electronically labeled and augmented physical entities, can contribute to the overall vision of the real time enterprise by utilizing different ubiquitous computing technologies. The main components of the smart items middleware are described.

Section III
Adaptability: What is (Not) Content?

This chapter gives an overview of how knowledge of the current context, that is, information characterizing the situation, can be represented and how this knowledge can be used for enhancing applications. The definitions of "context" and "context-aware applications" are given. The authors present guidelines on how to build a context-aware application and some challenges in using context information are discussed.

With respect to the important ubiquitous computing issue "context awareness," location is presently considered the most important and best supported context. Accordingly, the chapter starts with an overview of relevant location determination technologies. A thorough treatment of the physical and mathematical foundations of location determination follows. Both indoor and outdoor position are treated in detail. The chapter also provides insight into a broad range of available positioning systems.

Adaptation is needed to handle the increasing complexity in today's computing environments. The chapter focuses on the aspect of adaptation that puts the user into focus. It thus provides an important complement to the adaptation via context-awareness that is emphasized in the ubiquitous computing community and in the two preceding chapters. It introduces different adaptation types possible in ubiquitous computing, like interaction, content, and presentation. Basic requirements for appropriately modelling the users and approaches to personalize applications are presented.

Section IV
Liability: From IT Security to Liability

For IP-based communications, charging is used as a comprehensive term for metering or monitoring, accounting, pricing, charge calculation, and billing. These five actions are detailed in the chapter to provide a clear view on their interdependencies as well as their relations to distributed computing. The legal and contractual relationships between customers and providers as well as technological choices of protocols, mechanisms, and parameters define the area of interest here. With their background purpose of assuring and verifying exactly the flow of service provision and service remuneration intended, the concepts described represent an important ingredient of future liability concepts for ubiquitous computing

The chapter motivates the need for a dedicated treatment of security in the context of ubiquitous computing. It systematically discusses the particular security challenges and predominant security risks in the ubiquitous computing context. The major part of the chapter is dedicated to the description of sample solutions in order to illustrate the wealth of protection mechanisms required – and increasingly available. An overview of cryptographic tools is given.

The chapter focuses on the concepts of trust and accountability. The author first introduces the semantics of both concepts and then explains why trust is relevant for ubiquitous computing and what the main issues for dealing with trust in computer science are. Then, the chapter discusses how accountability can be achieved in distributed systems using reputation and micropayment mechanisms.

Section V
Ease-of-Use: Natural and Multimodal Interaction

Chapter XVII

This chapter is considered as a prerequisite for deeper understanding of the subsequent chapter. It gives an overview of the main architectures to enable speech recognition on embedded devices, including their characteristic features and properties. A description of the main challenges for the use of speech recognition on embedded devices—and thus, in the ubiquitous computing context—is given. The author provides a solid base for the selection of the most appropriate architecture for the business case of real time enterprises.

Chapter XVIII

Ubiquitous computing involves users on the move, suggesting hands-and-eyes-free operation, for which speech is an obvious choice. The chapter gives an overview of the challenges that have to be mastered in ubiquitous computing while working with audio, which is not easy to handle as a medium. To make things worse, mouth and ear interaction is often performed without focusing attention on the device. The author explains why audio-based interfaces are challenging to handle and shows how to master the challenges and to improve the quality of applications involving mouth and ear interaction.

Chapter XIX

While mouth-and-ears interaction is becoming more important for ubiquitous computing, hands-and-eyes interaction, especially in novel forms, remains essential. The chapter gives an overview of the broad range of pertinent interaction techniques. The chapter gives a short introduction to the fundamentals of human-computer interaction and the traditional user interfaces. It then surveys multi-scale output devices, gives a general idea of hands and eyes input, specializes them by merging the virtual and real world, and introduces attention and affection for enhancing the interaction with computers and especially with disappearing computers.

Chapter XX

The chapter introduces a set of general approaches for designing user interfaces with a special focus on the specific needs for ubiquitous computing scenarios. The author learns from good interface design for other—classical—devices and applies many of those user interface design principles to ubiquitous computing as well. A central aspect is the design process that helps to find the right sequence of steps in building a good user interface.

The authors first introduce some of the various modalities available for human-computer interaction. Then, they discuss how multimodality can be used both in desktop and mobile computing environments. The goal of the chapter is to familiarize scholars and researchers with the range of topics covered under the heading "multimodality" and suggest new areas of research around the combination of modalities, as well as the combination of mobile and stationary computing devices to improve usability.

Ubiquitous computing makes it necessary to supplant the desktop metaphor of graphical user interfaces by other kinds of user interfaces for a multitude of devices and interaction modalities. The chapter presents three different software engineering approaches that address this challenge: extensions to Web-based approaches, abstract user interface definitions that add a level of abstraction to the user interface definition, and model-based approaches that extend model-based application development to integrate user interface issues as well.

Ambient learning is a new area in ubiquitous computing, dealing with the different learning processes that occur between people and smart technology environments. The chapter provides a definition of what ambient learning is and discusses its relevance to ubiquitous computing. It presents the learning concepts behind ambient learning and a detailed example of training a user. The technological building blocks behind the smart products supporting their ability to learn from each other and assemble or "compose" their functionality are examined in detail.

Section V
Pilots and Trends at SAP Research

The chapter describes an example of ubiquitous computing technology in a corporate environment. The goal of the pilot was reduction of the risk in handling hazardous substances by detecting potentially dangerous storage situations and raising alarms if certain rules are violated. The lesson learnt: if employed in a shop floor, warehouse, or retail environment, UC technology can improve real-world business processes, making them safer and more efficient.

The goals and application scenarios of the PROMISE project are presented. The PROMISE project aims to close the information loop in product lifecycle management by employing product embedded information devices (PEIDs) in products. Special attention is given to the middleware design and implementation well as the role of universal plug and play (UPnP) as device-level protocol.

The chapter describes a new automatic vehicle location (AVL) system designed to take advantage of technologies that are currently gaining popularity in the enterprise, namely, online maps, real time GPS location tracking, and service-oriented architectures. The system uses a service-oriented architecture and Ajax-style user interface technology. The authors show that for Ajax technology to be widely adopted in the applications involving real time data updates, a server-side push mechanism is needed.

The authors introduce two example projects that contribute to meeting the challenges in adaptive security. The first project focuses on an architecture that allows for adaptive security in mobile environments based on security services whose adaptation is guided by context information derived from sensor networks. The second project addresses engineering aspects of secure ubiquitous computing systems through making security solutions accessible and deployable on demand and following emerging application-level requirements.

The Multimodal Warehouse Project is presented, which aims at applying multimodal interaction to a warehouse picking process. The authors provide an overview of the warehouse picking procedure as well as the overall architecture of the multimodal picking application and technologies applied to design the application. Then, they describe the execution of user tests of the picking application at a warehouse and present the results of these tests.

Foreword

WHAT'S IN A NAME IF IT IS ALL IN THE GAME?

When reading through the manuscript of this novel volume I was struck by the heroic attempt of the editors to position their book as a holistic approach to the subject of ubiquitous computing. I found their strong stand especially striking in this respect with respect to the use of nomenclature in the domain of ubiquitous computing. The editors acknowledge that there are many different notions presented in the literature addressing similar concepts as that of ubiquitous computing, but they argue that all these notions should be considered as a single approach to the topic of the disappearing computer. More specifically, the editors refuse to identify and describe the borderlines between different notions such as ubiquitous computing, pervasive computing, and ambient intelligence, following their strong conviction that it makes not much sense to quarrel about thin borderlines between major overlapping fields as their exploration is still open to a large extent.

As a convert to the concept of ambient intelligence for almost ten years now I must admit that I con-tinuously have felt the need in the past to explain these differences in an attempt to mark the borderlines. Evidently, most of these notions, which were developed during the late nineties of the past century, are rooted in the early ideas expressed by the late Mark Weiser, who was dreaming of a world that would be flooded with embedded devices, note pads, and electronic dust, which would soon become feasible as a result of the remarkable advances in the manufacturing of semiconductor devices and micro-systems. However, the developments that have been achieved over the past ten years have shown that there can be no doubt about the question whether or not Mark's dream will come true; it surely will. The remain-ing question however is related to the issue of which form it will take and how it can be configured in such a way that society and its participants maximally benefit from it. On the other hand, some of the innovation directions have changed in the meantime, which has opened new venues for research. Great inventions, such as ambient atmospheres through distributed solid-state lighting devices, virtual envi-ronments applying 3D interactive words such as Second Life, and ultimately "The Internet of Things" have made the discussion about the differences between the various notions artificial and esoteric. More interesting therefore is the question how far the advances in this domain have stretched the boundaries of what is currently feasible. And again the editors deserve a compliment as they have addressed this question in a most original way. Their S.C.A.L.E. classification provides a simple and most practical reference model for the description of the relevant topics in the field of ubiquitous computing. Further-more, they have succeeded in combining in the present book a most remarkable collection of research results representative of the advances in this domain. The many high-quality contributions reflect the scholarship and expertise of their authors. The book is definitely a mandatory reading for anyone who is professionally active in the field of ubiquitous computing, as it can be seen as a landmark approach to the description of the advances in this domain.

After more than ten years of breakthrough developments, ubiquitous computing can now live up to its expectation that it can change peoples' lives for the better through the promise of the disappearing computer.

Finally, I would like to thank the editors for providing me with the insight that the true progress achieved in our field if investigation is not reflected by names we attribute to our inventions, but merely by the games we play with it.

Emile Aarts

Emile Aarts *holds an MSc and a PhD degree in physics. For more than 20 years he has been active as a research scientist in computing science. Since 1991 he has held a teaching position at the Eindhoven University of Technology as a part-time professor of computing science. He also serves on numerous scientific and governmental advisory boards. He holds a part-time position of senior consultant with the Center for Quantitative Methods in Eindhoven, The Netherlands. Aarts is the author of 10 books and more than 150 scientific papers on a diversity of subjects including nuclear physics, VLSI design, combinatorial optimization and neural networks. In 1998 he launched the concept of ambient intelligence, and in 2001 he founded Philips' HomeLab. His current research interests include intelligent systems and interaction technology.*

Foreword

As computing has become more and more an integral part of our daily business and personal lives, the trend of ubiquitous computing will transform the way in which businesses will work and collaborate. The well-known fact of a huge community of users on the Internet (1,100 million users as of March 2007) will be complemented by at least one order of magnitude higher (10,000 millions of artificial users) instantiated by machines, sensors and things connected to the Internet. More precise data will be generated and accumulated that enable completely new business scenarios for the future. The fact of being connected to that universe of human users and artificial users will speed up decisions in business (real-time enterprise) and enable those who can master the infrastructure and the application services on top of the infrastructure to be more competitive than others. Application fields from logistics to e-health, from supply-chain management and manufacturing to public security will benefit from the fact that the "Internet of Things" and the "Internet of People" converge using an "Internet of Services" architecture.

I would like to congratulate Professor Mühlhäuser and Dr. Gurevych for their comprehensive overview of ubiquitous computing scenarios, real world examples and architectural blueprints that combine the various elements into insights into the vision of how the virtual world will interact with the physical world. I would also like to thank my colleagues from SAP Research and the SAP senior executives who have been supporting the research program of "smart items," which has produced many excellent results over the last eight years that are also reflected in this book.

Joachim Schaper

Joachim Schaper *received his Diploma (1988) and PhD (1995) from the Technical University of Karlsruhe. Since 1989, he worked for Digital Equipment Corp. in their European Research Center, CEC Karlsruhe. He became the manager of that center, which in turn became part of SAP AG Corporate Research (1999). In 2001, Schaper took over additional responsibilities as a founding manager of the Corporate Research Groups at SAP Labs France and SAP Africa. From 2003 to 2005, he managed the SAP Research Center in Palo Alto and a research group in Montreal. A vice president of EMEA, Schaper is responsible for all research activities of SAP in Europe, Middle East, and Africa, reporting to the head of corporate research and to the executive board. His research interests comply with the topics investigated in the SAP research groups on e-learning, smart items, mobile computing, and technology for application integration and advanced customer interfaces.*

Preface

ABSTRACT

The preface provides an introduction to and a definition of ubiquitous computing as a computer science field and relates it to the concept of real time enterprises. We describe the main challenges in ubiquitous computing and introduce the S.C.A.L.E. classification employed to organize the contents of the book. Finally, recommendations about using the book as a reference and teaching resource are given.

OUTLINE AND SUBJECT OF THIS BOOK

On the next couple of pages, we first want to provide an introduction to and a definition of ubiquitous computing (UC)—both as a scientific domain and as a technology area—and relate it to the concept of real time enterprises. We first define the scope of UC as a domain—in particular as covered in the present book. The question is raised whether UC is a research field in its own right; we also explain the required trade-off between breadth and depth of coverage concerning the contents of this book. The S.C.A.L.E. classification is introduced as probably the first attempt to provide a canonical structure and organization of the area. The present preface thus gives the reader a better idea about why this book is structured in a particular way and why it covers the range of topics selected by the editors. A "reader's digest" is provided, both as an overview of the chapters provided in this book and as a guide for readers with different backgrounds and interests.

So far, no single book exists which sufficiently covers ubiquitous computing in a holistic way. Many UC books restrict themselves to combinations of middleware, networking, and security. However, UC has lately extended beyond this focus and even beyond purely technical issues. In particular, understanding current developments in the field requires knowledge about pertinent algorithms and concepts in artificial intelligence and human-computer interaction. All-in-one reference books covering the foundations of ubiquitous computing and the areas mentioned above are missing; therefore, researchers, practitioners, and academics typically use collections of papers from the respective conferences and individual chapters from the books emphasizing a single area. This approach does not provide the target audience with a coherent view of the field. Also, the presentation of materials often presumes too much knowledge about the related topics.

As we will substantiate later, real time enterprises (RTE) are a key application area for UC. In fact, the authors of this book will show that RTE is *the* first application domain when it comes to the economic advantages of UC. Therefore, RTE can be considered a key driving force for large-scale deployment of UC technology. The last part of this book describes a selection of pilot projects and trend analyses concerning UC applied to RTE, provided by *SAP Research*. These chapters will strongly support the above-mentioned arguments. Note that most UC concepts and technologies described in this book are not restricted to RTE. Rather, readers should consider RTE as the first widespread, commercially successful area - they should also consider our RTE related examples as an aid for a better understanding of the value and usage of UC.

DEFINING UC

According to the Oxford English Dictionary, the word *ubiquitous* has two meanings: the first meaning is *(seemingly) present, everywhere simultaneously,* and the second meaning is *often encountered*. The seminal work by Weiser (1991) introduced the term ubiquitous computing, stating that it:

"represents a powerful shift in computation, where people live, work, and play in a seamlessly interweaving computing environment. Ubiquitous computing postulates a world where people are surrounded by computing devices and a computing infrastructure that supports us in everything we do."

Well, then what is *ubiquitous computing?*

One approach to an answer is the rough division of computer science into three consecutive eras:

1. Era number one was that of *mainframe computers,* where one computer was used by many users (1:N)
2. Era number two is about to end: the era of *personal computers* (PC), where one computer was used (owned) by one user (1:1), and
3. The third, dawning era is one in which many computers surround a single user (N:1)—almost anytime and anywhere.

Based on this approach, ubiquitous computing is nothing else than the third era cited above, that is, it is equivalent to the "Post-PC era."

We all experience this dawning era and realize that it brings about a proliferation of computers, with desktop PCs, laptops, PDAs and cell phones just being examples. The anytime-anywhere availability of computers indicates a shift away from pure desktop—and thereby, "isolated, full-attention"—computing to mobile (or rather, nomadic)—and thereby "integrated, shared-attention" computing. The term *integrated* alludes to the fact that the new computers interact with—or are even perceived as "part of"—their environment; the attribute *shared-attention* emphasizes the fact that users do not devote themselves to "sessions at the computer," but rather conduct an activity during which they "happen to interact with a computer, too."

Accordingly, the computers that surround us fall into two categories:

- Some are *worn or carried* in the sense that they move along with us, and
- Some are *encountered* in the sense that they are either part of the environment of our respective whereabouts, or worn or carried again, namely by people whom we meet.

The first category covers devices denoted as wearables or portable devices, respectively. The second category of devices encountered in the environment shifts from traditional PCs—which were somewhat alien to the environment and general-purpose in nature—to computers that are perceived as an integral part of the environment and that are rather special-purpose in nature (see the next section for concrete examples). More precisely speaking, the boundaries between general-purpose computers (formerly: servers and PCs) and special-purpose computers (formerly: microcontrollers) become blurred. On the one hand, computers become ever cheaper and can be dedicated to specific tasks. Power constraints and other resource limitations for portable and unattended computers increase this trend towards dedicated devices and favor "right-sizing." On the other hand, the required flexibility, adaptability, sophistication, and maintainability suggest devices that can be easily re-programmed. As a negative side effect, the latter trend introduces the curses of general-purpose computers—vulnerability (e.g., in the IT security sense) and limited reliability due to restricted maturity of devices with fast innovation cycles (cf., the fact that cell phones now have a far greater tendency to "crash," since they are based on full operating systems and software applications).

One is tempted to define UC simply as the era of portable and embedded specialized computers. However, embedded computers have existed for decades and have *already* become ubiquitous: they have become indispensable in washing machines and VCRs, and up to a hundred or even more of them are on duty in modern automobiles. *New* is the fact that these embedded devices are now:

- Networked, that is, cooperation enabled, Internet-enabled, and
- More flexible in terms of both maintenance/evolution and adaptation.

(Rather) new is also the insight that neither PCs—with their still unnatural and non-intuitive interfaces, interaction devices, and modes-of-operation (updates, re-boots, …)—nor embedded devices—with their increasing "featurism" (increasing sophistication that average users don't learn how to exploit)—scale well up to a world where hundreds of them would surround a user. Quantum leaps are required in terms of ease-of-use if ubiquitous computers are not to become a curse.

In summary, we can turn the rough definition "UC is the Post-PC era" into the following more elaborate one:

Ubiquitous computing is the dawning era of computing, in which individuals are surrounded by many networked, spontaneously yet tightly cooperating computers, some of them worn or carried, some of them encountered on the move, many of them serving dedicated purposes as part of physical objects, all of them used in an intuitive, hardly noticeable way with limited attention.

As a link to upcoming sections, readers should note that the definition given above buries two crucial issues:

1. Truly *integrative* cooperation: the path from mere connectivity of the "networked UC nodes" to true cooperation is long and arduous. Rapid deployment of all kind of networked sensors, appliances, labels, and so forth does not by itself lead to a meaningful "whole."
2. As to the last line of the definition above, it was already mentioned that a quantum leap in usability and dependability is required. We want to call this requirement a need for *humane* computing henceforth.

THE SIGNIFICANCE OF UC

The reader may want to get a feeling about the spatial and temporal significance of UC. By "spatial" we mean the spectrum from niche technologies to technologies that deeply influence an era. In this respect, it should soon become clear that UC is going to deeply mark our society over the years to come. By "temporal" we mean how visionary, that is, far off, UC actually is. In this respect, the quick answer, which we are going to substantiate further in the following, is as follows:

Figure 1. Overview of UC nodes

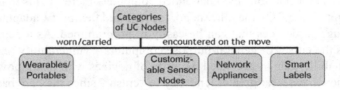

1. On one hand, *UC is already a reality* in the sense that the computer-based devices carried and encountered by users are already—and increasingly—networked.
2. On the other hand, *UC is still a big challenge* with respect to the required quantum leaps in *integrative* cooperation, as mentioned further previously, ("the whole must become way more than its parts") and *humane* behavior.

A few examples are cited for the first aspect, by providing a very selective list of four important categories of "UC nodes" in the global UC network:

1. **Wearables and portable devices** ("networked computers worn or carried" as mentioned in the UC definition), such as handhelds for warehouse picking, washable computer jackets, or companions like the so called *lovegetties* introduced in Japan almost ten years ago. These pocket size devices store their user's profile, that is, dating interests, and beep or vibrate when a "compatible" person—carrying a lovegetty—appears. In contrast to portable device, the term *wearable* denotes a degree of integration with a piece of clothing or clothing accessory that goes beyond that of mobile computing devices, up to a degree where the "computer nature" is hardly noticed by the user. MIT is known for influential research in the field (www.media.mit.edu/wearables). The examples given illustrate that this category of UC nodes is far larger than a simple extrapolation from the common representatives, that is, PDAs, cell phones, MP3 players, laptops, and so forth. Another example, namely body sensors, illustrates the possible seamless integration of "UC nodes worn or carried" and "UC nodes encountered." Body sensors are useful, for example, for activity monitoring (a basis for better context-aware applications) and health condition monitoring.

The last three of these categories are refinements of the "networked computers encountered on the move" from the definition of UC given in the last section (with exceptions like body sensors).

2. **Customizable sensor nodes** like the so-called *motes* developed by UC Berkeley and Intel. As opposed to traditional sensors, these nodes come with a fully programmable microprocessor and micro operating system (called *TinyOS* for *motes*), a variety of sensor options, and low energy networking. Mass production of these customizable nodes is intended to drive down cost such that easy customization and easy assembly of nodes into *sensor networks* are set to simplify application development. The Intel-funded company Crossbow (www.xbow.com) is commercializing motes. Companies like the German start-up *Particle Computer* (www.particle-computer.de) support the IEEE sensor network standard 802.15.4 known as *ZigBee* (www.zigbee.org). In 2003, UC Berkeley built the first single-chip successor to motes nicknamed *Spec*. They represent a major step towards almost invisible sensor networks with large quantities of nodes, often coined as *smart dust*.
3. **Networked appliances,** also called *Internet appliances* or *smart appliances*, which are mainly perceived by their users as tools, machines, devices, furniture, and so forth, rather than computers.

Apart from ever cheaper and more powerful embedded computers, affordable and energy-aware wireless technology is a key enabler not only for hand-held appliances, but also for fixed installations—which are much easier to deploy if network cabling can be spared on and if embedded "clients" can be easily combined with back office servers or gateways inaccessible to the public. One example is *smart vending machines*: the company USA technology (www.usatech.com) developed solutions for supporting online transactions (credit card payment, etc.) and for transmitting various information (fill status or out-of-stock events, out-of-change events, defects, customer behaviour patterns, etc.) to the operating agency. One step further, vending of physical and of digital goods start to converge: Coke vending machines are combined with vending of cell phone credits, ring tones, MP3 music, and so forth.

4. **Smart labels**, which identify physical objects and creatures vis-à-vis an IT-based system. Radio frequency identifiers *(RFIDs)* represent one important technology; *active badges* (e.g., for employees) denote a possible use case. Such labels may be thought of as Web addresses that serve as a "link" to data describing details about the identified object or person. Therefore, their on-board storage and processing capabilities can be very limited, even non-existent. In the application domain of *product identification*, RFIDs are set to complement (and later, replace) barcodes. Relevant barcode standards include the Universal Product Code UPC and (as a superset) the European Article Number EAN. For RFIDs, both are intended to be replaced by EPCglobal's Electronic Product Code EPC (www.epcglobalinc.org), which may contain a serial number in addition to the article number.

These few categories of ubiquitous computing nodes illustrate that specialized networked computers—most of them "hidden" in physical objects—are indeed penetrating the world.

Machine–to–Machine Communication

The example categories cited above illustrate yet another phenomenon of key importance: the advent of large volume machine-to-machine communication. Throughout the history of the Internet, its exponential growth has been boosted by communication with or among people. This development contradicted what protagonists of distributed parallel processing had envisioned, namely a boosting importance of distributed systems as replacements for parallel and super computers. While this use case for distributed systems—and thereby for the Internet—continues to play a non-negligible role (cf., recent advancements in Grid computing), it has never been, and probably will never be a reason for "exploding numbers of Internet nodes." Three "waves of Internet usages" have driven and are driving this explosion to date:

1. "E-mail" as a means for people-to-people communication, the major reason for the Internet to grow up to the order of 10 million nodes.
2. "The Web" as a major use case of people-to-machine communication. Under its increasing importance, the Internet passed the 100 million node mark
3. "The wireless Internet," which—after flops like WAP-based cell phones—currently drives the convergence of the Internet with cell phones (cf., UMTS in Korea), MP3 players, and other portable devices. This wave contributes heavily to the hit of 1 billion Internet nodes around 2008.

As we approach the order of magnitude of the world population, one might expect the Internet (number of nodes) to enter a phase of sub-exponential growth. Yet the predicted shift from people-to-machine to machine-to-machine communication is likely to lead to a continuation of the exponential growth: sensor

Figure 2. Growth rates: Internet vs. CPU power

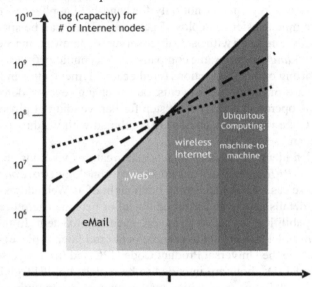

networks, networked appliances, and smart labels communicate autonomously and forward real-world events through the net.

A second important effect is illustrated in *Figure 2*: the growth rate of the Internet has constantly exceeded that of CPU power—measured, for example, in terms of the time that it takes for key indicators to double, like the number of Internet nodes or the processor speed (18 to 20 months for the latter one according to "Moore's Law").

This difference in growth rate has consequences for the Internet: the *relative* cost of distributed versus local processing decreases. Note, however, that this is only true for the wired Internet, for which the aggregated throughput per second (at least nationwide for the U.S.) and the typical bandwidth are all growing at roughly the same pace as the number of Internet nodes. Two reasons suggest more conservative predictions for wireless nodes: on one hand, there is no long term indication yet that the typical bandwidth will keep pace with the other Internet growth indicators mentioned above. Despite recent boosts in WLAN bandwidth, physical limits and frequency scarcity remain tough obstacles. But even if bandwidth keeps pace, wireless nodes are set to become more and more independent from the power line—and for mass deployment use cases like sensor nodes, even from battery replacement. A question mark must be placed here at least until revolutionary battery technology hits a breakthrough.

In summary, the reader should now understand that UC is the *key technology* that will deeply influence our society for three reasons:

1. UC describes *the* next era of computing. Since we live in the information (i.e., computer) society, the influence will be at least as pervasive as that of computer today. As a side remark, virtually every domain of computer science or IT is potentially impacted. This makes it difficult to be selective and concise for the present book—but not impossible, as we will show.
2. UC has potential impact on every facet of our lives. Computing is no longer "what we do when we sit at the computer" nor "what is encapsulated/hidden deep inside VCRs, and so forth."
3. UC is inevitable and "impossible" at the same time: the components are already developed and massively deployed, consult the four categories of UC nodes described. Since UC use cases are

becoming increasingly profitable, for example, the replacement of barcodes with RFIDs, the industry will push the use of UC technology. Nevertheless, the two top-level challenges remain "integrative cooperation" and "humane computing." Both must be solved in order for UC to become the envisioned helpful anytime-anywhere technology and not a nightmare.

THE CHALLENGES OF UC

As described in the last sentences above, UC is inevitable and probably very influential, even able to change our society—and it buries unresolved problems. Therefore, UC can be considered one of the biggest challenges of our times—an insight that led to the present book, for instance.

Conflicting Developments Due to Ubiquity of Networked Computers

The above sentences have also pointed out two top-level challenges in UC: "integrative cooperation" and "humane computing." Before we try to describe and define these challenges in more detail, as a basis for the structure and content of this book, we want to mention one more viewpoint of what has been already discussed: we will try to describe the upcoming "ubiquity" of networked computers as a problem space that is becoming increasingly challenging due to conflicting developments on four levels (see Figure 3):

1. **More sensitivity ↔ less protection:** As UC penetrates more and more areas of daily life and work life, more and more sensitive data, but also processes and activities, of privacy critical and liability critical nature depend on computers. As a conflicting development, the established IT security solutions are not fully viable in machine-to-machine scenarios, in particular if a subset of these machines acts autonomously as substitutes for humans or organizations. Further aggravation of the situation is due to the ever widening gap between the "in principle" availability of appropriate security measures and their acceptance, that is, application by users, even more so since IT related concepts—for example, of trust—do not easily match the concepts of trust that users are acquainted with from their real-life experience. Obviously, IT security research—in a broad sense, including trust models and other issues—must be stressed and focused on UC.
2. **More dependence ↔ less perfection:** if many actions and aspects of daily life are supported and controlled by ubiquitous computers, then these actions and aspects (and in turn the average human) become dependent on these computers. Obviously, this dependence becomes as ubiquitous as the computers, and is not restricted to desktop work anymore. As an increasingly critical source of

Figure 3. Overview of conflicting developments

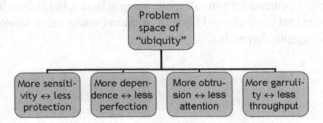

conflict, ubiquitous computing relies on cheap components and close to zero maintenance, a context in which the failure of nodes becomes a regular event as opposed to an exception. Furthermore, overall system dependability declines rapidly with the number of components involved under the assumption that the per-component dependability (and therefore, failure rate) remain constant and that all considered components contribute a crucial portion to the system. Obviously, research on system dependability must emphasize "over-provisioning" approaches where, for instance, a considerable number of components can fail without harmful consequences for system dependability. Complex biological and social systems exhibit this property and can serve as examples.

3. **More obtrusion ↔ less attention:** users are expected to be surrounded by ubiquitous networked computers for many purposes. In principle, each additional computer means an additional user interface. As a source of conflict, the move from desktop use to everyday use means that users have to share attention to computers with attention to their daily lives (human communication, driving, manual work, etc.). Altogether, this issue suggests a dramatic focus on "humane computing" as has been stated several times already. We will see below that such research must be understood in a broader sense than classical human-computer interaction (HCI) research.

4. **More garrulity ↔ less throughput:** the market for sensors is predicted to explode and the replacement of barcodes by RFIDs will lead to zillions of wireless nodes (in the longer term, after intermediate phases where only containers and expensive goods will be tagged). These two effects alone show how dramatically the number of wireless data paths around us will grow—and feed the wired network in turn. One may object to calling this development dramatic, since machine-to-machine communication can often be restricted to short binary messages, whereas computer-to-human communication tends to involve verbose data, media streams in particular. However, increasing performance of computer vision and voice recognition will increase the bandwidth famine on the sensor-to-backend path. Again, one may object that computer vision may be carried out locally and that only reduced information will be sent (intermediate results, i.e., recognized "features" of the scene observed, or the final result, i.e., a "semantic" description of what was recognized). However, computer vision is compute intensive and therefore not likely to be executed entirely on the sensor side. Increased sensor-to-backend bandwidth demands can therefore be expected at least for this kind of sensor.

The critical factor in this fourth dimension is the fact that sensor nodes must be built under extreme energy constraints, such as a grain size battery determining the lifetime of the entire sensor. Since wireless transmission tends to be the most energy hungry part of a sensor and since this hunger increases considerably as bandwidth is increased, we can state that the throughput of many UC nodes will remain far below that of an average PC even today. Similar arguments apply to smart labels: the widely used RFID tags are passive, that is, receive their transmitting energy from the reader (receiver). Portable readers are crucial for many application scenarios, and the required energy is a function of both bandwidth and distance—yet increased reading distance is supposed to be a key advantage over barcodes. All in all, there is a large demand for advancements not only in the energy/bandwidth tradeoff (and in battery capacity, of course, which we consider a non-computer science issue), but also in distributed architectures and distributed algorithms that optimize and trade off minimal resources at sensor nodes (and other UC nodes) and minimal throughput demands.

Integrative Cooperation and Humane Computing

The preceding observations provide further insight into the challenges of UC, which we described as "integrative cooperation" and "humane computing" on the top level. We now want to go one level deeper and divide each of these two challenges into two or three sub-issues.

As to "integrative cooperation," we want to distinguish two issues:

1. **Scalability:** We discussed several times that UC furthers the explosion of the Internet and that even many local networks (such as smart dust and RFID-tagged products in a warehouse) rather represent big assemblies of nodes (in particular in relation to the network bandwidth to be expected). This means that highly scalable solutions are required. The history of the Internet (especially in comparison to less successful networks) is a history of extreme scalability, and all standard textbooks about the Internet state that scalability was and is a key success factor. This applies even more to ubiquitous computing as the future nature of IT systems, depending on the Internet. Note that scalability is to be understood in a broad sense, as will be described further below.

2. **Connectivity:** Again, this term is a brief notion for a broad issue. We have identified scalability as a broad issue in its own right, but everything else that relates to the need to integrate UC nodes and to make them cooperate will be summarized under *connectivity*. In particular, tiny ("dumb," or at least special-purpose) nodes must be integrated into a meaningful whole based on spontaneous discovery and interaction. New, that is unforeseen, components or components that vary over time or usage context must be able to enter into meaningful cooperation with existing nodes. We will see later in the book that such connectivity issues are addressed and solved somewhat differently for different kinds of UC components today; for example, differently for software services than for smart labels. Various chapters of the book will reflect these differences that exist today. When it comes to the vision of "intelligent behavior" of the integrated, cooperating whole, we must deal with approaches that are also related to the scalability issue and to the ease-of-use issues treated below. This indicates that our classification (as always) is good for understanding the topic space, but not "ideal" in the sense that any issue could be classified as belonging to exactly one category (an issue that any taxonomy has to live with).

The residual three issues represent sub-challenges of "humane computing":

3. **Adaptability:** A key to dramatically reduced cognitive load (required in order to counter the "more obtrusiveness, less attention" dilemma described) is found in highly adaptive systems that interact "optimally"—with respect to the use case, user, situation, device or resource constraints, and so forth. A great deal of research in this respect has been carried out lately under the term "context-aware computing;" many of the respective activities tried to adapt software and particularly user interfaces to data retrieved from sensors with the users' locations being a number one context category. Other context types, like activities carried out by the user or data "hidden" in their files, are also important, but their integration into UC solutions is less well understood. Even less emphasized and understood today is adaptation to the users' state of knowledge.

4. **Liability:** As discussed with the issue "more sensitivity, less protection," IT security issues must be revisited under UC requirements and constraints. Moreover, the use of UC technology in everyday life makes UC-based physical and digital components an integral part of our society—and consequently of our economy. A majority of UC components or services will not be available for free. Even if they are free of charge to the end-user, someone will have to pay for their development

and execution. This means that UC services will have to respond to a number of "market rules," for instance: (i) users will want to make sure that "they get what they paid for," (ii) providers will want to make sure that "they get paid for what they provide," and (iii) users will want to be able to truly compare offerings based on prices and a variety of parameters describing the associated "value" of a UC service. Providers will want to be able to offer their "values" to users appropriately, and so forth. Since all these issues are tightly linked to financial, and thereby to legal issues, they are closely intertwined with the security issues mentioned above; altogether, we will summarize the respective issues as "liability."

5. **Ease-of-use:** Under this term, we want to emphasize HCI aspects in the more narrow sense. Maybe the single most important change brought about by UC in this respect is the proliferation of interaction devices and, thereby, modalities. In order to understand this issue, one has to note that throughout the history of computer science, software engineers and programmers were exposed to a single major interaction paradigm at any given time. It started with "holes in paper," that is, punch tapes and punch cards. Later teletype like devices came, followed by full screen terminals like the IBM 3270 and the DEC VT100, both being de facto industry standards. Finally, more than 15 years ago, Windows-based UIs and the WIMPS metaphor (windows, icons, menus, pointers, scrollbars) were introduced. In the UC world of special-purpose nodes, there is no longer any single dominating interaction paradigm: cooperative-use devices like interactive walls, speech-and-graphics devices, soft-key-based cell phones, physical-interaction appliances, and many more must be coped with. Accordingly, multimodal user interfaces—supposed to cater for this variety—are becoming crucial. At the same time, the "classical" graphical (or rather, hands-and-eyes) interfaces are currently experiencing rapid innovation and "voice" is recognized as a most natural way of interaction, in particular for users whose hands and eyes are busy with "real world activities." These and other issues must be addressed under "ease-of-use" in a UC related book.

The five sub-challenges treated above—scalability, connectivity, adaptability, liability, and ease-of-use—can be abbreviated by concatenating the first letter of each sub-challenge, leading to S.C.A.L.E. We will describe below how they represent the backbone structure for the present book—and a suggested structure for the emerging discipline.

THE FOCUS ON REAL TIME ENTERPRISES

This section addresses two questions: "What is a real time enterprise?" And, "Why and how does the present book emphasize this topic?"

First of all, in preparation of a "definition," one must understand that in many domains software has become more and more sophisticated over the years. Whatever domain is supported—it is represented as a machine-readable "digital model" as part of the software. For instance, *virtual reality* applications for the automotive industry, such as "digital mockups," contain not only three-dimensional representations of a yet-to-be-built car but also the materials' characteristics, laws of physics used to model the dynamics—to a degree that supports "virtual crash tests"—and much more. The same applies to enterprise application integration (EAI) software (at the core of real time enterprise approaches): almost the entire enterprise is "digitally modeled," including human resources, workflows, a whole spectrum of financial issues, product lifecycle management, customer relationships, and much more.

Despite the increasing sophistication of "digital enterprise models," the gap between this digital model and the "real enterprise" remains hard to bridge: events and changes in the real enterprise (goods arriving, stock being manipulated, products being manufactured, etc.) must be reflected in the digital model, and changes and decisions made in the digital model (work orders, production plans, route slips, etc.) must be forwarded to the "real enterprise." The gap is dominated today by *switches in media* (e.g., from machine-readable data to printed paper or vice versa) and *"analog transmission,"* mainly by means of humans and, again, paper as the "media."

This brings about three major "stress points:"

- **Medium cost:** The use of humans as media (i.e., human "manual" intervention) as well as the handling of large amounts of paper represent major cost factors in an enterprise. For instance, paper-based time sheets may be filled using pencils and turned into machine-readable formats afterwards. Even if this cycle is reduced, that is, timesheets are filled at a PDA or laptop, the manual task remains. Only UC technology offers novel ways of entirely avoiding manual entries.
- **Time lag:** The time required for printing and sending paper or for human-based transmission of information causes delays that may represent a major reason for revenue loss (e.g., due to a longer delay between raw material cost incurrence and end product revenue receipt).
- **Inaccuracy (errors, lacking and too coarse-grained information):** Manual processes are error prone. For instance, inventories are regularly made in order to match the "digital" stock data with the "real" one. Misplacements (by customers or employees) and theft are examples of lacking information here, and mistakes in the "analog transmission" are the major source of errors. Both errors and lacking information account for expensive differences between the real and the digital world (cf., the need for more conservative stock planning or missed business due to products out of stock). Moreover, the cost of manual (human) "data elicitation" (counting of goods in stock, provision of time sheets) is prohibitive for more fine-grained updates between real and digital models. For instance, workflow optimization might be achieved with more accurate and more fine-grained data, but the expected benefit may not justify the cost of fine-grained manual acquisition.

Obviously, electronic, that is, automated, ways of bridging the real-to-digital gap have a lot of potential in the business world. Many steps towards this goal have already been taken: a major step was the introduction of barcodes—not only on consumer products, but also on containers, temporarily handled goods like airport baggage, and so forth. Other approaches, like the introduction of handhelds, networked control of production machinery, and paperless business-to-business communication, are still emerging.

While such steps represent a certain degree of real-time behavior, the advancements possible by means of UC technology can be dramatically more far-reaching and more complete (with respect to getting rid of manual/analog gaps). Therefore, the application of UC technology as a means for advancing real time enterprises is extremely promising and buries a high economic potential.

With these explanations in mind, the reader may understand why we consider a definition found on a Microsoft Web site insufficient (http://www.microsoft.com/dynamics/businessneeds/realtime_enterprise. mspx, last retrieved on January 18, 2007): *"A Real Time Enterprise is an organization that leverages technology to reduce the gap between when data is recorded in a system and when it is available for information processing."* This definition focuses only on "time loss" as an optimization dimension and ignores "medium cost" and "inaccuracy" (a deficit probably due to the term "real-time" which buries a temptation to look at the time aspect only—yet a term which we keep using since it is widespread). Moreover, the definition above focuses on the *"inbound"* channel to the digital model—we regard the *"outbound"* channel as equally important: consider, for example, the digital model suggesting spontaneous changes to workflows and parts applied at a production plant, but the realization of these changes taking too much time and too much effort to cross the digital-to-real gap. In such a case, an electronic and automated transmission would make a huge difference (faster, more accurate forwarding of decisions might be achieved using the most appropriate media, such as computer-generated, detailed individual voice instructions sent to the respective employees' ears).

We will therefore use the following "definition" :

A real time enterprise is an organization that bridges the gap between digital enterprise models and the corresponding real world largely by means of ubiquitous computing technology—in both directions—in order to reduce time lags, medium cost, and inaccuracy.

Now that we have answered the question, "What is a real time enterprise?," we turn to the question "Why and how does the present book emphasize this topic?"

The rationale for emphasizing this application domain is simple: the paragraphs above provide hints about the very considerable and measurable economic potential of UC technology for real time enterprises. The editors have reasons to believe that real time enterprises presently represent the most profitable domain for UC technology. Other areas, such as smart homes or smart travel support, exhibit cost/benefit ratios worse than that. Therefore, the large-scale deployment of UC technology in the domain of real time enterprises will precede deployment in other areas. In turn, many innovations can be expected to lead to a breakthrough in this area, too.

The present book is divided into six parts, the last one of which is dedicated to pilot projects and trends. All short chapters included there treat the use of UC technology in real time enterprises. The pilots were carried out since participating industrial partners had successfully evaluated the related business opportunities; this backs the editors' decision substantially. Looking at *how* the present book emphasizes the topic *real time enterprise*, the core of the answer lies in the last book part: we will look at the most important use cases from this application domain and particular the aspects of UC technology in the real time enterprise context. However, apart from this, we will treat UC technology independent of application domains, such that the book will be useful for the readers interested in either the core technology or its application to any other domain.

THE S.C.A.L.E. CLASSIFICATION USED IN THIS BOOK

UC is the hot topic in computer science, as it describes where computer science as a whole is heading. Lectures and books about UC have outstanding opportunities, since they address the future of computing—but also considerable threats, which the editors face with their carefully devised approach. A major threat is to perceive UC solely as modern distributed computing and not as a vision that needs several major problem domains to be addressed simultaneously—issues of distributed computing, HCI, IT security, and so forth. Since UC draws from and influences many areas of classical computer science, the real challenge is to cover all fundamentals, that is, to avoid being one-sided, without getting lost in a "big world" and remaining shallow. The editors approach this challenge by organizing the book and the pertinent issues into five interrelated categories, which are systematically ordered and addressed under one umbrella:

1. **Scalability:** Solutions for huge networks/applications and support for global spontaneous interoperability;

2. **Connectivity:** Intelligent ad hoc cooperation of a multitude of (specialized) devices over unreliable wireless networks;
3. **Adaptability:** Adaptation to users and context-aware computing;
4. **Liability:** Novel problems in IT security like privacy/traceability tradeoffs, human-understandable trust models, legal binding of service users and providers, and so forth;
5. **Ease-of-use:** *User-friendliness* in human-computer interaction as a major concern

Another threat is the temptation to draw artificial lines between UC, pervasive computing, and ambient intelligence. Instead, these three terms are considered synonyms, an attitude that is backed by an extremely high degree of overlap in the concrete research agendas of research groups and labs that carry these different names. We will elaborate on the roots and meanings of these three terms further.

From a truly holistic point of view, UC is a multidisciplinary issue that concerns both social sciences and economics in addition to computer science. However, the five categories described above show that an all-encompassing treatment of the computer science issues in UC is already pushing the format of a serious reference book to its limits. Therefore, the present book does not include additional social sciences chapters, but keeps the contents within the limits of computer science, while emphasizing human-centric approaches within these limits. This decision is supported by the fact that several books about the social sciences aspects of UC already exist.

The "Preface," as well as the following "Introduction to Ubiquitous Computing," provides an overview of the history and visions of UC. They explicate the overall structure and the philosophy of the field required for understanding and relating the following in-depth chapters grouped into the five categories as stated above (S.C.A.L.E.) and a final part providing concise descriptions of the pilot projects in UC realized at SAP Research.

As a research field, ubiquitous computing touches almost every area of computer science. More than that, it is closely interwoven with many of them. Then, the question might arise: is it a research and teaching subject in its own right? We believe the answer to this question is "yes." As an analogy, we can look at the area of distributed systems that was at a comparable stage some twenty years ago. The area of distributed systems, too, involves a lot of issues from different computer science fields, coined as distributed simulation, distributed programming, distributed algorithms, distributed databases, distributed artificial intelligence, and so on. For some time, it seemed as if almost every branch of computer science would "go distributed." Today, the area of distributed systems has settled as a teaching and research subject in computer science in its own right. However, the boundaries with many other disciplines remain blurred; for example, distributed software engineering is taught in both software engineering and distributed systems. The analogy shows what the editors expect to happen with ubiquitous computing as a domain "in its own right." For the time being, ubiquitous computing is still an actively evolving topic, that is, not as well established as distributed systems yet.

According to the above analogy, we will have to cover topics in UC that reach out to a number of sub-disciplines within computer science and even beyond. Since different readers will have a background in different sub-disciplines, how can we treat the subjects without having to cover most of computer science, but also without "losing" our readers? In other words, the question arises: how can we achieve the most optimal trade-off between breadth and depth in the coverage of relevant UC topics? The only viable approach here is an attempt to provide the required background knowledge as briefly as possible to our readers, still leaving enough room to covering the UC specific issues. This was one of the major challenges for the contributing authors.

A second and related issue is the fact that UC as a field has never been organized into a canonical discipline before. Therefore, no "pattern" exists for structuring this research area in a concise way that would help authors and readers to form mindmaps of the discipline and organize the wealth of research issues and related concepts and approaches. We consider the present book as the first one to introduce such a canonical structure: the S.C.A.L.E. classification that was already discussed above. With the help of this taxonomy, we can first organize the problem space of ubiquitous computing in a set of distinct areas. Second, we discuss the contents of particular areas and emphasize some pertinent challenges within each of them. Often, such challenges either represent a truly new aspect in ubiquitous computing or well-known issues, which become particularly relevant in the context of ubiquitous computing.

We expect that a "normal" background in computer science would be sufficient to understand the most of the discussions in this book. Any additional background is hardly needed. However, readers will have to go deeper into particular topics at some places and learn more about the methods and algorithms of general computer science as their application in the context of UC is explained.

The readers might ask the question if this book is going to cover the entire field of ubiquitous computing. The answer to this question is really no, as the field is too broad to be covered completely within the given space limitations. However, this book is more complete than any other reference book on UC known to the editors. It covers not only the issues of networking and mobile computing, but also those of scalability, security and a wide range of topics in human-computer interaction. The editors have made every effort to make the chapters very comprehensive, comprehensible and to provide additional references to advanced research topics related to individual chapters. We also believe that using the book in UC courses will be greatly facilitated due to the organization of materials into distinct areas of the S.C.A.L.E. classification.

As UC is a rather new and rapidly evolving subject, we first tried to organize the problem space into coherent chunks of knowledge. This is approached in two different ways. On one hand, the S.C.A.L.E. classification was devised in order to provide a holistic view of the research areas pertinent to ubiquitous computing. This classification is employed throughout the book for structuring purposes and represents a major "guide" through the remaining book chapters. On the other hand, we attempt to provide a holistic view of the global UC network (or system) by introducing and explaining a reference architecture for designing ubiquitous computing systems. For this purpose, we picked out one particular example of a reference architecture for ubiquitous computing called Mundo, which was used as the design rationale for the MundoCore middleware (Aitenbichler, Kangasharju, & Mühlhäuser, 2006). As a reference architecture, Mundo can be thought of as a rough floorplan for an entire UC system, which helps the readers to understand and organize the field of ubiquitous computing. It can be used to show the differences in the definitions of distributed systems and ubiquitous computing as a field. Those are supposed to be approximated by the differences in their respective reference architectures.

In the following, we describe a set of challenges in ubiquitous computing as defined by the S.C.A.L.E. classification.

Part **S** stands for SCALABILITY in UC systems. It addresses two main issues: (i) Existing UC systems are typically limited to a certain number of components. The question arises how to scale the system to support the cooperation between zillions of components in open and growing ambient environments; (ii) Another aspect is the support of nomadic users around the globe as opposed to a single user interacting with the UC system.

Part **C** stands for CONNECTIVITY in UC systems. This area tries to provide answers to the questions, such as how to easily connect zillions of cooperating components. Here, several levels of abstraction are possible: (i) Wireless networks are a blessing and a curse at the same time: a blessing, due to the unique capabilities of data transmission without hardwiring the networks, a curse, due to the unreliable nature of the connection technologies existing today, posing many challenges for the operation of UC systems. (ii) Still, most issues in connectivity go definitely beyond the wired or wireless nature of the connection and significantly overlap with the issues in scalability. The questions, such as how to find and understand the peers on the network, how to enable zero configuration, and finally how to design networks for zillions of connections avoiding the bottlenecks of the architectures based on a central server belong to such topics.

Part **A** stands for ADAPTABILITY. This issue is crucial as UC systems are employed by people not only at their leisure, but also during their daily work. Therefore the users may be surrounded by hundreds of computational components, but do not want those components to significantly interfere with their working routines. Such users need as few interactions with the UC system as possible. One major approach to achieve this goal is context-aware computing. Context-awareness is a very important mechanism. It allows the design of a system in such a way that the number of automated tasks is maximized and the number of options that the user has to select explicitly is reduced to the minimum. Beyond that, adaptability means adapting to a particular user interacting with the system on the fly. It involves methods of acquiring and using the data about the user of a UC system. As to adaptability vs. adaptivity, the former comprises both the passive capability of "being adapted" and the active capability of "adapting oneself," while the latter is often associated with the passive variant only.

Part **L** stands for LIABILITY. As the term itself indicates, we must go beyond today's IT security solutions in ubiquitous computing. It should be noted that, while the goals of liability remain the same as the goals of security, special solutions need to be found. Such solutions should: (i) scale, that is, not depend on centralized components, and (ii) be human-centric, for example, flexibly consider conflicting goals, such as privacy and traceability, and related goals, such as dependability.

Part **E** stands for EASE-OF-USE. As stated above, adaptability has to ensure that the amount of interactions between the user and a UC system remain minimal; in contrast to this, ease-of-use means that interactions are optimal, which is related to but not the same as minimal. Optimizing the interaction means, for example, that the modalities are dynamically selected and combined and specific modalities are introduced to meet the requirements of a specific situation. A crucial issue in designing an optimal human-computer interface is understanding the natural input, that is, the ability of the system to derive the meaning of the input and represent it formally for further processing by the system. Mapping the input to such a semantic representation, for example, interpreting the natural language input of the user is a form of computational intelligence. It is currently better studied in limited domains, such as airplane ticket reservation. Scaling this kind of intelligence to unrestricted domains is rather an open research issue.

In the following, we describe each of the **S.C.A.L.E.** components in more detail. This will lay the foundations for understanding our recommendations on how to use the book in ubiquitous computing courses, as a reference, or for self-study.

Part S: Scalability. We consider *scalability* to be a top priority challenge in ubiquitous computing, which is also reflected in the first place it occupies in the acronym S.C.A.L.E. There are several dimensions of scalability that have to be considered in the context of ubiquitous computing for real time enterprises. In this book, we concentrate the discussion along two such dimensions, the technical scalability and the economic scalability.

The *technical scalability* leads to (potential) cooperation of "zillions" of devices. Thus, solutions have to be found that work efficiently with zillions of components. The most relevant areas for this, which are basically alternatives for addressing technical scalability, are:

- *Bionics*, that is, bio-analog computing, including the topics such as (i) neural networks and cooperating robots, which are only of marginal importance for ubiquitous computing, (ii) ant colonies, which are often simulated or executed on a single computer today, swarms and autonomous computing, and (iii) brain-like modeling of the human memory;

- *Event-based computing*, a more conventional paradigm of addressing the technical scalability in UC settings. It is fairly widespread; therefore, we will defer the discussion of it to the section on connectivity.

Economic scalability addresses, in the first place, the issues of global interoperability. It is attached to humans as the components encountered need to cooperate globally. One possible solution to this might be the introduction of standards. However, global standards will be insufficient in many cases and it is often unrealistic to assume that all parties participating in communication will adhere to them. Moreover, interface definition languages, such as remote methods or procedure calls, and so forth, only define the syntax, that is, the formal structure of expressions. Examples of this are typing, names of operations or operands exported in a particular interface. Such languages do not define, for instance, valid call sequences, preconditions, the cost or the quality of the operation and similar things. Though there exist partial solutions to these issues, it is still unclear how to specify the semantics of processes on a broad scale; for example, how to encode formally, that is, in a machine understandable manner, what an operation actually *performs*.

The most relevant areas providing at least partial solutions to the previously described challenges are:

- Web services and business processes, describing service-oriented architectures (SOA) as a promising paradigm to support large-scale UC environments in the business world;
- Ontologies as a key technology to formally capture the meaning of the processes. This is a holy grail for making UC components or services understand each other, giving the hope for a machine to "know" what the specific operation performs;
- Service discovery, taking into account service level agreements, the quality of service in the business sense of "get what you pay for," and further issues.

Part C: Connectivity. The issue of global interconnection of UC components is closely related to scalability. Two important issues that lead from networked computers to truly cooperating nodes are treated in the scalability part, but are related to connectivity: (i) previously unknown components must be able to join a cooperating system, and (ii) a high degree of autonomy of the nodes must be combined with a close cooperation that leads to a "meaningful whole." In the "Connectivity" part of the book, we will discuss further issues of scalable communication infrastructures and scalable cooperation infrastructures, such as spontaneous—that is, ad hoc—communication that must be possible without human intervention, such as configuration. More details follow below.

Scalable communication infrastructures cover wireless networks, which are often a pre-requisite for higher layers, and require the basic understanding of the pertinent technologies such as ZigBee or WiMax. Furthermore, scalable communication infrastructures involve event-based communication praised as the UC approach to connectivity. They operate according to the so-called "push" paradigm, which is an important pre-requisite for the scaleable open cooperation of components superseding the client/server architectural paradigm. Thus, such communication infrastructures constitute a significant contribution to the scalability of ubiquitous computing systems. It may very well be the case in the future that event-based communication will become superseded by the approaches inspired through bionics or socionics. As long as this remains an open research issue, event-based communication certainly represents the best choice. Issues such as advertising of services, the openness of component cooperation and the integration of other paradigms therefore have to be addressed. Appropriate UC middleware should be described including available services and tools.

Scalable cooperation infrastructures focus on issues beyond getting the bits across, such as:

- *Overlay networks,* which are special sub-networks on the Internet that can be classified by at least 3 classes: (i) peer-to-peer networks avoiding centralized bottlenecks and scaling fairly well, (ii) opportunistic networks, trying to correlate the proximity of communication nodes with the proximity of humans, and (iii) smart item networks, AutoID and beyond, representing the networks of "machines;"
- *Service discovery:* a prerequisite for zero configuration, that is, fully automated configuration;
- *Federations* where individual components must be integrated into ambient environments composed of many cooperating components; thereby, many components may be involved, for example, in the interaction of a user with a service or environment.

Scalable cooperation infrastructures may sound like a solution to "economic scalability" already mentioned above, but actually they are not. Many assumptions about the components are made, which really turns this into a connectivity issue on the whole.

Part A: Adaptability. The capability of a UC system to dynamically adapt its behavior according to the state of the environment is structured along two main dimensions: context awareness and user awareness. *Context awareness* is a term that means the adaptation of a system to the situation of use. The situation of use can thus be characterized by the different types of context, such as sensed context, modeled context and inferred context. Sensed context is represented by the data acquired with the help of various sensors. Some examples of measurements performed with the help of sensors are, for example, temperature, shock, location, and so forth. Modeled context can be obtained from other software or databases, where it must have been previously specified, for example, models of tasks or activities fall into this category. Finally, the context can be inferred, which means that some inferences are made and conclusions are drawn based on possibly multiple sources of contextual knowledge, either sensed, modeled or both. A GPS component, for instance, may sense the location of a particular entity to be a specific street in the town (sensed context). Another component consults the knowledge base with modeled contextual knowledge and determines that there is a co-located chemical plant. From these facts, it can be inferred that the entity is in a dangerous location (inferred context), so that appropriate actions can be taken to resolve this undesirable situation.

It should be noted that contextual models are subject to "aging," which means that they have to be continuously updated. Sometimes, the contextual evidence is uncertain, that is, it is provided given specific probabilities. The evidence obtained from different information sources may even be contradictory. For instance, the sensors may be imprecise, so that a calendar entry reports a different location as it is sensed by the GPS component. The most well investigated type of context is location. Therefore it will be described in particular detail in a special chapter of the book. This type of contextual information may be absolute ("X is room 253"), or relative ("voltmeter is with Mr. X").

User awareness denotes the ability of a UC system to adapt to human users. The notion of user should not be understood in the narrow sense of a system user. In the future, this could be, for example, also a provider of specific services in a UC environment. We will describe the technologies pertinent to user awareness, such as user models, user profiles and preferences, and user agents. A challenge here is to design models supporting a huge range of possible new types of users. For example, the users may be inexperienced, they may be limited in terms of interaction capabilities, such as hands/eyes free environments, or display restricted cognitive capabilities, such as limited attention. Appropriately supporting interaction with these kinds of users requires the modeling and understanding of their actions in an appropriate way. Specifically for UC applications, user models should become ubiquitous. Current UC systems contribute and use only a small fraction of this information to date.

Part L: Liability. This part discusses the protection of actors, that is, users of UC systems, and those concerned by actions, that is, peers, third parties and the society. Protection has to be realized in the presence of zillions of peers, which requires special extensions of the conventional concepts of security to make them scalable with respect to the number of parties and the open nature of communication. Scalable security pursues the old goals, for example, of ensuring privacy and authentication, but involves a set of new aspects discussed below.

Machine-to-machine communication & ad hoc (spontaneous) communication and interaction: *A priori*, UC settings are *un*managed domains. One cannot assume that in each and every setting hierarchical and managed security infrastructures, for example a PKI (public key infrastructure), are in place. Thus, to support ad hoc communication, including machine-to-machine communication without users involved, PKIs and the like are impractical. First, a PKI require powerful hardware to complete the cryptographic operations in a reasonable time. Second, every centralized approach scales badly in respect of zillions of peers, and the pre-requisite of being always reliably connected to a central and trusted third party is not given. An early approach to support secure ad hoc machine-to-machine interaction is the resurrecting duckling protocol (Stajano & Anderson, 1999).

End-to-end encryption is very hard to achieve in UC settings. One major question is: "How do we define an endpoint?" At one extreme a user and her interaction with the UC environment is the endpoint. But this requires the user to trust the very first device she is interacting with. Whether or not work on trusted computing helps is still unclear today.

Since UC places the human at its centre, we need anthropomorphic security methods and solutions that comply with human intuition while a user interacts with UC technology in her everyday life. This suggests intuitive and human understandable models of trust, risk, and recommendation, to name but a few concepts. In addition, security measures need to be accepted by a user. Therefore, a focus on user-friendliness (ease-of-use) is necessary.

Taking society as a whole into account, liability has to deal with conflicting goals and forces. For example, protection of an individual's privacy may conflict with a public/society goal to secure living together. This involves several scientific disciplines (law, society, computer science), but liability in UC needs to provide flexible solutions that comply with society rules and laws as well with individual needs. These solutions will always come with a tradeoff between the concerned parties.

In this context, liability is also related to the rules of an economy, or market: UC services are offered and used based on currencies, which both users and providers have to associate with the value of these services. Users want "to get what they pay for," providers want to "get paid for what they provide"—a matter of contracts *prior to* service use, and guarantees plus enforcement means *during* service use. A free economy must be based on competition, which in turn can only work if values and prices associated with goods (here: services) can be compared. The key question is the extent to which these economic concepts can be formalized and automated for software. There are concepts and mechanisms in current networks (telephony networks in particular), which provide a certain degree of contract/guarantee/enforcement-means and of comparability as described, either for Internet-based services (such as those following the Web service paradigm and standards) or for services offered in operator owned (e.g., telephony) networks. Major concepts to mention in this respect comprise: (i) the accounting and billing concepts used in telephony networks, (ii) "service level agreements" (SLAs) between service providers and users (a wealth of non-formal approaches to SLA exist for non-software, for example, call center or help-desk services, but some concepts have been formalized for software-based negotiation and control in the network services context), (iii) "quality-of-service" (QoS) concepts known from multimedia (transmission) services, and (iv) semantics-based descriptions of Web services based on, for example, the Web Service Modeling Language WSML.

Part E: Ease-of-Use. User-friendliness considers the optimal use and combination of modalities as well as the advancement of specific modalities given a particular application setting. The readers should note that, partially, ease-of-use is treated in the "Adaptability" part of the present book. In particular, the adaptability of the user interface treated there belongs within the scope of ease-of-use. In a nutshell, the user interface is reduced to what "makes sense" in a given situation.

We further discuss a variety of input and output devices in the ubiquitous computing world. Such devices are designed to enable multimodal interaction. A simple distinction in this context is made between hands and eyes and mouth and ear interaction. In advanced hands and eyes interaction, graphical displays and GUIs are typically predominant, though further developments are still needed at this point. Examples of hands and eyes interaction are focus + context displays, 3rd dimension (VR), 4th dimension (dynamic displays), immersion and narration. Mouth and ear interaction bears great potential as it allows the users to operate in a hands/eyes free manner. However, voice processing is still underdeveloped today. It requires understanding speech input, which is challenging due to multiple reasons, such as the quality of speech recognition, the necessity to adapt to a multitude of speakers, and generally the difficulty of generating semantic representations for unrestricted language.

Generally, a better integration of human-computer interaction and software engineering is desirable. So far, these two strands of computer science research have developed in parallel. Another important issue is multimodality, which goes beyond syntactic transformation (transcoding) of XML representations with the help of XSLT to generate device-specific variants of these XML representations. A more abstract interaction layer has to be introduced, so that the details concerning the use of a specific modality are decoupled from the core program. The advantages concerning the use of this particular modality, however, cannot yet be fully exploited. True multimodality also implies the use of multiple modalities simultaneously, giving the user a lot of freedom while interacting with the system. In this case, the inputs are subject to so-called fusion, that is, they are mapped to a single unified semantic representation of the user's input, while the outputs have to be fissioned, that is, distributed over a set of appropriate modalities for presentation. Furthermore, multimodality can be integrated with advanced user interfaces, which are context-sensitive, adapt to the user and behave pro-actively, making suggestions for actions to be taken in a specific situation. Finally, multimodality has to be enabled for federated devices, which involves determining the optimal use of multiple input and output devices currently surrounding the user. In this case, liability explained above becomes an important issue.

Ease-of-use in UC systems should approach human intuition. Thereby, a cross-cutting concern is to design post-desktop metaphors utilizing many of the aspects discussed above. For example, the task of sorting e-mails or documents into specific folders or directories is carried out by the user. In the future, all applications will be likely to adapt to the user's favorite structure. In a similar way, as metaphors have been invented for graphical user interfaces, appropriate ones have to be designed and introduced for voice, and so forth.

Users of UC systems should get used to and understand the probabilistic behavior of such systems as their inherent characteristic. Some amount of uncertainty is a natural consequence of scalability. Mass data emerge as the result of ubiquity; for example, digital recordings are swamping user disks due to digital cameras. The models of dealing with this problem today involve either reducing the amount of data, that is, deleting some pictures, classifying the data manually, or accepting the chaos. The future will make use of more intelligent methods, for example, modeling the human brain, whereby the data is classified and ranked automatically. During this process, it has to be (i) evaluated with respect to existing priorities, (ii) summarized, that is, reduced to a set of compact statements, and (iii) even forgotten, that is, deleted, if the data is no longer relevant.

Figure 4. Relationship to computer science research

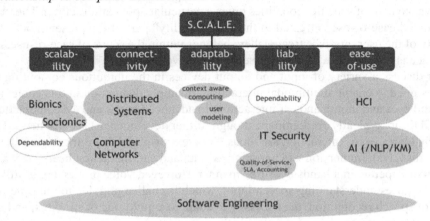

A further approach to ease-of-use is modeling human-computer interaction on human dialogues. Intelligent user interfaces should be capable of talking with the user in such a way as people would talk to each other. For this purpose, computational linguistics and natural language processing techniques have to be employed. Determining the meaning of language is, however, not a trivial task as stated above. Grammars used for natural language analysis are often limited to specific domains. To enable natural language understanding beyond phrases, large databases with world knowledge are required, which are difficult to obtain. Therefore, natural dialogues with computers are still a matter of ongoing research.

Another issue involving understanding natural language in UC systems involves integrating formal knowledge with informal knowledge sources. Formal knowledge is represented in structured semantically annotated documents, while informal knowledge is rather scattered over a huge number of information repositories. Examples of the information repositories with informal knowledge are e-mails, forums, Web sites, blogs, and so on. Analyzing such informal knowledge documents is especially challenging, as the language employed in electronic communication is often informal. For instance, it typically contains abbreviated expressions, which have to be resolved automatically.

To enable multimodal interaction with UC systems, the results of natural language analysis have to be combined with the analysis of other modalities, such as gesture or facial expressions. Note that the latter even involves the analysis of human emotions, whose interpretation is challenging even for people, let alone machines. Therefore, natural language processing alone would not suffice to enable natural human-computer interaction. Instead, it should be enriched with additional techniques to cover all forms of input.

As became evident from the previous discussion, the S.C.A.L.E. classification defining the scope of ubiquitous computing as a field is related to multiple areas of computer science. These relations are shown in the Figure 4.

- **Scalability**, although an issue in its own right, is not considered a scientific (sub-) discipline; therefore, only bionics and socionics are mentioned here as recognized disciplines. A number of other issues will be treated in this part, some of which have a long tradition (but are rooted in different areas that would really be a distraction if listed here). Dependability is marked as "half related" in the sense that new, scalable approaches must be looked for which depart from the idea that the dependability of individual components can ever reach a level of "perfection."

- **Connectivity** is largely rooted in computer networks and distributed systems—areas that some consider as the roots of UC as a whole, but that would underemphasize success critical issues such as "humane computing."
- **Adaptability** is a superset of the newly established area "context-aware computing." The book emphasizes the need for more elaborate user modeling than what usual context-aware computing approaches foresee, thus the inclusion of this second research domain in the figure.
- **Liability** as a major part of the book is largely dominated by IT security issues. More appropriate solutions for them must be found, such as anthropomorphic concepts and models, scalable schemes, and so forth. For turning UC into a global market, economic aspects must be handled, leveraging off sub-aspects of computer networks/distributed systems, such as QoS, SLA, and accounting/billing concepts.
- **Ease-of-use** finally is dominated by HCI research, but is also greatly influenced by the AI concepts used in natural language processing and computational linguistics, and by the concepts of knowledge management.

Software engineering is the basis for efficient and effective development of UC applications. Therefore it influences UC greatly—but must also itself be influenced by UC, since many software engineering methods, notations, and concepts must reflect the requirements imposed by UC.

READER'S DIGEST

The book will be interesting to many researchers and practitioners in industry and academia, whose interests lie in one or several of the five different axes of the S.C.A.L.E. classification, that is, scalability (AI algorithms, ontologies, services), connectivity (networks, peer-to-peer), adaptability (context and user models), liability (trust, security), and ease-of-use (multimodal interaction, intelligent user interfaces). In this case, they can learn the foundations of ubiquitous computing and how their area of interest can be readied for ubiquitous computing.

We believe that the book will serve not only as a practical reference book, but also as a reference book for academics in the area of ubiquitous computing. For students in advanced undergraduate and graduate programs, the book will be suitable as a course book in computer science, electrical and computer engineering, and information technology. It can be used in courses like distributed systems, computer networks, human-computer interaction, and IT security. Additionally, students doing specialized studies in areas like software engineering, media and communications engineering, ubiquitous computing/pervasive computing/ambient intelligence, or business process modeling will be able to use the book as supplementary material. It will provide not only foundational material and a description of the state-of-the-art, but bibliographic pointers for further readings and a discussion of the research issues, trends and the development of the field.

As to the introduction and five main parts, the book covers different aspects of ubiquitous computing in a manner that makes the book suitable for undergraduate courses. Concepts, methods and algorithms of ubiquitous computing are presented such that the book is "self-contained." This means that students can learn the foundations of ubiquitous computing from the book itself. In addition, each chapter provides an extensive list of bibliographic references and a discussion of research issues complementing the foundational material. This makes the book suitable as a reference for computer science practitioners and also as a reference book in advanced, for example, graduate, courses. For each part, a short introduction prepares the ground for the reader to understand and interrelate the following chapters. For all chapters, special care is taken not to remain shallow, but to cover long-term methodological knowledge (overview of the state-of-the-art with selected fundamental methods, algorithms, or concepts in detail) and to describe current problems and innovative solutions.

Finally, a supplementary part with the descriptions of ubiquitous computing projects at SAP Research complements the treatment of the subject by providing insight into real-life projects and problems that have to be dealt with while transferring UC technologies into industrial practice. SAP Research is the research division of SAP, the world's leading producer of business software (used, incidentally, by the top 100 companies worldwide). The main charter of SAP Research is the realization of the vision "real time enterprise." Thus, the digital world (company software) is connected online to the physical world: events and actions in one of these worlds are reflected without error-prone intermediate manual steps or switches in media in the other world in real time. This final part of the book is intended as the "grounding" that illustrates to what extent the approaches and research findings from the previous chapters are already on their way to practical use.

We believe that we have provided the first systematic, full-coverage book about ubiquitous computing (a.k.a., pervasive computing, a.k.a., ambient intelligence) that can serve as a reference book and a researcher and practitioner's guide.

REFERENCES

Aitenbichler, E., Kangasharju, J., & Mühlhäuser, M. (2006). MundoCore: A lightweight infrastructure for pervasive computing. *Pervasive and Mobile Computing, 3*(4), 332-361.

Stajano, F., & Anderson, R.J. (1999). The resurrecting duckling: Security issues for ad-hoc wireless networks. In *Security Protocols, 7th International Workshop*, Cambridge, UK (pp. 172-194).

Weiser, M. (1991). The computer for the twenty first century. *Scientific American*, 265(3), 94-104.

Acknowledgment

The editors of the book express their deep gratitude to the many people who provided crucial contributions to the success of this project. We will not try to provide a conclusive list at this point since the list is too long and there is a high risk that the many authors would forget a valuable contributor. Rather, the editors would like to mention a few names as examples of what it takes to compile a thirty chapter handbook for a scientific field that is still in the process of taking shape. It all starts with the research cooperation network that makes it possible to generate the "wealth-of-knowledge" accumulated in the present book. Special thanks are directed to all the colleagues involved, such as Kurt Rothermel (University of Stuttgart, Germany) and Terry Winograd (Stanford University), to people from closely cooperating institutions like Eurécom in France (Ernst Biersack, Ulrich Finger, Bernard Mérialdo, and others), and to those colleagues from SAP Research and from the Telecooperation Group at Technische Universität Darmstadt who did not contribute to the book directly as authors. The editors are deeply grateful to the various peer reviewers for their detailed work, to Piklu Gupta for proofreading, and to Karin Tillack, Elke Halla, and Dimitri Belski for their administrative support. Last but not least, this book would not have happened without the support of the editors' families, patiently waiting for the last page to be finished.

Chapter I
Introduction to
Ubiquitous Computing

Max Mühlhäuser
Technische Universität Darmstadt, Germany

Iryna Gurevych
Technische Universität Darmstadt, Germany

ABSTRACT

The present chapter is intended as a lightweight introduction to ubiquitous computing as a whole, in preparation for the more specific book parts and chapters that cover selected aspects. This chapter thus assumes the preface of this book to be prior knowledge. In the following, a brief history of ubiquitous computing (UC) is given first, concentrating on selected facts considered as necessary background for understanding the rest of the book. Some terms and a few important standards are subsequently mentioned that are considered necessary for understanding related literature. For traditional standards like those widespread in the computer networks world, at least superficial knowledge must be assumed since their coverage is impractical for a field with such diverse roots as UC. In the last part of this chapter, we will discuss two kinds of reference architectures, explain why they are important for the furthering of Ubiquitous Computing and for the reader's understanding, and briefly sketch a few of these architectures by way of example.

A BRIEF HISTORY OF UBIQUITOUS COMPUTING

Mark Weiser

The term ubiquitous computing was coined and introduced by the late Mark Weiser (1952-1999). He worked at the Xerox Palo Alto Research Cen-

ter (PARC, now an independent organization). PARC was more or less the birthplace of many developments that marked the PC era, such as the mouse, windows-based user interfaces, and the desktop metaphor (note that Xerox STAR preceded the Apple Lisa, which again preceded Microsoft Windows), laser printers, many concepts of computer supported cooperative work

(CSCW) and media spaces, and much more. This success is contributed (among other reasons) to the fact that PARC managed to integrate technology research and humanities research (computer science and "human factors" in particular) in a truly interdisciplinary way. This is important to bear in mind since a considerable number of publications argue that the difference between UC and Ambient Intelligence was the more technology/networks-centered focus of the former and the more interdisciplinary nature of the latter that considered human and societal factors. We do not agree with this argument, in particular due to the nature of the original UC research at PARC—and the fact that quite a number of UC research labs worldwide try to follow the PARC mindset. Indeed, Mark Weiser concentrated so much on user aspects that quite a number of his first prototypes were mere mockups: during corresponding user studies, users had to imagine the technology side of the devices investigated and focus on use cases, ideal form factors and desired features, integration into a pretend intelligent environment, and so forth.

Weiser's Vision of UC

Mark Weiser's ideas were first exposed to a large worldwide audience by way of his famous article *The Computer of the 21st Century,* published in *Scientific American* in 1991. A preprint version of this article is publicly available at: http://www.ubiq.com/hypertext/weiser/SciAmDraft3.html.

Maybe the most frequently cited quotation from this article reads as follows: "The most profound technologies are those that disappear. They weave themselves into the fabric of everyday life until they are indistinguishable from it." This was Mark's vision for the final step in a development away from "standard PCs", towards a proliferation and diversification of interconnected computer-based devices. A deeper understanding of Mark Weiser's visions can be drawn from his position towards three dominant, maybe overhyped trends

in computer science at his time: virtual reality, artificial intelligence, and user agents. With a good sense for how to raise public attention, Mark criticized these three trends as leading in the wrong direction and positioned UC as a kind of "opposite trend". We will follow Mark's arguments for a short while and take a less dramatic view afterwards.

UC vs. Virtual Reality (VR)

According to Mark, VR "brings the world into the computer", whereas UC "brings the computer into the world". What he meant was that VR technology is generally based on elaborate models of an existing or imagined (excerpt of the) world. This model contains not only 3D (geometric) aspects but many more static and dynamic descriptions of what is modeled. For instance, digital mockups of cars have been pushed to the point of simulating crash tests based on the car /obstacle geometry, static, and dynamic material characteristics, laws of physics, and so forth. As the sophistication of models grows, more and more aspects of the world are entered into the computer, finally almost everything happens in the virtual space and even the human becomes a peripheral device for the computer, attached via data gloves and head-mounted displays. Mark Weiser criticized mainly the central and peripheral roles of computers and humans, respectively. He proposed to follow the UC vision in order to *invert* these roles: by abandoning the central role of computers and by embedding them in the environment (in physical objects, in particular), room is made for the *human in the center.* In this context, he used the term "embodied virtuality" as a synonym for UC. The cartoons in Figure 1 were made by Mark Weiser and provided by courtesy of PARC, the Palo Alto Research Center, Inc.

UC vs. Artificial Intelligence (AI)

In essence, Mark Weiser criticized the overly high expectations associated with AI in the 1980's. In

Figure 1. Mark Weiser's cartoons about UC vs. virtual reality

Virtual Reality

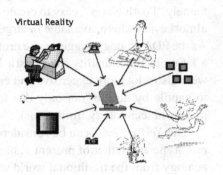

Embodied Virtuality
(Ubiquitous Computing)

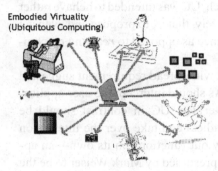

the late 1980's and early 1990's, that is, at the time when he developed his UC vision, AI research had to undergo a serious confidence crisis. The term AI had not been associated with a commonly accepted, reasonably realistic definition, so that the association with human intelligence (or the human brain) was destined to lead to disappointments. The AI hype had provided researchers with considerable funds—but only for a while. Mark Weiser proposed to take a different approach towards a higher level of sophistication of computer-based solutions (which had been the goal of AI at large). He considered it a more reasonable objective to concentrate on small subsets of "intelligent behavior" and to dedicate each computer to such a subset. Higher sophistication would be fostered by interconnecting the special-purpose computers and by making them cooperate. This reasoning lead to the term *smart,* considered more modest than the term *intelligent.* Sensor technology plays an important role in dedicating computers to a small subset of "understanding the world around us" (a key element of intelligent behavior). By widely deploying and interconnecting sensor-based tiny computers, one would be able to integrate environmental data (location, temperature, lighting, movement, etc.) and use this information to produce smart behavior of computers and computerized physical objects.

UC vs. User Agents (UA)

In contrast to virtual reality and artificial intelligence, the term *user agent* is not very prominent in the general public. At the time referred to, UAs were thought as intelligent intermediaries between the user and the computer world, that is, as an approach towards increased ease-of-use or better human-computer interaction. User agents were often compared to the common perception of British butlers who are very discreet and unobtrusive, but always at disposal and extremely knowledgeable about the wishes and habits of their employers. Following this analogy, UAs were installed as autonomous software components between applications and users, inspecting and learning from the user-software application. Mark Weiser challenged five requirements usually derived from this analogy for user agents and proposed UA as a better alternative for the first three; as to the last two, he judged the necessary base technology as immature:

1. UAs were supposed to give advice to their users based on what they had learned. Mark Weiser asked, in essence, why they would not do the job themselves—a promise that UC should fulfill;
2. UAs were supposed to obey the user, for example, by applying planning algorithms to basic operations with the aim to fulfill

the goals set by a user. In contrast to this approach, UC was intended to behave rather proactively, that is, to propose and even act in advance as opposed to *re*acting on command;

3. A third widespread requirement suggested that UAs should intercept the user-application interface. UC in contrast should be more radical and take over the interaction or carry out functions on its own—an approach presumed by Mark Weiser to be the only viable one if humans were to be surrounded by hundreds of computers;

4. A basic assumption about UAs was that they would listen to the (interactions of) the user. Mark Weiser considered natural language processing technology and speech recognition technology at his time to be far too immature to promise satisfying results in this respect;

5. UAs should learn the users' preferences, wishes, and so forth by observation. Again, the necessary (machine learning) technology was judged to be too immature to live up to this promise.

We will resume the VR / AI / UA discussion in the next large section.

Mark Weiser's Three Key Devices

We want to finish this lengthy but still extremely compressed, much simplifying and abstracting treatment of Mark Weiser's contributions by looking at three devices. These complementary UC devices were prototyped at his lab; investigated in the context of PARC's typical creative, team-oriented setting, all three were thought as electronic replacements for the common "analog" information appliances.

The *Xerox "Pad"* can be considered to be the prototype and father of present PDA's, introduced even before Apple's Newton appeared in 1993. The initial concept was that of an electronic

equivalent to "inch-size" information bearers, namely "PostIt Notes": easy to create and to stick almost everywhere, available in large quantities. As the PDA analogy suggests, the prototypes had a lot more functionality than PostIt Notes—but were also a lot more expensive and cumbersome to handle by design (not only due to short and mid-term technology limitations).

The *Xerox "Tab"* can be considered to be the prototype and father of present Tablet PC's. The analogy from the traditional world was that of a "foot-size" information bearer, namely a notebook or notepad. One may infer from the rather stalling market penetration of Tablet PC's that technology is still not ready for mass market "Tabs" today, but one may also expect to find a pen centric, foot size, handheld computer to become very successful any time soon. An interesting facet of the original Tab concept was the idea that Tabs would in the future lay around for free use pretty much as one finds paper notebooks today, for example, as part of the complementary stationery offered to meeting participants.

The *Xerox "Liveboard"* was the prototype of present electronic whiteboards. A PARC spinoff company designed and marketed such boards, and today many companies like Calgary-based SmartTechnologies Inc. still sell such devices. Liveboards represented the "yard-size" information bearers in the family of cooperating devices for cooperating people. In contrast to many devices sold today, Liveboards supported multi-user input pretty early on.

The developments and studies conducted at Mark Weiser's lab emphasized the combination of the three device types for computer supported cooperation, and cooperative knowledge work in particular.

While Mark Weiser was a truly outstanding visionary person with respect to predicting the future of hardware, that is, UC nodes (proliferation of worn and embedded networked devices, specialized instead of personal general-purpose computers, numbers by far exceeding the number of human users), two other people were more instrumental in generating awareness for the two remaining big challenges mentioned in the preface of this book, namely *integrative cooperation* and *humane computing*; the former of these challenges was emphasized by Kevin Kelly, the latter by Don Norman. A deeper analysis reveals that for the second aspect, humane computing, it is very difficult to argue about the true protagonists. Readers remember that Mark Weiser was actually placing a lot of emphasis on usability, by virtue of his education and mindset and in the context of the human focus of PARC. He also coined the exaggerated term "invisible" for mature technology. On the other hand, Don Norman was not advocating the humane computing challenge in all its facets yet. Nevertheless, we want to highlight him next as maybe the single most important advocate of this challenge.

The Book *Out of Control* by Kevin Kelly

In 1994, K. Kelly published a book entitled *Out of Control*. The thoughts expressed by Kelly were an excellent complement to Mark Weiser's publications. While the latter emphasized the emergence of networked small "neuron like" (i.e., smart) UC nodes, Kelly emphasized the integrated whole that these neurons should form. His starting argument was the substantiated observation that the *complexity of the made,* that is, of human-made systems or technology, approached the *complexity of the born*, that is, of "nature-made" systems, such as human or biological organisms, human or biological societies (cf. ant colonies), and so forth.

This observation led to the obvious requirement to investigate the intrinsic principles and mechanisms of how the born organized, evolved, and so forth. By properly adopting these principles to '"the made", this complexity might be coped with. Research about the organization and evolution of the born should be particularly concerned

with questions such as: how do they cope with errors, with change, with control, with goals, and so forth. For instance, beehives were found *not* to follow a controlling head (the queen bee does *not* fulfill this function), and it is often very difficult to discern primary from subordinate goals and to find out how goals of the whole are realized as goals of the individuals in a totally decentralized setting.

Kevin Kelly summarizes central findings and laws of nature several times with different foci. Therefore, it is not possible to list and discuss these partly conflicting findings here in detail. An incomplete list of *perceived central laws* "of God" reads as follows: (1) give away control: make individuals autonomous, endow them with responsible behavior as parts of the whole, (2) *accept* errors, even "build it in" as an essential means for selection and constant adaptation and optimization, (3) distribute control *truly*, that is, try to live with no central instance at all, (4) promote *chunks* of different kinds (e.g., hierarchies) for taming complexity, and (5) accept heterogeneity and disequilibrium as sound bases for survival.

The Book *The Invisible Computer* by Donald Norman

Don Norman emphasized the "humane computing" grand challenge described in the preface of this book. World renowned as an expert on usability and user-centered design, he published *The Invisible Computer* in 1999. He considered the usability problems of PC's to be intrinsically related to their general-purpose nature and thus perceived the dawning UC era more as a chance than a risk for humane computing. The intrinsic usability problems that he attributed to PCs were rooted in two main anomalies, according to Don Norman: (1) PCs try to be all-purpose and all-user devices—a fact that makes them overly complex, and (2) PC's are isolated and separated from daily work and life; truly intuitive use—in the context of known daily tasks—is therefore hardly possible. From this analysis, Norman derived various *design guidelines*, *patterns*, and *methodological implications*, which we will summarize again at an extremely coarse level:

1. He advocated UC nodes using the term "information appliances": dedicated to a specific task or problem, they can be far simpler and more optimized;
2. He further advocated user-centered development: especially with a specific user group in mind, "information appliances" as described previously can be further tailored to optimally support their users;
3. Norman stated three key axioms, that is, basic goals to be pursued during design and development: simplicity (a drastic contrast to the epidemic "featurism" of PC software), versatility, and pleasurability as an often forgotten yet success critical factor;
4. As a cross-reference to the second big UC challenge (integrative cooperation), he advocated "families of appliances" that can be easily and very flexibly composed into systems.

History Revised

The preceding paragraphs are important to know for a deeper understanding of the mindset and roots of UC. However, about 15 years after the time when the corresponding arguments were exchanged, it is important to review them critically in the light of what has happened since. We will first revise the three "religious disputes" that Mark Weiser conducted against AI, VR, and UAs. To put the bottom line first, the word "versus" should rather be replaced by "and" today, meaning that the scientific disciplines mentioned should be (and have, mostly) reconciled:

As to *UC and VR*, specialized nodes in a global UC network can only contribute to a meaningful holistic purpose if models exist that help to cooperatively process the many specialist purposes of the UC nodes. In other words, we need the computer embedded into the world and the world embedded in the computer. Real Time Enterprises are a good example for very complex models—in this case, of enterprises—for which the large-scale deployment of UC technology provides online connectivity to the computers embedded into the world, that is, specialized nodes (appliances, smart labels, etc.). In this case, the complex models are usually not considered VR models, but they play the same role as VR models in Mark Weiser's arguments. The progress made in the area of augmented reality is another excellent example of the benefit of reconciliation between UC and VR: in corresponding applications, real-world vision and virtual (graphical) worlds are tightly synchronized and overlaid.

As to *UC and AI*, Mark Weiser had not addressed the issue of how interconnected, smart, that is, "modest", specialized nodes would be integrated into a sophisticated holistic solution. If the difference between AI and the functionality of a single smart UC node (e.g., temperature sensor) was comparable to the difference between a brain and a few neurons, then how can the equivalent of the transition (evolution) from five pounds of neurons to a well-functioning brain be achieved? Mark Weiser did not have a good answer to that question—such an answer would have "sounded like AI" anyway.

Today, there is still not a simple answer yet. The most sophisticated computer science technology is needed in order to meet the integration challenge of how to make a meaningful whole out of the interconnected UC nodes. However, the state of the art has advanced a lot and our understanding for what can be achieved and what not (in short term) has improved. For instance, socionic and bionic approaches have become recognized research areas. A mature set of methods and algorithms is taught in typical "Introduction to AI" classes today and has replaced the ill-defined, fuzzy former understanding of the area. Thus the boundaries between AI and computer science are more blurred than ever and their discussion is left to the public and press.

As to *UC and UAs*, remember that Mark Weiser considered UAs as "too little" in terms of what they attempted (at least too little for the UC world envisioned by him), yet "too much" in terms of what the underlying technology was able to provide. This left doubts about how the even more ambitious goals of UC could be met, namely active (proactive, autonomous, even responsible) rather than reactive (obeying) behavior. In other words, Mark Weiser was right when he advocated active as opposed to reactive behavior, but he had little to offer for getting there. Luckily, the technologies that he had then considered immature (e.g., speech processing, NLP, machine learning) have advanced a lot since.

All in all, Mark Weiser's arguments from 15 years ago (1) provide a deep understanding of the field, (2) should be modified towards a more conciliatory attitude (in particular with respect to AI and VR / complex "world models"), and (3) have become more substantiated in certain respects since technology advancements make some of his more audacious assumptions more realistic (but most visions of his "opponents", too). In other words, Mark Weiser's visions were and still are *marking* the research and developments made by the UC community. His concepts and predictions were accurate to a degree that was hardly paralleled by any other visionary person. Restrictions apply as to his overly drastic opposition to VR, AI, and UAs: some of the exaggerated promises of these were repeated by him in the UC context - right when he denounced the over-expectations raised by AI and UAs! VR and AI in particular should be reconciled with UC. Maybe Weiser underestimated the two grand challenges of the UC era, namely "integrative cooperation" and "humane computing".

Kevin Kelly and Donald Norman emphasized these two challenges, respectively. Looking at the advancements in totally decentralized systems, Kelly's promises can be evaluated as too extreme today: bionics social science inspired, and autonomic (or autonomous) computing have advanced a lot. However, two restrictions still apply: (1) less decentralized systems still prove to be extremely viable in daily operation—it will be hard for fully decentralized systems to really prove their superiority in practice; (2) system-wide goals must still be planned by some centralized authority and—to a certain extent manually—translated into methods for fully decentralized goal pursuit; evolution-like approaches that would generate optimization rules and their pursuit automatically in a fully decentralized systems are still hardly viable. As a consequence, the present book will not only describe the above-mentioned computing approaches in part "Scalability", but also other aspects of scalability.

As to Don Norman, he was right to advocate simplicity as a primary and key challenge. However, he maybe underestimated the 'humane computing' problems associated with the nomadic characteristics and 'integrative cooperation' challenge of the UC era. The usability of the integrated whole that we advocate to build out of UC nodes is by far not automatically endowed with easy-to-use user interaction just because the participating appliances exhibit a high degree of usability. On the other hand, only the integration that is, federation of miniature appliances with large interaction devices (wall displays, room surround sound, etc.) may be able to provide the usability desired for an individual device.

As we conclude this section, we should not forget to mention that the UC era was of course not only marked by just three visionary people.

TERMS AND SELECTED STANDARDS

While there is a lot of agreement among researchers and practitioners worldwide that the third era of computing is dawning as the era of networked, worn/portable and embedded computers, there is not so much agreement about what to *call* that era. This fact is something of an obstacle, for instance for wider recognition in politics (the crowd does not scream the same name as one may put it). This situation is aggravated by the fact that partial issues and aspects of Ubiquitous Computing are also suffering from buzzword inflation. With this background in mind, one may understand why we list a considerable number of these buzzwords below and provide a short explanation, rather than swapping this issue out into a glossary alone. Knowledge of the following terms is indeed necessary for attaining a decent level of "UC literacy".

Synonyms for Ubiquitous Computing

First, we want to look at the terms that describe—more or less—the third era of computing as introduced:

- **Post-PC era:** The root of this term is obvious, it describes 'the era that comes after the second, that is, the PC era. We suggest avoiding this term since it points at what it is not (PC's) rather than at what it actually is.
- **Pervasive computing:** A distinction between the word ubiquitous and pervasive is difficult if not artificial. One could argue that the term pervasive eludes more to the process of penetration (i.e., to the verb pervade) whereas ubiquitous eludes more to the final state of this process. We suggest that pervasive computing and ubiquitous computing are synonyms, one (pervasive) being slightly more common in industry (its origin has been attributed to IBM), the other one (UC) being slightly more common in academia.
- **Ubiquitous computing:** The term may be interpreted as "computers everywhere". We are using it as the notion for the third era of

computing throughout the book and prefer it, among others, because we try to fight buzzword mania and dislike the invention of additional terms for a named concept. We therefore propose to stick to the first (reasonable) term invented and somewhat broadly accepted; since Mark Weiser is the first visionary person who sketched essential characteristics of the dawning era and since he invented the term UC, the question of what is the oldest well-known term should not be questionable.

- **Ambient intelligence:** This term was invented in particular in the context of the European Union's research framework programs (5, 6, 7). As a positive argument, one may say that the two words reflect the grand challenges of UC as stated in this book: ambient may be associated with the challenge of humane computing, making UC systems an integral part of our daily life. Intelligence may be interpreted as the challenge of integrative cooperation of the whole that consists of myriads of interconnected UC nodes. On the downside, one should remember that Mark Weiser had intentionally avoided the term "intelligence" due to the over-expectations that AI had raised. We suggest avoiding this term, too, because it is still burdened with these over-expectations and because it is still ill defined.
- **Disappearing / invisible / calm computing:** All three terms are less common than UC and pervasive computing. Their roots have been discussed in the historical context above. Obviously, disappearing describes again a process while "invisible" describes a final state. "Calm" emphasizes hearing as opposed to vision like the other two. In any case, the terms "invisible" and "disappearing" are not very well chosen (despite our tribute to Don Norman) since computers and interfaces that have totally disappeared cannot be commanded or controlled by hu-

mans any more. Since we doubt that 100% satisfactory service to the user can be paid at all without leaving the customer, that is the user, the option to explicitly influence the service behavior, we consider the term misleading. We favor again Mark Weiser's notion of computers that are so well interwoven with the fabric of our lives that we hardly notice them.

- **Mixed-mode systems:** This is a term used to describe the heterogeneity of UC nodes, in contrast to the rather resource rich, general purpose PC's of the last era. This term is even less common, but pops up every now and then like those previously discussed, and should not be used to describe UC as a whole since it emphasizes a particular aspect.

- **Tangible bits:** This term has found some currency in the Netherlands and Japan, but remained rather uncommon in general. It refers mainly to the fact that networked computers are becoming part of the physical world.

- **Real time enterprise:** This term has been explained in the preface of the book and is not thought as a synonym for UC, but rather as a very important and cutting-edge application domain that may drive down the learning curve, that is, prices of UC hardware and solutions.

It was mentioned in the preface that some authors argued in favor of one or the other of the UC synonyms, saying that their choice was more far-reaching in time (the other ones being intermediate steps) or space (the other ones only comprising a subset of the relevant issues). However, we cannot follow these arguments, mainly because research labs and projects around the world work on the same subjects, some more advanced or holistic, some less ambitious or more specialized, carrying the names UC, pervasive computing, and ambient intelligence rather randomly.

Towards a Taxonomy of UC Nodes

Throughout this book, UC nodes will be categorized according to different aspects. In the context of reference architectures further below, we will emphasize the role of UC nodes in a holistic picture. In the present paragraph, we want to try categorizing them as devices. It should be noted that in the preface of the book, we already provided a preliminary, light weight introduction. The difference between carried (worn, portable) and encountered nodes was emphasized and four preliminary categories (wearables, sensors, appliances, and smart labels) were briefly described. It soon became clear that smart labels attached to goods must be distinguished again from those attached to humans, although the base technology may be the same.

In a second, more serious attempt to categorize UC nodes as device categories, we propose the following distinction (see Figure 2):

1. **Devices attached to humans**
   a. **Devices carried:** Here we further distinguish three subcategories: (1) *mobile devices*, synonymous with portable devices, contain rather general purpose computers and range from laptops via PDA's to mobile phones and the like, (2) *smart badges*, that is, smart labels serve for identification, authentication and authorization of humans and possibly further purposes, and (3) *body sensors* of all kinds play an increasingly important role in particular in the fitness and health context;
   b. **Devices worn:** These wearables range from truly sophisticated, computer-augmented cloths and accessories to prototypes that are built from standard components (PDA in a holster with headset, etc.). A further categorization is not attempted since the spectrum is rather blurred;

c. **Devices implanted:** while there is a lot of hype about implanted RFID tags and networked health implants, the many issues (e.g., health, privacy, or dependability) around the necessary device-environment communication have not permitted this category to become widespread.

2. **Devices encountered**

a. **Smart items** denote computer-augmented physical objects. The terms "smart object" and "smart product" are used with subtle differences depending on the context to denote more sophisticated variants of smart items, such as smart items that proactively communicate with the users. We suggest treating smart items as the most general term and to distinguish the following subcategories: (1) *smart tags* as the least sophisticated variant: they can be considered to be mimicry for embedded computers: by attaching a smart tag to a physical object, a physically remote computer (often in proximity, though) can take over some of the functionality that would be embedded otherwise. This approach opens the door for turning even the cheapest products into UC nodes. The term "smart label" is sometimes used

synonymously; sometimes it is used as the comprehensive term for smart tags and smart badges (attached to humans, see earlier discussion). We suggest sticking to the term smart tag for the smart item sub-category described here; (2) *networked sensor nodes*, and (3) *networked appliances* denote the other subcategories of smart items. They were already introduced in the preface of this book.

b. **Smart environments** denote the surroundings of smart items, that is, the additional communication and compute power installed in order to turn an assembly of smart items into a local, meaningful whole.

The reader must be aware that all terms arranged in the taxonomy are not settled yet for a common understanding. For instance, one might argue whether a sensor network that computes context information for networked appliances and users should be considered a set of smart items (as we defined it) or a part of the smart environment. Nevertheless, we find it useful to associate a well-defined meaning with these terms and to apply it throughout the book (see Figure 2).

In addition, it should be noted that *smart environments* (with integrated smart items) constitute a particularly important research

Figure 2. Taxonomy of UC devices

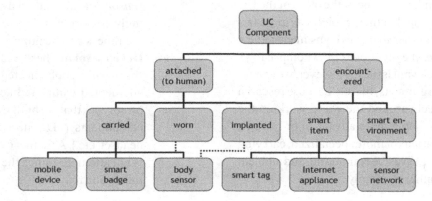

10

area—maybe because they permit researchers and project leaders to implement self-contained "little UC worlds" without a need for multiparty agreements about interoperability standards. In particular, "smart homes" were among the first subjects of investigation in the young history of UC. Prestigious projects in the smart home area were and are conducted by industry (Microsoft eHome, Philips AmbientIntelligence initiative, etc.) and academia (GeorgiaTech AwareHome, MIT House, etc.). HP made an early attempt to overcome the isolation of such incompatible islands by emphasizing standard middleware in the *Cooltown* project). Quite a number of projects about smart homes terminated without exciting results, not to the least due to insufficient business impact (note our argument in favor of Real Time Enterprises as a more promising subject). More recently, smart homes projects have focused on issues considered to be particularly promising, as was discussed in the preface to this book. Important areas comprise home security, energy conservation, home entertainment, and particularly assisted living for the aging society—a topic considered particularly interesting in Europe (1 year prolongation of independepnt living saving about half a billion Euros in Germany alone). Renowned large-scale projects were carried out, for example, in Zwijndrecht (Belgium) and Tønsberg (Norway) in this respect.

A Few More Relevant Terms

A few more UC terms—and sometimes, corresponding concepts—are worth mentioning.

- **Smart dust** is a term used for sensor networks if the emphasis is on miniaturization and the concept is based on one-time deployment and zero maintenance. Environment data sensors are often cited as an example, the vision then is to deploy them, for instance, from an aircraft, and let them monitor the environment until they fail. Environment-

friendly degradation is a major issue here, of course.

- **Things that think** was the name of an early UC project led by Nicholas Negroponte at the MIT media lab. Other authors have since hijacked the term.

- **Smart paper** denotes the vision of a display device that would exhibit characteristics comparable to traditional paper in terms of weight, robustness, readability, and so forth, and loadable with the content of newspapers, journals, books and so forth,. it would help to save paper and revolutionize the press distribution channels and more. Many projects that were not even close to this vision had, and continue to have, the name "smart paper".

- **Smart wallpaper** is a similar term to *smart paper* in that it extrapolates the above mentioned characteristics to wall-size devices.

- **Smart <you-name-it>:** virtually every noun has been associated with the attribute smart recently, not always alluding to the characteristics of UC nodes. For instance, smart materials are supposed to adapt to the context of use, with no IT involved. Most of the time though, smart <something> alludes to a physical object that has been augmented with an embedded computer.

- **The Internet of things** is a term favored by the press. It is not considered appropriate as a term for UC as a whole by the authors since it emphasizes the hardware side of UC as opposed to the human side, which was already described as crucial and as a major challenge (cf. humane computing). Most publications that favor this term concentrate on the two standards discussed in the following section.

The EPCglobal Standard

As mentioned at the beginning, we will only sketch two important standards in the UC context. Other standards are too unimportant, too immature, too specific (they might be treated in one of the focused parts of this book), or part of the background knowledge about well-established technology that this book cannot cover. The first standard to mention is EPCglobal and was mentioned in the preface of this book. As mentioned, it is meant to succeed the barcodes that encode the European article number or universal product code on current consumer products. The 96-bit Electronic Product Code EPC is usually stored on RFIDs (a subcategory of smart tags, as we can now say) and can be read:

- From a greater distance (e.g., 10m)
- With better reading accuracy
- With much less effort (e.g., en-passant by a RFID reader gate as opposed to carefully with line-of-sight connection by a barcode scanner)
- In bulk (RFID readers can read, for example, a hundred tags at once)

Since the EPC contains a 36-bit serial number, individual items can be tracked and traced. For instance, theft can be much more easily attributed to criminals, product life cycles can be recorded more accurately, product lots with manufacturing errors can be called back more specifically, etc. On the other hand, the serial number may in principle be used to trace an individual, too, if she carries

around an RFID tagged product. This privacy issue has raised many concerns in recent years and amplified the decision of the whole sales and retail industry to focus on tagging their containers, palettes, cases, etc., for a start. So-called item level tagging is only envisioned for highly valuable goods initially; it may enter the mass market when tag prices and system costs have come down and after settling the privacy issues.

Figure 3 depicts the functioning of EPC smart tags in an overall IT infrastructure. In step 1, an EPC code is read from a product. In the example, each carton on the palette could contain a number of tagged products. The residual example would then explain the action for just one such tag. Usually prior to reading the tag, the system has already searched and discovered servers capable of 'resolving' certain ranges of EPC code. Based on the results of this discovery process, the appropriate 'resolution node', called an ONS server, is asked to resolve the EPC code, that is to translate it into a global Internet address where the relevant product information is actually stored. The product information is encoded in a standardized way, using the so-called product markup language PML, an XML derivate.

The second generation of RFID tags introduced in 2006 features improved bulk reading (hundreds of tags simultaneously), size and cost improvements. "Printable" tags have become common: these paper labels with embedded RFID chips can

Figure 3. RFID / EPC scheme

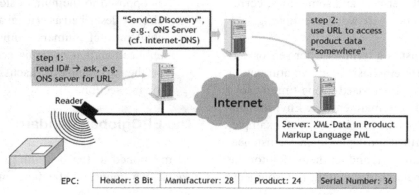

be custom imprinted with custom human-readable information. The chips themselves are not altered in the printer and they come with pre-assigned EPC codes from the manufacturer.

The OSGi Standard

The Open Services Gateway Initiative (OSGi) is an industry driven nonprofit consortium. OSGi standardized a Java virtual machine (JVM). This JVM can be considered a standardized virtual 'computer' that runs on any real computer and is capable of executing programs that are transmitted to it, so-called *bundles*. OSGi standardizes not only the format for bundles, but also the necessary protocols and procedures for authenticating and authorizing senders of bundles, for replacing and updating bundles (remote maintenance), for discovering other bundles, and so forth. OSGi bundles are particularly useful for controlling the functionality of networked appliances. Possible use cases include SetTopBoxes, Vehicles (note that car electronics today requires much shorter maintenance cycles than the mechanical parts, especially for software updates!), consumer electronics, and so forth. As to smart homes, the favored concept is that of a residential gateway that is connected to the global Internet and receives updates for smart home appliances via OSGi. The residential gateway may then forward bundle updates and so forth to the relevant appliances if needed.

OSGi has a number of deficiencies. For instance, it is not considered to be very resource effective. Nevertheless, it has tremendous impact as a de facto standard for dealing with some of the elementary aspects of coping with global UC systems in a platform and vendor independent way.

REFERENCE ARCHITECTURES FOR UBIQUITOUS COMPUTING

The Importance and Role of a Reference Architecture

A sophisticated distributed infrastructure is needed in order to make a myriad of networked UC nodes communicate and cooperate. If interoperability is to take on a worldwide scale, means for agreement among arbitrary participants must be provided. Ideally, the move from isolated proprietary UC solutions to a world of cooperating UC components is driven by so-called *reference architectures* which establish several *levels* of agreement: on level one, a common terminology and conceptualization of UC systems is established in order for researchers and practitioners to speak the same language and to work on the same global UC vision. On the second level, a common understanding of the ensemble and components of a typical UC system is established, including the potential roles of the components. On level three, basic functional principles can then be agreed upon. A fourth level is desirable but beyond the scope of reference architectures, that is concrete standards for intercomponent cooperation. This level is discussed in the introduction to the part Scalability.

Reference Architectures in a More Realistic World

In reality, a worldwide common understanding and corresponding standards have to be developed in a struggle for the best solution. Real life has a large impact on what becomes widespread. By "real life" we mean breaking research results, industry practice, experiences gained with proprietary prototypes and realizations, user acceptance, and not least business interests defended by global industrial players. Nevertheless, the exercise of proposing and refining reference architectures—in communication with the stakeholders mentioned—plays a key role in a struggle for globally interoperable solutions. Here reference architectures must be invented and published and then consolidated and reiterated based on feedback by the stakeholders.

Prominent Examples from the Past

The ISO reference architecture for open systems interconnection (OSI) was developed in the 1970s as an important step towards global networks. OSI was very successful in that it led to a common terminology and a common understanding of the components of computer networks including their roles. The fourth level aforementioned above: ISO standards for communication protocol, were not nearly as successful as the reference architecture itself. Rather, the Internet protocols TCP and IP took over almost the entire market. Nevertheless, the OSI reference architecture was extremely influential on the computer networking community as a whole and on the Internet in particular. Another ISO reference architecture is ODP (open distributed processing). It emphasizes complex distributed systems and applications. An influential contribution of ODP is its support for different viewpoints of various stakeholders. In particular, ODP emphasized the importance of enterprise modeling for application development. All too often, applications are modeled and built with a technology focus and thus neglect the (dynamically changing) organization they should support. ODP addresses important issues, but came at a time when distributed applications were usually rather simple: ODP was considered overkill.

Layered Architectures vs. Component Architectures

Before we introduce concrete reference architectures, it is worth recalling the two complementary flavors:

- **Layered reference architectures** serve as a blueprint for layered software architectures. Both arrange sets of functions into layers that act as virtual machines: only the "what" (provided functionality and how to access it) must be known to users in higher layers, whereas the internal "how" (realization) is hidden and can be independently modified. The layer stack represents the range from higher to lower function sets, where higher means "closer to what users and applications need" and lower means "closer to what hardware provides". Strict variants preclude higher layer components to access lower layers except for the one immediately below. Recent research has concentrated on approaches for automatic, selective custom configuration of the entire layer stack, according to the needs of applications—this trend is important in the UC world where dedicated, resource-poor UC nodes cannot host fat all-purpose layers.
- **Component reference architectures** take a birds-eye view on the world addressed. They define a number of cooperating components or rather component types, and specify inter-component cooperation at a certain level of detail. Again, a kind of art of right-sizing exists: too few component types do not really help to understand and discern relevant roles and specializations common to the world addressed, too many component types lead to overly complex architectures and problems in matching reference and reality.

Although we focus on the Computer Networks / Distributed Systems aspects of UC in the remainder of this chapter, readers should note that the entire book represents a holistic approach.

Why Component Reference Architectures are Important for UC

The OSI reference architecture assumes a network consisting of rather homogeneous nodes, namely general-purpose computers with 'sufficient' CPU and memory capacity. Accordingly, a common definition of a computer network reads as follows:

A computer network CN is a set of autonomous nodes AN, each of which disposes of CPU(s) and memory, plus a Communication Subsystem CSS capable of exchanging messages between any of the nodes: CN :== {AN} ∪ CSS.

In the definition, "all nodes are created equal". At a closer look, computer networks rely on four mandatory constituents of nodes (ANs):

1. **Communication capability:** The capacity of exchanging messages with other nodes through the CSS.
2. **Address:** A unique identifier that can be used to specify the recipient or sender of messages.
3. **Processor:** A general purpose CPU.
4. **Memory:** Means for storing—at least—incoming messages.

In a UC world, resource scarcity and the special-purpose nature of many nodes are key issues.

A holistic UC approach must scale from servers to sensors and support the consideration of smart labels etc. The definition of a UC node must be different from the one above—the four constituents now read as follows:

1. **Communication** is mandatory, but may be passive (cf. passive RFID tags)
2. **Address** is not necessarily a unique identifier; for example, in a sensor network, a random node out of a redundant set with identical address may provide a certain functionality
3. **Processor** becomes an *optional* constituent
4. **Memory** becomes an *optional* constituent, too

With the above modifications, not all nodes are *autonomous (ANs)* any more.

Proposed UC Component Reference Architectures

The definition introduces a first possibility for distinguishing nodes as components of an application, that is, from the component architecture point of view. However, it only discerns between existing versus missing fundamental characteristics. More interesting is the aspect of different roles that nodes can play in the network—not application specific roles, but fundamental roles in the set of cooperating resources. Thus UC systems will take on more complex node topologies than what was considered in the eras of simple interprocess communication and client-server computing. In addition, a holistic approach needed for UC systems raises issues such as security, which are important when trying to find important node types at different levels of granularity.

One of the first proposals for a UC component reference architecture was made by the Fraunhofer research institute FOKUS in Berlin. They did not distinguish different node types that would assume different roles, but identified important roles that *each* UC node may potentially assume. Their concept is coined *I-Centric Services* and achieved a certain level of influence on the industrial Object Management Group (OMG). In their view, a UC node (usually a software service) should provide standard interfaces for four major issues:

1. **Discovery** of peers in a spontaneous, configuration-free manner
2. **Maintainance**, i.e., software update and revision

3. **Reservation**, that is, pre-allocation of some of the node's resources as a basis for service guarantees

4. **Configuration** as a means for customizing the service for a dedicated role

Nodes that conform to these interfaces are called *super distributed objects (SDO)* in this proposal.

We will discuss another component architecture in some more detail since it attempts to discern between more specific roles of UC nodes. It was developed in the Telecooperation Group at the Technische Universität Darmstadt and is called Mundo, see Figure 4. Mundo distinguishes five different node types: Me, Us, It, We, and They.

Me (Minimal Entity): Mundo emphasizes the importance of a distinct personal UC node, that is the device tightly associated with its user: the Me. Every user uses exactly only one Me at any time. The rationale is rooted in the envisioned ubiquity of computer support in everyday life: if every step that one takes is potentially computer supported and controlled, then humans need a high level of trust that the computers "do the right thing". For instance, users will want to make sure that their actions are only recorded and disclosed to the degree they consent to or that is legally imposed. As another example, they want to be sure that they only trigger actions which they understand in their legal, financial, and other consequences and that they agree to. To this end, the Mundo researchers propose to conceptualize a single, truly owned UC node type that acts in the user's stead and controls when, how, and to what extent other UC node types are invited or chartered to participate in actions. Since computer use becomes ubiquitous, such a personally-owned node type must be carried along virtually at all times. This imposes strong requirements with respect to miniaturization, robustness, and the conflicting goals of (a) the impossibility to falsify or duplicate such a node, and (b) the possibility to replace it easily in case of theft or failure. An

important research questions is concerned with the minimum functionality of a Me.

Me nodes are considered as the representation of their users in the digital world—a digital persona involved in all user activities. It is a small wearable computer with minimal functionality. In order to support interaction with UC environments in a sensible way, the term *minimal* must be associated with a set of specific requirements regarding *size, identity, security, interaction, context awareness*, and *networking*. The design was guided by the principle that the minimal feature set of a system is determined by the worst-case environmental conditions under which the application must run satisfactorily (Satyanarayanan, 2001). This leads to a focus on speech based interaction and it is described in detail by Aitenbichler, Kangasharju, and Mühlhäuser (2004). Any Me can augment its capabilities through *association* with other entities of the Mundo architecture as described next.

Us (Ubiquitous aSsociable object): Minimization pressure will not permit feature-rich Mes. Hence, they must be able to connect to other mobile devices or devices embedded into the environment to offer more powerful services to their users, such as large display space. This process is called *association* and such devices are called *ubiquitous associable objects* (Us). A Us is a computing device that extends the user's *personal environment* by adding storage, processing capacity, displays, interaction devices, and so forth. During association, the Me sends authentication information to the Us, sets up a secure communication link, and personalizes the Us to suit the user's preferences and needs. For privacy reasons, any personalization of a Us becomes automatically unavailable if it is out of range of the user's Me.

It (smart ITem): There are also numerous smart items that do not support association that would classify them as Us. Vending machines, goods equipped with radio frequency IDs, and landmarks with "what is" functionality are just

Figure 4. Mundo reference architecture

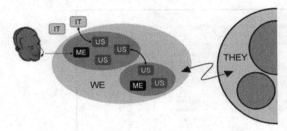

a few examples. Such devices are called *smart items* (ITs). An IT is any digital or real entity that has an identity and can communicate with a US or the ME. Communication may be active or passive. Memory and computation capabilities are optional (cf. the four constituents of a UC node described previously).

WE (Wireless group Environment): Ad-hoc networking is restricted to an area near to the user of a ME device, as connections with remote services will involve a non ad hoc network infrastructure. The functionality of a wireless group environment is to bring together two or more personal environments consisting of a ME and arbitrary US entities each. It enables cooperation between the devices and also allows for sharing and transferring hardware (e.g., US devices) and software or data between WE users.

THEY (Telecooperative Hierarchical ovErlaY) stands for the backbone infrastructure as part of the Mundo component architecture. It connects users to the (nonlocal) world, and delivers services and information to the user. The THEY integrates different physical networks and provides transparent data access to users. Frequently used data may be cached on US devices.

UC Layered Reference Architectures

Many actual UC projects are based on a layered architecture. Most of them are just first approaches to software architectures, only a few of them are intended to serve as a crystallization point for the community and future standards. Nevertheless,

one of them may turn out to be so successful that a future reference architecture will evolve from it. We will concentrate on a small selection of the few projects that have a general reference model in mind. They concentrate on different challenges or foci, that is their findings will have to be merged if a holistic layered architecture is to be derived.

A first focus is the enterprise modeling that ODP already addressed. A reference architecture worth mentioning here is ODSI, the so-called open distributed services infrastructure (Bond, 2001). Although already outdated, ODSI was influential since it fostered the move away from ODP's more top-down approach to a component-based, that is service based approach that supports the concept of applications being compositions of services.

Other reference architectures emphasize Smart Environments. Two facets are important and investigated—still—in different camps even as to the work on reference architectures: smart information spaces and smart physical spaces. By smart information spaces, we mean environments which concentrate on cooperative treatment of IT- and data/media centric work (cf. Mark Weiser's three initial UC devices). Smart physical spaces are often called smart spaces or more specifically smart houses, labs, offices, homes etc. Work on these kinds of environments emphasizes the tangible, physical (computer-augmented) objects to be handled.

As for smart information spaces, an interesting reference architecture was proposed in the LifeSpaces project in South Australia (Bright & Vernik, 2004). Their architecture incorporates some of the findings from ODSI and distinguishes four layers:

1. **Enterprise model:** This layer supports rules, processes, and organizational models of roles and services in the enterprise.
2. **Coordination and control including interaction support:** On this layer, a shared and persistent event space of limited capacity,

Figure 5. SmartSpace middleware layered reference architecture

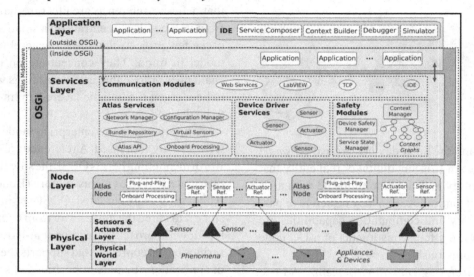

and an agent-based workspace infrastructure are offered.

3. **Enterprise bus:** This term refers to a communication layer based on the publish/subscribe paradigm.

4. **The service layer:** Here, the core functionality is represented by easily composable services. An *enterprise bus* is offered for services to communicate and cooperate; this bus connects so-called *peers* which host the services.

As for smart physical spaces, a prominent example is the reference architecture developed by the Gator Tech Smart House project of the University of Florida (see Figure 5). The reference architecture depicted is a more recent version of what was published by Helal, Mann, El-Zabadani, King, Kaddoura, and Jansen (2005) and is included by courtesy of the authors (the commercial version is called *Atlas* now). For more information, the reader may consult the group's Web Site at *www.*

icta.ufl.edu or the Atlas Web site at www.pervasa. com. The architecture emphasizes sensors (plus actuators) and networked embedded devices at the lowest layer as the hardware foundation of UC applications. The OSGI standard is exploited for customizing and maintaining these sensors and embedded devices in a dedicated second layer. The third layer contains three large parts which reflect major insights into the nature of the UC world (note that these insights have a large influence on the present book, too):

- **The context management layer** reflects the importance of context-awareness for UC as a whole, as discussed in the preface of the book;
- **The service layer** reflects services (and service-oriented architectures, SOA) as the dominating paradigm for building autonomous software components in a UC setting;

- **The knowledge layer** reflects the fact that large-scale service composition cannot rely on standardized interfaces that are distributed prior to software (service) development; rather, service discovery and service interaction must rely on machine readable descriptions of the service semantics available at runtime;
- Due to the strictly service-oriented concept used, application development boils down to service composition; **the top layer** offers corresponding tools.

In conclusion, it should have become clear that both a component based and a layered reference architecture, if widely accepted, would be important steps from UC islands towards truly global UC. The reference architectures presented could serve as a basis for better communication among the UC protagonists and for the necessary standards.

REFERENCES

Aitenbichler, E., Kangasharju, J., & Mühlhäuser, M. (2004). Talking assistant headset: A smart digital identity for ubiquitous computing. *Advances in pervasive computing* (pp. 279-284). Austrian Computer Society.

Bond, A. (2001). *ODSI: Enterprise service co-ordination*. In *Proceedings of the 3rd International Symposium on Distributed Objects and Applications DOA'01* (pp. 156-164). IEEE Press.

Bright, D., & Vernik, R. (2004). *LiveSpaces: An interactive ubiquitous workspace architecture for the enterprise in embedded and ubiquitous computing*. Springer (pp. 982-993).

Helal, S., Mann, W., El-Zabadani, H., King, J., Kaddoura, Y., & Jansen, E. (2005, March). *The Gator Tech Smart House: A programmable pervasive space. IEEE Computer, 38*(3), 64-74.

Satyanarayanan, M. (2001). Pervasive computing: Vision and challenges. *IEEE Personal Communications* (pp. 10-17). IEEE Press.

ADDITIONAL READING

Aarts, E., & Encarnaco J. L. (Eds.). (2006). *True visions. The emergence of ambient intelligenc.* Berlin, Germany: Springer.

Adelstein, F., Gupta, S. K. S. et al. (2004). *Fundamentals of mobile and pervasive computing.* New York: McGraw-Hill Professional Publishing.

Antoniou, G., & van Harmelen, F. (2004). *A semantic web primer.* Massachusetts: MIT Press.

Hansmann, U., Merk, L. et al. (2003). *Pervasive computing handbook. The mobile world.* Berlin, Germany: Springer.

Hedgepeth, W.O. (2006): *RFID metrics: Decision making tools for today's supply chains.* University of Alaska, Anchorage, USA

Helal, A.A., Haskell, B., Carter, J.L., Brice, R., Woelk, D., & Rusinkiewicz, M. (1999). *Any time, anywhere computing: Mobile computing concepts and technology.* Springer.

Huber, A. J. F. & Huber, J.F. (2002): *UMTS and mobile computing.* Artech House.

Jurafsky, D., & Martin, J. H. (2000). *Speech und language processing.* Upper Saddle River, NJ: Prentice Hall.

Lu, Y., Staff, L.Y., Zhang, Y., Yang, L.T., & Ning, H. (2008). *The Internet of things.* Taylor & Francis Group

McTear, M. F. (2004). *Spoken dialogue technolog.* London: Springer.

Moreville, P. (2005): *Ambient findability.* O'Reilly.

Riva, G., Vatalaro, F., Davide, F., & Alcañiz, M. (2005): *Ambient intelligence.* Amsterdam: IOS Press.

Sharp, H., Rogers, Y., Preece, J. (2002). *Interaction design: Beyond human-computer interaction.* J. Wiley & Sons.

Stajano, F. (2002). *Security for ubiquitous computing.* Cambridge: John Wiley & Sons, Ltd.

Weber, W., Rabaey, J. M., & Aarts, E. (Eds.). (2005). *Ambient intelligence,* Berlin, Germany: Springer.

Section I
Scalability:
Two Issues of Global Scale

Max Mühlhäuser
Technische Universität Darmstadt, Germany

GENERAL INTRODUCTION TO SCALABILITY

The notion of scalability has gained considerable attention mainly in two domains: a) interconnected computers (computer networks, telecommunications, and distributed systems) and b) software engineering. Both face increasingly large and dynamically growing systems.

Formal definitions for scalability must be restricted to narrow domains since they have to refer to well-defined elements of a corresponding world model. General definitions must remain informal. Our introductory approach reads: *Scalability is the ability to grow.*

This definition becomes more meaningful if we consider two issues:

1. *What* is growing? *Subjects of a solution.*
    By subjects, we mean parameter values, sets of entities considered, and so forth; for instance, the number of nodes, users, or data sets; the solution itself is usually given as an algorithm, a method, or the architecture of a system (which in turn may be a software system, platform, computer network, etc.).
2. What do we mean by *"ability to grow?"* Here we have to discern several aspects; the terms introduced below are not commonly accepted, but quite common in the literature (note that we will regroup the three categories into only two later in this introduction):
    a. **Mathematical scalability:** The ability to grow and remain *useful* in terms of performance; a first approach to better precision is to require that, as a "problem" grows, the resources required by the "solution" to solve the problem should not grow considerably faster—obviously, we will have to give a more precise definition.

b. **Technical scalability:** The ability to grow and remain *usable* in terms of the "handling cost" or "handling effort" associated; this facet may refer to installation efforts, to efforts needed for coping with the growth itself (changing configurations, i.e., adding, removing, updating a component), to efforts for migrating or re-using components or entire systems and so forth, or to other aspects of usability for either individual users or the organization chartered with "running" the solution (algorithm, system, …).

c. **Economic scalability:** As Wikipedia states (cf., http://en.wikipedia.org/wiki/Scalability), the term scalability is also wide spread in economics; it denotes the ability (or preparedness) of a *business* to grow; growth can relate to the turnover of a company or its geographic spread or something else; in the context of the present book, an emphasis is put on information technology related issues of economic growth.

Mathematical Scalability

Three different forms of mathematical scalability are worth mentioning here. The first two of them are only of marginal interest, but so fundamental that readers should be aware of them.

1. **Computational complexity** is treated in an elaborate theory that has evolved around the question of how algorithms and programs can cope with a growing size of the data set on which they operate; more precisely, complexity theory deals with the relative computational difficulty of computable functions; the so called Big-O Notation—a standard element of any university curriculum in computer science—is used to describe complexity growth as a function of data set growth, *O(N log N)* is a typical term in Big-O Notation.

2. **Speedup** describes the possible degree of parallelization on multiprocessor systems or computer networks as a function of the number of computing nodes involved. Two authors published popular theoretical considerations about this problem; the second one tried to contradict the first one, while the truth lies probably somewhere in between. The famous paper of the first author is found in the references as Amdahl (1967), the counter arguments provided by the second author are nicely laid out at http://www.scl.ameslab.gov/Publications/Gus/Amdahl-sLaw/Amdahls.html

a. **Amdahl's Law** leads to rather frustrating results; it is based on the partitioning of a program (intended for parallel execution) into a portion $p \in (0,1)$ that can be parallelized and a portion s that requires sequential computation; obviously, the following equation holds: $s + p = 1$, that is, $p = 1-s$. On N processors, p can be computed in time p/N; this yields an overall execution time of $s + p/N$. Since $s+p=1$, we can deduct a formula for the possible speedup by relating the execution time on one processor, $s+p$, to the execution time on N processors as above. We get:

$$\frac{s+p}{s+\dfrac{p}{N}} = \frac{1}{s+\dfrac{1-s}{N}}.$$

For large values of *N*, the term *(1-s)/N* approaches zero, such that the overall speedup approaches *1/s*. Imagine a program in which only 4% of the computation can *not* be parallelized. In this case, Amdahl's law tells us that the upper bound for speedup is 25 (1/0,04

= 25), even if thousands of nodes are implied in a computation.

b. **Gustafson's Law** is based on a fundamental critique of Amdahl's work: in the discussion above, we assumed an attempt to parallelize a problem of fixed size. Gustafson argues that, in reality, one will run small problems on small clusters and large problems on large clusters; in other words, one should assume that N grows with the problem size. Gustafson shows several examples of real problems for which the non-parallelizable part *s* of a program grows only marginally with the problem size; this means that there is hope for close to linear parallelization if the number of nodes grows linear with the problem size. For Grid Computing, where nodes on the Internet are rented as computational problems arise, this assumption sounds reasonable. The extent to which *s* remains small with growing problem size remains debatable.

3. **Message & computation complexity (in distributed systems):** the third kind of mathematical scalability discussed here is the only one that is fundamentally interesting for large, loosely coupled distributed programs and thus for ubiquitous computing; alas, it has not been consistently treated and denoted in the literature; we will use the term *message & computation complexity*. This issue deserves further investigation.

Message & computation complexity (in distributed systems) is concerned with growing "populations" in networks and extrapolates Gustafson's thoughts: the growth of the problem size is not only considered to *stimulate* the use of larger networks (that was Gustafson's argument); rather, the growth of the network is considered to *cause* the growth of the problem size. Thereby we consider distributed algorithms for which the number of participants in the network defines the problem size. Participants may be users, computers—that is, nodes, processes, and so forth—we will henceforth employ "nodes" as a comprehensive term. There is a wealth of pertinent problems such as synchronization, ordering, search or notification if it involves virtually every node of a system. (In UC reality, there will be many cooperating distributed algorithms involved in a large software system). A simple example of an inappropriate—that is, non-scaling—algorithm would be one in which every node needs to store information about every other node. The mention of storage indicates that *message & computation complexity* must take into account more than the normalized compute time as used for computational complexity [see (1) above]. On the one hand, we have to distinguish computation *amount* complexity (the sum of CPU times consumed for a computation) from computation *real time* complexity (the normalized time elapsing during a computation); on the other hand, we must consider the number, sequence, and size of messages required for a computation; it is difficult to turn these "message complexity" considerations into well-defined measures like "message number complexity" since the scalability may, for instance, depend on the degree to which multiple messages with *identical* content may be *broadcast* (as opposed to different content and unicast). In fact, alternative distributed algorithms for the same problem often represent a tradeoff between different variants of computational and message complexity. Two problems must be considered in an attempt to keep *message & computation complexity* low:

1. **Physical meshing:** A fully meshed network of N nodes requires ½*N*(N-1) bidirectional connections; generally speaking, the number of connections must grow at $O(N2)$ to avoid decreasing connectivity, that is, to maintain the same average distance (number of hops) between two nodes under growth. In the

Internet, this is impractical for technical and economic reasons. Rather, connections grow at O(N), that is, linear with the number of nodes. This means that the Internet gets "worse" as it grows. Attempts to counter this problem have been coined as "escaping from Flatland" (referring to a 19th century novella by E.A. Abbott); for local networks, compromises between "Flatland" and O(N2) were proposed, such as the Hypercube architecture, where the distance between two nodes grows at O(log N)—at the price of O(log N) connections added for each additional node; for the Internet, hierarchies of (sub)networks and hierarchies of routers are considered to be a decent means for keeping distances moderate. With the advent of modern peer-to-peer networks, distributed hash tables and other alternatives to this routing scheme are investigated.

2. **Logical meshing:** A solution's ability to grow is also inhibited if (almost) each node has to keep track of, or communicate with, (almost) every "added node" in a system; in this case, the size of data structures, the number or size of messages, and/or computation times explode despite the resources that are added with every "added node." This problem is countered, for example, by means of hierarchies as described for message routing above, with the KISS principle described later, and with several principles of distributed algorithms; to cite an example here, one such principle is called *aggregation:* instead of sending an interesting value from every node to every other one, only an accumulated value is computed in a first round of messages and announced to every node in a second round.

Technical and Economical Scalability

We start from the term "technical scalability" as initially explained. This term is much more difficult to categorize than mathematical scalability since many contradicting descriptions, terms, and definitions are used in the literature. In an attempt to summarize these diverging views, we distinguish three top-level categories of technical scalability:

1. **Openness:** Intuitively speaking, openness denotes the ability to cope with *spatial* diversification. On one hand, it should be possible to re-use components of various origins and to integrate them into various target systems; on the other hand, entire systems or solutions should also be usable or re-usable in various environments and contexts.

2. **Manageability under growth:** Until a few years ago, it was considered helpful to *concentrate* on aspects that require management efforts as systems grow—so called non-functional aspects in particular, such as reliability (via transactional behaviour, replication, etc.) and security (via authorization and authentication, etc.). Based on "separation of concerns," such aspects were isolated and concentrated, that is, offered for "one stop" management; related approaches range from "central configuration files" to "aspect oriented programming." More recently, this trend was inverted by an effort to *de-concentrate* such aspects by delegating the entire responsibility to the sub-systems themselves: such "autonomic computing" concepts rely on mechanisms in which the autonomous behaviour of components suffices for providing the required property of the entire system.

3. **Longevity:** This principle can be intuitively explained as the ability to cope with *temporal* diversification. As problems and solutions, that is, (software) systems, grow, it becomes difficult or even impossible to replace them. For instance, replacing the core Internet protocols with incompatible new versions would require a coordinated software update

on almost a billion computers. On the one hand, longevity must be assured as *plasticity*, that is, the ability to adapt to changing conditions. On the other hand, *durability* is needed: large and widely used systems must be particularly capable of surviving failures, "attacks," and so forth. *Adaptability* (or *evolutionary behavior)* and *safety* are more common terms than plasticity and durability, but the latter two nicely allude to potential conflicts between these goals.

At first sight, economical scalability does not seem to be closely related to computer science. At second sight, IT infrastructures have to grow as business grows—and in the UC context, growing business, and thereby a growing number of "business items" (tangible products, software as a product, or services, all of which will be computer based)—*inevitably* leads to growing computer and software service networks. Moreover, business growth means either geographical spread or diversification in products. The IT support structure must reflect the related growing variety of cultures, languages, legislations, market segments, customer "classes," and so forth. We

can conclude that, from a computer science perspective, economic scalability is closely related to technical scalability; if we look at the three aspects introduced above:

- We can extend *openness* towards the ability of business software to interact with components, systems, and environments "encountered" as the business diverges, scales up, and moves into other regions;
- We have to conserve *manageability* in spite of the many variants as mentioned; and
- We can extend *longevity*, too. In terms of plasticity, the adaptation to changing legislations and other contexts of the region or market segment is needed; in terms of durability, a typical requirement is 24/7 support, for example, due to global business.

Summary

We can now provide somewhat more rigorous definitions of scalability (cf. Figure 1). Given the close relation between technical scalability as defined and economical scalability in our context, we can unite these two in a single definition as follows.

Figure 1. Taxonomy of scalability

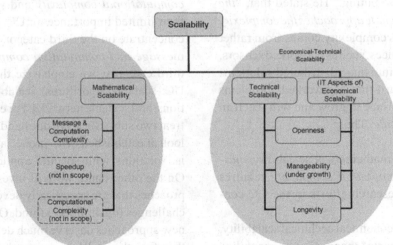

- **Mathematical scalability:** The ability of a solution to perform well under problem growth whereby, solution may be a system, method, or algorithm whereby, growth refers to nodes, users, or data whereby, performing well refers to the ratio of work load and required resources (storage, processor time, etc.)
- **Economical-technical scalability:** The ability to cope well with spread and is divided into *openness* (the ability to comprise, interact with, and be integrated into foreign technical or economic components/systems) and *manageability* (the ability to grow and be diversified without superlinear growth of technical or economical management cost) and *longevity* (the ability to both adapt to changing conditions and survive threats—again with respect to both technical and economical challenges.)

IMPORTANCE OF SCALABILITY FOR UBIQUITOUS COMPUTING

In order to understand why an entire part of the present book is devoted to the issue of scalability, we must remember what UC visionary Kevin Kelly mentioned in the chapter "Introduction to Ubiquitous Computing." He stated that, *"the complexity of the made approaches the complexity of the born."* This complexity comes from rather simple, smart devices, such as networked sensors, being integrated into huge distributed solutions. This means in turn that "networked" problems and solutions continue to grow and will reach an unprecedented *scale*. Thus:

- In terms of mathematical scalability, *message & computation complexity* requires particular research efforts in the UC context
- In terms of economical-technical scalability, all three *aspects (openness, manageability,*

and longevity) must be investigated with high priority

As the UC era advances, known approaches to all of the above are not sufficient. We will treat new approaches to mathematical scalability in the first part of the next section. With respect to economical-technical scalability, a look at the state-of-the-art and a comparison with predominant problems in UC suggest efforts towards the following major advancements, all of which will be briefly treated in the second part of the next section. At this point, the necessary advancements will only be mentioned by means of catchword phrases:

- **Openness:** From syntax to semantics (and to autonomy as below)
- **Manageability:** From isolation to autonomy
- **Longevity:** From perfection to abundance

SCALABILITY APPROACHES FOR UBIQUITOUS COMPUTING

Mathematical Scalability and UC

As indicated, we will largely ignore two "classical" categories of mathematical scalability, *computational complexity* and *speedup*, due to their limited importance for UC. Rather, we will concentrate on the third category as mentioned, *message and computation complexity*. For this third category, we emphasize three aspects for UC: scalable algorithms, scalable communications, and scalable networks. For each of these, we treat two sub-issues. On one hand, we will briefly look at established "UC-prone" approaches, that is, solutions with specific applicability to UC. On the other hand, we will investigate new approaches that are specifically developed with UC challenges (or similar) in mind. Obviously, these new approaches deserve much deeper treatment; therefore, they will be—more or less 1:1—mapped onto the book chapters in the present book part.

Scalable Algorithms – Known UC-Prone Approaches

UC prone approaches to mathematical scalability of algorithms (in a wide sense, including protocols, methods, etc.) can be found in the computer networks and distributed systems arena. We will only briefly mention a few fundamental principles here that provided scalability of a huge spectrum of approaches:

1. **Hierarchies:** Hierarchical structures provide an excellent means for taming exponential growth of "nodes," "users," "processes," and so forth involved in a problem and solution. For instance, Internet routing is a classical problem since the number of nodes on the Internet have been growing exponentially for decades and will continue to do so (see the chapter "Introduction to Ubiquitous Computing"). While decentralized (more or less "autonomous" in the sense below) routing algorithms have competed with more centralized ones and "full information broadcast" like ones without a clear winner, the Internet *did* survive exponential growth due to a hierarchical structure that comprises networks, sub-networks, and nodes on one hand, and hierarchical levels of gateways and routers on the other hand.

2. **KISS:** The general construction principle "*keep it simple, stupid!*" *(KISS,* opinions vary about what the acronym stands for) is a second success factor for the Internet, where it is usually translated into the specific principle "minimize the state information to be kept by a network node." For instance, the Internet IP protocol does not keep track of "connections" (information flows) between communicating processes; this ignorance comes at the cost of very limited support for and convenience of IP connections (e.g., erroneous packets are not retransmitted at the IP layer), but made IP outperform any

other network protocol as the Internet grew beyond billions of simultaneous connections.

3. **"Humane" ways of facing stress:** This principle is even more blurred and general than the first two. Nevertheless, it is a good abstraction for many principles found in optimizations of algorithms, particularly in computer networks and distributed systems. If humans do not have a chance (yet) to reorganize or delegate (which they usually do by means of forming or optimizing hierarchies), they consider scaling up as stress; the list of typical successful reactions comprises simplification, omission of the less important, laziness (attitudes of laziness are indeed often a good counter measure), and optimistic behavior (treating cases like "the frequent case" and looking at exceptions only as they occur).

Scalable Algorithms – Novel UC-Specific Approaches: Bionics

Since challenging UC systems represent huge networks of "smart items," it seems to be more appropriate to investigate patterns of scalability in huge networks of human beings than in individual human behavior as above. With Kevin Kelly in mind ("the complexity of the made approaches the complexity of the *born*"), one may look at huge networks of creatures in general. There has indeed been recent research that looked at humans or nature, respectively, as models for technology. *Bionics* as a discipline looked at animals and plants more than at humans in the past, and did not emphasize scalability in particular; a scientific field that looks at social behavior and its analogies in computer science is not well established in the global research community. In Germany, the term "Sozionik" has been coined in this context, and corresponding research efforts are ongoing; however, the term and its English equivalent, *socionics*, cause confusion since there is a branch of psychology by that name. Rather, aspects of social behavior in distributed systems are usually subsumed under the *distributed artificial intelligence* or *distributed agents* research fields.

Bionic approaches to scalability are indeed considered as very promising by the editors of the present book; especially the set of natural archetypes for UC solutions comprises humans. Therefore, the chapter "Bionics: Learning from the Born" of this book part will be devoted to bio-inspired scalability approaches.

Kevin Kelly takes a particular twist in his bio-inspired treatment of scalability: many of the fundamental principles that he cites ("give away control," "provide ample redundancy," "plan the unexpected"—a principle that he explains with examples of self-organization) may cause the reader to think that entirely decentralized, "autonomous" behavior is *the* general answer of nature to scalability. Autonomic computing is indeed a very important research field for UC and will be further discussed in the context of technical-economical scalability (it could be discussed here equally well since it serves both needs), but the editors would like to stress the fact that it is *not* the only successful scalability pattern for large networks; societies, for instance, add hierarchical and non-trivial cooperative structures with elaborate "negotiation" (in the widest sense) behavior and other sophisticated means.

Scalable Communication – Known UC-Prone Approaches

In an attempt to scale up communication paradigms, distributed systems had to evolve from the traditional peer-to-peer paradigms of early days: interprocess communication between *pairs* of processes did not scale up well. The *client-server* paradigm proved to be better suited and dominated the field for about two decades. Less noticed, there were also attempts to move multimedia-based communication in a similar direction, namely from point-to-point streaming to broadcast, or rather, multicast behavior (an attempt that is still not satisfactorily solved since modern digital media are rather interactive and personalized, a requirement that does not blend well with multicast). One should note that all approaches mentioned (and other less widespread ones) belong to the *"pull"* category of communication paradigms: the receiver or client determines the timing for information exchange. This pull principle has several major drawbacks in the UC context: (a) clients' need rather individual treatment on the server side in terms of time-to-serve since this time-to-serve is determined by each client (information sink) individually; (b) clients may easily get blocked if their timing expects a certain piece of information that is not readily available on the server side; in any case, the time-related synchronization of sender and receiver tends to be too tight; (c) at least one party needs to know the other in advance in order to establish a communication relationship.

Scalable Communication – Novel UC-Specific Approaches: Event-Based Pub/Sub

Publish/Subscribe, or Pub/Sub for short, is the most important communication paradigm in the *"push"* category; as one can guess, it aims at avoiding the three drawbacks just listed. The basis for Pub/Sub is *event-based* communication. Here information providers publish, that is, send information, at their own pace whenever it becomes ready. Information receivers have to specify their "interests" in a subscription prior to participating in information exchange; they subsequently receive information (asynchronously to their local thread of control) whenever an information publication matches their subscription(s). An "event routing middleware" takes care of forwarding publications efficiently and storing them until all subscribers have received them; obviously, the decoupling of sender and receiver is much better than in the "pull" category, the drawbacks a) through c) are considerably less serious: for instance, publishers usually do not "know" their subscribers at all. Evidently, the sophistication and efficiency of the event routing middleware is a key issue, and it is therefore treated extensively in the chapter "Event-Based and Publish/Subscribe Communication" in Section II of this book.

Scalable Networks – Known UC-Prone Approaches

As discussed with scalable algorithms, the scalability of the Internet has been its primary success factor to date—a scalability that relied largely on the principles for scalable algorithms used in the "core" of the Internet, the IP protocol. A major such principle being "KISS," the Internet evolved as a "virtual bit pipe" for the edges of the network, basically clients and servers like, for instance, Web browsers and Web servers. This principle of *pushing everything (processing, data, complexity, ...) to the edge* has been approaching its limits for quite some time. For instance, heavy Web traffic has made ISPs and the Internet providers in general investigate *Web caching* as a high priority area of emphasis. Today, many Internet routers serve as transparent caches; the old scalability approach "push everything to the edge" is increasingly violated—for scalability reasons.

Scalable Networks – Novel UC-Specific Approaches: Overlay Networks

The "modern" peer-to-peer systems (P2P for short, not to be confused with the early paradigm mentioned before) were mainly invented for digital music file sharing in an attempt to keep the clients and servers anonymous (contents exchanged were copyrighted) and to have every participant benefit and contribute (about) equal shares. This trend led to a wealth of approaches that can help to overcome another drawback of client-server systems:

the heavy traffic often experienced by (and on the links that surround!) servers. The scalability of P2P systems goes even further since it has built-in mechanisms that balance the amount of replicas in a tradeoff between update frequency, node and file availability, search time, and so forth. Moreover, the P2P principle represents one trend towards transforming the Internet from a huge virtual bit pipe into a huge ubiquitous distributed computer! The Web caching approaches already mentioned were pretty much the predecessors, along with early—scientific—*grid computing* approaches.

Grid computing can be thought of as a (flock-of) poor man's supercomputer. Instead of investing in a massively parallel computer, Internet users bundle their distributed resources to form a distributed virtual parallel machine. For a long time, grid computers were mainly limited to scientific experiments. Meanwhile, there is an increasing interest in "business grids:" Internet-based distributed systems offered as "virtual machines" to business clients who need compute and storage power—either temporarily or as an outsourcing concept. This trend strengthens the transformation of the Internet as indicated. As with P2P systems, the nodes of a grid form a logical (maybe globally distributed!) sub-network of the Internet called an *overlay network*

Other kinds of overlay networks include *opportunistic networks* that are established as mobile users form communities of interest based on spontaneous connectivity; yet another kind are communicating smart items that form a logical network (temporarily or permanently) with a specific (computational or business) goal.

All in all, overlay networks mark the trend from "the Internet as a bit pipe" to "the Internet as *the* ubiquitous distributed system, logically partitioned into communities of nodes." Overlay networks will be intensively treated in the chapters "Peer-to-Peer Systems," "Opportunistic Networks," and "Smart Items in Real Time Enterprises" in Section II of the present book.

Technical-Economical Scalability – Digression on Open Standards

Before we can look at UC-prone approaches to technical-economical scalability, we must briefly revise a long history of openness and standardization, which we will summarize as "syntactic standards" (explained below).

What is openness? Intuitively speaking, it is "the ability of independently developed 'things' to work together." This can only work out if the "independent" parties adhere to some common principles, specification, or other agreement—hence the close relation to standards. Obviously, the standardization body involved determines the "degree" of openness (global or national; vendor-independent or not, etc.).

Which entities are concerned? In the software context, openness and standards concern basically three categories of "things:" components, systems, and environments. Components may be modules, objects, assemblies, packages, protocol entities, agents, processes, and so forth. Systems denote the application or software solution under development, and environment denotes everything relevant for the system as it is deployed. The boundaries may be blurred (i.e., subject to interpretation). Hierarchical decomposition is paramount (a system may be a component of a larger system) but not always appropriate: aspect-oriented programming has systematically addressed the issue of "factoring out" cross cutting concerns orthogonal to hierarchical structures. The figure below illustrates the four most important *issues of openness:*

1. Interoperability of components;
2. Capability of systems to assimilate components;
3. Capability of components to assimilate to systems;
4. Capability of systems to assimilate to environments.

What must be standardized? At a first glance, standardization concerns the data, that is, messages exchanged between entities: what types of messages exist and how are they recognized by the receiver? How are they structured into parts, how is the content encoded –that is, how does the receiver derive its *meaning*? What are the permitted sequences of messages?

Besides data, the bits exchanged may represent "operations" (cf. *remote procedure call*) or code (cf. Java applets, mobile agents).

Syntactic vs. Semantic Openness

The "meaning" of message types and their parts is commonly defined as part of the standard itself. For example, one has to read the Internet IP standard in order to know the meaning of the bits in an IP packet. This up-front prescription limits openness. UC prone standards should support "semantic openness" by which entities can tell each other the meaning of messages. The *degree* of support for semantics can vary a lot, depending on how much prior knowledge about the common agreements is required and how "much" meaning can be exchanged (can one component tell another one how politics works?).

Humans, as an analogy, need a common language of some kind in order to engage in a communication: there seems to be no interoperability and no "exchange of semantics" without pre-established semantics. But then, what is this "bootstrap semantics" for newborn babies?

Selected Areas of Openness

In search of appropriate UC-prone approaches, one may consider the two disciplines concerned with openness in the past: computer networks and software engineering. As to the first one, the ISO "reference model for open systems interconnection" (OSI) has marked the scene and influenced the Internet. The openness issues (1) thru (4) mentioned above were all considered as part of OSI. However, most standards are purely

Figure 2. Issues of openness

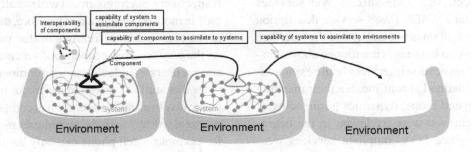

syntactic in the sense above with small exceptions: "interface definition languages" for remote procedure calls and notations like the abstract syntax notation ASN.1 support the definition of custom compound operations or messages, but not their meaning. Automata-based languages like SDL and rule-based languages like Estelle were standardized as a basis for defining meaning, but there is no known attempt to exchange meaning by exchanging SDL or Estelle programs.

As to openness in software engineering, self-contained components are the enabler for openness, re-usability, maintainability, and more, but had a tedious battle to fight against "spaghetti code" and "side effects" that were paramount in "efficient" programming languages. Since about 1970, there were four major "waves" of concepts for software components: *(i) abstract data types, (ii) objects, (iii) components* in the component-oriented programming sense, and lately *(iv) services* in the *service-oriented architecture (SOA)* or in the slightly different *WebServices* sense. The fourth of these waves usually lacks sophisticated object-oriented concepts (inheritance, polymorphism, late binding) for the sake of Internet wide scope; this global scope makes them an important UC concept, see below. Noteworthy approaches to semantic openness are only about to emerge with WebServices.

Technical-Economical Scalability and UC

Following the digression in the last section, we return to the three issues of technical-economical scalability (openness, manageability, longevity). We will see that the UC-prone approaches in this respect often serve several of these goals.

Openness, Services, and UC Challenges: Towards Semantics

Services are commonly considered *the* component paradigm for UC—a concept that is still evolving. Research emphasizes service-oriented concepts for both the components of the "digital world" (enterprise software in the real time enterprise sense of this book) *and* the computer/software-augmented components of the "real world" (appliances, sensors, etc., henceforth called smart items). The two lines of research, WebServices and service-oriented smart items, are still not very well synchronized, but the two areas reach out for each other. For the time being, we devote two different chapters of this book to these aspects. In the remainder of this overview, we will focus on WebServices since they represent the more wide spread service concept. We will now look at the four openness issues:

31

1. **Interoperability of components:** In this respect, the wide-spread WebServices standard WSDL (Web service description language) does not go beyond the interface definition languages mentioned above: custom "invocation interfaces" can be syntactically defined at runtime, but their meaning is beyond scope; dynamics (sequencing of invocations) were irrelevant in the beginning since SOA-compliant services were required to be stateless; meanwhile, stateful WebServices are considered and sequencing can be described by means of WSCI (Web services choreography interface).

2. **Capability of systems to assimilate components.**

3. **Capability of components to assimilate to systems:** In the WebServices world, the "systems" are the business processes as mentioned (WebServices that call a set of other WebServices in a coordinated way can be considered systems, too, but that does not lead to additional insights in our context); currently, a fairly syntax-oriented binding between business processes and WebServices is required, as for example, in the W3C standard BPEL (business process execution language); *Service Discovery* mechanisms can be applied in order to make an ad hoc choice among services (cf., W3C standard UDDI: Universal Description, Discovery and Integration), but they remain in essence on a syntactic level and match the WSDL-like service description of a service searched with that of services offered;

4. **Capability of systems to assimilate to environments:** In this respect, approaches to "autonomy" are most relevant; this will be discussed in the context of "manageability."

With the syntax-prone approaches described for issues (2) and (3), components must agree on much more than the "minimal common ground" explained earlier: interoperable services have to apply an almost identical syntax in describing the requested and the provided service invocations, respectively. Such agreement will usually happen only in industry syndicates. Therefore, the syntax-prone approach is currently a **major roadblock** on the way to a free economy of services, where service users would select among competitive services. For similar reasons, it is a major roadblock on the way to ad hoc cooperation of components in the "real world:" with the techniques mentioned, for example, a cell phone can only be integrated "ad hoc" with the multi-purpose control levers on a steering wheel if both the car manufacturer and the cell phone manufacturer adhere to the same standards.

Towards semantics: obviously, there is a long way to go from syntax-prone interface descriptions to truly semantics-based ones:

- **Level 0** are fixed message/operation formats, consult communication protocols
- **Level 1** are custom definitions of operations and data searched for/offered, without a means to express the semantics of these operations or data: this is the current standard with WebServices
- **Level 2** adds custom definition of operation dynamics, that is, sequencing; the Web service choreography interface (WSCI) is an approach in this direction
- **Level 3** adds means for exchanging and mutually understanding the "effects" of operation calls or data exchanges
- **Level 4** adds means for establishing a true service market; in this case, many issues of price/performance comparison, of legal contracts and business rules and laws, and so forth, must be added; this issue will be briefly addressed in the chapter "Accounting and Charging: Guarantees and Contracts" of Section IV in this book and omitted here.

Obviously, level 3 is the most interesting one. In this context, *ontologies* play a key role. At first sight, an ontology is an ordered set of terms that describe a cut-out of the real world—such as, all the terms related to automobiles and their relation to one another (synonyms, part-whole relationships and much more). In a next step, one can attempt to define the syntax of operations (sic!) by describing their effects on the ontology: obviously, this requires a rather detailed ontology and a kind of logic or programming language to specify the effects.

Ontologies can only overcome the roadblocks described if all (or at least, many) relevant "industry players and users" in the corresponding domain agree on the same ontology and on the same formal language for its description. W3C standards like RDF (resource description framework) and OWL (Web ontology language) are claimed to be such common languages, but OWL has considerable limitations—see the chapter "Ontologies for Scalable Services-Based Ubiquitous Computing" for details.

Since ontologies represent a formal description of the semantics of a certain domain, they are not fully sufficient. UC means that the entire world is gradually computerized and interconnected, so there is a need to formally describe the semantics of the whole world. Corresponding attempts were started more than 10 years ago and deemed a failure. However, there are several indications that this vision is not unrealistic anymore. Firstly, labor intensive projects for a handcrafted ontology that would specify world knowledge advanced slowly but they advanced; secondly, many detailed, handcrafted ontologies for narrower domains exist and techniques for their interlinking and merging have advanced; thirdly, so-called folksonomies (folk—taxonomies) like Wikipedia have emerged, and progress in *natural language processing* (NLP) gives rise to the hope that natural-language folksonomies (and ultimately, the wealth of knowledge buried in zillions of documents on the Web) can be automatically interpreted and turned into ontologies.

In parallel to these developments, there are increasing efforts to prepare the formal ground for specifying WebServices by means of ontological semantics. These efforts, often coined as Semantic

(or Intelligent) Web Services, have led to a number of proposed languages and standards, such as the Web Services Modelling Language (WSML), a corresponding framework WSMF and ontology WSMO—the latter represents an ontology about the domain "Web services" itself.

In summary, the above-made claim "*openness: from syntax to semantics*" should have become clear from the preceding paragraphs. Major ingredients for making the move happen have been explained above: *services* as a concept for globally distributed components—with *WebServices* and *Smart Items Services* hopefully converging—service discovery concepts and description languages for services and systems as a basis (UDDI, WSDL, BPEL, and others in the WebServices context), ontologies (RDF, OWL and beyond), and Semantic WebService description approaches (WSML, etc.). These and further aspects will be addressed in several chapters of the present book section, additional aspects (towards service marketplaces, even a software service economy) are treated in Part IV *(liability)* of the book.

Manageability and UC Challenges: Towards Autonomy

Earlier in this chapter, we discussed approaches towards isolation of cross cutting concerns, as attempts to keep them manageable and maintainable. Centralized configuration files and aspect-oriented programming were mentioned as attempts to define single points of change. In the UC context, even a single point of change is often unacceptable since components of systems "come and go" and change their behaviour at a high rate. One would like to go one step further and avoid any need for manual managerial tasks. The above-mentioned *service discovery* mechanisms were introduced as means for avoiding manual configuration needs. Their applicability is limited as explained above, but in areas where they can be applied, service discovery concepts and standards have been very successful. A special chapter of this book will be dedicated to this issue; therefore it will not be treated further here.

Service discovery provides autonomous (in the sense of non-human intercepted) behavior for a specific aspect, namely distributed system configuration. However, further cross cutting concerns are prone to human interception. Approaches to autonomous reflection of such cross cutting concerns (maintenance, security, etc.) have been carried out using different names like autonomic computing, self organization, and organic computing. IBM lists major sub-goals of autonomic computing, including self-configuration, self-healing (in case of faults), self-optimization, and self-protection (with respect to IT security). Similar sub-goals are listed in research projects about "self-organization." This term has long been established in psychology, chemistry, and economics. Wikipedia defines it as "a process in which the internal organization of a system, normally an open system, increases in complexity without being guided or managed by an outside source." Due to the many and partly overlapping sub-goals mentioned in the pertinent literature, the comprehensive term *self-X* has been coined. Prehofer & Bettstetter (2005) give an introduction to the field and show that the principle has long existed in computer networks and distributed systems.

Briefly speaking, self-organization establishes a "global," that is, system-wide property (such as order, safety, security, fairness, etc.), via purely "local" action: there is no central control, and components interact with "nearby" neighbours only—as Prehofer puts it, component behavior is based on local information only. Many concrete self-organization methods exhibit a number of patterns in common: for instance, optimal solutions are usually traded in against robust behavior and limited propagation of information, long term state information is avoided (e.g., due to the high probability of out-dating), and adaptation to changing conditions is an important design aspect.

Routing algorithms for ad hoc networks, the congestion control mechanism in the Internet TCP

protocol, and optimistic media access control (MAC) control schemes—for example, for wireless networks—are just a few examples that show the long tradition of self-organization in computer networks and distributed systems. Many examples from UC approaches to security, accounting, trust management, adaptation, and many more could be cited. Along with the many possible Xes in "self-X," this indicates that self-organization is an extremely cross cutting aspect, which we have to consider across pretty much all of the UC challenges treated in this book. Therefore, we will not dedicate a single chapter to it.

In summary, "autonomy" in the sense of the concrete concept of service discovery and in the sense of the vast cross cutting issue of "autonomic computing" or self-organization represent the roadmap for manageability in the light of UC challenges.

Longevity and UC Challenges: Towards Abundance

Finally, we want to revisit the longevity sub-issue of technical-economical scalability with respect to UC challenges. Early on in this chapter, we saw that long-lived systems were traditionally built in an attempt to introduce "perfection," that is, highly durable components and possibly mathematically proven correctness. In terms of software, the high complexity of typical long-lived systems (such as operating systems) makes "100% overall correctness" usually infeasible. Durability is always limited; therefore, redundancy is usually introduced. Since redundant systems multiply hardware cost and require sophisticated checkpoint/recovery/failover mechanisms, they are still not very common. After decades of research on 100% correct, safe, and secure code without really satisfying results, at the dawning of the UC era that will bring more computers than ever, an ever increasing degree of human dependence on computers, and ever increasing complexity of systems, we have to seek new ways to complement the striving for perfection with more radical redundancy approaches—we call such a degree of redundancy "abundance."

According to Kevin Kelly, nature takes a different approach to longevity: not only does it abandon perfection; it introduces abundance (a high degree of redundancy) and "build-in errors" (such as genetic recombination via chromosomal crossover) as a means for adaptability and optimization.

Alas, abundance as we put it is maybe the most unexplored and risky area of UC research. For the time being, it is out of the question to abandon the striving for perfection as Kevin Kelly's suggestions may be interpreted. Three of the many reasons are as follows:

- Nature, as described by Kelly, with its "planned-in" failure of components, accepts the eradication of planets, species, and so forth, a behaviour that we would have to "mask" in critical cases such as vital support functions for human patients; such a vital support system would have to behave like "nature as a whole," which is supposed to survive … but how? (and is that really true?)

- Natural evolution is based on incredible time factors (that differ from geology to biology, etc.); in the "controlled analogies in computer science" that exist today, namely genetic algorithms, the mapping of these time factors to the computer do not play a major role since the entire model is so much simplified that it can run and evolve as fast as possible; in a complex interweaving of "planned failure" and "adaptation to real world changes," this issue needs careful reconsideration,

- There have been decades of debates about the extent to which nature works in a chaotic fashion as opposed to the extent of built-in "laws" of all kinds; accordingly, there is little knowledge today about appropriate tradeoffs between "controlled behaviour"

(e.g., in the sense present in human society), "self-organizing behaviour" (in the sense described above), and "abundance," that is, chaotic behaviour based on planned errors.

In summary, the UC challenges indicate the necessity for longevity approaches to complement "perfection" concepts (code verification, etc.) not only with traditional fault tolerance concepts, but with more radical thinking that we call "abundance." There are indications that abundance blends well with autonomy, that is, self-organization. Due to the early state and many unresolved issues, we will not devote a self-contained chapter to abundance. Rather, the editors found it important to point to this issue at least in this introductory chapter; a reasonable coverage of this issue will be found in the chapter "Bionics: Learning from 'The Born;'" this chapter was mentioned in the context of UC approaches to scalable algorithms as part of mathematical scalability—an interesting coincidence because thus the "circle" of this chapter closes nicely.

OVERVIEW OF FURTHER CHAPTERS

The mapping of our overview chapter onto the detailed chapters was already discussed in the respective sections above. Therefore, we can remain very brief and relate the structure of the present book part to *Figure 3*. The principle taxonomy and issues illustrated on the upper part of *Figure 3* were treated in the present chapter, along with very brief treatments of those issues that do not need special care in the UC context (complexity theory, speedup). The widespread approaches have also been introduced in this chapter briefly. Therefore, the rest of this book can concentrate on advanced UC-related issues, denoted as layer "novel approaches appropriate for UC" in the figure.

As to mathematical scalability:

- The chapter, "Bionics: Learning from 'The Born,'" will elaborate on the most interesting approaches to novel scaleable algorithms
- The chapter "Event-Based and Publish/Subscribe Communication" will treat scalable communication for UC; it is more closely related to *connectivity,* therefore it appears in Part II of this book;
- The same applies to the chapter "Peer-to-Peer Systems" that treats scaleable networks in the UC sense; along with the treatment of other overlay networks—consult the chapters "Smart Items for Real Time Enterprises" and "Opportunistic Networks," also comprised in Section II; note that the latter are not comprised in *Figure 3* for simplicity reasons.

As to technical-economical scalability

- The three novel issues "semantic standards," "autonomy." and "abundance" as introduced

in the present chapter can not be easily mapped to book chapters; rather:

- "semantic standards" strongly affects the chapters on "Ontologies for Scalable Services-Based Ubiquitous Computing" and on "Ubiquitous Services and Business Processes;"
- "Autonomy" strongly affects the chapter on "Service Discovery" and, to a lesser extent, the chapter "Ubiquitous Services and Business Processes:" *self-organization* is treated as an orthogonal issue in many chapters (see the arguments about multiple roots and aspects of the topic as presented earlier);
- "Abundance" is still a rather far-reaching issue and is treated in the context of the chapter "Bionics: Learning from 'The Born.'"

REFERENCES

Amdahl, G.M. (1967). Validity of the single-processor approach to achieving large scale computing capabilities. In *AFIPS Conference*

Figure 3. Overview

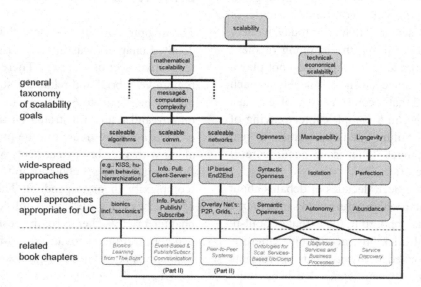

Proceedings (Vol. 30, pp. 483-485). Reston, VA: AFIPS Press.

Gustafson, J.L. (n.d.). *Reevaluating Amdahl's Law.* Retrieved May 1, 2007, from http://www.scl.ameslab.gov/Publications/Gus/AmdahlsLaw/Amdahls.html

Prehofer, C., & Bettstetter, C. (2005). Self-organization in communication networks: Principles and design paradigms. *IEEE Communications Magazine, Feature Topic on Advances in Self-Organizing Networks*, *43*(7), 78-85.

Scalability. (n.d.). Wikipedia. Retrieved March 1, 2007, from http://en.wikipedia.org/wiki/Scalability

Chapter II
Bionics:
Learning from "The Born"

Tobias Limberger
TU Darmstadt, Germany

ABSTRACT

In this chapter we will focus on distributed approaches to answer the scalability challenges in ubiquitous computing (UC) with so-called bio-analog algorithms. Based on decentralization via use of autonomous components, these algorithms draw their examples from the realm of biology. Following a motivating introduction to bionics and socionics, we will give an overview of bio-analog algorithms structured as follows. First we will have a look at algorithms based on phenomena found on the organism level of biological systems. Next we will examine algorithms imitating procedures on the cell level, then turn to algorithms inspired by principles found on the molecular level. Finally we will extrapolate bio-analog approaches to data management.

INTRODUCTION

Definition and Classification of Terms

Historically, the term "bionics", a combination of "biology" and "technics", was introduced by Steele (1995) at a 1960 congress in Dayton, Ohio. "Bionics" or "biomimetics" (Greek: bios = life, mimesis = mimicry) covers all approaches to finding solutions to technical problems by imitating nature. Bio-analog computing can be seen as just one field of bionics, and will be the one we will emphasize. Unless stated otherwise, we will therefore simply use the terms "bionics" and "bio-analog computing" as synonyms from now on. Other classifications consider bio-analog computing as strongly related to or as a subarea of fuzzy logic, soft computing, or artificial intelligence. "Socionics" on the other hand investigates political organisms. While it is often considered a scientific field of its own, bee hives and ant colonies are just two obvious examples of overlap with bionics. Therefore, socionics is sometimes also seen as a subarea of bionics.

Scope of this Chapter

The present chapter emphasizes the scalability problems in UC and how to counter them with decentralization and autonomy of components. From our common knowledge, we understand these concepts as approaches to providing components with the capability to form long-lived and highly scalable "composites". In such a "composite" the whole is far more than the sum of its components. Of course, serious studies reveal "decentralization" and "autonomy" to be quite complex and interwoven with other concepts. Nevertheless, they seem to be important for composite formation, suggesting them as promising bionic and socionic approaches for quantum leaps in scalability issues in UC. This is the main motivation for including the present chapter in the book. The reader should be aware, however, that we have to face three pragmatic constraints:

- We will have to introduce basic concepts of bionics as a foundation since we cannot assume them to be prior knowledge of the average reader. Therefore, the chapter has to be rather introductory;

- In order to provide a consistent picture of the field, relevant areas such as neural networks have to be introduced, but their treatment must remain much more superficial than their general importance would suggest;

- In most cases, concepts from biology or society are initially ported to computer science in the form of simulations. These simulations are typically executed on a single computer and compared to traditional computing methods. Therefore, much of what follows will not be recognizable as a scalability approach to distributed computing at first sight. In most cases, we will even have to restrict ourselves to coarse descriptions of how the state of the art can be extended towards solving UC specific issues.

Chapter Structure

In order to structure the contents of this chapter, we have to find a classification of bio-analog computing approaches. Since we identified bio-analog computing as a subarea of bionics, we will have to have a look at bionic approaches first. In fact, the principle of imitation for problem solving is definitely older than the term itself. The first bionic attempts are traceable back to 16th century, when Leonardo da Vinci designed aerofoils inspired by his studies of birds.

In doing so, da Vinci followed the *constructive approach* to bionics. He first identified biological paradigms, and then transferred them to technical domains in order to look for appropriate fields of application. That means that the constructive approach (also called bottom-up or abstraction bionics) seeks to first understand known natural methods in order to apply them to technical problems later on.

The *analytic approach* instead starts from problems in technical domains. It searches for feasible paradigms in nature in order to identify their essential features and use them to build a solution. So the analytic approach (also called top-down or analogy bionics) identifies known similarities in problems of both domains in order to get inspiration for solving the technical ones.

Since we are looking for alternatives to solve the scalability problems in UC, we start from a defined set of problem constraints. Therefore we will follow the analytic approach by looking for similarities in natural information handling. Basically, UC scalability problems stem from the limited capacities of devices regarding memory, computing power, communication range, and so forth. These in turn result from demand for characteristics such as small size, unobtrusiveness, low price, and so on. Solutions are typically based on countering these limitations by distributing algorithms over numerous devices.

Highly distributed concepts for information handling on the other hand can be found in many biological systems as well as societies. A conceivable classification of these concepts can be derived from hierarchies based on part-of relations. Components of biological systems can be interacting organisms (which also form natural societies), cells or biomolecules. Each organism consists of a number of cells which are in turn formed by molecules, suggesting a 3-tier hierarchy with the tiers respectively.

- Organism
- Cell
- Molecule

Typical distributed biological systems on the organism level (which could also be called natural societies) are animal communities, for example insect colonies and flocks of birds. Examples of coordinated activity on the cell level are clusters and networks of cells, one of the best-known examples being neural networks. On the molecular level, we have to distinguish between organic systems (such as genetic information handling) and inorganic ones (such as annealing matter). The latter do not fall into the realm of biology, but they are examples of molecule interaction in natural systems.

While other classifications of equal power can be defined, we will use the *3-tier architecture* as the foundation of the present chapter's structure. For each tier, we will briefly discuss the basics of a typical system, introduce a corresponding bio-analog algorithm, illustrate its mode of operation using pseudo-code and try to show how it can be extended towards solving UC scalability problems. The chapter's conclusion will be formed by an attempt to translate the idea of bio-analog computing (i.e., decentralized program control) to bio-analog data management (i.e., decentralized data maintenance).

BIO-ANALOG COMPUTING ON THE ORGANISM LEVEL

Basics

Finding good paths through graphs poses an enormous computational problem. The first probabilistic approach to solve this path-finding (i.e., routing) problem was inspired by the behavior of ant colonies searching for food. It was introduced by Dorigo (1992), who called it ant colony optimization (ACO). ACO is a typical member of the organism level of distributed biological systems. It is a meta heuristic that makes up the basis for most so-called "ant algorithms" known today. The first algorithm conforming to the ACO meta heuristic (Dorigo, Maniezzo, & Colorni, 1991) was called ant system (AS). Later on, ant algorithms were adapted to solve various sorts of optimization problems. Examples include the workings of Michel and Middendorf (1999), Stützle and Dorigo (1999) and Gambardella, Taillard, and Agazzi (1999).

The basic idea of an ant algorithm is to imitate the strategy of ant colonies for finding shortest paths between their nest and food sources. Real ants searching for food sources wander about randomly at the beginning of their search process. As soon as an ant has found a food source, it returns to the nest choosing the same way back. It marks its path with a certain amount of chemical secretions called pheromones. Other ants tend to prefer paths with high pheromone concentrations to those with lower concentrations. Since pheromones evaporate over time, they lose their ant-attracting effect gradually. Ants following longer paths cannot mark them as fast as those using the shorter ones. A short path therefore tends to accumulate pheromones faster. Consequently the chance that ants choose short paths grows over time, and ants doing so in turn further increase this chance. This is called an autocatalytic effect. Since an ant's decisions are influenced by pheromones, it is a semi-autonomous agent.

Bio-Analog Algorithm

Ant algorithm implementations rely on "artificial ants", simple agents imitating real ants' behavior to a certain degree. An artificial ant does not have much planning or memory capacity. It is just able to

- Choose its route at branching points of a graph
- Mark its path with pheromones
- Sense pheromone concentration at current alternatives for its next step
- Trace its way back "home"

In order to be worked on by artificial ants, problems and their constraints have to be translated into an adequate representation. For ant algorithms, this means defining a solution to a given problem by a finite number of variables x_i ($i = 1, ..., n$). Artificial ants find their way through solution space by successively choosing values for each of these variables from its respective domain J^i where J^i is a finite set of options. In order to set a variable, each possible value j is assigned a probability of choice $P(x_{ij})$. This probability is defined by:

- Pheromone concentration T_{ij}
- A priority rule V_{ij}
- Weight factors α and β, setting influence of pheromones and priority rule

A value is then chosen following the Monte Carlo method (a class of computational schemes relying on random or pseudo-random numbers, for a more detailed description see, for example, Robert & Casella, 2004) with individual probabilities:

$$P(x_{ij}) = \frac{T_{ij}^{\alpha} \cdot V_{ij}^{\beta}}{\sum_{k \in J^i} T_{ik}^{\alpha} \cdot V_{ik}^{\beta}} \ \forall \ i = 1..n, \ j \in J^i \qquad (1)$$

where the sum of all $P(x_{ij})$ equals 1.

Apart from choice of alternatives at branching points, pheromone excretion is the most important element of ACO algorithms. Real ants continuously produce pheromones, thus marking their routes while they follow them. Artificial ants are in contrast pooled in so-called iterations or generations. First all ants of generation g choose their complete paths, and then all of them mark their respective paths subsequently, influencing choice of ants of later generations $g + i$.

The amount of pheromones used to mark a path's elements is usually proportional to its quality or "length". A path x consisting of n elements x_{ij} of solution space can be assigned a quality and therefore corresponding pheromone amounts T_{ij} for all x_{ij}. The path's quality depends on a target function $F(x)$ measuring path length (where quality is usually an inverse of length).

Pheromone amounts can be computed in each generation as follows:

$$T_{ij} = T_{ij}(1-\rho) + \rho \cdot \begin{cases} 1/F(x) & \forall x_{ij} \in x \\ 0 & \forall x_{ij} \notin x \end{cases} \qquad (2)$$

where ρ indicates pheromone evaporation rate. The basic ant algorithm could therefore be described in pseudocode as follows:

```
translate solutions into paths [x_1j_1, x_2j_2, ..., x_nj_n]
in solution space;
repeat {
    create ant generation;
    for each ant a_m member of current
    generation {
        choose individual path [x_1m_1, x_2m_2,
        ..., x_nm_n] ;
        compute length F([x_1m_1, x_2m_2, ..., x_nm_n])
        of path;
        compute pheromone dose;
        mark elements x_im_i , i = 1.n with
        pheromone dose;
        return to nest (i.e., delete
        ant);
```

```
    }
}
until path with satisfactory quality/
length is found;
```

An example of the working basic ant algorithm can be seen in Figure 1. The figure's upper part shows the paths two ants (a black one and a white one) chose through a solution space. Assuming both ants are members of the same generation, they started at the same time at their nest.

All segments have a certain quality (shown by a number next to the segment). The quality of an ant's path is equal to the sum of all of its components' qualities. The black ant's path (shown by a dotted line) has a quality value of $3+2+1+2 = 8$. The white ant chose a path (the dashed line) with a quality of $1+2+1+2 = 6$. Each of them would mark all of its path's segments with a pheromone dose proportional to this quality value. The segments that were part of both paths would be marked by both ants. Let us assume that at the time when the ants started no segment was marked. After marking, the pheromone concentration on each of the segments would then be as shown in the lower part of the figure.

Variants of the basic ant algorithm include for example restricting the right to excrete pheromones to the ant which has found the best path. In our above example, this would mean that all

segments of the black ant's path would be marked with a pheromone dose of value 8. All other segments would not receive any pheromones. This variation leads to an even stronger preference of ants for shortest paths currently known. While this effect can speed up an ant algorithm significantly, it can also result in preference of a target function's local maxima over global ones.

Another common variant is based on different choices of evaporation rate ρ of pheromones. This modifies the measure of influence of earlier generations' choice of paths on later generations' decisions.

UC Implementation Issues

Due to their reliance on numerous simple agents, ant algorithms seem to be a rather promising approach to countering scalability problems in UC. They provide a paradigm for a simple yet robust method of device coordination. It is suitable for great numbers of devices with severely limited computing power and memory capacity, as artificial ants are also subject to these limitations.

The power of the ant algorithm's communication paradigm (Figure 2) lies in its independence of complex communication infrastructures. It has yet to be exploited for UC domain applications, especially interesting candidates being for example routing problems in ad-hoc networks

Figure 1. Ants marking their paths through solution space

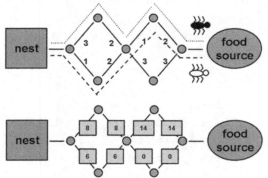

Figure 2. Communication paradigms

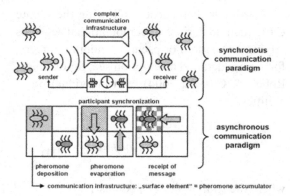

which involve finding paths in networks subject to dynamically changing topologies which therefore require robust methods. More on ad-hoc networks and their specific problems can be found in the chapters "Wireless and Mobile Communication" and "Opportunistic Networks".

In standard paradigms, communication means that a sender produces a message which is somehow routed to its receiver(s). This demands synchronization of sender and receiver plus allocation and coordination of a number of communication channels.

Ants' communication does not need synchronization of participants. Therefore its paradigm could be called asynchronous. It only requires some kind of evaporating pheromones, a "surface" able to hold those for a while and ant-type agents able to use and sense them. Since the surface provides message contents in a push and pop manner (each surface segment working like a mail box for pheromone messages), the number of participating devices is not an important factor of communication complexity.

Applied to the above-mentioned ad-hoc network routing problems, ant-based approaches would clearly benefit from this robustness and simplicity of asynchronous communication. No special error handling would be needed in case of a device breakdown. Ants could quickly react to the resulting loss of a communication link. Simply following their basic algorithm, they would search for a new path bypassing inactive segments. A corresponding ant-based UC implementation of asynchronous communication would be based on:

- Pheromones (or a digital equivalent, e.g., a "pheromone protocol")
- A surface (i.e., immobile devices able to hold pheromones and let them evaporate)
- Ants/agents (UC devices able to handle messages based on pheromone protocol)

BIO-ANALOG COMPUTING ON THE CELL LEVEL

Basics

Sets of cells within organisms can be seen as sets of simple components able to perform various tasks in a distributed manner. An excellent example of a distributed biological system on the cell level is the nervous system in humans and animals. It is a network of cells called neurons. The ability of neural networks to learn input patterns (stimuli) and corresponding outputs (reactions) makes them well suited for a broad palette of tasks. This palette includes pattern recognition in general, speech analysis, gaming and other tasks, many of which are relevant to UC. Networks of neurons, especially their ability to adapt to new situations by learning, were first described by Hebb (1949) in his book, *The Organization of Behavior*. A learning rule, the so-called Hebb rule, was followed by other workings by Minsky and Papert (1969) with their "Perceptrons", Kohonen's (1983, 1995) "Self-Organizing Maps" and others. One strength of neural networks is that they are able to learn patterns without having to abstract formal rules that define those patterns. Knowledge about patterns and corresponding reactions is stored within the entirety of neurons in a network, thus being truly distributed.

Neurons (or nerve cells), the basic components of neural networks, can be described as accumulators communicating via junctions of their cell bodies, the so-called synapses. Each neuron receives bioelectrical impulses at these synapses. These impulses are neural networks' means of communication. Synapses are able to biochemically modulate impulse strength and effect, but apart from this modulation, impulses are all-or-nothing, that is, binary. Information can be coded in temporal and/or spatial patterns of impulses. Neurons accumulate incoming impulses over time or over different synapses. Each impulse changes the electrical level of the cell body until it reaches a certain threshold. Once the threshold is reached, the neuron fires an impulse or series of impulses in turn.

Bio-Analog Algorithm

Thus, single neurons can be regarded as relatively simple components. This makes it possible to describe an artificial neuron (a natural neuron's technical equivalent) using a small number of mathematical functions.

A typical artificial neuron as shown in Figure 3 is defined by three different functions:

- An input or propagation function f_{prop}
- An activation function f_{act}
- An output function f_{out}

The propagation function defines how incoming impulses $w_x \times o_x$ (subject to output o_x of previous neurons and so-called weight factors w_x of connecting synapses) are accumulated. Most often the sum $\Sigma_k (w_k \times o_k)$ of incoming impulses is chosen. The activation function is used to compute the new state $s(t + 1)$ of the neuron subject to input and old state $s(t)$:

$$s(t+1) = f_{act}(f_{prop}(w_x, o_x), s(t)) = f_{act} (\Sigma_k (w_k \times o_k), s(t))$$
(3)

Figure 3. Model of an artificial neuron

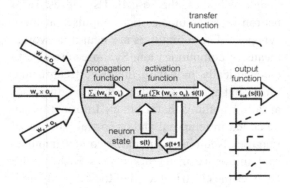

Neuron output is an equivalent of firing rate described by the output function of a neuron. It depends on neuron state in turn representing an electrical level. Output functions (as seen in the lower right of Figure 3) can be linear (meaning output activity is proportional to electrical level), threshold-type (full output or none at all) or sigmoid. Sigmoid functions are the most accurate of these three approximations of real neuron behavior. Activation and output function are sometimes merged into the so-called transfer function.

The output o_x of a neuron x is modulated by a weight factor w_x of the corresponding synapse before it arrives at the next neuron. Weight factors can be positive or negative, in the latter case simulating a so-called inhibitive synapse. Additionally, they are a means of long-term information storage in a neural network. The function a given network computes varies with its weight values.

The power of the approach is considerably affected by the number of neurons involved. Modern artificial neural networks can involve five-digit numbers of neurons (which is roughly the same as the nervous systems of some snails). The human brain in contrast consists of up to 100 billion neurons. The effective computing power of such a large network is greater than the sum of individual neuron capabilities of all its cells.

SOMs

A good example for operating neural networks is the so-called self-organizing map (or SOM). SOMs were initially developed in order to augment understanding of brain organization, which was observed to heavily rely on topographic structures. They are also called "Kohonen cards".

SOMs are an approach to classification problems based on unsupervised learning. This means they are able to learn unknown target functions. The output of an SOM is generated by a set of neurons in the so-called output layer. Depending on input patterns, different neurons of the output layer react. The neurons in the output layer form a two-dimensional field. Their distribution with regard to their output is a topographic map.

This means that neighboring neurons in the output layer react to similar input patterns. The neurons of the input layer in contrast form a single row. Input is fed to the network in the form of vectors. These vectors have as many components as there are neurons in the input layer. Simple SOMs often work with binary input vectors. The algorithm implemented by these simple SOMs has the following basic structure (presented in pseudo-code):

```
for x = 1...input length
    feed input layer neuron n_ix component
    i_x of input vector;
for each neuron n_oy of output layer {
    feed n_oy input vector via synapses
    w_xy;
    compute Euclidean distance
```
$$\sqrt{\sum_{z=1}^{input\ length}(i_z - w_{zy})^2};$$
```
}
find minimum
```
$$\min_j \sqrt{\sum_{z=1}^{input\ length}(i_z - w_{zj})^2};$$
```
mark n_oj as winning neuron;
for each synapse w_xj of winning neuron
    set w_xj = w_xj × (1 − α) + i_x × α;
    // where α is the SOM's learning fac-
    tor;
```

Thus each neuron in the input layer receives input via exactly one synapse. The corresponding synapse weight equals 1. The propagation function is $f_{prop}(i_x) = 1 \cdot i_x = i_x$. Since $s(t)$, $f_{act}(i_x, s(t))$ and $f_{out}(s(t))$, and along with them the transfer function also equal i_x, the input layer neurons do nothing but propagate components i_x of the input vector. Output layer neurons, in contrast, receive input from multiple synapses and use more complex propagation, activation and output functions.

An SOM's learning method involves change of weight values as mentioned above. For each

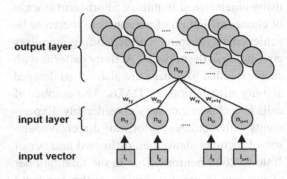

Figure 4. A self-organizing map

input, the SOM computes the winning neuron within the output layer. The winning neuron is the individual with a minimal Euclidean distance between its incoming synapse weight vector and input vector (computed using the above-mentioned complex functions). The network adapts this neuron's incoming synapse weights. It reduces each one's difference to the corresponding input vector component. The degree of adaptation is defined by a so-called learning factor. Sometimes the incoming synapse weights of neighboring neurons are also adapted (but, usually, to a lesser degree than the winning neurons). A schematic depiction of a SOM can be seen in Figure 4.

UC Implementation Issues

While a critical factor for a neural network's computing power is the number of neurons in it, their mode of cooperation is also essential for the approach. Each neuron can (as a simple accumulator) be seen as a cheap, multipurpose device. This means that it has no fixed tasks.

In a natural neural network, the neurons seem to cooperate on a temporal basis. They build neuron clusters via aggregation based on the tasks at hand. A cluster of neurons can be thought of as a sub-network that is temporarily dedicated to a specific task. The aggregation of neurons based on a synchronization using semistable patterns of bioelectric activity.

All data exchange in a neural network is done using bioelectrical impulses. Short-term storage of cluster affiliation of neurons can therefore be achieved by keeping corresponding impulses circulating in the network. Activity patterns with such extended life spans are also called delayed activity distributions or DADs. The number of cells in a cluster can vary considerably. Experiments with monkeys performing direct comparison of pictures showed an estimated number of 1000 to 2000 neurons. Due to the total number of neurons in monkey brains on the one hand and the estimated number of DADs on the other, some activity distributions must also overlap. A further interesting characteristic of DADs is their robustness. A DAD is saved even if single neurons in a cluster do not contribute to the correct reproduction of its activity pattern. Only severe distortion of patterns (which could in UC scenarios be caused by fragmentation of a network due to breakdown of communication links) can destroy DADs and therefore prematurely end cluster synchronization.

UC applications would benefit from such cheap-to-produce, multipurpose devices using a robust, dynamic method of coordination. This is especially true with regard to scalability issues. The example of the SOM shows that neural networks are—among other fields of application—a good approach to pattern recognition as we stated at the beginning of this section. Pattern recognition in turn is an important factor of UC processes such as speech recognition (see the chapter "Mobile Speech Recognition"). In order to implement the neural network paradigm within the UC domain, we need:

- **Cells:** Devices that are small, cheap, and multipurpose, which is a basic UC requirement
- **Synapses:** In form of interfaces for fast device-to-device communication
- **DADs:** Circulating messages telling devices which task/network they belong to and what its working cycle is

BIO-ANALOG COMPUTING ON THE MOLECULAR LEVEL

Basics

One of the most prominent members of the molecular level of algorithmic prototypes inspired by nature is the so-called genetic algorithm. Genetic algorithms are heuristic methods based on works on cellular automata (see, for example, Adami, 1998). They are among the best-known members of a class of methods called evolutionary algorithms (Bäck, 1999).

Formal genetic algorithms were first introduced by Holland (1962, 1973) and De Jong (1985). The term "genetic algorithm" dates from one of Bagley's early works (1967). The basic idea of a genetic algorithm is to transfer the strategy known as "survival of the fittest" to optimization problems. To this end, genetic algorithms translate the descriptions of problems and potential solutions into a so-called genetic language.

The scheme of a genetic algorithm is based on mixing the designs of two parent individuals (candidate solutions). Thereby it produces new child individuals possessing a slightly different feature palette. If the children are fitter than their parents (i.e., the newfound solutions are better than the original ones) they are used for further mixing (called "breeding").

The breeding procedure (called the "crossover") is shown in Figure 5. This algorithm is usually executed until a satisfactory solution quality has been reached.

Since the breeding procedure can be executed in a highly distributed manner (meaning it is an example for massive parallelism), genetic algorithms lend themselves to a closer inspection with regard to scalability problems in UC.

Bio-Analog Algorithm

Basically, each genetic algorithm's structure can be described by a simple five-step scheme. The

Figure 5. Binary chromosome crossover

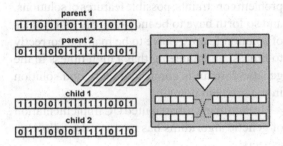

first step of this scheme initializes the algorithm while the other four are repeated cyclically. The five steps are as follows:

- Creation of starting population;
- Selection of "fittest" individuals;
- Crossover (or recombination);
- Mutation;
- Next generation.

Genetic algorithms work on a set of potential solutions to a specific problem. A solution set is called a "population".

Before the genetic algorithm can work, problem and candidate solutions have to be translated into a suitable form.

Typically, an individual solution is defined by a vector which is called a "chromosome".

Each index of a chromosome codes the value of a solution feature. In the simplest case, features are binary, that is, an index codes presence or absence of a corresponding feature. Population size depends on the nature of the problem, but a typical population contains several hundreds or thousands of possible solutions.

Using pseudo-code, we can define a basic genetic algorithm as shown in Box A.

Variants of this basic algorithm include binary contest selection and alternative mutation procedures, among others. Binary contest selection is based on working with two populations simultaneously, alternating between them. In each cycle, the solutions of the active population are compared pairwise, choosing the best one respectively. The winners are copied to the inactive population, which becomes the active one in the next cycle.

The form of mutation shown above is the simplest one, called bit flip mutation. More complex alternatives are mutations flipping several randomly chosen bits or even bit strings. The alternative procedures are compared in Figure 6. Note that mutation is included in genetic algorithms in order to guarantee genetic diversity and thus maximize the chances of finding the best solutions. It does not necessarily produce fitter individuals.

UC Implementation Issues

The basic form of a genetic language is the binary presentation of presence or absence of single features, as mentioned above. Due to this simple code, operations on chromosomes neither require much storage capacity nor advanced computing power. The power of the genetic algorithms' paradigm on the other hand is based on the number of potential solutions that can be worked on simultaneously. Since individual chromosomes are independent of each other except for crossover, populations can be easily distributed. Researchers commonly apply genetic algorithms to scheduling problems (which are characteristic of the multiprocess systems with limited resources in UC scenarios) with success. The interested reader will find more about scheduling and planning problems in the chapter "Ambient Learning". For these two reasons, genetic algorithms seem to be predestined for implementation in distributed UC scenarios.

The simplicity of artificial genetic languages does in fact mirror real life genetics. The genetic code of organisms exists in the form of molecule chains called DNA (deoxyribonucleic acid). The chains are in turn composed of pairs of bases. A group of three pairs of bases is called codon. Codons code either an amino acid or a special start or stop sequence which guides molecules "reading" or "writing" DNA. There are four types of bases (called adenine, guanine, cytosine, and thymine), so the genetic language knows only $4^3 = 64$ "words".

The main problem of genetic algorithms on the other hand also stems from their simple coding paradigm. A correct translation from the technical domain to the genetic domain is most often not trivial. "Correctness" of translation in this context covers mainly two aspects. *First*, all problem constraints, possible features of solutions, and so forth have to be included. *Second*, values of solution features have to be mapped correctly to fitness, guaranteeing that a high fitness in the genetic domain is connected to a good solution in the problem domain.

In summary, a distributed UC implementation of genetic algorithms has to cover the following aspects:

Box A.

```
// initialization
for  x = 1..population_size  {

        generate candidate solution  s_x  by randomly

        choosing features  fx_1..fx_n ;

        if  ( s_x ∉ P_0 )

                add candidate solution  s_x  to population  P_0 ;

        else

                return to "generate candidate solution";

}
cycle = 0;
while (no satisfactory quality solution  s_sat  found) do {

        // selection

        for all solutions  s_x ∈ P_cycle  {

                compute fitness  f(s_x) ;

                // choose solutions for further breeding

                // "survival" depends on fitness

                if  ( f(s_x) < random_value )  delete  s_x ;

        }

        // fill vacant positions w/ copies of randomly

        // chosen solutions  s_rand

        if  ( size(P_cycle) < population_size )  {

                for  ( x = size(P_cycle) + 1..population_size )

                        copy  s_rand  to  s_x ;

        }

        // crossover

        P_rest = P_cycle ;
```

continued on following page

Box A. continued

```
for (x = 1..population_size/2) {
    // cross each member exactly once, choosing
    // random pairs (s_rand_1, s_rand_2)
    select s_rand_1 ∈ P_rest; delete s_rand_1 from P_rest;
    select s_rand_2 ∈ P_rest; delete s_rand_2 from P_rest;
    // generate children c1, c2
    select index i_rand;  // random index i_rand
```

$$c_1 = (frand\_1_1 .. frand\_1_{i_{rand}}, frand\_2_{i_{rand}+1} .. frand\_2_n);$$

```
    add c1 to P_cycle+1;
```

$$c_2 = (frand\_2_1 .. frand\_2_{i_{rand}}, frand\_1_{i_{rand}+1} .. frand\_1_n);$$

```
    add c2 to P_cycle+1;
}
// mutation
for x = 1..population_size {
    // mutate? decide for each solution s_x
    if (random_number_x > random_threshold) {
        select random index i_random of s_x ∈ P_cycle+1;
        // flip feature bit of s_x
        if (fx_{i_random} = 1) then fx_{i_random} = 0;
        else fx_{i_random} = 1;
    }
}
// next generation
cycle = cycle+1;
}
// end of procedure
```

- Translation (of the UC problem at hand into a "genetic" representation);
- Definition of a fitness function (with the above-mentioned characteristics);
- Mutation and crossover operations (replacing the original UC algorithm).

BIO-ANALOG DATA MANAGEMENT

Basics

We saw in the sections discussing bio-analog computing on the cell level that a network of neurons knows two methods of data storage. Bioelectrical impulses are its means of short-term storage and

Figure 6. Alternative mutation procedures

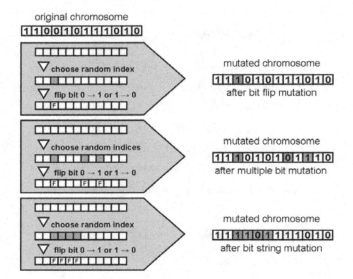

communication. Long-term storage, on the other hand, is based on the biochemical modulation of these impulses. The biochemical features of synapses are therefore a biological equivalent of digital memory.

We know from practical experience that this biological memory is capable of real time mass data management. Sensory organs such as eyes and ears produce continuous streams of input which have to be handled fast enough to react to potential threats and urgencies. Simultaneously, our memory is able to retrieve important data with appropriate speed and accuracy.

In UC, we are already facing similar problems. Powerful and almost ubiquitous multimedia recorders assume the role of sensory organs. Due to the progressive miniaturization and price-reduction of such devices, we could soon have a massive information oversupply, where important data are untraceable within huge amounts of garbage. This is what can be called the mass data problem (Limberger, 2006).

In the previous sections we tried to demonstrate the benefits of bio-analog computing based on various levels of biological systems for dealing with scalability problems in UC algorithms. We will now show how bio-analogy can be utilized not only in an algorithmic sense, but also to counter UC data management problems. In this case, the biochemical features of synapses will provide us with inspiration, and the decentralized nature of their operating mode will again lead us to a highly distributed approach.

Bio-Analog Algorithm

According to a neuropsychological theory of memory called "levels-of-processing theory" (Craik & Lockhard, 1972), data in biological memories is not fixed. It fades away over time if not stimulated by regular access.

Since data are accessed as they are needed for processing, the frequency of being accessed is closely related to their level of processing. Therefore, data with a deep level of processing tend to remain in memory. Data which are not as deeply processed in contrast lose detail, eventually fading from memory. This thesis of the levels-of-processing theory mirrors the fact that synapses' biochemical features can also degrade over time if they are not stimulated by bioelectrical impulses. The process of stimulation is also called consolidation.

Due to the spatial distribution of neurons and synapses in neural systems, data are also distributed over a network. Even so, they are embedded in interconnected systems of storage units. Whenever neurons receive an impulse over their synapses, the synapses' features are consolidated in the biochemical process. At the same time, summation of impulses gives rise to further bioelectrical activity, starting the same consolidation process in other neurons "downstream" (see Figure 7).

Consequently, the data contained in a synapse can be thought of as directly connected to data contained in synapses of neighboring neurons. The farther we go in terms of neuron-to-neuron "hops", the looser the connection becomes.

As a result of this interconnectivity of distributed data fragments, we have a "neighborhood" concept or context for each fragment. A context-oriented storage paradigm has several consequences. *First*, access of data is executed in an associative way. As we all know, it is easier to remember facts if we have a clue, that is, another fact which is closely related. *Second*, consolidation

effects spread out over associative connections. If a data fragment in memory is consolidated, closely related fragments are also consolidated. As a consequence, whole complexes of information tend to remain in memory when relevant parts of them are processed. Likewise, complexes of less interesting data which are seldom accessed tend to fade from memory collectively. This mechanism acts as a filter, keeping interesting data in memory and filtering out less important content. It is therefore exactly what we need to counter the mass data problem. A pseudo-code implementation of access-driven consolidation could look like in Box B.

An important question is how to implement reduction of detail level or resolution as the digital equivalent of fading memory fragments. In the case of many multimedia data types recorded by the above-mentioned UC devices, this is easy. The corresponding data types (video, audio, and graphics) all have one or more resolution dimensions.

This can be resolution in time (applicable for video and audio) or graphic resolution (for video and graphics). Data can be reduced with regard to these resolutions, directly mirroring biological fading of details without loss of a whole data

Figure 7. Consolidation effects spreading out in a network

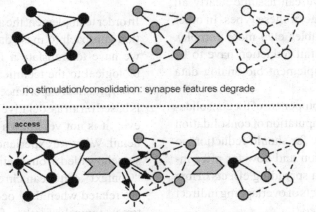

no stimulation/consolidation: synapse features degrade

stimulation: consolidation effects spread out, features are saved

Box B.

```
main loop (executed for the life time of a specific
data base D ) {
        // first compute consolidation activity
        for all data fragments  frag_x ∈ data base D {
                if ( is_accessed( frag_x ) ) then {
                        mark_as_directly_consolidated( frag_x ) ;
                        for all
                        frag_y : ∃ synapse syn_xy connecting frag_x and frag_y )
                                mark_as_indirectly_consolidated( frag_y ) ;
                }
        }
        // then compute consolidation effects
        for all data fragments  frag_x ∈ data base D {
                if ( not_consolidated( frag_x ) )
                        // greatly reduce detail
                        reduce_resolution ( frag_x , great_extent) ;
                else if ( indirectly_consolidated ( frag_x ) )
                        // moderately reduce detail
                        reduce_resolution ( frag_x , some_extent) ;
        } // directly consolidated fragments unchanged
} // end of main loop
```

fragment. We are focusing on scalability issues of UC scenarios, so we can assume nearly all relevant data to be of one of these types. In other cases (such as texts, tables etc.) more complex methods of gradual detail reduction have to be defined in order to implement bio-analog data management.

A second essential component of the consolidation approach is the computation of consolidation effect summation. How far should reduction go after direct consolidation and how far after indirect consolidation via spreading effects? How could the combined effects of overlapping indirect consolidations be defined?

UC Implementation Issues

In order to implement the access-driven consolidation approach to mass data management in UC, we have to translate a further factor from the biological to the technical domain. It is evident from practical experience that biological memory is based on an associative access paradigm. However, it is not yet known how this is realized in detail. What we experience through our senses is somehow filed in our brain on the basis of context. "Context" can mean chronological (experiences are related when they occur at similar points in time), topical or other forms of neighborhood relationship.

Figure 8. Mapping data fragments to graphic representation

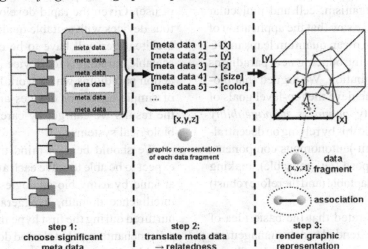

Let us assume that we want to implement a system that is able to manage mass data through a combination of fading and consolidation. To this end, we have to register users' access to data fragments. Further, we have to compute consolidating effects of this access and how they spread through our database. In order to do so, we embed the data into a space that is spanned by our definition of relatedness. This definition in turn can only be based on what we know about our data, that is, on metadata. The expectedly high-dimensional data space has to be presented to users in a comprehensible form they can work with. This usually means translation to a low-dimensional representation, preferably a graphic one. These prerequisites imply a three-step mapping of data to accessible context-embedded data fragments (as shown in Figure 8).

First, significant metadata types have to be chosen for each data fragment. These should represent the fragment well with respect to its context. *Next*, the metadata chosen must be mapped to axes (i.e., 1-dimensional rooms), preserving relations. If, for example, "date" was chosen, fragments stored at similar dates get mapped to neighboring points. In a *third step*, graphic equivalents for axes should be chosen. These equivalents could be spatial (an axis would become the x-, y- or z-axis

of our graphic representation) or of a different kind (the metadata could be translated to size, color, form, or any other aspect of a fragment's graphic representation).

Resuming what we said above, we can define the components necessary for managing UC mass data in a bio-analog way (based on fading and access-driven consolidation):

- Recording devices (complementing data with metadata for embedding in contexts);
- Associative filing paradigm for data fragments;
- Graphical user interface (for gathering access to data within its context);
- Method for computing consolidation effects (especially patterns of their spreading and summation of overlapping indirect activation effects);
- Reduction function for non-consolidated data.

SUMMARY

Following the analytic approach of bionics, we identified a number of bio-analog distributed algorithms matching UC scalability problem constraints in this chapter. By means of examples from the organism, cell and molecular levels respectively, we saw that the application of these algorithms can mean quantum leaps in UC scalability issues by introducing new paradigms of algorithmic distribution. We argued that bio-analog approaches achieve the top-level goals of (technical) scalability, *openness*, *manageability* and *longevity*. They do this by relying on decentralized systems of (semi-)autonomous components which are multipurpose (i.e., reusable), making complete systems adaptable (and therefore robust) in turn.

We also demonstrated that the basic idea of bio-analogy can be extended to data management scalability problems, resulting in truly distributed flow of control and data as promoted by K. Kelly (1994) in his book "Out of Control". Finally we briefly discussed which foundations have to be laid in order to apply bio-analog algorithms to UC scalability problems.

FUTURE RESEARCH DIRECTIONS

In the course of the discussion mentioned above, we saw that there is no trivial mapping of natural societies' or systems' solutions to computational problems in UC. As the term analogy already implies, following a bio-analog approach does not mean copying biological strategies and concepts and reusing them in the technical scenario at hand, regardless of the latter. In fact researchers have to identify valuable basic ideas implemented in biological systems and try to map them to feasible algorithms, for example in the UC domain. This means an imitation of behavior, not functionality.

However, the use of bio-analogies can provide valuable impulses for future UC paradigms. Examples for serviceable bio-analog algorithms already in existence include among others Ant-Net (Di Caro & Dorigo, 1997, used for adaptive routing tasks in communications networks) and JGAP (a Java framework for genetic algorithm

use, see http://jgap.sourceforge.net/ for examples of use). Given the rapid development of ubiquitous devices with suitable qualities, existing UC architectures will have to be complemented by scalable paradigms for device interaction. Interaction paradigms which work for huge numbers of simple agents or devices are in turn one of the results we can get by careful inspection of biological systems.

We should bear in mind that we could not expect to be able to solve each and every problem at hand by using bio-analogies. In the artificial intelligence domain, exaggerated expectations nurtured during the first hype in the 1960's led to a disenchantment that slowed down development considerably until recently. In order not to repeat this error, we have to approach bionics (within the UC context as well as beyond) with more realistic visions. By realistic, we mean that we can indeed expect to get the inspiration for more elegant and efficient solutions to some of our current and future problems. The emphasis of this statement is on the term efficient as almost all biological systems are optimized for a satisfactory performance with minimal complexity. Good examples are motion (where for example sharks have a skin structure that minimizes skin friction and thus can move through their environment with minimal effort. This effect was successfully transferred to cargo ships, thus lowering freight costs) and information handling (where biology uses the genetic minimal language as described in the section "bio-analog computing on the molecular level"). Thus bionics (and socionics) will be not the holy grail of UC, but they can nonetheless provide valuable ideas and impulses that help in implementing the UC vision.

REFERENCES

Adami, C. (1998). *Introduction to artificial life*. New York: Springer-Verlag.

Bäck, T. (1996). Evolutionary algorithms. *Theory and practice: Evolution strategies, evolution-*

ary programming, genetic algorithms. Oxford University Press.

Bagley, J. D. (1967). *The behavior of adaptive systems which employ genetic and correlation algorithms*. Unpublished doctoral dissertation, University of Michigan.

Craik, F. I. M., & Lockhard, R. S. (1972). Levels of processing. A framework for memory research. *Journal of Verbal Learning and Verbal Behavior, 11*, 671-684.

De Jong, K. A. (1985). Genetic algorithms: A 10 year perspective. In *Proceedings of the 1st International Conference on Genetic Algorithms* (pp. 169-177). Lawrence Erlbaum Associates, Inc.

Di Caro, G., & Dorigo, M. (1997). *AntNet: A mobile agents approach to adaptive routing* (Tech. Rep. IRIDIA/97-12). Universit Libre de Bruxelles, Belgium.

Dorigo, M. (1992). *Optimization, learning and natural algorithms*. Unpublished doctoral dissertation, Politecnico di Milan, Italy.

Dorigo, M., Maniezzo, V., & Colorni, A. (1991). *Ant system: An autocatalytic optimizing process* (Working paper No. 91-016). Politecnico di Milan, Italy.

Gambardella, L. M., Taillard, E., & Agazzi, G. (1999). MACS-VRPTW: A multiple ant colony system for vehicle routing problems with time windows. In D. Corne, M. Dorigo, & F. Glover (Eds.), *New ideas in optimization*. Maidenhead, UK: McGraw-Hill Ltd.

Hebb, D. O. (1949). *The organization of behavior: A neuropsychological theory*. New York: Wiley.

Holland, J. H. (1962). Outline for a logical theory of adaptive systems. *Journal of the ACM, 9*(3), 297-314.

Holland, J. H. (1973). Genetic algorithms and the optimal allocation of trials. *SIAM Journal on Computing, 2*(2), 88-105.

Kohonen, T. (1983). *Self-organization and associative memory*. Berlin: Springer.

Kohonen, T. (1995). *Self-organizing maps*. 3. Berlin: Auflage Springer.

Kelly, K. (1994). *Out of control*. New York: Addison-Wesley.

Limberger, T. (2006). *Interaktionsgestützte bioanaloge Konsolidierung von Datensammlungen*. Unpublished doctoral dissertation. Technical University of Darmstadt, Tectum-Verlag Marburg.

Michel, R., & Middendorf, M. (1999). An ACO algorithm for the shortest common supersequence problem. In Corne, D., Dorigo, M., & Glover, F. (Eds.), *New ideas in optimization*. Maidenhead, UK: McGraw-Hill.

Minsky, M., & Papert, S. (1969). *Perceptrons* (Enlarged edition, 1988). MIT Press.

Robert, C. P., & Casella, G. (2004). *Monte Carlo statistical methods* (2nd ed.). New York: Springer-Verlag.

Steele, J. E. (1995) How do we get there? In C. Gray (Ed.) *The Cyborg Handbook* (pp. 55-60). New York: Routledge.

Stützle, T., & Dorigo, M. (1999). ACO algorithms for the traveling salesman problem. In Miettinen, K., Mäkelä, M. M., Neittaanmaki, P., & Periaux, J. (Eds.), *Evolutionary algorithms in engineering and computer science* (pp. 163-183). Wiley.

ADDITIONAL READING

Alba, E. (2005). *Parallel metaheuristics: A new class of algorithms*. Wiley-Interscience.

Arbib, M. A. (2002). *The handbook of brain theory and neural networks* (2nd ed.). MIT Press.

Back, T. (1996). *Evolutionary algorithms in theory and practice: Evolution strategies, evolutionary programming, genetic algorithms.* Oxford University Press.

Bishop, C. M. (1996). *Neural networks for pattern recognition.* Oxford University Press.

Bosque, M. (2002). *Understanding 99% of artificial neural networks: Introduction & tricks.* Writers Club Press.

Chambers, L. D. (2000). *The practical handbook of genetic algorithms* (2nd ed.). Chapman & Hall/CRC.

Dorigo, M. (Ed.). (2006). *Ant colony optimization and swarm intelligence* (1st ed.). Springer.

Dorigo, M., Di Caro, G., & Sampels, M. (Eds.). (2002, September 12-14). In *Proceedings of Ant Algorithms: Third International Workshop, ANTS 2002,* Brussels, Belgium.

Fausett, L. V. (1994). *Fundamentals of neural networks.* Prentice Hall.

Gallant, S. I. (1993). *Neural network learning and expert systems* (Bradford Books). MIT Press.

Goldberg, D. E. (1989). *Genetic algorithms in search, optimization, and machine learning.* Addison-Wesley.

Gurney, K. (1997). *An introduction to neural networks.* CRC.

Gwiazda, D. T. (2006). *Genetic algorithms reference.* Tomasz Gwiazda.

Hassoun, M. H. (1995). *Fundamentals of artificial neural networks.* MIT Press.

Haupt, R. L., & Haupt, S. E. (2004). *Practical genetic algorithms* (2nd ed.). Wiley-Interscience.

Haykin, S. (1998). *Neural networks: A comprehensive foundation* (2nd ed.). Prentice Hall.

Heaton, J. T. (2005). *Introduction to neural networks with java.* Heaton Research, Inc.

Davis, L. (1987). *Genetic algorithms and simulated annealing* (Research Notes in Artificial Intelligence). Morgan Kaufmann.

Langdon, W. B., & Poli, R. (2002). *Foundations of genetic programming* (1st ed.). Springer.

Mehrotra, K., Mohan, C. K., & Ranka, S. (1996). *Elements of artificial neural networks* (Complex Adaptive Systems). MIT Press.

Miki, T. (2001). *Brainware: Bio-inspired architecture and its hardware implementation.* World Scientific Publishing Company.

Mitchell, M. (1998). *An introduction to genetic algorithms* (Complex Adaptive Systems). MIT Press.

Olariu, S., & Zomaya, A. Y. (Eds.). (2006). *Handbook of bioinspired algorithms and applications* (Chapman & Hall/CRC Computer & Information Science). Chapman & Hall/CRC.

Rossmann, T., & Tropea, C. (Eds.). (2006). *Bionik: Aktuelle Forschungsergebnisse in Natur-, Ingenieur- und Geisteswissenschaft* (1st ed.). Springer.

Salamon, P., Sibani, P., & Frost, R. (2002). *Facts, conjectures, and improvements for simulated annealing (SIAM monographs on mathematical modeling and computation) (Monographs on mathematical modeling and computation).* Society for Industrial and Applied Mathematic.

Chapter III
Ubiquitous Services and Business Processes

Alistair Barros
SAP Research, Australia

ABSTRACT

In the commercial world, the value of ubiquitous computing applications is proportional to the range of business services that can be accessed in device-consumptive ways. Services originate in legacy applications of organizations, and are developed and operated typically in heterogeneous environments. Service-oriented architecture (SOA), supported by a complex stack of Web services standards, addresses ways in which software components of diverse applications can be homogeneously interacted with and composed. Thus, SOA provides a crucial mechanism for making services accessible to ubiquitous computing applications. In this chapter, we shed light on what SOA entails, based on Web services interfaces and messaging, and service composition through single-party process orchestration and multiparty choreography languages. For the latter, concrete patterns are used to describe the capabilities of prospective standards. Ways in which SOA needs be extended to allow wider and more flexible service trading, typified in current developments through service marketplaces, are then discussed. Such extensions, we argue, converge with directions in ubiquitous computing through so-called ubiquitous service networks and service ecosystems.

INTRODUCTION

Over recent years, service-oriented architecture (SOA) has gained mainstream acceptance as a strategy for consolidating and repurposing legacy applications to dynamic market needs through self-contained, reusable and configurable services. As fostered through the *Web Services*

standards, services, once in place, can interoperate with other services and be composed into long-running business processes spanning intra- and inter-organizational boundaries.

As Web services technologies mature, and commercial-scale SOAs shift from early adoption to mainstream development, a new revolution of service-orientation is emerging. Beyond the coordination of Web services in supply and value chains, a strategic trend for flexibly trading Web services into new and unforseen markets is emerging. This development is shaping ubiquitous computing (UC) initiatives such as digital communities, service marketplaces and dynamic trading networks.

In this chapter, we provide insights into the ways in which Web services support the development of SOA, and how these need to evolve in the more ambitious UC setting.

In section "Service-Oriented Architecture Fundamentals", we present a background on SOA and details of *software interfacing* through Web services interface definition (WSDL) and *messaging* through simple object access protocol (SOAP). In section "Web Services Composition", we look at mechanisms for supporting the composition of Web services through business processes. Insights into intra-organizational, process *orchestration* are presented in terms of the widely referenced Web services business process execution language (WS-BPEL) and its support of workflow patterns. The inter-organizational process *choreography* layer is discussed through currently developing modelling concepts, service interactions and insights into a particular standards effort Web services choreography definition language (WS-CDL). In section "Scaling SOA for UC Applications", we chart the vision of SOA for UC applications, discussing how the recent developments of software-as-as-service applications are giving rise to wide-spanning UC service networks and service ecosystems. Accordingly, we discuss some open issues and future challenges which identify where present capabilities of SOA need scaling for UC. Finally, the chapter is concluded with a summary.

SERVICE-ORIENTED ARCHITECTURE FUNDAMENTALS

Fundamentals

Broadly speaking, there are two aspects of software architectures which impact the development and operation of applications. The first is software layering made possible by decoupling application functionality into separate and stand-alone parts known as software components (Szyperski, 2004). This fosters flexible reuse of otherwise unwieldy application monoliths, through independent deployment of individual components and their composition into more value-added service offerings. The second aspect is keeping applications focussed on business logic and relying on dedicated middleware to support platform functions such as naming and directory service, remote procedure calls, security, messaging, and persistence.

Distributed computing frameworks such as CORBA and, over recent years, J2EE and .NET based application servers have emerged in support of enterprise application integration (EAI) strategy. Through EAI, standard mechanisms are available for accessing and interacting with applications functions in different and heterogeneous environments in the enterprise's IT landscape. In addition, related functions across different applications, for example, for purchase order processing, are grouped to yield coherent and reusable business components.

With the proliferation of Web services, we nowadays speak increasingly of service-oriented architectures (SOA). Naturally the question arises as to whether Web services and SOA are substantially different from what has come before. As trite as it may sound, the answer is: yes and no. Understanding this lies at the heart of the whole posit of Web services. Consider collaborating partners (e.g., retailer, supplier, and shipper) in a supply chain with shared business processes spanning different applications operating in the

Figure 1. Software layering in a service-oriented architecture

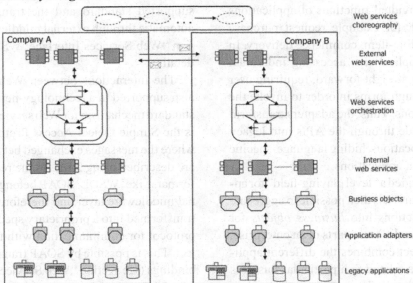

separate IT environments. To coordinate the processes in the supply chain, different applications need to interoperate. However, the mechanism for interoperability is not obvious because of the variety of middleware products (for naming and directory service, remote procedure call and the like) operating at the different partners.

One possibility is for point-to-point middleware integration between each pair of partners. Each partner provides adapters for its middleware and those of other partners. Clearly, as the number of partners increases, the middleware becomes more heterogeneous, making this approach cumbersome (considering also different middleware versions for supporting different software releases). A further complication is that software invocations across business boundaries are more long-running unlike invocations within applications which are generally short-lived. In the supply chain example, when a purchase order is issued by a retailer to a supplier, the supplier may have to check availability of line-items, which it cannot supply through other suppliers. In this situation, it cannot immediately respond to the retailer. The retailer's process does not

block and wait for the response *synchronously*, but continues with other activities and waits for the response *asynchronously*.

Thus, Web services came into being, precisely because of the problems of interoperability between applications *across* different environments. The Web, and more particularly, URL, HTTP and XML becoming widely adopted, made it possible to develop a set of standards constituting an *external* middleware layer (Alonso, Casati, Kuno, & Machiraju, 2004) that can interoperate with the *internal* middleware of companies. Applications shared between collaborating partners are coded against the external middleware while translations to internal middleware functions take place under the "hood".

To illustrate how SOA works in terms of Web services and software layering over legacy applications, consider Figure 1.

At the bottom of the stack are *legacy applications* coded in different languages and running in different environments. To standardize access mechanisms to these, a layer consisting of *application adapters* is provided that exposes the application programming interfaces (API). The operations in the APIs are structured in a way that allows individual functions of applications to be accessed, for example request purchase order, allocate line-item, commence delivery. In large legacy applications, accessing individual functions is not straight-forward, requiring user navigation through forms in order to invoke the required functions. Thus, the adapters transform invocations made through the APIs into legacy application invocations, hiding language-specific logic from client applications.

Having provided a "level playing-field" for application structure, it is then possible to aggregate application functions into *business objects* for software reuse in different parts of an enterprise. A business object combines the different application functions related to a particular business artefact, for example the functions of creating, modifying, approving and deleting purchase orders are combined into a purchase order object. The value-proposition of business objects is that they run in an application server, relying on the container for middleware functionality. So for example, remote access to a business object is considerably simplified, because the container generates the required code for remote procedure calls (RPC) into corresponding proxy objects. Note, for a seminal explanation of RPC, the reader is referred to (Birrel & Nelson, 1984).

The next level of integration, typically within wide-spanning organizations like banks and government agencies, is establishing *internal Web services* to allow loose-coupled interactions between decentralized units of an organization. Web services provide a standard way of interfacing distributed software components implemented in different languages. This is supported through the XML-based standard interface definition language, Web Services Definition Language (WSDL[1]). Following the convention of the Web, the address of a Web service is described through URL. Much like the strategy for application adapters, external interfaces are transformed into language-specific business object interfaces.

However with Web services, WSDL is a widely supported standard and the transformation is automatic through external middleware (see section "Web Services Interface: WSDL" for more details).

The interactions between Web services are also supported in a technology-neutral way. The standard mechanism for Web services interaction is the Simple Object Access Protocol (SOAP[2]), where the messages exchanged between services are described using XML in the required SOAP format. Like, WSDL, SOAP belongs at the external middleware layer and therefore needs for be transformed into a proprietary specific transport protocol for communication with the target object. This is possible by SOAP transport protocol bindings (see section "Web Services Messaging: SOAP" for more details).

As more complex and externally interactive services are needed, a layer for *external Web services* is created. These services are visible outside an organizational boundary and are required to be amenable for external discovery. A standard naming and directory service is available for Web services so that clients can discover and interact with services. This is the Universal Description and Directory Service (UDDI) Chapter "Service Discovery", provides a detailed insight into the UDDI specification and its extensions.

To allow better technical controls over message exchange outside organizational boundaries, a number of *quality-of-messaging* specifications have been developed on top of SOAP and WSDL. WS-Reliability[3] ensures reliable message delivery (e.g., when a message is received, an acknowledgment is sent to sender's transport server avoiding the need for programmers having to code up message acknowledgments or performing checks to avoid repeated message sends). WS-Atomic-Transaction[4] and WS-Business-Activity[5] specifications support basic transactional controls (e.g., when a number of parties need to be sent a message, the transport engine should guarantee that all messages are sent, in an "all-or-nothing" fashion). WS-Addressing[6] allows for more sophisticated message routing than basic request-response messaging between senders and receivers. For instance, "carbon-copies" of a message may be sent to other parties (through "cc" fields in extended SOAP headers). Furthermore, a party may issue a request with a referral to another party that acts on its behalf as to where responses to the request should be sent to.

A major requirement for applications inside and outside enterprises is *service composition*. Here Web services are not executed individually but are coordinated through business processes. A business process description captures an execution order of activities through control flow dependencies between these. Examples of control flow are: sequences, decision points, parallel paths, synchronization, and looping. These are described in a flowchart-like notation. Web services are said to be composed together because activities in the process can be assigned to Web services. The execution of the process, one activity after the next, leads to execution of Web services, one after the next. This removes the need for users to know what service (operation) to execute next in a multistep business task like the following: first check purchase orders for stock, then allocate stock, next assign resources for shipments, and finally schedule shipment and notifying the customer about delivery. The form of service composition related to single party processes is popularly called *Web services orchestration*. Web Services Business Process Execution Language (BPEL) specification supports an XML-based language for executing business processes (see section "Web Services Composition" for more details).

The highest level of service composition is known as *Web services choreography*. Here the focus is not on detailed descriptions of processes, but rather the collaboration between partners (e.g., retailer, supplier, and shipper) in wider process settings like value-chains. The collaboration captures the messages and the order of their exchange: for example first a retailer sends a purchase order request to a supplier; next the supplier either confirms or rejects intention to investigate the order; then supplier proceeds to investigate stock for line-items and sends a confirmation or rejection back; during this period the retailer can send requests to vary the order, and so forth. Here we see a prescribed *conversation* between the partners. It precludes arbitrary service invocation, for example if a retailer could send a variation of a purchase order immediately after sending the initial request, this would cause problems in processing at the supplier's side. A conversational order captured in choreography models should be reflected in the process orchestration models of each partner, to safeguard correct interoperation of these remote processes. Indeed, from a choreography specification, it should be possible to derive the process interfaces of each party's process (details later). This work has been playing through the development of the Web Services Choreography Definition Language (WS-CDL[7]) specification, a successor of previous attempts at defining choreography languages.

To illustrate how current technologies support the EAI stack, consider the approach of J2EE in the following.

- At the lowest level of the application stack, a homogeneous adaptation mechanism to legacy applications is possible through the Java Connector Architecture (JCA). The specific languages and protocols used in an enterprise's disparate applications are hidden in this adaptation layer, through which applications can be connected to.
- Application functionality can then be aggregated into standard business components using Enterprise Java Beans (EJB) such that the business logic can be coded without cumbersome middleware programming. An EJB provider codes the bean class, its business interface, and various configurations through annotations for the type of bean,

whether the bean can be accessed remotely and so on. References to bean interfaces can be obtained through Java Naming and Directory (JNDI) look-up removing the need for clients to "hard-wire" addresses of beans, thus allowing locations of beans to change. Using the business interface, the EJB container generates an implementation for the interface, "injecting" container functionality for transaction, persistence, security, and so forth. Calls to the business methods in this generated bean implementation are delegated to the provider's bean class. User-interface presentations are separated from EJBs through Java Server Pages (JSP) and Servlets.

- Web service interfaces can be generated for EJB business interfaces, as specified through the EJB standard
- The composition of components along the lines of business processes is possible through use of different business process management (BPM) and workflow products, where the coordinated activities of a process are assigned objects at the presentation or business tier depending on whether they involve human actors or direct computation respectively.

It should be noted there are more detailed variations of EAI through different application servers such as SAP Netweaver, IBM Websphere, Oracle Application Server and .NET. Some application servers have been developed in the context of having to support large-scale products like enterprise resource planning business applications, for example SAP Netweaver (Woods & Word, 2004). The vast range of products and different requirements for EAI support mean that different mechanisms and levels for service interfaces and composition are available. For example, not one but several workflow tools are supported for different types of business processes, for example human-oriented versus automated workflows.

Another example is the different degrees of interface and composition: core services which expose elementary operations but are not visible to business users, business objects using core services which are visible to business users, and composite applications aggregating several business objects into a value-added application.

To elaborate on details, we now describe some of the core standards of Web services, namely service messaging through SOAP (section "Web Services Messaging: SOAP") and service interfaces through WSDL (section "Web Services Interface: WSDL"). The topic of service composition including Web services orchestration and choreography is discussed on the assumption of understanding these (section "Web Services Composition"). Note that details of a core aspect of service discovery may be found in the separate chapter "Service Directory".

Web Services Messaging: SOAP

SOAP is the protocol for message exchange between interacting Web services. It is designed to utilize a variety of underlying transport protocols. To support business-to-business (B2B) interoperability, it is asynchronous (as discussed above), implementing request-response interactions out of combinations of one-way interactions. It defines a message format for transmission of data between a sender and receiver, and intermediary nodes that receive and forward the message. However, it is stateless in that it imposes no persistent storage of messages and is agnostic to the semantics (i.e., business meaning) of the message being exchanged.

A SOAP message consists of an envelope containing the following:

- **Header:** Which is optional, containing control information for propagating a message between sender, ultimate receiver and intermediaries along the way. Instructions for processing a message are stored in header blocks designated to different roles on the message route. Other forms of header control relate to quality-of-messaging like security, reliability, and transactional control (as discussed above);

- **Body:** Which is mandatory, containing the message payload.

Essentially, the interaction style and encoding rules determine how the header and body of a message are structured. There are two forms of message interaction through SOAP, described as follows and illustrated in Figure 2:

- **Document-style interaction:** The parties agree on the type and structure of business documents and the order of their interaction. For example, a client creates a purchase order document, containing the all line items and quantities in the body. The header provides sufficient contextual information to identify the client to the supplier. In response, the supplier must send either an acknowledgment document that contains the order number conveying confirmation of the order or it

sends a rejection document. SOAP middleware translates the asynchronous document exchanges into invocations using the relevant transport protocol. Note, these may be asynchronous or synchronous depending on the conventions of the transport protocol;

- **RPC-style interaction:** The parties communicate through standard request and response messages, with the structure of the messages following method invocations. The request contains the method name and the input parameters, while the response contains the return value. SOAP middleware translates the method signature to the XML formats of SOAP messages.

In order for a client and server to interoperate, both need to agree on how the contents of a SOAP message are encoded. SOAP 1.2 defines how data structures such as integers, strings, arrays and so on are serialized in XML—known as *SOAP encoding*. For greater flexibility, two applications agree on an XML Schema defining the required data structures, and this serves as the lexicon for serializing the SOAP messages—known as *literal encoding*.

Figure 2. Message interaction styles in SOAP

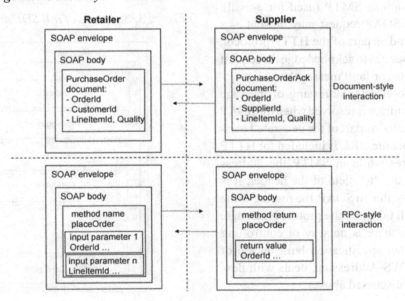

The header provides control information about what nodes receive a message between sender and ultimate receiver and whether they are allowed to process a message. Processing of header blocks may involve adding or removing header data and performing actions such as logging. To allow for this kind of data flow along the routed path of a message, a block in a SOAP header specifies one of the following:

- That it should not be directly processed by any node receiving the message (*none* role);
- That it is intended for the ultimate receiver but not intermediaries (*ultimateReceiver* role);
- That it is intended for intermediaries and the ultimate receiver (*next* role).

The body of a message is only processed by the ultimate receiver. As discussed above, SOAP needs to be mapped to a transport protocol. This is otherwise known as the *binding* of transport protocol. It means the message is marshalled using the transport protocol, based on the protocol's structure and primitives. HTTP is the typical choice although binding to other protocols are possible, for example SMTP (used for e-mail). For example, a SOAP request may be sent as a HTTP POST, and as part of the HTTP protocol, the receiving node has to acknowledge the request (an RPC response or fault message).

Binding also effects addressing of message recipients: the address is resolved when the SOAP message is included as part of the generated message, for example the URL is included for HTTP request messages while in SMTP the address is contained in the "to" field of the header. It is important to note that in SOAP, the routing is the same as the path taken by the protocol message. In other words, there is no way of controlling routing. A further specification built on top of SOAP, namely WS-Addressing, deals with flexible routing (as discussed above).

Web Services Interface: WSDL

WSDL provides an XML-based way for invoking operations on Web services, regardless of how the services are implemented. As such, WSDL can be seen as an interface definition language (IDL) that has been used in middleware technologies, however there are significant differences. Conventional middleware is centralized in that clients access interfaces to components through addresses located using the middleware's naming and directory service. In contrast, Web services operate in decentralized environments and so the address of a Web service needs to be made explicit. What is more, Web services involve reciprocated message exchanges, not simply RPC interactions, meaning different interaction mechanisms need to be supported in WSDL. As discussed above, conventional middleware operates through the same access mechanisms, for example an RPC based protocol, however for Web services, different protocols are available and should be specified in the Web service interface.

A WSDL specification has an abstract and a concrete part, as depicted in Figure 3.

Figure 3. Structure of a WSDL document

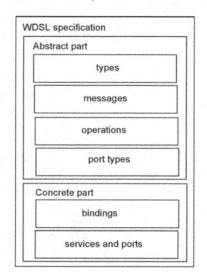

The interface aspect is contained in the *abstract part* while implementation aspects of the abstract interface are stored in the concrete part. Interfaces to services are described as *ports* (known also as endpoints), each containing a group of logical *operations* on the service. Each port defines an inbound or outbound exchange of a message. *Types* are captured for data elements of messages used in operations. Typing is based on XML Schemas (supporting built-in simple data types and more complex user-defined types) by default, although the WSDL document is free to use a different type system. *Messages* are built out of parts of a name and a type.

Four basic modes of operations are available in WSDL:

- In a *one-way* operation, a service receives a message only;
- In a *notification*, a service sends a message only;
- In *request-response*, a service (receiving a request) specifies the inbound message for a client invocation and the outbound message for the service's response.
- In *solicit-response*, the service (sending a request) specifies the outbound request to another services and the corresponding inbound response.

Ports are then assembled out of groups of operations and can be extended from other port types (thereby inheriting operations from those port types).

In the *concrete part* of a WSDL document, the protocol bindings (e.g., RPC- or document-style), message encodings for all operations in a port type and access points to operations and their service groupings are defined. An operation can be declared to communicate using SOAP and HTTP or SMTP bindings (as described in the previous section), although nonSOAP protocols could be used as well. Message encodings are *literal* where the WSDL types defined in XML Schemas are "literally" used to represent the message payload. *SOAP encoding* takes XML Schema definitions and translates them into SOAP using SOAP encoding rules. Literal encoding is typically used for document-style interactions while SOAP encoding is used for RPC-style interactions.

Implementations of ports are also defined in the concrete part of a WSDL document. Here, ports are combined with interface bindings of operations with network addresses (specified as a URI) to declare where a particular port implementation can be accessed from. Finally, groups of different ports are assigned to services. Services may group ports at the same address or the same port having different implementations. This feature allows the same functionality to be accessed using different transport protocols and interaction styles.

Tying this back to SOAP (discussed earlier), if messages defined in WSDL are exchanged using SOAP, then the interface bindings contain all information to construct the SOAP messages. For example, if the interaction style is RPC then the input message of an operation determines the procedure name and input parameters for an RPC call. Figure 4 illustrates how WSDL is used in conjunction with SOAP.

In the figure, a WSDL document is generated for the API of a service provider's application. For client-service interactions with the Web service, stubs and skeletons (i.e., proxies) are generated at the service consumer and provider respectively, using WSDL compilers. This allows the interactions between the client-side application object and the server-side application object (related to the WSDL) to be executed as they are local. The calls are in fact made against the stubs and skeletons. These invoke SOAP engines to generate the required SOAP messages. The SOAP messages are in turn marshalled into the relevant transport protocol messages based on the protocol bindings of the SOAP messages (which in turn are derived from the bindings captured in the WSDL document). Figure 4 shows HTTP as an example of a specific protocol binding.

Figure 4. Structure of a WSDL document

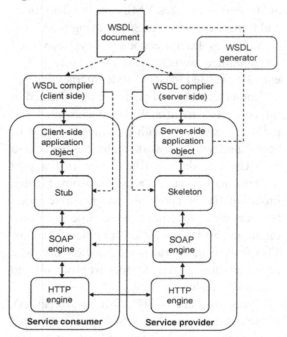

Thus we can see the distinctive and yet dependent relationship between external Web services middleware and internal middleware: SOAP and WSDL act as wrappers over existing protocols and description mechanisms, providing an additional tier for service interfaces and communication, which leverage existing interoperability mechanisms. The reader should bear in mind that there is much more to SOAP and WSDL interoperability than the details provided here. Production-scale communication needs to factor in fault scenarios, versioning, events and semantics. A further consideration is the legacy of existing interoperability investments through widely adopted standards such as Electronic Data Interchange (EDI) and Swift, which make use of specialized infrastructure. For these, we believe that WSDL is unlikely to replace the existing basis for interoperability, but to offer an additional interoperability tier.

WEB SERVICES COMPOSITION

This section provides details of Web services composition through two perspectives. The first is Web services orchestration or the way Web services are coordinated through business processes of a single party, and WS-BPEL in particular. The second is Web services choreography offering a multiparty way of understanding the way partners collaborate through ordered message exchanges.

Single-Party Process Orchestration: WS-BPEL

WS-BPEL[8] is an XML-based executable process language specification developed through the OASIS standards body. It has support from IBM, SAP, Oracle, Microsoft, BEA among other players. As an executable process language, it can support different graphical process modelling languages used at design-time. Popular examples of such languages are Business Process Modelling Notation (White, 2004) and Activity Diagrams from the Unified Modelling Language framework (Eriksson & Penker, 2000). Providing that modelling languages have a mapping to WS-BPEL—that is say their constructs map to WS-BPEL constructs—the design-time models can be transformed into WS-BPEL models. Here, they are refined with implementation detail and executed.

WS-BPEL addresses service composition meaning that processes can interact with other Web services which in turn may be implemented as processes. Hence, WS-BPEL is said to address Web services *orchestration*. However, WS-BPEL focuses on the perspective of a single process. Thus, the context in which a process operates including its collaborating parties and service endpoints needs to be captured somehow, in order for the process to be sufficiently defined.

There are two levels of processes in WS-BPEL: *abstract processes* and *process implementations*. An abstract process is analogous to a software interface while a process implementation is like a class implementing an interface. Abstract processes provide the external message exchanges between a process and its collaborating partners without revealing the process logic behind message sending and receiving. Since processes are long-running, the execution order between these activities is captured using different control flow constructs (which we describe below). The process implementation provides the activities local to a process, hidden from external view. A process implementation, as such, refines an abstract process, detailing the computational activities relating to message sending and receiving.

To illustrate how WS-BPEL processes are structured, consider an example depicted in Figure 5. It shows a process, PurchaseOrderProcess, whose activities (boxes) involve communication or internal actions. The activities involving communication (orange boxes) do so with outside processes (Buyer, Shipper and Warehouse) through service operations on port types (black "lollypops"). Internal activities are also involved (green boxes). An abstract WS-BPEL process would have

communication actions only (the orange parts) while process implementations include internal processing (orange and green parts).

For external communication, invocations are not made directly against port types. Rather *partner links* (grey boxes) are defined for each pair of collaborating partners. The partner link type identifies the roles (light grey rounded boxes, e.g., Buyer, Shipper) of the parties exchanging messages and the required WSDL port types (interface symbols, e.g., PO port type, Shipper port type) that the services bound to these roles should implement. Partner links provide the context for collaboration but do not require the services to be nominated. This is an especially useful because it allows the definitions of business processes to be used in multiple deployments: different services supporting the required port types can be introduced.

With partner link types in place, details of each process can be defined. Following on from partner link types, *partner links* define the services bindings of roles. The definition of a partner link identifies the following:

Figure 5. WS-BPEL in a collaboration context

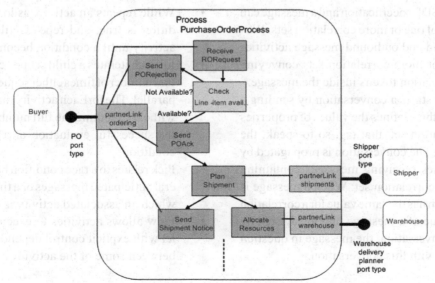

- The partner link type
- The role played by the process
- The one played by the partner

The actual service endpoints can be assigned to the partner link as part of deployment or during run-time. Indeed, endpoint assignments can be made more than one in WS-BPEL code. This is useful in situations where different instances of the same type need communication, for example different suppliers for a particular stock item. For example:

```
<partnerLink name="orderingPL"
    partnerLinkType="ordering"
    myRole="Supplier"
    partnerRole="Buyer">
</partner>
```

The logic of a process can then refer to partner links, and not to explicit services. A process defines partner links, the messages exchanged, correlation sets, fault and exception handling and process logic. *Correlation sets* are the mechanism in WS-BPEL for supporting identification of properties with messages, and relating these to processes and conversations. A correlation set is implemented as special fields (of simple XML types) in a WSDL specification and a message can carry tokens of one or more correlation sets. WS-BPEL inbound and outbound message activities specify one or more correlation sets conveying relevant correlation tokens inside the message.

A process starts a conversation by sending a message and thus defines the values of properties in the correlation set, that tag, so to speak, the conversation. The conversation is propagated by other processes receiving messages containing values of the correlation set. When a message is received which has the same value for a correlation set as the value of a message previously sent by a running conversation, the message in question is associated with this conversation.

A WS-BPEL process essentially consists of the execution order (essentially a partial order) of activities. Activities are either *basic* relating to elementary operations, or *structured* meaning they contain other basic or structured activities. Some salient basic activities are as follows:

- Invoke of an operation on a Web service;
- Receive of a message from an external party;
- Reply to an external party;
- Assign relating to updates of variables, and validate of values of variables against their XML and WSDL data definitions;
- Throw an exception that will be caught in a scope;
- Terminate of an entire process instance.

Structured activities form the basis for process logic by allowing different forms of control flow dependencies between activities. Some salient structured activities are as follows:

- Sequence, defining a strict execution order between activities;
- If, for selecting only one activities from a set based on conditions associated with activities;
- While repeats an activity as long as a condition is true, and repeatUntil repeats an activity until a condition becomes true;
- forEach iterates a child scope activity a certain number of times either sequentially or in parallel. The forEach activity may complete without executing the full number based on the successful evaluation of a completion condition;
- Pick relates to a race condition between several anticipated messages or a timeout, after which an associated activity is executed;
- Flow allows activities to execute in parallel with explicit control dependencies used between some of the activities;

- Scope defines a nested activity with its own partner links, message exchanges, variables, correlation sets, and execution handlers which we have not discussed (fault handlers, compensation handlers termination handlers and event handlers).

A useful basis for understanding the expressiveness of WS-BPEL's control flow and to compare it against other business process and workflow languages is the set of *workflow patterns*; see (van der Aalst et al., 2002) for the original set of workflow patterns and (Russell, ter Hofstede, van der Aalst, & Mulyar, 2006) for a recently revised set. A comprehensive evaluation of BPEL 1.4 against the workflow patterns can be found in (Wohed, van der Aalst, Dumas, & ter Hofstede, 2003). For the limited purposes of our discussion of WS-BPEL in this section, we summarize in Table 1 the original workflow patterns and WS-BPEL (version 2) support for these. Below, we elaborate on some solutions for a more detailed insight into WS-BPEL's process logic.

Classical synchronization: This process structure widely available in business process languages is reflected in the *parallel split* (WP2) and *synchronization* (WP3) patterns: at a point in a branch (of one activity or more than one activity running in a sequence), a split occurs of branches that run in parallel. These branches converge after they all execute into a single branch. In BPEL, this can be straightforwardly captured through defining activities inside a flow activity. The activities will thus execute in parallel. After the flow, the activity is defined and it will run after all these activities complete. In the listing which follows, we illustrate a solution that makes use of control links (introduced above). Inside flow f, two activities a1 and a2 are defined to execute in parallel. A further activity x is also defined to execute after synchronization of a1 and a2. In order to implement synchronization, two links l1 and l2 are defined having as source a1 and a2 respectively, and both having as target x. In

order to ensure that both a1 and a2 complete before x is enabled, an "AND" joinCondition is defined for x:

```
<flow-name="f">
    <links>
        <link name="l1"/>
        <link name="l2"/>
    </links>
    activitya1
        <source linkName= "l1"/>...
    activitya2
        <source linkName= "l2"/>...
    Activityx
        <joinCondition="l1 AND l2"
        <target linkName= "l1"/>
        <target linkName= "l2"/>...
</flow>
```

Choice-merge: The merging of branches, not all of which have been taken is also required in business process languages. Hence, we use the notion of merging (like merging of cars in a traffic lane) instead of synchronization. A basic form of merging arises from an *exclusive choice* (WP4) used to model decision points in business processes. One of an alternative set of branches is taken based on guards (conditions) evaluated for the branches. For example, if one branch relates to purchase orders above a certain amount and another branch for orders below the limit, then only one branch will be enabled for a particular purchaser order case. At some point downstream in the process, the branches may need to merge for common process logic. When alternative branches merge, only the active branch triggers the subsequent branch. This is described through the *simple merge* pattern (WP5). In BPEL, a choice-merge (WP4 and WP5) structure can be supported through control links on activities in a flow, as shown in the listing that follows. The guards are defined through transition conditions c1 and c2. These are defined for links l1 and l2 that have as targets the (alternative) activities a1

Table 1. Summary of BPEL 2 support of workflow patterns

Workflow pattern	Description	BPEL support	BPEL support strategy
WP1 Sequence	An activity is enabled after completion of another activity in the same process.	+	**sequence** activity.
WP2 Parallel split	Split of a branch into multiple branches executed in parallel, allowing activities to be executed in parallel.	+	Activities defined inside a **flow** activity without any links between them.
WP3 Synchronization	Convergence of multiple branches into single branch, thus synchronizing the completion of a number of activities executed in parallel.	+	Implicit join through activity that follows a **flow** with activities defined inside it. An alternative solution is an explicit join defined inside a **flow** through an ("and") **joinCondition** of the synchronizing activity using links.
WP4 Exclusive choice	One of several branches are chosen based on decision or control data.	+	Activities with guards (**case condition**) execute inside an **if** activity. Alternatively, links are defined between guards (**transitionCondition**) and activities in a flow. In both solutions, the guards should be exclusive.
WP5 Simple merge	Two or more alternative branches come together without synchronization; only one of the branches is assumed to be active.	+	Following from a simple merge **if**, an activity follows the if. Alternatively, an ("or") **joinCondition** is used as part of the merged activity.
WP6 Multichoice	One or more of several branches are chosen based on decision or control data.	+	Same solutions as those for exclusive choice (WP4), except that guards are not exclusive.
WP7 Synchronizing merge	Two or more branches come together. If one branch is active the subsequent branch is triggered (i.e., merge semantics). However if more than one branch is active, synchronization of all active branches takes place. A branch which has been active cannot be re-activated for the same merge.	+	Same solution as simple merge except that guards are not exclusive. BPEL implementations use true/false tokens to determine active and dead paths and thus can perform synchronizations for all branches.
WP8 Multimerge	Two or more branches merge without synchronization. For each active branch, the subsequent branch is executed.	-	Not supported because BPEL does not allow multiple activations of the same branch.
WP9 Discriminator & WP10 N-out-M join	One of several incoming branches causes the subsequent branch to be triggered. The remaining incoming branches complete but are ignored. The discriminator is a special case of the N-out-of-M join.	-	Not supported because a **joinCondition** requires all incoming branches to complete.
WP11 Arbitrary cycles	Looping over a part of a process which is not limited to one entry point and one exit point.	-	Not supported as BPEL loops (**while, forEach** and **repeatUntil**) operate in structured cycles.
WP12 Implicit termination	A sub-process is terminated when there is nothing left to do, that is explicit termination is not required	+	No explicit termination is required for BPEL processes.
WP13 Multiple instances without synchronization	New threads in a process can be created, each running independent of each other.	+	**invoke** activity inside a loop. Although the loops are structured, the invoked activities run in parallel.
WP14 Multiple instances with synchronization, having design-time knowledge	A number of activities are executed a required number of times and after all complete the rest of the process continues.	+	The activity is replicated for the required number of times inside a **flow**.

continued on following page

Table 1. continued

Workflow pattern	Description	BPEL support	BPEL support strategy
WP15 Multiple instances with synchronization, having static run-time knowledge	A number of activities are executed without synchronization, where the number is known at during execution prior to the initiation of the activities.	+/-	No direct support. One solution provided in (Wohed et al., 2003) is to execute a **pick** in an loop with three messages: one for the indicating that a new instance is required, one indicating that a previous one has completed and one that no more instances are required.
WP16 Multiple instances with synchronization having dynamic run-time knowledge	A number of activities are executed without synchronization, where the number can change prior to the last instance running.	+/-	No direct support and only covered through approach of multiple instances with synchronization, having static run-time knowledge (WP15).
WP17 Deferred choice	One of several alternative branches is chosen based on information not available at the decision point. Choice is based on event occurrence.	+	Racing incoming messages in **pick** determines which activity is executed.
WP18 Interleaved parallel routing	For a set of activities in a process, each is executed in any order, one at a time.	+	Serializable scopes—an activity of type scope whose **containerAccessSerializable** is set to "yes".
WP19 Milestone	An activity can only be enabled if a milestone has been reached. The milestone is the state of another activity in the same or different process being completed and its successor not yet started.	+/-	Not direct support. A workaround suggested in (Wohed et al., 2003) involves using a deferred choice.
WP20 Cancel activity & WP21 cancel case	Cancel activity involves terminating a running instance while cancel case involves all activities within a process being terminated.	+	**terminate** activity

and a2. In turn, a1 and a2 are sources of links l1-x and l2-x for the merging activity x. An "OR" join condition is defined for x based on these links.

```
<flow>
 <links>
   <link name= "l1"/>
   <link name= "l2"/>
   <link name= "l1-x"/>
   <link name= "l2-x"/>
 </links>
 <empty>
   <source linkName= "l1" transitionCondition
="c1"/>
    <source linkName= "l2" transitionConditio
n="c1"/>
 </empty>
 activitya1
   <target linkName="l1">
   <source linkName="l1-x">
```

```
 activitya2
   <target linkName="l2">
   <source linkName="l2-x">
 activityx
   joinCondition="l1-x OR l2-x"
   <target linkName="l1-x">
   <target linkName="l2-x">
</flow>
```

Of course, the choice-merge that we have described involves guards with *exclusive* conditions. The designer is responsible for ensuring exclusivity. In business processes, there are situations where not all branches are exclusive. Consider a branch which deals with vehicles in general and one that deals with prestige cars in particular. A case involving a Ferrari will result in both branches being enabled while one involving a boat will result in the first branch only. Such a pattern is supported through the *multichoice* pattern (WP6). Now the question is how do we know whether to synchronize (if all branches were enabled) or merge (if only one branch was enabled)?

The solution to this is defined through the *synchronizing merge* pattern (WP7). In BPEL, it turns out that the solution for multichoice and synchronizing merge is the same as choice-merge (described above). This is because BPEL relies on *dead path elimination* to determine when to synchronize or merge; in BPEL it does not matter whether conditions are exclusive or inclusive as the same "OR" join activity is used. More precisely, if a branch is enabled, a true token is sent down the branch, otherwise BPEL sends a false token. Using true and false tokens, it tracks which branches are active and which are dead. This allows BPEL to determine whether to synchronize or merge for "OR" join activities.

Ambiguity can arise if a divergent branch is re-enabled for the same merge. If, for example, there is loop upstream, several invocations of a branch can occur. In this situation, it should be noted that BPEL does not support multiple invocations of branches. Thus the *multimerge* pattern (WP8) is not supported.

Partial synchronization: A form of partial synchronization is described through the *discriminator* pattern (WP9). It requires that for multiple incoming and active branches, the first triggers the subsequent branch while the remaining branches are allowed to complete but are ignored. As an example, a search is undertaken through different sources, and the first result continues the process while the others are allowed to complete without cancellation. The *N-out-M join pattern* (WP10) provides a generalization of the discriminator: after N out M incoming branches arrives, the subsequent branch is enabled. From our description of BPEL's "OR" join mechanism, we can see that these patterns are not supported because a joinCondition is evaluated against all incoming, active branches. Thus, all would have to arrive at the "OR" join activity.

Multiple instances: As a final insight into BPEL support of the workflow patterns, we discuss multiple instances patterns. Multiple instances relate to a number of activities which are instantiated and run in parallel: for example, for a large number of line-items in a purchase order, their checks for stock availability may be executed in parallel for efficiency. *Multiple instances with synchronization* (WP13) is straightforwardly implemented through a parallel forEach side a flow for the number to be instantiated. After the loop terminates after all instances complete. A rather crude alternative is to include the required number of activities in a flow.

Multiple instances without synchronization come in different patterns: the number of activities is known at design-time (WP14); the number is known at run-time before the first instance runs (WP15); and the number can change at any time prior to the last running instance completing (WP16). BPEL does not directly support for these patterns, and coded solutions are required. In the listing that follows, we address the last and most complex of these patterns. The solution, inspired from (Wohed et al., 2003), relies on a pick which waits for a number of messages and upon arrival of the first executes an activity. In the solution, the pick executes in the context of a while loop which iterates when further instances can still be requested (furtherProcessing variable) or created instances are still executed (counter variable). The pick waits for one of three messages: NewActivity in which case a new instance of activity a is created and counter incremented; FinishedActivity where counter is decremented; and StopProcessing which disables furtherProcessing:

```
furtherProcessing:=True
counter:=0
<while furtherProcessing OR counter>0>
    <pick>
        <onMessage NewActivity>
            invoke activitya
            counter:=counter+1
```

```
        </onMessage>
        <onMessage FinishedActivity>
            counter:=counter-1
        </onMessage>
        <onMessage StopProcessing>
            furtherProcessing:=False
        </onMessage>
    </pick>
</while>
```

We note in passing that in the above solution is an example of the *deferred choice* pattern (WP17) through the pick, of racing incoming events.

Multiparty Process Choreography

We have seen that when using an orchestration language like WS-BPEL, inter-organizational domains are captured with the focus of one process at a time. This is sometimes described as a "hub-spoke" approach for integrating processes of collaborating partners because each process is designed is isolation with message exchange to remote processes. An alternative approach is to design the "big picture" of collaborations across partners first, and then reflect collaboration needs into the individual processes. This is the subject of *multiparty choreography* modelling.

A choreography model describes collaboration between a set of partners to achieve a common goal. It constitutes their agreement about the order in which they invoke each other's services. A choreography model does not describe any internal action that occurs within processes of the partners. Rather it focuses solely on *message exchanges* for interoperability at the highest level in the SOA stack. All partners are involved in the design of a choreography model. This is in contrast with detailed process orchestration models (of WS-BPEL) which have the perspective of one partner only.

Choreography models, as such, play a crucial role in describing the domains of a wide-spanning value-chains like sales and logistics. An illustra-tion of the different domains of a global sales and logistics value-chain is illustrated in a Figure 6, together with a high-level decomposition of the logistics domain. This decomposition shows the different partners involved and their interaction dependencies (double-headed arrows). An interaction dependency means that the partners share message exchanges.

To provide an impression of collaborations that take place, one scenario related to Figure 6 is described. It relates to a single stock replenishment event in a supply contract that might operate in a significant time-period (like one year):

The Retailer notifies the Manufacturer about the next delivery, confirming delivery details such as Consignee (delivery point) and finalizing any variations to the order. The Retailer notifies the Consignee (i.e., the delivery warehouse which may be a Retailer Distribution Centre or Retailer Store) about the scheduled delivery. At same time, the Supplier sends a number of Shippers requests-for-quotation, passing on requirements for shipment including ordered stock and destinations. From the quotation, a specific Shipper is selected and sent the order details. A Shipper includes the order into a number of shipments (an order can result in many shipments while a shipment transports several orders). Although not obvious from the figure, line items of orders can packaged into different shipment pellets (and are traceable to these pellets). The Shipper establishes one or more physical shipments with the relevant Air, Sea, Rail and Land Carriers while also obtaining additional insurance as required. Land Carriers subscribe to Locative Services (traffic monitoring) and Break-Down services. The different shipments are transported to their Transient Nodes along the way to the destination Consignee. Transients Nodes are warehouses and regulation authorities in Customs/Quarantine.

This rather simple depiction highlights the need for careful planning through choreography models to safeguard the integration of complex business operations. Trying to accomplish this

Figure. 6. High-level role-based choreography depiction for logistics domain

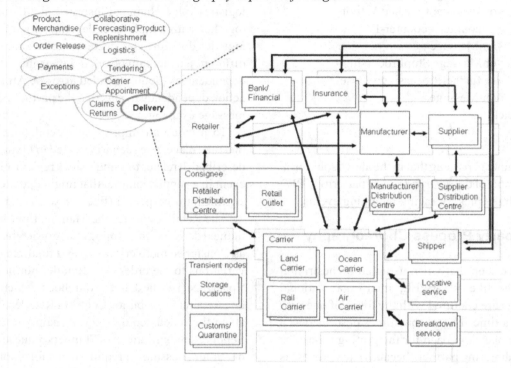

task through "hub-spoke" process design of processes could proceed more reliably with such a multiparty agreement in place.

Choreography languages have received attention is recent years in the BPM and Web services and communities. Process modelling languages in UML, UMM (developed through the UN/CEFACT consortium), BPSS, and BPMN support multiparty collaborations as informal analysis contexts. These are refined by designers into detailed process models per party. More recently, the modelling language Let's Dance (Zaha, Dumas, ter Hofstede, Barros, & Decker, 2006) based on insights from service interaction patterns (Burros, Dumas & ter Hofstede, 2004) capturing recurrent scenarios in bilateral and multilateral collaborations.

In terms of the Web services composition layer, the most advanced of choreography developments in the form of WS-CDL, "grew" out of fledgling developments in WSCI, WSCL, BPEL and BPSS.

This W3C effort seeks to provide greater sophistication for a design-time, global message exchange contract such that templates of individual participants, abiding by the global contract, are generated. As such, WS-CDL is neither a modelling nor execution language. It sits in between, as a design-to-execution transition language, allowing choreography modelling languages to be mapped to an intermediate specification that contains detailed implementation issues.

To provide insights into the nature of choreography specifications, consider Figure 7. It shows a particular choreography model, in UML Activity Diagrams, for the replenishment aspect of the logistics domain.

The figure shows that four roles are involved in this choreography: Consignee, Buyer (a role of Retailer), Supplier and Shipper. The elementary actions in the diagram represent interactions involving message send/receive exchanges across the role types: an action inside the "lane" of a

Figure 7. Choreography model for replenishment scenario in logistics

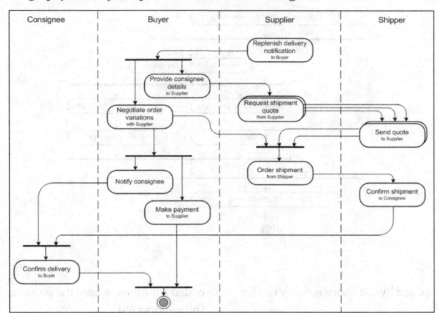

role together with an arc leading to another role denotes a message sent from that role to the other. Thus, Replenish delivery notification in the Supplier captures a message sent from the Supplier and a corresponding message receive in Buyer. Choreographies also involve branch splitting and joining, as with classical BP and workflow languages, but related to message interaction. In the figure, the Buyer triggered interactions, Provide consignee details to Buyer or Negotiate order variations with Supplier follow Replenish delivery notification to Buyer. A choice of these interactions is apparent in the diagram. Noteworthy are the multicast interactions depicted through Request shipment quote from Supplier and Send quote to Supplier.

To implement partner-specific processes (in a language like WS-BPEL); behavioural interfaces for the processes need to be created based on the interactions defined in a choreography model. A *behavioural interface model* captures the dependency of interactions from one partner's perspective. These can be derived from a choreography model and can be implemented using abstract WS-BPEL processes (see earlier).

To illustrate the correspondence between choreography and behavioural interfaces for processes, consider Figures 8. It depicts a behavioural interface related to the Supplier role in the choreography of Figure 7. In the model, send or receive actions are derived from the choreography interactions, reflecting that partner's side of the interaction. Thus we can see that first communication action for the Supplier is Send replenish delivery notification (to the Buyer). Following this is a Receive consignee details (from the Buyer). Multiple instances of Send request for quote (to roles of Shipper) and corresponding Receive quote then follow. Finally, the parallel branches are synchronized for the Send shipment order to the (selected) Shipper.

The example illustrates the fact that in a given B2B collaboration, a role in a choreography description may be associated with multiple behavioural interfaces (and thus multiple WSDL interfaces). It should also be noted that given a choreography and a role within this choreography, a number of processes may be defined that would "fit" (or "conform to") the behavioural

Figure 8. Supplier's behavioural interface for replenishment choreography

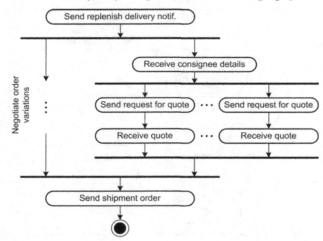

constraints imposed by the choreography on that particular role.

Given the prominence of WS-CDL in the Web services arena, we summarize in Table 2 its capabilities with respect to the service interaction patterns. The reader is referred to (Decker, Overdick, & Zaha, 2006) for an assessment of WS-CDL for the service interaction patterns and coded solutions, where the patterns are partly or fully supported.

Scaling SOA for UC Applications

While much of the promise of SOA has been on modular decomposition and repurposing of legacy applications to dynamic market needs, a new frontier for Web services is emerging. This is

Table 2. Summary of WS-CDL support of service interaction patterns

Service inter-action pattern	Description	WS-CDL support	WS-CDL support strategy
SIP1 Send SIP2 Receive SIP3 Send/receive SIP4 Receive/send	A party sends a message to another party; a party receives a message from another party; a party sends a message to another party and then receives a message from that party; a party receives a message from another party and sends a message to that party.	+	**interaction** structure defines message exchanges between two roles over channel in **request-only**, **response-only** or **request-response** modes
SIP5 One-to-many send	A party sends messages to a set of parties in parallel. The number of recipients may be known at design- or run-time.	+/-	Number of recipients known at design-time: send interactions are placed in **parallel** structure. Number of recipients known at run-time, involves sequential solution: send interactions are placed in a repeated **work unit** and a counter is used to determine how many sends have taken place. Alternatively, send interactions can be placed in a sub-choreography which are spawned off through a nonblocking **perform** action (nonblocking means that synchronization is not required after the instances complete)

continued on following page

Table 2. continued

Service inter-action pattern	Description	WS-CDL support	WS-CDL support strategy
SIP6 One-from-many receive	A party receives messages in a timeframe from a set of parties in parallel. The number of parties may be known at design- or run-time.	+	A receive interaction within a repeated work unit, which is configured for correlation of the receives. The timeframe is supported through the timeout structure in CDL.
SIP7 One-to-many send-receive	A party sends messages to a set of parties in parallel. Subsequently, the party receives responses from the parties. The number of parties may be known at design- or run-time.	+/-	Ditto SIP5 solution, where interactions are send followed by receive.
SIP8 One-from-many receive-send	A party receives messages from a set of parties in parallel. Subsequently, the party sends responses to the parties. The number of parties may be known at design- or run-time.	+/-	Ditto SIP6 and SIP5 solutions.
SIP9 Competing receive	A party sends a request to a set of parties and accepts only the first response.	+	Receive interactions involving the same recipient in a **choice** structure.
SIP10 Contingent request	A party sends a request to another party. If the party has not responded within a certain time, the party issues the request to another party, without cancelling the first request. The time-out of the new request may be different from the previous one. The process of contingent requesting continues until a final request is issued. If at any time, a response arrives the open requests are cancelled.	+/-	Only direct support is available for case where responses from previous request-response are ignored (which does not meet the requirement of the pattern). Alternatively, each request-response is executed in parallel through blocking work units (activated after time-out of previous request-response). Blocking allows time-out for the next interaction. However, recipients can only be known at design-time.
SIP11 Multiresponse	A party sends a request to another party and after that accepts responses until either party indicates that no further responses are to occur.	+	Repeated work unit containing response interaction.
SIP12 Atomic multi-cast request	A party send a request to a set of parties requiring that all should receive the request. If a between a minimum and maximum number of recipients indicate interest, full details of the request are sent to these, otherwise no further interaction occurs. Nested structures should be possible in this atomic multicast.	-	No support. Coded solution involving parallel blocking work units and house-keeping variables.
SIP13 Request with referral	A party A sends a request to party B indicating that responses should be sent to a set of parties, P1 … Pn.	-	Interaction structure contains **exchange** structure with specification of a **channelType**.
SIP14 Referred request	A party A sends a request to party B which delegates the request to other parties PI … Pn. B is allowed some monitoring of interactions between A and P1 … Pn.	+	All responses are expressed in one-way interactions. A is notified of delegated request through SIP13 solution. Where interactions need to involve B as well, respective interactions are executed in parallel.
SIP15 Dynamic routing	A request is routed between different participants, depending on conditions evaluated following previous interactions. Conditions may themselves be dynamic. The next "step" of dynamic routing may involve several recipients.	-	No supported.

where widely-sourced Web services are procured and traded outside their traditional governance and operational boundaries. The benefits of service-enablement, in other words, extend beyond the service provider's ability to deliver services. Under this new frontier for Web services, services once enabled can be aggregated by third parties, delivered through new intermediaries and accessed through a new generation of applications. Indeed, service consumption increasingly takes through devices in wide-spanning sensor networks, where services are ubiquitous. This is precisely, where the field of service-oriented computing meets the field of UC. In this section, we discuss how service-oriented architectures need to scale as service platforms underpinning UC networks.

The most prominent examples of "pooling" together Web services from wide-ranging sources can be seen through "dotcom" service ventures *software-as-a-service*:

- **Salesforce.com,** with around seven hundred thousand subscribers, rapidly expanded its initial Customer Relationship Management portfolio of Web services through its *AppExchange*[9] marketplace, in which the community of open developers are able to offer their software solutions for integration through Salesforce services.
- **NetSuite,** another of a growing number of on-procurement initiatives, integrates Salesforce services with its ERP and portals solutions, thereby competing with Salesforce's value-added layer. More sophisticated procurements can be seen through more general service marketplace solutions.
- **StrikeIron's** repertoire of marketplace functions like customer account management, wizard-based software-as-a-service publishing, search/discovery, purchasing, authentication, billing, payment, and systems monitoring is supplemented through third parties intermediaries, for example PayPal.

A service provider is able to service-enable, deploy and deliver endpoints to different business channels without having to factor in hosting and service delivery functionality. Indeed, Salesforce services like tele-call listing can be ordered through StrikeIron, and StrikeIron enables value-added extensions through US government services for address, phone number, and taxation type of verifications.

In addition, prominent Internet players in Amazon, eBay and Google are making their move. In July 2005, Amazon filed a patent application for "Web Service Marketplaces", and recently has offered some of its infrastructure and business functionality through Web services (e.g., stand-alone queuing and software hosting services). For some time, eBay has hosted a growing number of vertical *service* marketplaces using ChannelAdvisor portals, recasting its auctioning and subscriptions features of its goods marketplace to services. Google has moved beyond pure text search to a growing set of commodity services. It plans to harmonise the Web by unifying information, desktop/office, geospatial, social networking—and service—worlds.

To understand how business applications can exploit environments where Web services and processes in ubiquitous networks, consider the following two motivating examples:

- **Dynamic trading networks:** Today's supply chains are managed through BPM technology coordinating processes ranging from market analysis and collaborative forecasting, contract planning, logistics and transportation, and feeding all the way back to product merchandizing. Typically, these processes do not operate under the assumptions of linear process pipelines, but need to respond flexibly to asynchronous events generated through the distributed nature of collaborating parties. A major source of asynchronous events impacting processes are unforseen exceptions. Under current conceptions of processes in supply chains, exceptions are typically handled "out-of-band" from the process context. Take the situation of *resource scarcity* arising at a storage warehouse due to an adverse transportation delay, like a strike or air/sea carrier mal-function. The warehouse would now have to store stock longer than expected while having to also cater for oncoming stock scheduled. Another source of exceptions is *resource surplus*, caused because stock is no longer needed, for example a project is cancelled. In such situations, the processes could continue to manage affairs if they could detect services within ubiquitous networks which could offer alternative processing paths. In the warehouse example, a tender could be issued to conveniently locate warehouse services to offload additional storage, by a query into a registry listing warehouse providers undertaking tenders

to determine the cheapest service on offer. Similarly, in the cancelled stock example, the process could "demand-sense" other retailer services which have advertised need of that type of stock. In short, today's relatively rigid trading networks could become "real-world" aware and adaptive by operating in the context of ubiquitous service networks.

- **Digital communities:** The second example, illustrated in Figure 9, emphasizes the proliferation of device-sensitive Web applications built through wide-ranging services exposed through ubiquitous service network. Prominent examples of this can be seen in initiatives of digital communities or digital city[10]. Here Web services are published on-mass through different and domain-specific registries. It is then possible for Web applications to be developed, which make use of services translating these into communal and economic benefit.

Figure 9. Vision of the digital city

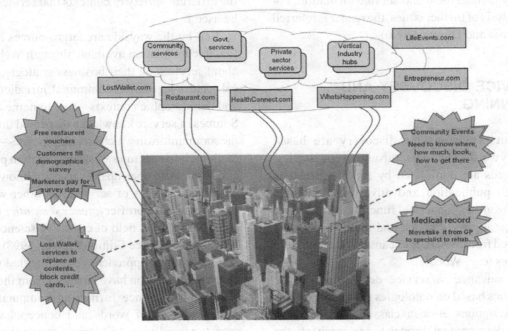

Figure 9 shows two such initiatives in actual operation. Postal services in some countries offer a *LifeEvents.com* portal through which sources are determined that need notification for events such as birth, marriage and change-of-address. *Restaurent.com* operated through eBay for restaurants in Chicago which increased business by issuing free vouchers during certain periods. The vouches were subsidized by market planners who required that survey data be filled by customers as vouchers were issued. The planners collected market data cost-effectively, restaurants prospered through stagnant periods and customers enjoyed free *souffle*.

Given this vision, the question now turns to the implications for support required for service-oriented architectures to scale in ubiquitous service networks, where services are extended to digital media delivery. This is receiving considerable attention by technology platform players seen in Microsoft's Connected Services Framework[11] and service delivery platforms (for a state-of-the-art survey, see Campman et al. (2004). In the next sections, we restrict our attention to three aspects of SOA: service discovery and planning, service quality management and service mediation. For an analysis of further issues, the reader is referred to Barros and Dumas (2006).

SERVICE DISCOVERY AND PLANNING

Current provisions for discovery are based on keywords searches through repositories. Keywords are nominated by service providers through publication and advertising features of software-as-a-service functions. Details of message inputs, outputs, and methods are also captured from WSDL file scans and factored into searches (e.g., Woogle).

An advance in service descriptions is the semantics based on ontologies (essentially terms and descriptions service as classification schemes). This is development through the research into the Semantic Web, aimed at improving the technology to organize, search, integrate, and evolve Web resources by using rich, machine-understandable abstractions for the representation of resource semantics. By combining elements from Web services and Semantic Web technologies, the "semantic Web services" trend promises to make a step forward in the area of Web services engineering by providing the foundation to enable automated selection and composition of web services that exploit rich semantics captured in service descriptions.

Such discovery techniques are suitable for tightly-coupled and well-scoped domains, where service consumers can determine what services offer and how they can be independently utilised from search results. In other words, users are expected to know what they want when they search. Within the setting of more widespread UC service networks involving greater heterogeneity, this assumption breaks down. The wider the domain, the more general search schemas are. Therefore, the greater onus is on providers of services to enrich service descriptions including nonfunctional properties that can be queried for the different variety of contexts that services can be used in.

Left by the wayside are large sources of textual documentation available through Web sites about services, in their business strategic, tactical, legal or legislative, communal, jurisdictional, and demographic contexts—just to name a few. Sources of service knowledge dispersed through the communities in which services operate—jurisdictions, business missions, consumption points, and so on—can open up the variety of known and unknown contexts of services. In other words, these documents proffer *latency semantics* to use a notion from the field of cognitive science, see for example (Pierce Edition Project, 1998).

Quantitative approaches to semantic knowledge representation have emerged from the field of cognitive science furnishing computational representations of words and concepts which seem to accord with equivalent human representation (Gardenfors, 2000). Applied logic provides pragmatic mechanisms for reasoning with such knowledge. Validity is not the goal, but rather producing inferences that are relevant to a given service discovery *agenda*.

A distinctive feature of the approach taken in the project is logical *abduction* (Pierce Edition Project, 1998) (proposed originally by philosopher Charles Pierce and relatively recently entering computer science via artificial intelligence). The value of abduction over classical deduction is that new facts can be introduced (i.e., hypothesized). That is, abduction has the potential to produce ``creative'' inferences, which could then be justified through deduction. Deduction (and logical induction for that matter) do not generate new facts, but essentially proceed from known facts. The value-proposition of abduction is that it would provide greater support for knowledge extraction and reasoning about service descriptions—in unstructured form.

Increased knowledge from a variety of sources captured and indexed through automated techniques, opens up the possibility for search *agents* to guide users from a fuzzy starting point (e.g., "how do I open up a coffee shop") through the variety of contexts (regulated registration tasks, market analysis, logistics of resourcing a business, etc.) to hone in on the users' agenda. Logical abduction (Gabbay & Woods, 2005) could be opened as a suggestion-based mechanism through searches to determine search agendas.

Service Quality Management

In wider spanning service ecosystems, several service providers may offer functionally replaceable services that differ in their extra-functional characteristics such as usage terms and quality of service delivery. Service providers need to be responsive, potentially in real-time, to negotiated variations of service delivery requirements (e.g., price, deliverable timetable). Service ecosystems should therefore explicitly support the negotiation process, reducing noncritical human involvement

and providing decision-makers with the information they require to formulate and assess service offers.

In particular, automated support for negotiation over services is needed for comparing requirements and preferences of prospective service users against capabilities and terms of usage of service providers. This calls for languages and tools supporting the capture of nonfunctional, business-oriented service properties including: temporal and spatial availability, pricing models, payment mechanisms, trust, reputation, promises, penalties, escalation and dispute resolution mechanisms, just to name a few. For a comprehensive, state-of-the-art classification of nonfunctional service properties, see (O'Sullivan, Edmond, & ter Hofstede, 2002).

In many industry sectors, service contracts are put in place that include precise definitions of service reliability and responsiveness guarantees and penalties that apply when these guarantees are breached. Capturing these contracts in a machine-understandable way allows the associated guarantees and penalties to be automatically monitored and enforced and facilitates the comparison and matchmaking of service offerings with respect to customer requirements.

Techniques for matching customer requirements and preferences against possibly parameterised service offers can build upon explicit representations of such properties. Making these nonfunctional service properties explicit is crucial for the capture service level agreements and more broadly service contracts. Being able to link these agreements to collaborative process coordination models allows these contracts to be automatically monitored.

Service Mediation and Adaptation

The availability of services from wide-spanning sources presents major integration development and maintenance costs. Service providers need to effectively compose their services with other services if they are to engage in oncoming market opportunities and situations. Further up the supply/distribution chain, if services are to be brokered and delivered through other intermediaries (e.g., for authentication, payment, device-specific service presentations), they need to be interfaced with service delivery components that operate in various ways. Thus, one can expect that services will have to interact with one another in ways not necessarily foreseen during their development or deployment.

A key challenge in this setting is *service mediation*: the act of repurposing existing services so that they can interact in unforeseen manners by intercepting, storing, transforming, and (re-)routing messages going into and out of these services. A prominent sub-problem of service mediation is that of service interface adaptation (Bimetallic et al., 2005). Here the goal is to keep interfaces as generic as possible while functions peculiar to implementation or prone to change are adapted to. As a basic example, consider a procurement service which, after sending a Purchase Order (PO) to a supplier's order management service, expects to receive one and only one response. Now, consider the case where this procurement service engages in collaboration where the order management service sends responses for line-items of purchase orders.

Figure 10. Mismatch of required and provided behavioural interfaces

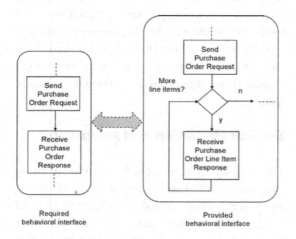

Required behavioral interface

Provided behavioral interface

This example shows that a service may be required to participate in multiple collaborations such that in each of them, a different interface is expected from it. Implementing, testing, deploying, and maintaining adapters to deal with the multiplicity of interfaces required from a service may be costly and error-prone. This calls for specialised tool support based on high-level concepts, as opposed to implementing adapters using programming languages extended with basic message manipulation primitives.

SUMMARY

After several years of intensive research, development and standardization efforts, the expanse of SOA technologies, spread-headed through Web services specifications, is considerable. Indeed the range of specifications developing through W3C and OASIS now makes the familiar WS stack quite difficult to depict comprehensively. In this chapter, we described the key technologies having widespread take-up in current SOA investments and which give concrete insight into the way SOA needs to be adapted for the next revolution of service-orientation playing out in the UC arena.

Conventionally, reusable application components layered over legacy applications of an organization are developed using the adopted middleware technology. From a B2B standpoint however, technology-neutral interfaces for services and interactions are needed which can be used over the technology-specific choices of the collaborating parties. The interface definition language for Web services is WSDL, and it captures the structural aspects of a Web service (messages, data types, operations, and operation groups or ports) and the transport protocol bindings for ports. Thus, WSDL permits one or more application components (coded in different languages) to be interacted with using different transportations. The interactions involve message exchanges, which for loose-coupled B2B applications, are asynchronous; synchronous send-receive and receive-send are mapped into two corresponding asynchronous exchanges. The message exchanges are described through a technology-neutral communication protocol, SOAP. SOAP encodes different interaction mechanisms into XML documents, together with the required transport protocol bindings.

A strategic business trend has been for value-chains to be better coordinated through explicitly described business process of collaborating partners. The Web services stack has seen considerable development with WS-BPEL allowing complex business process descriptions using execution dependencies between activities, along the lines of classical workflow constructs. While WS-BPEL has considerable expressiveness, seen through its support of most the widely-referenced workflow patterns, it operates in well-formed block structures which do not permit arbitrary cycles and multiple merge invocations. As an execution language, companies investing in WS-BPEL need to adopt higher-level graphical languages like BPMN and UML Activity Diagrams to allow business processes to be captured from a less technical, conceptual design perspective.

To complete the internal process view of WS-BPEL process orchestration, the Web services choreography is being crafted to focus solely on message exchanges between collaborating partners. This provides the "big picture" of collaboration, which can then guide the more detailed development of processes related to individual partners. As yet, a convergent standard, let alone standards development, is to be reached.

While the higher levels of service composition unfold, a new revolution has taken off in the Web services world, seen through disruptive business models from software-as-a-service initiatives. These herald repurposing services in an altogether new way: services can be deployed and delivered well outside the boundaries of their original providers and can be accessed in flexible ways through wide-spanning sensor networks. This calls for a convergence between classical SOA technologies and UC.

For procurement of UC service networks, traditional assumptions no longer hold. Keyword or ontology-based searching suits discovery of services within well-scoped domains, however in larger settings like service marketplaces and digital communities, consumers need a richer exposure of semantics and support of fuzzier search goals. If services are to be independently delivered, their nonfunctional properties like geospatial and temporal availability, methods of charging and payment, security, trust, rights and penalties need to be carefully described. Without intervening developers, automated assistance will be required by prospective Web service suppliers to "instantly" integrate their services with other services and service delivery components. These are just to name a few of the challenges posed by the new frontier of service-orientation.

FUTURE RESEARCH DIRECTIONS

Significant research challenges are posed by the extensions required of SOA to scale as the underpinning for ubiquitous service networks and service ecosystems. Some of these have been described in the previous section of this chapter.

Considered as a whole, the capabilities of SDPs need to be extended beyond classical client/server models of service delivery. This should reflect more dynamic ways in which Web services can be procured into new applications and business channels, outside their traditional governance boundaries. The classical SOA strategy, as we have seen, supports technology-independent service interfaces, remote service access and service composition. Third parties can thereby aggregate services and recast value-added services into new settings. However, expectations are emerging for further forms of service provisioning. For example, it should be possible to allow services to be discovered, ordered, paid for, authenticated and authorized against, rights-protected during access and execution, and finally evaluated for usage (trust-ranked)—through third-parties.

In the business sense, such functionality would be supportive of a service broker (like a mortgage broker or an "iTunes" for services). Service brokers focus on making service offerings more lucrative for the market through different pricing models. They should have mechanisms at their disposal to discount services, for example through use of advertising. Thus, further insights are required to identify specialist roles of service supply like service broker, and to support these through SDPs. This entails understanding the contexts in which these roles operate and the extent of service delivery control that can be relinquished to a role so that particular interactions (like collection of payments and usage metering) are controlled by it. In general, the fostering of service ecosystems featuring flexible delivery outsourcing to various specialist service delivery roles is required.

Given such a diverse and diffuse service landscape, service quality through service level agreements (SLA) are crucial. Whereas current research addresses the formalization of SLA, the dependencies on the delivery of a service are largely centralized. As different services are aggregated and as the different layers of service supply are introduced, like service brokerage, the influences of service quality are clearly distributed. Thus, ways of determining the impacts on promises and obligations of collective service delivery need to be understood given the diffuse components of the service within their different and perhaps conflicting SLAs.

In addition, the classical service interactions need to incorporate service negotiations so that similar services and delivery roles can be selected based on price, location, time, reliability, and other factors. Thus, nonfunctional aspects of service interactions and composition need to be factored in current composition mechanisms supporting process orchestration and choreography.

REFERENCES

Alonso, G., Casati, F., Kuno, H., & Machiraju, V. (2004). *Web services: Concepts, architectures and applications.* Springer-Verlag.

Barros, A. P., Dumas, M., & ter Hofstede, A. H. M. (2005). Service interaction patterns: Towards a reference framework for service-based business process interconnection. In *Proceedings of the Third International Conference on Business Process Management 2005 (BPM'2005).* Nancy, France.

Barros, A. P., & Dumas, M. (2006). The rise of web service ecosystems. *IEEE IT Professional Magazine, 8*(5), 31-37.

Barros, A. P., & Bruza, P. (in press). Augmenting web services discovery with cognitive semantics and abduction, SAP Research Technical Report. *Journal of Web Semantics.*

Benatallah, B., Casati, F., Grigori, D., Motahari-Nezhad, H., & Toumani, F. (2005). Developing adapters for web services integration. In *Proceedings of the International Conference on Advanced Information Systems Engineering 2005 (CAiSE'2005),* Porto, Portugal (pp. 415-429). Springer-Verlag.

Birrel, A. D., & Nelson, B. J. (1984). Implementing remote procedure calls. *ACM Transactions on Computer Systems (TOCS), 2*(1), 39-59.

Campman, M. et al. (2004). *Service delivery platforms and telecom web services* (Tech. Rep. Moriana Group). Retrieved October 8, 2007, from http://www.morianagroup.com/graphics/reports/ The Moriana Group SDP Operator Guide to SDP June 2004.pdf.

Decker, G., Overdick, H., & Zaha, J. M. (2006). On the suitability of WS-CDL for choreography modeling. In *Proceedings of Methoden, Konzepte und Technologien für die Entwicklung von dienstebasierten Informationssystemen, EMISA 2006,* Hamburg, Germany.

Eriksson, H. E., & Penker, M. (2000). *Business modelling with UML.* New York: OMG Press.

Gabbay, D., & Woods, J. (2005). The reach of abduction: Insight and trial. *Vol. 2: A Practical logic of cognitive systems.* Elsevier.

Gardenfors, P. (2000). *Conceptual spaces: The geometry of thought.* London: MIT Press.

O'Sullivan J., Edmond, D., & ter Hofstede, A. H. M. (2002). What's in a service? Towards accurate description of non-functional service properties. *Distributed and Parallel Databases, 12,* 117-133.

Pierce Edition Project (Ed.). (1998). The nature of meaning. *Essential peirce: Selected philosophical writings, 2 (1893-1913),* (pp. 208-225). Indiana University Press.

Russell, N., ter Hofstede, A. H. M., van der Aalst, W. M. P., & Mulyar, N. (2006). *Workflow control-flow patterns: A revised view* (BPM Center Report BPM-06-22). Retrived October 8, 2007, from, BPMcentre.org.

Szyperski, C. (2004). *Component software: Beyond object-oriented programming.* Addison-Wesley.

van der Aalst, W. M. P., ter Hofstede, A. H. M., Kiepusweski, B., & Barros, A. P. (2003). Workflow patterns. *Distributed and Parallel Databases, 14*(3), 5-51.

White, S. (2004). Process modelling notations and workflow patterns. In L. Fischer (Ed.), *Workflow handbook 2004* (pp. 265-294). Lighthouse Point, FL: Future Strategies Inc.

Woods, D., & Word, J. (2004). *SAP netweaver for dummies.* New Jersey: Wiley Publishing Inc.

Wohed, P., van der Aalst, W. M. P., Dumas, M., & ter Hofstede, A. H. M. (2003). Analysis of web services composition languages: The case of BPEL4WS. In I.Y. Song, S.W. Liddle, T.W. Ling, &

P. Scheurmann (Eds.), In *Proceedings of the 22nd International Conference on Conceptual Modeling (ER 2003).* Vol. 2813 of Lecture Notes in Computer Science, (pp. 200-215). Berlin: Springer-Verlag.

Zaha, J. M., Dumas, M., ter Hofstede, A. H. M., Barros, A. P., & Decker, G. (2006). Service interaction modelling: Bridging global and local views. In *Proceedings the International Conference on Enterprise Distributed Object Computing 2006, EDOC'2006,* Hong Kong.

ADDITIONAL READING

Barros, A. P., Grosskopf, A., & Decker, G. (in press). Complex events in business processes, SAP research technical report. *International Conference on Business Information Systems, BIS 2007.*

Barros, A. P., Decker, G., Dumas, M., & Weber, F. (in press). Correlations patterns in service-oriented architectures, SAP technical report. *Fundamental Approaches to Software Engineering, FASE 2006.*

Bussler, C. (2003). *B2B integration.* Springer-Verlag.

Casati, F., & Shan, M.-C. (2001). Dynamic and adaptive composition of e-services. *Infosystems, 24*(3), 211-238.

Davenport, T. H. (1992). Process innovation: Re-engineering work through information tecnology. Boston: Harvard Business School Press.

Fielding, R. (2000). *Architectural styles and the design of network-based software architectures.* Unpiblished doctoral thesis, University of California, Irvine.

Gottschalk, K., Graham, S., Kreger, H., & Snell, J. (2002). Introduction to web services architecture. *IBM Systems Journal, 41*(2), 170-177.

Hauck, R., & Reiser, H. (2000). Monitoring quality of service across organizational boundaries. Trends in distributed Systems: Towards a universal service market. In *Proceedings of the 3rd International IFIP/GI Working Conference, USM 2000.*

Hohpe, G., & Woolf, B. (2004). *Enterprise integration patterns: Designing, building and deploying messaging solutions.* Addison-Wesley.

Jablonski, S., & Bussler, C. (1996). *Workflow management: Modelling concepts, architecture and implementation.* International Thompson Computer Press.

Kaye, D. (2003). *Loosely-coupled: The missing pieces of web services.* RDS Press.

Kindler, E., Martens, A., & Reisig, W. (2000). Inter-operability of workflow applications: Local criteria for global soundness. In W. M. P. van der Aalst, J. Desel, & A. Oberweis, (Eds.), *Business process management: Models, techniques, and empirical studies. Vol. 1806 of Lecture Notes in Computer Science* (pp. 235-253). Berlin: Springer-Verlag.

Leymann, F., & Roller, D. (1999). *Production workflow: Concepts and techniques.* Upper Saddle River, NJ: Prentice-Hall PTR.

Luckham, D. (2002). *The power of events: An introduction to complex event processing in distributed enterprise systems.* Boston: Addison-Wesley

Lynch, N. (1997). *Distributed algorithms.* Morgan Kaufmann.

Madnick, S., et al. (2000). *Surviving and thriving in the new world of web aggregators* (Tech. Rep. v20). Sloan School of Management: MIT Press.

Milner, R., Parrow, J., & Walker, D. (1992). A calculus of mobile processes. *Information and E. Computation, 100*, 1-40.

Reijers, H. A. (2003). Design and control of workflow processes: Business process management for the service industry. *Vol. 2617 of Lecture Notes in Computer Science.* Berlin: Springer-Verlag.

Russell, N., ter Hofstede, A. H. M., Edmond, D., & van der Aalst, W. M. P. (2005). Workflow data patterns: Identification, representation and tool support. In L. Delcambre et al. (Eds), In *Proceedings of the 24th International Conference on Conceptual Modeling, ER 2005. Vol. 3716 Lecture Notes in Computer Science* (pp. 353-368). Berlin: Springer-Verlag.

Russell, N., van der Aalst, W. M. P., & ter Hofstede, A. H. M. (2006). Workflow exception patterns. In E. Dubois & K. Pohl (Eds.), In *Proceedings of the 18th International Conference on Advanced Information Systems Engineering, CAiSE '06. Vol. 4001 of Lecture Notes in Computer Science (pp.* 288-302). Berlin: Springer-Verlag.

Snir, M., & Gropp, W. (1998). *MPI: The complete reference* (2nd ed.). MIT Press.

van der Aalst, W. M. P. (1997). Verification of workflow nets. *Vol. 1248: Lecture notes in computer science, Application and theory of petri nets* (pp. 407-426). Springer-Verlag.

van der Aalst, W. M. P, Dumas, M., & ter Hofstede, A. H. M. (2003). Web service composition languages: Old wine in new bottles? In G. Chroust & C. Hofer (Eds.), In *Proceedings of the 29th EUROMICRO Conference: New Waves in System Architecture* (pp. 298-305). IEEE Computer Society, Los Alamitos, California.

Worah, D., & Sheth, A. (1997). Transactions in transactional workflows. In S. Jajodia & L. Kerschberg (Eds.), *Advanced transaction models and architectures.* New York: Kluwer Academic Publishers.

ENDNOTES

[1] Specification of Web Services Definition Language: http://www.w3.org/TR/2001/NOTE-wsdl-20010315

[2] Specification of Simple Object Access Protocol: http://www.w3.org/TR/2003/REC-soap12-part1-20030624/

[3] Specification of Web Services Reliability http://docs.oasis-open.org/wsrm/ws-reliability/v1.1/wsrm-ws_reliability-1.1-spec-os.pdf

[4] Specification of Web Services Atomic Transaction: http://docs.oasis-open.org/ws-tx/wsat/2006/03/wstx-wsat-1.1-rddl.htm

[5] Specification of Web Services Business Activity: http://www.oasis-open.org/apps/group_public/download.php/16447/Microsoft%20Word%20-%20wstx-wsba-1.1-spec-wd-02.pdf

[6] Specification of Web Services Addressing: http://www.w3.org/ Submission/ws-addressing

[7] Specification of Web Services Choreography Definition Language: http://www.w3.org/TR/ws-cdl-10/

[8] Web Services Business Process Execution (WS-BPEL) version 2: http://www.oasis-open.org/committees/download.php/10347/wsbpel-specification-draft-120204.htm

[9] "An eBay for Business Software", Business Week Online, 19 September 2005: http://www.businessweek.com/magazine/content/05_38/b3951097.htm

[10] A prominent example is Intel's Digital Communities being planned for Palo Alto, US. See http://www.govtech.net/dcarchive06/story.php?id=100383 for more details

[11] Microsoft's Connected Services Framework vision paper - http://download.microsoft.com/download/7/7/5/775cb839-a749-49a7-b735-edaf05ca1501/CSF%2025%20Overview%20WP_Final.pdf

Chapter IV
Ontologies for Scalable Services–Based Ubiquitous Computing

Daniel Oberle
SAP Research, CEC Karlsruhe, Germany

Christof Bornhövd
SAP Research, Research Center Palo Alto, USA

Michael Altenhofen
SAP Research, CEC Karlsruhe, Germany

ABSTRACT

This chapter discusses scalability problems and solutions to services-based ubiquitous computing applications in real time enterprises. The scalability problems are (1) identifying relevant services for deployment, (2) verifying a composition by a logical rule framework, and (3) enabling the mapping of required services to the "best" available device. We argue that ontologies can help to counter these challenges. Subsequently, we provide a detailed introduction to ontologies. We focus on the ontology languages emerging from the corresponding W3C Semantic Web activity. The W3C recommendations have a high impact on future tools and the interoperability of ontology-based applications. We contrast the pros and cons of ontologies at a general level and demonstrate the benefits and challenges in our concrete smart items middleware.

INTRODUCTION

Ubiquitous computing for real time enterprises calls for novel approaches to distributed applications since both the *economic* and *technical* scale of these applications will increase dramatically. Regarding the *economic* scale, applications grow beyond enterprise boundaries and potentially involve frequently changing, partly unknown participating entities. Therefore, much more open approaches are desired. In the world of enterprise computing, service-oriented architectures and Web services are considered important steps on the road to economic scalability as discussed in the chapter "Ubiquitous Services and Business Processes."

The concepts and technologies of service-oriented architectures can be fruitfully applied to ubiquitous computing for real time enterprises to counter the economic scale. However, the *technical scale* of services-based ubiquitous computing, which concerns the number of nodes and processes involved, still remains a challenge. We discuss the use of ontologies as a possible means of countering the scalability problem, and evaluate their promises and limitations for services-based ubiquitous computing applications.

Services-based ubiquitous computing applications are highly distributed applications that run in the form of cooperating services on a variety of possibly heterogeneous devices. The devices run services that can be combined, that is, "composed," into more complex services or applications. Such a services-based approach to the development of ubiquitous computing supports the distribution of functionality across the set of available devices, enables better reusability of components in new or different applications, and the division of the overall functionality into independent services with clearly defined interfaces that can be developed and tested separately.

However, the capability to decompose business processes into individual services and to deploy them on different smart devices poses new technical challenges. In particular, the services to be executed on the devices need to be modeled and described for identification and selection, mapped to appropriate smart devices, remotely deployed, configured, and monitored. The reason for such additional tasks is the heterogeneity of the underlying hardware platforms in terms of different communication protocols and technologies.

To facilitate such tasks, a service composition model tailored to smart device interaction is required. The service composition model has to enable the explicit modeling of the heterogeneities of different device platforms and has to support the identification, deployment, and composition of services for smart devices. While the identification, deployment, and composition are fairly simple with a small number of services and devices, the challenge of coping with such tasks increases with the number of devices and services.

In the remainder of this chapter, we show how ontologies may counter the fundamental scalability challenges of: (*1*) identifying relevant services for deployment, (*2*) verifying a composition by a logical rule framework, and (*3*) enabling the mapping of required services to the "best" available devices.

We begin by detailing the scalability challenges in a service-oriented smart items middleware. The chapter continues by introducing the reader to ontologies. We focus on the recent W3C recommendations RDF(S) and OWL that, for the first time, provide standard languages for ontology specification. These recommendations have a high impact on future tools and the interoperability of ontology-based applications. We proceed by contrasting the pros and cons of ontologies on a general level. Finally, we sketch how ontologies are used to counter challenges (*1*)-(*3*) in a service-oriented smart items middleware.

CHALLENGES IN SERVICE-ORIENTED SMART ITEMS MIDDLEWARE

As mentioned in the introduction, the technical scale of services-based ubiquitous computing applications struggles with the heterogeneity of the underlying smart devices, and the inherent complexity of a system that requires automatic or semi-automatic monitoring and deployment of services. In this section, we refer to the service-oriented smart items middleware presented in the chapter "Smart Items in Real Time Enterprises" and detail where such challenges occur. We argue that ontologies should be used to describe services and devices. Ontologies provide the means to identify available services, verify given service compositions, and guide the deployment of services.

Smart Items Middleware

The architectural overview of smart items middleware in the chapter "Smart Items in Real Time Enterprises" introduces five logical system layers. The technical scalability challenges occur in both the *Device Layer* and *Device Level Service Layer*. We would like to recap these layers in the following paragraphs.

The *Device Layer* comprises the actual smart item devices, the communication between them, and the presentation of the available hardware services to the next higher layer. Available devices usually provide different communication means and operating systems. For example, in the case of RFID, the reader always initiates the communication and the tags cannot directly communicate with each other. In case of wireless sensor networks, simple services can be pushed and executed on them and tasks can be accomplished in cooperation, since the sensor devices have integrated processing power and are able to use peer-to-peer communication.

The *Device Level Service Layer* manages the deployable services used by the device layer. It contains a service repository that stores a service description and one or more service executables for each service. Compound services rely solely on other services to fulfill their task and have a service composition description that is stored in the service repository. Atomic services, on the other hand, are associated with directly executable code. Since a service may be deployable on different platforms, an atomic service may have more than one service executable—one for each device platform.

Running Example

In order to illustrate the challenges in the smart items middleware, we first describe a running example (see Figure 1). We assume we are in a warehouse, where goods are tagged with RFID chips and shelves are equipped with RFID readers. The RFID readers feature both Ethernet and encrypted WLAN communication. Further, we assume that temperature sensors and gateways nodes are deployed at strategic locations within the warehouse. The gateway devices are linked to the RFID readers in the smart shelves via Ethernet cables and are equipped with antennas for wireless communication with the temperature sensors (e.g., via 433MHz) and for nonencrypted WLAN (about 2.4 GHz). Every warehouse employee is equipped with a PDA. The PDAs are integrated into a WLAN and provide an adapter for communication with the sensor devices.

Warehouse employees should be informed via their PDAs whether perishable goods are on shelves where the measured temperature exceeds a predefined threshold. The implementation and deployment of the corresponding services in the middleware can take place in the following three main steps. In the first step, a developer chooses the services from the middleware service repository required for our application. In the second step, the developer implements the new application by composing services and device types.

Figure 1. Running example: Goods, RFID, and temperature sensors in a warehouse

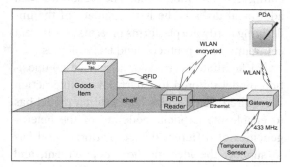

Finally, the services of the verified composition plan are mapped to the appropriate devices. Each of the three steps is afflicted with fundamental scalability challenges.

Fundamental Scalability Challenges

As the number of services and devices increases, identifying required services, verifying service compositions, and mapping services to devices becomes correspondingly more complex for the system developer. In the following section, we discuss three fundamental scalability challenges of the smart items middleware, which occur independently of any application. A technical scalability challenge is one that increases with the number of services and devices. Tool support is required because the developer can no longer handle the challenges manually.

Challenge 1: Service Identification

The descriptions of services available for deployment in the smart items middleware are stored and maintained in the middleware's service repository. At system deployment or during service composition, relevant services must be selected from the repository. The challenge here is to enable selection based on the semantics or behavior of the available services, rather than on the available interfaces or service signatures.

In our running example, the developer should be able to conveniently search for a "temperature sensing" service rather than having to conduct the tedious task of checking and examining all the services' interfaces.

Challenge 2: Verification of Service Compositions

Services available in the service repository can be composed into new, more powerful, services or applications. However, when composing services at the level of smart devices, heterogeneities of the underlying hardware platforms need to be addressed (Ziekow, Avanes, & Bornhövd, 2006). Heterogeneities concern different communication protocols and technologies as well as different programming models. An abstraction to a common, homogeneous service platform is not possible due to the limited computing capabilities of typical smart devices. The challenge here is to verify a composition plan with respect to the heterogeneities of the underlying hardware.

In our running example, the gateway devices can be used with a service that informs all PDAs about perishable goods that are too warm. As an alternative, the PDAs could also directly receive and evaluate the sensor values, and could request the required RFID data. However, in the setting described, there is no communication channel shared by RFID readers and PDAs. Composition plans for both situations can be specified, but only the first one can be implemented.

Challenge 3: Intelligent Service-to-Device Mapping

In addition to manual deployment using dedicated deployment tools, the system should be able to automatically map required services onto the most suitable available devices, or relocate services from one device to another based on changing system conditions. Such automatic deployment of services is essential to manage the increasing complexity of a distributed smart items solution (Ziekow et al., 2006).

In our running example, it would be worthwhile to define a deployment constraint that the temperature filter service gets deployed on only 30% of the nodes, and that these nodes also have to have a certain amount of battery power left. This constraint imposes the need to remap services, if some sensor nodes are running out of power.

In the remainder of this chapter we argue that ontologies can help to counter these challenges. Therefore, the section "Ontologies and Semantic Web Specifications" continues with a general introduction to ontologies. We focus on the ontology languages emerging from the corresponding W3C Semantic Web Activity. The W3C recommendations have a high impact on future tools and the interoperability of ontology-based applications.

ONTOLOGIES AND SEMANTIC WEB SPECIFICATIONS

One of the primary goals of ontologies is to enable information integration between humans, computers, or both. In essence, ontologies are similar to object-oriented or conceptual database schemas. In fact, they can be seen as the resulting next step from such technologies. The most cited definition of an ontology is the one from (Gruber, 1995): "*An ontology is an explicit specification of a conceptualization.*"

More recently, much emphasis has also been put on the fact that the conceptualization is "shared" (Studer, Benjamins, & Fensel, 1998). This means that a user group agrees on the way of modeling, to facilitate mutual understanding and information integration. In this section, we explain the notions of *conceptualization* and *explicit specification*. We clarify both notions by revisiting our running example. For more concise discussions, the reader may refer to Oberle (2006) or Staab and Studer (2004).

What is a Conceptualization?

A conceptualization is a representation of a relevant domain in a more or less formalized model expressed via cognitive modeling primitives. Modeling primitives are cognitive, when they resemble the way humans think and conceive of the world. Ontologies usually provide classes, relations between classes, and instances as cognitive modeling primitives[1]. The backbone of every conceptualization, and thus, each ontology is a hierarchy of classes (also called a taxonomy). This

means that sub- and superclass relations are very prominent in ontologies and that special modeling primitives are devoted to them.

Let us model the domain of our running example to clarify this notion. We start by identifying relevant classes in the warehouse domain and putting them into a taxonomy. In the section "Running Example" we learn about Ethernet cables, antennae, RFID chips, sensors, gateways, and so forth. As a first categorization we introduce the classes Specification, Communication Means, and Node. The three classes become direct subclasses of Entity (the most general class). In turn, we classify Antenna and Cable underneath Communication Means, and Sensor, Gateway, Reader, and PDA underneath Node. Furthermore, we introduce the relation describes between Specification and Communication Means as well as accesses between Node and Communication Means, as shown in Figure 2.

With a set of instances, we are able to capture a specific setting in our domain. Figure 3 depicts a specific situation where we can find specific Nodes, viz., *Gateway#1*, *RFIDReader#1*, and *PDA#1*. All of them are linked to their respective Communication Means via the accesses relation. In turn, concrete Specifications, that is, *WLAN*, *WLANencrypted*, *Ethernet*, describe the Communication Means. The reader might wonder, however, where to start and when to stop modeling. This leads us to the following requirements for a conceptualization:

Relevance

The conceptualization must represent only relevant classes, relations, and instances. Relevance depends on what we want to achieve with the conceptualization. In our case, we would like to counter the three challenges mentioned in the previous section. For this purpose, it is unnecessary to represent the warehouse as a class, for instance. With respect to these criteria, all classes and relations depicted in Figure 2 are relevant.

Figure 2. Sketch of the ontology for our running example

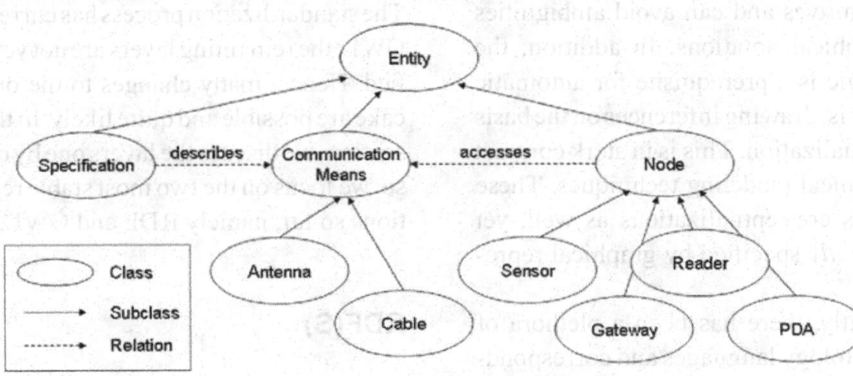

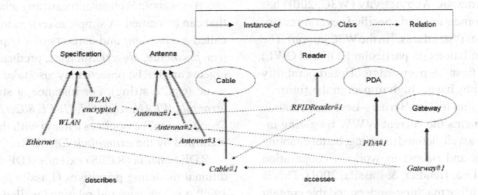

Figure 3. Instances of our running example corresponding to the ontology of Figure 2

Completeness

The conceptualization must represent all relevant classes, relations, and instances. In the running example, Specifications, Communication Means, and Nodes are all relevant, but will not suffice to address the three challenges. Thus, the conceptualization depicted in Figure 2 is not complete. We have skipped many details for the sake of brevity. The interested reader may refer to Oracle (2006) and Spieß, Bornhövd, Haller, Lin, and Schaper (2007) for the details.

Correctness

The conceptualization must reflect the domain in a consistent way. That means each class, rela-

tion, and instance must have counterparts in the domain. This requirement holds for the conceptualization shown in Figure 2.

This way of modeling a domain is very similar to UML class diagrams (Booch, Jacobson, & Rumbaugh, 1998) in object-orientation or entity relationship models (Chen, 1976) in database design. However, ontologies require an explicit, logic-based representation of the domain, as explained in the next section.

What is an Explicit Specification?

The definition of an ontology as given by Gruber (1995) requires an explicit specification of the conceptualization. This means that ontologies must be specified in a formal, logic-based language.

Such languages typically provide a wealth of modeling primitives and can avoid ambiguities bound to graphical notations. In addition, the underlying logic is a prerequisite for automatic reasoning, that is, drawing inferences on the basis of the conceptualization. This is in stark contrast to purely graphical modeling techniques. These can be seen as conceptualizations as well, yet are only *implicitly* specified by graphical representations.

Until recently, there has been a plethora of logic-based ontology languages and corresponding tool suites in research and academia which do not allow any interoperability. However, the W3C's Semantic Web Activity (W3C, 2001) has gained momentum and specified several recommendations ("standards," in the W3C jargon). The recommendations (in particular RDF and OWL) are a significant step towards tool interoperability and will thus have a high impact in the future.

According to Tim Berners-Lee, the semantic Web augments the current WWW by giving information a well-defined meaning, better enabling computers and people to work in cooperation (Berners-Lee, Hendler, & Lassila, 2001). This is done by adding machine-understandable content to Web resources. The result of this process is metadata, usually described as data about data. Descriptions such as this acquire semantics by referring to an ontology. The semantic Web's vision is that once all the layers shown in Figure 4 are in place, we will have an environment in which we can place trust that the data we are seeing, the deductions we are making, and the claims we are receiving have some value. The goal is to make the user's life easier through the aggregation and creation of new, trusted information from the Web, to enhance search functionality, and, in the ideal case, to infer additional knowledge.

Figure 4 depicts the original "layer cake" proposed by Tim Berners-Lee (Berners-Lee et al., 2001). The role of Unicode, URIs, XML, and Namespaces is limited to that of a syntax carrier for data exchange. An XML Schema defines simple data types such as string, date, or integer. The standardization process has currently reached OWL: the remaining layers are not yet fully specified. Hence, many changes to the original layer cake are possible and quite likely. In the following section, we discuss the layers one by one. In doing so, we focus on the two most stable recommendations so far, namely RDF and OWL.

RDF(S)

The resource description framework (RDF) (Lassila & Swick, 1999) can be used to make simple assertions about Web resources or any other entity that can be named. A simple assertion in RDF is called a *statement* and consists of a triple (*subject, predicate, object*). Subjects, predicates, and objects are URIs; objects may also take a literal value (e.g., a string). For instance, a statement (*example:WLAN, rdf:label, "IEEE 802.11 WLAN Specification"*) associates a name with the entity identified by the *example:WLAN* URI.

RDF Schema (RDFS) extends RDF with additional modeling primitives (Lassila & Swick, 1999), viz., classes and relations (called properties in RDFS) that can be specified, put into hierarchies, and interlinked to specify simple ontologies. For example, the classes, relations, and instances shown in Figures 2 and 3 can be

Figure 4. The Semantic Web "layer cake" as proposed by Tim Berners-Lee (Berners-Lee et al., 2001)

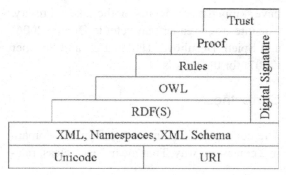

specified by a set of RDF(S) statements. Below, we list the statements that define the Specification class, the describes relation, and the *example: WLAN* instance.

(example:Specification, rdf:type, rdfs:Class)
(example:Specification, rdfs:subClassOf, example:Entity)
(example:describes, rdf:type, rdfs:Property)
(example:describes, rdfs:domain, example:Specification)
(example:describes, rdfs:range, example:Communication-Means)
(example:WLAN, rdf:type, example:Specification)
(example:WLAN, example:describes, example:Antenna2)
(example:WLAN, example:describes, example:Antenna3)

OWL

RDF(S) has one SQL-like query language, which is called SPARQL (Prud'hommeaux & Seaborne, 2006). However, the lack of a formal logical underpinning of RDF(S) prevents automatic reasoning tasks. In addition, the RDF(S) modeling primitives are limited with respect to expressiveness. Therefore, the W3C has come up with a dedicated set of logic-based languages called OWL (Web ontology language) (McGuinness & Harmelen, 2004). This set of languages allows the explicit specification of conceptualizations by logical theories, making intelligent reasoning tasks possible. For instance, using OWL, relations can be specified as transitive, and the transitive closure of the relation can be inferred automatically. OWL consists of:

OWL Lite

OWL Lite is the simplest variant of OWL. Its modeling primitives are a strict subset of the OWL DL modeling primitives. The modeling primitives were chosen using an 80:20 rule: OWL Lite contains the modeling primitives which are most often required. Furthermore, OWL Lite's reduced expressiveness leads to more efficient reasoners.

OWL DL

OWL DL is the most prominent variant of OWL. It is based on an older variant of Description Logic (DL) (Baader, Calvanese, McGuinness, Nardi, & Patel-Schneider, 2003) which essentially has been made Web-compliant. Description Logics are a family of knowledge representation languages which can be used to represent the terminological knowledge of an application domain in a structured and formally well-understood way. Web compliance means that URIs are used for identification, XML schema datatypes are introduced, and there is an RDF serialization for representing OWL DL ontologies. Below, we list the modeling primitives that exceed the expressiveness of RDF(S)[2]. The additional modeling primitives can be leveraged to specify our conceptualization more precisely:

- **Transitive Relations:** If a relation P is specified as transitive, then $P(x,y)$ and $P(y,z)$ implies $P(x,z)$.
- **Symmetric Relations:** If a relation P is tagged as symmetric, then $P(x,y)$ holds if $P(y,x)$.
- **Functional Relations:** If a relation P is tagged as functional, then $P(x,y)$ and $P(x,z)$ implies $y = z$.
- **Inverse Relations:** If a relation P_1 is tagged as the inverse of P_2, then $P_1(x,y)$ holds if $P_2(y,x)$.
- **Inverse Functional Relations:** If a relation P is tagged as inverse functional, then $P(y,x)$ and $P(z,x)$ implies $y = z$.
- **allValuesFrom:** The *allValuesFrom* modeling primitive restricts the range of a relation to a (complex) class. In our running example, we would restrict accesses to Communication Means, for instance.
- **someValuesFrom:** The difference between this and *allValuesFrom* is that there must exist at least one instance in the range of the specified relation.

95

- **Cardinality:** The *cardinality* primitive permits the specification of exactly the number of elements in a relation.
- **hasValue:** The *hasValue* primitive allows us to specify classes based on the existence of particular relation values.
- **equivalentClass:** The *equivalentClass* primitive is used to indicate that two classes have precisely the same instances.
- **equivalentRelation:** In order to tie relations together in a similar fashion, we use *equivalentRelation*.
- **Identity between Instances:** This primitive is similar to that for classes, but declares two instances to be identical.
- **Different Instances:** This primitive provides the opposite effect from the previous.
- **Complex Class Definitions:** OWL DL provides additional primitives for forming complex classes. The basic set operations, namely *union*, *intersection*, and *complement*, are provided. Additionally, classes can be defined by *enumeration*, and it is also possible to assert the *disjointness* of classes.

OWL Full

As the name suggests, OWL Full supersedes the expressiveness of OWL DL. For example, the distinction between classes and instances is no longer strict. Instances can also be classes simultaneously, and can have instances themselves. In essence, OWL Full equals first-order logic (also called predicate logic), which is known to be undecidable. This means that sound and complete reasoners cannot be constructed for this logic, which makes it very impracticable.

The explicit specification, that is, logical representation, of a conceptualization is a prerequisite for automatic reasoning tasks. Reasoners (also known as inference engines) enable such tasks, as they are implementations of logic calculi. Examples of OWL reasoners are KAON2 (Motik, Sattler, & Studer, 2004), FaCT (Horrocks, 1998)

and Racer (Haarslev & Möller, 2001). Next, we give a partial overview of typical OWL DL reasoning tasks:

- **Class satisfiability:** A class is satisfiable with respect to an ontology if the ontology can be interpreted such that the extension of the class is nonempty, that is, the class can potentially have an instance.
- **Ontology consistency:** An ontology is consistent if all of its classes are satisfiable.
- **Class subsumption:** A class X subsumes a class Y with respect to an ontology if any instance of Y is also an instance of X, no matter how the ontology is interpreted. A pairwise subsumption test of all classes in the ontology obtains an automatic classification of the taxonomy.
- **Class equivalence:** A concept X is equivalent to a class Y with respect to an ontology if X and Y subsume each other.
- **Class disjointness:** Two classes are disjoint with respect to an ontology if they do not have a common instance.
- **Instance retrieval:** Instance retrieval specifies which instances in the ontology are subsumed by a query.
- **Instance realization:** Instance realization specifies to which classes an instance belongs.

Rules

The Rule Layer provides an interoperable language for describing the sets of deductions one can make from a collection of data, that is, how, given a ontology-based information base, one can derive new information from existing data. At the time of writing this chapter, SWRL, the Semantic Web Rule Language (Horrocks, Patel-Schneider, Boley, Tabet, Grosof, & Dean, 2004), F-Logic (Kifer, Lausen, & Wu, 1995), and Business Rule approaches (Morgan, 2002), are in discussions for standardization within the context of the W3C Rule Interchange Format (W3C, 2005).

In our running example, we can specify a rule which automatically infers whether there is a communication channel between two nodes. This is the case when two nodes access a communication means with identical specification. The corresponding rule is depicted next, and can be leveraged for countering challenge (2) as detailed in the section "Ontologies for Verification of Service Composition." *channel*(*Gateway*#1,*PDA*#1) would be inferred because both nodes access the same Ethernet cable. A counterexample would be *channel*(*RFIDreader*#1,*PDA*#1) because the nodes access antennae with incompatible WLAN specifications.

$$channel(x,y) \leftarrow Node(x) \wedge Node(y) \wedge accesses(x,a)$$
$$\wedge accesses(y,b) \wedge Specification(z) \wedge describes(z,a)$$
$$\wedge describes(z,b)$$

Proof, Trust, and Digital Signatures

The Proof language will provide a way of describing the steps taken to derive a conclusion from the facts. Proofs can then be passed around and verified, providing shortcuts to new facts in the system without requiring each node to make the deductions on it's own. The vision of the Trust layer on top is to create an environment in which we can place trust on the data we are seeing, the deductions we are making, and the claims we are receiving. For reasoning to be able to take trust into account, the common logical model requires extension to include the keys with which assertions have been digitally signed. The Proof and Trust layers, as well as the Digital Signatures, are not yet specified.

BENEFITS OF ONTOLOGIES

In the previous section, we introduced ontologies and focused on recent W3C recommendations emerging from the Semantic Web Activity. The latter are likely to have a high impact on future tools and the interoperability of ontology-based applications. In this section, we discuss the general benefits of ontologies. We give concrete examples of the benefits in the section "Ontologies for Improving the Smart Items Middleware", where we detail how ontologies can be used to counter the three challenges introduced in the section "Fundamental Scalability Challenges".

Benefits through Conceptual Modeling (Conceptualization)

The first set of benefits concentrates on conceptual modeling. All the advantages are conceivable at first sight. However, they are hard—or sometimes even impossible—to measure.

Reuse, Flexibility, and Maintainability

With modeling techniques, such as UML, ERM, or ontologies, we make the conceptual model underlying a specific application explicit. In our running example, we analyze the domain of smart devices, identify relevant classes and their relations, and represent this knowledge explicitly. Thus, the ontology can be reused in other applications in the same domain, and can be used to facilitate communication with domain experts. The alternative would be to hard-code domain knowledge, resulting in an inflexible application with high maintenance costs (every change of the domain knowledge would require code adaptation and recompilation).

Reuse of Best Practice for Conceptual Modeling

Recent developments allow us to talk about the quality of ontologies as well as ontology design patterns. In addition to purely structural approaches, for example, the normalization of relational data models, the ontology design patterns consider the conceptual level (Gangemi, 2005). For example, a simple participation pattern (including objects taking part in events) emerges in domain ontologies as diverse as enterprise models, legal norms, software management, biochemical pathways, and fishery techniques. Ontology design patterns are useful to acquire, develop, and refine an ontology.

Standardization

We already learned in the section "Section Ontologies and Semantic Web Specifications" that the standardized ontology languages of the W3C are a significant step towards tool interoperability and will thus have a high impact in the future. So far, there have been a plethora of ontology languages in research and academia without any interoperability. In addition, the Object Modeling Group (OMG) is currently developing an Ontology Definition Metamodel (IBM, Sandpiper, 2006). Once established, ODM will allow using UML tools to specify OWL ontologies as well.

Benefits from Explicit Specification

The second set of benefits focuses on the explicit specification, that is, advantages that are a consequence of the logic-based representation. As with the aforementioned benefits, the following ones are also hard to substantiate in numbers.

Unambiguous, Formal Representation of Shared Meanings of Terms

The advantage of ontologies over other conceptual modeling techniques is the decreased ambiguity of the modeling. This is due to the increased formality of the logic-based representation. For instance, relations can be defined as symmetric, transitive, or inverse. A reasoner can leverage the formal representation to infer additional knowl-

edge, perform consistency checks, and so forth. A user of the ontology can leverage the increased formality to avoid ambiguity. Depending on the expressiveness of the ontology language, one might add further rules or integrity constraints. While something similar can be done with approaches such as OCL (the Object Constraint Language in UML), ontologies demand agreement at the modeling level. All this results in a formal, machine executable description of the shared meaning of terms and relations.

Reasoning Saves Development Efforts

We discussed in "Ontologies and Semantic Web Specifications" that ontology languages are based on logics, possibly with a rule mechanism on top. Reasoners let us leverage the advantages of the logics and offer powerful functionality, such as instance retrieval (all instances of a class x), subsumption checking (is a class x subsumed by a class y?), automatic classification of an ontology, consistency checking, and potentially a rule mechanism. This means that such functionality does not have to be developed from scratch.

Many problems can be reduced to such functionality. For example, the matching of services can be reduced to the subsumption problem. A detailed example follows in the section "Ontologies for Improving the Smart Items Middleware," where we apply rules to realize a verification mechanism. In essence, we can say that ontological modeling and the associated reasoning capabilities can be used to save development efforts.

Standardization

So far, there has not only been a plethora of ontology languages in research and academia, but also a multitude of existing ontology editors, stores, and reasoners. Hence, standardization also comes in handy for interoperability between such tools.

LIMITATIONS OF ONTOLOGIES

Despite all the benefits discussed in the previous section, every ontology-based application encounters limitations. In the following section, we proceed by giving a general explanation of each limitation. We give concrete examples of the limitations in the section "Ontologies for Improving the Smart Items Middleware."

Theoretical Limitations

The first set of limitations is of a theoretical nature. Among them is the fundamental trade-off between expressiveness and efficiency, as well as the widely known frame problem.

Expressiveness vs. Efficiency

Representation languages for ontologies encounter a trade-off between expressiveness and efficiency. The search for expressiveness is an elaborate process of finding consensus on what modeling primitives might be required most urgently by potential users. Requirements for more modeling primitives, that is, expressiveness, must be traded off against efficiency or even decidability of the corresponding reasoner. In essence, we can say that the more modeling primitives the language provides, the less efficient the respective reasoners are. The decision for the right language has to be taken on a case-by-case basis: if expressiveness is important, use a language with many modeling primitives but with a less efficient reasoner. If fast run-time reasoning is important, use a less expressive language.

The most recent example of this trade-off is shown by the three increasingly powerful variants of OWL, viz., OWL Lite, OWL DL, and OWL Full. OWL Lite and OWL DL are languages from the family of description logics (DL) and, thus, strict subsets of first-order logic. If chosen carefully, as are OWL Lite and OWL DL, they are decidable, which means that sound and complete reasoners can be constructed. OWL Full equals full first-order logic which is known to be undecidable, that is, no sound and complete reasoner exists for this language.

The Frame Problem

Ontologies are ideally suited to categorize the entities in a relevant domain and to capture their interrelationships, as well as specific situations, via instances. User groups can agree on the ontology with the ultimate goal of information integration and mutual understanding. However, ontologies exhibit fundamental limitations when describing the behavior of entities. As an example, consider the preconditions, post conditions, and the functionality of a service. All theses aspects are required for semantic service discovery, yet their representation via ontologies is severely limited. The reason is to be found in the logic-based representation and is called the *frame problem*.

Put succinctly, the frame problem in its narrow, technical form is this: Using mathematical logic, how is it possible to write formulae that describe the effects of actions without having to write a large number of accompanying formulae that describe the obvious noneffects of those actions? This means that in standard first-order logic, one would need to describe the properties that change as the result of an action as well as the properties that *do not* change (Baader, 1999). The challenge is to find a way to capture the noneffects of actions in formal logic. What we need is some way of declaring the general rule-of-thumb that an action can be assumed not to change a given property of a situation unless there is evidence to the contrary. The main obstacle to doing this is the monotonicity of classical logic. In classical logic, the set of conclusions that can be drawn from a set of formulae always increases with the addition of further formulae. This makes it impossible to express a rule that has an open-ended set of exceptions. The solution to the frame problem requires special logic languages which are, however, not aligned with common ontology languages, for example (Levesque, Pirri, & Reiter, 1998).

Practical Limitations

Unlike the theoretical limitations, which are rooted in the fundamentals of ontologies, the limitations discussed in this section typically occur when ontologies are applied in practice.

Development vs. Modeling Efforts

In the section "Benefits from Explicit Specification," we learned that reasoning could be used to reduce the development efforts. Reasoners provide us with powerful functionality, such as consistency checks, automatic classification of an ontology, rules, and so forth. A specific problem might be reduced to the services offered by the reasoner. Therefore, one is able to avoid developing a solution from scratch.

The drawback here is that we have to invest modeling efforts to apply the reasoner. First of all, developers have to be skilled enough to build an ontology and rules. While building the actual ontology is a one-off effort, every relevant entity has to be modeled via the ontology as well. This is a linear effort based on the number of entities. Finally, we cannot expect the ontology to remain stable over time. Changes will be necessary, and will lead to maintenance efforts.

In our example, we have to come up with the ontology depicted in Figure 2 and extensions for specific domains. While this is a one-off effort, it is not to be underestimated. The ontology has to be built in such a way that the rules can be efficiently applied. This requires a lot of expertise from the ontology engineer. Furthermore, all entities in our example have to be classified and modeled via the ontology. As shown in the section "Ontologies and Semantic Web Specifications," the *WLAN* instance has to be classified as an instance of the Specification class and has to be related to the ontology shown in Figure 3. As

mentioned before, this is a linear effort based on the number of entities we have to model. In addition, the rules must be modeled, which requires detailed domain expertise.

In conclusion, there is a trade-off between development and modeling efforts. On the one hand, we save development efforts by reducing specific problems to the functionality provided by reasoning. On the other hand, we have to invest modeling efforts in order to model the ontology and relevant entities. Modeling is a prerequisite for using the reasoner. Identifying the sweet spot between both efforts is a difficult undertaking, because it is hard to measure. Therefore, the trade-off must be made on a case-by-case basis.

Modeling Scope

Ontologies are afflicted with several other problematic aspects, which we subsume under the term "modeling scope". First, ontologies formalize the shared understanding of a user group to enable information integration. However, different user groups will use different ontologies: we cannot expect the usage of an all-encompassing ontology. Manual reconciliation or sophisticated ontology mapping algorithms will be required. (Ehrig, 2006) discusses several different approaches to ontology mapping. Most of them are probabilistic and require manual revision. Another approach is to use a common foundational ontology to align the ontologies (Guarino, 1998). The foundational ontology can be seen as a generic modeling basis which is used for several domain-specific ontologies. It is expected that having a common basis facilitates mapping between domain-specific terms. However, this has not been proven so far.

Second, ontologies model a specific domain. There have been attempts for an all-encompassing ontology, but they have failed, typically because of the lack of agreement and because of the rapidly changing and expanding universe of discourse. One of the most prominent examples of the past has been the CYC project (Guha & Lenat, 1990).

In our example, we also encounter expansions of the universe of discourse, that is, the ontology must account for future technologies.

ONTOLOGIES FOR IMPROVING THE SMART ITEMS MIDDLEWARE

In this section, we leverage the advantages of ontologies to counter the challenges (*1*) - (*3*) presented in the section "Fundamental Scalability Challenges." Of the three challenges, we sketch solutions to (*1*) and (*3*) and discuss (*2*) in more detail. Furthermore, we highlight which of the benefits and limitations apply.

Ontologies for Service Identification

Descriptions of services available for deployment in the smart items middleware are stored and maintained in the service repository. At system deployment or during service composition, relevant services must be selected from the repository. This selection usually takes place based on the available interfaces or service signatures, rather than on the semantics or behavior of the offered services. Ontologies can be used as the common vocabulary for the semantic description of services in the repository. They provide the formal basis for the mapping of a service request to available services (cf. benefits *unambiguous, formal representation of shared meanings of terms* as well as *reuse, flexibility, and maintainability*). However, such semantic service descriptions do not include the specification of the operation performed, for example, provision of temperature readings or the filtering of incoming sensor readings, as well as pre and post conditions of a service (cf. limitation *frame problem*).

In our running example, a developer chooses the services from the service repository required for our application. A request for a "temperature sensing" service gets translated by the repository into a request based on the common vocabulary

used to describe the semantic inputs and outputs of the available services. Through a couple of refinement steps, the system enables the developer to identify the required services. In a similar way, the developer identifies the desired device types based on their profile and availability.

Ontologies for Verification of Service Composition

Ontologies provide the means to conceptually model the heterogeneities of different device platforms. Software, platform, and device components must be enriched by additional information about the communication technologies they apply. The biggest challenge in modeling is the heterogeneity of communication aspects of different device types that must be represented. Required attributes may range from shapes of plugs to frequencies of radio signals. For example, to model applications for a system using different types of data cables, details about plug shapes and their specifications must be represented in the ontology. Also, in order to make the ontology adaptable to details of every application domain and to enable extensions for future technologies, it must be extensible.

The problem with this flexibility is in finding verification algorithms that work in spite of changes in the structure of the ontology. This problem can be solved by using the rather generic ontology depicted in Figure 2. This ontology serves as the basis on which more specific domain ontologies can be defined.

Combining the modeled information, the required and provided technologies for cross device interaction can be automatically derived and used to verify composite applications by a reasoner. The verification is achieved by compatibility rules for composition validation defined only on the basis of classes and relations in the ontology. Consequently, these rules apply to all descriptions that are based on this ontology. We have already seen an exemplary rule in the section "What is an Explicit Specification?" Therefore, it is ensured that the descriptions can be adapted to the required level of granularity and can be extended in the future. For example, new protocol standards to access upcoming generations of RFID tags must be included in the ontology once they become available. As long as the generic ontology is respected, no changes in the verification algorithms are needed. With this solution, we leverage the benefits of *reasoning saves development efforts* as we do not have to realize the verification from scratch. The drawback of this approach is that we have to expend efforts for modeling the ontology and rules, which can only be done manually (cf. limitation *development vs. modeling efforts*).

A Prototypical Implementation

Ziekow et al. (2006) provides a first prototype of a verification tool that can be used to compose and verify service compositions for smart device applications. As input, it uses an ontology together with verification rules. In addition, the tool requires descriptions of compositions (composition plan). These are models of functional components, for example, services or devices, and a specification of how these components are combined into a more complex service or application.

The verification tool includes a reasoner that checks the rules against the given composition plan. In this way, the correctness of the modeled composite service or application is determined. The tool returns a report about the check results. This can include errors and warnings or may just indicate a correct composition. In case of an error, information about the cause of a failure is provided to support the correction of the encountered problems.

During the verification process, intermediate results of composition steps are created. These are models of composite components resulting from the respective composition step. These models are also part of the verifier's output and describe already-verified combinations of components, which can be stored and reused for future compositions.

In this way, the tool supports the development and utilization of composite services or applications for collaborative smart devices. Detailed knowledge about the low-level communication issues is modeled once and automatically used by the tool. Another system component or a human can use the described tool to check for correctness of a composition, leaving the burden of considering details of the communication layer to the tool.

Revisiting our Running Example

In our running example, the developer might want to reduce energy-intensive communication. For deployment on the nodes, a service is chosen which identifies and filters temperature readings to the gateway when they exceed a specified threshold. For the gateways, a service is selected that issues read-requests to the RFID readers if more than 15% of the sensors report temperature readings above the threshold. Based on the RFID data, it can be determined if perishable products are on the shelves. Another service on the gateways informs all PDAs about perishable goods that are too warm. The specified composition of services

Figure 5. Verification tool for composite services for smart devices (Ziekow et al., 2006)

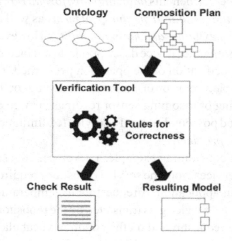

and device types can now be validated based on the service description and device profiles.

From a software perspective, an alternative implementation without using gateway devices would have been possible. The PDAs could directly receive and evaluate the sensor values, and could request the needed RFID data. However, in the setting described, there is no communication channel shared by RFID readers and PDAs. Although both have WLAN access, the RFID readers use encrypted communication whereas the PDAs do not. Consequently, their alternative composition plan would be falsified by the verification tool and rejected in the implementation process.

Ontologies for Service-to-Device Mapping

In addition to manual deployment using dedicated deployment tools, the smart items middleware should be able to automatically map required services onto the most suitable available devices, or to relocate services from one device to another based on changing system conditions. Such automatic deployment of services is essential to manage the increasing complexity of distributed large-scale smart items solutions or scenarios, where available devices change frequently.

An automatic "intelligent" mapping of required services to the most suitable available device requires a formal description of the service requirements (e.g., CPU power, available main memory, or communication means) as well as the capability profiles of the available target devices. Ontologies can provide the formal description means for the specification of service requirements (which can be stored together with the semantic service description in the service repository) and the device profiles (cf. benefit *unambiguous, formal representation of shared meanings of terms*). Based on this foundation, reasoning can be used to specify appropriate metrics to identify the "best" target device for a given service to be deployed

(cf. benefit *reasoning saves development efforts*). Note, however, that significant modeling efforts (for the ontologies as well as for the rules) have to be expended before the benefits can be reaped (cf. limitation *development vs. modeling efforts*).

In our running example, services of the verified composition plan are mapped to appropriate devices. Services chosen for the gateways, RFID readers, and PDAs are to be installed on all those devices that have appropriate locations and properties (e.g., sufficient memory). Also, at this point, deployment constraints are specified (e.g., that the temperature filter service gets deployed to only 30% of the nodes, which are also required to have a certain amount of battery power left). This constraint imposes the need for a remapping of services if some sensor nodes are running out of power. The service mapper then maps the given services to the most suitable devices available by taking into consideration a formal specification of these mapping constraints and the service and device profiles. The actual service deployment is done by a service injector component which installs the respective service binaries for the respective platform.

CONCLUSION

The chapter introduced the reader to ontologies with the focus on the recent W3C recommendations RDF(S) and OWL that, for the first time, provide standard ontology languages. The recommendations have high impact on future tools and the interoperability of ontology-based applications. We further contrasted the pros and cons of ontologies on a general level and showed where ontologies can be used to counter fundamental challenges to enable scalable services-based ubiquitous computing applications in real-time enterprises.

FUTURE RESEARCH DIRECTIONS

One future research direction of this work is the collaboration between the nodes of the sensor network. By using collaborative algorithms, the nodes are able to perform business processes autonomously and independently from the back-end, only reporting exceptional situations (such as a dangerous constellation or the change of a monitored value). The expected outcome is a system that is highly autonomous, fault-tolerant, and scalable. Powerful tools will be developed, that allow business professionals to model the business logic to be executed by the nodes, simply by combining basic services.

Another area of future work is concerned with closing the information loop for the manufacturer of a product over the whole product lifecycle. At the beginning of the life of a product (including design and production), the manufacturer has detailed information available. However, once the product is delivered and used (middle of life), as well as at the end of its life (when it is recycled or refurbished), the information available to the manufacturer is scarce. By attaching product embedded information devices (PEIDs, such as rewritable RFID-Tags, embedded systems, or sensors) to the goods that can gather and store information during their lifetime, the information loop can be closed. This will allow business applications that are integrated in complex business processes to uniformly access data stored on or gathered by PEIDs in real time. This also enables the applications to configure and control PEIDs and update their memory.

Finally, there is a body of work in research and academia around what is called Semantic Web Services (McIlraith, Son, & Zeng, 2001). The principal objective of Semantic Web Services is a wide-reaching formalization that allows full automation of the Web service management tasks, such as discovery and composition. The core of the proposals lies in creating semantic standards for the markup of Web services. Hence, another research direction is to evaluate whether the existing proposals can be used to also counter the technical challenges of our domain. The existing proposals are OWL-S (Martin, Burstein, Hobbs, Lassila, McDermott, & McIlraith, 2004), WSMO (Fensel & Bussler, 2002), and WSDL-S (Akkiraju, Farrell, Miller, Nagarajan, Schmidt, & Sheth, 2005).

REFERENCES

Booch, G., Jacobson, I., & Rumbaugh, J. (1998). *The unified modeling language user guide* (Vol. 1). Addison-Wesley.

Chen, P. P.-S. (1976). The entity-relationship model – Toward a unified view of data. *ACM Transactions on Database System, 1*(1), 9-36.

Gruber, T. R. (1995). Toward principles for the design of ontologies used for knowledge sharing. *International Journal of Human Computer Studies, 43*(5-6), 907-928.

Guha, R. V., & Lenat, D. (1990). Cyc: A mid-term report. *AI Magazine, 11*(3), 32-59.

Haarslev, V. & Möller, R. (2001). RACER system description. In R. Goré, A. Leitsch, & T. Nipkow (Eds.), In *Proceedings of the International Joint Conference on Automated Reasoning, IJCAR'2001, June 18-23,* Siena, Italy (pp. 701–705).

Horrocks, I. (1998). The FaCT system. In H. de Swart (Ed.), In *Proceedings of the 2nd Int. Conference on Analytic Tableaux and Related Methods (TABLEAUX'98): Vol. 1397. Lecture Notes in Artificial Intelligence* (pp. 307-312). Springer.

Motik, B., Sattler, U., & Studer, R. (2004). Query answering for OWL-DL with rules. In *Proceedings of the 3rd International Semantic Web Conference (ISWC 2004),* Hiroshima, Japan.

Oracle (2006, February). *Enterprise information architecture for RFID and sensor-based services.* White Paper.

Spiess, P., Bornhövd, C., Haller, S., Lin, T. & Schaper, J. (2007 March). Going beyond auto-ID: A service-oriented smart items infrastructure. *Journal of Enterprise Information Management, 20*(3), 356-370.

Studer, R., Benjamins, R., & Fensel, D. (1998, March). Knowledge engineering: Principles and methods. *Data & Knowledge Engineering, 25*(1-2), 161-198.

Ziekow, H., Avanes, A., & Bornhövd, C. (2006). Service composition and deployment for a smart items infrastructure. In *Proceedings of the 14th International Conference on Cooperative Information Systems, COOPIS'06,* Montpellier, France.

ADDITIONAL READING

Akkiraju, R., Farrell, J., Miller, J., Nagarajan, M., Schmidt, M.-T., Sheth, A., & Verma, K. (2005). Web service semantics - WSDL-S (Tech. Rep.). IBM Research and LSDIS Lab, University of Georgia.

Baader, F. (1999). Logic-based knowledge representation. In M. Wooldridge & M. M. Veloso (Eds.), *Artificial intelligence today: Col. 1600. Recent trends and developments* (pp. 13-41). Springer.

Baader, F., Calvanese, D., McGuinness, D., Nardi, D., & Patel-Schneider, P. (Eds.). (2003). *The description logic handbook.* Cambridge University Press.

Berners-Lee, T., Hendler, J., & Lassila, O. (2001, May). The Semantic Web. *Scientific American,* 34-43.

Bornhövd, C., Lin, T., Haller, S., & Schaper, J. (2004). Integrating automatic data acquisition with business processes – Experiences with SAP's Auto-ID infrastructure. In *Proceedings of the 30th International Conference on Very Large Databases (VLDB'04),* Toronto, Canada.

Ehrig, M. (2006). Ontology alignment—Bridging the semantic gap. *The Semantic Web and beyond* (Vol. IV). New York: Springer.

Fensel, D. & Bussler, C. (2002). The web service modeling framework WSMF. *Electronic Commerce: Research and Applications, 1,* 113–137.

Gangemi, A. (2005). Ontology design patterns for semantic web content. In Y. Gil, E. Motta, V. R. Benjamins, & M. A. Musen (Eds.), *The semantic web -ISWC 2005.* In *Proceedings of the 4th International Semantic Web Conference: Vol. 3729. ISWC 2005,* Galway, Ireland.

Guarino, N. (1998). Formal ontology in information systems. In N. Guarino (Ed.), *Formal ontology in information systems* (pp. 3-15). In *Proceedings of FOIS'98,* Trento, Italy. Amsterdam: IOS Press.

Horrocks, I., Patel-Schneider, F., Boley, H., Tabet, S., Grosof, B., & Dean, M. (2004). SWRL: A semantic web rule language combining OWL and ruleML. *W3C member submission.* Retrieved October 8, 2007, from http://www.w3.org/Submission/SWRL/

IBM, Sandpiper (2006). *Ontology definition metamodel sixth revised submission to OMG/ RFP ad/2003-03-40.* Retrieved October 8, 2007, from http://www.omg.org/ontology/

Kifer, M., Lausen, G., & Wu, J. (1995). Logical foundations of object-oriented and frame-based languages. *Journal of the ACM, 42*(1), 741–843.

Lassila, O., & Swick, R. (1999, February). Resource description framework (RDF) model and syntax specification. *W3C recommendation.*

Retrieved October 8, 2007, from http://www.w3.org/TR/1999/REC-rdf-syntax-19990222/

Levesque, H., Pirri, F., & Reiter, R. (1998). Foundations for the situation calculus. *Electronic Transactions on Artificial Intelligence, 2*(3-4), 159-178.

Martin, D., Burstein, M., Hobbs, J., Lassila, O., McDermott, D., McIlraith, S., Narayanan, S., Paolucci, M., Parsia, B., Payne, T., Sirin, E., Srinivasan, N., & Sycara, K. (2004). *OWL-S: Semantic markup for web services.* Retrieved October 8, 2007, from http://www.daml.org/services/owl-s/1.1/

McIlraith, S. A., Son, T–C., & Zeng, H. (2001). Semantic web services. *IEEE Intelligent Systems, 16*(2), 46–53.

McGuinness, D. L., & Harmelen, F. van. (2004, February). Web ontology language (OWL) overview. *W3C recommendation.* Retrieved October 8, 2007, from http://www.w3.org/TR/owl-features/

Morgan, T. (2002). Business rules and information systems: Aligning IT with business goals. *Addison-Wesley professional* (1st ed.).

Oberle, D. (2006). Semantic management of middleware. *The semantic web and beyond* (Vol. I). New York: Springer.

Prud'hommeaux, E. & Seaborne, A. (2006). SPARQL query language for RDF. *W3C working draft.* Retrieved October 8, 2007, from http://www.w3.org/TR/rdf-sparql-query/

Staab, S., & Studer, R. (2004). *Handbook on ontologies.* Heidelberg: Springer.

W3C (2001). *Technology and society domain. Semantic Web activity.* October 8, 2007, from http://www.w3.org/2001/sw/

W3C (2005). *Technology and society domain. Semantic web activity, Rule interchange format.* Retrieved October 8, 2007, from http://www.w3.org/2005/rules/

ENDNOTES

[1] Depending on the specific language used, classes are also called concepts or universals, relations are also called properties or roles, and instances are also called individuals or particulars.

[2] Note that many of these primitives are also part of the OWL Lite language. Furthermore, Web compliance as described above holds for all three OWL variants.

Chapter V
Service Discovery

Gerhard Austaller
Technische Universität Darmstadt, Germany

ABSTRACT

The chapter "Ubiquitous Services and Business Processes" discussed the benefits for real time enterprises of service oriented architectures (SOA) in terms of reusability and flexibility. Web services are one incarnation of SOA. This chapter gives a brief introduction to SOA. It discusses the attributes that define SOA, the roles of the participants in a service oriented environment. The essence of SOA is that clients use services offered by a service provider to get a task done. For the moment we simplify service to "a software component with network connection". Services are offered with a description at well-known "places" (also called registries, repositories), where clients choose services according to their needs. The chapter discusses several approaches to describe services and to look for them. Moreover, some well-known systems, and also current research, are discussed.

INTRODUCTION

We live in a service society and every day we are able to make use of many services because of the specialized training people have in different service areas. We need our damaged cars repaired and our hair cut, so we use the yellow pages to find feasible service providers and eventually negotiate with some of them to make a final decision of whom to use. This kind of specialized business has many advantages for consumers; the service providers are specialists, therefore they do the job faster, better, and cheaper than we could ourselves.

And if not satisfied, another service provider will be chosen next time.

Not surprisingly, this pattern to handle portions of work can also be found in distributed computer systems, namely "service oriented Architectures" (SOA) or "service oriented computing" (SOC). Applications are built of services, where each service fulfills a task for the application. Services are either implemented in software or act as proxies ("bridge") to hardware, for example printers or light switches. In contrast to software components, services run on different computers and communicate over networks with their clients.

SERVICE ORIENTED ARCHITECTURES

Although the general idea of service-oriented architectures is well understood, there are two competing views on SOA. Firstly, there are definitions that emphasize the "sum of operations provided by an object" (e.g., like in the "Open Distributed Processing" standard). A concrete technology then implements this model as shown in Figure 1. Secondly, there are definitions that already refer to the implementations or instances of a concrete technology as service (e.g., "Web Service Technology").

Depending on the model and the implementation of SOA, the terminology may vary, but there are common elements to all of them:

- Service is the sum of operations or actions provided by a service provider to a service client.
- (Service) Provider provides one or more services.
- (Service) Client uses services.
- Service Implementation is the technical realization (implementation) of the service.
- Client Implementation is the technical realization (implementation) of the client.
- Computational Interface is a mapping of the service to a concrete technology or programming language to use the service implementation.
- Network is used for communication between provider and client.

Another rarely used definition of "service" emerged with dynamic web pages for human users such as shops, route planning applications, search engines. In this case, the action offered on these Websites is referred to as a service, for example "selling a book" and "searching for a term". This case is out of the scope of this chapter. In our definition clients of services are (normally) other services or applications, but not human users. Of course, the Web pages mentioned can also offer a computational interface. This would also make them services according to our definition. Well-known examples are google.com or amazon. com. They can be accessed through Web pages by human users, but also through SOAP by other Web services.

Finding Services

Service client and service provider may not know each other at runtime and therefore a mechanism for them to find each other has to be provided. This is another part of defining SOAs.

Figure 2 gives an overview of the roles in SOA. The service provider announces (registers) its services at a service registry (repository). Depend-

Figure 1. Service model

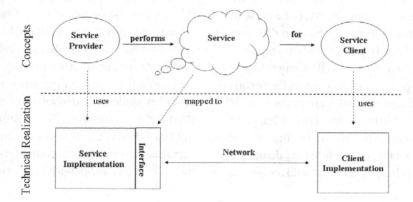

Figure 2. Roles in SOA

ing on the technology, the announcements vary in their expressiveness ranging from a key/value pair to an ontology-based description, as will be discussed later in section "Description". A client queries the registry (also called service broker or service mediator) to find required services. The query is structurally similar to the description. Therefore, different types of queries are discussed in section "Description", too. Further, the organization and implementation of registries may differ, as well as discussed later in section "Discovery and Lookup".

SERVICE DESCRIPTION AND DISCOVERY

This section gives an overview of different methods for describing a service ("service description") and finding them ("service discovery"). Any implementation introduced later in the chapter is based on these methods.

Service Description

Services, even if they are of the same type, can be realized in different ways. Therefore, there must be means to characterize the service further. A printer service, for example, may define that it is a grayscale printer that can print 12 pages per minute. In a company there may be a wide range of different printers and a client specifies which attributes must be fulfilled. We now discuss some types of service descriptions and query mechanisms that rely on them.

Key/Value & Strict Value Comparison

In this approach, attributes characterizing a service are a collection of key/value pairs. In a query for a service, it is only possible to specify the exact value of an attribute or a wild card to indicate that the attribute does not matter at all. One example is Jini, as will be discussed in section "Jini".

Key/Value & Query Language

Service attributes are modeled as in the first approach, but the query is more expressive. Attribute values can be compared to required values using operators such as >, <, =. Each comparison forms an expression. Expressions can be further combined using Boolean operations. So it is possible to query for a printer with a resolution of at least 600dpi, but at most 1200dpi. The service location protocol that will be discussed in section "service location protocol (SLP)" supports this kind of query.

Template-Based Description

With the increasing use of semistructured languages like XML, such languages are also used for service description. Although XML documents can be viewed as "keys" (elements) containing "values" (data), which can be nested, sometimes service descriptions based on such languages are referred to as template-based description. A schema defines strictly the structure of the document. This implies that the structure of the description is very strict. An example is UPnP, discussed in section "Universal Plug and Play (UPnP) and Simple Service Discovery Protocol (SSDP)".

Semantic Description

Inspired by the idea of the semantic Web, many companies and researchers started to work on semantic services based on Web service technology or other SOA technology using ontologies. Ontologies are used to provide a strict and unambiguous description of a service. Furthermore, inference engines are used to find the most appropriate services. Often, further aspects like context-awareness are taken into account for service discovery. Some current research is discussed in section "Research" of this chapter.

Service Discovery and Service Lookup

The terms discovery and lookup are often used in the context of service selection. Though similar in their meaning, there exist some differences. Service discovery typically refers to a completely spontaneous method without any (centralized) servers holding service description information. In contrast, service lookup refers to methods that use lookup servers, where services register with their description and clients can query for appropriate services. Some systems first use discovery to find the registry and then use the registry for service lookup.

There are several approaches to finding services that can be classified as follows.

Centralized Registry

There is a centralized repository storing all information. Centralized refers to an organizational or a technical unit. Organizational means one repository may exist for a department or a company. A technical unit refers to the realization and implementation. Sometimes the design of the service discovery protocol and the technology used to implement it imposes requirements on the environment where it will be used. For instance, there must be a repository within a network subnet, where service discovery should be possible.

A service publishes its description to the registry and clients can lookup there for required services. Depending on the implementation,

descriptions are registered with an "expiration date", a so-called lease. The service renews this information periodically. If a service crashes or quits without deregistering, the description becomes invalid after some time and the stale information disappears from the registry.

Federated Registry

Centralized registries can be federated. This means that the registries hold information about other registries. A client can get this information and browse through several other registries also. In more transparent modes, a registry forwards client queries automatically to other registries, gathers the responses and sends them back to the client. This process is completely transparent to the clients.

Distributed Registry

Distributed registries go further than federated registries and almost work in a peer-to-peer like style. In this case, any client node holds a local part of the registry. This local part holds information about local services and caches frequently used services and may even hold redundant information from other registry parts. Queries are distributed across the other registry parts transparently to the clients.

Without Registry

Some service discovery protocols do not rely on any registry, but make use of and rely on the mechanisms of the underlying network. One example is multicast of IP networks. Services announce their existence periodically on well-defined multicast channels to which clients listen. The multicast messages are sent periodically, so clients that join the network later also get the announcements. In some protocols, clients may also send multicast messages for triggering services to immediately announce themselves. Clients then do not have to wait for the periodic announcement.

Besides the organization of the registries there is another aspect, namely the communication pattern. There are two types of communication patterns.

Query/Pull

Clients have to query for services. This can reduce communication overhead, if the relationship between clients and services is very stable for a long time.

Notification/Push

Clients can register and be notified if a new and appropriate service appears. This mode is very feasible in mobile and ubiquitous environments. In a pull mode, a client has to query for new services periodically. The question remains of what is the right "period" in order not to miss an important service? If the period chosen is too long, there is a great deal of unnecessary communication that consumes energy and bandwidth and might incur costs. If it is too short, an important service could be missed.

SERVICE DISCOVERY SYSTEMS

This section describes some existing service discovery systems. Special attention is paid to their importance for Real Time Enterprises and availability.

Universal Plug and Play (UPnP) and Simple Service Discovery Protocol (SSDP)

Universal Plug and Play (UPnP) is a joint effort of the UPnP Forum, an industry initiative, "to enable simple and robust connectivity among stand-alone devices and PCs from many different vendors" (UPnP(TM) Forum, 2006). Initiated by Microsoft, the name UPnP suggests making connecting networked devices as easy as Plug&Play for computer peripheral devices.

In contrast to other efforts, the UPnP Forum defines a complete standard not only for the discovery of services, but also for controlling them. This standard is built upon IP that is used for communication between devices and uses established technologies like HTTP and SOAP (XML) for discovery, description, and control of devices.

UPnP (UPnP(TM) Forum, 2003) defines:

1. Addressing (assigning IP addresses to devices);
2. Discovery (announcing the existence of devices and services and finding appropriate services);
3. Description (describing the capabilities of devices and services);
4. Controlling (using services);
5. Eventing (getting notifications about the state changes of a service);
6. Presentation (enabling human users to control the service through a Web page).

Controlling, eventing, and presentation are not discussed further, since these topics are out of the scope of this chapter.

Architecture

UPnP defines two roles: controlled devices (or simply "devices") containing services and control points, which use these services. Both can be implemented in a single, physical device.

A physical device may contain several services (functional units) or further logical devices as shown in Figure 3. The logical devices can be organized as devices within one container (a so called "root device") or as several root devices.

Figure 3. A UPnP example device

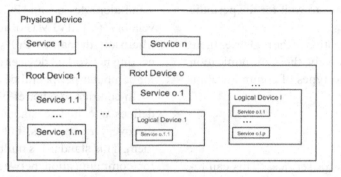

A root device contains services and, if needed, further embedded devices. This means that one physical device may contain one or more root device with each of them containing embedded devices. Physical and embedded devices contain services.

Every root device has a device description containing the description for the embedded devices. It does not matter whether there is only one root device or several root devices on one physical device.

Addressing

UPnP is based on IP. Therefore, physical devices plugged into the network have assigned IP addresses. UPnP defines two methods for that. The first method is requesting an IP address via DHCP. If no DHCP server is available, the IP address is determined by AUTO-IP like Bonjour (see 3.2). Several mechanisms ensure unique IP addresses for the devices and automatically resolve conflicts. Conflict resolution is not only done at device startup, but at any time during runtime of the device.

Devices can register a host name for DNS name resolution at a DNS server even though the host name is unimportant for discovery. Still, the device itself has to ensure that the name is unique.

Discovery

After a device is assigned an IP address, it uses the Simple Service Discovery Protocol (SSDP) to advertise itself, embedded devices and its services to control points. These advertisements only contain information about the device or service types and links to the descriptions, but no detailed descriptions. SSDP messages are HTTP requests over multicast UDP, also called HTTPMulticast. Due to the unreliable nature of UDP, discovery messages should be sent several times but not more than three times. Advertisements also have expiration times. That requires periodic retransmission of the messages. Devices and services should also deregister when they are about to leave the network. SSDP also allows control points to search for services when added to the network.

Figure 4 depicts the request line (first line) and the content of the message header of the request sent by a device added to the network.

The NOTIFY request determines the method for sending notifications. The second argument specifies the target of the request and the last argument determines the protocol version. The example request applies to no specific resource and the protocol is HTTP version 1.1. HOST determines the multicast channel used. In the example case, it is 239.255.255.250:1900. CACHE-

Figure 4. Notify message containing NTS ssdp: Alive

```
NOTIFY * HTTP/1.1
HOST: 239.255.255.250:1900
CACHE-CONTROL: max-age=seconds until advertisement
expires
N: URL for UPnP description for root device
NT: search target
NTS: ssdp:alive
SERVER: OS/version UPnP/1.0 product/version
USN: advertisement UUID
```

Figure 5. Search request

```
M-SEARCH * HTTP/1.1
HOST: 239.255.255.250:1900
MAN: "ssdp:discover"
MX: seconds to delay response
ST: search target
```

CONTROL specifies the time, for which the advertisement is valid. The UPnP specification recommends renewing the advertisement after about half of the time. LOCATION contains the URL for the description of the root device. NT determines the notification type. The value depends upon the notification advertising a device, root device, embedded device or service. NTS determines the notification subtype. The subtype in the example is "ssdp:alive", which is used to advertise the existence of a device or service. Another subtype is ssdp:byebye. This should be sent before a device leaves the network. SERVER specifies the operating system of the device and further device specific information. And USN finally defines a unique ID for the instance of a device or service.

SSDP defines two more messages to search for services (search request) and to respond to a search request. Figure 5 shows an example of a search request in the first line and the request header.

The M-SEARCH specifies the method for the search request. The second argument specifies the target of the request and the last argument determines the protocol version. The example request applies to no specific resource and the protocol is HTTP version 1.1. HOST determines the multicast channel used. SSDP compliant devices must use 239.255.255.250:1900. MAN is required by the HTTP extension framework and must be "ssdp: discover" according to the UPnP specification. MX defines the maximum waiting time in seconds. A device should wait for a random time between

1 and this value, before sending the response. ST defines the search target. It defines what type of device or service the control point is interested in. There is no further possibility for a control point to specify a more detailed query. The control point has to download the description from the device and then compare it with its requirements to choose the most appropriate service.

If a device or a service receives a M-SEARCH query and the query matches their descriptions, they send their UDP responses to the source IP address of the search request. It contains similar information as the NOTIFY message. The header of the response message includes the MAN attribute with the value "ssdp:alive" and the LOCATION attribute with a URL for the service description.

Description

During the process of discovery, control points gather URLs to service descriptions of the service types they are interested in. The URLs are then used in the next step to learn more about the services through the analysis of the descriptions. Service descriptions are XML documents that are requested through HTTP from the device or service. The UPnP Forum defines a couple of descriptions typically used in companies and in private. The descriptions range from those of printers to those of entertainment systems, for example CD players (UPnP(TM) Forum, 2006).

The organization of devices and services is reflected in the service description. The device description contains vendor specific information, a list of services and a list of embedded devices as shown in Figure 6 from (UPnP(TM) Forum, 2003).

The vendor specific part contains information such as the model number, the manufacturer, the model name, a human readable device description, and a serial number. Every service part contains

URLs for several aspects of the service: a URL for the service description, a URL for eventing and a URL for controlling the service. The device list contains again a device description for every embedded device. The service description finally defines the actions that a service can perform. This definition is similar to a computational interface including function names and expected parameters.

Figure 6. UPnP device description

```xml
<?xml version="1.0"?>
<root xmlns="urn:schemas-upnp-org:device-1-0">
  <specVersion>
     <major>1</major>
     <minor>0</minor>
  </specVersion>
  <URLBase>base URL for all relative URLs</URLBase>
   <device>
    <deviceType>urn:schemas-upnp-org:device:deviceType:v</deviceType>
    <friendlyName>short user-friendly title</friendlyName>
    <manufacturer>manufacturer name</manufacturer>
    <manufacturerURL>URL to manufacturer site</manufacturerURL>
    <modelDescription>long user-friendly title</modelDescription>
    <modelName>model name</modelName>
    <modelNumber>model number</modelNumber>
    <modelURL>URL to model site</modelURL>
    <serialNumber>manufacturer's serial number</serialNumber>
    <UDN>uuid:UUID</UDN>
    <UPC>Universal Product Code</UPC>
    <iconList>
       <icon>
          <mimetype>image/format</mimetype>
          <width>horizontal pixels</width>
          <height>vertical pixels</height>
          <depth>color depth</depth>
          <url>URL to icon</url>
       </icon>
       XML to declare other icons, if any, go here
    </iconList>
    <serviceList>
       <service>
          <serviceType>urn:schemas-upnp-org:service:serviceType:v</serviceType>
          <serviceId>urn:upnp-org:serviceId:serviceID</serviceId>
          <SCPDURL>URL to service description</SCPDURL>
          <controlURL>URL for control</controlURL>
       <eventSubURL>URL for eventing</eventSubURL>
       </service>
       Declarations for other services defined by a UPnP Forum working committee (if any) go here
       Declarations for other services added by UPnP vendor (if any) go here
    </serviceList>
    <deviceList>
       Description of embedded devices defined by a UPnP Forum working committee (if any) go here
       Description of embedded devices added by UPnP vendor (if any) go here
    </deviceList>
    <presentationURL>URL for presentation</presentationURL>
  </device>
</root>
```

Figure 7. Architecture of Bonjour

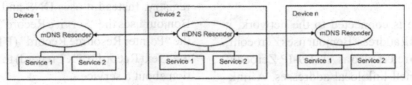

Bonjour

Normally, IP-based intranets in companies are maintained by administrators. They assign addresses to the computers or IP-enabled devices either directly on the device itself or through DHCP and set up DNS for the name resolution.

With more and more consumer devices developed for private use by untrained users (consumers), it is no longer possible to manually configure all devices. Consumer devices should work instantly, be interoperable, consumers should not have to understand how IP works, and of course should not have to set up a DNS or a DHCP server.

Apple considers Bonjour (Apple, 2006) to be a solution for this problem. Bonjour has emerged from the work of the IETF ZEROCONF Working Group (Zeroconf Working Group, 2006). In particular, Bonjour covers:

- Addressing (assigning unique IP addresses to devices);
- Naming (mapping unique names to IP addresses);
- Service discovery (finding appropriate services).

Bonjour does not define new protocols or interfaces for services. Instead, it uses existing ones.

General Architecture

Apple stresses that the focus of Bonjour is on service browsing in contrast to device discovery. The user specifies the type of service that is needed and then gets a list of available services. Next, the user selects the service and uses it. The hosts for services are devices that run one or more services. For instance, today there are many so-called multifunction devices that can print, scan and copy. In terms of Bonjour, the hardware device runs three services. There is often a close relationship between hardware and service. A "printing service" needs a printer hardware/device or even runs on that very device, so that sometimes there is no distinction made between the service and the device.

Some services are not bound to a particular piece of hardware, but can be purely virtual. A file sharing service can run on any computer, and even a camera could offer its pictures through a file sharing service.

Figure 7 depicts the general architecture and the interaction between the components. Clients, either users or other services, must be able to find services. Bonjour uses Multicast DNS (mDNS), in which DNS queries are sent over the local network using IP multicast. Services that encounter a query containing their DNS name should respond to this request. To avoid every service having to understand DNS, Apple suggests implementing a simple mDNS Responder that runs on a device. This responder handles the DNS requests for all services running on that device as depicted in Figure 6. Apple further provides an mDNS Responder daemon for some operating systems and APIs to register services with Bonjour.

Addressing

When a device is connected to the network, it needs a unique IP address. Bonjour uses Zeroconf, sometimes also referred to as AUTO-IP. Zeroconf uses self-assigned link-local addresses. A link-local address is an IP address in the range from 169.254.1.0 to 169.254.254.255 and can be seen as a private address range within the global IP address space. Any network can use this range, as IP packets from and to these addresses are not routed outside of the local network. This implies that Bonjour-enabled devices have to be in the same network segment and must not be separated by routers.

A device gets an IP address by choosing one from the link-local address range. Then, it sends an ARP (Address Resolution Protocol) query with that IP onto the network to see if another device already has this address. If there is no response, the IP is assigned to the device, otherwise another IP is selected, and the procedure is repeated until the device has chosen a free IP address.

Naming

After a device has chosen a unique IP address, it needs a unique host name. This process works like the assignment of a unique IP address to a device. The device sends an mDNS query for that name. If another device answers, the device has to choose a different name. If no other device answers, the device keeps the name. If a software service uses the Bonjour API to register with Bonjour, Bonjour renames the service by default. Bonjour further introduces a pseudo top level domain "local". Addresses in this domain resolve only to IP addresses in the local domain through mDNS.

Service Announcement

Bonjour introduces neither a new mechanism for service announcements (sometimes also called "service publication") nor a Bonjour specific registry. Instead it uses DNS and DNS records. Bonjour uses the "Service Record" (SRV record), the "Pointer Resource Record" (PTR record) and the "Text Record" (TXT record) to store information about a service.

The SRV record scheme as defined in RFC 2782 (RFCs specify standards for the Internet community (Postel, 1989)) is not sufficient for encoding several instances of one type of service. Therefore, the Internet draft "DNS-Based Service Discovery" (Cheshire & Krochmal, 2005) proposes the naming convention as follows: <Service Instance Name> = <Instance>.<Service>.<Domain> to address individual service instances in a SRV record. Depending on the source, either the proposed Internet draft or other technical references from Apple, the "service" is more correctly called "service type". The format of the SRV record is then:

<Instance>.<Service>.<Domain><TTL><Class> SRV <Priority> <Weight> <Port> <Target>.

Instance is the unique instance name of the service. The name is intended to be human readable. The Service entry consists of a pair of DNS labels, following the established convention for SRV records (Gulbrandsen, Vixie, & Esibov, 2000). The first label of the pair is the application protocol name with a preceding "_" like "printer" or "ipp". The second label is either "_tcp" or "_udp", depending on the transport protocol used by the service. Domain is the DNS domain name or "local". TTL (Time to Live) defines the validity time of the record. The Class field has to be "IN" for Internet. SRV is a constant expression to indicate that the entry is a SRV record. Priority defines the priority of the service. Services with a lower number should be used in preference to higher numbered services. Weight determines how services with the same priority should be selected. Services with equal priority should be selected randomly in proportion to their relative weights.

Port defines the UDP or TCP port where the service can be accessed. Target is the domain name of the device running the service. An example of a printer description looks as follows:

PrintsALot._printer._tcp.local 120 IN SRV 0 0 515 blackhawk.local

The information in the SRV record alone is not expressive enough for service discovery that enables clients to browse through a list of services to choose the most feasible one. Further entries in the PTR (Pointer Resource Records) and TXT resource records (Rosenbaum, 1993) are needed.

PTR records are normally used in DNS for reverse lookup, which means to get the domain name for a given IP address. In Bonjour, PTR records enable service discovery by mapping the type of the service to a specific instance of that type of service. The format of a PTR entry in Bonjour is:

<ServiceType>.<Domain> <TTL> <Class> PTR <Service Instance Name>

Figure 8 gives a client looking for local printer a pointer to a printer instance in the SRV resource record.

The TXT resource record finally can be used to store further information about the service:

<Service Instance Name> <Class> <TTL> TXT "<attribute name>=<attribute value>"

The attribute and values are service specific.

Service Discovery

Discovery is straightforward. Normal DNS queries can be used to get information from SRV

records or PTR records and to resolve service names into IP addresses. As mentioned, any mDNS responder reacts to queries concerning its entries. Queries for "_printer._tcp", for example, return every printer service running on any device in the local network.

Bluetooth Service Discovery Protocol (SDP)

Bluetooth is a short-range technology for wireless communication originally designed to replace cable connections between fixed and mobile devices. Therefore, Bluetooth defines a stack from media access ("air") to logical connections for applications or higher layer protocols.

The physical layer provides four types of channels. These channels are characterized by an RF frequency combined with temporal parameters and restricted by spatial considerations. One of these channels is the "inquiry scan channel" used for device discovery. Service discovery in contrast uses L2CAP. L2CAP offers reliable communication between services and applications.

Bluetooth devices organize themselves into so-called "piconets". A piconet can at most consist of eight active devices whereas one of them acts as master. Several piconets can exist in the same place.

Architecture

Many protocols are built upon a specific technology like IP and use IP-specific features like

Figure 9. The Bluetooth stack

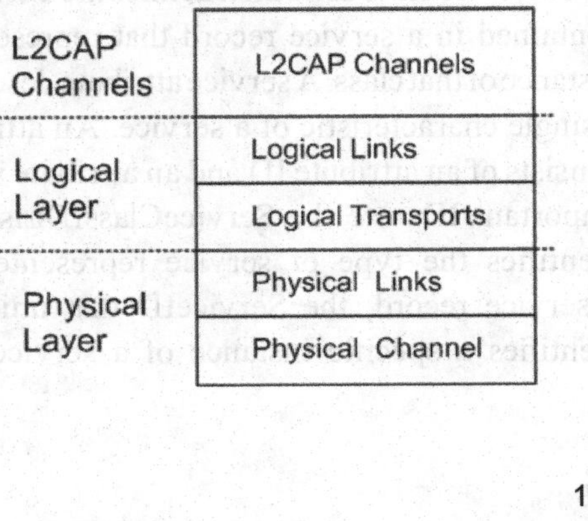

L2CAP Channels	L2CAP Channels
Logical Layer	Logical Links
	Logical Transports
Physical Layer	Physical Links
	Physical Channel

Figure 8. Printer description in PTR record

_printer._tcp.local. 28800 IN PTR PrintsAlot._printer._tcp

multicast for service discovery. IP is on layer 3 (network layer) in the OSI/ISO layered model and already provides much abstraction from the underlying network technology.

Bluetooth's device discovery works on the physical layer using the inquiry scan channel. In order for a device to discover other devices, it iterates (hops) through all possible inquiry scan channel frequencies in a pseudo-random fashion, sending an inquiry request on each frequency and listening for any response. Devices remain passive until they receive an inquiry message. The inquiry scan is mandatory in a Bluetooth network to become part of a piconet. After a device becomes part of a piconet, the service discovery protocol is used to find services.

Description

In Bluetooth "a service is any entity that can provide information, perform an action, or control a resource on behalf of another entity. A service may be implemented as software, hardware, or a combination of hardware and software" (Specification of the Bluetooth System, 2003). Information about services is stored in SDP servers in service records. SDP servers run on devices that provide services. Devices that do not provide services do not have to run an SDP server. A service record identified by a service record handle (32-bit number) consists of a list of service attributes. The record handles are unique within a SDP server but not across SDP servers. One exception is the predefined handle with value 0x00000000. It identifies the SDP servers on a device.

A service class definition defines the attributes contained in a service record that represent an instance of that class. A service attribute describes a single characteristic of a service. An attribute consists of an attribute ID and an attribute value. Important IDs are the ServiceClassIDList that identifies the type of service represented by a service record, the ServiceID that uniquely identifies a specific instance of a service, the

ProtocolDescriptorList that specifies the protocol stack(s) that may be used to utilize a service, and the ProviderName which is a textual name of the individual or organization that provides a service. The attribute type and value depends on the attribute ID. Attribute values may be represented by literals or by IDs.

Discovery

Once the SDP server of a device is discovered, a client can query the SDP server for services specified in "service search patterns". A service search pattern is a list of IDs used to locate matching service records. A service pattern matches, if all IDs are contained in the service's attribute values. The capability search for service records based on the values of arbitrary attributes is not provided. Of course, the client can still query the attributes of a service record, compare the attribute values locally and decide whether the service is appropriate.

Furthermore, service browsing is supported. This means clients can query for all available services or services belonging to a "topic" (group). If there are many services on a device, they can be grouped according to a topic like "entertainment" or "news".

JINI

Jini envisions a world, where every device and service is represented through a proxy object that implements Java interfaces to access the service. Services register proxies with a description in a registry. A client queries the registry and gets a collection of proxies that match the query. The services can then be accessed through these proxies (Edwards, 1999; Venners, 1999).

Architecture

Although Jini makes use of Java-specific concepts, a service can be virtually anything and does not have to be implemented in Java at all. Nor do devices providing a service have to run Java. This is because in Jini there is a strict distinction between the service and the Java proxy object that is used to access the service. Consider a network printer that supports "lpr" and that should become Jini enabled. The proxy object implementation can use the lpr protocol to communicate with the printer. The printer itself does not have to run any Java at all.

Although it is not a strict requirement, it is good practice for the proxy to implement service specific Java interfaces. A client can then access any service implementing this interface, no matter how the proxy is implemented.

Consider printer manufacturers, who want to Jini enable their printers. They agree on a common Printer Java interface. The clients looking for services implementing this interface no matter how the proxy implementation was realized, can later use any printer proxy object implementing this interface.

Clients and services are not aware of each other in advance. Therefore, a service lookup service is part of Jini. Services register their proxies there including a description and clients use the registry to get appropriate services. Registering a proxy also includes code upload to the lookup service, because clients later need the proxy implementation to "run" the proxy.

Discovery of Lookup Service

Services and clients have to find the lookup service before they can use it. There are three protocols for this:

- Multicast request protocol (on UDP);
- Multicast announcement protocol (on UDP);
- Unicast discovery protocol (on TCP).

The multicast request protocol is used, when a service or client starts up and wants to find lookup services. A multicast message is sent via UDP multicast to the multicast address 224.0.1.85 at port 4160. The Jini specification suggests sending the message seven times because of the unreliable nature of UDP. The message contains the version number of the request protocol, the unicast port number, where the lookup service has to reply to the client or service, several groups that the client or service are interested in, and a list of lookup services that already had responded to the request. This is because request messages are sent several times a lookup service can get a couple of them from the same client. If the receiving lookup service is already listed in the message, it should not respond to the message.

If a lookup service receives a request message from a client/service for the first time, it answers on the port defined in the message. The message contains the protocol version, its proxy object and the list of groups that it belongs to.

Multicast announcement protocol is used by the lookup service to announce itself after startup and periodically. UDP multicast messages are sent to the address 224.0.1.85 at port 4160. The message contains the protocol version, the name of the host, the port number, on which the lookup service waits for incoming unicast discovery requests, and its unique identifier. Further more, it contains a list of groups, of which the lookup service is a member. Service and clients get this message and use the information to initiate a unicast discovery with the lookup service.

Unicast discovery protocol is used when the address of the lookup service is known. In this case, the client or service directly connects to the lookup service over TCP at port 4160 if no other port is configured and sends the request. The request only contains the protocol version number. The lookup service responds according to the multicast request protocol.

The unicast discovery protocol is also used, if a client or service learned the IP addresses of lookup services from the Multicast announcement protocol. New lookup services announce themselves after startup and afterwards periodically. Clients and services can then use the unicast discovery protocol to directly communicate with them.

The unicast discovery protocol can also be used to connect to lookup services that cannot be found with the multicast request protocol because, for example, the lookup service is in another network segment and routers may block multicast messages.

Service Description

Services register their proxies including a description in terms of so-called "attributes". These attributes are Java-serializable objects that implement the Entry interface and have a nullary constructor. Jini already provides a couple of standard attributes, but any service provider may implement a new set of attributes. Standard attributes contain information about the service, such as human readable name and description of the service, physical location of the service and so on. Printer manufacturers could define their own attributes describing the printer capabilities such as technology used (dot matrix, ink, or laser), type (grayscale or color), duplex printing support, and number of trays. Figure 10 demonstrates a minimal attribute for a printer.

When a service registers its proxy and the attributes, it also sets a lease (expiration time) for the registration. This means the registration is only valid for a certain time. After the time

has expired, the registration becomes invalid. This ensures that even when services crash, their registrations are invalidated and no stale information is left in the registry. On the other hand, it requires the services to renew the leases periodically. With the first registration a service also gets a unique identifier. Every time the service renews the registration or reregisters after a restart, the service has to register with this ID.

Service Lookup

After clients have discovered one or more lookup services, they use them to obtain services that match their requirements. They specify the requirements in ServiceTemplates that consist of three parts as shown in Figure 11 (constructors and methods omitted).

Each of these three parts has to match, whereas each part can be null. Null acts as a wildcard which means that this part is not taken into account for discovery.

In the serviceID field, a client can specify a known unique service identifier (serviceID) to get a particular service. The identifier given here has to exactly match the serviceID of the service. This may be useful if a client always wants to get the same instance of a service. In the serviceTypes array, the template contains a list of interfaces the service proxy has to implement. The proxy object has to implement each of these interfaces.

The attrSetTemplates array contains a list

Figure 10. Description for printer

```
enum Technology {DOT_MATRIX, INK, LASER};
public class PrinterDescription implements Entry {
    public Integer numberOfTrays;
    public Boolean isDuplex;
    public Boolean supportsColor;
    public Integer numberOfColors;
    public Technology prinitingTechnology;
    public PrinterDescription(){
            // Initialize fields.
    }
}
```

Figure 11. ServiceTemplate Class

```
public class ServiceTemplate implements Serializable {
    public ServiceID serviceID;
    public Class[] serviceTypes;
    public Entry[] attrSetTemplates;
}
```

of attribute templates that are matched with the service attributes. Attribute templates are nothing else than attributes but the fields get "different semantics" when used as a template. For a successful match, for every service attribute there must be at least one matching entry for each attribute template.

The matching of attributes and attribute templates is quite limited. The values in the service attribute have to be exactly the same as in the template attribute. No other operations than for equality are available except that fields in the template entries may be null and act as wildcards. This means that the fields do not have to match.

For example, to search for a printer that supports duplex printing, a new object from the class PrinterDescription would be created and the field isDuplex set to true, all other fields left null.

Service Location Protocol (SLP)

Service Location Protocol (Guttman, 1999; Guttman, Perkins, Veizades, & Day, 1999) is a RFC for service lookup in IP-based intranets. Unlike other technologies, it does not define the IP address assignment to services. This is done manually or through DHCP.

SLP defines three types of agents that act on behalf of the services or client software:

- User Agents (UA) perform service discovery on behalf of client software;
- Service Agents (SA) advertise the location and attributes on behalf of services;
- Directory Agents (DA) aggregate service information into what is initially a stateless repository.

SLP also supports the absence of directory agents. User agents can find service agents when no directory agents are available.

Directory Agent Discovery

There are several ways for service agents and user agents to get the address of the directory agent. First, the DA address can be configured statically and UA and SA read it from a well-known resource like a configuration file. Second, the DA address can be obtained from DHCP. DHCP servers, configured by network administrators, can use DHCP Option 78 to distribute the addresses of DAs to hosts that request them. The third possibility is multicast discovery that exists in two flavors, the active and passive method.

In active mode, SAs and UAs send a multicast DA Discovery request message at startup. By the answer of the DA, SAs and UAs learn the IP address of the DA. Multicast convergence similar to Jini is used to find all DAs. DAs not only answer to requests, but also further announce themselves periodically. In passive mode, SAs and UAs do not send requests as in active mode, but wait for the periodic announcements of the DAs to get the IP addresses of the DAs.

Service Advertisement

A service is advertised with a so-called service: URL specifying where and how to access it and attributes characterizing the service. Both URL schemas and attributes are defined in service specific service type templates (Guttman, Perkins, & Kempf, 1999).

Service: URL = "service:" service-type ":" site url-path is the general form of a service: URL. The prefix "service:" is mandatory, followed by the service type. The site specifies the node (device, computer, …) where the service is running. The url-path finally is service specific and defines access and service specific attributes. Figure 12 gives an example for a printer.

Attributes for a networked printer as specified in Pierre, Isaacson, and McDonald (2002) could specify the characteristics of the printer further

Figure 12. SLP service URL for printer

```
service:printer:lpr://<address of printer>/<queue name>
```

Figure 13. SLP service attributes for networked printer

```
scopes = tum, bmw, administrator
printer-name = lj4050
printer-model = HP LJ4050 N
printer-location = Room 0409
color-supported = false
pages-per-minute = 9
sides-supported = one-sided, two-sided
```

as shown in Figure 13. For readability, the attributes are not encoded into the URL as they would be in reality.

Service Request

Service requests (Veizades, Guttman, Perkins, & Kaplan, 1997) specify the services needed. The general form is:

<srvtype>[.<na>]/[<scope>]/[<where>]/

The "srvtype" refers to the service type. For each type of service available, there is a unique service type name string. The "na" is the naming authority. This string determines the semantic interpretation of the attribute information in the where part of the service request. Scope is a string used to restrict the range of the query. The scope mechanism in the Service Location Protocol enhances its scalability. The primary use of scopes is to provide the capability to organize a site network along administrative lines. A set of services can be assigned to a given department of an organization, to a certain building or geographical area or for a certain purpose. The "where string" is the where-clause of the request. It contains a query that allows the selection of those service instances in which the User Agent is interested in. The query includes attributes, Boolean operators and keywords.

Figure 14.

```
lpr//(& (pages-per-minute >= 12)
        (UNRESTRICTED_ACCESS)
        (printer-location == 12th FLOOR))/
```

Figure 14 gives an example of a service request for a printer on the 12th floor of the building with unrestricted access printing at least 12 pages per minute.

UNIVERSAL DESCRIPTION, DISCOVERY AND INTEGRATION (UDDI)

Universal Description and Discovery (UDDI) has a different focus than the other systems. It was designed for Internet scale service discovery. "Service" in this context refers also to nontechnical realizations. The access point to a service can also be an email address to a person that provides the service. But UDDI became well known in conjunction with Web services.

Web services are based on a couple of different XML-based standards for system and programming language independent service access. These are the simple object access protocol (SOAP) for service access and the Web service description language (WSDL) for describing the computational interface. UDDI specifies the registry entries in XML for publishing Web services and an API to publish and look for services.

UDDI directories support several kinds of entries as shown in Figure 15 from (UDDI Version 3.0.2, UDDI Spec Technical Committee Draft, Dated 20041019, 2004).

- So-called White Pages hold information about the business partner like business name, text description, contact information. The businessEntity structures in a UDDI registry store this information.
- Yellow Pages contain information about the kind of business according to business

Figure 15. UDDI registry structures

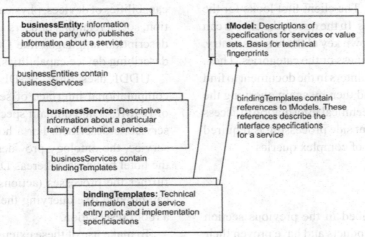

categories. Three standard taxonomies are supported: North American Industrial Classification System (NAICS); Universal Standard Products and Services Classification (UNSPSC); Geographic Classification System (GCS). The businessService structure contains this information.

- Finally, Green Pages contain the information describing how to do business with the service partner. The bindingTemplates and tModels contain this information.

Description

UDDI uses XML to specify the structures used to store information. Therefore, elements may have attributes. A bindingTemplate may have optional attributes, namely the bindingKey and the serviceKey. The bindingKey is a unique ID. A bindingTemplate is registered with this unique ID in the UDDI registry. The serviceKey contains the ID of the businessService that contains the bindingTemplate.

The elements of the bindingTemplate are:

- **UDDI:** Description contains textual information about the template.

- **UDDI:** AccessPoint is a string that contains the access point of the service. This may be the URL where a Web service can be invoked. Because UDDI is designed as a general registry for service, this could also be an email address to get in contact with the business partner.

- **UDDI:** HostingRedirector is a deprecated element and should not be used any more. It is just for backward compatibility.

- **uddi:** tModelInstanceDetails may contain one or more tModelInstanceInfo elements to provide a technical fingerprint of the Web service. This may include the URL of the WSDL document of the Web service.

- **UDDI:** CategoryBag contains a list of categorizations. Each of them describes a specific aspect of the bindingTemplate and is valid in its own category system.

- **UDDI:** Signature may be used to digitally sign the template.

UDDI API

UDDI defines an API for accessing registries through SOAP. There are several APIs for publishing information and searching the different entries of the registry. The general approach is the browse pattern. The client first looks for the appropriate business. In the query, the clients can specify the well-known key of the business entry, the name of the business or the categories. Then, the client uses the pointers in the document to find feasible services and then by again querying the registry to find the technical information to access them. So much client side processing is required because of the lack of complex queries.

Research

The systems described in the previous section are used in many products and have proven their suitability for the purpose, for which they have been designed. But for use in a large scale ubiquitous computing scenario each of the systems lacks some features. Some of them do not scale either in the amount of devices they can handle or geographical extent. Context-aware computing, for instance does not only mean finding services nearby, but perhaps also services at very distant places to where a client will soon move. Further service providers want to control who may use services and clients want to be able to compare the quality of services that they want to use and perhaps have to pay for. Many research projects are trying to address these challenges. This section discusses some examples.

Extending UDDI with Context-Aware Features Based on Semantic Service Descriptions

UDDI uses t-models to refer to taxonomies and service classification systems. But these classifications are mostly quite coarse grained and the exact specification is only provided by normal text that has to be interpreted by a human being. Therefore they are not suitable for automated service discovery. (Pokraev, Koolwaaij, & Wibbels, 2003) discusses a possibility to use ontologies in UDDI and further make use of context to constrain the search.

The context ontology contains concepts for capabilities of devices, physical context like location, social relations of users and so on. Existing description languages like CC/PP are used for describing device capabilities.

UDDI uses only WSDL to describe the computational interface of services. By means of DAML-S and domain specific ontologies the service is described. For a hotel room booking service, the ontology provides the concepts for the hotel business, whereas DAML-S describes further the processes (actions) that the service can provide like querying the prices or making a room reservation.

To make use of these extensions an enhanced UDDI server was implemented. The server offers additional interfaces to register services with their semantic descriptions and clients can search for services. A query for a service is the description for an "ideal service". The server returns the services that match this ideal service best.

Semantic Extensions to Bluetooth SDP and Jini

As already discussed, SDP and Jini have limited means of expressing queries. By use of ontologies and inference engines it is possible to formally express the capabilities of a service and by use of inference engines it is possible to find services that do match the query exactly, but are still acceptable (Avancha, Joshi, & Finin, 2002; Chakraborty, Perich, Avancha, & Joshi, 2001). This means, for example, that a client application is offered a gray scale printer if it is the only printer available, even though the applications need a color printer. This is because having any printer is in most cases preferable to having no printer at all.

The ontology based on DAML+OIL (the predecessor of OWL) contains a rich set of concepts (classes) to describe the capabilities and functionalities of services. The class component forms the root of the hierarchy and contains properties containing the describing elements.

For use with Jini, an enhanced lookup service was implemented that is almost fully compliant with the Sun lookup service, but was additionally able to handle ontological description. Jini objects instantiated from Entry classes store the service description. Therefore, a new entry class (attribute) to hold the ontological description was defined. So, with the normal means of Jini the service can be registered at the lookup service. The modified lookup service stores the description. When a client sends a "semantic service discovery request" message to the server, the message contains the DAML query. The query is processed by means of a Prolog interpreter and a set of matching services sent back to the client.

A similar approach was taken to enhance Bluetooth service discovery. Services are described with an ontology and stored in XML files on the device. Like any other Bluetooth service, the service gets a universally unique 128-bit identifier (UUID). Furthermore, an XSB engine that supports XSB, a variant of Prolog, and supports small footprint devices, runs on the device. When a client sends a semantic query, this engine processes the queries and returns the UUIDs of matching services.

FUTURE RESEARCH DIRECTIONS

This chapter gave an introduction to service oriented architectures and common approaches to service description and discovery. In SOA, service providers register services in registries with service descriptions. Service clients search in the registries to find feasible services. There are several ways of describing services as discussed in the chapter. Closely related to the descriptions are the means for finding services. They range from simple and exact comparisons to query languages with logical operators.

There are several different approaches dealing with the organization of the service registries. Some systems depend on centralized registries, whereas others implement distributed registries. Some do not need any registry at all.

Next, some popular systems were explained in more detail. This includes the standards for service description, the query language and initial discovery of the registries. Finally, research on service description and discovery was discussed.

The mainstream service description and discovery systems have a well-defined scope. Scope means where the systems are used and who uses them. But current approaches do not scale for a worldwide UC-environment, where anybody may offer services with a multitude of services and clients. So there are two research objectives for the near future: adding semantics to service descriptions and finding efficient ways to distribute service descriptions and search for services. Semantics includes information about the kind of service, how to access a service and where it makes sense to use the service. This research will be influenced by the Semantic Web and Semantic Web Services.

Research on peer-to-peer or pub/sub systems may influence research on service discovery. Both peer-to-peer and pub/sub are well suited to efficiently distributing information, in terms of UC and the service descriptions in SOA. The main challenge will be to integrate filter or query mechanisms and discovery mechanisms that take into account the semantics of the service descriptions.

REFERENCES

Apple (2006, April). *Bonjour overview*. Retrieved October 9, 2007, from http://developer.apple.com/documentation/Cocoa/Conceptual/NetServices/NetServices.pdf

Avancha, S., Joshi, A., & Finin, T. (2002). Enhanced service discovery in Bluetooth. *Computer, 35*(6), 96-99.

Chakraborty, D., Perich, F., Avancha, S., & Joshi, A. (2001). Dreggie: Semantic service discovery for m-commerce applications. In *Proceedings of the Workshop on Reliable and Secure Applications in Mobile Environment, 20th Symposiom on Reliable Distributed Systems.*

Cheshire, S., & Krochmal, M. (2005, June). *DNS-based service discovery.* Retrieved October 9, 2007, from http://files.dns-sd.org/draft-cheshire-dnsext-dns-sd.txt

Edwards, W. K. (1999). *Core Jini.* Prentice Hall.

Gulbrandsen, A., Vixie, P., & Esibov, L. (2000). *RFC 2782: A DNS RR for specifying the location of services (DNS SRV).*

Guttman, E. (1999). Service location protocol: Automatic discovery of IP network services. *IEEE Internet Computing, 3*(4), 71–80.

Guttman, E., Perkins, C., & Kempf, J. (1999). *RFC 2609: Service templates and service: Schemes.*

Pierre, P. S., Isaacson, S., & McDonald, I. (2002). *Printer service template.* Retrieved October 9, 2007, from http://www.iana.org/assignments/svr-loc-templates/printer.2.0.en

Pokraev, S., Koolwaaij, J., & Wibbels, M. (2003, June). Extending UDDI with context-aware features based on semantic service descriptions. In *Proceedings of the International Conference on Web Services, ICWS'03* (pp. 184–190). Las Vegas, Nevada.

Postel, J. (1989). *RFC 1111: Request for comments on Request for Comments: Instructions to RFC authors.*

Rosenbaum, R. (1993). *RFC 1464: Using the domain name system to store arbitrary string attributes.*

UPnP(TM) Forum (2006). *Welcome to the UPnP(tm) forum!* Retrieved October 9, 2007, from http://www.upnp.org/

Veizades, J., Guttman, E., Perkins, C., & Kaplan, S. (1997). *RFC 2165: Service Location Protocol.*

Venners, B. (1999). *The Jini technology vision.* Retrieved October 9, 2007, from http://java.sun.com/developer/technicalArticles/jini/JiniVision/jiniology.html)

Zeroconf Working Group (2006). *Zero configuration networking (Zeroconf).* Retrieved October 9, 2007, 2006, from http://www.zeroconf.org/

ADDITIONAL READING

Bettstetter, C., & Renner, C. (2000). A comparison of service discovery protocols and implementation of the service location protocol. *Sixth EUNICE Open European Summer School: Innovative Internet Applications.*

Campo, C., Muñoz, M., Perea, J. C., Marin, A., & Garcia-Rubio, C. (2005). PDP and GSDL: A new service discovery middleware to support spontaneous interactions in pervasive systems. *PerCom Workshop* (pp. 178-182).

Chinnici, R., Gudgin, M., Lewis, A., Schlimmer, J., & Weerawarana, S. (2004). *Web services description language (WSDL) Version 2.0 Part 1: Core language.* Retrieved October 9, 2007, from http://www.w3.org/TR/2004/WD-wsdl20-20040803

Doulkeridis, C., Loutas, N., & Vazirgiannis, M. (2006). A system architecture for context-aware service discovery. *Electronic Notes in Theoretical Computer Science, 146*(1), 101-116.

Edwards, W. W. (2006). Discovery systems in ubiquitous computing. *IEEE Pervasive Computing, 5*(2), 70-77.

Guttman, E., Perkins, C., Veizades, J., & Day, M. (1999). *RFC 2165: Service Location Protocol, Version 2.*

Specification of the Bluetooth System (2003). Retrieved October 9, 2007, from http://www.bluetooth.org/foundry/adopters/document/Core_v2.0_EDR/en/1/Core_v2.0_EDR.zip

The OWL Services Coalition (2004). *OWL-S: Semantic markup for web services (1.1 Release)*. Retrieved October 9, 2007, from http://www.daml.org/services/owl-s/1.1/overview/

UDDI version 3.0.2, UDDI spec technical committee draft, dated 20041019. (2004).

UPnP(TM) Forum (2003). *UPnPn(tm) device architecture v1.0*. Retrieved October 9, 2007, from http://www.upnp.org/resources/documents/CleanUPnPDA101-20031202s.pdf

Zhu, F., Mutka, M. W., & Ni, L. M. (2005). Service discovery in pervasive computing environments. *IEEE Pervasive Computing, 4*(4), 81-90.

Section II
Connectivity:
Tapping into Humans and Items

Max Mühlhäuser
Technische Universität Darmstadt, Germany

Erwin Aitenbichler
Technische Universität Darmstadt, Germany

GENERAL INTRODUCTION TO CONNECTIVITY

Two well-established disciplines of computer science form the background for this part of the present book: *computer networks* and *distributed systems.*

Computer networks is concerned with engineering communication systems for computers. Networks are built from a variety of transmission media, including wire, cable, fiber, and wireless channels; hardware devices, such as routers, switches, bridges, hubs, repeaters, and network interface cards; and software components, including drivers and protocol stacks. The principles on which computer networks are based include protocol layering, packet switching, routing, and data streaming. The major example for a computer network is the Internet.

Distributed systems are the software infrastructures built on top of computer networks. This discipline has a more abstract view on communi-cation aspects. It considers hardware or software components located at networked computers that communicate and coordinate their actions only by passing messages. Distributed systems are concerned with interprocess communication, distributed objects and remote invocation, resource sharing, replication, distributed file systems, coordination and agreement, transactions and concurrency control, and security aspects.

In the remainder of this introduction, we will refer to six layers of computer networks plus distributed systems as shown in Figure 1. Note that there is no common understanding about a specific layering in the literature.

From a coarse-grained point of view, these six layers have the following responsibilities:

Layer 1 (Meshing): At the *meshing* level, adjacent computers are interconnected, mostly by wired connections. In the beginning, computers were often interconnected in bus topologies, using shared media. Since the 1990s and with the advent of higher transmission speeds, computers

Figure 1. Coarse layer architecture

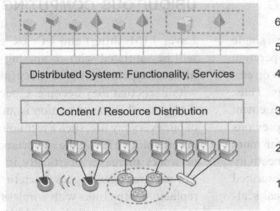

have usually been connected to central switches using a star topology.

Layer 2 (Nodes): Computers provide the resources of the distributed system, for example, in terms of processing power or storage. *Nodes* are mostly considered to be homogeneous, with their resources being controlled by the respective owner of the computer. On the Internet and in business applications we often distinguish between clients and servers. However, what appears to be a single server at the logical level (e.g., www. google.com) is often implemented as a distributed system in reality.

Layer 3 (Overlay Network): An *overlay network* forms a logical network topology on top of the underlying (IP) network. One example of an existing effective overlay network on the Internet is the Akamai content delivery network. It dynamically replicates content on various servers nearer to those requesting the content. In this way, it allows for the main servers of content providers to have less traffic and prevents congestion on the network links to popular providers.

Layer 4 (Platform): The *platform* consists of operating system and middleware software that provides application developers with a "powerful and easy-to-use" distributed system. Services common to all distributed applications are directly provided by the platform, for example, interprocess communication, remote invocation, service location, coordination, concurrency control, transactions, encryption, or authentication.

Layer 5 (Communication Abstraction): Communication abstractions define the interfaces between platform and applications. An abstraction provides a conceptual description of the communication and synchronization operations available. This determines how communicating processes will be coupled in terms of space, time, and program flow. It is crucial for programmers that a platform offers the abstractions necessary to implement an application's requirements. Today, we mainly encounter information pull and the client/server paradigm.

Layer 6 (Distributed Application): The distributed applications themselves are situated at this level. Today, such applications are in fact "closed." Apart from the common communications-related services provided by the platform, there is almost no reuse of application-specific components.

IMPORTANCE OF CONNECTIVITY FOR UBIQUITOUS COMPUTING

Ubiquitous computing does not build on a single device—its power emerges from the cooperation of many devices, either carried by users or embedded into our everyday environments. Thus, communication is a very fundamental requirement in UC. The layer model described in the previous section points out that connectivity is far more than just interconnecting computers. Connectivity is a major scalability issue in UC, as described in the Flatland analogy and mathematical scalability in Part I.

As computers become ubiquitous and special purpose, UC developers and applications want to draw on the special abilities and knowledge of the devices. This requires open and extensible platforms. UC also needs to integrate very resource-poor nodes, which contradicts the resource requirements of today's platforms. Beside ubiquitous connectivity, UC aims to provide ubiquitous availability of resources, thereby driving the paradigm shift from "the network as a universal bit pipe" to "the network as a universal computer."

The predominant communication paradigm in the Internet is *pull*, that is, clients initiate the communication and request information from servers. UC aims to bridge the gap between the physical and the digital world. To do so, UC systems utilize various sensors to monitor the physical environment. Here, the sensors, for example, RFID readers or location tracking systems, are the initiators of communication and *push* information into the UC system. Thus, to properly support the new communication patterns found in UC, novel communication paradigms are required.

Two major classes of applications arise in UC: applications around "everyday objects" that are augmented with smart items, and applications around "everyday humans" that are exchanging information using opportunistic networks.

CONNECTIVITY APPROACHES FOR UBIQUITOUS COMPUTING

Layer 1 (Meshing) and UC: UC environments will be saturated with computing and communication capability, yet so gracefully integrated with users that they become a "technology that disappears." Because motion is an integral part of our everyday life, such a technology must support mobility. Hence, the importance of wireless networks increases drastically in this context. The research agenda goes much further than just replacing wired links with wireless links. Meshing must support self-X capabilities, including resource discovery, spontaneous and secure link formation, zero-configuration, and fault tolerance. Wired networks will still remain important as part of the fixed infrastructure in the future, because of their greater reliability and bandwidth.

Layer 2 (Nodes) and UC: UC introduces a variety of new computing devices, vastly different in their characteristics. Smart tags will only have very limited computational resources and no independent power supply. Hence, it can no longer be assumed that nodes are homogeneous "peers." An example for a new class of such nodes is smart labels, like RFID tags, representing handles to the "digital shadow" of an everyday object. Another example is a federated computer, consisting of multiple nodes for computer core, input devices, output devices, and so forth, "assembled" together in an ad hoc manner. For this kind of "resource socialization" we also require grouping concepts for nodes.

Layer 3 (Overlay Network) and UC: While overlay networks are only used for special applications on the Internet, their use will be the standard case in UC. In peer-to-peer systems, each participating computer is a "servent," that is, it has the role of a server and a client at the same time. Every peer-to-peer system, for example, for file sharing, software distribution, messaging, telephony, and so forth, is based on overlay networks. Grid computing aims to make access to computing or storage resources as simple as how we obtain power from the power grid today.

Layer 4 (Platform) and UC: Compared to today's middleware, UC platforms must face several additional challenges:

- Nodes are no longer always entire computers consisting of CPU, memory, input, and output devices. Smart labels may only provide memory and not even have an independent power supply. A platform must also be able to accommodate such "node fragments" to enable the federation of nodes.
- Nodes differ vastly in their capabilities. When deploying services in a distributed system, the platform must take resource constraints of nodes into account.
- Platforms must enable the deployment of zillions of nodes with zero effort. Manual pairing processes as required by Bluetooth are not feasible in UC environments.
- In presence of many, competing middleware systems, the vision of ubiquitous interoperability will not come true. Interoperability requires protocol and interface standards, or novel concepts for service composition.
- The automatic composition of services from multiple different vendors must take liability issues into account.
- In today's distributed systems, the IP stack is part of the operating system running on each node. UC requires more flexible communication architectures and platforms also have to support devices that are too small to host an IP stack. Does the IP stack live below layers 3 and 4, or alongside them?
- Services commonly required by UC applications should be integrated directly into the platform. For example, almost any UC application will require processing of context information and would benefit from a common context service.

- Platforms must be scalable and support a large number of nodes.

Layer 5 (Communication Abstractions) and UC: While the *pull* model serves well on the Internet, the dominating model in UC will be *push*. An effective API must provide functions to programmers suitable for their specific application scenarios. In context-aware and other information-driven systems, event-based communication is a good abstraction for distributing information, because it supports multicasting and decouples data producers from data consumers. Having the right abstractions offered by the middleware leads to reduced application development time and reduced size of application code. A need for the pull model still remains, because UC will also require client/server-type interactions and stateful connections to dedicated peers. Communication does not have to be either push or pull – arbitrary mixed forms of push and pull can be implemented. More scalable and more efficient event routing algorithms might also be inspired by bionics.

Layer 6 (Distributed Applications) and UC: UC applications will be more decentralized and require a new dimension of openness: users can encounter new services while they walk through smart environments and applications should automatically discover and take advantage of these services. To properly support the development of UC applications, current software development processes must be extended with new methods and tools. New aspects in UC include the modeling of device properties, context information, environments, and multimodal user interfaces, semantic services, sensor simulation, monitoring, and testing.

OVERVIEW OF FURTHER BOOK CHAPTERS

Figure 2 depicts both a summary of the last section (discussion of the six layers) and its relation to the corresponding book chapters, in particular with respect to the "connectivity" part of this book.

We conclude this introduction by giving the reader pointers to literature that covers communication aspects in ubiquitous computing. The short list presents a selection of survey work with a focus on open issues and challenges.

ADDITIONAL READING

Satyanarayanan, M. (2001). Pervasive computing: Vision and challenges. *IEEE Personal Communications Magazine, 8*(4), 10-17.

Borriello, G. (2002). Key challenges in communication for ubiquitous computing. *IEEE Communications Magazine—50th Anniversary Commemorative Issue, 40*(5), 16-18.

Prehofer, C., & Bettstetter, C. (2005). Self-organization in communication networks: Principles and design paradigms. *IEEE Communications Magazine, Feature Topic on Advances in Self-Organizing Networks, 43*(7), 78-85.

Figure 2. Relation between connectivity issues and book chapters

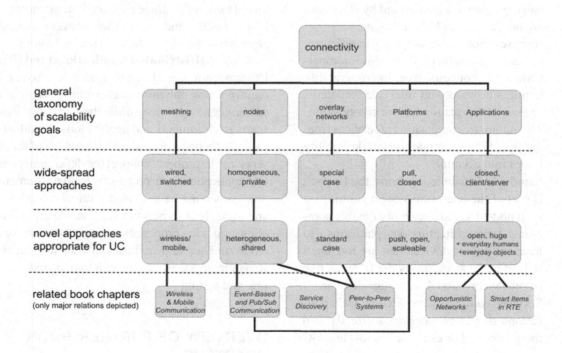

Chapter VI
Wireless and Mobile Communications

Jochen H. Schiller
Freie Universität Berlin, Germany

ABSTRACT

This chapter introduces different wireless and mobile communication systems that represent an important technological basis for ubiquitous computing applications. Different communication systems co-exist and vary with respect to many parameters, such as transmission range, data rates, cost, mobility, power consumption, scalability in the number of users, and so forth. The introduction gives a quick chapter overview of prominent communication systems. Next, the necessary minimal knowledge required about wireless transmission and media-sharing technologies is provided. The core of the chapter then provides brief introductions to the classes of wireless networks that are most relevant for ubiquitous computing, in particular wireless wide area networks and wireless distribution, local area, personal area, and sensor networks. A brief description of current convergence efforts follows. Readers should be aware that the wealth of technologies to be considered requires this chapter to remain rather survey-like.

INTRODUCTION AND FOUNDATIONS

Figure 1 gives a rough overview of some prominent wireless communication systems focusing on the two parameters gross data rate and relative speed between sender and receiver. Assuming a mobile end-user connected to a stationary transceiver station, the points on the (non proportional) speed axis resemble nonmoving persons, pedestrians, cars downtown, cars outside cities, and cars on a highway, respectively. Note that high-speed trains and airplanes cannot be accommodated by most technologies without specialized equipment.

In the range suitable for higher speeds, we find typical mobile telecommunication systems offering mainly voice service and covering whole countries (see Schiller (2003) for a comparison). The most successful system is GSM (global system for mobile communication) with its successor UMTS (universal mobile communications system) for higher data rates. While GSM can be enhanced for higher data rates with GPRS (general packet radio service) and EDGE (enhanced data rates for global evolution), UMTS with its new enhancements HSDPA (high speed downlink packet access) and HSUPA (high speed uplink packet access) can deliver even higher data rates of 10 Mbit/s and more per radio cell. Digital broadcast systems, such as DVB (digital video broadcasting), DAB (digital audio broadcasting), and DMB (digital multimedia broadcasting) play a special role as they are (at least *a priori*) conceived as unidirectional broadcast systems. Their key benefits are extreme scalability and suitability for higher speeds. For bidirectional applications, these technologies are often complemented with GSM or UMTS back channels. Systems for higher data rates typically trade off this advantage with sensibility to higher speeds and with lower transmission ranges, requiring antennas to be more close-by i.e. more densely distributed. Prominent examples for this class of systems are WPANs (wireless personal area networks) following the standard IEEE 802.15, such as the Bluetooth and ZigBee substandards, and WLANs (wireless local area networks) following IEEE 802.11. Especially the latter has initiated a revolutionary new way of ubiquitous access to the Internet by forming the basis of thousands of hot-spots world-wide. While offering higher data rates than, for example, GSM or UMTS, WLANs usually apply randomized,

optimistic media access control schemes, that is, ways for sharing the available bandwidth among all active users within a hot spot. Such schemes adapt well to the bursty data rates characteristic for Internet use (as opposed to mobile phone use), but usually cannot cope well with accumulated bandwidth demands close to or beyond available bandwidth. WSNs (wireless sensor networks) form a wireless systems class of their own as they focus on energy conservation rather than on high data rates; among others, energy consumption calls for low transmission reach, such that sensor nodes are expected to act as routers for neighboring sensors—a function that consumes energy! The above-mentioned ZigBee standard is considered a basis for WSNs, too. Wireless distribution systems, finally, could replace DSL (digital subscriber line) in residential areas. They follow the IEEE 802.16 standard known as WiMAX (worldwide interoperability for microwave access). The initially lacking mobility support is added under IEEE 802.16e; WiMAX cooperates and competes with IEEE 802.11 at higher data rates.

Figure 1. Overview of wireless communication technologies relevant for UC

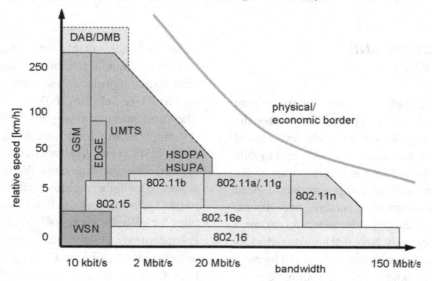

Figure 2. Overview of different frequencies occupied by communication systems

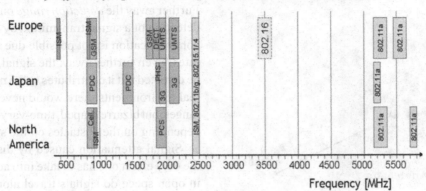

It is either not feasible due to physical limitations or simply too expensive to implement systems with high data rates that can also operate at higher relative speeds. Although new technologies are pushing this border further up, it is not going to be totally removed.

The following sections describe the technical basics for wireless communication systems, such as frequencies, transmission ranges, signal propagation characteristics as well as basic architectures and the effects of mobility. The next sections then present the five wireless network technologies as introduced earlier. These five classes were selected due to their importance for ubiquitous computing (UC) applications. Wireless wide area networks comprise GSM and UMTS, while the upcoming distribution networks following the WiMAX standard are establishing an alternative to DSL connections. WLANs and WPANs brought wireless technology to everybody as they can be operated without the need for a network operator. For all technologies the sections describe key characteristics, benefits, and drawbacks. The fifth technology, WSN, comprises technologies for environmental monitoring, industrial control, total asset management, and so forth. Note that no sharp borderlines exist; for example, WiMAX may replace both UMTS in urban areas and WLAN for high data rate demands. Finally, a section about convergence and the path to the fourth generation of wireless and mobile communication systems

shows key characteristics of a unified approach, but highlights also the problems along the way. The summary emphasizes the key thesis of this chapter—there is not going be a single technology, but an increasing convergence of technologies.

WIRELESS DATA TRANSMISSION

In order to fully understand the limitations and challenges of mobile and wireless communication systems one has to understand the fundamental basics of wireless transmission. All wireless communication systems use radio waves for data transmission. The frequencies of these waves depend on the desired characteristics of the systems and many regulations. Generally speaking, the higher the frequency, the higher the potential data rate, but also the worse the capability to penetrate material such as walls. The lower the frequency, the better can radio waves penetrate different materials, but also the larger the antennas have to be. Figure 2 gives an overview of typical transmission frequencies of prominent wireless communication systems. It shows that the frequencies in use may differ from continent to continent, even from country to country. Only very few systems can be used world-wide at the same frequency. One example is WLANs and WPANs operating in the license-free band (often called ISM for industrial, scientific, medical)

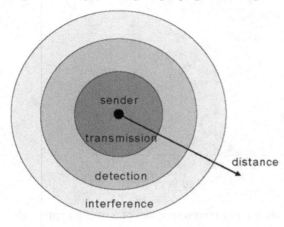

Figure 3. Simplified signal propagation ranges

at 2.4 GHz, such as 802.11b/g and Bluetooth. WLANs following 802.11a already have to use different frequencies and follow different regulations when used in different countries. Mobile phone systems, thus, comprise the capability to automatically switch to the right frequency depending on the country they are used in. GSM, for example, can be used in four different bands. Even for the 3G (Third Generation) systems it was not possible to establish the same frequency bands worldwide due to national restrictions and legacy systems occupying the frequencies. Additional ISM bands are used for industrial control, WSNs, and so forth. For new systems following IEEE 802.16 the frequencies have not yet been finally allocated; the frequency band at 3.5 GHz is being considered in Germany, the ISM bands and additional frequencies in the US.

Even under ideal conditions in a vacuum, transmitted wireless signals lose energy proportionally to the squared distance d^2. In realistic environments this attenuation effect is much worse; signals weaken proportional to d^3, d^4 or worse depending on obstacles they have to penetrate. This effect leads to a completely different signal propagation characteristic compared to wired transmission where attenuation is linear, that is, proportional to d. Figure 3 shows a very simplified signal propagation scheme with three ranges. Within *transmission range* communica-

tion is possible since error rates are low enough. Further away the *detection range* only allows the detection of a signal transmitted by a sender, but communication is not possible due to high error rates. Even further away, the signal cannot even be detected but it contributes to the noise level. In real environments there would never be circular ranges, but bizarre shaped, time-varying polygons depending on the obstacles on the signal path.

Signal attenuation caused by distance is not the only effect one has to take into account. Only in open space do signals travel along a straight line called LOS (line-of-sight). Real environments comprise buildings, trees, cars, people, rain, clouds etc. that may get in the way of a signal and that may thus influence it. Figure 4 shows the most prominent effects that influence a signal on its path. Note that without reflection mobile telephones would hardly work, as there is rarely an LOS to a sender. Further effects depicted comprise:

- Refraction, which is caused when signals travel through media with different densities
- Diffraction, which is caused when signals travel along edges, and
- Scattering, which is caused when signal waves hit smaller objects.

The previous mentioned effects on signal propagation do not only weaken the signal, they also influence the paths along which a signal travels. Most antennas send their signals either omnidirectionally (i.e., in all directions) or directed (i.e., focused on a certain sector). In both cases, the antenna emits waves that may reach the receiver via different paths as shown in Figure 5.

Figure 4. Effects on signal propagation

Figure 5. Multipath propagation

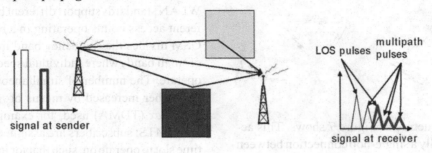

The shortest path is obviously the LOS. Other possible paths are formed by (multiple) reflections and the above-mentioned effects. This leads to a spreading of a signal in time at the receiver. For each pulse emitted by the sender, the receiver receives a first "copy" that traveled on the shortest path, plus multiple (weaker) pulses. The effect of this multipath propagation is an interference of symbols that were emitted at distinct times by the sender. This interference can be avoided by observing sufficient temporal displacement, which directly limits the maximum data rate of a communication system. Means for limiting interference while allowing high symbol frequencies represent an important research topic.

Apart from effects related to wireless transmission, *mobility* contributes to system complexity. In wireless mobile networks, powerful antennas are deployed for sending and receiving signals from mobile devices; one or more antennas are controlled by a so-called base transceiver station (BTS) that is, relay station that mediates between mobile users and the residual network (often the a wired network). Most networks common

Figure 6. Typical handover scenarios

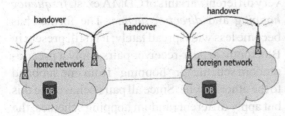

today are called *cellular:* they support multiple BTS. Figure 6 shows an abstract architecture of a mobile communication system consisting of two cells. A mobile device may move from one *cell* to another, a process called *roaming*. If roaming occurs while a phone call or data connection is active, a so-called handover is required: the active connection must be carried over to the new cell. In the US, the term handoff is more common than handover; both are synonymous. Handovers may take place between antennas of the same operator or between different operators. Handover support was first introduced for mobile phone systems such as GSM, then for WLAN and other technologies. Newer developments support handover between different technologies for seamless connectivity. Each network has to keep track of the mobile devices currently attached to its antennas using databases. Most systems differentiate between a subscriber's home networks (often called home location register), and a foreign or "visitor" network i.e. the network a mobile device or a mobile subscriber is visiting. The databases are also needed for localization of devices and subscribers, for forwarding of data, for authorization and for accounting. Possible effects of handover are service interrupts, more complicated forwarding of data from a sender to a mobile receiver, and addressing problems if receivers are roaming within foreign networks.

Wireless communication systems can be classified according to their architecture. Most systems only offer wireless access to an otherwise

Figure 7. Infrastructure vs. ad-hoc networks

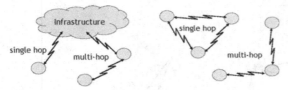

fixed infrastructure as Figure 7 shows. This access is typically a single-hop connection between the mobile device and the network. Examples for this architecture are GSM, UMTS, but also most WLANs. New developments allow for wireless multihop access to an infrastructure. This complicates the system architecture but offers a range extension. A third class of systems is called ad-hoc networks as shown on the right-hand side of Figure 7: they do not rely on a fixed infrastructure at all. Currently popular systems, such as WLANs in ad-hoc mode or Bluetooth, require single-hop connectivity between all devices. Newer developments allow full flexibility by supporting multi-hop communication as well. Support for highly mobile nodes dramatically increases the complexity as the topology keeps changing dynamically; note that multihop networks require sophisticated routing algorithms.

MULTIPLE ACCESS SCHEMES

One of the most thoroughly researched issues in wireless communication systems is *multiple access (MA)* that is, the coordination of multiple senders and receivers that operate both within a certain frequency band used by the network and within a region of potential signal interference. The two important subclasses of MA schemes are discussed below: *multiplexing* and *concurrent access*.

Multiplexing schemes are often abbreviated *M* instead of *MA*. The most common variant is *frequency multiplexing* (FDMA: frequency division multiple access, or FDM) that is, the

separation into different sub-bands. For instance, WLAN standards support different bands for different access points operating in a building, and GSM divides the frequency band into hundreds of small bands where individual speech channels operate. The number of simultaneous users can be further increased by means of *time division multiplex* (TDMA) used, for example, in GSM and UMTS: subscribers are assigned a band *and* time slot to operate on, such that for instance eight phone calls can be time multiplexed on a single carrier frequency. Somewhat at odds with these two principles, the term *space division multiplex* (SDMA) is applied if disjoint sets of carrier frequency bands are used in neighboring cells. Again a hardly comparable concept, code division multiple access (CDMA; Groe, & Larson, 2000) denotes the latest of the four multiplex schemes, which makes it possible for multiple sender-receiver pairs to occupy the same band without a need for *a priori* coordination (such as band or timeslot assignment as with FDMA / TDMA); the co-occupied bandwidth roughly equals the (average) required bandwidth of each participant multiplied by the number of simultaneously active participants so that there is no advantage over the other schemes at first sight. At second sight, the ad-hoc participation of users and the demand driven (instead of pre-assigned and fixed-size) bandwidth use are invaluable advantages for data-centric (as opposed to formerly voice-centric) networks. CDMA can be mixed with FDMA if the overall frequency band is divided into relatively large carrier frequency bands each of which accommodates a group of users as described. Even a combination with TDMA is possible and UMTS applies all four schemes mentioned so far. Two very different variants of CDMA exist: *frequency hopping* and *direct sequence*. The former has become less widespread lately; it is still present in Bluetooth: sender-receiver pairs apply a pseudo-random scheme for "hopping" from one subband to the other in sync. Since all pairs behave like this but apply different random hopping schemes, the collision risk is kept low. In the *direct sequence* variant of CDMA, applied in WLANs and UMTS, each sender-receiver pair applies a characteristic and relatively large sequence of symbols (called *chips*) to transmit a single bit (the characteristic chip sequence signals a "1", the inverse sequence a "0"). Despite considerable deformation of the chip sequence due to interference from other chip sequences traveling in the same band, the receiver can detect the original bit by means of mathematical correlation. Obviously, the chip rate divided by the chips-per-bit determines the peak bit rate of a sender-receiver pair. In UMTS, pairs can dynamically allocate more 'space' in the overall space of possible chip sequences and thereby temporarily increase their peak bandwidth as required.

Complementary to multiplexing schemes as described, a second set of MA schemes provides random concurrent access at the risk of signal collision. Such schemes permit anytime access to the medium provided it is not currently occupied—the stations are requested to apply the so-called "listen-before-talk" scheme *LBT*. Limited packet size ensures a timely end of 'the currently active transmission' for stations waiting to transmit. LBT sounds simple, but the devil is in the details. On the one hand, collisions cannot be fully avoided since a station that applies LBT may not *yet* recognize an ongoing transmission that started just milliseconds ago, that is, for which the "first bit" did not travel the distance yet. This sounds like a rare coincidence, but it is not: several stations may produce packets ready-to-transmit during an ongoing transmission: they all apply LBT, that is, wait for the ether to become free and may start almost simultaneously after the end of the ongoing transmission. To make things worse, collisions cannot be detected *during* transmission in wireless networks since high signal attenuation as described earlier prohibits received-signal detection during signal transmission on the same frequency—note that such "listen-while-talk" (LWT) is possible in wired networks. Thus, collisions can only be detected

at higher layers of the communication stack (e.g., an expected acknowledgement times out), making them expensive. Yet another aggravating effect is called *hidden terminal*: the sender may not observe an ongoing transmission via LBT, but the receiver may still experience signal interference due to a sender "on the other side" (far away from the first sender). For satellite channels, LBT is virtually impossible due to the directed signal path: all competing stations transmit up into the sky. A specific and fairly advanced MA scheme for WLAN will be described further below.

THE FIVE MAJOR MOST RELEVANT CLASSES OF WIRELESS NETWORKS

Wireless Wide Area Networks

The growth of wireless wide area networks was—and continues to be—one of the greatest success stories in mobile communications. Today, almost two billion people worldwide use these systems for telephony, Internet access, surveillance, or remote control. The most prominent examples for this category are GSM (Eberspächer, Vögel, & Bettstetter, 2001) and nowadays UMTS (Muratore, 2000). The technical advancements are best reflected in the user data rates offered. While the 2G system GSM started with 9.6 kbit/s (later 14.4 kbit/s) it was enhanced by GPRS (Grasche & Walke, 1997) to offer typical data rates of 53 kbit/s on the downlink (from the network to the mobile device) and 28 kbit/s on the uplink. This 2.5G system can even be further enhanced using different modulation and coding schemes standardized as EDGE. This system is particularly useful in areas without 3G coverage, such as rural areas, and offers data rates up to 384 kbit/s. A 3G system such as UMTS offers up to 384 kbit/s per user from the beginning. Further enhancements, such as HSDPA, raise the data rate to 1.8 Mbit/s and later on to 3.6 and 7.2 Mbit/s, respectively.

Figure 8. Basic architecture of GSM networks

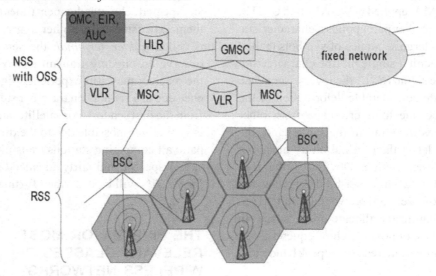

However, the actual data rates depend heavily on the mobility pattern of a user, on her speed, on the direction of communication ("uplink" to the BTS or "downlink"), on the current signal strength (and thus also error rate) and even on the current load of the cell.

A prominent example of the evolution from 2G to 3G is the "cdma family" of networks applying various cdma schemes, starting with cdmaOne as a 2G system, followed by cdma2000 1X as a 2.5G system, and finally followed by the 3G system cdma2000 1X EV-DO (evolution-data optimized). While UMTS is installed by almost all operators that already use GSM (more than 600 in over 200 countries), cdma2000 is the natural choice for operators using cdmaOne technology (mainly in the US, Japan, Australia, South Korea). Due to the bandwidth limitations even of 3G systems and the increasing demand for multimedia services, unidirectional systems like DVB and DMB are currently deployed to satisfy the demand. GSM and UMTS then act as the backward channel for interactive multimedia streaming, while DVB and DMB offer several

video streams broadcast to larger regions independent of individual receivers.

GSM is definitively the most prominent 2G system with far more than 1 billion subscribers in more than 200 countries resulting in a market share of more than 70%. Furthermore, the architecture of GSM can be seen as a template for many other mobile communication architectures. Figure 8 gives an overview of the GSM architecture. Mobile phones connect to the BTS that represents their cell; cells are typically drawn as hexagons although in reality they look like bizarrely shaped polygons, even with holes and islands. Several cells are controlled by a BSC (base station controller). Cells with their BTSs and BSCs together form the RSS (Radio Subsystem). Several BSCs are attached to a MSC (mobile service switching center), which is basically an ISDN (integrated services digital network) switching system with mobility enhancements. MSCs are connected to one another via a fixed network. A GMSC (Gateway MSC) provides connectivity to other networks, such as the classical telephone network or the Internet. Each operator has at least

Figure 9. New features of UMTS networks

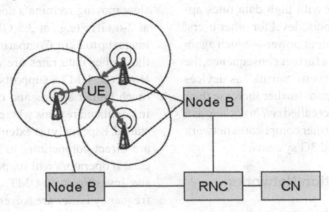

one HLR (home location register) comprising all subscriber data, such as contract data and current location. For inactive users, this location refers to a so-called location area, that is set of cells, not to a single cell since book-keeping on the cell level would generate too much overhead in this case. For active users, that is those making phone calls, the HLR keeps track of users on the cell level. The VLRs (visitor location registers) monitor visiting subscribers within a certain location area. HLR and VLR together with the switching components, that is MSCs and GMSCs form a so-called network subsystem (NSS). Additionally, GSM needs security and maintenance related components forming the operation subsystem (OSS). The operation and maintenance center (OMC) monitors and controls the whole network. Important authentication data per subscriber is stored in the authentication center (AUC). Finally, the equipment identity register (EIR) keeps track of the identity of each mobile device; for instance, it enables blocking of stolen devices.

Mobility in GSM is supported by hard handovers between antennas. Hard refers to the fact that a device can only be connected to exactly one BTS at the same time. UMTS, in contrast, offers soft handovers: it supports the simultaneous connection of a mobile device to up to three

different BTSs. Noticeable service degradation, interruption, or even disconnection can be avoided with much higher probabiliy. UMTS in its initial release is often built on top of a GSM/GPRS infrastructure by adding CDMA. Figure 9 shows a part of the UMTS architecture. Major differences with respect to GSM are as follows. Due to a more intelligent and dynamic SDMA scheme, all UMTS cells of an operator can use the same frequencies; multipath propagation is treated similarly to receiving a signal from different senders. The BTS is called *Node B* and can control several antennas, an RNC (radio network controller) can control several Node Bs and connects to the core. RNCs and Node Bs have the capability to merge data streams they receive via different antennas (and, conversely, to split them).

While UMTS enables much higher data rates per user, it also comes with the drawback of higher system complexity and the requirement of tight sending power control (1500 times per second) since all signals from different devices must reach the receiving antenna of a base station with roughly the same energy, a prerequisite for the correlation-based detection of the original vs. inverted CDMA chip sequences as described above. Furthermore, in contrast to GSM systems different users within the same or neighboring cells can now heavily influence each other's performance. Sending with high data rates appears as an increased noise level for other users, thus requiring more output power—which again leads to more noise. As a further consequence, the radio cell virtually starts to "shrink" as devices at the edge of a cell cannot further increase their output power. This effect called *cell breathing* as a function of cell load further complicates network design in CDMA-based 3G systems.

Wireless Distribution Networks

While many people enjoy DSL connectivity and high-speed backbone networks usually crisscross all major cities in the developed countries in the form of copper wires and fiber optics, many regions are still not reached by high data rate lines. Reasons vary and include sparse population, regulations, or lagging deployment. Additionally, quite often competitors want to deploy alternative networks without the burden and cost of either digging wires into the ground or paying high tolls for using "last mile" cables operated by large telecom operators, usually the former national monopolists. The IEEE 802.16 family of standards (IEEE, 2004a) known as WiMAX (Ghosh, Wolter, Andrews, & Chen, 2005) offers an alternative for wireless distribution of data. (The so-called WiMAX Forum fosters this family of standards.) These systems typically operate in the frequency range 2-10 GHz, but also far above 10 GHz for directed microwave point-to-point connections. The latter setting can reach data rates of above 100 Mbit/s. Typical user data rates are in the range of 1-5 Mbit/s as the medium is shared among several subscribers—in any case, WiMAX is targeting data rates superior to WLAN (see next section).

While the basic 802.16 standard focuses on fixed senders and receivers—in accordance with the initial target to compete with DSL on the "last mile to the subscriber at home and in business", 802.16e introduces mobility and therefore competes with UMTS and WLAN. With this standard, slow moving terminals are supported operating at 2-6 GHz (e.g., at 3.5 GHz in Germany) with ranges up to 2 km. Comparing 802.16e with UMTS the higher data rates are clearly an advantage. However, UMTS supports terminal mobility at much higher speeds and offers better coverage in populated regions where UMTS is already installed. Especially the extensions HSDPA/HSUPA are direct competitors to 802.16e and it is not clear if operators will support 802.16e after massive investments in UMTS. Furthermore, not all frequency issues are solved regarding WiMAX. Nevertheless, one may imagine WiMAX "success stories" in the context of national deployment in developing countries or city-wide deployment in audacious US cities, and a delayed adoption in areas where UMTS takes the lead today.

Wireless Local Area Networks

No other technology has made Internet access simpler for the masses than WLANs. Many public spaces, restaurants, schools, universities, libraries, and millions of private homes are covered by WLAN technology. Almost all WLANs follow the IEEE 802.11 standard family (IEEE 1999)—with 802.11b/g (cf. IEEE, 1999b; IEEE, 2003) being the most prominent versions offering up to 54 Mbit/s gross data rate per channel operating at 2.4 GHz. Most installations use the technology for accessing a wired-network infrastructure via "access points", but the IEEE 802.11 standard offers a mode for single-hop ad-hoc networks, too: a set of devices within direct reach can all be tuned to a network that is spontaneously defined (by someone "inventing" its name and some basic parameters) and that does not have a "master device". The ad-hoc mode is used by, for example, portable game consoles for connecting gamers. Typical modes of operation do not offer any service guarantees and are based on a best effort medium access scheme.

As mentioned at the end of the section *Multiple Access Schemes* above, we will describe the

Figure 10. Basic medium access mechanism of IEEE 802.11 WLANs

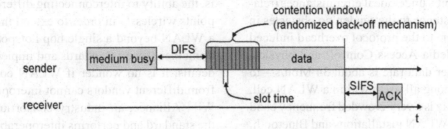

CSMA/CA (Carrier Sense Multiple Access with Collision Avoidance) scheme for concurrent access as used in WLANs today, since it is one of the most sophisticated and effective schemes known to date, cf. Figure 10. Each sender ready to transmit data has to listen into the medium before sending (LBT, see above, also called "carrier sense"). If the medium is sensed as busy, the sender has to wait until the medium is free again. CSMA/CA attempts to control the "dangerous" time right after a transmission (cf. the section above as mentioned), where several stations may want to access the medium concurrently. But before the actual concurrent scheme becomes operational, expedited traffic (e.g., for network management purposes) is allowed; the corresponding time interval is called Distributed coordination function Inter-Frame Spacing (DIFS). The subsequent concurrent access is based on a so-called randomized back-off mechanism (see Figure 10). A basic and well-known companion concept is the introduction of slots: the slot length equals the maximum signal latency between the remotest possible users of a cell; transmissions are allowed at the beginning of a slot only, such that any cell member will have detected an ongoing transmission (based on LBT, see above) before the first transmission slot elapsed and before a transmission planned for the subsequent slot would start—due to LBT, such a ready-to-fire transmission would be cancelled.

With CSMA/CA, a so-called *collision window* is defined as "slot length times *N*" where *N* reflects the "typical" number of concurrently waiting senders for a given network and period of use (*N* is dynamically adjustable). Each sender draws a random number that is mapped onto a beginning-of-slot as the scheduled start-of-transmission. During waiting time a sender applies LBT, that is, senses the medium to see if another sender (with an earlier scheduled slot) started sending. If the waiting time is over and the medium was still free, transmission starts.

This randomization of starting times avoids collisions of senders waiting for a free medium. However, senders may still collide if they randomly chose the same start-of-transmission slot. This illustrates the nondeterministic nature of 802.11: there is no guarantee that medium access is possible within a certain time limit. A certain degree of fairness is provided by the fact that deferred stations get credited for the waiting time elapsed when competing for the next transmssion. Since wireless transmission is quite error prone compared to wire based transmission, WLANs actually implement the per-hop acknowledgement mechanism 'theoretically' present in all LAN standards: the receiver on the "wireless hop" of a network path is supposed to immediately reply by means of an acknowledgement (ACK). More precisely, the ACK is sent with DIFS, see above; even more precisely, the ACK may be send within the Short Inter-Frame Spacing interval SIFS, which is shorter than DIFS. While the MA scheme described is identical for all 802.11 WLANs, the substandards differ with respect to the physical layer. While 802.11b and 802.11g operate at 2.4 GHz, 802.11a uses frequency bands at about 5

GHz. Both 802.11g and 802.11a offer a gross data rate of 54 Mbit/s under ideal circumstances (relatively low distance to the sender, no obstacles in the LOS). Due to the protocol overhead induced by MAC (Media Access Control) and physical layers the user data rate is about 34 Mbit/s—to be shared among all users within a WLAN cell. While 2.4 GHz is a very crowded frequency band due to many WLAN installations and Bluetooth, the frequency bands at 5 GHz offer not only more channels for transmission but also less interference. The big drawback is the lower range due to the higher frequency.

WLANs following 802.11 comprise optional modes of operation. One is the RTS/CTS (Request to Send/Clear to Send) mechanism which helps to overcome the hidden terminal problem described above. RTS packets can be considered to be small "probe" packets sent by stations willing to transmit. If an RTS gets through to the sender, it survived both potential collisions and potential hidden terminals—and the "true" packet is guaranteed to get through since a CTS packet sent by the potential receiver (usually an access point) announces this "true" packet and reserves the ether. If, however, the RTS packet does not get through (due to either collision or hidden terminals), then the required counter measures can be applied much faster: only a small packet is lost and the timeout (for the expected CTS packet) can be set to a value much smaller than the one for (variable length) data packets.

As the basic 802.11 WLAN does not provide any *quality-of-service*, a new standard 802.11e introduces prioritized medium access, providing for jitter sensitive applications such as VoIP (Voice over Internet Protocol). *Security* is a prime concern in wireless networks. Since the security mechanisms provided with early 802.11 standards were insufficient, 802.11i introduces new ones (IEEE 2004). As more and more applications need higher data rates and all users have to share the bandwidth of a WLAN radio cell, 802.11n defines *high-speed WLANs* at rates above 100

Mbit/s. 802.11s introduces mesh networks, that is, the ability to interconnecting different access points wirelessly in order to extend the range of a WLAN beyond a single hop hotspot. Considering these many standards and implementation details, it is no wonder if WLAN components from different vendors cannot interoperate. The WiFi Alliance, an industry consortium fosters the standard and performs interoperability tests, bringing together different vendors and ensuring interoperability.

Wireless Personal Area Networks

The main purpose of WPANs is the wireless connectivity of people and devices within a limited radius of 10-20 m. Systems belonging to this category comprise Bluetooth and ZigBee, both members of the IEEE 802.15 family of WPANs (sometimes also called body area networks), cf. (IEEE, 2002). Key characteristics compared to WLANs are the much lower data rate but also lower power consumption making them the ideal candidate for battery driven devices. Currently, many new systems belonging to this category of wireless networks are being announced. Examples are ZWave focusing on building automation, "Wireless USB" as a USB cable replacement, and several other systems for special purposes. The systems also comprise new transmission technologies like UWB (ultra wideband transmission), see (UWB, 2002). There is no clear boundary between WPANs and sensor networks (WSNs) since the former provide WSN prone characteristics like ultra low power hardware, self-configuration and multihop capabilities. There is also no clear boundary to WLANs as new WPAN standards strive for higher data rates and broader ranges.

Bluetooth is currently the most prominent WPAN technology example (Bluetooth, 2004). Its main usage is cable replacement for peripheral devices such as headsets. Bluetooth offers a synchronous transmission service for voice streams and an asynchronous data service. Currently,

Figure 11. Bluetooth pico network

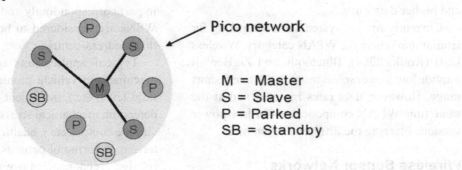

Bluetooth chips are integrated in many mobile phones, laptops, PDAs, and cameras bridging distances up to typically 10 m. Bluetooth operates at 2.4 GHz offering gross data rates of less than 1 Mbit/s. Figure 11 shows the basic topology of a Bluetooth network, called a piconet. Each piconet is controlled by a single master. Up to seven slaves can simultaneously participate in the piconet, other devices may be parked. Nonparticipating devices are on stand-by. Several low-power modes prolong battery lifetime.

The master of the piconet controls medium access by strict polling of slaves. Furthermore, the master defines the frequency-hopping scheme that all slaves have to follow. Different networks use different hopping sequences derived from the master's unique address and a clock. This mechanism guarantees a very low probability of collisions of two piconets as collisions only occur if two piconets are using the same frequency at the same time in the same space. As the frequency is changed 1600 times per second the overlapping time would be quite short anyway.

Typical data rates of Bluetooth V1.1 are 433 kbit/s for symmetric connections and 723 kbit/s combined with 57 kbit/s for asymmetric connections. As wireless transmission and the capability of wireless device access pose a security risk, Bluetooth comprises several security mechanisms. Devices that never met before have to be paired first. This pairing requires user interaction (i.e.,

the entering of a number). After this procedure both paired devices store a link key for further use. For each communication session an encryption key is generated which then creates a cipher key for encryption of the data stream.

A service discovery protocol helps Bluetooth devices to detect services in the close environment. To enable interoperability between different Bluetooth devices many profiles have been defined. Examples are object push, imaging, and fax. While the Bluetooth consortium mainly deals with higher layers and applications, IEEE standardized the MAC and physical layer in the standard 802.15.1. Additionally, 802.15.2 tries to ensure coexistence of Bluetooth with WLANs as both operate in the same 2.4 GHz ISM band. However, as Bluetooth does not use carrier sensing before medium access it might cause heavy interference with WLAN devices politely using carrier sensing.

Based on the IEEE 802.15.4 standard, ZigBee focuses on a low-rate wireless transmission system enabling devices with multi-year battery lifetime. Potential applications are interactive toys, smart badges, remote controls, or home automation. Typical data rates are in the range of 20 to 250 kbit/s with a very low latency of down to 15 ms. The relation of the ZigBee alliance to 802.15.4 is similar to that of Bluetooth to 802.15.1—it provides the higher layers, profiles, and application interfaces. Alternative physical layers are provided by 802.15.4a that includes ranging capabilities and higher data rates.

Currently several systems are competing for similar markets in the WPAN category. Wireless USB (Kolik, 2004), Bluetooth, and ZigBee all provide low-power solutions with relatively short range. However, data rates increase and at the same time WLAN components offer low-power versions blurring the difference even more.

Wireless Sensor Networks

Although at first glance WSNs have much in common with WPANs, there are certain key characteristics that make them form a category of their own. WSNs are always deployed in a physical environment; they are often used to measure certain parameters in this environment, which they may influence by means of on-board actuators. The network itself is self-organizing and typically very energy efficient. The potentially high number of nodes should come at very low cost per node. Willig (2005) provides a good overview of existing WSN systems and technologies.

A main difference to wLANs, wPANs or other classical ad-hoc networks is the usually clear application orientation of WSNs—almost all performance parameters depend on the application to ensure the best adaptation to a problem. Furthermore, device power in WSNs is very limited and, thus, data rates are rather low. Since WSNs potentially comprise thousands of nodes, indi-

vidual nodes are considered rather dispensable; in part correspondingly and in part additionally, WSNs are considered to be data-centric rather than address-centric.

Typical applications of WSNs comprise machine and vehicle monitoring (temperature, fluid level, etc.), intelligent buildings (intrusion detection, mechanical stress detection, precision climate control, etc.), health and medicine (long-term monitoring of patients, intensive care with relative freedom of movement, etc.), logistics (total asset management, etc.) and environmental monitoring (wildlife, waste dumps, demilitarized zones, etc.). WSNs are quite often complementary to fixed networks.

Figure 12 shows a typical topology of a WSN. Many sensor nodes *SN* monitor and control the environment. The nodes also process and forward data via other nodes towards gateways. The gateways *GW* connect the WSN to different other networks. Furthermore, the gateways themselves may form a wireless mesh backbone to allow for greater flexibility.

WSNs still face many challenges for widespread deployment. First of all, WSNs have to be integrated into real world applications. Examples come from emergency and rescue applications, monitoring and surveillance, as well as from gaming and tourism. In order to be used by laymen WSNs must be self-configuring. Research must develop robust routing algorithms, self-healing capabilities, as well as data aggregation and pre-

Figure 12. Basic topology of a wireless sensor network

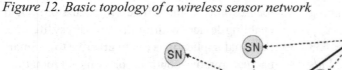
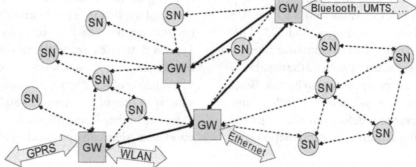

cise localization methods. For everyday usage it is important to have tools for managing WSNs, for example, for reprogramming and update distribution. Further research must come up with WSNs that can really be embedded and never touched again. This includes the use of environmental energy sources to avoid battery replacement.

Currently, there are many WSN platforms available. A coarse distinction can be made between research platforms and industrial platforms. Research WSNs comprise less robust components, but offer many more features and have a higher complexity. Furthermore, many different programming paradigms are available (procedural, role based, rule based, etc.). The most prominent example is the *mote* family of sensors developed at the University of California in Berkeley with many derivatives; other examples comprise BTnodes, ScatterWeb, SmartITs etc. Industrial platforms must follow different rules. All components must be certified following different national and international regulations for consumer electronics, radio transceivers, lead free production, and so forth. Robustness and reliability are prime issues and, thus, these industry components typically come with fewer features. Additionally, the companies typically do not publish the precise mechanisms for, for example, self-configuration, energy conservation, and so forth. Prominent examples are components from Coronis, Dust Networks, Ember, ScatterWeb, and so forth.

In addition to the sensor nodes, all WSNs need different gateways for network integration (e.g., GSM/GPRS, UMTS, Bluetooth, etc.), but also programming interfaces to common development platforms (e.g., Visual Studio, Eclipse, LabView).

CONCLUSION

The five classes of networks introduced above were selected due to their importance for UC.

The reader should be aware that further classes like those listed below may well be used in the UC context but will remain restricted to special use cases:

- Paging Systems, which are still prominent in the US, but useful for niche UC applications only due to limited bandwidth and interactivity and due to the broadcast nature of the infrastructure
- Trunk networks, which are and will be in use, for example, for customer premises (field) networks and public security/emergency services (fire brigades, police, etc.); the technological basis of the system leads to restrictions comparable to those mentioned for paging networks; in addition, the focus on closed user groups is somewhat in contrast to "ubiquity".

The summary of this chapter should read *"one size does not fit all"*. The chapter presented five different classes of wireless communication systems. Each of them has its specific characteristics that cannot simply be replaced by another technology. Systems have different ranges, different data rates and latencies; they differ in their robustness or power consumption. While some overlap exists and some technologies may take on applications from other technologies, the future will see more different wireless systems rather than fewer ones. A good example for the differences relates to voice transmission over GSM vs. WLAN. As GSM was built for that purpose, it offers certain service guarantees to ensure voice quality with minimal interference. One key feature for this is guaranteed medium access independent of other users based on heavy use of *multiplex* as introduced. WLAN on the other hand has a much higher bandwidth, can be used for mass data download—but still suffers from its nondeterministic medium access scheme when it comes to voice transmission and the radio cell is loaded by other users (since concurrent-access schemes are heavily used as introduced above).

Figure 13. Future architecture of 4G networks

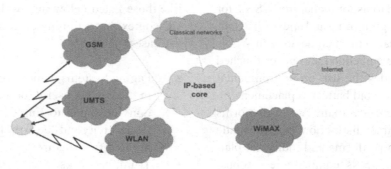

Applications for wireless and mobile systems have to take into account performance fluctuations of the networks. While wired networks typically offer the same quality-of-service all the time, mobile networks may experience service interrupts, suffer from spontaneous resource bottlenecks, and exhibit lower performance under heavy load.

While at least some convergence in the core of the network is foreseeable, applications still have to adapt to many different technologies. Users do not really care about the underlying network technology; they simply want to use their applications. Thus, applications have to work independently from the access technology or core network design. While the convergence to a common network layer based on IP will help in many respects, there are still many unsolved issues such as security, reliability, quality-of-service, and, last but not least, charging models.

FUTURE RESEARCH DIRECTIONS

Considering the many different wireless transmission systems presented in this chapter, the main question is: What will the future look like? In line with the conclusion above, we cannot expect all systems to converge to a single technology. Therefore, mainstream research and development will emphasize a converged fourth generation of wireless networks (Mähönen & Polyzos,

2001) coined as *Always Best Connected (ABC)*. Many different wireless and mobile systems will coexist due to physical limitations, application requirements, regulations, power consumption and economic issues, where the latter range from equipment cost to network provider tariffs for provider-operated vs. license-free technologies. Figure 13 gives a very high level overview of the future converged networks. A mobile device may chose from available networks (here: GSM, UMTS, and WLAN) depending on its requirements. For instance, for voice applications GSM may be sufficient and preferrable due to high coverage. For reliable video streaming UMTS may be the better choice, while for downloads WLAN offers the highest bandwidth.

An obvious move towards convergence is the attempt to "hide" the different access technologies under the Internet IP protocol. As an important move towards this goal, many provider-operated networks are evolving towards an "IP-based core network" (also called IP-based signalling network). This core network is used for transmitting "dialing" information, management data, and so forth. Today, different core technologies make, for example, handovers between different access networks difficult. A unified core helps to reduce complexity. Another important step towards "all IP" is the ongoing move towards the IPv6 version of the IP protocol that can accommodate billions of subscribers without nasty address translation schemes (cf. NAT (Network Address Translation)) as used in the current IPv4. However, a still open issue is the reliability and quality-of-service support of the IP technology. Classical networks will remain for some time, such as the classical telephone network and the classical Internet. By classical Internet we denote the existing basic structure that is highly dominated by fixed systems and considers mobile users as "special cases at the fringe". Tomorrow's Internet will be dominated by mobile and wireless access. The development will soon be boosted in developing countries where mobile Internet access is not a luxury add-on but *the* preferable solution for initial Internet access; this situation applies for millions of people in Asia and Africa, both outside and inside rural areas (cf. WiMAX).

It is foreseeable that current big network operators will also operate the new technologies. After some initial hesitation, the big classical fixed network operators are currently also the world's biggest hotspot operators and mobile network operators—and will be the operators for whatever technology may prove beneficial from an economical point of view.

The following key features will shape the technology of 4G networks.

- Improved radio technology and antennas: Smart antennas that can form a beam and follow individual devices will replace omnidirectional antennas. Software-defined radios will replace fixed hardware that can communicate only via certain preconfigured standards. Mobile devices will be able to download new transmission technologies, learn to communicate on different frequencies following different, new, and flexible standards. Furthermore, the spectrum will be allocated dynamically following the current demand and not fixed rules.

- Core network convergence: An IP-based, but quality-of-service enhanced, network core will connect the different access technolo-

gies. For some applications mobile IP will be provided.

- Ad-hoc technologies will be integrated: In order to support spontaneous communication and to save energy, current networks will be complemented by ad-hoc components. This also increases the redundancy and thus robustness of networks.

- Simple and open service platform: Similar to today's Internet, future mobile communication systems should push the intelligence to the edge of the network rather than make the network itself more intelligent. This enables many more service providers besides the network operators. It remains open if the current network operators support this development.

For a good insight into these and further research challenges, see (Shakkottai & Rappaport 2002).

REFERENCES

Bluetooth (2004). Specification of the Bluetooth system—Vol. 1: Architecture & terminology Overview; Vol. 2: Core system package; Vol. 3: Core system package, Version 2.0+EDR. Retrieved October 9, 2007, from http://www.bluetooth.org

Brasche, G., & Walke, B. (1997). Concepts, services, and protocols of the new GSM phase 2+ general packet radio service. *IEEE Communications Magazine, 35*(8).

Eberspächer, J., Vögel, H.-J., & Bettstetter, C. (2001). GSM—Switching, services and protocols. John Wiley & Sons.

Ghosh, A., Wolter, D. R., Andrews, J. G., & Chen, R. (2005). Broadband wireless access with WiMAX 802.16: Current performance benchmarks and future potential. *IEEE Communications Magazine,* February 2005.

Groe, J. B., & Larson, L. E. (2000). *CDMA mobile radio design.* Artech House.

IEEE (1999). *Standard 802.11: Wireless LAN Medium Access Control (MAC) and Physical Layer (PHY) Specifications, 1999.* New York: IEEE Press.

IEEE (1999b). *Standard 802.11b: Wireless LAN Medium Access Control (MAC) and Physical Layer (PHY) Specifications: High-speed physical layer extension in the 2.4 GHz band, 1999.* New York: IEEE Press.

IEEE (2002). *IEEE P802.15. The working group for WPAN. The Institute of Electrical and Electronics Engineers.* New York: IEEE Press.

IEEE (2003). *Standard 802.11g: Wireless LAN Medium Access Control (MAC) and Physical Layer (PHY) Specifications: Further high-speed physical layer extension in the 2.4 GHz band, 2003.* New York: IEEE Press.

IEEE (2004). *Standard 802.11i: Wireless LAN Medium Access Control (MAC) and Physical Layer (PHY) specification, Amendment 6: Medium Access Control (MAC) security enhancement, July 2004.* Retrieved October 13, 2007, from http://www.ieee.org

IEEE (2004a). *IEEE 802.16: IEEE standards for local and metropolitan area networks: Part 16. Air interface for fixed wireless access systems, October 2004.* Retrieved October 14, 2007, from http://www.ieee.org

Karl, H., & Willig, A. (2005). *Protocols and architectures for wireless sensor networks.* John Wiley & Sons.

Kolik, R. (2004). Wireless USB brings greater convenience and mobility to devices. *Technology@ Intel Magazine,* February 2004. Retrieved October

14, 2007, from http://wwwp.intel.com/technology/magazine/communications/wi02041.pdf

Mähönen, P., & Polyzos, G. (2001). European R&D on fourth-generation mobile and wireless IP networks. *IEEE Personal Communications, 8*(6).

Muratore, F. (Ed.). (2000). *UMTS: Mobile communications for the future.* John Wiley & Sons.

Schiller, J. (2003). *Mobile communications* (2nd ed). Addison-Wesley.

Shakkottai, S., & Rappaport, T. S. (2002). Research challenges in wireless networks: A technical overview. In *Proceedings of the 5th International Symposium on Wireless Personal Multimedia Communications* (pp. 12-18). IEEE Press.

UWB (2002). *Ultra-wideband working group.* Retrieved October 14, 2007, from http://www.uwb.org

ADDITIONAL READING

Abramson, N. (1996). Wideband random access for the last mile. *IEEE Personal Communications, 3*(4).

Adachi, F., Sawahashi, M., & Suda, H. (1998). Wideband DS-CDMA for next-generation mobile communications systems. *IEEE Communications Magazine, 36*(9).

Adelstein, F., Gupta, S. K. S., Richard, G. G., & Schwiebert, L. (2005). *Fundamentals of mobile and pervasive computing.* McGraw Hill.

Akyildiz, I., Su, W., Sankarasubramaniam, Y., & Cayirci, E. (2002). *Wireless sensor networks: A survey.* Computer Networks, Elsevier Science, 38(2002).

Alesso, H. P., & Smith, C. (2001). *The intelligent wireless web.* Addison Wesley Longman, Inc.

Arroyo-Fernandez, B., DaSilva, J., Fernandes, J., & Prasad, R. (2001). Life after third-generation mobile communications. *IEEE Communications Magazine, 39*(8).

Barry, J. R. (1994). *Wireless infrared communications*. Kluwer Academic Publishers.

Dahlman, E., Gudmundson, B., Nilsson, M., & Sköld, J. (1998). UMTS/IMT-2000 based on wideband CDMA. *IEEE Communications Magazine, 36*(9).

Dornan, A. (2002). *The essential guide to wireless communications applications*. Prentice Hall.

DVB (2002). *DVB project office*. Retrieved October 13, 2007, from http://dvb.org

Jamalipour, A., & Tekinay, S. (2001). Fourth generation wireless networks and interconnection standards. *IEEE Personal Communications, 8*(5).

Lewis, T. (1999). UbiNet: The ubiquitous internet will be wireless. *IEEE Computer, 32*(10).

Ojanperä, T., & Prasad, R. (1998a). An overview of third-generation wireless personal communications: An European perspective. *IEEE Personal Communications, 5*(6).

Pahlavan, K., & Krishnamurthy, P. (2002). *Principles of wireless network*. Prentice Hall.

Pahlavan, K., Krishnamurthy, P., Hatami, A., Ylianttila, M., Makela, J.-P., Pichma, R., & Vallström, J. (2000). Handoff in hybrid mobile data networks. *IEEE Personal Communications, 7*(2).

Peterson, R., Ziemer, R., & Borth, D. (1995). *Introduction to spread spectrum communications*. Prentice Hall.

Proakis, J. G. (1989). *Digital communications* (2nd ed). McGraw-Hill International Editions,.

Santamaria, A., & Lopez-Hernandez, F. (1994). *Wireless LAN systems*. Artech House.

Stallings, W. (2001). *Wireless communication and networks*. Prentice Hall.

Stavroulakis, P. (2001). *Third generation mobile telecommunication systems*. Springer.

Tisal, J. (2001). *The GSM network. GPRS evolution: One step towards UMTS* (2nd ed). John Wiley & Sons.

UMTS Forum (2002). Retrieved October 13, 2007 from http://www.umts-forum.org

Viterbi, A. (1995). *CDMA: Principles of spread spectrum communication*. Addison-Wesley.

Wisely, D., Eardley, P., & Burness, L. (2002). *IP for 3G, Networking technologies for mobile communications*. Wiley.

WiMAX Forum (2006). Mobile WiMAX—Part 1: A Technical Overview and Performance Evaluation, February 2006.

Wong, D., & Lim, T. (1997). Soft handoffs in CDMA mobile systems. *IEEE Personal Communications, 4*(6).

Yaghoobi, H. (2004). *802.16 broadband wireless access—The next big thing in wireless*. Presentation at Intel Developer Forum, September 2004.

Chapter VII
Event–Based and Publish/ Subscribe Communication

Erwin Aitenbichler
Technische Universität Darmstadt, Germany

ABSTRACT

Ubiquitous Computing assumes that users and their computing devices are highly mobile. Because it is unlikely that mobile networks will be equally available in the same quality everywhere, there may be varying levels of connectivity, ranging from full network availability through low-bandwidth connectivity, to no connection at all. As a consequence, software components in the system cannot assume that the connections between them are static and always available. The event-based style is essential for ubiquitous computing, since it offers a good decoupling of the communicating entities in terms of space, time, and program flow. This chapter starts with an introduction to the different interaction models found in distributed systems. Next, a classification of publish/subscribe-systems is presented. We then describe a formal data and filter model that allows us to precisely define the semantics of event filters. Based on this model, we discuss different routing algorithms for the efficient distribution of event notifications in a network. Finally, a number of examples for publish/subscribe systems are presented.

INTRODUCTION

The communication models found in distributed systems can be classified according to the following two attributes: who initiated the communication and how the communication partner is addressed. The resulting four models are shown in Table 1. Provider-initiated communication is also often called *push* communication and consumer-initiated communication is also often called *pull* communication.

Table 1. Taxonomy of communication models

	Consumer-Initiated ("pull")	Provider-Initiated ("push")
Direct Addressing	Request/Reply	Callback
Indirect Addressing	Anonymous Request/Reply	Event-Based

Request/Reply: The most widely used model is request/reply. Any kind of client-server communication or remote procedure call belongs to this class. The initiator is a client, which requests the execution of an operation or the delivery of data. The provider is a server that processes the requests issued by clients. Servers are directly addressed by clients, resulting in a tight coupling of the cooperating entities.

Anonymous Request/Reply: builds on request/reply as basic action, but without specifying the provider directly. Instead, requests are delivered to an arbitrary provider or a set of providers automatically chosen by the communication system. For example, the IP Anycast mechanism routes a packet to the nearest member of a group of destinations without resolving the target IP address in advance.

Callback: In this model, consumers register their interest in certain events directly with specific, known providers. Providers maintain lists with the consumers' addresses and notify them when an event of interest has occurred. Thus, this model introduces a tight coupling between the communicating entities. The *Observer Design Pattern* is a well-known example for this interaction.

Event-based: In the event-based model, providers publish notifications and consumers subscribe to notifications by issuing subscriptions, which are stateless event filters. Communication between providers and consumers is decoupled by a broker. Consumers can have multiple active subscriptions, and after a client has issued a subscription, a message broker delivers all future matching notifications that are published by any provider until the client cancels the respective subscription.

The event-based communication style has been used for decades in the area of graphical user interfaces. It is now also increasingly being applied to widely distributed and critical systems such as real-time, automotive, traffic control (including air and rail), e-commerce, logistics, workflow, and mobile computing. The acceptance of this paradigm is also witnessed by its incorporation into such widespread standards as CORBA and Java Enterprise Edition.

Events, Notifications, and Messages

Any phenomenon in the real world or any kind of state change inside an information system can be an *event*. However, it must be observable and some component in the information system must observe it in order to notify parties interested in the event.

The reification of an event is called *notification*. Observers create these notifications. Notifications represent the data describing events. They contain precisely formatted data to notify interested parties in the distributed systems about the occurrence of events. The content of a notification is usually application-dependent. It may simply indicate the occurrence of an event, or may as well contain additional information about the object observed and its context.

For example, consider a room that is equipped with a badge-based location system (see the chapter "A Focus on Location Context" in this book). Now, if *a person enters the room*, we call this occurrence an event. The badge system is able to observe this event and publishes an event *notification* to inform interested parties about this occurrence. This notification is a data structure that would typically contain the event type, the identifier of the badge, the identifier of the receiver, and a timestamp. The most common data models for notifications are typed name-value pairs, semistructured data (i.e., XML), or objects of some programming language.

Messages are transport containers that carry data between communication endpoints. In the event-based model, the endpoints are *publishers* and *subscribers*. Beside request and reply messages, notifications are messages with a special purpose. They inform subscribers that an event has occurred.

Decoupling

Event-based communication decouples providers, or more specifically, producers and consumers in terms of the following three aspects:

Space decoupling: Producers do not individually address consumers while publishing messages. Instead, they publish messages through a message broker and subscribers receive these messages indirectly through this broker. Publishers do not usually hold references to the consumers and they are not aware of how many consumers are participating in the interaction.

Time decoupling: Producers and consumers do not need to actively participate in the interaction at the same time. In particular, a subscription causes messages to be delivered even if producers join after the subscription was issued. In a plain publish/subscribe system, notifications are retained only as long as it takes to distribute them to current subscribers. Some brokers deliver messages to consumers through a queue. This gives consumers the ability to temporarily disconnect from the system. The message broker will dispatch all messages that it stored while the consumer was offline upon reconnect.

Flow decoupling: The production and consumption of messages does not block the flow of control of the producing and consuming application, respectively. Publish operations do not put the publisher on hold, as they are nonblocking. The actual publication of the message may be handled in a different thread at a later time. Consumers are asynchronously notified about an arriving message.

Concepts

The following basic concepts can be used to build event-based systems.

Notifications: Event-based systems are often emulated using multiple remote method calls and the callback model described earlier. This involves the following steps. First, the consumer performs a call to register with the producer. Among other data, the consumer must pass a callback reference to itself. Once the producer observes an event which the consumer registered for, it asynchronously notifies the consumer using the callback reference. In this type of interaction, the consumers register their interest directly with producers which manage subscriptions and send events. This scheme is a distributed version of the *Observer* design pattern. It is specified in the Java Distributed Event Specification and used in many Java applications. Notifications provide flow decoupling by notifying subscribers asynchronously. Yet they still remain closely coupled in time and space. Subscription management has to be handled by the publisher itself. As a result, the code for subscription management, event publication, and error handling is usually duplicated in each publisher.

Message queuing: In this concept, producer and consumer are decoupled by a message queue (Figure 1). Messages always pass through queues on their way from the producer to the consumer. Each message is addressed to a specific queue, and consumers extract messages from the queues established to hold their messages. If the queue is empty, then the *dequeue* operation blocks until a new message becomes available. Queues retain all messages sent to them until the messages are consumed or until the messages expire. This scheme has the following characteristics:

- Each message has only one consumer.
- Producer and consumer of a message have no timing dependencies. The consumer can fetch the message regardless of whether or not it was running when the producer sent the message.

Thus, Message Queuing offers space decoupling, time decoupling, and flow decoupling on the producer side.

Publish/Subscribe: A publish/subscribe system consists of *publishers*, *subscribers*, and an *event service*. Publishers produce event notifications and pass them to the event service. Subscribers express their interest in certain events by defining stateless message filters, called *subscriptions*, and issue them to the event service.

Figure 1. Message queuing: Producers send messages asynchronously to the queue while consumers dequeue messages synchronously

The event service is a message broker responsible for distributing messages arriving from multiple publishers to its multiple subscribers. The publish/subscribe paradigm fully decouples publishers and subscribers in terms of space, time, and program flow.

PUBLISH/SUBSCRIBE

Publish/subscribe systems can be classified according to the subscription mechanisms, addressing schemes, data models, and filter models they employ. Both publishers and subscribers are denoted as clients in the following.

Subscription Mechanisms

Subscription-based: A subscription-based publish/subscribe system supports the following operations:

pub(X, n)	Client *X* publishes notification *n*
sub(X, F)	Client *X* subscribes with filter *F*
unsub(X, F)	Client *X* unsubscribes with filter *F*
notify(X, n)	Client *X* is notified about notification *n*

Clients register their interest in specific kinds of notifications by issuing subscriptions via the *sub(X, F)* operation. From that time on, all notifications matching the filter parameter *F* are delivered to the client. The event service calls the *notify(X, n)* operation of the client and passes the notification as a parameter so that the client can process it. Each client can have multiple subscriptions. A client can revoke subscriptions individually using the *unsub(X, F)* operation.

Advertisement-based: An advertisement-based publish/subscribe system extends subscription-based systems with the notion of advertisements. Advertisements are issued by publishers to indicate that they have the intention of publishing certain kinds of notifications. An advertisement-based publish/subscribe system supports the following operations:

adv(X, F)	Client *X* advertises with filter *F*
unadv(X, F)	Client *X* unadvertises with filter *F*
pub(X, n)	Client *X* publishes notification *n*
sub(X, F)	Client *X* subscribes with filter *F*
unsub(X, F)	Client *X* unsubscribes with filter *F*
notify(X, n)	Client *X* is notified about notification *n*

Before a publisher can start to publish a notification via the *pub(X, n)* operation, it has to advertise this via *adv(X, F)*. The parameter *F* is a filter that matches *n*. Likewise, the operation *unadv(X, F)* is invoked when the client is no longer interested in publishing notifications matching *F*. If a publisher fails to correctly advertise a notification, advertisement-based systems do not guarantee that clients will be notified.

Addressing

Topic-based addressing: The simplest publish/subscribe addressing scheme is based on the notion of topics or channels. Participants explicitly publish notifications to one or more topics, which are identified by a name. The publish/subscribe system defines how proper names look. Often they are simple strings or URL-like expressions. Each notification also carries exactly one topic identifier. The event service compares the topic identifiers of subscriptions and of notifications for equivalence in order to match subscriptions and notifications. This is the only part of a notification understood by the event service—the remaining payload is opaque. Since there is no interplay between different topics, each topic can be considered as an event service of its own. Figure 2 shows the components of a topic-based publish/subscribe system with advertisements.

This abstraction is equivalent to the one provided by a mailing list or an IP multicast group address. Topic-based publish/subscribe systems are functionally equivalent to a reliable multicast with a one-to-one mapping between topic identifiers and multicast addresses. Many industrial solutions, like JMS (Hapner, 2001) and the CORBA Event Service (OMG, 2004) implement topic-based architectures.

Subject-based addressing: Some systems extend the concept of topic-based addressing with a more flexible matching mechanism. In these systems, the topic of a notification is called "subject" and it is possible to use operations other than equality to match notifications and subscriptions. A subscription specifies some sort of expression that is evaluated against this subject string, for example, a regular expression. Consequently, a single subscription can express interest in multiple subjects. Also, two subscriptions might match two overlapping sets of notifications. This would not be possible in topic-based systems.

While the topic-based scheme only offers flat addressing with separate event spaces, subject-based addressing allows the organization of topics into a hierarchy corresponding to containment relationships. A subscription made to some node in the hierarchy will match all notifications

published to the corresponding topic and all its subtopics.

JMS (Haase, 2002), SwiftMQ (IIT, 2005), as well as the USENET News System support a subject-based subscription mechanism.

Type-based addressing: In topic-based and subject-based systems, notifications with similar content usually are grouped together with a common subject. Often, such similar notifications share the same internal structure and therefore the same data type. For that reason, the name-based topic classification model can be replaced by a scheme that filters events according to their type (Eugster, 2001; Eugster, 2003).

In systems with type-based addressing, a notification matches a subscription if the type of the notification is equal to or a subtype of the type specified by the subscription. If one allows type inheritance, where subtypes are instances of one supertype, it is possible to model hierarchies. With multiple inheritance, the subject tree is extended to a type lattice which allows for different rooted paths to the same node.

Because the kind of an event is directly coupled with the type of the notification, a closer integration with object-oriented languages is possible. With proper language extensions, all possible type mismatches can already be detected at compile time.

Content-based addressing: Content-based addressing is the most general scheme and ex-

Figure 2. Publish/subscribe with topic-based addressing

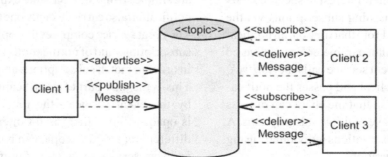

tends the domain of filters to the whole content of notifications. While the schemes previously described are easier to implement and route, a major drawback is that the publisher has to explicitly specify the data that is used for filtering. To select a suitable channel, or type, or to generate a subject string, one has to categorize the messages in some way. By doing this categorization, the publisher makes assumptions about the possible interests of subscribers.

In content-based publish/subscribe systems, the publisher does not generate additional attributes like topic names or subject strings. Filters can operate on the entire content of the notification messages. For that reason, this scheme offers the best flexibility and extensibility. A large part of this chapter is dedicated to the theory, algorithms, and implementation challenges of content-based systems.

Concept-based addressing: Concept-based addressing extends content-based addressing by attaching meta-information to event publications and event subscriptions. In doing so, concept-based addressing provides a higher level of abstraction to describe the interests of publishers and subscribers.

In CREAM (Cilia, 2003), a concept is understood as an abstraction of characteristics common to a set of real world phenomena. By associating specific concepts with notifications and filters, their correspondence with real world phenomena is described. This information allows the event service to transform notifications between different semantic representations, based on ontologies. For more information, see the chapter "Ontologies for Scalable Service-Based Ubiquitous Computing" in this book.

Data Models

Depending on the addressing scheme and the chosen filter model, the data model underlying notifications varies considerably. For example, a topic-based event service uses the channel name, which is a distinguished attribute, to route messages. It treats the notification as opaque data and does not make any assumptions about its internal structure. In contrast, a content-based service has to apply event filters on notifications. Consequently, the data contained in the notification must have a well-defined structure. The structure of notifications ranges from simple to complex, usually consisting of a name and additional, user-definable parameters. Examples of data models are:

- A single string representing the event name, without any additional parameters.
- A set of attributes, similar to records in programming languages. In untyped models, each attribute is a tuple of name and value. In typed models, each attribute is a triple of name, type and value. The set of available types is often limited to basic data types. A table in an SQL database is an example for this data model.
- A set of attributes that is hierarchically structured. A name can map to an atomic value or to a nested set of attributes. An XML document is an example for this data model.
- An object specific to some programming language, consisting of a set of attributes as described above and a set of methods.

Structured notifications are not only well defined and expressive, but also enable the use of event filters as introduced in the next section.

Filter Models

Subscribers are usually only interested in a subset of all events that are published. They express their interest in certain kinds of events by defining appropriate filters. Simple addressing schemes rely solely on special properties (e.g., topic names) for filtering, while more complex models allow the defining of filters on the whole content of a notification.

Filters are passed to the event service along with a subscription. Before notifications are propagated, they are matched against the filters and are only delivered to those subscribers that are interested in them. There are several different approaches for defining filters and the expressiveness of different filter models ranges from limited to powerful. Different content-based publish/subscribe systems vary strongly in their approach to defining filters. Some examples are:

- A set of attribute filters. In untyped models, each attribute filter is a triple of name, operator and value. In typed models, each attribute filter is a quadruple of name, type, operator and value.
- A declarative filtering language similar to database or document query languages. Examples are SQL-like filter languages and XPath.
- Program code that directly implements filtering methods in the classes of notification objects. In distributed systems, this model requires *mobile code* to define and propagate new filters.

In the next section we will focus on data and filter models that are particularly suitable for distributed event-based systems.

DISTRIBUTED EVENT-BASED SYSTEMS

A distributed event-based system (DEBS) is realized by one or more interconnected event brokers that route notifications through the network. Distributed systems operate effectively and efficiently at many different scales. The smallest practicable distributed event-based system consists of two clients and one message broker. Larger ones may be comprised of several hundred clients and many brokers. The size of the distributed system can change dynamically over time. DEBS provide considerable mathematical scalability in the sense of chapter "Introduction to Part I: Two Aspects of Global Scale" in this book. For distributed event systems, the parameters that may vary include:

- The number of clients (i.e., publishers and subscribers),
- The number of event brokers,
- The number of subscriptions and advertisements, and
- The number of notifications per second.

For building scalable publish/subscribe systems, it is imperative to condense the size of routing tables either by distribution (e.g., using *Distributed Hash Tables*), or by *filter merging*. As described earlier, filter models may have different levels of expressiveness. Simple models that only support exact string or value matches are not very expressive, but it is easy to implement filter-merging algorithms. Unfortunately, more expressive filter models increase the complexity of filter merging. For example, mobile code is most expressive and extensible, but along with the many issues regarding code portability in heterogeneous environments, code mobility, safety, and security, it is difficult to apply filter merging to filters based on mobile code. Choosing the right filter model for a given application is often referred to as the "expressiveness/scalability tradeoff" problem (Carzaniga, Rosenblum, & Wolf, 1999).

In the following, we consider a data and filter model for *structured records*, because it provides a good tradeoff between expressiveness and scalability. One indication of the suitability of this filter model is that many systems model notifications similarly to structured records. Examples are SIENA (Carzaniga, 1998), REBECA (Mühl, 2006), Gryphon (Bhola, 2003), JMS (Haase, 2002), the CORBA Notification Service (OMG, 2004), and MundoCore (Aitenbichler, 2006).

Data Model

A notification consists of a nonempty set of attributes $\{a_1, ..., a_n\}$. An attribute is a tuple $a_i = (n_i, v_i)$, where n_i is the name of the attribute, and v_i is the value.

While this model looks very simple at first glance, it is possible to map all data models discussed earlier to this tuple-based representation. To avoid the introduction of special filter operators for hierarchical records, using a dotted naming scheme can flatten them. For example, the notification:

$$\{(pos,\{(x, 1), (y, 2)\})\}$$

can be rewritten as

$$\{(pos.x, 1), (pos.y, 2)\}.$$

Any arbitrary object graph can be transformed into a hierarchical message by transforming the graph into a tree. For example, this is accomplished by numbering the graph nodes and storing node numbers in the referencing nodes, instead of using extra edges.

Filter Model

An attribute filter is a simple filter that imposes a constraint on the value and type of a single attribute. It is defined as a triple $A = (n, op, c)$, where n is the name of the attribute to test, op is the test operator, and c is a constant that serves as a parameter for the operator op. The match relation between the attribute a and the attribute filter A is defined as follows:

$$a \mathbin{E} A : \Leftrightarrow n_A = n_a \wedge op_A (v_a, c_A)$$

A filter F is a predicate $F(n) \to \{true, false\}$ that is applied to a notification n. If $F(n)$ evaluates to *true*, we say that the notification *matches* the filter. A filter is a Boolean expression that consists of one or more attribute filters, combined by Boolean operators (e.g., and, or, implication). Filters that only consist of a single attribute filter are called *simple filters*, and filters containing multiple attribute filters are called *compound filters*.

Compound filters of the form $F = A_1 \wedge ... \wedge A_n$ that only contain conjunctions, are called conjunctive filters. A notification *matches* a filter iff it satisfies all attribute filters:

$$n \mathbin{E} F : \Leftrightarrow \forall A \in F : \exists a \in n : a \mathbin{E} A$$

The filter model described here is restricted to conjunctive filters. This limitation may have an impact on efficiency, but not on the expressiveness of the model, because compound filters can always be broken down into multiple conjunctive filters. For example, the filter $F = A_1 \vee A_2$ can be split up into two subscriptions with $F_1 = A_1$ and $F_2 = A_2$. Generally speaking, one must transform logical expressions into *conjunctive normal form* before issuing subscriptions. Doing so, the filter models described earlier can be mapped into this tuple representation as well.

Subscriptions and Advertisements: Filters are specified with subscribe and advertise operations. A subscription filter F_S specifies the interests of the client. It will receive all notifications that match this filter. An advertisement filter F_A expresses which messages a client intends to emit. A client may only emit messages that match the filter specified in the advertisement.

Covering: The covering relation between two attribute filters A_1 and A_2 is defined as follows:

$$A_1 \sqsupseteq A_2 : \Leftrightarrow n_1 = n_2 \wedge L_A (A_1) \sqsupseteq L_A (A_2)$$

where L_A is the set of all values that cause an attribute filter to match:

$$L_A (A_i) := \{ v \mid op_i (v, c_i) = true \}$$

Given two conjunctive filters F_1 and F_2 with at most one attribute filter per attribute, F_1 covers F_2, iff for each attribute filter in F_1 there exists an attribute filter in F_2 that is covered by the attribute filter in F_1:

$$F_1 \sqsupseteq F_2 : \Leftrightarrow \forall_i \exists_j : A_{1,i} \sqsupseteq A_{2,j}$$

For example, consider the following two filters. The filter F_1 covers filter F_2:

$$F_1 = \{(x, \geq, 2), (y, >, 5)\}$$

$$F_2 = \{(x, =, 5), (y, >, 9), (z, =, 1)\}$$

The covering relations are required to identify and merge similar filters.

Overlapping: The overlapping relation between two attribute filters A_1 and A_2 is defined as follows:

$$A_1 \sqcap A_2 : \Leftrightarrow \neg (n_1 = n_2 \wedge L_A(A_1) \cap L_A(A_2) = \varnothing$$

Given two conjunctive filters F_1 and F_2 with at most one attribute filter per attribute, the filters F_1 and F_2 are overlapping, iff

$$F_1 \sqcap F_2 : \Leftrightarrow \neg \exists i, j : A_{1,i} \sqcap A_{2,j}.$$

This relation is required to implement advertisements. If an advertisement filter F_A overlaps with a subscription filter F_S, we say that "F_A is relevant for F_S". As a consequence, all notifications published by the client that advertised with F_A must be delivered to the client that subscribed with F_S. An example for an overlapping advertisement filter F_A and a subscription filter F_S is:

$$F_A = \{(x, \geq, 2), (y, >, 5)\}$$

$$F_S = \{(x, <, 5), (y, <, 7)\}$$

If the same attribute is constrained in both filters and the corresponding attribute filters are disjoint, then the filters are also disjoint, that is, not overlapping.

$$F_A = \{(x, \geq, 2), (y, >, 5)\}$$

$$F_S = \{(x, <, 1), (y, <, 7)\}$$

Next, we will show different topologies of router networks and then describe how the relations presented for filters are used in routing algorithms.

ROUTER TOPOLOGIES

A distributed event system is realized by one or more interconnected event brokers that route notifications through the network. We distinguish between the following network topologies.

Centralized

A centralized system consists of a single event broker and its clients, which can be publishers and subscribers. A client-to-broker protocol is used between the broker and the clients to transport subscriptions, advertisements, and notifications. It is obvious that with an increasing number of clients, the single broker and its network connection become a bottleneck.

The end-to-end paradigm dictates keeping the network infrastructure as simple as possible and implementing advanced functionality at the edge of the network, and the organizational barriers existing between different companies make it difficult to deploy a distributed system of proprietary event brokers on a large scale. For these reasons, the centralized model is highly relevant for the Internet. Clustering can increase the capacity of centralized systems. Such clusters consist of multiple event brokers and behave in a very similar way to distributed broker networks.

Hierarchical

In the hierarchical model, event brokers are organized into a tree. An event broker can treat all subordinate entities as clients, regardless of whether they are real clients or other event brokers. For that reason, the hierarchical model does not require any protocol extensions compared to the client-to-broker protocol in the centralized model.

Each broker that receives a subscription or unsubscription request from a subordinate client or a broker updates its subscription table and passes the request on to its parent broker. Hence, all requests are propagated up the tree until they reach the root. A client producing a notification passes it to the local broker, which forwards it up the tree. Each broker that receives a notification checks its descendants, passes the notification on to any descendant that has issued a matching subscription and then forwards the event to its parent broker. Thus, events are also propagated up the tree until they reach the root. This strategy ensures that all relevant nodes receive all subscription, unsubscription and event messages.

Because brokers higher up in the tree receive all messages from subordinate entities, these brokers and their network links will turn out to be bottlenecks when new clients and brokers are added to the system. Another issue is that every broker is a critical point of failure for the whole system. In fact, the failure of one server partitions the tree into two subtrees and disconnects all contained clients from each other.

Peer-to-Peer

In the peer-to-peer topology, brokers communicate with each other as peers. A special broker-to-broker protocol is required in this case to facilitate a bidirectional flow of subscriptions, advertisements and notifications.

Acyclic peer-to-peer: Connections among brokers form an acyclic graph. The path along which notifications are routed through the network has to be acyclic, because otherwise notifications could circle infinitely in the network. If the connection graph is already acyclic, this condition is fulfilled for all possible routing paths. Similar to the hierarchical topology, this topology suffers from the lack of redundancy in the connection graph, which makes the system susceptible to node and link failures.

Generic peer-to-peer: The connection graph may contain cycles and therefore multiple paths between brokers may exist. The advantage of this topology is that its redundant links make it more robust to failures of single brokers. On the other hand, routing algorithms must handle redudant connections specially to avoid infinitely cycling messages.

It was shown that the distributed peer-to-peer topology offers a better scalability compared to centralized or hierarchical topologies (Carzaniga, 1998).

Routing

The routing tasks in publish/subscribe systems can be organized into two separate layers that build on each other.

Overlay management and request routing: This layer is responsible for the low-level tasks like discovering neighbor brokers, maintaining the overlay network of brokers, and request routing. Such requests include notifications but also various kinds of control messages internally required by the brokers. The routing algorithms provided depend on the network topology. Examples are flooding, routing based on spanning trees, or distance vector routing.

Publish/subscribe routing: Publish/subscribe routing is concerned with higher-level aspects and will be described in the following.

Routing Principles

In order to save communication and computational resources, routing algorithms should obey the following two principles.

Upstream filtering: Filters should be applied upstream, i.e., as close as possible to the sources of messages.

The example in Figure 3 shows a network of event routers 1-6 and the clients *A-C*. The clients *B* and *C* issue subscriptions using filter F_x. Now if client *A* publishes a notification n_y that does not match filter F_x, the notification is already dropped at router 1, because nobody in the network is interested in this notification.

Downstream duplication: A notification should be routed as a single copy as far as possible. If it has multiple subscribers, it should be replicated downstream, that is, as close as possible to the subscribers.

The example in Figure 4 shows a network of event routers 1-6 and the clients *A-C*. The clients *B* and *C* issue subscriptions using filter F_x. Now if client *A* publishes a notification n_x that matches filter F_x via router 1, the notification is forwarded to the routers 1, 3, 4, 5, 6, and finally reaches the clients *B* and *C*. The optimal place for duplicating the notification is router 4. Every other solution would require more packets to be sent and would therefore be less efficient.

Routing in Subscription-Based System

In a subscription-based publish/subscribe system, each broker maintains a subscription table T_S to route notifications based on subscriptions.

The following discussion is limited to routing between brokers, because the implementation of the communication between a broker and its clients is straightforward.

Routing of notifications: A notification n is forwarded to a broker *S*, iff:

$$\exists\, (S, F) \in T_S : n \in F.$$

Routing of subscriptions: When a subscribe or unsubscribe request is received, the table T_S is updated. After that, the broker has to forward subscribe and unsubscribe requests according to the underlying routing algorithm to a subset of its neighbors. There are different algorithms for updating routing tables and there are also different algorithms for forwarding. In general, we can distinguish between *unstructured* and *structured* overlay networks:

- In unstructured overlays, requests have to be forwarded to all neighbors with the exception of the neighbor that sent the request.
- In structured overlays, subscriptions are stored at defined locations. Consequently, requests are routed toward this location and only have to be passed to the next-hop neighbor.

For more information about overlay networks, see the chapter "Peer-to-Peer Systems" in this book. In addition, there are several strategies for reducing the number of (un)subscribe requests between brokers, for example, by using advertisements or filter merging. Both concepts will be described.

Figure 3. Upstream filtering

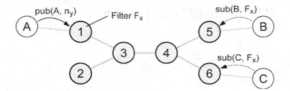

Figure 4. Downstream duplication

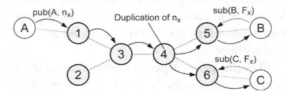

In the following, we only consider a very simple update and forwarding strategy. It is assumed that each filter F has a unique ID and that filters issued by different clients have disjoint sets of IDs. This ID is used to identify a filter when it is added to or removed from a table. When a broker receives a subscribe request from a broker S, it adds an entry to its subscriptions table:

$$T_S \leftarrow T_S \cup \{(S, F)\}$$

When a broker receives an unsubscribe request from a broker S, then the corresponding entry is removed from the table:

$$T_S \leftarrow T_S \setminus \{(S, F)\}$$

Finally, the broker forwards the subscribe or unsubscribe request to all neighbors $N \neq S$. Thus, these requests are flooded into the broker network such that they reach every broker.

Routing in Advertisement-Based System

For advertisement-based publish/subscribe, each broker maintains two routing tables. One subscription table T_S to route notifications based on subscriptions, and one advertisements table T_A to route subscriptions based on advertisements.

Routing of notifications: As before, a notification n is forwarded to a subscriber S, iff:

$$\exists (S, F) \in T_S : n \in F$$

Routing of subscriptions: When a subscribe or unsubscribe request is received, the table T_S is updated as before. However, subscribe and unsubscribe requests with a filter F_S are only forwarded to a broker A, iff:

$$\exists (A, F_A) \in T_A : F_S \sqcap F_A$$

Routing of advertisements: When a broker B receives a new advertisement with a filter F_A from a neighbor A, it

- Forwards all subscriptions to A that came from a destination $S \neq A$, overlap with F_A, and do not overlap with any previous advertisement from A:

$$M_S \leftarrow \{(S, F_S) \in T_S \mid S \neq A \wedge F_S \sqcap F_A \wedge \\ (\neg \exists (A', F'_A) \in T_A : (A' = A \wedge F_S \sqcap F'_A))\}$$
for all $(S, F_S) \in M_S$ send *subscribe* (B, F_S) to A

- Adds the advertisement to T_A:

$$T_A \leftarrow T_A \cup \{(A, F_A)\}$$

- Forwards the advertise request potentially to all neighbors $N \neq A$, according to the underlying routing algorithm.

If a broker B receives an unadvertisement request with a filter F_A from a neighbor A, it:

- Removes the advertisement from T_A:

$$T_A \leftarrow T_A \setminus \{(A, F_A)\}$$

- Removes all routing entries from T_S of all neighbors $S \neq A$, for whose filter there is no other advertisement from any other broker $A' \neq S$ that overlaps:

$$T_S \leftarrow T_S \setminus \{(S, F_S) \in T_S \mid S \neq A \wedge \\ (\neg \exists (A', F'_A) \in T_A : (S \neq A' \wedge F_S \sqcap \\ F'_A))\}$$

- Forwards the unadvertise request potentially to all neighbors $S \neq A$, according to the underlying routing algorithm.

Assuming an unstructured overlay and a simple update and forwarding strategy, an advertisement-based system floods advertisements into the broker network. However, subscriptions only have to be propagated along the reverse paths of advertisements. It depends on the application, if subscription-based or advertisement-based publish/subscribe is more efficient. For example, if the join and leave rate of subscribers is significantly higher compared to the join and leave rate of publishers, then advertisement-based publish/subscribe is usually the better choice.

Filter Merging

If multiple clients subscribe at the same event router using the same filter, then the router can merge these filters into one and the router only has to forward the subscription once to its peers. Filter merging reduces routing table sizes and saves network traffic. Merging does not require filters to be equal, although this is the simplest case. A merged filter must at least cover all its constituent filters, as described by the following definition.

Merging: F_M is a merge of F_1 and F_2 iff:

$$F_M \sqsupseteq F_1 \wedge F_M \sqsupseteq F_2$$

In general, we distinguish between perfect and imperfect merging. A perfect merge only covers its constituent filters and no more.

Perfect merging: F_M is a perfect merge of F_1 and F_2 iff :

$$F_M \sqsupseteq F_1 \wedge F_M \sqsupseteq F_2 \wedge \neg \exists\, F_3 : (F_3 \sqcap F_1 \wedge F_3 \sqcap F_2 \wedge F_M \sqsupseteq F_3)$$

Figure 5(a) shows the perfect merging of the two filters $F_1 = \{1 \leq x \leq 3 \wedge 1 \leq y \leq 3\}$ and $F_2 = \{1 \leq x \leq 3 \wedge 3 \leq y \leq 4\}$ into the filter $F_M = \{1 \leq x \leq 3 \wedge 1 \leq y \leq 4\}$.

Imperfect merging: All øther merges are called imperfect merges. Figure 5(b) shows an imperfect merging of the two filters $F_1 = \{1 \leq x \leq 3 \wedge 1 \leq y \leq 3\}$ and $F_2 = \{2 \leq x \leq 4 \wedge 3 \leq y \leq 4\}$ into the filter $F_M = \{1 \leq x \leq 4 \wedge 1 \leq y \leq 4\}$.

Figure 5. Examples for filter merging

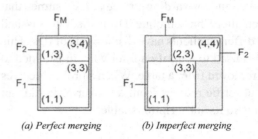

(a) Perfect merging   (b) Imperfect merging

Imperfect merging seems to be less promising at first glance, but in situations where perfect merging is either too complex or not computable it is often a good compromise. In addition, there exists a tradeoff between filtering effort and network resource consumption. Imperfect merging can help to reduce control traffic and to keep advertisement and subscription tables small. On the other hand, it results in notifications being forwarded that do not match any of the original subscriptions.

In order to use imperfect merging, heuristics are necessary that define in what situations and to what degree it should be carried out.

Routing in Structured Peer-to-Peer Networks

Structured peer-to-peer networks build on the notion of distributed hash tables or similar. (For details, see the chapter "Peer-to-Peer Systems" in this book.) In such distributed data structures, the location of a data item in the network is determined by its unique hash value. Publish/subscribe systems use this concept to implement rendezvous points between publishers and subscribers that are distributed over the network. The subscriber list for a certain channel or a set of subscriptions is stored at such a rendezvous point.

In channel-based publish/subscribe systems, the necessary hash value can be obtained by calculating the hash value of the channel name.

In content-based publish/subscribe systems, it is not easy to determine such a hash value, since this very attempt opposes the idea of specifying advertisements and subscriptions independently. The term *channelization* denotes the process of deriving a unique key for a subscription or advertisement. For example, in the Hermes system (Pietzuch, 2004), the hash value is derived from the notification type.

DEBS IN UBIQUITOUS COMPUTING

Distributed event-based systems are particularly useful for ubiquitous computing. An important application area is context-aware computing, because context-aware systems are often distributed systems that have to interface with a multitude of sensors and other event sources (see the chapter "Context Models and Context Awareness" in this book). UC applications may require, for example, the following extensions to the DEBS concept for improved mobility and quality of service support.

Disconnected operation: With the concept of durable subscriptions, messages to consumers are dispatched through queues (Figure 6). This allows consumers to temporarily disconnect from the system without missing messages during times they are disconnected. All messages stored while the consumer is offline are dispatched upon reconnect. Durable subscriptions are supported,

for example, by JMS (Hapner, 2001) and Gryphon (Bhola, 2003).

Redundant connections: If the router network has a generic peer-to-peer topology, then only an acyclic subgraph is used for the dissemination of notifications in the network. But unlike the acyclic peer-to-peer topology, when a link breaks, the system can adapt and switch over to one of the previously redundant links between routers.

Clustering: In peer-to-peer systems with a distributed subscription database, the departure of a router from the network means that subscriptions are lost. The resilience of such networks can be improved by organizing routers into clusters. Each cluster is made responsible for a specific partition of the subscription database and every router in the cluster holds a replica.

Quality of service requirements are fairly application-specific. For example, a service delivering events from RFID readers in a logistics application must support guaranteed delivery. Distributed event systems are also a good basis for distributing sensor, audio, or video data streams in a network, because such streams are often multicast to multiple receivers. In this case, the event system should deliver the stream packets with a low latency, while losing single packets is tolerable.

Transactions: Because of the decoupled nature of publish/subscribe, an event service cannot guarantee end-to-end delivery of notifications. However, *local transactions* can provide

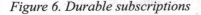

Figure 6. Durable subscriptions

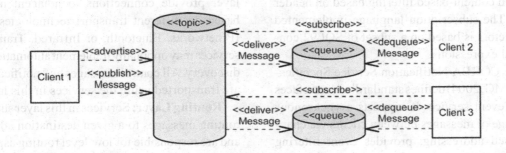

some delivery guarantees. Local transactions are transactions between the publisher and the event service, or between the event service and the subscriber. Between publisher and event service, a local transaction groups a series of publish operations into an atomic unit of work. Between event service and subscriber, a local transaction groups a series of receive operations into an atomic unit of work.

EXAMPLES OF PUBLISH/ SUBSCRIBE SYSTEMS

REBECA (Mühl, 2006) and SIENA (Carzaniga, 1998) are academic prototypes for content-based publish/subscribe systems. Gryphon (Bhola, 2003) was developed by IBM Research and is aimed at distributing large volumes of data throughout large public networks. Because data is sent through public networks, fail-safe routing and security features, like authentication, access control, and encryption needed to be implemented. The integration of Gryphon into the IBM WebSphere MQ Event Broker (IBM, 2005) indicates that this event service is mature and has been successfully deployed.

The Java Message Service (JMS) (Haase, 2002) is an API specification provided by Sun Microsystems for its Java platform. Its publish/subscribe system is based on topic-based addressing. A message in JMS has three parts: a header, properties, and a body. The message body is completely opaque to the message broker. JMS defines message selectors that can be used to perform content-based filtering based on header fields. The subscription language implemented by selectors is based on a subset of SQL92 conditional expressions.

The CORBA Notification Service Specification (OMG, 2004) defines standardized interfaces for an event service. It supports asynchronous exchange of messages between clients via channel-based addressing, provides event filtering

capability, and the ability to configure quality of service parameters.

System Example: MundoCore

MundoCore (Aitenbichler, 2006) is a communication middleware specifically designed for ubiquitous computing. It is based on a modular architecture and can be dynamically reconfigured to suit different application needs. MundoCore provides a common set of APIs for different programming languages (Java, C++, Python) on a wide range of different devices (small embedded systems to servers). The architectural model addresses the need for proper language bindings, different communication abstractions, peer-to-peer overlays, different transport protocols, different invocation protocols, and automatic peer discovery.

The services in MundoCore are arranged into five layers: transport, routing, brokering, language binding, and application. The roles of the routing and brokering layers have already been described in this chapter. The routing layer is concerned with the routing of requests to a single destination, which is *directly addressed* by its globally unique node ID. The brokering layer contains the publish/subscribe routing services, which permit *indirect addressing*. Below the routing layer, the transport layer interfaces with different communication APIs of operating systems. Above the brokering layer, the language binding layer implements the APIs enabling applications to access the publish/subscribe system.

Transport Layer: Services on the transport layer provide connections to adjacent nodes, based on different transport technologies, e.g. IP networks, Bluetooth, or Infrared. Transport services may optionally implement automatic peer discovery. All control messages and notifications are transported using the services in this layer.

Routing Layer: Services in this layer support routing messages to a given destination address and are responsible for low-level routing aspects.

The abstraction provided by this layer makes routing independent of the underlying transport services and configuration parameters, such as network addresses. This facilitates seamless handovers. The optimal routing strategy for a given application depends on the structure and stability of the network. Three examples are described in the following.

- **Single-hop:** In a single-hop network, each node communicates with each other node directly. This network structure is usually the best choice if the network is highly dynamic, like in spontaneous collaborations, and the number of nodes does not exceed a few dozen clients.
- **Distance vector:** A larger number of clients can be supported by introducing super-nodes. Super-nodes should be highly available and rather static in terms of location. For example, a smart environment has embedded computing resources and can easily provide such static super-nodes. Variants of distance vector routing are often used in such networks.
- **Structured peer-to-peer:** Unstructured networks only scale up to a certain degree, because the size of routing tables grows proportionally with the size of the network. Structured peer-to-peer networks are more suitable for large-scale deployments, because they basically allow the sizes of routing tables at individual nodes to be constant.

Brokering Layer: Services in this layer support routing messages that are indirectly adressed to their targets, and are responsible for high-level routing. When using topic-based publish/subscribe, the sender of a message specifies the topic name as target address. Interested parties subscribe to the same topic at the broker. The broker takes care of distributing notifications arriving from a topic's multiple publishers to its multiple subscribers. Content-based publish/subscribe does not use explicit address information; only the content of a message determines its recipients.

Language Binding Layer: The language-binding layer offers convenient interfaces to application programmers for the services provided by lower layers. It supports remote method calls, parameter marshaling, and object externalization. MundoCore supports a subset of the XQuery language for content-based subscriptions. The following example subscribes to all messages whose text field contains the substring IMPORTANT.

```
XQuery xq = new XQuery();
xq.parse("for $o in $msg where contains($o/text,
'IMPORTANT')");
subscriber = ContentSubscription.
subscribe(session, xq.getMapFilter());
```

Subscriptions can also be made using filter classes. Filter classes can be automatically generated by a precompiler for all serializable classes. The following example shows the same subscription as above, but with filter classes:

```
ChatMessageFilter filter = new ChatMessage-
Filter();
filter.text = "IMPORTANT";
filter._op_text = filter.CONTAINS;
subscriber = ContentSubscription.
subscribe(session, filter);
```

Finally, the application-specific services reside on the application layer. MundoCore is freely available under an open-source license and can be downloaded from the Telecooperation Group, Darmstadt University of Technology.

FUTURE RESEARCH DIRECTIONS

This chapter provided an introduction to distributed event-based systems. A large part was dedicated to content-based publish/subscribe with data and filter models based on structured records. The description of routing algorithms was limited to rather simple algorithms. Mühl, Fiege, and Pietzuch (2006) describe more data and filter models, a more extensive formal model, and efficient routing algorithms. Event-based communication has been applied for a long time in many disciplines of computer science. Because there was the desire to capture the general concepts of event-based systems and to collect the knowledge scattered among disciplines, event-based systems emerged as a research area of its own about a decade ago. Some particular areas where research is currently active and is likely to remain active in the near future are:

- **Expressiveness/scalability tradeoff:** Simple filter models that only support exact string or value matches are not very expressive, but it is easy to implement filter-merging algorithms. More expressive filter models increase the complexity of filter merging. The choice of a suitable filter language depends on the application area. In general, however, we aim for a language that is as general and expressive as possible, which can still be executed efficiently.
- **Overlay network optimization:** This chapter described the basic routing strategies in unstructured and in structured broker networks. In terms of the overlay structure, these are two extremes. In the classic routing schemes (e.g., Carzaniga, 1998), the overlay structure optimally matches the (geographical) topology of the underlying network. However, the size of routing tables grows with the size of the system. Consequently, such systems only scale up to a certain degree (without using merging strategies). Structured networks, on the other hand, are scalable in this respect. However, their overlay structure does not efficiently match the structure of the underlying network.
- **Scoping:** All basic event-based systems operate on a single global namespace. This

is not unlike working with a programming language that only supports global variables. Consequently, large-scale deployment of event-based systems raises the need for modularization concepts. There are several applications for scoping. First, each scope can have its own namespace. Scopes can be used to limit the distribution of notifications, for example, for security or privacy reasons. Routers placed at the borders of multiple scopes can filter notifications or translate between different data representations.

REFERENCES

Aitenbichler, E. (2006). *System support for ubiquitous computing*. Aachen: Shaker Verlag.

Bhola, S., Zhao, Y., & Auerbach, J. (2003). Scalably supporting durable subscriptions in a publish/subscribe system. In *Proceedings of the International Conference on Dependable Systems and Networks (DSN)* (pp. 57-66).

Carzaniga, A. (1998). *Architectures for an event notification service scalable to wide-area networks*. Unpublished doctoral dissertation, Politecnico di Milano, Milano, Italy.

Carzaniga, A., Rosenblum, D. S., & Wolf, A. L. (1999). Challenges for distributed event services: Scalability vs. expressiveness. In *Proceedings Engineering Distributed Objects '99*, Los Angeles, California (Online proceedings).

Cilia, M., Bornhoevd, C., & Buchmann, A. P. (2003). CREAM: An infrastructure for distributed, Heterogeneous event-based applications. In *Proceedings of the International Conference on Cooperative Information Systems (CoopIS03)* (Vol. 2888, pp. 482-502).

Eugster, P., Felber, P., Guerraoui, R., & Kermarrec, A.-M. (2003). The many faces of publish/subscribe. *ACM Computing Surveys, 35*(2), 114-131.

Eugster, P. T., Guerraoui, R., & Damm, C. H. (2001). On objects and events. In *Proceedings of the Conference on Object-Oriented Programming, Systems, Languages, and Applications* (p. 254-269).

Haase, K. (2002). *Java message service API tutorial, Version 1.3.1*. Retrieved October 14, 2007, from http://java.sun.com/products/jms/tutorial

Hapner, M., Burridge, R., Sharma, R., & Fialli, J. (2001). *Java message service* (Tech. Rep.). Sun Microsystems.

IBM Corporation, (2005). *WebSphere MQ (MQ-Series)*. Retrieved October 14, 2007, from http://www-306.ibm.com/software/integration/wmq

IIT Software (2005). *SwiftMQ: Smart, fast, reliable JMS*. Retrieved October 14, 2007, from http://www.swiftmq.com/index.html

Mühl, G., Fiege, L., & Pietzuch, P. R. (2006). *Distributed event-based systems*. Heidelberg: Springer.

OMG—The Object Management Group Inc. (2004). *CORBA notification service specification (Vol.2)*. Retrieved October 14, 2007, from http://www.omg.org/technology/documents/formal/event_service.htm

Pietzuch, P. R. (2004). *Hermes: A scalable event-based middleware*. Unpublished doctoral dissertation, Computer Laboratory, Queens' College, University of Cambridge.

ADDITIONAL READING

Abadi, D., Carney, D., Cetintemel, U., Cherniack, M., Convey, C., Lee, S., Stonebraker, M., Tatbul, N., & Zdonik, S. (2003). Aurora: A new model and architecture for data stream management. *The VLDB Journal, 12*(2), 120-139.

Aguilera, M., Strom, R., Sturman, D., Astley, M., & Chandra, T. (1999). Matching events in a content-based subscription system. In *Proceedings of the 18th ACM Symposium on Principles of Distributed Computing (PODC 1999)* (pp. 53-61).

Altinel, M., & Franklin, M. J. (2000). Efficient filtering of XML documents for selective dissemination of information. In *Proceedings of the 26th International Conference on Very Large Data Bases* (pp. 53-64).

Arasu, A., Babu, S., & Widom, J. (2003). *The CQL continuous query language: Semantic foundations and query execution* (Tech. Rep.). Stanford University.

Bacon, J., Moody, K., Bates, J., Hayton, R., Ma, C., NcNeil, A., Seidel, O., & Spiteri, M. (2000). Generic support for distributed applications. *IEEE Computer, 33*(3), 68-76.

Banavar, G., Chandra, T., Mukherjee, B., Nagarajarao, J., Strom, R. E., & Sturman, D. C. (1999). An efficient multicast protocol for content-based publish/subscribe systems. In *Proceedings of the 19th IEEE International Conference on Distributed Computing Systems* (pp. 262-272).

Campailla, A., Chaki, S., Clarke, E., Jha, S., & Veith, H. (2001). Efficient filtering in publish/subscribe systems using binary decision diagrams. In *Proceedings of the 19th Conference on Software Engineering* (pp. 443-452).

Caporuscio, M., Inverardi, P., & Pelliccione, P. (2002). *Formal analysis of clients mobility in the SIENA publish/subscribe middleware* (Tech. Rep.). Department of Computer Science, University of L'Aquila.

Carzaniga, A., & Fenkam, P. (2004). In *Proceedings of the 3rd International Workshop on Distributed Event-Based Systems (DEBS'04)*.

Cilia, M., Fiege, L., Haul, G., Zeidler, A., & Buchmann, A. (2003). Looking into the past: Enhancing mobile publish/subscribe middleware. In *Proceedings of the 2nd International Workshop on Distributed Event-Based Systems (DEBS'03)*.

Crespo, A., Buyukkokten, O., & Garcia-Molina, H. (2000). Efficient query subscription processing in a multicast environment. In *Proceedings of the 16th International Conference on Data Engineering (ICDE)* (p. 83).

Crowcroft, J., Bacon, J., Pietzuch, P., Coulouris, G., & Naguib, H. (2002). Channel islands in a reflective ocean: Large-scale event distribution in heterogeneous networks. *IEEE Communications Magazine, 40*(9), 112-115.

Cugola, G., Di Nitto, E., & Fugetta, A. (2001). The JEDI event-based infrastructure and its application to the development of the OPSS WFMS. *IEEE Transactions on Software Engineering, 27*(9), 827-850.

DeLucia, D., & Obraczka, K. (1997). Multicast feedback suppression using representatives. In *Proceedings of INFOCOM'97* (pp. 463-470).

Dingel, J., & Strom, R. (2005). In *Proceedings of the 4th International Workshop on Distributed Event-Based Systems (DEBS'05)*.

Eugster, P., Guerraoui, R., & Sventek, J. (2000). *Type-based publish/subscribe* (Tech. Rep. DSC ID:200029). Lausanne, Switzerland: EPFL.

Fabret, F., Jacobsen, A., Llirbat, F., Pereira, J., Ross, K., & Shasha, D. (2001). Filtering algorithms and implementation for very fast publish/subscribe. In *Proceedings of the 20th International Conference on Management of Data (SIGMOD 2001)* (pp. 115-126).

Fiege, L. (2005). *Visibility in event-based systems*. Unpublished doctoral thesis, Technical University of Darmstadt, Germany.

Fiege, L., Gärtner, F. C., Kasten, O., & Zeidler, A. (2003). Supporting mobility in content-based publish/subscribe middleware. In *Proceedings of the ACM/IFIP/USENIX International Middleware Conference (Middleware 2003)* (LNCS 2672, pp. 103-122).

Fiege, L., Zeidler, A., Buchmann, A., Kilian-Kehr, R., & Mühl, G. (2004). Security aspects in publish/subscribe systems. In *Proceedings of the 3rd International Workshop on Distributed Event-Based Systems (DEBS'04)*.

Fitzpatrick, S., Kaplan, S., Mansfield, T., David, A., & Segall, B. (2002). Supporting public availability and accessibility with elvin: Experiences and reflections. *Computer Supported Cooperative Work, 11*(3), 447-474.

Gruber, R., Krishnamurthy, B., & Panagos, E. (2000). READY: A high performance event notification service. In *Proceedings of the 16th International Conference on Data Engineering* (pp. 668-669).

Hohpe, G., & Woolf, B. (2003). *Enterprise integration patterns: Designing, building, and deploying messaging solutions*. Addison-Wesley.

Huang, Y., & Garcia-Molina H. (2003). Publish/subscribe tree construction in wireless ad-hoc networks. In *Proceedings 4th International Conference on Mobile Data Management (MDM 2003)* (Vol. 2574 of LNCS) (pp. 122-140).

Jacobsen, H. A. (2003). In *Proceedings of the 2nd International Workshop on Distributed Event-Based Systems (DEBS'03)*.

Jaeger, M. A., & Mühl, G. (2005). Stochastic analysis and comparison of self-stabilizing routing algorithms for publish/subscribe systems. In *Proceedings of the 13th IEEE/ACM International Symposium on Modeling, Analysis and Simulation of Computer and Telecommunication Systems (MASCOTS 2005)* (pp. 471-479).

Liu, H., & Jacobsen, H. A. (2002). A-ToPSS – A publish/subscribe system supporting approximate matching. In *Proceedings of the 28th VLDB Conference*.

Ma, C., & Bacon, J. (1998). COBEA: A CORBA-Based event architecture. In *Proceedings of the 4th Conference on Object-Oriented Technologies and Systems (COOTS-98)* (pp. 117-132)

Meier, R. (2000). *State of the art review of distributed event models* (Tech. Rep.), University of Dublin, Ireland.

Mühl, G. (2002). *Large-scale content-based publish/subscribe systems*. Unpublished doctoral thesis, Darmstadt University of Technology, Germany.

Opyrchal, L. (2004). *Content-based publish/subscribe systems: Scalability and security*. Unpublished doctoral thesis, University of Michigan.

Opyrchal, L., Astley, M., Auerbach, J., Banavar, G., Strom, R., & Sturman, D. (2000). Exploiting IP-multicast in content-based publish/subscribe systems. In *Proceedings of the IFIP/ACM International Conference on Distributed Systems Platforms (Middleware 2000)*, (Vol. 1795 of LNCS) (pp. 185-207).

Parzyjegla, H., Mühl, G., & Jaeger, M. A. (2006). Reconfiguring publish/subscribe overlay topologies. In *Proceedings of the 5th International Workshop on Distributed Event-Based Systems (DEBS'06)*.

Picco, G. P., Cugola, G., & Murphy A. L. (2003). Efficient content-based event dispatching in the presence of topological reconfiguration. In *Proceedings of the 23rd International Conference on Distributed Computing Systems (ICDCS 03)* (pp. 234-243).

Segall, W., & Arnold, D. (1997). Elvin has left the building: A publish/subscribe notification service with quenching. In *Proceedings of the 1997 Australian UNIX Users Group*, Brisbane, Australia.

Zhao, Y., Sturman, D., & Bhola, S. (2004). Subscription propagation in highly-available publish/subscribe middleware. In *Proceedings of the 5th ACM/IFIP/USENIX International Conference on Middleware* (pp. 274-293).

Chapter VIII
Peer–to–Peer Systems

Jussi Kangasharju
University of Helsinki, Finland

ABSTRACT

Peer-to-peer systems have become extremely popular on the Internet in recent years. However, peer-to-peer systems are not limited to Internet applications, but are also of significant interest to ubiquitous computing. This is because both peer-to-peer systems and ubiquitous computing are based on collaboration between independent, autonomous entities. Peer-to-peer systems are built around resource sharing and in this chapter, we will look at the different aspects of this resource sharing, from the types of resources to be shared to how the peers are connected to each other and on to how the resources can be located in these different kinds of networks. This chapter is organized as follows. First we provide a definition of what peer-to-peer is and discuss its relevance to ubiquitous computing in more detail. The section "Current Systems" gives an overview of currently deployed and used peer-to-peer systems. Then, we will present a classification of peer-to-peer systems according to how resources are located. In the section "Resource Location in Peer-to-Peer Networks" we will present algorithms for locating resources in peer-to-peer networks. Finally, the chapter discusses the future of peer-to-peer systems.

INTRODUCTION

Peer-to-peer technologies (or P2P for short) have broken through in recent years as an attractive alternative to the traditional client-server-based architectures and systems. A lot of the attention paid to peer-to-peer systems has been caused by the widespread use of P2P file sharing networks, where (often illegal) media content is being distributed. Recently deployed peer-to-peer systems however demonstrate that the peer-to-peer concept extends to other applications as well and can also be used in commercial scenarios.

In this chapter, we will present a definition of what peer-to-peer is and what it means as a communication paradigm. In many ways, peer-to-peer is the opposite of the traditional client-server communication paradigm, since in peer-to-peer networks all nodes are more or less equal in terms of their duties and privileges. We will give an overview of currently deployed peer-to-peer systems and analyze how they exhibit the peer-to-peer properties.

Later, we will present a classification of peer-to-peer systems, based on how resources in the networks are located. Although this classification is only one of many possibilities, it is also one of the most commonly used classifications of peer-to-peer systems. Based on this classification, we will take a closer look at search algorithms in peer-to-peer networks. In a large network, where the resources are distributed over a large number of peers, being able to locate the required resources efficiently is of great importance. We will therefore dedicate the bulk of this chapter to discussing search algorithms in peer-to-peer networks.

DEFINITION OF PEER-TO-PEER

There exist many different definitions of what peer-to-peer is in the community (Oram, 2001; Steinmetz & Wehrle, 2005, Subramanian & Goodman, 2005). However, many of the current definitions have several points in common, which we have distilled and combined below.

In our definition, peer-to-peer systems exhibit the following characteristics:

- **Autonomy from central servers:** Peer-to-peer systems typically have no central, controlling components in them. However, as we will see in Section "Unstructured Peer-to-Peer Systems", some peer-to-peer networks (most notably Napster (Napster, 2001) and BitTorrent (BitTorrent, 2007) to a lesser extent) are based on a central coordinator, but the actual work of the system *always* happens directly between the peers, without any need to involve the coordinator.
- **Sharing resources at the edge of the network:** Peers in a peer-to-peer network offer their resources for others to use and they use resources provided by other peers. We will discuss the types of resources in more detail below. An open question in peer-to-peer networks is whether all peers should be forced to contribute to the system (e.g., BitTorrent and Skype (Skype, 2007)), or whether the system should tolerate peers which are not contributing. Such non-contributing peers are also called free-riders (Adar & Huberman, 2000), since they only consume resources on other peers without providing any.
- **Individual nodes have intermittent connectivity:** Individual peers in a peer-to-peer network are typically fully independent, since they are under the control of the individual users. A peer joins the network when it wants and can leave at any time. Typically, there are no guarantees about when peers are online; instead, the system relies on a large number of participants, so that it does not matter what individual peers do.

The above characteristics already point out some of the advantages and disadvantages of peer-to-peer systems. The main advantages of peer-to-peer systems, compared to traditional client-server systems are that peer-to-peer systems typically scale well to a large number of participants, up to several millions of simultaneous users. Furthermore, thanks to the large number of participants, peer-to-peer systems are robust against failures, and practice has shown them to also be very efficient in performing the task they were designed to do. Peer-to-peer systems can also have the advantage of not requiring dedicated and expensive servers, since the individual peers can offer the same resources at a much lower (monetary) cost. The costs of a using a peer-to-peer solution are independent of the number of users, whereas the costs of a centralized client-server system scale up with the number of users.

However, replacing a client-server system, for example, a file server, with a peer-to-peer solution also brings out the disadvantages and shortcomings of current peer-to-peer systems. Because the individual peers are autonomous and can disconnect whenever they want, it is extremely hard to offer strong guarantees about the services delivered by a peer-to-peer system. This lack of quality guarantees, or service level agreements, is one of the reasons why peer-to-peer systems have experienced only limited success outside of the file-sharing domain. Furthermore, the success of the file sharing networks has, in some cases, given peer-to-peer a bad reputation because they have been mainly used for illegal sharing of copyrighted material; however, new applications, such as Skype, already show that the potential of peer-to-peer systems extends beyond file sharing.

Resources in Peer-to-Peer Systems

As defined above, peer-to-peer systems are based on sharing resources from nodes located at the edges
of the network. Most of the time, these resources are typical computing resources, such as CPU cycles, memory, storage, or bandwidth. However, some systems are based on sharing human presence, in order to enable interpersonal communications. According to the resources being shared, peer-to-peer systems can be classified into three different classes.

Data Sharing

Data sharing systems are systems where the main resources being shared are storage space on the nodes and the bandwidth of the nodes. Classical examples of such systems are the peer-to-peer file sharing systems, such as eDonkey (eDonkey, 2007) and BitTorrent. In these systems, individual nodes offer their local storage to the network and also their bandwidth for others to fetch the data they share. Note that in these networks, it is the owner of the node who decides what the node will share.

CPU Sharing

In some peer-to-peer networks, the main resources being shared are the computation capabilities of the nodes. Examples of such systems are all of the distributed computation initiatives, such as SETI@Home (SETI@Home, 2007) and BOINC (Berkeley Open Infrastructure for Network Computing, 2007). In these systems, a central authority delegates parts of a computation-intensive task to the peers, who then independently compute their parts and send the answers back to the central authority. Although CPU sharing systems are often based on a central authority, we classify them as peer-to-peer systems, because the actual computation resources are provided by the individual peers, who share most of the characteristics of our peer-to-peer definition from above.

Presence Sharing

Presence sharing systems are systems which, instead of sharing traditional computer resources, are based on sharing human presence. In this case, the human presence refers to the users of the computers. Examples of this category of applications are all instant messaging systems, and peer-to-peer telephony applications, such as Skype (Skype, 2007). These systems aim at enabling direct communications between the users, by exploiting the network built up by the peers.

PEER-TO-PEER AND UBIQUITOUS COMPUTING

From our definition of peer-to-peer systems above, we can easily draw the parallels with ubiquitous computing and see why peer-to-peer systems appear attractive for solving problems in ubiquitous computing. In both cases, we are faced with a system with many independent entities, acting autonomously and collaborating with other entities to deliver the services to the user (or other entities). This obvious similarity makes peer-to-peer technologies a logical possibility for building ubiquitous computing systems. In the rest of this chapter, we will look at different aspects of peer-to-peer systems, in particular how peers are organized and how resources are located in different peer-to-peer systems. At the end of the chapter, in the section "Peer-to-Peer and Ubiquitous Computing Revisited", we will return to the question of how suitable peer-to-peer systems are for ubiquitous computing.

CURRENT SYSTEMS

On the current Internet, the main use of peer-to-peer systems is still in the area of file sharing. We will now give a brief overview of some of the existing peer-to-peer systems and highlight their main characteristics. We cover traditional file sharing systems, peer-to-peer content distribution, and other, emerging peer-to-peer systems.

In Table 1 we provide an overview of the systems which we will cover in this section, classified according to what resources they share.

File Sharing

Peer-to-peer file sharing was started by Napster in 1999. Napster was based on a simple, central-

Table 1. Existing peer-to-peer systems

Shared resource	Systems	Application domain
Data sharing	Napster, Gnutella, Kazaa, eDonkey	File sharing
	BitTorrent	P2P content distribution
CPU sharing	SETI@Home, BOINC	Distributed computing
Presence sharing	AIM, Jabber, MSN Messenger, Yahoo Messenger	Instant messaging
	Skype	Internet telephony

ized architecture and gained popularity at a very rapid pace. Because Napster was being used for sharing MP3 files of copyrighted works without permission, it was shut down by the courts after record companies had sued them for copyright infringement (von Lohmann, 2003).

Napster was quickly followed by other file sharing systems, and one of the first was Gnutella (Gnutella, 2007). In contrast to Napster, Gnutella was based on a fully distributed architecture. However, partly because of the poor performance of Gnutella (see Section "Resource Location in Peer-to-Peer Networks") and partly because of the arrival of new solutions, Gnutella never experienced wide popularity. Recently, the Gnutella2-proposal has been gaining momentum, based on an architecture similar to KaZaA.

The third wave of file sharing systems was originally launched by KaZaA (Kazaa, 2007). It has later been joined by eDonkey (eDonkey, 2007) and the above-mentioned Gnutella2. All of these systems are examples of so-called hybrid peer-to-peer systems. Hybrid systems attempt to combine the positive aspects of centralized and distributed systems, such as an efficient centralized search and the robustness brought about by a fully distributed system.

Peer-to-Peer Content Distribution: BitTorrent

BitTorrent (BitTorrent, 2007) is a new and popular form of peer-to-peer content distribution. It is especially used for delivering large files, such as Linux distributions (Izal, Urvoy-Keller, Biersack, Felber, Al Hamra, & Garcés-Erice, 2004). BitTorrent differs from the file sharing networks in the sense that BitTorrent builds one peer-to-peer network for *each* file that is being distributed. In this sense, we have classified BitTorrent as peer-to-peer content distribution, since it competes more with traditional content distribution systems (e.g., Akamai (Akamai, 2007) and CoralCDN (Freedman, Freudenthal, & Mazieres, 2004)) than with file sharing systems.

A BitTorrent network works as follows. Originally, the file to be distributed is available from one server, called *seed*. In addition to the seed, there is a *tracker* server which keeps track of all the clients in the network. A client which wants to download the file needs to get the so-called "torrent-file" which contains metadata about the file (length, checksums, etc.) and the address of the tracker for that file.

The client then contacts the tracker and receives a list of peers which are currently downloading that file (also called *leechers*) or have already downloaded it and are still connected to the network (known as *seeds*). The client then picks some peers from this *peer set* and starts downloading chunks from them. BitTorrent uses a tit-for-tat policy, so that a client serves chunks to other peers which are serving chunks to it. A client will try to find a set of peers from which it can download the fastest. The set of candidates is enlarged through a process called *optimistic unchoking*, where a peer randomly picks a peer from its peer set and uploads a chunk to this peer. This process has been observed to improve the performance of the download because it allows the client to use all of its downstream bandwidth (Rodriguez & Biersack, 2002). For a detailed description of how BitTorrent works, see (Izal, et al., 2004).

Newer Applications

Although file-sharing applications have received the bulk of the attention in the peer-to-peer domain, other applications are also slowly emerging. Most of the popular instant messaging systems are also peer-to-peer networks, since the messages are sent directly between the end-users. In fact, instant messaging systems are very similar to the original Napster in their setup, since they also have a central server for coordinating the peers (i.e., keeping track of who is online), while the actual resource usage happens directly between the peers (exchange of files in Napster, exchange of messages in instant messaging).

Another peer-to-peer application which has become extremely popular is the Internet telephony application Skype (Skype, 2007). Skype is in essence a peer-to-peer network for voice-over-IP (VoIP) telephony on the Internet. Logging into the system happens via a central server run by Skype, but the maintenance of information about who is online and the routing of calls happens on the individual peers.

CLASSIFICATION OF PEER-TO-PEER SYSTEMS

Peer-to-peer systems are typically classified according to how the resources in the systems are placed and located. Every peer-to-peer system is based on an overlay network, which forms a logical network topology on top of the underlying IP network. This overlay network can be constructed in several ways, and the type of the overlay network serves as the basis for our classification of peer-to-peer systems. This classification puts the systems into one of two categories: unstructured or structured (Steinmetz & Wehrle, 2005). In an unstructured network, any peer is free to offer any resources, and resources are located by *searching* for a peer which can provide the resource. In contrast, in structured peer-to-peer systems, resource placement follows certain rules and resources are *addressed* instead of searched for. Next, we will give an overview of the different peer-to-peer systems and how they fit into these two classes.

Unstructured Peer-to-Peer Systems

Almost all of the widely deployed peer-to-peer systems are unstructured systems. As mentioned above, the focus in unstructured networks is on how to locate the peers with the desired resources. Unstructured peer-to-peer systems can be divided into three classes, depending on how the search for resources is handled: centralized, distributed, and hybrid systems.

Figure 1. Centralized peer-to-peer system

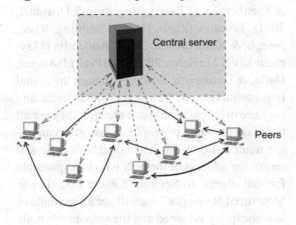

Figure 2. Distributed peer-to-peer system

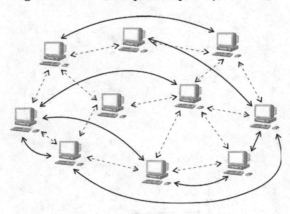

A centralized system is based on a centralized indexing server or a server farm. An example of such a system is shown in Figure 1. In the figure, dashed lines refer to overlay maintenance traffic and queries, while the solid lines refer to actual file transfers. The original Napster system was based on a centralized architecture. A centralized architecture has the advantage that searching is very efficient and the results are guaranteed to be correct. Because the index server knows about all the files in the network, it can give complete answers in any situation. Note that the index server only participates in searching; all file transfers happen directly between peers.

In a fully distributed peer-to-peer system, all peers are equal. An example is shown in Figure 2. The original Gnutella network was based on a fully distributed architecture. The main weakness of a fully distributed system is that its search performance is very low. Typically searches have to be flooded with a certain radius and only files within the radius can be discovered. The advantage of a fully distributed system is that it is very robust against failures because no node has a special role in the network (Saroiu, Gummadi, & Gribble, 2002).

A hybrid peer-to-peer system, as shown in Figure 3, combines elements from both the centralized and distributed architectures. The system is based on the so-called *superpeers* (shown as larger peers in Figure 3) which manage a certain number of normal peers (children) and act as a centralized hub for their children. The superpeers communicate among themselves using a distributed network, like Gnutella. Searching for resources happens so that a peer will send a request to its superpeer. The superpeer knows which of its children has the resource, if any. It can also send queries to other superpeers which answer for their children. As with the centralized and distributed architectures, file transfers happen directly between peers.

Structured Peer-to-Peer Systems

In contrast to the unstructured systems, structured peer-to-peer systems assign clear responsibilities to the peers in terms of what resources they should serve. For example, whereas in an unstructured file sharing system, any peer is free to offer any files for downloading, in a structured system files

Figure 3. Hybrid peer-to-peer system

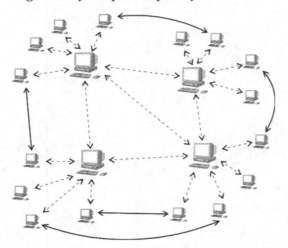

would be placed on specific nodes and requests for the files would be directed to these nodes. Hence, the main challenge in structured peer-to-peer systems is on how to route the user requests to the responsible nodes and how to maintain an overlay structure which allows for efficient routing. Structured networks have not yet been widely deployed in real-world use. A notable exception to this is the Overnet structured network which is used in the eDonkey file sharing system (eDonkey, 2007).

Structured peer-to-peer systems are often also called *distributed hash tables* (DHT), since they are based on the same idea as conventional hash tables. Each peer has a unique identifier which is calculated as a hash function from some property of the peer (e.g., IP address). Similarly, each object is mapped to the same hash space, for example, by calculating the hash value of the object's name. A peer is responsible for objects that are mapped "near" to its place in the hash space. The definition of the metric for proximity, that is, what is "near" depends on the actual implementation of the DHT.

There have been several proposals for different structured peer-to-peer systems. Examples are Chord (Stoica, Morris, Karger, Kaashoek, & Balakrishnan, 2001), Content Addressable Net-

work (CAN) (Ratnasamy, Francis, Handley, Karp, & Shenker, 2001), Pastry (Rowstron & Druschel, 2001), Tapestry (Zhao, Huang, Stribling, Rhea, Joseph, & Kubiatowicz, 2004), Kademlia (Maymounkov & Mazieres, 2002), and P-Grid (Aberer, Datta, & Hauswirth, 2005). Although the actual implementations of the systems are different and they use different hash space metrics, they are all based on the same principle. When given an object name as input, the distributed hash table will return the address of the peer who is responsible for that object. In Section "Object Location in Structured Networks", we will see an example of how the query is routed and the responsible node is determined in the Chord network.

CLASSIFICATION OF EXISTING SYSTEMS

Table 2 shows the systems mentioned in Section "Current Systems", classified into unstructured and structured systems. The large majority of file sharing systems are based on the hybrid unstructured architecture, thanks to its good scalability, performance, and robustness. In contrast, fully distributed unstructured systems are not widely used, mainly due to their low performance due to the need for flood queries. Centralized architectures were the first ones to be used, but recently they have been mainly used for nonfile-sharing systems. One of the reasons is that a centralized system gives a better overview of the systems and makes management easier. This makes them attractive for systems like SETI@Home or Skype which require exact knowledge about the available resources.

At the end of the following section, we will take a closer look at the properties of unstructured and structured systems and compare them. In the section "Suitability for Ubiquitous Computing", we will then analyze them in terms of their suitability and applicability for ubiquitous computing.

Table 2. Classification of existing peer-to-peer systems

Type	Example systems
Unstructured/Centralized	Napster, SETI@Home, BOINC, Skype
Unstructured/Distributed	Gnutella
Unstructured/Hybrid	Kazaa, eDonkey
Structured	Chord, CAN, Pastry, Tapestry, Kademlia, P-Grid

Before this analysis, we will take a closer look at how resources are located in unstructured and structured systems.

RESOURCE LOCATION IN PEER-TO-PEER NETWORKS

We now turn our attention to an important topic in peer-to-peer networks, namely how to locate the resources provided by the peers. As mentioned earlier, in unstructured networks resources must somehow be located, since we do not know where they are being offered. In contrast, in structured networks we "know" where the resources are, but we need to locate the peer responsible for the resource. In other words, unstructured networks are based on *searching*, while structured networks are based on *addressing*.

This difference between searching and addressing brings up a fundamental difference in how unstructured and structured networks are used. Because unstructured networks are based on searching, for example, by flooding a query, we do not need to know the exact name of a resource; instead we can use any standard search techniques, for example, wildcard queries, to locate the resources. In contrast, because structured networks require us to know the exact name of the resource before it can be mapped to the hash space, advanced searches are typically not easy or even impossible in structured networks.

Searching in Unstructured Networks

Unstructured networks locate resources by allowing the users to send search queries and matching these queries to the resources provided by the peers. The differences between the networks depend on how and where this matching is done. In the original Napster, the central server performed this matching and therefore all search results were fully reliable. If no matches to a query were returned, then no matching file was currently available in the network.

Recall that the original Gnutella network was a fully distributed network. In this network, queries were flooded throughout the network by the peers. The peer originating the query would send it to all its neighbors which would then forward it to all of their neighbors (except the one having sent the query to them), and so on. Queries had a unique identifier to prevent peers from forwarding the same query multiple times. Such query flooding will eventually deliver the query to all the peers, but it is extremely expensive in terms of network bandwidth and query processing load. Hence, Gnutella queries were typically limited to a certain radius, or number of hops that the query could be forwarded. While this decreases the effectiveness of the query (a match might be found one hop beyond the limit), the overall savings were considerable enough, that the small possibility of not finding the file was acceptable.

Kazaa, being a hybrid system, combined the two search features of Napster and Gnutella. As mentioned earlier, peers in Kazaa belong to a superpeer (Kazaa calls them supernodes) which acts as a Napster-like hub for its children. When a peer wants to get a file, it sends the query to its superpeer which knows if any of its children has the file and send a list of those peers back to the requesting peer. At the same time, the superpeer will forward the query to its neighbor superpeers which all form a Gnutella-like network. The other superpeers will send answers for their own peers and forward the query to their neighbors (again, up to a certain radius). This query mechanism attempts to strike a balance between the efficient-but-vulnerable Napster model and the robust-but-inefficient Gnutella model. A good comparison of search strategies in unstructured networks can be found in (Lv, Cao, Cohen, Li, & Shenker, 2002).

Object Location in Structured Networks

As mentioned in the previous section, structured networks are not actually based on searching for resources, but on addressing them. We will now give an example of how the overlay structure is maintained and how resources are located in the Chord network (Stoica et al., 2001). We mentioned several other structured networks earlier and although the practical details of each of them are different, the same fundamental principles apply to all of them.

Chord assigns each peer and object an m-bit identifier using some hash function (e.g., SHA-1 which gives 160-bit identifiers). All objects and peers are assumed to have unique, well-known names, for example an IP address for a peer and a URL for an object. These identifiers are mapped on to an identifier circle modulo . This circle is also called the Chord ring. Object identifier k is mapped to the first peer whose identifier is equal to or follows the identifier of the object on the circle. This peer is called the *successor* of k. Each peer is required to keep track of its successor at all times. Figure 4 shows an example of a Chord ring with 3-bit identifiers, three nodes (0, 1, and 4) and three objects (1, 2, and 6). The arrows point to the successors of each of the objects.

When a peer wants to locate an object, it first computes the hash function on the name of the object and discovers the point on the identifier circle where the object maps. In case the peer itself happens to be responsible for that point, the search has ended. However, this is very unlikely since a real network would have several thousands or even millions of nodes and objects.

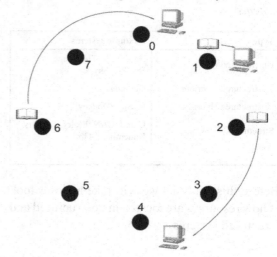

Figure 4. Chord ring with 3-bit identifiers

In the case that the peer wanting the object is not responsible for that object, it will send the request to its successor on the ring. The successor will check if it is responsible and if not, it will forward the request to its own successor. In this way, the request will eventually arrive at the peer which is the successor of the identifier of the requested object and that peer can then send a reply back to the requesting peer.

Although this approach can be proven to find the responsible node (Stoica et al., 2001), it does not scale to a large number of peers. This is because on average we have to traverse half-way across the circle to find the correct peer and if the circle has several thousands of peers, this means that we also need to send several thousands of messages to locate the right peer.

Chord solves this problem by letting each peer know about a few other peers, in order to speed up the lookup process. Note that this additional information is not required for correctness, which is ensured by peers knowing their successors.

Chord maintains this additional information in the so-called *finger table*. A finger table is a table with m entries in an m-bit identifier space. The entry in the finger table of peer p contains the address of the peer that succeeds p by at least on the ring, that is, the entry is the successor

Figure 5. Chord finger tables

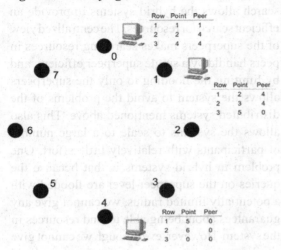

peer of the key (modulo). The first entry in the finger table is the peer's successor. Figure 5 shows the same Chord ring as in Figure 4, but with the finger tables added for each of the three nodes. The finger tables show the row, the starting point of the finger interval (i.e., position of the node plus for row *i*), and finally the successor of the starting point.

For example, consider the finger table for node 0. The first row should have the successor of key , i.e., node 1. Likewise, row 2 has the successor of key , or node 4. Finally, row 3 has the successor of key which is again node 4.

Note that with finger tables, each peer knows about some (up to *m*) other peers, but it does not have enough information to determine the successor of an arbitrary object key. Also, due to the way the finger tables are constructed, peers know more about other peers nearby, but always know some peers that are far away, up to a half of the ring.

Object lookup with fingers works as follows. When a peer *p* wants to retrieve an object with key *k*, it will check in its finger table for a peer *q* which immediately precedes *k*. Then, peer *p* asks *q* for a peer which is closer to *k*. The lookup will proceed in this way, until the responsible peer

has been found. For example, if node 4 wants to locate object 1, it will look in its finger table for the node which is the last one it knows before identifier 1. In our case, this is node 0. Node 0 will again perform the same search in its finger table, and return node 1, which is also the correct responsible node.

Because the distance between the finger table entries doubles, each step in the lookup process will halve the distance to the responsible node. Hence, in a network with *N* peers, Chord with finger tables is able to find the responsible node in $O(\log(N))$ message hops. The proof of this claim can be found in (Stoica et al., 2001).

Each of the other structured peer-to-peer systems mentioned in the section "Structured Peer-to-Peer Systems" also has similar lookup properties. This means that the number of messages needed to discover the responsible peer typically grows with the logarithm of the network size. This comes at the additional cost of having to maintain state information for several other peers. Again, the amount of state information typically also grows logarithmically with the size of the network.

Comparison of Unstructured and Structured Networks

Table 3 shows an overview of the advantages and disadvantages of unstructured and structured networks. Centralized unstructured networks use a single, central server to locate the resources in the system. In this case, searching is easy to implement in an efficient manner, since all the relevant data is available on the central server. For this reason, the central server also always has a consistent view of the system, that is, which peers are online, where are they located, what resources they provide, and so forth. A disadvantage of such a centralized solution is that the central server can become a bottleneck, and represents a single point of failure.

Table 3. Advantages and disadvantages of un-structured and structured networks

Network Type	Advantages	Disadvantages
Unstructured/ Centralized	Fast and efficient searching; Consistent view of network	Single point of failure
Unstructured/ Distributed	Robust against attacks; "Truly" P2P	Inefficient search; No guarantees
Unstructured/ Hybrid	Efficient searching; Very scalable	No guarantees
Structured	Efficient location; Provable guarantees	Maintenance overhead; Resources may disappear; Low performance

In a distributed unstructured system, all peers are equal and no single point of failure, such as the central server, exists. This gives the systems a large degree of robustness against system failures and attacks. Also, this equality of peers makes such systems in one sense truly peer-to-peer, in the sense of our definition in the introduction of this chapter. However, because queries need to be flooded into the system, such distributed systems are not very efficient in searching for content, and typically must limit the search radius in order to keep the number of messages in the system manageable. These limited queries also imply that not all resources in the system are discoverable, thus there are no guarantees about being able to find resources, even if they are being provided by some peers.

Hybrid unstructured systems attempt to strike a balance between centralized and distributed systems. The superpeers provide efficient searching, since each superpeer has a consistent view of a (small) part of the whole system. The superpeers typically build an unstructured distributed network between them for discovering resources located in the peers handled by other superpeers.

This combination of centralized and distributed search allows the hybrid systems to provide an efficient search for resources. The centralized view of the superpeers makes searching resources in peers handld by a single superpeer efficient, and by limiting the flooding to only the superpeers allows the system to avoid the problems of the distributed systems mentioned above. This also allows the systems to scale to a large number of participants with relatively little effort. One problem in hybrid systems is that because the queries on the superpeer-level are flooded with a potentially limited radius, we cannot give any guarantees about being able to find resources in the system. However, even though we cannot give similar guarantees as we can for the centralized systems, hybrid systems are still better at locating resources than fully distributed systems.

Structured systems present a stark contrast to unstructured systems. Due to the well-defined placement of objects on peers, we are always able to find the peer which provides the resource (or which *should* provide the resource). Furthermore, the structure of the systems often allows us to actually prove the correctness of the resource location in the system (see for example, Stoica et al. (2001)). The downsides of structured systems are the maintenance overhead required by the structure and their low performance. Because all the peers in the system have a well-specified place and well-specified neighbors, we need to update the neighbors when new peers join the system or current peers leave the system. This can lead to large amounts of maintenance traffic and to a possibly inconsistent state of the system where resources might not be discoverable for some period of time. Because some peers might abruptly leave the network (e.g., because the peer crashed or suddenly lost its network connection), it is possible that resources stored on the peer which has disappeared might be lost to the system. In order to avoid this, resources in structured networks are typically replicated to guarantee their availability. A further problem with structured networks is their low overall performance for certain types of applications. Even though the number of messages needed to locate a resource typically grows logarithmically with the number of nodes, this can still mean that several messages must be sent from one peer to others to locate a resource. In contrast, a centralized unstructured system needs only two messages to locate a resource (query and answer). How much this really affects the system depends on what kind of an application we are building on top of the structured system.

SUITABILITY FOR UBIQUITOUS COMPUTING

We now turn our attention to looking at the suitability of peer-to-peer systems for ubiquitous computing. In particular, we will concentrate on analyzing how well the different unstructured and structured systems would fit the requirements of ubiquitous computing, as described in the introduction of this book.

Ubiquitous computing environments are often highly dynamic, with the capabilities of the participating devices varying widely, from small sensors to servers. This means that if we want to use a peer-to-peer communication system between the devices and entities, we should select a system which is able to handle the high dynamics and heterogeneity present in the environment. We will analyze all the four types of systems from Section "Classification of Peer-to-Peer Systems" in order from least suitable to the most suitable. Note that this analysis is of a very general nature and the particularities of any given ubiquitous computing application might change the ranking.

An unstructured centralized system is, a priori, the least suitable system for ubiquitous computing. A centralized server could help alleviate the amount of work needed to be done by the individual entities, which would help low-resource devices such as sensors, yet it is hard to guarantee that every device would always be able to connect to the central server, due to the dynamic nature of ubiquitous computing environments. Even if this connectivity problem can be solved, a further problem is the scalability of the central server for handling all the related devices. We could try to solve this scalability problem by having several such servers and have each server take care of only a part of the environment. This would bring us close to a hybrid solution, which we will discuss in more detail below.

The second least suitable alternative would be structured networks. Given the need to maintain the network structure when peers join or leave, the requirements for communication are likely to be too high for most ubiquitous computing applications. Furthermore, structured networks typically consider all peers to be equal and are not in a good position to exploit the heterogeneity of the devices. However, they do have the advantage over the purely centralized solutions in that we do not need any additional servers, but all the devices in communication range could build their own structured network. Structured systems could be used in the backbone network, but are unlikely to be very practical for other ubiquitous computing scenarios.

Unstructured distributed systems are quite attractive for ubiquitous computing. This is because the communications in such networks are relatively lightweight (especially compared to structured systems), and we do not need any additional servers. However, their one weakness is that all peers are typically considered equal, which neglects to account for the inherent heterogeneity of ubiquitous computing. In addition, as with Gnutella, they suffer from scalability problems, but in smaller systems this would not be a problem.

Finally, the a priori most suitable systems for ubiquitous computing known to date are the structured hybrid systems. As already mentioned above, we could try to scale a purely centralized solution by having several servers take on different responsibilities and then network the servers

Table 4. Suitability of peer-to-peer systems for ubiquitous computing

Type of system	Most suitable for
Unstructured/Centralized	Small environments
Unstructured/Distributed	Relatively homogeneous situations
	As interconnection network for superpeers
	Small-scale systems
Unstructured/Hybrid	Most ubiquitous computing scenarios
Structured	As interconnection network for superpeers
	Low dynamics situations

in some way between themselves. This allows us to use the more powerful devices as superpeers and let the other devices organize themselves under the superpeers. Hence, the hybrid system appears to be the most suitable for ubiquitous computing.

One issue with hybrid systems is how the superpeers are connected among themselves. Existing Internet-based systems like Kazaa or eDonkey use an unstructured distributed system for this interconnection. If the superpeers are well-connected to each other and relatively stable, then we could also envision building a structured network to manage the superpeers.

FUTURE OF PEER-TO-PEER SYSTEMS

Peer-to-peer systems are currently widely used, however, most of that use is concentrated around file sharing systems. New applications, such as Skype, have only recently started making inroads in actual use. Still, peer-to-peer applications have so far mostly failed to make the jump from file sharing to other applications. We will now analyze some of the key points and requirements which are needed in order to make peer-to-peer systems more widely applicable. We divide our analysis into two parts: quality guarantees of peer-to-peer systems and their general applicability as solutions.

Quality of Peer-to-Peer Systems

One serious shortcoming of peer-to-peer applications is their best-effort nature. Much like the Internet, on which peer-to-peer applications are built, which does not offer any quality guarantees beyond a simple best-effort service, most peer-to-peer applications also lack the ability to give any guarantees about the service they perform. Apart from the original, centralized Napster, no file-sharing network is able to guarantee that it will find all the copies of files matching the user's request. While best effort service is sufficient for general Internet usage and simple applications like file sharing, it is not sufficient for building sophisticated applications.

Consider, for example, a storage system built on top of a peer-to-peer network. Due to the intermittent connectivity of the peers, data would have to be widely replicated in order to guarantee a certain level of availability (Kangasharju, Ross, & Turner, 2007). Yet no peer-to-peer system beyond research prototypes (Haeberlen, Mislove, & Druschel, 2005; Rhea, Eaton, Geels, Weatherspoon, Zhao, & Kubiatoqicz, 2003) offers any guarantees. The same argument about lack of quality guarantees applies to many aspects of peer-to-peer systems.

This lack of quality guarantees is one of the biggest hurdles standing in the way of a wider adoption of peer-to-peer applications in serious, commercial usage, for example. Note, however, that this does not imply that peer-to-peer systems would have to be engineered to provide extremely high quality service in all cases. In many cases, it would be sufficient to give users a certain, *predictable* quality, so that users and applications would know what to expect. Improving the quality of peer-to-peer systems is a topic of on-going research in the community.

Applicability of Peer-to-Peer Systems

Another important question when building peer-to-peer systems is what parts of the system can, or should, be made to work in a peer-to-peer fashion. Centralized solutions exist for many problems and they are well-understood. While a peer-to-peer solution might remove the need to operate a server, it could easily turn out that the peer-to-peer solution is not able to offer the same services as the centralized solution. For example, Skype maintains the information about which users are online on the peers, but requires all users to login through their centralized server, which also handles billing for calls into the normal telephone network. Although it would likely be possible to implement the login and billing in a peer-to-peer fashion, the unanswered question is how much security would potentially be lost in such an implementation.

Peer-to-Peer and Ubiquitous Computing Revisited

Given the two weaknesses of peer-to-peer systems mentioned above, we now turn to revisiting the issue of how suitable peer-to-peer systems are for ubiquitous computing applications. Given the large heterogeneity of both peer-to-peer systems and ubiquitous computing applications, we can only give some general rules of thumb; the developer of a particular application must analyze the situation herself to see which technologies would be most appropriate for that particular case.

Our classification in Table 4 shows that all the main types of peer-to-peer systems are applicable for some ubiquitous computing scenarios. However, the most suitable solutions seem to be the hybrid and fully distributed solutions. This is because both of these systems are able to exploit the natural heterogeneity of the peers.

The lack of quality guarantees in peer-to-peer systems need not be a problem for ubiquitous

computing applications. For example, consider a sensor which sends its reading every 5 seconds to the system. If one such transmission is lost because of an unreliable network subsystem, it takes only 5 seconds more to get the next reading and most applications would likely be robust against such situations. However, consider a case where the user has to be authenticated to use a specific service. In this case, we cannot afford to have an unreliable authentication mechanism, but instead require that all messages are transmitted reliably. If we want to use a peer-to-peer system as a basis for such applications, we must be able to guarantee that the peer-to-peer system is able to perform at the level required by the application. For some applications, a statistical, predictable quality level might suffice; others might require more stringent guarantees.

FUTURE RESEARCH DIRECTIONS

The research area of peer-to-peer networks and systems is currently very active. It combines elements from the networking and distributed systems communities. One of the main future challenges in the area of peer-to-peer systems is investigating what fundamental properties set peer-to-peer systems apart from the traditional client-server systems. In particular, it remains to be seen what the real limits of peer-to-peer systems are, and how far these limits can be pushed.

Some particular areas where peer-to-peer research is currently active and is likely to remain active for the near future are:

- **Peer-to-peer content distribution:** As shown by BitTorrent and other current examples, there is considerable demand for efficient delivery of large files to a large number of customers.
- **Peer-to-peer media delivery:** One particular area of interest in content distribution is the delivery of media content to the users.

This can take either the form of media downloads, such as film or music downloads, or the form of streaming. In the first case, we are likely to see an increase in demand due to the online media stores, which are opening, but the actual delivery technologies are likely to be based on the more traditional peer-to-peer content distribution technologies. In the case of streaming, which is needed for live content, there is still considerable amount of work to be done.

- **Peer-to-peer communication:** As exemplified by Skype and instant messaging systems, peer-to-peer-based communication architectures are showing their strengths. Such systems are likely to gain in popularity and importance in the future, but they also present several fundamental research questions, regarding how the resources in the systems should be managed and allocated.

REFERENCES

Aberer, K., Datta, A., & Hauswirth, M. (2005). Peer-to-peer systems and applications. *Chapter P-Grid: Dynamics of self-organizing processes in structured peer-to-peer systems*, (pp. 137–153). Springer.

Adar, E., & Huberman, B. A. (2000). *Free riding on Gnutella* (Tech. Rep.), Internet Ecologies Area, Xerox Palo Alto Research Center.

Akamai. Retrieved October 14, 2007, from http://www.akamai.com

Berkeley Open Infrastructure for Network Computing. Retrieved October 14, 2007, from http://boinc.berkeley.edu

BitTorrent. Retrieved October 14, 2007, http://www.bittorrent.com

eDonkey. Retrieved October 14, 2007, from http://www.edonkey2000.com

Freedman, M. J., Freudenthal, E., & Mazieres, D. (2004). Democratizing content publication with Coral. In *Proceedings of Symposium on Networked Systems Design and Implementation*, San Francisco.

Gnutella. Retrieved October 14, 2007, from http://www.gnutella.com

Haeberlen, A., Mislove, A., & Druschel, P. (2005). Glacier: Highly durable, decentralized storage despite massive correlated failures. In *Proceedings of Symposium on Networked Systems Design and Implementation*, Boston.

Izal, M., Urvoy-Keller, G., Biersack, E. W., Felber, P., Al Hamra, A., & Garcés-Erice, L. (2004). Dissecting BitTorrent: Five months in a torrent's lifetime. In *Proceedings of Passive and Active Measurements*.

Kangasharju, J., Ross, K. W., & Turner, D. A. (2007). Optimizing file availability in P2P content distribution. In *Proceedings of IEEE Infocom*, Anchorage, AK.

Kazaa. Retrieved October 14, 2007, from http://www.kazaa.com

Lv, Q., Cao, P., Cohen, E., Li, K., & Shenker, S. (2002). Search and replication in unstructured peer-to-peer networks. In *Proceedings of the 16th annual ACM International Conference on Supercomputing*, New York.

Maymounkov, P., & Mazieres, D. (2002). Kademlia: A peer-to-peer information system based on the xor metric. In *Proceedings of International Workshop on Peer-to-Peer Systems*, Cambridge, Massachusetts.

Napster. Retrieved October 14, 2007, from http://www.napster.com

Oram, A., (Ed.). (2001). *Peer-to-Peer: Harnessing the power of disruptive technologies*. O'Reilly.

Ratnasamy, S., Francis, P., Handley, M., Karp, R., & Shenker, S. (2001). A scalable content-addressable network. In *Proceedings of ACM SIGCOMM*, San Diego, California.

Rhea, S., Eaton, P., Geels, D., Weatherspoon, H., Zhao, B., & Kubiatoqicz, J. (2003). Pond: The oceanStore prototype. In *Proceedings of the USENIX Conference on File and Storage Technologies*, San Francisco.

Rodriguez, P., & Biersack, E. W. (2002). Dynamic parallel-access to replicated content in the Internet. *IEEE/ACM Transactions on Networking, 7*(1), 67-78.

Rowstron, A., & Druschel, P. (2001). Pastry: Scalable, distributed object location and routing for large-scale peer-to-peer systems. In *IFIP/ACM International Conference on Distributed Systems Platforms (Middleware)*, Heidelberg, Germany.

Saroiu, S., Gummadi, K. P., & Gribble, S. D. (2002). A measurement study of peer-to-peer file sharing networks. In *Proceedings of Multimedia Computing and Networking*, San Jose, California.

SETI@Home. Retrieved October 14, 2007, from http://setiathome.berkeley.edu

Skype. Retrieved October 14, 2007, from http://www.skype.com

Steinmetz, R., & Wehrle, K. (Eds.). (2005). *Peer-to-peer systems and applications*. Springer.

Stoica, I., Morris, R., Karger, D., Kaashoek, M. F., & Balakrishnan, H. (2001). Chord: A scalable peer-to-peer lookup service for Internet applications. In *Proceedings of ACM SIGCOMM*, San Diego, California.

Subramanian, R., & Goodman, B. D. (Eds.). (2005). *Peer-to-peer computing: The evolution of a disruptive technology*. Hershey, PA: Idea Group Publishing.

von Lohmann, F. (2003). Peer-to-peer file sharing and copyright law: A primer for developers. In *Proceedings of International Workshop on Peer-to-Peer Systems*, Berkeley, California.

Zhao, B. Y., Huang, L., Stribling, J., Rhea, S. C., Joseph, A. D., & Kubiatowicz, J. D. (2004). Tapestry: A resilient global-scale overlay for service deployment. *IEEE Journal on Selected Areas in Communications, 22*(1), 41-53.

ADDITIONAL READING

Al Hamra, A., & Felber, P. A. (2005). Design choices for content distribution in P2P networks. *Computer Communications Review, 35*(5), 29–40.

Biersack, E. W., Rodriguez, P., & Felber, P. (2004). Performance analysis of peer-to-peer networks for file distribution. In *Proceedings of Fifth International Workshop on Quality of Future Internet Services*, Barcelona, Spain.

Breslau, L., Cao, P., Fan, L., Phillips, G., & Shenker, S. (1999). Web caching and Zipf-like distributions: Evidence and implications. In *Proceedings of IEEE Infocom*, New York.

Cohen, E., & Shenker, S. (2002). Replication strategies in unstructured peer-to-peer networks. In *Proceedings of ACM SIGCOMM*, Pittsburgh, Pennsylvannia.

Cox, R., Muthitacharoen, A., & Morris, R. (2002). Serving DNS using a peer-to-peer lookup service. In *Proceedings of International Workshop on Peer-to-Peer Systems*, Cambridge, Massachusetts.

Dabek, F., Kaashoek, M. F., Karger, D., Morris, R., & Stoica, I. (2001). Wide-area cooperative storage with CFS. In *Proceedings of ACM Symposium on Operating Systems Principles*, Banff, Canada.

Felber, P. A., & Biersack, E. W. (2004). Self-scaling networks for content distribution. In *Proceedings of Self-**, Bertinoro, Italy.

Iyer, S., Rowstron, A., & Druschel, P. (2002). Squirrel: A decentralized peer-to-peer web cache. In *Proceedings of ACM Symposium on*

Principles of Distributed Computing, Monterey, California.

Kangasharju, J., & Kangasharju, J. (2006). An optimal basis for efficient peer-to-peer content distribution. In *Proceedings of 15th International Conference on Computer Communications and Networks*, Arlington, Virginia.

Kangasharju, J., Ross, K. W., & Turner, D. A. (2003). Secure and resilient peer-to-peer email: Design and implementation. In *Proceedings of 3rd International Conference on Peer-to-Peer Computing*, Linköping, Sweden.

Kangasharju, J., Ross, K. W., & Turner, D. A. (2007a). Optimizing file availability in P2P content distribution. In *Proceedings of IEEE Infocom*, Anchorage, Alaska.

Kangasharju, J., Schmidt, U., Bradler, D., & Schröder-Bernhardi, J. (2007b). ChunkSim: Simulating peer-to-peer content distribution. In *Proceedings of 10th Communications and Networking Simulation Symposium*, Norfolk, Virginia.

Karagiannis, T., Rodriguez, P., & Papagiannaki, K. (2005). Should Internet service providers fear peer-assisted content distribution? In *Proceedings of Internet Measurement Conference*, Berkeley, California.

Kubiatowicz, J., Bindel, D., Chen, Y., Czerwinski, S., Eaton, P., Geels, D., Gummadi, R., Rhea, S., Weatherspoon, H., Weimer, W., Wells, C., & Zhao, B. (2000). OceanStore: An architecture for global-scale persistent storage. In *Proceedings of International Conference on Architectural Support for Programming Languages and Operating Systems*, Boston.

Kumar, R., & Ross, K. W. (2006). Peer-assisted file distribution: The minimum distribution time. In *Proceedings of HotWeb*, Boston.

Maymounkov, P., & Mazieres, D. (2002). Kademlia: A peer-to-peer information system based on the xor metric. In *Proceedings of International Workshop on Peer-to-Peer Systems*, Cambridge, Masachusetts.

Qiu, D., & Srikant, R. (2004). Modeling and performance analysis of BitTorrent-like peer-to-peer networks. In *Proceedings of ACM SIGCOMM*, Portland, Oregon.

Rhea, S., Eaton, P., Geels, D., Weatherspoon, H., Zhao, B., & Kubiatoqicz, J. (2003). Pond: The oceanStore prototype. In *Proceedings of the USENIX Conference on File and Storage Technologies*, San Francisco.

Rowstron, A., & Druschel, P. (2001). Storage management and caching in PAST, a large-scale, persistent peer-to-peer storage utility. In *Proceedings of ACM Symposium on Operating Systems Principles*, Banff, Canada.

Saroiu, S., Gummadi, K. P., & Gribble, S. D. (2002). A measurement study of peer-to-peer file sharing networks. In *Proceedings of Multimedia Computing and Networking*, San Jose, California.

Schiely, M., Renfer, L., & Felber, P. (2005). Self-organization in cooperative content distribution networks. In *Proceedings of IEEE International Symposium on Network Computing and Applications*, Cambridge, Massachusetts.

Sen, S., & Wang, J. (2004). Analyzing peer-to-peer traffic across large networks. *IEEE/ACM Transactions on Networking, 12*(2), 219-232.

Sit, E., & Morris, R. (2002). Security considerations for peer-to-peer distributed hash tables. In *Proceedings of International Workshop on Peer-to-Peer Systems*, Cambridge, Massachusetts.

Stoica, I., Adkins, D., Zhuang, D., Shenker, S., & Surana, S. (2002). Internet indirection infrastructure. In *Proceedings of ACM SIGCOMM,* Pittsburgh, Pennsylvania.

Terpstra, W. T., Behnel, S., Fiege, L., Kangasharju, J., & Buchmann, A. (2004). Bit zipper rendezvous: Optimal data placement for general P2P queries. In *Proceedings of International Workshop on Peer-to-Peer Computing & Databases*, Heraklion, Greece.

Yang, W., & Abu-Ghazaleh, N. (2005). GPS: A general peer-to-peer simulator and its use for modeling bittorrent. In *Proceedings of MASCOTS.*

Yang, X., & de Veciana, G. (2004). Service capacity of peer-to-peer networks. In *Proceedings of IEEE Infocom*, Hong Kong.

Chapter IX
Opportunistic Networks

Andreas Heinemann
Technical University of Darmstadt, Germany

ABSTRACT

This chapter introduces opportunistic networks. Such networks support spontaneous interaction between mobile users carrying mobile devices with them. After having been presented with the motivation for this new type of network, the reader will learn the underlying concepts, including an opportunistic network definition. Next, this chapter discusses what makes opportunistic networks different to mobile peer-to-peer networks and mobile ad hoc networks; two network types that are closely related. We present a number of applications with a focus on data dissemination. As a sequel to that, the chapter discusses human factors that are important for opportunistic networks, namely privacy preserving techniques and an incentive scheme. The chapter concludes with an overview of future research issues by naming a number of open and unsolved problems.

INTRODUCTION AND MOTIVATION

A predominant concern in ubiquitous computing (UC) is the natural and effortless interaction of humans with a *smart* environment in order to carry out a certain task or simply to make life easier. Often, interaction is bootstrapped with a user's personal, mobile device. Such a device may carry a digital representation in form of a user profile and a key pair that serves as a digital identity. Examples of devices are personal digital assistants (PDAs) or mobile phones. Especially the mobile phone plays a prominent role since it

has conquered our everyday life and is basically *ubiquitously* available for the user.

More and more mobile phones and PDAs are equipped with short range wireless communication capabilities. In most cases, either Bluetooth (Bluetooth SIG Inc., 2003-2005) or 802.11b WiFi technology (IEEE, 1999) is integrated. The prevalent use of wireless connectivity is to synchronize personal data between a mobile device and a desktop computer (via Bluetooth) or have easy access to an institution's network (via a 802.11 WiFi Wireless Access Point) and further to the Internet. But in addition, with the integration of short-range wireless communication technology into these devices a new network type called *opportunistic network* and its corresponding applications based on *spontaneous* interaction and collaboration among devices and users is emerging.

Opportunistic networks are closely related to two other network types: mobile peer-to-peer networks and mobile ad hoc networks (MANETs). The latter operate mainly on the networking layer and provide novel types of infrastructure for all kinds of applications. Some underlying principles of the two types of networks can be found in the chapters "Wireless and Mobile Communication" and "Peer-to-Peer Networks" of this book, respectively. Later in this chapter, we will compare the two network types to opportunistic networks, which we concentrate on in the remainder. Opportunistic networks may be considered the least emphasized of the three in the literature, but as the chapter will show, they offer unique and promising opportunities for the dawning ubiquitous computing era.

Opportunistic network applications take advantage of the fact that mobile, personal devices are able to discover and communicate with each other whenever they are nearby. We motivate opportunistic networks with a concrete application example.

Example: *At a computer science conference site, researchers from all around the world stay together for 2-3 days to discuss recent advances in their fields. Due to the limited time, each attendee tries to make his stay as beneficial as possible, for example, by talking to colleagues during coffee breaks. For novices in research there might be the question "Who should I talk to?" or "Which other attendees are working on similar research problems?" By carrying a Bluetooth enabled mobile phone, the device is able to communicate with nearby devices carried by others in order to look for interesting conversational partners. Once the devices have discovered a match in research*

interests, the devices notify their owners and the owners are able to switch to a face-to-face communication due to the short communication range.

The devices might also exchange information, for example, paper reading lists, without user notification. By this, each attendee would learn about what other researchers are currently working on.

After the conference is over, this information is carried back home and the attendee might share this information with colleagues at his research institute, again, by using his mobile phone and without notice.

The example emphasizes two things. First, opportunistic networks help to make people physically aware of each other and second, opportunistic networks support data dissemination very similar to *word of mouth* communication among humans.

The remainder of this chapter is organized as follows. In the next section the reader will learn the underlying ideas and concepts of opportunistic networks. After that, a comparison to mobile peer-to-peer and MANETs is done. The section "Opportunistic Network Applications" presents typical applications for this network type with a focus on data dissemination mechanisms. As seen in the previous example, an opportunistic network node consists of a human with a personal device. Thus human factors need to be considered in opportunistic network application design. This is addressed in the penultimate section. The final section summaries this chapter and, being a fairly new topic in UC, gives directions for possible future issues and challenges. The chapter closes with a list of pointers to literature for those who want to dig deeper into opportunistic networks.

UNDERLYING IDEAS AND CONCEPTS

Opportunistic networks have several roots. Similar ideas can be found in work that combines *peer-to-peer networking* concepts with *mobile ad hoc networking* (Datta, 2003; Ding & Bhargava, 2004; Goel, Singh, & Xu, 2002; Hayes & Wilson, 2005; Hu, Das, & Pucha, 2003; Klemm, Lindemann, & Waldhorst, 2004, 2003; Lindemann & Waldhorst, 2005, 2002). Some authors recognize delay tolerant networks (DTNs) as a superset of opportunistic networks (Leguay, Lindgren, Scott, Friedman, & Crowcroft, 2006), while others regard opportunistic networks to be more general than DTNs (Pelusi, Passarella, & Conti, 2006). At the time of writing, the term opportunistic networks is gaining a foothold, but other terms, such as *en-passant communication* (Görgen, Frey, & Hutter, 2005), *pocket switched networking* (Hui, Chaintreau, Gass, Scott, & Crowcroft, 2005; Hui, Chaintreau, Scott, Crowcroft, & Diot, 2005; Scott, Hui, Crowcroft, & Diot, 2006), *spontaneous networking* (Aldunate, Nussbaum, & Gonzalez, 2002; Schwotzer & Preuss, 2002) or *mobile ad hoc information system* (Kortuem, 2002; Kortuem, Schneider, Preuitt, Thompson, Fickas, & Segall, 2001; Kortuem, Segall, & Thompson, 1999) can also be found in the literature. However in all cited work the following ideas and concepts are present:

- **User vicinity exploitation**: An obvious necessity for short-range communication to happen is the *co-location* of devices and thus their owners at a certain time and place. This vicinity sharing raises the opportunity for users to meet *face-to-face* and make personal contact. In addition, to some extent, the usefulness of an application increases, since nearby users share the same physical context and the likeliness might be high that these users share a common interest. For example, users attending a pop concert have a similar taste in music. Their devices being close enough for communication may help to introduce the users to each other. This assumption might not be true for every encounter, for example, people meeting by accident on a public bus. But even in these kinds of situations, close vicinity enables getting to know new people with the help of the users' devices.

- **Profile based user interest expression**: After two devices have discovered each other, there needs to be a way to determine if it is beneficial for a device and thus for the user to communicate further. This is often achieved by employing a user profile on the device. A user profile expresses personal interests and knowledge. At the bottom line, a user wants to satisfy his interest and is committed to sharing his knowledge

- **Data dissemination:** Wenever Alice's knowledge that is stored on her device matches the interest of user Bob (by user profile matching), this knowledge is transferred from Alice's device to Bob's device. Given a number of users with the same interest, we observe a data dissemination process. This process is additionally supported by the user's mobility, that is, users physically carry the data stored on their devices while they move around.

- **Open and unrelated user group:** Opportunistic network applications do not make any assumptions about their participating users. Thus, except for a few exceptions discussed later, users are *unknown* to each other, act *independently* and might pursue *solely personal* interests.

- **Unpredictable communication pattern:** Communication and information exchange takes place between mobile users that accidentally happen to be close-by. A user cannot rely on opportunistic network applications to satisfy his interest at all. Opportunistic networks (as implied by the term *opportunistic*) solely provide *best effort* functionality. This restricts opportunistic networks to a certain kind of applications. We will illustrate typical applications later.

The predominant use of opportunistic networks is the distribution of data by making use of human mobility and local, that is, one-hop, forwarding techniques. Information is stored on the device and passed further when an appropriate contact is met. The section "Opportunistic Network Applications" presents the data dissemination mechanism in *iClouds*, an opportunistic network prototype developed at the Technical University of Darmstadt.

A Definition for Opportunistic Networks

As already mentioned, *opportunistic networks* as a term are not yet clearly defined, neither is the scope of this concept. This section gives a first definition that underpins the following assumptions: An opportunistic network is formed by mobile users carrying mobile devices. These devices are able to connect to each other using a wireless link. Together they communicate in a *spontaneous* manner and build a mobile network. In addition, fixed nodes, mounted at dedicated places, may extend the usefulness of an application by acting as intermediates or by offering localized services.

Opportunistic network definition: *An opportunistic network is a network of wireless connected nodes. Nodes may be either mobile or fixed. Communication range between two connected nodes is within walking distance, that is, ≈ 100–300 meters. The network topology may change due to node mobility or node activation and node deactivation. The nodes provide the following functionality:*

- *Node discovery: A network node is able to discover other network nodes in direct communication range.*
- *One-hop message exchange: A node is able to send and receive arbitrary data in form of a message to or from any other node in direct communication range.*

This definition emphasizes that in an opportunistic network there is an *opportunity* for nodes (devices) to recognize other nodes in physical proximity and to *talk* to them. Our view on opportunistic networks supports only *one-hop* message exchange due to a missing relation and a missing common goal among nodes. We elaborate on this in the section in which we compare opportunistic networks to MANETs.

Opportunistic network node definition: *An opportunistic network node consists of a device with short-range wireless communication capabilities. The device operates an opportunistic network application that uses a data sharing protocol for data dissemination. The data sharing protocol uses (1) node discovery and (2) one-hop message exchange.*

An opportunistic network node can be a mobile device carried by a human or a fixed device. This is reflected in the next two definitions.

Mobile node definition: *A mobile node (or node for short) consists of a user carrying a mobile device that acts as an opportunistic network node.*

Information sprinkler definition: *An information sprinkler (abbreviated IS) is a fixed opportunistic network node within the network. It is a device placed at a dedicated location, thus it is not mobile and not under direct user control. The information sprinkler uses the same data sharing protocol as other opportunistic network nodes.*

An IS can operate in a *sprinkler* mode, meaning information is only dispersed, or in a *sink* mode, meaning information is only collected, or in both modes together. An Information Sprinkler may also be connected to a *backbone* network. The backbone network may be a wired network that connects a set of Information Sprinklers and synchronizes their operation. For example, data that is collected at one Information Sprinkler is available at all other sprinklers shortly after.

Vertical Architecture

The definitions lead to a vertical architecture as depicted in Figure 1. The Figure shows three Information Sprinklers and an *optional* sprinkler backbone. A connection link between nodes is indicated by a black dotted line. This link indicates that two adjacent nodes are close enough to exchange messages with each other. If they communicate at all after they have discovered each other depends on the application. As discussed in the next section, there is no multi-hop communication support in opportunistic network. Thus, there is no direct message exchange between distant nodes.

Communication ranges are depicted as dashed spheres. Note that in practice the communication range of a node is not an ideal sphere due to communication signal interference with the surroundings.

DIFFERENCES TO MOBILE P2P AND MANETS

As mentioned in the introduction, opportunistic networks are closely related to mobile ad hoc networks and mobile peer-to-peer networks. Due to their inherent dynamic nature, all network types exhibit a number of self-organizing functionality. We will discuss this issue and compare it to opportunistic networks in the following two sections.

Opportunistic Networks vs. MANETs

Since opportunistic network nodes are either mobile or fixed (cf. Information Sprinkler) and communicate over a wireless link, there is a relation to mobile ad hoc networks (MANETs). The MANET Definition (Wikipedia, 2005) says:

Figure 1. Opportunistic network example

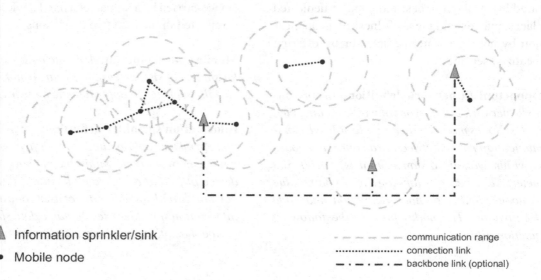

▲ Information sprinkler/sink

● Mobile node

– – – – – communication range
·················· connection link
– · – · – · backbone link (optional)

Mobile ad hoc network definition: *A mobile ad hoc network (MANET) is a self-configuring network of mobile routers (and associated hosts) connected by wireless links—the union of which form an arbitrary topology. The routers are free to move randomly and organize themselves arbitrarily; thus, the network's wireless topology may change rapidly and unpredictably. Such a network may operate in a stand-alone fashion, or may be connected to the larger Internet.*

Obviously, MANETs are similar to opportunistic networks: both network types do not rely on a central component, for example, a central server. Their architecture is decentralized by definition and takes node mobility into account, that is, nodes connect and disconnect since they move in and out of communication range. Connection and disconnection may also happen because devices are turned on or off unpredictably. Thus, in a given MANET, the node community may change during operation. Given by the physical presence of nodes and a limited communication range, typically a few hundred nodes constitute a MANET. This is similar to opportunistic networks.

MANETs reside on the network layer and take special care about routing—an aspect that is deliberately left aside in opportunistic networks (see next section). Routing allows end-to-end communication of network nodes via intermediates. Since MANETs have been investigated in the context of military networks, emergency response, and mobile sensor networks, all applications considered have several assumptions in common that are a prerequisite for routing: All nodes expose a close node relationship. Nodes trust each other and share a common goal they want to accomplish.

In contrast, opportunistic networks are formed between unrelated nodes, and users might even be anonymous and therefore unknown to each other. This has an important impact on routing. Consider the situation in Figure 2 with *A*, *B*, and *C* as mobile nodes, in other words, individuals

Figure 2. Multi-hop communication

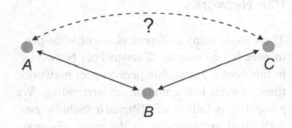

equipped with a mobile device. *A* is in communication range of *B*, but not in range of *C*, who, on the other hand, is in communication range of *B*. If *A* wants to communicate with *C*, all messages have to be routed via *B*. Bearing in mind that *A*, *B*, and *C*, a priori do not know each other, two questions arise:

1. What is the *incentive* for node *B* to route messages between *A* and *C*? Why should node *B* be willing to donate part of his battery power to enable communication between *A* and *C*?
2. Why should node *A* and *C* *trust* and *rely* on node *B* for their communication? Node *B* could easily eavesdrop, manipulate, or just reject messages.

These questions cannot be easily answered. Therefore, any routing schemes for MANETs appear to fall short of providing for communication in opportunistic network settings. What are missing are incentives for users to forward messages and suitable security mechanisms.

Thus, opportunistic networks solely expose a wireless *one-hop* communication scheme, where only directly connected nodes exchange messages if they benefit from the communication, for example, by learning about information they where looking for. This implies that opportunistic networks reside on the application layer.

Opportunistic Networks and Mobile P2P Networks

There exist many different views of what peer-to-peer is (see chapter "Peer-to-Peer Networks" in this book). For *mobile* peer-to-peer networks, there is even less common understanding. We present the definition of P2P used in (Schollmeier, 2001) that corresponds to the more elaborate definitions given in the above mentioned chapter of this book.

Peer-to-Peer Definition: *A distributed network architecture may be called a Peer-to-Peer (P-to-P, P2P) network if the participants share a part of their own hardware resources (processing power, storage capacity, network link capacity, printers, etc.). These shared resources are necessary to provide the service and content offered by the network (e.g., file sharing or shared workspaces for collaboration). They are accessible by other peers directly, without passing intermediary entities. The participants in such a network are thus resource (service and content) providers as well as resource (service and content) requesters (Servant-concept).*

Although not explicitly included, the definition above was given with Internet based P2P applications in mind, as stated in the abstract of (Schollmeier, 2001). Therefore, node mobility is not assumed. In addition, if we consider the Internet as the default P2P environment, a P2P network size is several orders of magnitude higher as compared to opportunistic networks.

Opportunistic networks and peer-to-peer networks have the integration of client and server functionality into one node or peer in common. Looking at the most prominent P2P application, file sharing on the Internet, a P2P node consumes files from other nodes that match a search query and allows other nodes to access locally stored files. Similarly, the main purpose of opportunistic network nodes is to initiate collaboration. Thus,

by providing information, opportunistic networks nodes take the role of a server, and, by consuming information of other nodes, they take the role of a client as well. Having stated this, opportunistic networks fall within the definition of peer-to-peer networks.

However, in P2P networks which do not rely on a central component (sometimes called *pure* P2P networks), peers build a so-called overlay network (managed in the application layer) for searching resources or content. Although peer relationship is basically not present on the Internet, P2P networks count on a cooperative behavior of peers in order to maintain the overlay network structure. Thus, individual peers forward search requests to adjacent nodes. This works well on the Internet, where online costs and peer energy consumption are not a predominant issue, and although nodes join and leave a P2P network at will, the size of the P2P network remedies this dynamic and unpredictable peer behavior.

For *mobile* P2P networks (MP2P), resource sharing without a returned benefit raises the same problems as presented in the last section, namely incentives, trust and reliability. These problems are largely ignored by the current research in mobile P2P networks. Peer-to-peer concepts are simply mapped onto mobile networks. There exists no coherent view of what is to be understood by mobile P2P. The only thing in common is node mobility and, therefore, nodes are equipped with wireless communication technology. Implementations range from *MP2P over mobile ad hoc networks* (Datta, 2003) to *MP2P over cellular based networks* (Hoßfeld, Tutschku, & Andersen, 2005a; Hoßfeld, Tutschku, & Andersen, 2005b). Application scenarios include pedestrians with mobile devices (Hayes & Wilson, 2005) or vehicles with wireless communication capabilities (Xu, Ouksel, & Wolfson, 2004).

Closing this section, Table 1 summarizes similarities and differences between the discussed network types. We recapitulate major points: the most notable difference to P2P and MANET

Table 1. Self-organizing networks

Network Type	Layer	Routing/Msg. Forwarding	Focus Node Mobility	Network Size	Community Dynamics	Node Relation-ship
P2P	*Application*	*YES*	*NO*	*HIGH*	*HIGH*	*LOW*
MANET	*Network*	*YES*	*YES*	*LOW–MEDIUM*	*MEDIUM*	*HIGH*
Opp. network	*Application*	*NO*	*YES*	*LOW*	*MEDIUM*	*LOW*

is the missing routing support in opportunistic networks. This corresponds to the low (maybe even nonexistent) relationship between nodes and the missing incentives and reliability among nodes. The medium community dynamics in both, MANETs and opportunistic networks, reflects the fact that nodes need to be physically present at a certain location in order to take part in the network. This location may vary. For example, a node may be seen at different city spots, but not change arbitrarily. At the bottom line, opportunistic networks are a little closer to MANETs than to P2P.

OPPORTUNISTIC NETWORK APPLICATIONS

With the *best effort* functionality of opportunistic networks in mind, one could identify two main application domains:

1. **Active Collaboration (AC):** AC exploits the physical proximity of users. In addition to the exchange of digital information with users nearby, this allows for use of the device as a *link* to the user him or herself. Via nonintrusive user notification, such as for example, a subtle device vibration, users are made aware of each other. This may lead to *face-to-face* collaboration, for example, a conversation or pursuing a common goal in the real world.

    Active Collaboration has the advantage that the user's knowledge does not need to be stored on the device as a whole. A short summary or some keywords are sufficient.

Deeper knowledge about a topic may be exchanged by other means, after an initial contact between users has been made by their devices.

2. **Passive Collaboration (PC):** PC collects and passes any kind of information from and to other users within communication range. This happens *without any* user interaction. Passive collaboration leads to autonomous information dissemination. In other terms, it is a form of digital *word-of-mouth* communication, for example, similar to the way rumors spread by word-of-mouth.

    Since user devices act without user control and interference, an incentive scheme might be crucial for application acceptance due to the fact that users share private resources (memory, battery, CPU). Otherwise, a user might not be interested in taking part in an application at all. In addition, depending on the application and the shared information, privacy preserving mechanisms may also be an important issue.

    For passive collaboration, most work is the subject of research and focuses on data dissemination mechanisms. We will compare selected research contributions in the section "Passive Collaboration" and show similarities in approaches.

    The active collaboration domain is already populated by a number of technically mature prototypes and commercial products. The next section, without claiming to be exhaustive, lists a number of systems to illustrate the usefulness and variety of active collaboration.

197

Active Collaboration

The following applications focus on mutual device and thus mutual user awareness in order to stimulate active collaboration:

- **Lovegety** (Iwatani, 1998) is a small mobile device to introduce people to each other that happen to be in close proximity (approximately 5 meters). The device knows three different states. Whenever another device is found that is set to the same state, both devices beep and the holders may search for each other.
- **SpotMe** (Shockfish SA Switzerland, 2003) is a collaboration system and tool for conferences, symposia, corporate meetings, and the like. Using a special purpose handheld device, users are able to search for interesting conversation partners nearby. The device allows users to exchange information in a spontaneous manner A SpotMe device is personalized during a registration process. This step includes taking a photo of the attendee and other contact information. The information is stored on the device itself but also in a database for post event services. On the spot, users can query this database. Thus, they learn who is participating. The so-called *radar* function allows a user to scan all other attendees in a range of 30 meters. With this information, a user is able to identify the people sitting nearby at lunch. A user can specify special interest in another user. The device will then give a notification when this other user is nearby. This may help to start a conversation.
- **Nokia Sensor** (Nokia, 2005) is a Bluetooth based application for Nokia cellular phones. A user specifies a profile on the device, for example, taste in music, and allows other Nokia Sensor users to search for her device. This allows people to form spontaneous social circles or instant communities and

networks. In addition, it allows users to share files. Using Bluetooth, the communication range is limited and thus only users in walking distance see each other.

Passive Collaboration

Most work in the passive collaboration domain has focused on data dissemination between mobile and wireless connected nodes. We will compare selective work now.

Datta, Quarteroni, and Aberer (2004) describe a selective information dissemination mechanism called *autonomous gossiping* (A/G) for mobile, wireless connected mobile devices. Devices own a profile that expresses a user's information interest. A device profile is modeled as a set of fixed categories. This profile is advertised, that is, broadcast locally to surrounding devices. In addition, each data item owns a profile. A profile for a data item is described as a tuple of its categories, its utility value, and its target location. A so-called *similarity* function is used for the replication and migration decision respectively.

A data item tries to identify suitable nodes for migration or replication based on its own profile and the node's advertised profile. The underlying idea reflects an ecological and economic paradigm. Mobile nodes form habitats for the data items. The data items compete among themselves for limited resources, for example, device memory.

Görgen et al. (2005) describe an information dissemination protocol based on *single hop* communication between mobile devices. Devices form single hop peer-to-peer overlay networks according to interest in certain information categories. A simple quiz game application called *UbiQuiz* shows the feasibility of their communication scheme. In UbiQuiz, a user has to answer questions that are either stored on the device or received from other users devices. The application aims to help students preparing exams. New questions are collected in a software component called *InformationPool*. Questions and interest in questions are put in the *InformationGate*, another component that manages outgoing messages in a FIFO manner. UbiQuiz makes use of user profiles to express interest in certain question categories.

Khelil, Becker, Tian, and Rothermel (2002) investigate an epidemic model for information diffusion in MANETs. Inspired by the way an infectious disease spreads among individuals; a mobile node is either in *susceptible* state or in *infective* state. A susceptible node has interest in an information entity and an infective node has already received an information entity and passes this entity further to other susceptible nodes.

Summarizing, all authors make use of node profiles, with the work of Khelil being a subtle variation. In Khelil's work the profile is implicit, that is, all nodes are interested in all information entities. The next section discusses another profile based data dissemination mechanism in greater detail.

Example: Data Dissemination in *iClouds*

iClouds (Heinemann, Kangasharju, Lyardet, & Mühlhäuser, 2003b; Heinemann, Kangasharju, Lyardet, & Mühlhäuser, 2003a) is another opportunistic network reference architecture and prototype developed at the Telecooperation Group, Computer Science Department, at Technical University of Darmstadt. iClouds support active and passive collaboration applications.

We will now look more closely at the profile based data dissemination mechanisms proposed in *iClouds*. For this purpose, an iClouds node maintains a node profile that consists of the following components, so-called *information lists* (iLists):

- **iHave-list (information have list):** The iHave-list holds all the information the node wants to contribute to other nodes. A single entry on the iHave-list is called an information item.

- **iWish-list (information wish list):** In the iWish-list, the node specifies what kind of information it is interested in. A single entry on the iWish-list is called information wish or wish.

The proposed data sharing protocol is based on exchanging information lists between connected nodes. Items on the iWish-lists are matched against items on the iHave-lists. Given a match, information items move from one iHave-list to the other.

Consider two nodes, Alice and Bob, who meet on the street. When the nodes discover each other, they might exchange their iHave-lists and match them locally against their iWish-lists. If an item on Bob's iHave-list matches an item on Alice's iWish-list, her device will transfer that item onto her iHave-list.

For two nodes that are in communication range, there are two communication methods for transferring the iLists. Nodes can either *pull* the iLists from other nodes or they can *push* their own iLists to nodes they encounter. In addition, either of these two operations is applicable to both lists, which gives us four distinct possibilities of communication.

In each of the four cases shown in Table 2, the matching operation is always performed on the peer who receives the list (Alice's in pull and Bob's in push). Each of the four possible combinations corresponds to some interaction in the real world:

- **Standard search:** *Alice pulls iHave-list from Bob.* This is the most natural communica-

Table 2. Information flow semantics (from Alice's point of view)

	Pull (from Bob)	Push (to Bob)
iHave-List	Standard search	Advertise
iWish-List	Active service inquiry	Active search

tion pattern. Alice asks for the information stored on Bob's device and performs a match against her information needs (specified in her iWish-list) on her device. We can also see the user as just passively "browsing" what is available.

- **Advertisement:** *Alice pushes her iHave-list to Bob.* This is a more direct approach. Alice gives her information items straight to Bob and it is up to Bob to match this against the things he is interested in. As an example, consider an Information Sprinkler mounted on shopping mall doorways transmitting advertisements to customer devices when they enter the building.

- **Active service inquiry:** *Alice pulls iWish-list from Bob.* This is similar to shopping clerks. They learn at an early stage what their customers are interested in. An example of this query could be: "Can I help you? Please show me what you are looking for".

- **Active search:** *Alice pushes her iWish-list to Bob.* With active search, we model the natural "I'm looking for X. Can you help me?" question. This is similar to the standard search mechanism, except that the user is actively searching for a particular item, whereas in the standard search the user is more passive.

Depending on where and how the matching occurs, we distinguish three different sub-classes of data dissemination. These are presented below:

Information Pass

The basic mechanism is called *information pass* and is illustrated in Figure 3. As the name suggests, some information is passed from one node to another. For this, the following conditions must be fulfilled:

- Nodes must be within communication range

Figure 3. Information pass

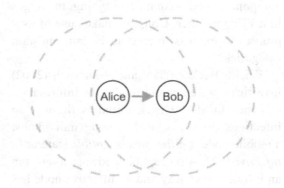

- Node Alice offers information that node Bob is interested in.

For any two nodes that are within communication range, we can conclude that the nodes are in close proximity at the same time. Basically, they are at the same place at the same time. According to the information exchange protocol used, two nodes match their profiles. If an entry on the iHave-list of Alice matches an entry on the iWish-list of Bob this entry (information) is passed from one node to the other.

In Figure 3, Alice is in communication range to Bob and passes information to Bob (indicated by the arrow). This may also happen in the other direction simultaneously.

Time-Shifted Information Pass

A variation of *information pass* is called *time-shifted information pass*. This mechanism uses an Information Sprinkler enabling users to share information who are at the same place but at a different time. As an example, consider a user Alice who goes to a local coffee bar at 10 a.m. every morning. User Bob visits the same place each afternoon. Alice and Bob will never meet and thus come into communication range while visiting that coffee bar. In this situation, the installation of an Information Sprinkler helps. The sprinkler is set up in the bar and collects all information of users visiting the bar. This allows

Figure 4. Time-shifted information pass

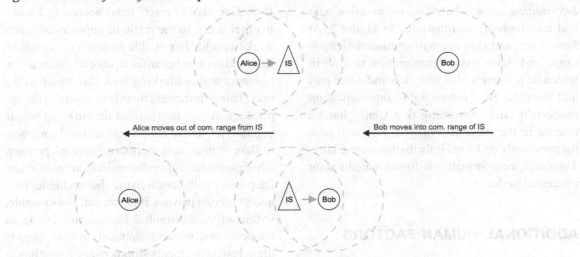

Alice to leave her information at the sprinkler in the morning and Bob to learn about this information from Alice in the afternoon. Figure 4 depicts this mechanism.

In order to reduce communication costs and storage capacity at the Information Sprinkler, the mechanism might be optimized in the following way. Bob leaves his information wishes at the sprinkler. Later Alice asks the sprinkler for new wishes and matches these against her information.

Figure 5. Information move

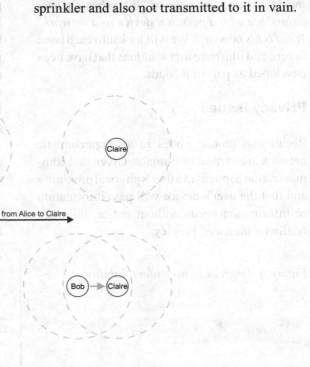

Then, the successful matches are passed from Alice to the sprinkler. Assuming, that Bob visits the coffee bar in the afternoon and his information wishes have not changed since the last visit, the sprinkler can now pass the information from Alice to Bob. Therefore, storage for information that Bob is not interested in is not wasted at the sprinkler and also not transmitted to it in vain.

Information Move

Information move is based on *information pass* and user mobility as illustrated in Figure 5. At first, Alice and Bob are within communication range and Alice passes information to Bob in which he is interested. Then, Bob and Alice part and later on Bob comes into communication range of Claire. Assuming that Claire has an interest in the same information, Bob will pass the previously collected information on to Claire. Therefore, the information is disseminated among interested nodes.

ADDITIONAL HUMAN FACTORS

Since humans are heavily involved in opportunistic networks, this section covers two advanced issues, namely privacy and incentives. User privacy is an important issue since opportunistic networks are formed by humans carrying a *personal* device and potentially pass sensitive information. In addition, the use of a personal device leads to incentive issues in terms of *"Why should a user contribute with a personal device to a network? What is his benefit?"* We will look into each issue in turn and illustrate first solutions that have been developed as part of iClouds.

Privacy Issues

Recall that mobile nodes in an opportunistic network are carried by humans. Given that communication happens in a user's physical proximity and that the user's device will pass information or information needs without notice, this may conflict with users' privacy.

Privacy is the ability of a user to prevent information about herself from becoming known to other users. In the realm of opportunistic networks it should be possible for a user to express an information need or offer a piece of information to others without linking back this action to the user. This requirement mainly depends on the application. An application that aims to bring people together (cf. active collaboration) needs one way to identify users and, therefore, to breach privacy, while pure information dissemination applications (cf. passive collaboration) may have a higher user acceptance, if privacy is protected. For example, within adPASS (Straub & Heinemann, 2004), an opportunistic network application that spreads digital advertisements among users, a user has to express her interest in a certain kind of product. As regards user acceptance of adPASS, it makes a difference, whether an observer learns that *"A user in my vicinity is interested in DVD players"* or *"A user named Alice in my vicinity is interested in DVD players"*. The second statement leads towards learning something about Alice. If it is possible to link this information to, for example, her postal address, this could be used to estimate her living standards and so on. Whether this extra information is purely used to offer Alice additional accessories for her DVD player or it is used for other more dubious actions is irrelevant at this point. Privacy protection should be an integral part of opportunistic network applications.

In order to breach the user's privacy, data gathered has to be linked to the human being in the real world. This involves identifying the person.

Figure 6. Degrees of user identifiability

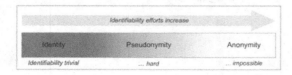

Figure 7. Anonymity strategy

```
activeNodes := 0;
for each node in communication range do
  if (node is alive) then
    activeNodes++;
  if
done
if (activeNodes > k) then
  /* start taking part in OppNet application */
else
  /* stay silent */
endif
```

There are three distinct degrees of classifying user identifiability as depicted in Figure 6:

- **Identity:** A user that communicates with others and reveals any piece of information that can be used to clearly identify him is said to work under his *identity*. Examples are the full name of a user (if not too common) or his social security number.
- **Pseudonymity:** This is the ability to prove a consistent identity without revealing a user's real identity, instead using a *pseudonym*. This is very frequent on the Internet, for example in chat rooms or with electronic mail. Users are free to choose a nickname as a pseudonym and identify themselves with that.

  Whether a pseudonym can be linked to the real identity of a user depends on a variety of factors. For example, while it may be impossible for you to identify other members in a chat room, this may be trivial for an Internet Service Provider.

  The harder it is to reveal the pseudonym of a user, the closer we are to the state of not being identifiable at all, thus acting anonymously.
- **Anonymity:** Anonymity is the ability to remain unidentifiable within a set. A user acts *anonymously* if it is impossible to reveal his identity.

Different applications demand different degrees of user identifiability. In addition, some applications may ask for anonymity and provableness

simultaneously. The incentive scheme presented in the next section depicts such an example. In order to achieve these goals, an adPASS node combines 3 technical solutions that correspond well with *one-hop* communication:

- *A node waits for a minimal amount k of users in its proximity before taking part in information sharing (goal: anonymity).* This approach is outlined in Figure 7.

If there is a minimal set of nodes active at the same place and time, it's harder for an attacker to deduce the source of a certain piece of information or interest in a certain piece of information respectively.

- *A node changes its network identifier frequently (goal: anonymity).* Since the network is based on *one-hop* communication and does not use routing or any other multi-hop message exchange, it is feasible for a node to generate its network identifier by itself and to change this identifier periodically. Thus, it is harder for an attacker to map communication behavior to one particular node over the course of time. This approach also defeats user movement tracking that would otherwise be possible with a unique device id once an attacker has revealed a user's name.
- *A node uses asymmetric key-pairs as aliases (goal: anonymity and provableness).* A node generates a set of asymmetric key-pairs. Each message exchange is tagged with a

Figure 8. Incentive scheme: Basic idea

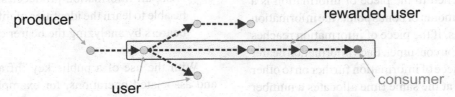

public key as an alias and signed with the corresponding private key. A signing operation, in which the private key is used, may be carried out later to prove the legitimate ownership of the public key.

The next section presents the incentive scheme used in adPASS. It is based on self-generated asymmetric key-pairs that allow anonymity and provableness, at first sight two contradictory issues, to coexist.

Incentive Scheme: An Example

Opportunistic networks exploit private resources of users, mainly battery power and device memory, so the question arises why a user should take part in an application at all?

An obvious benefit for the user is the potential fulfillment of his information needs. The device collects only information the user is interested in. In return, this information is shared with others.

In addition, opportunistic networks can be extended with an incentive scheme to stimulate and thus increase user participation. In short, the proposed incentive scheme allows users to gain some kind of benefit in the form of bonus points by passing information on to other users. We now present the basic idea, roles and security issues.

Basic Idea and Roles

The incentive scheme rewards users who partly help to carry a piece of information from an *information producer* to an *information consumer*.

Figure 8 illustrates this. There are several roles: An *information producer* passes information to an *information bearer* in communication range. Attached to the piece of information is a maximum amount of bonus points the information bearer issues, if the piece of information reaches an information consumer. Each information bearer passes the piece of information further on to other bearers and at the same time allocates a number of bonus points for himself. The information is passed on from node to node until it reaches an *information consumer* that uses the information for his benefit. Thus, all nodes framed in the box (Figure 8) are rewarded by the information producer since they helped in bringing them together. For this purpose, the allocated bonus points are utilized. The set of nodes framed in the box is called a *bearer chain*.

Security Goals and Solutions

The incentive scheme raises a number of security issues. We will discuss the most important ones.

- **Authentication:** For all nodes taking part in the incentive scheme, *authentication* of a piece of information provides the nodes with assurance that the information was issued by the claimed information producer and not forged. This prevents nodes from sharing their personal resources in vain, since the information producer commits himself to issue a reward.

- **Nonrepudiation:** This goal prevents an information producer from denying that he has issued a certain piece of information.

- **Integrity:** First, the information itself, for example, price information about an advertised product, should be kept safe from manipulation. Second, the integrity of the bearer chain that holds information about the bonus point claims needs to be ensured.

- **Anonymity:** Information bearers should be able to take part in the incentive scheme without revealing their identities to each other. This would hold off an attacker from being able to create user profiles of that person's preferences and protects a user's privacy. Also, an information producer should not be able to learn the identities of information bearers by analyzing the bearer chain.

With the use of a public key infrastructure and associated operations, for example, digital signing of information, the relevant security goals are solved.

First, the use of a public key infrastructure allows network nodes to authenticate information. For this, an information producer m is required to use a key pair (P_m^-, P_m^+) that is certified by a certification authority (CA) under a certain policy. The certificate $Cert_{P_m^+}$ issued for the public key P_m^+ is called a *qualified* certificate. For a qualified certificate, the identity of the public key owner is verified in the real word. Now, during the initial dissemination of information π, an information producer m binds his certificate to π and signs both:

$$S_{P_m^-}(\pi, Cert_{P_m^+}) := P \qquad (1)$$

From now on, this tuple is called payload P. Whenever a node receives this payload, it is able to check whether:

1. The information π was issued by m and no one else.
2. The information π was not modified during the dissemination process. For example, the price of an advertised product has not been altered.

Thus, (1) and (2) hold as long as the signature verification succeeds. Second, it derives from (1) that authentication and nonrepudiation is achieved and from (2) follows information integrity.

If an information producer does repudiate the dissemination of a piece of information, the

relevant information bearer and information consumer need to take legal action. Here, the usage of qualified certificates will help them to prove their claims.

To prevent a malicious node from manipulating the bearer chain, a chain from node m (information provider) to node c_{i_k} (information consumer) via nodes c_{i_0} to $c_{i_{k-1}}$ (information bearer) is secured by the following equation:

$$[S_{P_m^-}((P_m^+, P_{c_{i_0}}^+, b_{m,c_{i_0}})),$$
$$S_{P_{c_{i_0}}^-}((P_{c_{i_0}}^+, P_{c_{i_1}}^+, b_{c_{i_0},c_{i_1}})),$$
$$S_{P_{c_{i_1}}^-}((P_{c_{i_1}}^+, P_{c_{i_2}}^+, b_{c_{i_1},c_{i_2}})), \qquad (2)$$
$$...$$
$$S_{P_{c_{i_{k-1}}}^-}((P_{c_{i_{k-1}}}^+, P_{c_{i_k}}^+, b_{c_{i_{k-1}},c_{i_k}}))]$$

Here $b_{c_{i_l},c_{i_m}} := b(c_{i_l}, c_{i_m})$ denotes how many bonus points c_{i_0} passes to c_{i_1}. The general structure for one entry in the bearer chain is

$$(S, R, b) \text{ signed by } S \qquad (3)$$

where S is an alias for the sender, R is an alias for the receiver and b is the number of bonus points passed from S to R. Both sender and receiver use public keys as aliases. With the difference that the first sender, i.e., the information producer, uses the public key certified in the payload P (cf. equation 1), all other participants in the chain use a public key out of a set of self generated key pairs as an alias. This method enables a participant to stay anonymous within the bearer chain and, at the same time, allows a participant to rightfully claim bonus points later on. The proof of possession of the corresponding private key is used here.

Table 3 summarizes techniques employed in order to achieve the desired security goals. Note that most of the techniques are based on public key cryptography, which in turn demand sufficient CPU power on a mobile device.

Due to lack of space, this section does not cover all incentive scheme aspects. The bonus point redemption and usage that introduces a trusted

Table 3. Summary of protection goals and techniques

Goal	Technique
Integrity	Digital signature operation
Authentication	Certificates
NonRepudiation	Qualified signatures and certificates
Anonymity	Multiple key pairs as aliases

third party called *mediator* is not covered. For a complete description see (Straub & Heinemann, 2004; Heinemann, Ranke, & Straub, 2004; Heinemann et al., 2003a).

RESEARCH OUTLOOK

Research in opportunistic networks is still in its infancy and raises a number of research questions that have not been discussed in this chapter. We will mention three of them here:

Since opportunistic network applications rely on a user profile, there needs to be an elegant and effortless way to fill this profile with useful data. Given the limited user interface of mobile devices, a user will probably not wish to type in his detailed taste in music by providing a list of all band names etc.

The usage of user recommendation and trust mechanisms might be needed to avoid the dissemination of useless of deliberately incorrectly labeled data. But given the highly volatile nature of opportunistic network applications, that is, users might encounter each other just once in a lifetime, will trust mechanisms work?

Finally, given an application is a success, this soon would ask for sophisticated and fine grained filtering mechanisms to keep the application useful by filtering out unwanted information.

REFERENCES

Aldunate, R., Nussbaum, M., & Gonzalez, R. (2002). An agent-based middleware for supporting spontaneous collaboration among co-located, mobile, and not necessarily known people. In *Proceedings of the Workshop on Ad-hoc Communications and Collaboration in Ubiquitous Computing Environments',Conference on Computer Supported Cooperative Work (CSCW)*.

Bluetooth SIG Inc. (2003-2005). *The official bluetooth membership site*. Retrieved October 14, 2007, from http://www.bluetooth.org

Datta, A. (2003). MobiGrid: Peer-to-peer overlay and mobile ad-hoc network rendezvous - A data management perspective. In *Proceedings of the Caise 2003 Doctoral Symposium, In Conjunction with the 15th Conference on Advanced Information Systems Engineering*.

Datta, A., Quarteroni, S., & Aberer, K. (2004). Autonomous gossiping: A self-organizing epidemic algorithm for selective information dissemination in wireless mobile ad-hoc networks. *Lecture Notes in Computer Science, 3226*, 126-143.

Ding, G., & Bhargava, B. (2004). Peer-to-peer file-sharing over mobile ad-hoc networks. In *Proceedings of the 2nd IEEE International Conference on Pervasive Computing and Communications-Workshop on Mobile Peer-to-Peer Computing*.

Goel, S. K., Singh, M., & Xu, D. (2002). Efficient peer-to-peer data dissemination in mobile ad-hoc networks. In *Proceeding of the International Conference on Parallel Processing Workshops* (pp. 152-158).

Görgen, D., Frey, H., & Hutter, C. (2005). Information dissemination based on the en-passent communication pattern. In *Proceedings of the Kommunikation in Verteilten Systemen (KIVS 2005)* (pp. 129-141).

Hayes, A., & Wilson, D. (2005). Peer-to-peer information sharing in a mobile ad hoc environment. In *Proceedings of the Sixth IEEE Workshop on Mobile Computing Systems and Applications (WMCSA'04)* (p. 154-162).

Heinemann, A., Kangasharju, J., Lyardet, F., & Mühlhäuser, M. (2003a). Ad hoc collaboration and information services using information clouds. In T. Braun, N. Golmie, & J. Schiller (Eds.), *Proceedings of the 3rd workshop on applications and services in wireless networks, (ASWN 2003)* (pp. 233-242). Bern, Switzerland: Institute of Computer Science and Applied Mathematics, University of Bern.

Heinemann, A., Kangasharju, J., Lyardet, F., & Mühlhäuser, M. (2003b). iClouds—Peer-to-peer information sharing in mobile environments. In H. Kosch, L. Böszörményi, & H. Hellwagner (Eds.), *Proceedings of the 9th international euro-par conference, (EURO-PAR 2003)* (Vol. 2790, p. 1038-1045). Klagenfurt, Austria: Springer.

Heinemann, A., Ranke, J., & Straub, T. (2004). Zur rechtsverträglichen Technikgestaltung anhand einer M-Commerce-Anwendung. In K. Pousttchi & K. Turowski (Eds.), *Mobile Economy—transaktionen, Prozesse, Anwendungen und Dienste, Proceedings zum 4. workshop mobile commerce* (Vol. P-42, pp. 162-177). Augsburg, Deutschland: GI.

Hoßfeld, T., Tutschku, K., & Andersen, F.-U. (2005a). Mapping of file-sharing onto mobile environments: Enhancement by UMTS. In *Proceedings of the Mobile Peer-to-Peer Computing MP2p, In Conjunction with the 3rd IEEE International Conference on Pervasive Computing and Communications (PERCOM'05)* (pp. 43-54).

Hoßfeld, T., Tutschku, K., & Andersen, F.-U. (2005b). Mapping of file-sharing onto mobile environments: Feasibility and performance of eDonkey with GPRS. In *Proceedings of the Wireless Communications and Networking Conference, 2004 (WCNC 2005)*

Hu, Y. C., Das, S. M., & Pucha, H. (2003). Exploiting the synergy between peer-to-peer and mobile ad hoc networks. In *Proceedings of Hotos'03: 9th Workshop on Hot Topics in Operating Systems* (p. 37-42).

Hui, P., Chaintreau, A., Gass, R., Scott, J., & Crowcroft, J. (2005). Pocket switched networking: Challenges, feasibility, and implementation issues. In *Proceedings of the Autonomic communication* (Vol. 3854).

Hui, P., Chaintreau, A., Scott, J., Gass, R., Crowcroft, J., & Diot, C. (2005). Pocket switched networks and human mobility in conference environments. In *Proceedings of the WDTN '05: Proceeding of the 2005 ACM SIGCOMM Workshop on Delay-Tolerant Networking* (pp. 244-251).

IEEE (1999). *IEEE 802.11 wireless specification, ISO/IEC 8802-11*. Retrieved October 14, 2007, from http://standards.ieee.org/getieee802/802.11.html

Iwatani, Y. (1998). *Love: Japanese style*. Retrieved October 14, 2007, from http://www.wired.com/news/culture/0,1284,12899,00.html

Khelil, A., Becker, C., Tian, J., & Rothermel, K. (2002). An epidemic model for information diffusion in MANETs. In *Proceedings of the MSWIM '02: Proceedings of the 5th ACM International Workshop on Modeling, Analysis, and Simulation of Wireless and Mobile Systems* (pp. 54-60), New York, NY.

Klemm, A., Lindemann, C., & Waldhorst, O. P. (2003). A special-purpose peer-to-peer file sharing system for mobile ad hoc networks. In *Proceedings of the IEEE Semiannual Vehicular Technology Conference (VTC 2003-Fall)*, Orlando, Florida.

Klemm, A., Lindemann, C., & Waldhorst, O. P. (2004). Peer-to-peer computing in mobile ad hoc networks. *Performance tools and applications to networked systems: Revised tutorial lectures* (Vol. 2965, pp. 187-208).

Kortuem, G. (2002). *A methodology and software platform for building wearable communities*. Unpublished doctoral dissertation, University of Oregon.

Kortuem, G., Schneider, J., Preuitt, D., Thompson, T. G. C., Fickas, S., & Segall, Z. (2001). When peer-to-peer comes face-to-face: Collaborative peer-to-peer computing in mobile ad hoc networks. In *Proceedings of the First International Conference on Peer-to-Peer Computing (P2P'01)* (p. 75-93).

Kortuem, G., Segall, Z., & Thompson, T. G. C. (1999). Close encounters: Supporting mobile collaboration through interchange of user profiles. In H.-W. Gellersen (Ed.), *Handheld and ubiquitous computing, first international symposium, HUC'99* (Vol. 1707, pp. 171-185) Karlsruhe, Germany.

Leguay, J., Lindgren, A., Scott, J., Friedman, T., & Crowcroft, J. (2006). Opportunistic content distribution in an urban setting. In *Proceedings of the Chants '06: Proceedings of the 2006 SIGCOMM Workshop on Challenged Networks* (pp. 205-212).

Lindemann, C., & Waldhorst, O. P. (2002). A distributed search service for peer-to-peer file sharing in mobile applications. In *Proceedings of the 2nd International Conference on Peer-to-Peer Computing (P2P 2002)* (p. 73-80), Linköping, Sweden.

Lindemann, C., & Waldhorst, O. P. (2005). Epidemic data dissemination for mobile peer-to-peer lookup services. *Peer-to-peer systems and applications* (Vol. 3485, p. 435-455). Springer Verlag.

Nokia (2005). *Nokia sensor.* Retrieved October 14, 2007, from http://www.nokia.com/sensor

Pelusi, L., Passarella, A., & Conti, M. (2006). Opportunistic networking: Data forwarding in disconnected mobile ad hoc networks. *IEEE Communications, 44*(11), 134-141.

Schollmeier, R. (2001). A definition of peer-to-peer networking for the classification of peer-to-peer architectures and applications. In *Proceedings of the 1st International Conference on Peer-to-Peer Computing (P2P 2001)* (pp. 101-102), Linköping, Sweden.

Schwotzer, T., & Preuss, T. (2002). Knowledge exchange in spontaneous networks - Towards ubiquitous knowledge. In *Proceedings of the E-World Syria- From Technology to e-Business (ET2EB 2002)*.

Scott, J., Hui, P., Crowcroft, J., & Diot, C. (2006, January 18-20). Haggle: A networking architec-

ture designed around mobile users IFIP WONS 2006. Les Menuires, France (invited paper). In *Proceedings of the IFIP WONS 2006*.

Shockfish SA Switzerland (2003). *The SpotMe homepage.* Retrieved October 15, 2007, from http://www.spotme.ch

Straub, T., & Heinemann, A. (2004). An anonymous bonus point system for mobile commerce based on word-of-mouth recommendation. In L. M. Liebrock (Ed.), *Applied computing 2004. In Proceedings of the 2004 ACM Symposium on Applied Computing* (pp. 766-773). New York: ACM Press.

Wikipedia - The Free Encyclopedia (2005). *Mobile ad-hoc network.* Retrieved October 15, 2007, from http://en.wikipedia.org/wiki/Ad-hoc_network

Xu, B., Ouksel, A., & Wolfson, O. (2004). Opportunistic resource exchange in inter-vehicle ad-hoc networks. In *Proceedings of the 2004 IEEE International Conference on Mobile Data Management (MDM'04)* (pp. 4-12).

ADDITIONAL READING

Aalto, L., Göthlin, N., Korhonen, J., & Ojala, T. (2004). Bluetooth and wap push based location-aware mobile advertising system. In *Proceedings of the 2nd International Conference on Mobile Systems, Applications, and Services* (pp. 49-58).

Almeroth, K. C., & Garyfalos, A. (2004). Coupons: Wide scale information distribution for wireless ad hoc networks. In *Proceedings of the IEEE Global Telecommunications Conference (Globecom) Global Internet and Next Generation Networks Symposium* (pp. 1655-1659).

Anastasi, G., Borgia, E., Conti, M., & Gregori, E. (2004). Wi-Fi in ad hoc mode: A measurement study. In *Proceedings of the Second IEEE Inter-*

national Conference on Pervasive Computing and Communications (PerCom'04) (pp. 145-155).

Awerbuch, B., Patt-Shamir, B., Peleg, D., & Tuttle, M. (2004). Collaboration of untrusting peers with changing interests. In *Proceedings of the EC '04: Proceedings of the 5th ACM Conference on Electronic Commerce* (pp. 112-119).

Bassoli, A., Moore, J., & Agamanolis, S. (2004). tunA: Synchronized music-sharing on handheld devices. In *Adjunct Proceedings of UbiComp 2004 Sixth International Conference on Ubiquitous Computing.*

Bassoli, A., Moore, J., & Agamanolis, S. (2006). Consuming music together: Social and collaborative aspects of music consumption technologies (Vol. 35), *Computer supported cooperative work.* Springer Verlag.

Beale, R. (2005). Supporting social interaction with smart phones. *IEEE Pervasive Computing, 4*(2), 35-41.

Becker, C., Bauer, M., & Hähner, J. (2002). Usenet-on-the-fly – Supporting locality of information in spontaneous networking environments. In R.Liscano, & G. Kortuem (Eds.), *Workshop on ad hoc communications and collaboration in ubiquitous computing environments.* New Orleans: ACM Press.

Borg, J. (2003). *A comparative study of ad hoc & peer to peer networks.* Unpublished master's thesis, University College London, Faculty of Engineering, Department of Electronic & Electrical Engineering.

Chaintreau, A., Hui, P., Crowcroft, J., Diot, C., Gass, R., & Scott, J. (2006). Impact of human mobility on the design of opportunistic forwarding algorithms. In *Proceeding of the IEEE INFOCOM 2006.*

Coatta, T., Hutchinson, N., Warfield, A., & Wong, J. (2004). A data synchronization service for ad hoc groups. In *Proceedings of the IEEE Wireless Communications and Networking Conference (WCNC),* (Vol. 1, pp. 483–488).

Conti, M., Gregori, E., & Turi, G. (2004). Towards scalable P2P computing for mobile ad hoc networks. In *Proceedings of the Second IEEE Annual Conference on Pervasive Computing and Communications Workshops* (pp. 109-114).

Crowcroft, J., Gibbens, R. J., Kelly, F. P., & Östring, S. (2004). Modeling incentives for collaboration in mobile ad hoc networks. *Performance Evaluation - Selected Papers from the First Workshop on Modeling and Optimization in Mobile, Ad Hoc and Wireless Networks (WiOpt'2003), 57*(4), 427-439.

Dammer, S. M., & Hinrichsen, H. (2003). Epidemic spreading with immunization and mutations. *Physical Review E, 68*(016114).

Davies, N., Cheverst, K., Mitchell, K., & Friday, A. (1999). Caches in the air: Disseminating tourist information in the guide system. In *Proceedings of the IEEE Workshop on Mobile Computing Systems and Applications, 1999 (WMCSA '99)* (pp. 11-19).

Duran, A., & Shen, C.-C. (2004). Mobile ad hoc P2P file sharing. In *Proceedings of IEEE Wireless Communications and Networking Conference (WCNC)* (Vol. 1, pp. 114-119).

Eugster, P. T., Guerraoui, R., Kermarrec, A.-M., & Massoulie, L. (2004). Epidemic information dissemination in distributed systems. *IEEE Computer, 37*(5), 60-67.

Garyfalos, A., & Almeroth, K. C. (2004). Coupon based incentive systems and the implications of equilibrium theory. In *Proceedings of the IEEE International Conference on E-Commerce Technology* (pp. 213-220).

Golle, P., Leyton-Brown, K., Mironov, I., & Lillibridge, M. (2001). Incentives for sharing in peer-to-peer networks. In *Proceedings of the Electronic Commerce: Second International Workshop,*

(WELCOM). Lecture Notes in Computer Science (Vol. 2232, pp. 75-87).

Huang, E., Crowcroft, J., & Wassell, I. (2004). Rethinking incentives for mobile ad hoc networks. In *Proceedings of the PINS '04: Proceedings of the ACM SIGCOMM Workshop on Practice and Theory of Incentives in Networked Systems* (pp. 191-196).

Kindberg, T. (2003). The zen of everyday encounters: Spontaneous interaction in ubiquitous systems. *Lecture Notes in Computer Science, 2795*, 15-16.

Lueg, C., & Mahmood, O. (2004). Hochschulverband für Informationswissenschaft [Combining mobile data transport and mobile data recharging to address public transport information maintenance problems in rural and remote Australia]. *Proceedings des 9. Internationalen Symposiums für Informationswissenschaft(ISI 2004)*, volume 42 of *Schriften zur Informationswissenschaft* [In *Proceedings of the Information Zwischen Kultur und Marktwirtschaft]*.(pp. 337-348).

Mannak, R., de Ridder, H., & Keyson, D. V. (2004). The human side of sharing in peer-to-peer networks. In *EUSAI '04: Proceedings of the 2nd European Union symposium on Ambient intelligence* (pp. 59-64).

Neyem, A., Ochoa, S. F., Pino, J. A., & Guerrero, L. A. (2005). Sharing information resources in mobile ad-hoc networks. *CRIWG* (Vol. 3706, pp. 351-358). Springer.

Papadopouli, M., & Schulzrinne, H. (2000). Seven degrees of separation in mobile ad hoc networks. In *Proceedings of the IEEE Conference on Global Communications (GLOBECOM)* (pp. 1707-1711), San Francisco, California.

Pentland, A., Fletcher, R., & Hasson, A. (2004). DakNet: Rethinking connectivity in developing nations. *Computer, 37*(1), 78-83.

Ranganathan, A., & Campbell, R. H. (2002). Advertising in a pervasive computing environ-ment. In *WMC '02: Proceedings of the 2nd international workshop on Mobile commerce* (pp. 10-14). ACM Press.

Ratsimor, O., Finin, T., Joshi, A., & Yesha, Y. (2003). eNcentive: A framework for intelligent marketing in mobile peer-to-peer environments. In *Proceedings of the ICEC '03: Proceedings of the 5th International Conference on Electronic Commerce* (pp. 87-94).

Rudström, Å., Svensson, M., Cöster, R., & Höök, K. (2004). MobiTip: Using bluetooth as a mediator of social context. In *Proceedings of the UbiComp 2004: Ubiquitous Computing: 6th International Conference, Adjunct Proceedings (demo)*.

Tamminen, S., Oulasvirta, A., Toiskallio, K., & Kankainen, A. (2003). Understanding mobile contexts. *Lecture Notes in Computer Science, 2795*, 17-31.

Teng, C., Chu, H., & Hsu, J. (2004). Making use of serendipity: A new direction for pervasive ccomputing from a sociological view. In *Advances in pervasive computing* (pp. 303-308). Austrian Computer Society (OCG).

Terry, M., Mynatt, E. D., Ryall, K., & Leigh, D. (2002). Social net: Using patterns of physical proximity over time to infer shared interests. In *Proceedings of the CHI '02: CHI '02 Extended Abstracts on Human Factors in Computing Systems* (pp. 816-817).

Winer, D. (2000). P2P is bigger. RetrievedOctober 15, 2007, from http://davenet.scripting.com/2000/09/13/p2pIsBigger

Zurita, G., & Nussbaum, M. (2006). An ad-hoc wireless network architecture for face-to-face mobile Collaborative Applications. In *Architecture of Computing Systems—ARCS 2006: 19th International Conference, Frankfurt/Main, Germany, March 13-16, 2006 Lecture Notes in Computer Science*, (Vol. 3894, pp. 42-55).

Chapter X
Smart Items in Real Time Enterprises

Zoltán Nochta
SAP Research, SAP AG, Germany

ABSTRACT

This chapter deals with the idea of how—as we call them—"smart items" can contribute to the overall vision of the real time enterprise by utilizing ubiquitous computing (UC) technologies. First, an overview of functionality is given that smart items can offer to improve enterprise business processes. The discussed capabilities making everyday objects or goods "smart" are grouped into categories called Information Storage, Information Collection, Communication, Information Processing and Performance of Actions. This is followed by an overview of ways in which enterprise businesses processes can profit from these capabilities. The consistent and reliable integration of smart items into traditional enterprise software systems requires the implementation of a middleware layer. An important goal of the middleware is to hide technology specifics of ubiquitous computing systems from the applications that rely on them. The approach described is service orientation which allows the consistent encapsulation and standardized usage of the required functionality in a given business process.

INTRODUCTION

As you may know, in today's enterprises many business processes are supported by software systems. Just think of a system that automatically orders machine spare parts ensuring continuous production, and at the same time optimizes warehouse utilization and asset costs of the given company. Traditional enterprise software systems rely on manual collection of data. Since manual data collection is in many cases error prone (think of mistyped product codes, for example), software systems often do not have the correct information

to take the best decisions in a given situation. Consequently, this has a negative effect on the quality of the business processes they implement. Examples are delayed order fulfillment, trouble with customers, increasing storage costs, or out of stock situations.

When using UC technologies, this situation can be improved: UC technology may help the company capture the status of the enterprise more adequately, or even exactly in the ideal case, and represent in software systems what is happening in reality.

To reach this goal, physical items of the real enterprise environment, such as machine spare parts, and also warehouse shelves and gates, can provide some "smart" functionality extending the entire software system landscape down to the point of action. For example: When arriving at or leaving the warehouse, machine spare parts can automatically reveal their identity to the respective warehouse gate without any human interaction. Based on this information, warehouse inventory can always be up-to-date, helping avoid the "out of stock" nightmare.

To turn this vision into reality, there are many technical problems to solve. This includes the seamless integration of UC technologies and devices into companies' overall IT system landscape. There are many different ways to achieve this goal. In this chapter we stress a service-oriented middleware approach that helps span the technological gap between smart items and the targeted enterprise software systems.

The chapter is organized as follows: First, we take a closer look at smart items and categorize their functionality they can offer for business processes. This is followed by a definition of the term business process and the description of generic ways that business processes can profit from smart items functionality. Afterwards we motivate the service-oriented handling and integration of UC technologies in real enterprise environments. An important technical prerequisite for that is the implementation of a proper middleware layer, which we will describe in detail. Special emphasis will be placed on how to invoke and execute services provided by one or more smart items. Another aspect will be how services can be deployed and managed during all day operation.

SMART ITEMS

Continuous technological progress towards cheaper, smaller and faster hardware enables the construction of miniature computers that can be embedded in real world objects (Mattern, 2005). The resulting "smart items" consist of a physical component (that is the object itself) and an information-processing component, which enables the object to act in some sense intelligently.

There is a broad range of possible smartly acting things, including funny toys or components of intelligent homes. In enterprise environments—which we focus on—some possible objects include:

- Production machinery components
- Transport and storage containers, such as bottles, boxes, or pallets
- Shelves in warehouses or on shop floors
- Buildings including doors, gates, or rooms
- Any product items, including consumer goods
- Vehicles, such as trucks, cars, locomotives, air planes, or any of their parts

"Smart" items or more precisely, the miniature computers attached to or embedded into them, should provide functionality useful for the given business. Therefore, in order to complete the definition of what a smart item is, and thus what it is good for, we collected and classified the most relevant functionalities smart items can offer in five main categories. These are information storage, information collection, communication, information processing, and performance of actions.

It is important to note that a smart item can offer any meaningful subset and combination of these functional elements depending on given requirements, technical possibilities and affordable costs.

Information Storage

In companies operating with traditional information systems, data about business objects is usually stored in large centralized databases. Normally, there is no direct linkage between a physical object and the backend datasets associated with it. Smart items can help to change this situation and establish the linkage by storing and revealing information either about the object itself, or its environment.

The information an item stores can be pre-determined and static, or it can be dynamically updated during the life cycle of the item. Depending on requirements, different types of memory components might be used to store the respective data, such as read-only, write-once-read-many, or write-many-read-many memory modules. Descriptive information about objects can also be stored in printed labels, such as linear barcodes or two-dimensional data matrices. However, compared to smart tags the storage capacity of such printed labels is very limited.

The most relevant static information a smart item can hold and reveal is its identifier (Strassner & Schoch, 2002). Identifiers or names can be used to uniquely distinguish between single items of the same type of object (item-level identification). Once objects are identifiable, companies can determine their current position and also trace their movements. In many cases, however, it might be sufficient to determine only the type of the given object without knowing its exact identity (product-level identification).

There are many standardized numbering schemas for both item and product level identification. One example in this area is the Electronic Product Code (EPC) with a typical length of 96 bits. Its main application area currently is to track and trace movements of boxes or pallets through a supply chain (Schuster, Stuart & Brock, 2007).

Besides identity, that is, name, objects can store more static descriptive information about themselves, such as weight, color, manufacturer, price, or expiry date. If the item's memory is capacious enough, whole documents, for example manuals or repair instructions, may be stored as well.

Furthermore, smart items can be knowledgeable about their semantic relationships with other items. Important relations to mention are "consists of", "is part of", or "is a" (Römer & Schoch, 2002). A production machine made up of several parts could know what parts it consists of, for example, by storing the list of identifiers of its components. Conversely, each smart part of a machine could know which machine it belongs to. We can also think of machines that know the items they are currently processing (this dynamically changing relationship could be named as "working on") or trucks that know exactly what they are transporting.

An example of dynamically changing information a smart item can store is its history. In many application scenarios it is useful to have information about things that happened to an item in the past. For example, a machine can store its long-term maintenance history to monitor its aging process, or the list of buildings where it was installed.

Information Collection

A smart item may also be able to autonomously gather information either about itself, or its environment. Observation of the different dynamically changing parameters is carried out with various sensors that have to be integrated with the computer held by the object:

- **Location:** One of the most important observable parameters of a potentially moving item is its location. By knowing the identifier and current location of a given object, huge potential for optimizing business processes opens up. Some practical examples are: Based on real time location information of multiple moving assets in a company, maintenance processes can be optimized. Smart items can observe in a collaborative way whether storage regulations are met at a certain location. Movements of smart goods along supply chains can be monitored, and the resulting location information can help detect illicit trading activities, such as diversion of pharmaceuticals.

The concept of location, however, comes in many different flavors. Important location properties are absolute position in a given coordinate system and orientation. Depending on the needs of the application, the required accuracy of location must also be determined. For example, to locate trucks on the road, geographic position data delivered by a GPS system is of appropriate accuracy. Whereas locating objects within a warehouse requires much more accurate location methods, such as the usage of ultrasonic waves, or ultra wide band radio waves. For more details on location techniques please refer to the chapter "A Focus on Location Context".

Besides the ability to determine objects' locations in many cases, it is of interest to monitor their physical state. Measured by appropriate special sensors, temperature, speed, acceleration, motion, pressure, humidity, pressure, light intensity, or mechanical stress might be of interest.

- **Temperature:** Temperature sensors can be used to monitor the conditions of products during transport or storage. This is important for temperature sensitive, dangerous, or perishable goods. The information about a product's temperature history might be used to adjust the expiry date or to decide about the disposal of items.
- **Acceleration:** Some products, for instance hard drives, might be sensitive to acceleration rates and be damaged if the acceleration during transport is too high. The acceleration information might be used to prove who (e.g., carrier or distributor) is responsible for those damages.
- **Speed:** It is also possible to determine the speed at which items travel or are transported. This can be used for calculations about arrival time and resource optimization, or in cases where goods are damaged because they were transported too slowly, to prove who caused the damage.

- **Motion:** Abstracting from the concepts of speed, acceleration, and also location, a business process might be interested in the simpler fact of whether an item is currently moving or not.
- **Pressure:** Monitoring the pressure, for instance within chemical drums, is useful to determine transport and storage conditions, to prevent damage caused by too much pressure and to find the responsible party if a damage occurs.
- **Humidity:** Humidity sensors attached to an item can help monitor the condition of food, for example the humidity in a "smart" ham.
- **Light intensity:** Sensors measuring light intensity can be used to monitor the state of photo chemicals. Using them it is also possible to detect intruders in a sealed smart box, a container, or a room, by detecting that the item was opened when light intensity inside of it changed.
- **Mechanical stress:** Mechanical stress values, such as vibration, are of importance for preventive or condition-based maintenance applications.

With today's sophisticated sensor technology it is also possible to determine and continuously monitor chemical properties of goods, mainly of fluids and gases. It is feasible to determine their composition and also the presence of chemicals residing in a "smart" sensor equipped container, room, or a chimney. This information can be useful for emissions management or also to monitor chemical processes that take place in a barrel or container during transportation or storage and which may lead to dangerous compounds.

Communication

A fundamental capability of smart items is, of course, the ability to communicate. Communication, that is, information exchange between two or more parties, is required whenever an item should interact either with other items in its surroundings, or with a business software system.

- **Item-to-item communication:** In the majority of smart items systems known to us, items communicate with each other wirelessly, but wired solutions can also be found in practice.

In wireless systems, usually radio waves over various frequency bands are used as communication medium. Other examples of media used to transmit information wirelessly are light waves, such as infrared light, and also sound waves.

Data exchange between items is usually message-based, whereas messages can be sent and received in a unicast, multicast or broadcast manner.

From the logical topology viewpoint, smart items can form decentralized peer-to-peer networks, i.e., networks without a master node that controls traffic. In those systems smart items also implement data routing mechanisms to find the best hop-by-hop path between sender and receiver. However, there are also examples for centralized star topologies with a central message hub, and also ring as well as bus topologies are used. Communication protocols used in smart items systems are highly vendor and standard specific. Consequently, items supporting a specific communication protocol cannot interact with other items designed for using another protocol. For more details on communication aspects in smart environments please refer to the chapter "Wireless & Mobile Communication" and to the chapter "Peer2Peer Networks".

- **Communication with the outside world:** To ensure smart items' connectivity to enterprise processes there is a need to abstract from the medium, protocol, and topology used on the technical item-to-item level.

Application developers are interested in exchanging information with the items in a transparent and at best standardized way, instead of having to deal with various proprietary protocols.

Information exchange between applications and smart items can be implemented by following the request-response scheme. Typically, the application is the requesting party. It expects responses from the items either in a synchronous, or an asynchronous mode. In the first case, the targeted smart items have to guarantee a certain response time, since the requesting application will wait until the response arrives. An example for request-response communication is querying one or more sensor equipped smart items for previously measured room temperature values in a building.

Another common way of interaction is sending unidirectional messages from smart items to the backend system. These messages are important building blocks of notification and alerting scenarios. In an example case, a smart room would only contact the backend system when the room temperature has reached or exceeded a certain pre-configured threshold. Notification-based scenarios are often combined with publish-subscribe mechanisms: A fire alarm application may subscribe to receive an alert when temperature reaches a critical higher value. A heating regulation system can be informed about relatively slight room temperature changes.

Information Processing

With the increasing number of smart items in a given environment especially the problem of how to handle the amounts of collected data may arise. In order to overcome such problems, smart items might (pre-) process the gathered information autonomously. Based on information processing capabilities provided by an integrated microprocessor or microcontroller, smart items may also adapt their state or behavior to the current context and environmental conditions. For instance, an item can automatically determine its expiry date in accordance with monitored storage conditions.

The basic set of functionality needed to process information comprises arithmetic and logical operations, and the capability to compare values. Statistical computations directly carried out by the item may also be of interest. These help handle a series of values of a given parameter over time, such as to determine the average time of operation of a machine part, which can be useful for preventive asset maintenance and error diagnosis purposes.

In addition to computational tasks, items may also be requested to aggregate the potentially huge amounts of data they collect. The aim of data aggregation can be to deliver only the piece of information required by the relying business process. This can also be supported by filtering, i.e., the selection of data based on rules and conditions. For example, for a business process ensuring food quality, only warehouse temperatures higher than five degrees centigrade are of interest. In such cases, items equipped with temperature sensors would filter out, that is, not communicate, any other measured value.

Information processing can also be carried out in a distributed and collaborative manner. Think for example of multiple items in the same room, each equipped with light, sound, and temperature sensors. Based on the measured values, items can jointly find out whether there is an intruder in the room. In such application cases, single items only provide fragments of the data required to make the respective decision and draw conclusions, such as to alert the police.

Performing Actions

Some smart items are not only able to capture and process information, but also to actively change their own state or the state of the real world by performing physical actions. This capability becomes obvious when considering embedded systems, which are specifically designed to operate and control real-world objects, for example, to change the room temperature or to adjust the rotation speed of an engine. Proper actuators allow smart items to actively perform movements, for example, in response to changing environmental conditions. Smart items can also interact with human beings: human readable information may be shown on a display and optical or acoustic warnings can be issued.

BENEFITS FOR BUSINESS PROCESSES

Many competing definitions exist for business processes in the literature; see, for example (Davenport, 1993; Hammer & Champy, 1994; Scheer, 2006; van der Aalst, van Hee, & Houben, 1994). The aim of business processes is to use and transform input resources, such as materials, energy, information, manpower, and so forth, in order to achieve a measurable business relevant outcome. In a particular business area a process outcome may be a physical product or a service, but it can also be an intermediate component which contributes to the creation and delivery of products or services, either directly or indirectly. A business process can be seen, that is, modelled as a sequence of logically related process tasks, called activities or subprocesses.

An example business process in the context of a high-tech company is the assembling of computers from components delivered by different suppliers. Such a company typically also runs several other interlinked business processes, for instance to manage its supplier network, customer relationships, warehouses, or the monthly transfer of its employees' salaries.

Enterprise software systems are used to plan, execute, and monitor the company's business processes. For example, the previously mentioned

Figure 1. Smart items usage patterns

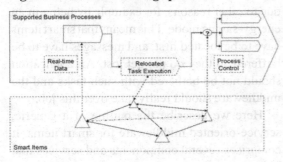

company can run a software system to allow customers to define their favorite hardware configuration via the Internet. Receiving an order might trigger the related production lines including the linked warehouse management systems. These can send orders to the company's suppliers early before the given component is out of stock.

The usage of smart technologies can motivate several changes within a given process landscape and thus can lead to useful modifications in the application logic of existing systems. Here we discuss three different usage patterns called *Real time Data Delivery, Process Control* and *Relocated Task Execution* as shown in Figure 1:

- **Real time data delivery:** In many application cases, back-end processes need a huge amount of information about the current or even past status of business relevant items or their environment. In those cases, smart items basically collect and deliver data in near to real time to the backend systems. Here, smart items play the most passive role from the business process execution point of view.

- **Process control:** Since smart items are placed at the point of action, there is potential to influence and indirectly or directly control the flow of the supported business processes that are implemented by backend systems. Depending on the current situation and context, as it is "seen', for instance, by distributed sensors, smart items can autonomously provide decisions to start or stop the right process at the backend at the right time.

- **Relocated task execution:** The most complex usage pattern allows for well-defined parts, i.e., task or sub-processes, of the business process to be directly executed by smart items. The term "execution" basically means that data collection and transformation steps corresponding to the relocated process tasks are completely carried out by (collaborating) smart items.

One important technical prerequisite of the utilization of the previously described smart functionality is to connect smart items to the enterprise software systems. A possible way to do so is to offer smart items functionality by means of services. In our concept, a smart items service *does:*

- Support a given, well-defined *Functionality* for the relying application,
- Provide a well-defined *Interface* that the Service can be called/invoked through,
- Run transparently from the user's point of view (*Black-Box*),
- Not depend on the context or state of other services (*Independency*).

The executable part of a service, that is, a piece of software code executed by a smart item, is called the service executable. Once a given service is executed, the corresponding copy of the service code is called service instance.

A SMART ITEM MIDDLEWARE

When a backend system talks to a smart item, in fact it talks to the device that is embedded in the real product. However, a direct connection is impossible in most cases, since the machines on which an application is running use different protocols and communication channels than the smart items. Most smart items do not have a USB plug that can be easily connected to a workstation. Despite the fact that both kinds of systems are computing platforms, there are huge differences between them regarding their computational capabilities, energy and storage resources, user interfaces, and system management support. The task of a smart items middleware is to provide a bridge across this gap and seamlessly integrate both worlds.

One of the most important problems such a middleware has to address is the issue of how to address smart items from within an application. First, the application has to learn which smart items exist at all. The middleware provides an inventory containing a long list of smart item network addresses (for example, in IPv6 format), but which of them are relevant to the application in the current situation? The middleware should also support an application in finding out the important ones. Once they are identified, service calls, responses, and notification messages in different formats have to be routed back and forth between them and the application. However, smart items are

mobile or may be unavailable to communication due to other reasons, for example by being in an energy-saving mode. This means that smart items have to be located first, and messages have to be buffered so they do not get lost. An application should not be bothered with such tasks and the middleware should really take over this job.

Here we describe the outline of a generic, service-oriented middleware for smart items. It comprises several components and services that hide the details of smart item device management and communication while providing applications and their developers with all the necessary interfaces to interact with smart items. We concentrate on the part that covers functionality common to most device platforms that are used for smart items. Necessarily, there will be components that are unique to certain platform architectures. We will describe their interfaces and the functionality they must provide, but their inner workings will be subject to the requirements of a specific vendor.

We describe the components of the middleware in terms of services, that is, loosely coupled, distributed components providing explicitly stated functionality through well-defined interfaces. Accordingly, the functionality of smart items

Figure 2. Smart items middleware component overview

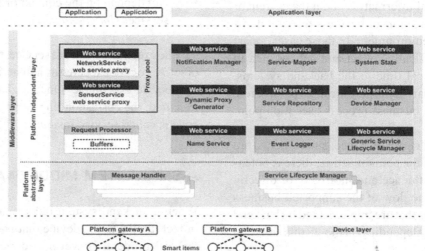

is also described in terms of services. Smart items and services are in an *n:m* relationship: A smart item can provide a variety of services, and a specific service may be implemented on a multitude of smart items. We do not consider the set of services implemented by a smart item as fixed per se. Rather, we assume the point of view that the functionality of a smart item can be updated and adapted to the needs of the context it is currently being used in.

The major active components of our example middleware are the following, see Figure 2:

- **Device Manager:** The Device Manager keeps a list of all registered smart items that may be available in the network. For each entry in the list, it stores a record of data describing the type and the capabilities of the respective device, such as its identifier (network address), hardware architecture, amount of memory, offered functionality, system software version, and so forth. New entries can be entered manually, or by discovery mechanisms that automatically register devices that appear in the network (e.g., UPnP, see the subsequent section).
- **System State:** A component which we call "System State", keeps track of the operational state of smart items. This may include information about when the last message from the device was received, whether the last service call could be successfully delivered, at which location the item was last seen, what its current battery level is, or which other items are in its neighborhood.
- **Notification Manager:** The Notification Manager implements a publish/subscribe mechanism for event messages. Smart items continuously monitor their environment and their own state. Whenever a significant change occurs, they emit spontaneous messages. These are collected and filtered by the notification manager and further distributed to interested parties. Applications can reg-

ister themselves for relevant notifications, for example a sudden temperature drop in a certain location.

- **Dynamic Proxy Generator:** In order to make smart items first-class objects in a service-oriented architecture, the Dynamic Proxy Generator creates interfaces over which an application can directly access the functionality of smart items. Proxy generation happens dynamically in the sense that whenever a novel type of service appears in the network, a proxy representing it is instantiated. This view has several implications. First, if an application wants to speak to a specific device, it nevertheless has to invoke a service interface (qualifying the device by its network address). Second, a service may still be callable through its proxy even if no devices implementing it are currently available.
- **Request Processor:** The Request Processor acts as a mediator between service proxies and the device layer. If a smart item is currently not connected to the network, the request processor is able to buffer requests to that device and deliver them when the device reconnects. The Request Processor also selects the correct message handler that is able to process messages for the hardware platform addressed.

The following components implement functionality that is vendor-specific and adapted to the given hardware architecture. They are, however, required to implement standard interfaces in order to interact with other middleware components.

- **Message Handler:** For the supported hardware architectures there are Message Handlers that transform messages into a format required by devices of the targeted hardware platform. For example, messages on upper layers may be encoded in an XML-based format, which is usually too heavy-weight for smart items. Such messages must be converted and may be pre-processed by the message handler. Conversely, messages emitted by smart items must be converted into the more elaborate format before they are passed on to other components.

- **Service Lifecycle Manager:** A Service Lifecycle Manager component can also be associated with a given hardware architecture. This component is responsible for keeping service implementations running on smart items up-to-date. This includes the removal of outdated or superseded implementations. The service lifecycle manager is usually not triggered by common business applications but by dedicated management applications.

- **Platform Gateway:** Platform Gateways establish the physical connection to smart items. These are network bridges translating between different protocols and networking technologies. These are usually not considered as part of the middleware as they are completely vendor-specific and provide no standard interface to other middleware components.

Device Abstraction

There is a wide variety of useful electronic devices, which could be even more useful if they could be integrated into a network where they would be able to exchange data, collaborate, or operate under central control. A popular example is home automation: devices for entertainment (such as audio and video systems), photo printers, lights, and the heating system could all be interconnected and be adapted to the residents' activities automatically or even autonomously. Similar requirements exist in business-oriented environments such as warehouses or factories. A pre-condition for such scenarios is a networking technology that allows the devices to interact with each other and their environment.

Today, the most commonly used network protocols are based on Internet standards such as TCP/IP, HTTP and SOAP. Adding that functionality to devices is relatively inexpensive. Additionally, a network infrastructure, either wired or wireless, is required. However, this basic functionality barely enables devices to communicate on a very basic level which is insufficient, for instance, to make them collaborate in a meaningful way. It is easy to create a message and send it to some device using, for example, HTTP. But before this can be done, two things have to be sorted out: What is the address of the desired target device, and what should the content of the message look like in order to achieve a certain effect? Therefore, additional protocols are necessary for describing and discovering the services being offered by devices and for exchanging data and control messages. They have to abstract from specific features but really provide a homogeneous view on a wide range of device types.

A number of standards exist today that provide the means for describing the capabilities of devices in a unified way. A prominent example is UPnP (Universal Plug and Play) (Jeronimo & Weast, 2003), which is supported, for example, by the Microsoft Windows operating system. UPnP is useful for setting up networks of smart items as well.

As a prerequisite, UPnP requires each UPnP device to have an IP address, which can be dynamically acquired through a DHCP server or via Auto-IP. Devices are then able to communicate in a client/server fashion. There is the concept of control point in UPnP, which is the client side of a device. This concept can be implemented by any device that potentially makes use of the services of other devices. It may be, for example, a DVD player that talks to the video screen. Or, it may be implemented simply as a piece of software running on a PC that controls all the home appliances.

Once all the devices are part of the IP network, UPnP facilitates the following fundamental operations:

- **Discovery:** Multicast messages are used by a device to announce its own sub-devices and services. These announcements are registered by all parties (control points) that are potentially interested in using these services. Control points can also look for devices by issuing search messages via multicasting (using the Simple Service Discovery Protocol, SSDP) (Golden, 2002; Kempf & St. Pierre, 1999). Devices that match the search criteria will then respond directly to the inquiring control point. The most important part of an announcement is the *location* field, which contains a URL referencing the description of the device's capabilities. For more details on service discovery, please refer to the chapter "Service Discovery".

- **Description:** After the discovery phase, a control point retrieves the description of a device and the services it offers. This enables the control point to decide whether the device can be used for a specific task. The device description contains basic information about the device itself, such as vendor-specific information and a URL for retrieving an HTML-based presentation, as well as URLs for controlling the device and retrieving events from it. All services offered by the device are listed and the available actions (including their arguments) and state variables are given. The descriptions must follow a prescribed XML scheme, which is a precondition for working with diverse device types.

- **Control:** This comprises the actual operational phase, where devices talk to each other. A control point making use of a service can do so in two ways. First, the control point can invoke an action that is offered by the service, giving parameters and retrieving results similar to a remote procedure call. The transport protocol for such invocations is SOAP, that is, the messages are XML-encoded. The second type of interaction is querying the state of a service by retrieving the values of its state variables. This is done similarly to an action invocation, but is slightly simpler. During such interactions, errors might occur, such as when an action cannot be performed since the current state of the service prevents it (but the client did not know about it). Therefore, an error code may be returned instead of a valid result, and the client must take appropriate action to deal with the error.

- **Eventing:** By eventing, an asynchronous, continuous type of interaction between a control point and a service is understood, as in publish/subscribe systems (Zeidler, 2004). A service may have special state variables that are "evented" meaning that every time the value of such a variable changes the new state is pushed to the subscribers of the service (subscribers always get the values of *all* evented variables, selective subscriptions are not allowed). UPnP supports all necessary operations for managing subscriptions, that is, the renewal of subscriptions (which have a limited lifetime), and their cancellation.

- **Presentation:** This is an important function for manual interactions with devices. Upon request, a UPnP device returns a HTML page representing a user interface for itself. There, the current state of its services could be displayed, and direct interaction between a user and the services is possible. In the context of smart items, where most interaction takes place without human intervention, this is the least used feature of UPnP.

The emergence of web services as a new paradigm for interaction on the Internet created the desire to facilitate the integration of devices in such environments. Therefore, a new specification has been created, which is supported in the latest version of Microsoft Windows, called Device Profile for Web Services (DPWS) (Microsoft, 2006). Basically, DPWS provides the same functionality as UPnP, which is already service-based, but is more extensible and relies even more on web service technologies.

While UPnP and DPWS have their focus on the communication between control points and devices, and are agnostic to the way the services on a device are implemented, the Open Services Gateway Initiative (OSGi) specification is concerned with the lifecycle management of these services (Osgi Alliance, 2003).

Unlike the others, OSGi is a Java-centered technology, drawing heavily on the dynamic aspects of Java, such as class-loading. It allows the loading of devices with new OSGi bundles, which are Java classes that support a well-specified, OSGi-specific API through which new services can be registered and instantiated, as well as stopped and unloaded. OSGi is thus well suited for Java-enabled devices that require capabilities for updating and extensions. Since UPnP is language-independent, OSGi can be used to manage services that are being offered through UPnP.

Request Processing

The Request Processor component of the middleware shown in *Figure 2* is responsible for the execution of service invocations targeted at device services, i.e., service requests that have to be responded to by smart items, or for which information has to be retrieved from a smart item. Responses may be cached by the Request Processor in order to speed up multiple similar invocations. It therefore checks for every invocation, whether the response from a previous call is already available.

Usually, a web service invocation is carried out by wrapping the service request and response in a SOAP message and performing a SOAP message exchange. This procedure is not entirely sufficient for handling service invocations whose target is located on a smart item. Underlying assumptions may not be met in such an environment, such as connectedness of the service provider (which is

a physical device, in our case). Also, the usual service fault tolerance and recovery mechanisms are not directly applicable to smart items. Request processing for smart items has to take this extended failure model into account.

There are the following failure modes specific to smart items with which the Request Processor has to deal:

- An item may not be immediately available for dealing with a request, for example due to temporary disconnectedness from the network during transportation, or due to other pending requests.
- An item has failed but will recover, for example due to a reset after a software failure. This case is typically not distinguishable from the previous one.
- An item has failed and is unable to recover (e.g., due to battery exhaustion or physical destruction). In such situations there are two basic options:
  1. Another smart item is able to take over the service provisioning for the failed item. Future service requests have to be redirected. This is a typical recovery mechanism in redundant systems.
  2. No other item can take over service provisioning. The service will not be available in the future anymore. An example for such a case would be the failure of a device that is responsible for reporting the temperature in a room, which has been deployed without redundancy.
- A service is not available on, or has been removed from the addressed smart item. This might occur if an application erroneously issues a service request to the wrong item.

The Request Processor has two major mechanisms to react to such failures. The first is buffering requests that cannot be immediately processed, and re-issuing them at a later time, which is de-

Figure 3. Operation of request processor

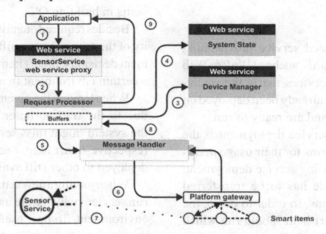

termined based on the assumed recovery time. The second is periodic re-issuing of requests until a response is successfully retrieved. Service requests are not indefinitely re-issued. After a timeout period, the service request is cancelled and the requesting client application is notified about the failure.

The Request Processor has to take precautions against an overloading of its request buffer. If too many requests are pending, new requests are immediately rejected. Applications can retrieve status information from the Request Processor in order to take own measures for avoiding the effects of unsuccessful service invocations, for example by notifying the user early.

The operation of the Request Processor is schematically shown in Figure 3. We describe the control flow during request processing where the steps are numbered according to the figure.

1. A client application invokes a smart item service by issuing a *request* to the respective web service proxy.

2. The request is forwarded to the Request Processor. Here, the request may be buffered if the addressed item is currently not available. After a timeout, the Request Processor assumes that an item has failed and notifies the application of that error.

3. The Request Processor uses the Device Manager to determine which Message Handler is associated with the addressed item. This is necessary since each hardware platform requires a distinct Message Handler.

4. The Request Processor determines the current state of the addressed smart item by consulting the System State component. If the Request Processor finds the state of the item different from what is recorded in the System State, for example, if no answer is received from a supposedly active item, it sends an update to the System State.

5. The service request is eventually handed over to the Message Handler responsible for the addressed smart item.

6. The Message Handler transforms the request message and forwards it to the Platform Gateway.

7. The Platform Gateway sends a message in platform-specific format to the network of smart items, where the message is routed to the addressed node.

8. The response generated by the smart item is routed along the same path as the request, only in reverse direction.

SMART ITEMS SERVICE DEPLOYMENT

The previously discussed service provisioning technologies and standards, such as UPnP or Web Services, assume that services, that is, the executable service code, have already been deployed on the executing devices and are ready to run.

The main task of service deployment is the preparation of smart items for their usage in different applications. During service deployment, service executable code has to be transferred to individual smart items. In order to do so, the question of which smart item should run which services has to be answered. The answer, that is, the automated construction of a proper answer, can depend on domain or application specific constraints, which we highlight below.

An item can be linked to more than one application at the same time, and applications might require the services of multiple smart items, too. For instance, a service providing room temperature data might be of interest for a heating control system and also for an automated fire alarm system within the same company. Obviously, fire alarms should not be raised just because one probably buggy sensor reports heavily increased room temperatures. Instead, such decisions should rely on temperature values sent by more than one item placed at the same location. The required number of service hosting smart items (a.k.a. service coverage) can be expressed in different ways, for example "Service A must run on every smart item within the warehouse", or "Service B can run on five to eight sensor nodes in room P"

or "Service C should run on at least 75% of the items in building Q".

Besides required quantity, the spatial dynamicity of the scenarios can influence service deployment decisions: Smart items might join and leave a certain environment in an ad-hoc manner.

When leaving the given scenario, for instance, due to the transportation of intelligent goods, the system might miss services provided by the respective smart item. Such services have to be deployed to other still available items.

When joining a new setting, a smart item might run services which were used only in its previous environment. To be a useful service provider in the new setting as well an update of the newbie's services is required.

In addition to the above, a smart deployment system should take resource constraints into consideration as well. Smart items have usually very limited computation power and much less memory than a PC, and very importantly a limited battery lifetime. Due to the limited amount of its memory, a single smart item might not run every required service to fulfill the needs of an application. In such cases, if applicable, service functionality can be brought by multiple items, each running a subset of the required service executables. For example, one item might measure and store long-term temperature values, while another item in the same area captures and analyzes humidity data.

By reaching a certain low-power battery status, services running on the item might be redistributed to other items with sufficient energy. This can lead to a prolonged lifetime of the entire smart system.

Figure 4. Service deployment process steps

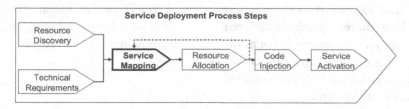

To handle situations sketched above in a systematic way, one can consider the following service deployment process as depicted in Figure 4:

- **Gathering technical requirements:** An important prerequisite to carry out successful service deployment is the collection of technical requirements that the given service needs for proper operation. Obviously, hardware related requirements have to be collected, such as minimum required memory, requested bandwidth of radio module, processor type, required set of sensors, and so forth. Besides required hardware capabilities of single items, further service-specific constraints, such as the required service coverage can be of interest. These requirements can be described by proper metadata attached to service executables. The metadata as well as the service executables are stored in the Service Repository (see *Figure 2*).

  In addition to service-specific requirements, deployment might have to take more global technical constraints into account: A typical requirement (which is usually hard to fulfil) is the maximization of remaining free resources, such as remaining battery or memory, after service executables are deployed on smart items.

- **Resource discovery:** The second necessary input to make deployment decisions is information about currently available capabilities of smart items in a given setting. To provide this information, monitoring of various static (e.g., CPU type, memory size, etc.) and dynamically changing parameters of smart items (e.g., remaining battery, available memory, CPU usage, network load, etc.) is required. It is also useful to see which services a given node actually hosts and which of them are currently running. This information as well as the functionality to

gain it is provided by the component called System State (see *Figure 2*). Continuous monitoring assumes that the items also spend resources on it. Therefore, it seems to be a good strategy to use eventing mechanisms to detect only relevant changes within an already known setting. One example is to raise an event when smart items join or leave the monitored setting. Another event might occur when a critical threshold of (low) battery power is exceeded.

- **Service mapping:** Based on technical requirements and currently available smart items resources determined during the above described preparatory steps, the Service Mapper component provides a set of decisions regarding which nodes can run which service(s).

- **Resource allocation:** In the optimal case, during service mapping a feasible configuration can be found that fulfils all the defined requirements by using available resources. However, service mapping might be unsuccessful due to the lack of available free resources. As a possible consequence, resources need to be re-allocated by actively stopping and/or removing some of the already deployed services. Which service should be sacrificed might depend on previously defined priorities: The service with a lower priority will be stopped; its freed resources will be further used by another service with higher priority.

- **Code injection:** After successful mapping of services to smart items and the allocation of resources, service executables have to be transferred to the corresponding smart items. This step can be implemented in different ways.

One strategy is to establish and use a *centralised* service injection component that sends instructions to individual smart items (e.g., remove Service A and deploy Service B) and, if required, the corresponding code as well (e.g., the service executable code of the new Service B). Clearly, this approach is simple to implement but it is not the best in terms of scalability and fault tolerance. When deploying the same service on multiple items, the same code would be sent multiple times to the target items.

Another approach (that works well in peer-to-peer-like sensor networks) is to instruct items to autonomously "infect" the specified smart items with the service executable code to run. During code infection, smart items can send the received executables to their direct neighbours.

SUMMARY

In this chapter we described and categorized functionality that real world objects may offer, in order to play an active role in enterprise business processes. The resulting smart items can help provide traditional enterprise software systems with real time data directly from the point of action. They can control and trigger the execution of business process tasks depending on their current status as well as the conditions of their surroundings. Furthermore, backend software system functionality can be distributed to smart items, which allows the handling of situations locally without the need of contacting a remote backend system. The integrated usage of smart items in an enterprise setting can potentially lead to reduced processing and transactional costs, to improved response times in business-, or even safety-critical situations, and also to enhanced quality of process results.

Due to the current diversity and incompatibility of the enabling UC technologies with today's enterprise software systems technologies, the consistent, reliable and safe integration of smart items requires the implementation of a middleware layer. Here, we described the architecture and main components of an exemplary middleware that helps hide technology specifics of UC sys-

tems from the respective business applications, in a service oriented way. In particular, service request processing as well as service deployment were discussed in more detail. The middleware approach has already found its applications in several real world trial implementations, such as the cases described in the chapters "PROMISE: Product Lifecycle Management and Information Tracking using Smart Embedded Systems" and "Safer Handling of Hazardous Substances through Automatic Surveillance of Storage Regulations".

FUTURE RESEARCH DIRECTIONS

Research in the systematic and in the same time economically beneficial usage of UC technologies in the enterprise business application area is of course not restricted to the aspects discussed in this chapter.

The potential impact of UC on business processes is enormous, but it is not fully understood yet how the usage of these novel technologies may change the way we build enterprise business software systems. The middleware can help manage communication with heterogeneous smart items systems, deploy the right piece of software on the right items, monitor the overall system, and so forth.

An open research relevant question is how the targeted business software systems may handle the expected high volume of real world data typically transferred in a large number of relatively short messages and guarantee acceptable response times whenever actions on the application side are required. Just imagine a large warehouse with millions of goods. In a critical situation each of those items may report valuable information (which should not be filtered out) to the warehouse management system which has to determine and start the proper action.

Another aspect we would like to highlight is research on modelling allowing application developers to model real world scenarios, such as the movements of goods, their interactions with each other, etc. This would, for instance, allow the (semi-)automated generation of the required executable service code as well as interfaces for both smart items as well as the relying applications.

We also clearly see the need for more research on the systematic creation as well as validation of economically beneficial business cases for smart items in enterprise settings. Systematic approaches can greatly help decision makers see improvements of business processes when they start utilize smart items, such as reduced costs, time, and so forth.

REFERENCES

Davenport, T. H. (1993). *Process innovation: Reengineering work through information technology*. Boston: Harvard Business School Press.

Golden, G. R. (2002). *Service and device discovery: Protocols and programming* (1st ed). McGraw-Hill Professional.

Hammer, M., & Champy, J. (1994). *Reengineering the corporation – A manifesto for business revolution*. London: Nicholas Brealey Publishing.

Jeronimo, M., & Weast, J. (2003). *UPnP design by example: A software developer's guide to universal plug and play*. Intel Press.

Kempf, J., & St. Pierre, P. (1999). *Service location protocol for enterprise networks: Implementing and deploying a dynamic service finder*. John Wiley & Sons.

Mattern, F. (2005). Ubiquitous computing: Scenarios from an informatised world. In A. Zerdick, A. Picot, K. Schrape, J.-C. Burgelman, R. Silverstone, V. Feldmann, Ch. Wernick, & C.

Wolff (Eds.), *E-merging media - communication and the media economy of the future* (p. 145-163). Springer.

Microsoft (2006). *Devices profile for web services*. Retrieved October 16, 2007, from http://specs.xmlsoap.org/ws/2006/02/devprof/devicesprofile.pdf

Osgi Alliance (2003). *OSGi service platform: The OSGi alliance*. IOS Press.

Römer, K., Schoch, T. (2002). Infrastructure concepts for tag-based ubiquitous computing applications. In *Proceedings of the Workshop on Concepts and Models for Ubiquitous Computing, Ubicomp 2002*.

Scheer, A.-W. (2006). *ARIS - Business process modeling* (3rd ed). Springer.

Schuster, E. W., Stuart, A. J., & Brock, D. L. (2007). Global RFID: The Value of the EPCglobal Network for Supply Chain Management. Springer.

Strassner, M., & Schoch, T. (2002). Today's impact of ubiquitous computing on business processes. In Mattern, F., Naghshineh, M. (Eds.), In *Proceedings of the Pervasive computing, first international conference, Pervasive 2002*, Zürich, Switzerland.

van der Aalst, W. M. P., van Hee, K. M., & Houben, G. J. (1994). Modelling workflow management systems with high-level petri nets. In G. De Michelis, C. Ellis, & G. Memmi (Eds.), In *Proceedings of the Second Workshop on Computer-Supported Cooperative Work, Petri Nets and Related Formalisms* (p. 31-50).

Zeidler, A. (2004). *A distributed publish/subscribe notification service for pervasive environments*. Unpublished doctoral thesis, Department of Computer Science, Darmstadt University of Technology, Darmstadt, Germany.

ADDITIONAL READING

Aberer, K., Hauswirth, M., & Salehi, A. (2006a). *The global sensor networks middleware for efficient and flexible deployment and interconnection of sensor networks* (Tech. Rep. No. LSIR-REPORT-2006-006). Laboratoire de Systèmes d'Information Répartis, Ecole Polytechnique Fédérale de Lausanne.

Aberer, K., Hauswirth, M., & Salehi, A. (2006b). Middleware support for the internet of things. In P. J. Marrón (Ed.), In *Proceedings of the 5th GI/ITG KuVS Fachgespräch Drahtlose Sensornetze* (p. 1-6).

Anke, J., Müller, J., Spieß, P., & Chaves, L. W. F. (2006). A service-oriented middleware for integration and management of heterogeneous smart items environments. In B. Koldehofe (Ed.), In *Proceedings of the 4th MiNEMA Workshop in Sintra* (p. 7-11).

Beigl, M., Krohn, A., Zimmer, T., & Decker, C. (2004). Typical sensors needed in ubiquitous and pervasive computing. In *Proceedings of the First International Workshop on Networked Sensing Systems*, Tokyo, Japan: Verlag.

Bornhövd, C., Lin, T., Haller, S., & Schaper, J. (2004). Integrating automatic data acquisition with business processes - Experiences with SAP's auto-ID infrastructure. In M. Nascimento, M. T. Öszu, D. Kossmann, R. Miller, J. Blakeley, & K. B. Schiefer (Eds.), In *Proceedings of the 30th International Conference on Very Large Databases* (p. 1182-1188). Toronto, Canada: Morgan Kaufmann.

Chaves, L. W. F., Anke, J., Souza, L. M. S. de, & Müller, J. (2006). Service lifecycle management infrastructure for smart items. In S. Michiels & W. Joosen (Eds.), In *Proceedings of the International Workshop on Middleware for Sensor Networks* (p. 25-30). New York: ACM Press.

Delicato, F. C., Pires, P. F., Rust, L., Pirmez, L., & Rezende, J. F. de. (2005). Reflective middleware for wireless sensor networks. In L. M. Liebrock (Ed.), In *Proceedings of the 2005 ACM Symposium on Applied Computing* (p. 1155-1159). New York: ACM Press.

Finkenzeller, K. (2003). *RFID handbook: Fundamentals and applications in contactless smart cards and identification* (2nd ed). Chichester, UK: John Wiley and Sons.

Hightower, J., & Boriello, G. (2001). A survey and taxonomy of location systems for ubiquitous computing. *IEEE Computer, 8*(34), 57-66).

Heinrich, C. (2005). *RFID and beyond: Growing your business through real world awareness.* Indianapolis, IN: John Wiley and Sons.

Mouël, F. L., Ibrahim, N., Royon, Y., & Frénot, S. (2006). Semantic deployment of services in pervasive environments. In *Proceedings of the 1st International Workshop on Requirements and Solutions for Pervasive Software Infrastructures*.

Römer, K., Schoch, T., Mattern, F., & Dübendorfer, T. (2003). Smart identification frameworks for ubiquitous computing applications. In *Proceedings of the First IEEE International Conference on Pervasive Computing and Communications* (p. 253-264). Fort Worth, Texas: IEEE Computer Society.

Uribarren, A., Parra, J., Uribe, J. P., Makibar, K., Olalde, I., & Herrasti, N. (2006). Service oriented pervasive applications based on interoperable middleware. In *Proceedings of the 1st International Workshop on Requirements and Solutions for Pervasive Software Infrastructures*.

Weiser, M., & Brown, J. S. (1998). The coming age of calm technology. In P. J. Denning, & R. M. Metcalfe (Eds.), *Beyond calculation: The next fifty years of computing* (p. 75-85). New York: Springer.

Section III
Adaptability:
What is (Not) Context?

Iryna Gurevych
Technische Universität Darmstadt, Germany

Max Mühlhäuser
Technische Universität Darmstadt, Germany

WHAT IS CONTEXT?

According to the Webster's, the word *context* is derived from the Latin *contextus*, which means "connection of words, coherence," and from *contexere* "to weave together." For natural (and formal, see below) languages, the word *context* denotes the parts of a discourse that surround a word or passage and can throw light on its meaning. In a much more general sense, it denotes the interrelated conditions in which something exists or occurs.

In science, the term *context* is relevant to a set of different academic disciplines, such as agent-based and multi-agent systems, artificial intelligence, context-aware applications, linguistics, natural language processing and inter-agent communication, neuroscience, philosophy, psychology, software engineering, ubiquitous computing, World Wide Web and Semantic Web applications.

Many of these disciplines belong to computer science. Specifically, in context-aware computing, we use the term context to refer to *the circumstances under which a specific computational program is being executed,* such as the current occupation of the user while some device is being used, or the current state of the environment.

In the introduction, we will use the term context awareness to denote the property of computer programs to have information about the circumstances under which they operate, and to react accordingly based on the relevant information. In the chapter "Context Models and Context Awareness," a set of formal definitions will be given and discussed in more detail. So far, we will state that context awareness may be of different kinds. The system can adapt to context in the sense of current conditions, or it can adapt to the long-term kind of context, that is, context extended along some temporal dimension, such as user preferences.

WHY IS CONTEXT IMPORTANT?

In ubiquitous computing, context awareness is relevant to various kinds of application scenarios concerned with the presentation of information, execution of actions, or adapting to the user. Context awareness is utilized to design new user interfaces, whereby context-aware devices try to make assumptions about the user's current situation based on their knowledge about the domain or circumstances under which they are operating. For example, a context-aware mobile phone may know that it is currently in a meeting room, and that the user has sat down. The phone may conclude that the user is currently in a meeting and reject any unimportant calls.

Another class of context-aware applications focuses on a business sector as a whole. In this case, ubiquitous computing systems are monitoring some assets, such as goods or equipment. Sometimes, this ability is described by the term *remote asset monitoring*. It provides the capability to network equipment and various devices, collect data about them, and derive some inferences from aggregating the data, for example, about the performance of devices. For example, a specific activity can be triggered upon that to correct a problem or an alert can be sent to the service stuff. Remote asset monitoring can be employed in different application domains, such as oil and gas drilling fields, heating and cooling equipment, manufacturing and retail operations.

In general, modelling and using context in ubiquitous computing appears to be the key to such fundamental problems as explanations tailored to users, the acquisition of knowledge in its context of use, and the learning capability of systems as an intrinsic part of their task. "Context-aware," "context-based," "context-sensitive," or "context-supported" smart devices are the basis for the design and development of intelligent assistant systems. Advanced solutions are needed to apply context, for example, to cope with the fuzziness of context information and especially because of the mobility in rapidly changing environments and unsteady information sources.

HOW TO CREATE "CONTEXT AWARENESS"?

In ubiquitous computing, there exist numerous classifications of context types depending on their specific property as the classification basis. One possible example of such a classification is given in Table 1. This table gives an overview of: (i) different types of context pertinent to ubiquitous computing systems, (ii) the content that they represent, and (iii) the knowledge store where the corresponding information is stored within the system.

Introducing context into ubiquitous computing applications requires the addressing of a number of various issues. Examples of such issues are presented in Figure 1 and will further be explained in individual following chapters.

The first step in building context-aware applications is the acquisition and management of context. Context information about the environment is typically acquired by physical sensors and can be classified into different categories, for example, light, proximity, temperature, mechanical force, and so forth. The acquisition of location context is enabled by the movement and location sensors. Additional sources of location context information are, for example, the Outlook calendar of the user or the processing of visual information. However,

Table 1. Types of context in ubiquitous computing systems

Type of context	Examples of content	Knowledge store
Environment	State of environment, temperature, etc.	Environment model
Location	Place, etc.	Location model
User	Properties of the user	User model
Interaction	Interaction history	Interaction model

Figure 1. Issues in creating context-aware applications

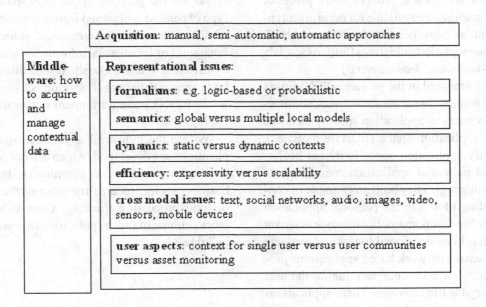

Acquisition: manual, semi-automatic, automatic approaches

Middleware: how to acquire and manage contextual data

Representational issues:

formalisms: e.g. logic-based or probabilistic

semantics: global versus multiple local models

dynamics: static versus dynamic contexts

efficiency: expressivity versus scalability

cross modal issues: text, social networks, audio, images, video, sensors, mobile devices

user aspects: context for single user versus user communities versus asset monitoring

the latter is rarely employed in real-life systems and is still far more in the domain of research due to the complexity of processing. Acquiring and utilizing context information about the user has a lot of different dimensions. Some of them are widely used, such as user profiling; other areas such as recognizing human emotions and moods are also still at the research stage. The model of user interaction is particularly relevant to user-centric ubiquitous computing systems. As the interaction with the system has a dialogic character, previous interactions have to be accounted for during the interaction.

Context acquisition presents a number of challenges, which have to be addressed during the design of context-aware systems. Firstly, context information in ubiquitous computing is typically distributed over heterogeneous devices, which can be either mobile or fixed. Secondly, it is distributed over different domains, such as the

domain of application, the user, and so forth. As a result, various sources of highly dynamic and error-prone information have to be integrated. With an increasing number of context sources and context sensors, large amounts of data are generated. Then, scalability becomes an issue, as the data has to be efficiently transmitted, stored and retrieved. In this case, special middleware has to be employed.

One particular example of such a middleware is the context management framework (CMF) implemented in the project MobiLife (http://www.ist-mobilife.org/). CMF is implemented as an enhanced Web service platform. It is designed to describe, discover and manage context providers, whereby multiple heterogeneous information sources are integrated. Furthermore, selected context elements can be related to context ontologies. One part of the context management framework is the context representation framework. It provides a standard API for context providers, context consumers, and context brokers. Some pieces of implementations are available for rapid prototyping as well as conversion tools and a cookbook with implementation guidelines (http://www.lab. telin.nl/~koolwaaij/showcase/crf/).

The central goal of the project e-SENSE was to build a context-aware sensor network architecture in a variety of application spaces, such as a personal application space (lifestyle assistant), community application space (wireless healthcare), and industrial application space (remote asset monitoring). They built an example of context-building blocks in the personal application space. Within this domain, the lifestyle assistant concept has been developed to test and evaluate wireless sensor network based applications provided through a 3G mobile terminal to the user in her everyday life activities. These applications range from mood-based services, to entertainment and nutrition services.

Table 2 gives an overview of context-building blocks for the personal application space. Each type of context is obtained from the combination of different sources of contextual information. Each source of contextual information is captured by different sensors classified into three types: body sensor networks (BSN), object sensor networks (OSN) and environment sensor networks (ESN).

Within the industrial application space, applications are developed, which are not centered on the user and users' community, but on a business sector, such as the store of the future, or food processing tracking. Context-building blocks enhancing such applications are presented in Table 3.

Table 2. Acquisition of contextual information in personal application space

Category	Context Information	Examples	Sensors	Sensor network
Identity	User Profile	Personal information, biometry	RFID tag, Retina sensor, fingerprint sensor	BSN, ESN
Physiology	Physiological information	Skin conductance	Skin conductance sensor	BSN
		Heart Rate, Heart Rate Variability and Pulse	Heart rate sensor	BSN
		Breathing Rate	Chest strap	BSN
		Facial Muscles	Electromyogram sensor	BSN
Presence and Location	Socio-Psychological information	Number of people around and their relationship	Audio/Video, infrared, RFID tag	BSN, ESN
	Location information	Position	Triangulation	BSN
Mood	Movement information	Orientation	Gyros	BSN
		Position	Triangulation	BSN
		Acceleration	Accelerometer	BSN
		Motion	Motion detector	BSN, ESN
Facial	information	Eyes distance	Camera	ESN
		Eyebrows shape	Camera	ESN
		Mouth shape	Camera	ESN

Table 3. Acquisition of contextual information in industrial application space

Context	Context Information	Context Data	Sensors	Category
Product description	Product information	Content, production date, expiration date, production site, price, number of calories	RFID/bar code reader	OSN
Product Tracking	Movement information	Position	Collaborative localisation	ESN
		Acceleration	Accelerometer	OSN
		Fall	Fall detector	OSN
		Motion	Motion detector	OSN
Product transportation	Stability information	Acceleration	Accelerometer	OSN
		Shock	Shock detector	OSN
		Vibration	Vibration detector	OSN
Load (strain) information	Force	Strain gauge sensors	OSN	
		Weight	Weight sensors	OSN
Environmental Conditions	Environmental information	Temperature	Thermometer	OSN, ESN
		Humidity	Humidity sensor	OSN, ESN
		Location	GPS, 3G/satellite receiver	ESN
		Pressure (air)	Pressure Sensors, barometer	OSN, ESN

STRUCTURE OF PART "ADAPTABILITY"

The part "Adaptability" comprises three chapters. The chapter "Context Models and Context Awareness" presents different definitions of context and discusses the features of context-aware systems in ubiquitous computing. After that, the ways of building context-aware applications and middleware architectures are presented. The chapter "A Focus on Location Context" places a special emphasis on location as an essential type of context for ubiquitous computing systems and discusses location-aware systems in detail. The main topic of the last chapter in this part of the book is adapting to use. Having given an overview of personalization and user modelling, different approaches to adapting the system are discussed there. This involves adapting the user interface and adapting the interaction.

Suggested Further Readings A comprehensive Web site of the context community can be found here: http://context-web.org/. The Web site col-lects information about important events such as conferences, links to bibliographies and further resources.

The Web site http://www.cs.cmu.edu/~anind/context.html contains information about the context toolkit. This toolkit is an example of middleware created to facilitate the development and deployment of context-aware applications. Thus context is understood as environmental information, which is part of an application's operating environment and can be sensed by the application. The Web site provides links to published papers and the documentation accompanying the toolkit.

Several projects funded as part of Information Society Technologies (IST) Program by the European Union are described on their corresponding Web sites:

- e-SENSE, a project that enables capturing of ambient intelligence for beyond 3G mobile communication systems through wireless sensor networks at http://www.ist-e-sense.org/.

- MobiLife, addressing problems related to different end-user devices, available communication networks, interaction modes, applications and services with a strong user-centric focus at http://www.ist-mobilife.org/.
- SPICE (Service Platform for Innovative Communication Environment), working on the still unsolved problem of designing, developing and putting into operation efficient and innovative mobile service creation and execution platforms for networks beyond 3G at http://www.ist-spice.org/.

More theoretical works about modelling and using contextual information in ubiquitous computing systems can be found in the articles by Dey (2001) and Porzel, Gurevych, and Malaka (2006).

REFERENCES

Dey, A.K. (2001). Understanding and using context. *Personal and Ubiquitous Computing Journal*, 5(1), 4-7.

Porzel, R., Gurevych, I., & Malaka, R. (2006). In context: Integrating domain- and situation-specific knowledge. In W. Wahlster (Ed.), *SmartKom: Foundations of multimodal dialogue systems* (pp. 269-284). Heidelberg: Springer Verlag.

Chapter XI
Context Models and Context Awareness

Melanie Hartmann
Technische Universität Darmstadt, Germany

Gerhard Austaller
Technische Universität Darmstadt, Germany

ABSTRACT

To support users in performing their tasks, applications need a better understanding of the current situation they are being used in. This chapter gives an overview of how knowledge of the current context, that is, information characterizing the situation, can be represented and how this knowledge can be used for enhancing applications. We discuss what is actually meant by "context" and "context-aware" applications. Further, we describe what has to be considered when building a context-aware application. We thereby focus on the representation of context information and how to deal with its unreliable nature. This chapter should sensitize the reader to the difficulties of using context information and give guidelines on how to build an application that benefits from knowing its current context.

INTRODUCTION

Humans use all kinds of information characterizing their current situation, like time, location and identity of persons nearby, to adapt their behavior to the situation and to make decisions. For example, when we speak to a person, we adapt what we say and how we say it to the social rank of the person (e.g., most people would not say "that's nonsense" to their boss, but would to a friend). All this information is not easily captured, represented and processed by a computer. However, this information can help to build more user-friendly applications that adapt and respond to the user's current situation. If the computer were aware of the user's context and its interpretation, it would be able to make decisions on behalf of the user, anticipating user needs like another human would. For example, it would be possible to provide the user only with information relevant to the current situation and thus reduce the cognitive load. This is especially necessary in the area of ubiquitous computing (UC), where the user has to deal with a multitude of different computers, and thus with a multitude of possible distractions. To enable all these devices disappear into background, they have to anticipate the user's future demands and adapt to the user's context to reduce the amount of interaction needed.

The word "context" has its origins in the Latin word "contextus" meaning: "to weave together", originally denoting the construction of a text. Nowadays, the term is loaded with a variety of different meanings. According to Merriam-Webster's Collegiate Dictionary, context is defined as "the interrelated conditions in which something exists or occurs". Even in computer science itself, context is used with a number of different meanings. For example, context in context-free or context-sensitive grammars refers to the symbols that surround a placeholder and determine which strings can replace it. In contrast, "context" in the area of context-aware computing refers to any information that can be used to enhance an application, especially the interaction with the user.

The term "context-aware computing" became popular in the middle of the 90s, when researchers started to develop applications that incorporated the current location of users. By then, location-awareness was regarded as the most important subset of context-awareness. These applications used the location as auxiliary information to improve interaction with the user by adapting it to the user's needs; thus context-awareness was more or less regarded as synonymous with adaptivity.

Adaptivity thereby comprises principally:

- Restricting the user interface to the relevant input possibilities and relevant data;
- Adapting dynamically to the user's context how the information is presented and how it can be accessed, for example, use of audio output instead of visual output if the user is currently driving;
- Automating actions for the user, for example, prefilling data.

However, there were also a growing number of applications, such as navigation systems, that did not regard location as auxiliary but rather as mandatory information. These applications require location information in order to provide their normal functionality and cannot operate without this information. As location-awareness was still regarded as a subset of context-awareness, the latter lost its connotation of using auxiliary information for enhancing the interaction. Thus, the term context became even more difficult to define as the discussion in the section "*What is Context?*" illustrates.

Nowadays, context-aware applications go beyond using context for adapting the interaction with the user. For example, they use it as an additional information source for facilitating the later retrieval of data. In the section "*What are context-aware applications?*", we list the various features making an application context-aware. Further, we discuss the difficulties that have to be faced when using context. In the section "*How to build a context-aware application*", we describe the design process for building a context-aware application and show how context information can be acquired, represented, accessed and managed. A middleware can be used to support the developer in building the application. We describe the different layers of such a middleware in the section "*Middleware Architectures*". As context information is highly dynamic and error-prone in comparison to traditional information sources, we have a closer look how to handle uncertainty in context-aware applications in the section "*Dealing with uncertainty*".

WHAT IS CONTEXT?

Which constituents of all this information surrounding us can be used to improve an application and thus should be regard as context for this application? Many researchers have given a definition for the concept of context, but none of them are really widely accepted. In this section, we give an overview of the most commonly used ones.

We illustrate the problem of defining context with an example application of a booking process for train tickets. In Figure 1, we list some information that is available when using the booking application. Some of this information is mandatory

Figure 1. Available information sources when using an example booking application

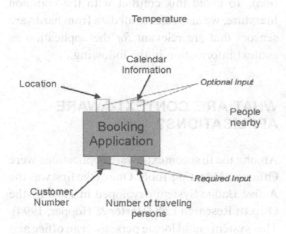

for the normal functionality of the system (the customer number and how many persons want to travel), some information cannot be processed by the application (the temperature and which people are near the user) and some is optional as it is just used as additional information source (the user's current location and her calendar information). The latter information is used to prefill the station of departure and arrival and travel times.

The simplest definitions of context are given by enumerating all constituents of context. For example, Schilit, Adams, and Want (1994) attempted to define context by specifying three categories of context:

- **Computing context:** For example, network connectivity, communication bandwidth, nearby resources like printers, displays;
- **User context:** For example, user's profile, location, emotional state, people nearby, current activity;
- **Physical context:** For example, lighting, noise level, traffic conditions, temperature.

Chen and Kotz (2000) extended this definition by the *time context* (e.g., time of day, season of the year).

A common problem of these definitions is that they do not specify a bound, for which information can be referred to as context. According to these definitions everything that fits into one of the categories can be named context, no matter whether or not it has any relevance for the application. In our example application the temperature and the people nearby would also be referred to as context for the application, even though the application cannot make use of it.

One of the most prominent context definitions (Dey, 2001) solves this problem by limiting the context to all information that is relevant to the interaction between user and application:

Context is any information that can be used to characterize the situation of an entity. An entity is a person, place, or object that is considered relevant to the interaction between a user and an application, including the user and applications themselves.

In our example, all information that can be processed by the application would be referred to as context (see "Relevant Information" in Figure 2). However, the definition has the shortcoming of defining context by means of other ill-defined terms such as "situation" or "relevance". Moreover, it limits the usage of context to the interaction between user and application. Thus, the definition does not take into account applications that do not directly interact with the user, for example a peer-to-peer application that can use additional information like the current load of the peers to adapt the route over which incoming packages are routed.

Another problem that arises from Dey's definition is that even information that the application needs to fulfill its tasks, like in our example the customer number and the number of people traveling, can be referred to as context. Thus, every application could be called context-aware.

To sum up, we need a context definition that defines an upper and a lower bound for what we

Figure 2. Classification of the different information sources from Figure 1

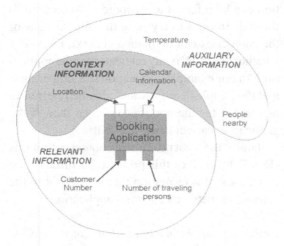

call context of an application. The upper bound is needed to exclude information that is irrelevant for the application, and the lower bound is needed to exclude information that is mandatory for its normal functionality. Therefore, we give our own definition of context that tries to overcome the limitations of Dey's definition:

Context characterizes the actual situation in which the application is used. This situation is determined by information which distinguishes the actual usage from others, in particular characteristics of the user (her location, task at hand, etc) and interfering physical or virtual objects (noise level, nearby resources etc). Thereby, we only refer to information as context that can actually be processed by an application (relevant information), but that is not mandatory for its normal functionality (auxiliary information).

Thus, we refer to context as the intersection of "Relevant Information" and "Auxiliary Information" as visualized in Figure 2.

However, it is common to call applications context-aware that consider location information or any other information retrieved from physical sensors, even if this information is mandatory for

the proper functioning of the application (e.g., a navigation system depends on location information). To avoid this conflict with the common literature, we also refer to all data from hardware sensors that are relevant for the application as context information in the following.

WHAT ARE CONTEXT-AWARE APPLICATIONS?

Among the first context-aware applications were Office and Meeting Tools. One of the first was the Active Badge System developed in 1990 by the Olivetti Research Lab (Harter & Hopper, 1994). This system could locate persons in an office and forward calls to a nearby phone. To locating the people, they used badges that transmitted IR-signals, which were picked up by a sensor network placed around the office building.

Another area for applying context-awareness is memory-aids. They provide the user with context-dependent information, for example by providing notes that might be relevant in the current context (Remembrance Agent by Rhodes (1997)) or by recording where the user is, who the user is with, whom the user phones, and so forth to facilitate later retrieval (Forget-Me-Not by Lamming & Flynn (1994)).

The most popular type of context-aware applications are systems that make use of location information: this comprises applications such as travel guides (e.g., GUIDE system developed at the University of Lancaster (Cheverst, Davies, Mitchell, & Friday, 2000)) or route planning tools.

The difference to traditional applications is on the input-side that they deal with information sources that need special handling, because they are more error-prone, dynamic and heterogeneous than traditional information sources like databases. Due to the dynamic input, the output of the application often also has to be adapted frequently. Thus, the focus of most context-aware applications is the high adaptability that is not the main point of most traditional applications.

Features of Context-Aware Applications

The goal of context-aware applications is to respond to context changes to enhance the computing environment for the user. Similar to the problem of defining the term *context*, researchers have tried to specify the features characterizing a context-aware application. We focus here on a categorization suggested by Dey (2001) and expand it with the feature "Adaptation" that is listed by some other categorizations (Schilit et al., 1994; & Pascoe, 1998):

- *Presentation* of information and services to a user;
- Automatic *execution* of a service for a user;
- *Tagging* of context to information to support later retrieval;
- *Adaptation* of application's behavior and appearance.

In the following, we present these four features of context-aware applications in more detail.

Presentation

An application supporting this feature is able to provide information to the user that is adapted to her context in order to optimally satisfy her current need. Further, it is also possible to display commands or services available in the current context. The presentation of relevant data can be performed proactively by the application or can be triggered by a user request. This feature therefore only focuses on what information is presented and not on how it is displayed.

Examples for this kind of application are tourist guides that provide the user with information depending on her current location, or ContextPhone (Raento, Oulasvirta, Petit, and Toivonen (2005), see Figure 3) that presents context information for the user's contacts (such as

Figure 3. Presentation of context information by the ContextPhone (Raento et al. 2005)

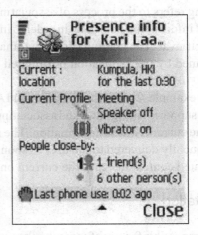

location, phone use activity, people present, and phone alarm profile). Another application is to display reminders depending on the context, for example a context-aware application could inform the user that she had intended to buy bread when she passes a bakery.

Execution

Context-triggered actions can be specified by IF-THEN rules that determine which operations should be automatically executed if the context changes according to the given condition. Here it is very important for this feature to have a predictable behavior; otherwise the user will not feel in control of the system and mistrust the whole application.

An example of the automated execution of an action is the PARCTAB System (Adams, Gold, Schilit, Tso, & Want, 1993): every room is equipped with a virtual workspace, like a virtual whiteboard, that can be used to exchange information between the persons present in the room. Thus, the location information is here used as context. As soon as a person enters a room, the mobile devices are automatically bound to this whiteboard.

Tagging

Tagging refers to the process of associating contextual information with data, in order to improve later retrieval. The tagging can be automatically performed by the application or initiated by the user.

For example, CybreMinder by Dey and Abowd (2000) supports taking notes and associating them with the current context information. The note is subsequently delivered to the user as soon as the associated context matches the current one.

Adaptation

Another possible feature of context-aware applications is to adapt their behavior or their appearance to a given context. The adaptation thereby does not refer to what information is presented, but how it is displayed.

The relevance of the data presented is considered for example in context-aware applications that support the user in searching for physical or virtual objects. These applications therefore emphasize those objects that best fit the current search criteria. An important issue here is how the information can be presented so that its relevance for the user is implicitly visible. One solution is to use different font sizes as illustrated in Figure 4.

Context-aware applications that adapt to the user's situation can, for example, increase the size of buttons on a PDA if the user is wearing protective gloves or they can delay notifications

Figure 4. Example of a user interface technique used for adapting the presentation (adapted from Schilit et al. (1994))

Name	Room	Distance
Paul	S202 / E118	85m
Max	S202 / A113	25m
Iryna	S202 / B103	35m
Daniel	S202 / A124	5m

about occurring events to minimize the adverse effect of an interruption. Deferment thus depends on the user's activity and on the importance of the notification.

Adaptive context-aware applications have to face some problems resulting from frequent context changes. It may be distracting for the user or impractical due to performance issues to adapt to every single change. Further, certain adaptations can lead to confusion, especially if a false context has been reported or if the user is not aware of why the application adapts. Another problem that has to be considered is whether and how the application should adapt while the user is actually interacting with it.

Difficulties in Using Context

Most available applications do not take context into account and existing context-aware applications cover only a very limited number of types of context information, like location. The main reason for this is that context is difficult to use. The following properties distinguish them from most other data sources used in traditional applications:

- Context is gathered from *heterogeneous sources* that are seldom traditional devices such as mouse or keyboard. Most developers have only limited experience with such context sources as, for instance, location sensors.
- Context is *dynamic*: Context changes must be detected in real time and applications must adapt to constant changes.
- Context is *error-prone*: Context is often acquired by external sensors that can get out of reach, completely fail or report unreliable data.

A uniform representation of context information that can be easily exchanged between sensors and applications (discussed in the section "How to build a context-aware application") would help to facilitate working with heterogeneous context sources. When dealing with context information, the application developer has to consider how the system should cope with the uncertainty and inaccuracy of context data. This is relevant if you, for example, deal with several sources to gain information about the same context (e.g., using several detection systems to determine the user's position). Furthermore, it has to be considered that the data loses its validity over time as long as it is not refreshed. This uncertainty of context data is discussed in more detail in the section "Dealing with uncertainty".

Due to the above mentioned properties of context information, the designer of a context-aware application has to take scalability and robustness into account.

- **Scalability** means that the application should be able to cope with a multitude of different sensors and users.
- **Robustness** comprises stability and reliability of results, the ability to adapt to new situations, resistance to frequent changes in the environment, to component failure, and to disturbing factors like noise.

HOW TO BUILD A CONTEXT-AWARE APPLICATION

Several steps have to be performed in order to make an application context-aware. The design process can be defined as follows (adapted from Abowd, Dey, Orr, & Brotherton, 1997):

- **Specification:** What context-aware behavior should be implemented? Which context is required for that purpose?
- **Acquisition:** Which sensors can be used to retrieve this context?
- **Delivery and Reception:** How is the context represented, managed and exchanged?

- **Action:** Which actions should be taken corresponding to the captured context?

We illustrate the design process with a simple example of a context-aware telephone exchange in an office environment. First we have to *specify* our problem being addressed and the context we therefore need:

Example: *Incoming calls should be forwarded to the phone that is closest to the called person. If no information about the current location of the called person is available, the caller is forwarded to the phone at the workplace of the person being called.*

The context needed for this application is the identity of the persons in the office and their locations.

In the following step of the design process, *acquisition*, we need to specify which sensors to use to gain our context data. The categorization of context data and their corresponding sensors is discussed in Section "Context Sources".

The third step, *delivery and reception*, deals with making context information available for the context-aware application. Therefore, we need

- A *representation* for the context information, and we have to define how it should be interpreted (e.g., how the GPS location of a person can be transformed to a room number) or aggregated (e.g., inferring a person's location from the data of various location sensors) (see the section "Context Representation and Inference").
- To specify *access* mechanisms and communicating protocols (see the section "Accessing Context").
- To *manage* the context information (see the section "Context Storage and Management"). This comprises the discovery and location of available context sources, and the context storage to compensate for sensor

failures or to allow later retrieval (context history).

In the fourth and final step, *action*, the developer needs to implement the context-aware behavior that should be performed according to the reported context. The most important steps that are necessary for building context-aware applications are discussed in the remainder of this section.

Context Sources

Most applications use different sources of context information and combine them to gain further context information. Therefore, we distinguish between two types of context information:

- **Sensed context** is information that can be derived by querying physical sensors or applications (virtual sensors). This data is often highly dynamic or at least frequently updated in response to periodic sensor output. Much inaccuracy can arise due to sensing errors or because the context information is completely unknown or stale. Sensors can also fail or networks can become disconnected, leading to a delay in the distribution process of the sensor data.
- **Inferred** or **derived context** is information that is gathered by combining context data. For example, the activity of a person could be inferred by her motions, her location and the people nearby. The persistence and the quality of this data depend on the sensors used as input and on the derivation mechanism.

Context information also varies in the level of *dynamics* and thus, in how often an update is necessary to maintain the quality of the context data. The location of a pedestrian is a highly dynamic context, whereas the ID assigned to a person hardly ever changes. This context informa-

Table 1. Overview of context-types and sensors

Context-type	Sensor
Sensed	Physical
	Virtual
Inferred	Logical

tion that persists almost forever is mostly used to enrich other context data, for example floor plans can be used to convert a GPS coordinate into a symbolic room number.

Context information is captured by sensors, with sensor not only referring to sensing hardware, but to every source that can provide an application with context information. Sensors can be subdivided into three groups regarding the way in which they capture the data:

- **Physical sensors** are hardware sensors that can capture physical data, for example, acceleration, light, noise and location.
- **Virtual sensors** retrieve their context data from software applications or services, for example, by capturing keystrokes, by querying a database or Outlook™.
- **Logical sensors** combine data from several sensors to gain inferred context information. For example, such a sensor can infer from the user's location and the time, that the user is now probably having dinner in the cafeteria.

Thus, physical and virtual sensors provide sensed context, whereas the inferred context is retrieved from logical sensors (see Table 1).

Example: *For simplification purposes, we assume that every room is equipped with exactly one phone. Thus, in order to determine the phone closest to the user, we need the room the user currently resides in. For that purpose, we use a location sensor (physical sensor) called ID-Location Sensor based on an infrared system that assigns user ids to rooms. Further, we need to know which id*

Figure 5. Illustration of the sensors needed for inferring the users' location in our example scenario

belongs to which user. This can be provided by a virtual sensor that provides the static mapping from id to username (Mapping Sensor). The data from these two sensors has to be combined in a logical Person-Location Sensor that delivers the room number for a given username. The required sensors are illustrated in Figure 5.

Context Representation and Inference

After identifying the context information needed and the sensors that could deliver it, we have to specify how context is represented, interpreted and exchanged between different components. Due to the heterogeneity of context sensors and varying requirements of the application, it is often necessary to transform the context information from one representation to another. For example, the user's location can be represented by absolute (e.g., "49°52′ N 8°39′ E"), relative (e.g., "5m north of the sensor") or symbolic coordinates (e.g., "Room S202/A124"). Further, we have to define how inferred context can be derived from the given context information. In this section we give an overview of context modeling approaches and discuss their drawbacks and advantages.

Context Models

A good context model is essential to allow the exchange of context information between different components (and even applications), and for the reusability of the context sensors. The model represents the semantics the components agreed upon that is necessary to understand the context information. Due to the heterogeneity and the wide range of available context data, it is a challenging task to define a context model that covers all types of context.

It is often insufficient to state only the type and value of context information. Additional information comprises:

- **Timestamp** when the context data was sensed. This can be used to create a context history or to determine how fresh and thus how valid the context information is. Furthermore, this information resolves sensing conflicts: If several sensors provide the same context data, but report different values for it, the freshest value can be prioritized.
- **Source** that actually sensed the context data. It can be used to resolve sensing conflicts, for example by preferring data from a specific sensor.
- **Quality** reflects the accuracy and uncertainty of the context information. The uncertainty is due to sensing errors or delays in the context capture. The quality and richness of information can differ among sensors and vary over time.

Besides providing a useful set of attributes, a good context model should allow us to specify relations between pieces of context information, such as the relation "close to".

Another valuable property of a context model is to provide the possibility to state constraints on the context information. These constraints are used to validate both the correctness of its structure and the actual data. Further, the model should address the issues of incompleteness and ambiguity. Most context information used in UC environments is incomplete or ambiguous due to sensor failure or because several sensors provide values for the same context type. For example, a person can be located with several location detection systems (GPS, RFID tags) or even the person's Outlook™ calendar. Therefore, the model should also cover how to cope with such sensing conflicts, and how to gain missing data from other sources, for example, by estimating it from available values.

Moreover, it should be possible to model the context in a modular manner. The encapsulation of parts of the context representation enables the hiding of details of context processing from other components and facilitates the reuse and extensibility of the components.

In the remainder of this section, we present the most relevant context modeling approaches (Strang & Linnhoff-Popien (2004) provide a more detailed overview of these models). Which model to choose depends on the application that uses it. For an application that needs only simple context information and that uses sensors that have only limited bandwidth for transmitting the information, a key-value model would be the right choice. For an application that infers a great deal of context information, a model based on logical expressions would be advantageous. Often several models are combined into a hybrid model. This is also necessary because some models do not necessarily specify a data serialization for submitting the data (e.g., Object Based Models). There exist mappings between several models (e.g., from Ontology Based Models to Logic Based Models). We illustrate each model with the representation of the context provided by the Id-Location Sensor of our example: it reports the room number A12 and the ID 44 (representing a person in this room) with a confidence of 80%.

Key-Value Models

The simplest way of describing context is to model it as a set of key-value pairs. The representation of our example is shown in Figure 6. Such a model is easy to manage, but it does not support rich context information such as specifying attributes of context information or relations between them. Furthermore, it normally does not allow checking

the context data against a model, for example, against allowed ranges, and it is not easily extendible. It is often used in service frameworks to describe the capabilities of a service (see chapter "Service Discovery").

Markup Scheme Models

Markup Scheme Models have a hierarchical data structure consisting of markup tags with an arbitrary number of attributes and content (Figure 7 illustrates a possible XML representation of our example). These models allow type and range checking for numerical values to some degree. For example, a lower and upper bound can be specified, but it is not possible to state that one value has to be greater than another.

Markup Scheme Models are typically used for modeling profiles (e.g., for device capabilities), mostly as XML serializations. The attributes and tags can be interpreted according to their position in the data tree, due to the hierarchical structure of the profiles. Hence, unambiguous naming across the whole model is not necessary.

Ontology Based Models

An ontology consists of concepts or classes (e.g., concept of a room describing all actual rooms in a building), attributes (e.g., name of a room), relations (e.g., located in) and instances (e.g., room A12) (for more details see the chapter "Ontologies for Scalable Services-Based Ubiquitous Comput-

Figure 6. Key-value representation of data from the location sensor (see Figure 5)

```
Room = A12
ID = 44
Confidence= 80%
```

Figure 7. Markup scheme representation of data from the location sensor (see Figure 5)

```
<Location confidence="80%">
    <Room>A12</Room>
    <ID>44</ID>
</Location>
```

ing"). An ontology can be represented in RDF statements (Resource Description Framework). RDF statements consist of triples of the form (subject, predicate, object) and are often serialized as XML representations. A possible ontological representation of our example is illustrated in Figure 8.

The importance of ontologies in computer science has increased in recent years, due to developments like the Semantic Web. The advantage of Ontology Based Models is to provide a uniform way of specifying a model's core concepts. They make it easy to share knowledge between different applications by defining a common vocabulary.

Object Based Models

Object Based Models, such as UML, represent data structures as objects (classes) with different attributes (see Figure 9 for our example representation). The objects can inherit attributes from other objects. Attributes can for their part also consist of objects. Thus, object based models allow the specification of arbitrary attributes, but they do not directly support relations between objects other than the "part-of" and "is-a" relation. However, some of the Object Based Models, like UML, have the advantage that they support global constraints, also on the objects' data.

Object Based Models take advantage of encapsulating and reusing parts of the model to cover

some problems arising from the highly dynamic nature of context data. Many details of data collection and fusion are hidden from higher-level components to simplify the handling of the context information.

Logic Based Models

Logic Based Models build a formal system based on facts (e.g., tall("Peter") stating that Peter is tall), terms (e.g., A∧B, i.e., A and B, or nextTo(A,B) being true if A is next to B) and rules (e.g., A➔B, i.e., if A is true than B is also true) to describe the context information (see Figure 10 for a possible representation of our example). These models are used by adding, updating and deleting context information from the logical system and inferring new context information by applying the specified rules on them. The abstract mathematical properties of such a system are useful for applications in the area of artificial intelligence. However, it does not contain a straightforward representation for any kind of meta-information, like quality attributes.

Context Inference

We illustrate the inference of context with the example of simplified inference in predicate logic,

Figure 9. Object based representation of data from the location sensor (see Figure 5)

Location
Room = A12
ID = 44

Figure 8. Ontology representation of data from the location sensor (see Figure 5). loc: is thereby the namespace of the location sensor (e.g., http://example.com/ontology/location/)

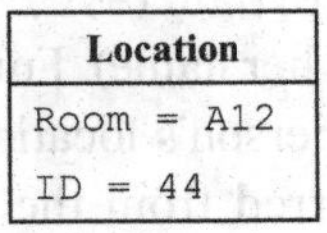

Figure 10. Logic based representation of data from the location sensor (see Figure 5). Thus the function locatedAt has three slots: the first represents the user's id, the second is the room number and the third the confidence of this mapping.

```
locatedAt("44", "A12", 80%)
```

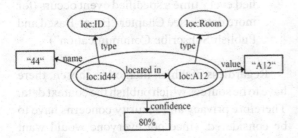

because most context models can be transformed into this representation. The basic syntactic elements of predicate logic are:

- *Variables* that stand for objects (often denoted by x,y,z...)
- *Predicate variables* or *relations* with an arity ≥ 1 (often denoted by P,Q,R...)
- *Functions* with an arity ≥ 1 (often denoted by f,g,h...)
- *Constants* for example "john"
- *Logical operators:* ↔ (logical biconditional), → (logical conditional), ∧ (logical and), ∨ (logical or), ¬ (logical not)
- *Quantifier:* ∀ (universal quantifier, i.e., for all), ∃ (existential quantifier, i.e., there exists)

For example, the expression ∀x.outside(x)∧¬covered(x)→wet(x) means that all objects that are located outside and that are not covered will get wet. The left-hand side of the rule (outside(x)∧¬covered(x)) is called its *premise* and the right-hand side (wet(x)) its *conclusion.*

In our example, we want to derive the location of a person by his name (Person-Location Sensor), given the location of a person's id (ID-Location Sensor) and the mapping of id to names (Mapping Sensor). We model the location sensor with the predicate idLocatedAt(a,b) (with a being an id and b a room number) and the mapping with the predicate mapping(a,c) (with a being a person's id and c her name). Further, we specify a rule for how a person's location (inferred context) can be inferred from the given data. The person's location is modeled with the predicate personLocatedAt(c,b) (with c being the person's name and b the person's location). Assume our knowledge base contains the following expressions:

```
idLocatedAt("44", "A12")
mapping("44", "Max")
```

$$\forall x \forall y \forall z.\text{idLocatedAt}(x,y) \wedge \text{mapping}(x,z)$$
$$\rightarrow \text{personLocatedAt}(z,y)$$

For a human being, it is obvious that the expression personLocatedAt("Max", "A12") can be inferred from this knowledge base. In order to enable the computer to draw such conclusions, we have to formalize the inference process. At first, we need to find a substitution for the variables in the premise idLocatedAt(x,y)∧mapping(x,z) to make it identical to expressions already in the knowledge base. In our case, we substitute x with "44", y with "A12" and z with "Max". This assignment makes the premise of the rule true and, thus, the resulting conclusion personLocatedAt("Max", "A12") can then be added to the knowledge base.[1]

Accessing Context

Having specified the context representation, the application designer has to decide on the access mechanisms for the context data and the communication protocols between the different components. In this section, we give a brief overview of access mechanisms, for more details about communication protocols see Tanenbaum (1996) and the chapter "Wireless and Mobile Communications" for wireless protocols.

As a matter of principle, there are two ways for an application to retrieve context data:

- **Queries:** the application requests context information via a remote method call (for example, specified in an SQL-like syntax)
- **Event Subscription:** the application is notified every time a specified event occurs (for more details see Chapter "Event-Based and Publish/Subscribe Communication")

Regardless of which method is chosen, there have to be sources which publish the context data. Therefore privacy and security concerns have to be considered, since not everyone would want every user to be able to look up the user's current location or activity. One possibility to cope with these issues is to allow the user to control the access to her context. This is for example realized by using localized location computation (LLC). This means that objects compute their current location on their own, and thus are the only ones that know their actual location. Hence, no entity can get the information about the location of an object, unless the object decides to publish it. For example, the navigation system of a car computes its location by using the signals of GPS satellites. The satellites therefore have no knowledge about who uses their signals and thus cannot compute the location of the car. Another possibility for protecting context data is to specify domain dependent policy rules used for access control.

Example: *In our example, we need to know in which room the user is currently located. We need the information only on demand if someone is calling. Thus, it is sufficient to realize a query interface for the different sensors, and no subscription system is needed. This also relieves us of storing all context data in the Person-Location Sensor and from keeping track of whether the context data is still up-to-date. The query from the application to the Person-Location Sensor contains the name of the person that is to be located. Then, the Person-Location Sensor queries the Mapping Sensor for the id of this person and sends this id to the Id-Location sensor to retrieve the user's location. This location is then sent back to the application.*

Context Storage and Management

Now that we know how to model and access context information, we need a way to store and manage it.

The *context storage* can provide a context history for later retrieval. Moreover, it can be used to establish trends, predict future context values and identify interrelations between context data. At least a context buffer is necessary for most applications. If a sensor fails, the buffer can report the last known value on its behalf, but it has to be considered that the data soon becomes outdated depending on the dynamics of the context information. For this reason, we need *context management* that determines when a context value should be updated or deleted. Further, the context manager has to ensure that all context consumers that subscribed to the context information are informed whenever the context changes depending on their subscriptions.

These mechanisms have to be available for every sensor. Therefore, it is often advantageous to have a global management system that takes care of these issues. Such an infrastructure can also provide a mechanism for discovering sensors. This is necessary if the application does not only use built-in sensors. This *discovery service* has to keep track of all currently available sensors and help the context consumers to find appropriate sensors (see also the chapter "Service Discovery"). This is especially important due to frequent changes in the number and kinds of available sensors during runtime: sensors fail, get out of reach, new ones become available etc. To ensure that a sensor is still operating and reachable, the discovery mechanism can ping the sensors regularly and remove them from its list if they do not respond to several consecutive pings. Most approaches use a central registry component for service discovery that has to be notified by all context producers about their presence, their capabilities and about their contact possibilities.

An architecture with global management could also undertake the task of *inferring context* from sensed context information, so that it relieves the programmer of implementing separate sensors for every type of inferred context information. In the following section, we discuss some models for managing context information.

Context Management Models

Several models have been proposed for coordinating the interaction between applications and context data and for managing context data. Winograd identified three main architectures (Winograd, 2001):

Widget

Just as GUI widgets relieve the UI designer of some presentation concerns, context widgets relieve the application designer of context acquisition concerns by hiding low-level details of sensing. Widgets provide a public interface to context data and are usually controlled by a widget manager. The different widgets can be easily exchanged at design-time or reused because of the encapsulation of low-level details of sensing. However, due to the tightly coupled approach, it is not robust to component failures. An example for this architecture is the Context Toolkit (Dey, Salber, & Abowd, 2001) discussed in the section "Middleware Architectures".

Networked Services

This approach allows heterogeneous processes to connect to a network service that provides the desired context data. This service-based approach provides discovery techniques for finding the appropriate components. The context sources are independent of each other without a global component (apart from a discovery service) that keeps track of the services and their connections. Thus, this approach is more flexible and robust than the widget approach, but less efficient and more complex. This is due to the higher communication costs and the independence of components, which have to contain code for handling connections, failures, and so forth.

Blackboard Model

The Blackboard Model focuses on the data itself and not on how it is processed. The context sources post their values to a common blackboard, and applications can subscribe to be notified of events that match a specific pattern. The advantage of this approach is its simple extensibility. The drawbacks are the need for a centralized server and the increased communication costs, as two hops per information exchange are needed.

Building a Context-Aware Application: Summary

In this section, we gave an overview of how to develop a context-aware application step-by-step. First, the developer has to specify the context-aware behavior she wants to implement and which context information she needs for that purpose (*Specification*). Next, she has to decide which sensors can deliver this context and install them (*Acquisition*) and then decide how the context information should be represented, accessed and managed (*Delivery and Reception*). Last of all, she has to implement the context-aware behavior according to the captured context (*Action*).

The step *Delivery and Reception* is similar for every context-aware application, thus, it can be taken over by a middleware infrastructure. The general architecture of such a middleware is discussed in the next section. Further, if the application just needs sensors that are already available for use by applications, the step *Acquisition* can also be skipped. Hence, with sufficient support for building context-aware applications, the developer just has to specify and implement desired context-aware behavior and is relieved of dealing with details of context retrieval.

MIDDLEWARE ARCHITECTURES

The task of developing context-aware applications can be facilitated by separating the acquisition and usage of context data by using a middleware. The middleware also eases extensibility and reusability. Thus, the application developer can focus on how to use context and not on how to acquire and manage it.

Most approaches use a layered architecture as depicted in Figure 11 consisting of the following layers:

- **Raw data retrieval:** This layer queries the available virtual and physical sensors by using appropriate drivers for physical sensors and APIs for virtual sensors, respectively. Providing a common interface for all sensors responsible for the same kind of context information makes the sensors exchangeable. For example, with a common location interface, RFID location data could be replaced by GPS data without major modifications to the upper layers.

- **Preprocessing:** The "Raw data retrieval" layer often returns technical data that is not appropriate to be used by an application developer. Therefore, the preprocessing layer is responsible for interpreting the contextual information and reasoning about it. The logical sensors (see Section "Context Sources") providing inferred context are located in this layer. The following techniques are used to process the context:

  - **Context aggregation/fusion:** Information from several context sources is combined to inferred context information. If several sensors report the same kind of context, its fusion can increase the quality and reliability of the data, but it can also lead to sensing conflicts that have to be solved by this layer.

  - **Context filtering:** Unnecessary technical data can be filtered or the resolution of the context data can be decreased.

  - **Context interpretation:** The context data can be interpreted by combining its value with the information from some other data source. For example, the context data gained from location detection systems can be turned into a symbolic position by combining it with the knowledge from a map.

Figure 11. Layers of a middleware for building context-aware applications

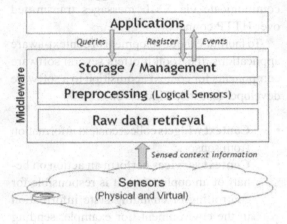

- **Management:** This layer manages the gathered data and offers a public interface to the client applications. As mentioned before, there are two principal ways to access context data: via querying the middleware or subscribing for specific events. The management layer is responsible for answering these queries and for notifying applications about occurring events. Further, this layer takes care of storing the context history and for keeping track of the available sensors. Most common approaches use a central component to manage and maintain distributed components (e.g., SOCAM (Gu, Pung, & Zhang, 2004)).

Example Framework: Context Toolkit

The most referenced example of a middleware to help building context-aware applications is the Context Toolkit framework (Dey et al., 2001), developed at Georgia Tech. It is a widget architecture that allows retrieval of contextual information through queries and subscriptions.

The Toolkit consists of context widgets and an infrastructure hosting the widgets. Context widgets can automatically store all the contextual information they gather. Thus, if a sensor cannot deliver current data, the widget can provide stored context information. The different components communicate via XML messages transmitted over HTTP connections.

To facilitate the development of context-aware applications, the Toolkit offers several software components for context acquisition to a software developer (see also Figure 12):

- **Context widgets** collect context information from sensors;
- **Context services** perform an action on behalf of an application. It is responsible for controlling or changing state information in the environment, for example, sending an email;
- **Context interpreters** are used to convert context between different representations;
- **Context aggregators** combine data from several widgets and interpreters;
- **Discoverers** maintain a registry of all available widgets. They are informed by new components of their presence and capabilities.

Figure 12. Example configuration of context toolkit components

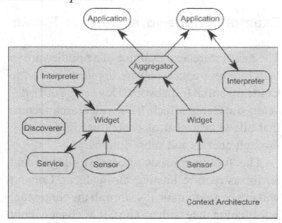

DEALING WITH UNCERTAINTY

Context-aware applications have to deal with context data that is imprecise or is acquired by unreliable sources. Sensing conflicts can occur meaning that several sources report different values for the same context information. For these reasons, it is important that context-aware applications take the uncertainty of context data into account.

The uncertainty of context data has to be handled in three areas:

- **Sensing context information:** Sensed context data is mostly afflicted with error, especially if it comes from a physical sensor. For example, location-sensing systems can only report the location to certain accuracy (see the section "Selected Positioning Systems" in the chapter "A Focus on Location Context"). Other sensors, like biometric authentication devices, give a measure of confidence for the reported data.
- **Inferring context information:** If the sensed context used for inferring context is uncertain, the derived context data will also be uncertain. Thereby, the resulting uncertainty is not necessarily worse than the basic values. For example, if two different location detection systems report the same location for the user, the trust in the provided data increases.
- **Using context information:** Applications have to determine how they cope with uncertain data. For example, they can specify a confidence level that has to be reached for authenticating a user. If an application does not want to deal with the probability distribution of different context values, they can assume that only the one with the maximum probability is valid. The more critical an application is, the more confidence in the context data used is needed.

An important factor that influences the validity of sensed context data is its freshness: The relevance of context data decreases over time. One possibility to cope with this issue is to specify relevance functions depending on the time difference to the capturing event. Figure 13 illustrates an example of a relevance function: At acquisition time t_0 the relevance R of the captured information is 1. The relevance decreases until its relevance reaches 0 at time t_{max}. Such a relevance function can also be specified for other proximity relations (e.g., spatial vicinity).

In the next section, we show an example of how the uncertainty of sensed context information is processed to infer context in form of a probability distribution.

Particle Filtering

Particle filters are used to estimate a dynamic system's state from noisy observations. Their main application area is location estimation. Particle Filters enable fusion of data from different sensors, enabling the developers to write applications independent of the sensors used.

Particle filters represent the probability distribution over different states of the world (for example over the different locations of a person) by a discrete distribution of samples. The set of samples S_t represents the system's possible states (e.g., user's location) at time t. The more samples report a particular state, the higher is its probability. Each sample $s_i \in S_t$ consists of its current state $x_t^{(i)}$ and a nonnegative weight $w_t^{(i)}$ representing the importance of the sample. The weights of all samples sum up to one. Thus, S_t with n samples is defined as follows:

$$S_t = \{(x_t^{(i)}, w_t^{(i)}) \mid i=1, \ldots, n\}$$

We illustrate the algorithm with an example for determining the user's position. We assume that the user is located at one of four possible positions: A, B, C or D (see Figure 14a).

At first, the particle filtering algorithm creates an initial population S_0 of n samples taken from the prior distribution at time 0. If the initial situation is unknown the weights are uniformly distributed over the state space. For our example, we use a set of 10 samples with 3 samples in state A and B and 2 samples in state C and D (all with weight 0.1) as illustrated in Figure 14a.

The reliability of the state determination improves by taking further observations into account. In order to be able to estimate how well the current sample set represents the real state, we need a measure for the likelihood of each state according to the observed event. This observation likelihood is denoted by the environmental model $P_o(e|x_i)$ with e being the current observation.

The determination of the most probable current state improves with every new observation.

Figure 13. Example of a relevance function

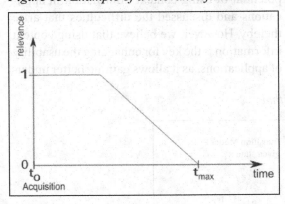

Figure 14. (a) Initial sample set representing the user's initially unknown position and (b) transition model of the different positions

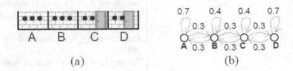

Figure 15. Update Cycle for the particle filtering algorithm

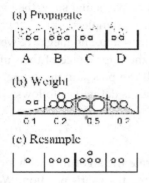

As this takes some time and the probability of the states is not static (e.g., the person to be located can move), we need a model of how the states change over time. Therefore, the transition between different states is specified in a transition model (for locations it is also called motion model) containing all conditional probabilities $P_c(x_i \mid x_j)$, where $P_c(x_i \mid x_j)$ denotes the probability that the system in state x_j at time t will be in state x_i at time $t+1$.

In our example, the user moves with a probability of 30% to an adjacent position resulting in the transition model illustrated in Figure 14b).

The update of the sample set is performed by the following three actions that are repeated for each time step. The brief version of this algorithm is shown in Figure 16.

- **Propagate:** Each sample is forwarded to the next state using the transition probabilities

$P_c(x_i \mid x_j)$ given in the transition model. Figure 15a illustrates the propagation of our initial samples.

- **Weight:** The samples' weights are adjusted and normalized according to the likelihood of the observation e. In other words, the weight of a sample represents the probability with which it could have been measured with respect to the current observation. In our example, we measure a location signal that indicates that the user's position is most probably position C (50%), followed by B(20%), D(20%), A(10%). This probability distribution leads to the weighted samples illustrated in Figure 15b (the corresponding probability distribution P_o is indicated by the grey area in the background).

- **Resample:** A new set of n samples is generated by weighted random selection from the current sample set. The probability that a particular sample is selected is proportional to its weight. The new samples all have the same weight. The new sample set for our example is illustrated in Figure 15c.

FUTURE RESEARCH DIRECTIONS

In this chapter, we gave an overview of the area of context-aware computing. We showed the potential of using context information in applications and discussed the difficulties that arise thereby. However, we believe that using context information is the key for enhancing the usability of applications, as it allows gaining better under-

Figure 16. Brief version of the particle filtering algorithm

> **Particle Filtering Algorithm**
> Given: Sample Set S_t with n samples, Transition Model $P_c(x_i \mid x_j)$,
> likelihood $P_o(e \mid x_i)$ of observation e given state x_i.
> Result: Sample Set S_{t+1}
>
> Propagate: $x_{t+1}^{(i)} \leftarrow$ sample from $P_c(x_j \mid x_t^{(i)})$
> Weight: $w_{t+1}^{(i)} = P_o(e \mid x_{t+1}^{(i)}) / \sum_j P_o(e \mid x_{t+1}^{(j)})$
> Resample: $x_{t+1}^{(i)} \leftarrow$ sample from S_{t+1} according to weights w_{t+1}
> $\quad\quad\quad\quad w_{t+1}^{(i)} = 1/n$

standing of the user's situation when she interacts with the application.

As we saw in the section "What is Context?" it is a very challenging task to clearly define what context actually is and which features characterize a context-aware application. However, more important than having a proper definition of context and context-awareness is to have a *common representation* of context-information to allow the exchange of context information between different applications and to facilitate the reuse of sensors. This is especially important as the amount of context types used increases, as research has moved away from focusing on location information alone. More and more different sensors are used, for example acceleration sensors the user is wearing can be used to determine her current activity.

When building context-aware applications, we have to consider the properties that distinguish context from traditional information sources: heterogeneity of context sources, dynamic and error-proneness of context information. Thus, we need a context representation that also models the *quality of context information* and states how to deal with incomplete or ambiguous data. Further, a middleware is needed that takes care of all these issues and thus relieves the developer of considering details of acquiring and processing context. A good context model is also necessary for specifying how context information can be automatically inferred without requiring the developer's intervention. There exists also context information that cannot be derived by specifying a rule, it has to be learned by observation. For example, the type of movement of a person, like "running" or "climbing stairs", can be learned by recording data from several acceleration sensors. This data is labeled with when the user performed which movement. Then machine learning techniques are applied to retrieve the patterns that characterize the different movements. The labeling process is mostly done manually, but research is being done on automating the process.

To sum up, a variety of context information will be available for a context-aware application. It will be easy for the developer to integrate this information in the application as most tasks can be performed by a middleware. Therefore, most applications will become context-aware and thus increase the usability of applications.

REFERENCES

Abowd, G. D., Dey, A. K., Orr, R., & Brotherton, J. A. (1997). Context-awareness in wearable and ubiquitous computing. *ISWC*, (pp. 179-180).

Adams, N. I., Gold, R., Schilit, B. N., Tso, M. M., & Want, R. (1993). An infrared network for mobile computers. In *Proceedings of the USENIX Symposium on Mobile and Location Independent Computing* (pp. 41-51). Cambridge, MA.

Chen, G., & Kotz, D. (2000). *A survey of context-aware mobile computing research* (Tech. Rep. TR2000-381), Department of Computer Science, Dartmouth College.

Cheverst, K., Davies, N., Mitchell, K., & Friday, A. (2000). Experiences of developing and deploying a context-aware tourist guide: The GUIDE project. In *Mobile Computing and Networking*, (pp. 20-31).

Dey, A., Salber, D., & Abowd, G. (2001). *A conceptual framework and a toolkit for supporting the rapid prototyping of context-aware applications*.

Dey, A. K. (2001). Understanding and using context. *Personal and Ubiquitous Computing, 5*(1), 4-7.

Dey, A. K., & Abowd, G. D. (2000). Cybreminder: A context-aware system for supporting reminders. *HUC Journal*, 172-186.

Gu, T., Pung, H., & Zhang, D. (2004). *A middleware for building context-aware mobile services*.

Harter, A., & Hopper, A. (1994). A distributed location system for the active office. *IEEE Network, 8*(1), 62-70.

Lamming, M., & Flynn, M. (1994). Forget-me-not: Intimate computing in support of human memory. In *Proceedings FRIEND21 Symposium on Next Generation Human Interfaces*.

Pascoe, M. J. (1998). Adding generic contextual capabilities to wearable computers. In *ISWC*, (pp. 92-99). Los Alamitos, CA, USA. IEEE Computer Society.

Raento, M., Oulasvirta, A., Petit, R., & Toivonen, H. (2005). Contextphone: A prototyping platform for context-aware mobile applications. *IEEE Pervasive Computing, 4*(2), 51-59.

Rhodes, B. J. (1997). The wearable remembrance agent: A system for augmented memory. In *Proceedings of The First International Symposium on Wearable Computers (ISWC '97)* (pp. 123-128), Cambridge, Massachusetts.

Russel, S., & Norvig, P. (1995). *Artificial intelligence: A Modern Approach* (2nd ed). Englewood Cliffs, NJ: Prentice-Hall.

Schilit, B., Adams, N., & Want, R. (1994). Context-aware computing applications. In *Proceedings of the IEEE Workshop on Mobile Computing Systems and Applications*, Santa Cruz, California.

Strang, T., & Linnhoff-Popien, C. (2004). *A context modeling survey*. Workshop on Advanced Context Modelling, Reasoning and Management.

Tanenbaum, A. S. (1996). *Computer network* (3rd ed). Prentice Hall.

Winograd, T. (2001). Architectures for context. *Human-Computer Interaction, 16*, 401-419.

ADDITIONAL READING

Akman, V., & Surav, M. (1997). The use of situation theory in context modeling. *Computational Intelligence, 13*(3), 427-438.

Antifakos, S., Schwaninger, A., & Schiele, B. (2004). Evaluating the effects of displaying uncertainty in context-aware applications. In *Ubicomp*, (pp. 54-69).

Baldauf, M., Dustdar, S., & Rosenberg, F. (2007). A survey on context-aware systems. *International Journal of Ad Hoc and Ubiquitous Computing, 2*(4), 263-277.

Chen, H. (2004). *An intelligent broker architecture for pervasive context-aware systems*. Unpublished doctoral thesis, University of Maryland.

Chen, H., Finin, T., & Joshi, A. (2003). Using OWL in a pervasive computing broker. In *Proceedings of the Workshop on Ontologies in Agent Systems, AAMAS-2003*.

Dey, A. K., & Abowd, G. D. (2000). Towards a better understanding of context and context awareness. In *Proceedings of the CHI 2000 Workshop on The What, Who, Where, When, Why, and How of Context-Awareness*.

Dürr, F., Hönle, N., Nicklas, D., Becker, C., & Rothermel, K. (2004). Nexus–A platform for context-aware applications. In J. Roth (Ed.), *1. Fachgespräch Ortsbezogene Anwendungen und Dienste der GI-Fachgruppe KuVS* (pp. 15-18). Hagen: Informatik-Bericht der FernUniversität Hagen.

Fox, D., Hightower, J., Liao, L., Schulz, D., & Borriello, G. (2003). Bayesian filtering for location estimation. *IEEE Pervasive Computing, 2*(3), 24-33.

Held, A., Buchholz, S., & Schill, A. (2002). Modeling of context information for pervasive computing applications. In *Proceedings of the 6th World Multiconference on Systemics, Cybernetics and Informatics (SCI2002)*.

Henricksen, K., & Indulska, J. (2004). Modelling and using imperfect context information. In *Proceedings of the PerCom Workshops*, (pp. 33-37).

Henricksen, K., & Indulska, J. (in press). Developing context aware pervasive computing applications: Models and approach. *Pervasive and mobile computing.*

Henricksen, K., Indulska, J., & Rakotonirainy, A. (2003). Generating context management infrastructure from context models. In *Proceedings of the 4th International Conference on Mobile Data Management (MDM), Industrial Track Proceedings*, (pp. 1-6), Melbourne, Australia.

Hightower, J., & Borriello, G. (2004). Particle filters for location estimation in ubiquitous computing: A case study. In *Proceedings of the Sixth International Conference on Ubiquitous Computing (Ubicomp 2004) Lecture Notes in Computer Science* (Vol. 3205, pp. 88-106).

Hightower, J., Brumitt, B., & Borriello, G. (2002). The location stack: A layered model for location in ubiquitous computing. In *Proceedings of the Fourth IEEE Workshop on Mobile Computing Systems and Applications (WCSMA 2002)* (pp. 22-30), Callicoon, New York.

Indulska, J., Robinson, R., Rakotonirainy, A., & Henricksen, K. (2003). Experiences in using CC/PP in context-aware systems. In *Proceedings of the MDM '03: Proceedings of the 4th International Conference on Mobile Data Management* (pp. 247-261), London, UK.

Kaenampornpan, M., & O'Neill, E. (2004). An integrated context model: Bringing activity to context. In *Proceedings of the UbiComp 2004 Workshop on Advanced Context Modelling, Reasoning and Management.*

Loke, S. W. (2006). Context-aware artifacts: Two development approaches. *IEEE Pervasive Computing, 5*(2), 48-53.

Mayrhofer, R. (2005). An architecture for context prediction. *Schriften der Johannes-Kepler-Universität Linz* (Vol. C 45). Trauner Verlag.

Pascoe, J., Ryan, N., & Morse, D. (1999). Issues in developing context-aware computing. In *Proceedings of the HUC '99: Proceedings of the 1st international symposium on Handheld and Ubiquitous Computing* (pp. 208-221), London, UK.

Ranganathan, A., Al-Muhtadi, J., & Campbell, R. (2004). Reasoning about uncertain contexts in pervasive computing environments. *IEEE pervasive computing.*

Schmidt, A. (2002). *Ubiquitous computing - Computing in context.* Unpublished doctoral thesis, Lancaster University.

Schmidt, A., Aidoo, K. A., Takaluoma, A., Tuomela, U., Laerhoven, K. V., & de Velde, W. V. (1999a). Advanced interaction in context. In *Proceedings of the 1st International Symposium on Handheld and Ubiquitous Computing (HUC'99)* (Vol. 1707).

Schmidt, A., Beigl, M., & Gellersen, H.-W. (1999b). There is more to context than location. *Computers and Graphics, 23*(6), 893-901.

Schmidt, A., & Laerhoven, K. V. (2001). How to build smart appliances. *IEEE Personal Communications*, pages 66-71.

Strang, T., Linnhoff-Popien, C., & Frank, K. (2003). CoOL: A context ontology language to enable contextual interoperability. In *Proceedings of 4th IFIP WG 6.1 International Conference on Distributed Applications and Interoperable Systems (DAIS2003), Lecture Notes in Computer Science (LNCS)* (Vol. 2893, pp. 236-247), Paris/France.

Wang, X. (2004). Ontology-based context modeling and reasoning using OWL. In *Proceedings of the Context Modeling and Reasoning Workshop at PerCom 2004.*

ENDNOTE

[1] This is a very simplified form of this algorithm. For more details refer to (Russel & Norvig, 1995)

Chapter XII
A Focus on Location Context

Erwin Aitenbichler
Technische Universität Darmstadt, Germany

ABSTRACT

This chapter adds an in-depth description of location context, because location is the most prominent context property and the associated tracking technology is increasingly deployed in industry. First, we motivate a number of application areas for this technology in industry, healthcare, tourism, and more. We first describe the different physical properties location sensors can measure and then the principles and algorithms to calculate the locations of mobile entities based on this sensor data. Several commercial location systems and research prototypes are described as implementation examples. Finally, with the help of location models, the raw location information is processed to derive higher-level information meaningful to application services.

INTRODUCTION

One of the most important physical context parameters is location, because most other physical and situational context properties can be determined as functions of place and time. There are numerous applications for location tracking technology in real-time enterprises, healthcare, tourism, etc. Currently, especially the market for Local Positioning Systems is growing. Services that can adapt to the user's location are also often called location based services (LBS). A few application areas are listed below.

- **Navigation:** GPS-based navigation systems virtually belong to the standard equipment of new cars.
- **Enhanced 911 services:** The Federal Communications Commission requires wireless carriers to locate cell phones with an accuracy of 50-300 meters in case of emergency calls.
- **People tracking:** For example, child tracking in amusement parks, security personnel in enterprises, hospital patients, prison inmates, or employees in office buildings.

- **Asset tracking** to keep a real-time inventory of assets and their locations to make items easier to find when they are needed. Various types of equipment can be tagged, including vehicles, inventory in a manufacturing line, containers, forklifts, shopping carts, or medical equipment.
- **Buddy finder:** Instant messaging applications on mobile devices can not only reveal when friends are online, but also where they are and alert users when friends are nearby.
- **Conference assistant:** Whenever the user enters a conference room, the assistant uses the location and the conference schedule to identify the current speaker and the presentation title.
- **Advertisement:** Special offers from nearby stores or restaurants can be displayed on cell phones.
- **Mobile patient monitoring:** Dementia patients need constant monitoring. LBSs can prevent patients from leaving hospital wards or buildings by automatically locking doors or notify the nursing staff.
- **Theft protection:** Retailers typically experience annual loss of ~15% for shopping carts. By tracking equipment both in store and in the parking lot, retailers can reduce theft.
- **Safety:** If an emergency happens at a large building or tunnel construction site, the supervisor must be able to quickly get a list of people at unsafe locations and the locations where they have been seen last.
- **Security:** Certain chemicals react with each other and may not be stored in the same area. A tracking system can monitor the warehouse and alarm the staff when storage regulations are violated.
- **Tour guides** automatically present information to the user based on the user's location.

This chapter is organized as follows. We first describe the basic principles to determine one's location from various kinds of sensor data. Next, the signal propagation characteristics of electromagnetic waves are discussed. In the context of positioning systems, the different bands of the electromagnetic spectrum have vastly different properties. Understanding these characteristics is essential for the construction and selection of systems. We then describe a number of positioning systems with their properties. With the help of sensors and positioning algorithms, we are able to determine the position of people or objects in a representation that is specific to the location system. To derive information more meaningful to applications, for example, the location within a building, or the location relative to other people or objects of interest, we need location models.

POSITIONING PRINCIPLES

A positioning system consists of *navigation sources* and *users*. The locations of the navigation sources are known. The locations of the users are unknown and should be determined. A positioning system uses sensors to measure certain physical properties and calculate the users' positions based on this data. Essentially, we distinguish between the following kinds of sensor information:

- Binary information if communication between source and user is possible.
- Received signal strength (RSS), bit error rate (BER) or read success rate. These values give an indication of the quality of the communication link between source and user.
- Time of arrival (TOA). TOA is a measure for the absolute distance between source and user.
- Time difference of arrival (TDOA). In TDOA systems, only the differences of multiple TOA measurements to different sources are known.

- Angle of arrival (AOA). The angles of signals arriving at sources or users are measured.

The positioning principles described in the following sections are used to calculate the user's position from raw sensor readings.

Proximity

The simplest method for locating a mobile device is to estimate its position to be the same as the position of a navigation source, that is, some (stationary) landmark. Such landmarks are receivers or transmitters and communicate over wireless links with the mobile devices. A location system based on this principle can work in two ways: either the mobile terminal receives the identifier of the landmark and calculates its position by using a database of landmark positions, or the landmark receives the identifier of the mobile terminal and the position is determined in the network infrastructure.

For example, this principle can be used to determine the position of a terminal based on the Cell ID of a WLAN or GSM network. To do so, the terminal uses the Cell ID of the closest access point, that is, the access point with the highest RSS indication, and queries a database to obtain the position of that access point.

Fingerprinting

In this approach, the strength of a radio signal is measured at the receiver. In open spaces, the signal strength is inversely proportional to the square of the distance of the transmitting antenna to the receiving antenna. Alternative methods to determine the quality of a radio link between sender and receiver is to measure the Bit Error Rate (BER) of a transmission or to measure the success rate of multiple communication attempts.

Location fingerprinting, also referred to as RF pattern matching, is often used in conjunction with RSS sensing. The propagation of radio waves in indoor environments is influenced by many obstacles, like walls, furniture, movement of people, change of temperature and humidity. These effects lead to signal attenuation, occlusion, reflection, and multipath effects. For that reason, it is not possible to describe a direct relationship between RSS and distance in an accurate manner. Location fingerprinting captures the static properties of an environment in RSS maps that have to be created beforehand, either manually by users or by using robots.

For example, consider the RSS map for a WLAN location system in Figure 1. It shows the locations of four access points and a number of reference points. Each reference point is described as a tuple $(x, y, rss_1, rss_2, rss_3, rss_4)$, where (x, y) is

Figure 1. Locations of access points and reference points (circles)

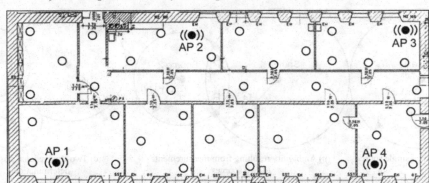

the 2D-position of the reference point and rss_i is the signal strength value at this location of the respective access point AP_i.

From this map, we can construct an n-dimensional space containing the RSS vectors of the reference points. n is the number of access points: for the example shown in Figure 1, $n=4$. The position of a mobile terminal can now be obtained by measuring an RSS vector and then searching the RSS space using one of the following methods.

- **Nearest neighbor:** This algorithm compares the observed signal strength vector with the signal strength vectors of all reference points, usually by calculating the root mean square errors. It returns the position of the closest match as the terminal's position. The drawback of NN is that it might require a large number of reference points, because a reference point is needed for each point-of-interest.
- **Multiple nearest neighbor:** The MNN algorithm finds the k (e.g., three) closest reference points in RSS space. It averages the x and y coordinates of all found reference points and returns the result as the terminal's position. Similar to NN, MNN requires a large number of reference points.

- **Interpolation:** Similar to MNN, this algorithm first finds the three closest reference points in signal space. It then uses (linear) interpolation on the obtained triangle to determine the terminal's position. Compared to NN and MNN, interpolation provides a higher accuracy with less reference points. Because interpolation works best in open space, reference points should be located close to walls.

Lateration

Lateration determines the position of an object by measuring its distance to multiple reference positions. In 2D space, this method requires distance measurements to three noncollinear points, and in 3D space, it requires distance measurements to four noncoplanar points.

Trilateration

Trilateration is used to determine the relative position of an object using the geometry of triangles. This method requires absolute distance measurements, as provided by Time-of-Arrival (TOA) ranging. TOA ranging is based on measuring the time it takes for a signal transmitted by an emitter (e.g., an (ultra)sound source) to reach

Figure 2. Time-of-arrival ranging

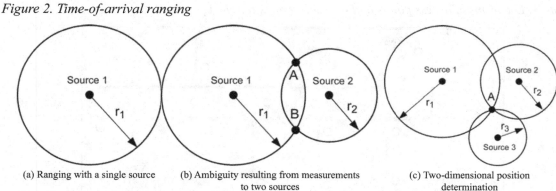

(a) Ranging with a single source   (b) Ambiguity resulting from measurements to two sources   (c) Two-dimensional position determination

a receiver. The distance from emitter to receiver can then be obtained by multiplying this time interval, referred to as the signal propagation time, with the propagation speed (e.g., speed of sound). Using this principle, a mobile user can determine her position by measuring the distance to multiple known locations.

As an introductory example, consider a mariner at sea determining the vessel's position from a foghorn (Kaplan, 1996). We assume a global clock, that is, both vessel and foghorn are equipped with accurate clocks that are synchronized. The foghorn whistle is now sounded precisely on the minute mark and the mariner notes the elapsed time from the minute mark until the foghorn whistle is heard. The measured propagation time multiplied by the speed of sound (approximately 340 m/s) is the distance from the foghorn to the mariner. With one measurement, we know that the vessel is somewhere on a circle with radius r_1 centered around the foghorn (Figure 2(a)).

When the mariner simultaneously measures the range from a second foghorn in the same way, the vessel would be at range r_1 from foghorn 1 and at range r_2 from foghorn 2, as shown in Figure 2(b). Therefore, the vessel is at one of the two circle intersection points A or B. This ambiguity can be resolved by making a third measurement, as shown in Figure 2(c). With three measurements we have the following equations:

$$(x - x_1)^2 + (y - y_1)^2 = r_1^2 \quad (1.1)$$
$$(x - x_2)^2 + (y - y_2)^2 = r_2^2 \quad (1.2)$$
$$(x - x_3)^2 + (y - y_3)^2 = r_3^2 \quad (1.3)$$

Setting equations (1.1) and (1.2) equal yields:

$$x = \frac{2y(y_2 - y_1) + x_1^2 - x_2^2 + y_1^2 - y_2^2 - r_1^2 + r_2^2}{2(x_1 - x_2)}$$

$$(2.1)$$

Similar expressions can be found by intersecting circles 2 and 3, or 1 and 3. Setting equations (1.2) and (1.3) equal yields:

$$x = \frac{2y(y_3 - y_2) + x_2^2 - x_3^2 + y_2^2 - y_3^2 - r_2^2 + r_3^2}{2(x_2 - x_3)}$$

$$(2.2)$$

Finally, we can combine (2.1) and (2.2) and solve for y:

$$y = \frac{\dfrac{x_2^2 - x_3^2 + y_2^2 - y_3^2 - r_2^2 + r_3^2}{2(x_2 - x_3)} - \dfrac{x_1^2 - x_2^2 + y_1^2 - y_2^2 - r_1^2 + r_2^2}{2(x_1 - x_2)}}{\dfrac{y_2 - y_1}{x_1 - x_2} - \dfrac{y_3 - y_2}{x_2 - x_3}}$$

$$(3)$$

To obtain the coordinate (x, y) of the intersection point, we first calculate the value of y using equation (3). Then, the value of x is calculated using equation (2.1) or (2.2). If divisions by zero occur, then the equations must be combined differently. There are also other techniques to calculate the intersection point, for example, by using the Newton-Raphson root-finding method.

In three-dimensional space, the position can be determined by calculating the intersections of multiple spheres. If one navigation source is used and the distance between source and user is determined as described before, we know that the user is located on the surface of a sphere centered about the position of the navigation source. Adding a second navigation source gives the information that the user is also located on the surface of a second sphere. The intersection of two spheres results in a plane and the user would be located somewhere on the perimeter of this intersection plane (i.e., a circle) or at a single point tangent to both spheres (i.e., where the spheres just touch). A third sphere would intersect the intersection circle determined by the first two spheres at two points. Therefore, in the general case, at least four navigation sources are required to determine the position in 3D space without ambiguity.

Multilateration

TOA assumes that all navigation aids and the user to locate have access to a globally synchronized clock. Whether this assumption is feasible or not depends very much on the signal propagation speed. While time measurements of signals that propagate with the speed of sound can be made with standard quartz-based clocks and simple synchronization protocols, the measurement of signals that propagate with the speed of light typically requires atomic clocks. For that reason, *Time difference of arrival (TDOA)* removes that requirement that the exact time must be known by the user.

Multilateration, also known as hyperbolic positioning, is used to determine the relative position of an object when only relative distances are known, for example, provided by TDOA. Given two reference positions and a TDOA, the possible object positions lie on a hyperboloid. 2D or 3D object coordinates are obtained by intersecting multiple hyperboloids (Figure 3). Consider a multilateration system comprising three reference stations at known locations and a mobile station at an unknown location (x, y), which we wish to locate.

The travel time t_i of a signal from a reference station i to the mobile terminal is given by

Figure 3. Intersection of two hyperbolas to determine the user's 2D position

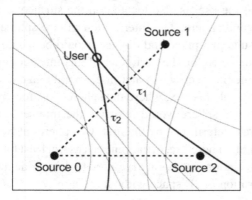

the distance divided by the signal propagation speed v:

$$t_0 = \frac{1}{v}\sqrt{(x-x_0)^2 + (y-y_0)^2} \qquad (4.1)$$

$$t_1 = \frac{1}{v}\sqrt{(x-x_1)^2 + (y-y_1)^2} \qquad (4.2)$$

$$t_2 = \frac{1}{v}\sqrt{(x-x_2)^2 + (y-y_2)^2} \qquad (4.3)$$

If reference station 0 is taken to be at the co-ordinate system origin, then equation (4.1) can be reduced to:

$$t_0 = \frac{1}{v}\sqrt{x^2 + y^2} \qquad (5)$$

The mobile station does not know the absolute values of t_0, t_1, and t_2. It is only able to obtain the time differences:

$$\tau_1 = t_1 - t_0 = \frac{1}{v}(\sqrt{(x-x_1)^2 + (y-y_1)^2} - \sqrt{x^2 + y^2})$$
$$(6.1)$$

$$\tau_2 = t_2 - t_0 = \frac{1}{v}(\sqrt{(x-x_2)^2 + (y-y_2)^2} - \sqrt{x^2 + y^2})$$
$$(6.2)$$

Equations (6.1) and (6.2) must now be solved for x and y. All other values are known. The unknowns in this nonlinear equation system can be determined by employing either closed form solutions (Awange, 2002; Bancroft, 1985), iterative techniques based on linearization (Kaplan, 1996), or Kalman filtering (Kaplan, 1996).

Angulation

Angulation is similar to lateration, but uses angles instead of distances to determine an object's position. In general, 2D angulation requires two angle measurements and one length measurement, which typically is the distance between the two stations measuring the angles. 3D angulation re-

Figure 4. Position determination with AOA

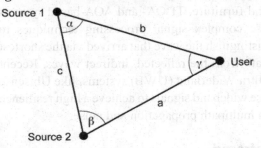

quires three angle measurements and one length measurement.

This technique measures the *angle of arrival (AOA)* of the signals sent by the mobile user at two or more base stations. Each angle determines a line between base station and user. The intersection point gives the user's location (Figure 4). The accuracy of AOA diminishes with an increasing distance between base stations and user.

Using the triangle sum formula and the law of sines, we can state the following equations:

$$\gamma = 180° - \alpha - \beta \qquad (7.1)$$

$$a = c \frac{\sin \alpha}{\sin \gamma} \qquad (7.2)$$

$$b = c \frac{\sin \beta}{\sin \gamma} \qquad (7.3)$$

SIGNAL PROPAGATION

In most cases, the communication between navigation sources and mobile stations is based on electromagnetic waves. The different parts of the electromagnetic spectrum have vastly different propagation characteristics. Thus, the communication frequency of a system largely determines

Table 1. Electromagnetic spectrum utilized by location systems

Band	Frequency	λ	Principles	Examples	
LF	30 kHz –	100 km –	RSS	125 kHz	Elpas LF
	300 kHz	10 km		<135 kHz	RFID (ISO 18000-2)
HF	3 MHz –	100 m –	RSS	13.56 MHz	RFID (ISO 18000-3)
	30 MHz	10 m			
UHF	300 MHz –	1 m –	RSS	433 MHz	RFID (ISO 18000-7)
	3 GHz	10 cm			Elpas RF
				860-960 MHz	RFID (ISO 18000-6)
				2.4 GHz	Bluetooth
					WLAN 802.11b/g
					RFID (ISO 18000-4)
			RSS,	820-960 MHz	GSM 850, 900
			AOA	1.7-2 GHz	GSM 1800, 1900
			TDOA	1.2-1.6 GHz	GPS, GLONASS, Galileo
SHF	3 GHz –	10 cm –	TDOA,	6-7.2 GHz	Ubisense
	30 GHz	1 cm	AOA		
NIR	120 THz –	2.5 µm –	RSS	880 nm	IR Badge Systems
	380 THz	780 nm	AOA	880 nm	ART, Polaris, IRIS
Visible	380 THz –	780 nm –	AOA		AR Toolkit
Light	780 THz	380 nm			Image-based Trackers
			TDOA		Laser Trackers

its range, accuracy, and robustness. Table 1 shows the parts of the electromagnetic spectrum used by various location systems.

Radio Frequency

The propagation of radio waves is influenced by many factors, such as wave frequency, terrain, humidity, velocity of sender and receiver, and effects caused by obstructions. Radio waves encounter various outdoor objects, such as mountains, trees, or buildings, and indoor objects, such as walls, furniture, or people. These objects attenuate and reflect the waves, thereby affecting the signal strength as well as the propagation time from sender to receiver. As a result, a signal reaches the receiver through multiple different paths, leading to constructive and destructive interference effects, and phase shifting of the signal.

Waves are attenuated when they pass through obstructions. In general, the amount of attenuation is a function of the frequency. While Low Frequency (LF) and High Frequency (HF) waves can be transmitted over long distances and then received inside buildings, waves in the upper part of the Ultra High Frequency (UHF) and the Super High Frequency (SHF) band already have quasi-optical properties and virtually require a direct line-of-sight between sender and receiver. For that reason, GPS does not work indoors. Its 1.5 GHz carrier signal is severely attenuated even by the thinnest roofing materials.

In many cases, devices concurrently make use of the same spectrum in one of the license-free ISM (Industrial, Scientific, and Medical) bands. For example, 802.11b/g/n WLANs experience severe interference from Bluetooth devices or microwave ovens.

These radio propagation effects are particularly relevant to location sensing, because they may influence the measured signal strength, signal time-of-flight and angle-of-arrival (caused by multipath). RSS-based systems often use special maps to capture the attenuation caused by walls and furniture. TDOA- and AOA-based systems use complex signal processing techniques to distinguish the wave that arrived via the shortest path from the reflected, indirect waves. Recent Ultra WideBand (UWB) systems, like Ubisense use wideband signals to achieve a high resilience to multipath propagation and noise.

Infrared

Infrared (IR) is commonly used in remote controls for TV sets and other consumer electronic products. IR-based systems are either based on proximity detection or on optical tracking.

For proximity detection, IR tags emit so-called beacon messages, modulated with their identification codes. The tags are then attached to objects of interest and users can receive the signals sent by tags with their mobile devices. The roles of senders and receivers can also be swapped. Depending on the hardware design, infrared systems can bridge a distance of some tens of centimeters up to about 10m. Because IR radiation does not penetrate walls, it can be inferred from the reception of a beacon that sender and receiver reside in the same room.

Infrared optical tracking systems use IR emitters or reflectors as tags and one or multiple IR cameras to determine the 3D positions of tags. Because monochrome CCD or CMOS cameras are also sensitive in the Near InfraRed (NIR) spectrum, the necessary IR cameras can be built out of ordinary cameras combined with IR filters. IR optical tracking systems require a direct line-of-sight and can achieve a very high accuracy down to the submillimeter range.

Infrared systems are limited to indoor use, because sunlight has a strong infrared component. This severely degrades the communication range. In contrast to that, IR radiation is low indoors. Also, fluorescent lights do not emit a considerable amount of IR.

Optical

In general, optical systems are based on passive sensing. Because the visible spectrum is "reserved" for humans, the use of active tags or large barcode markers would be disturbing. Optical systems rely on cameras and computationally intensive image processing methods, for example, for face recognition, object recognition, or the recognition of specialized markers (2D barcodes).

Ultrasound

Ultrasound location systems are based on time-of-flight measurements. Because sound waves are slower than electromagnetic waves by six orders of magnitude, the necessary time measurements can easily be done with current microprocessor technology. However, ultrasound is attenuated significantly in air, which limits the maximum distance between sender and receiver to approximately 5 m. This makes the installation of such systems cumbersome. For example, the Active Bat system requires the installation of a sensor grid on the ceiling that has to be laid out precisely. Like RF-based approaches, ultrasound-based systems suffer in their accuracy from reflections and obstacles between senders and receivers.

Magnetic

Electromagnetic tracking is one of the oldest methods and was initially developed for military applications. It offers a high resolution but is limited to a small and precisely controlled environment. Thus, it is mainly used for Cave Automatic Virtual Environment (CAVE) applications. Because such systems are sensitive to metal in the surrounding walls and floors, CAVEs are often constructed completely out of wood.

SELECTED POSITIONING SYSTEMS

Resolution (or precision) and accuracy are important properties of positioning systems. They are two orthogonal aspects and have a significant impact on the applicability of a system for a specific location-based service scenario (Figure 5).

The resolution of a system is limited by the underlying technology, such as radio links used, or sensor resolution. For example, an IR badge system has room resolution because either communication between badge and reader is possible, or not. WLAN hardware only distinguishes about 100 discrete RSS indications. Assuming that an access point has a range of 25 m and linear attenuation, the resulting distance has a resolution of no better than 25 cm.

Accuracy is another matter. It describes the deviation of the calculated position from the real position of an object. For systems providing geometric coordinates, the accuracy is usually specified as the maximum deviation for 95% of all measurements, that is 95 of 100 measurements lie within a circle (or sphere/ellipsoid) having the radius of the specified accuracy.

An infrared badge system is an example for a system with low resolution, but high accuracy. On one hand, the system does not provide information about where a tag inside a room is, but on the

Figure 5. Resolution vs. Accuracy

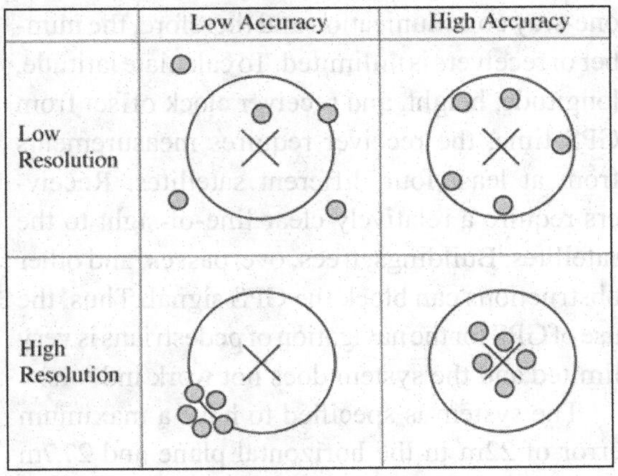

other hand, IR cannot pass through walls, which makes false positives nearly impossible.

GPS can be considered as a system with high resolution, but low accuracy. However, it is possible to correct the error in accuracy, because the deviation is a slowly changing function of location and time that can be compensated with the DGPS method (see the next section).

Global Positioning System (GPS)

GPS is a satellite-based positioning system with a worldwide coverage that was designed for the navigation of land, water, and air vehicles. It was installed by the United States Department of Defense (DOD) and has been fully operational since 1994. GPS is based on 24 satellites in a middle earth orbit that are equally distributed among six circular orbital planes. The orbits are designed such that at least six satellites are always visible from almost anywhere on the earth.

GPS is based on a global clock with each satellite having a highly accurate, synchronized atomic clock onboard. The satellites broadcast a navigation signal containing a satellite identification component, a position component, and a time component. The position component describes the satellite's position at the time of transmission. The time component is a ranging code to determine the satellite-to-user range.

A GPS receiver employs DTOA ranging to determine its position. The system is based on one-way communication and therefore, the number of receivers is unlimited. To calculate latitude, longitude, height, and receiver clock offset from GPS time, the receiver requires measurements from at least four different satellites. Receivers require a relatively clear line-of-sight to the satellites. Buildings, trees, overpasses, and other obstructions can block the GPS signal. Thus, the use of GPS for the navigation of pedestrians is very limited and the system does not work indoors.

The system is specified to have a maximum error of 22m in the horizontal plane and 27,7m in elevation for 95% of measurements, but in practice it is more accurate. The GPS Error Budget (Kaplan, 1995) contains a list of factors influencing the accuracy of the system and predicts a total error of only 6,6m. Signal delays in the Ionosphere and Troposphere constitute a large part of this error and depend on parameters such as sunlight intensity, temperature, or humidity. Reference stations on the ground are required in order to compensate for these atmospheric effects. The correction data can then be forwarded to receivers by the satellite system or via a separate communication link between ground station and receiver. The Differential GPS (DGPS) system is based on the latter. Here, the positioning accuracy is improved by removing correlated (i.e., common) errors between two or more receivers performing range measurements to the same satellites. A stationary reference receiver determines the current GPS deviation and broadcasts it to the mobile receivers.

The National Marine Electronics Association (NMEA) defined a standard protocol for the communication between GPS receiver and host (NMEA-0183), and WGS84 defines the coordinate system. For example, a GPS receiver that has determined a fix at 47°35,5634' north, 7°39,3538' east, at 19:14:10 UTC, on Nov 12, 2006 would generate the following record:

$GPRMC,191410,A,4735.5634,N,00739.3538,E,0.0,0.0,181106,0.4,E,A*19

GPS is free for civilian use, since 2000 even with full accuracy. However, the DOD has the ability to disable the public GPS services for specific areas of the world in case of a crisis, without affecting its own military systems. To date, GPS is the only existing satellite navigation system that is fully functional. Anticipated competitors in the future are the European Galileo system and the Russian GLONASS system. From a technical point of view, there are no significant differences to the constantly evolving GPS.

Cell Phone Location (Network-Based)

The location of a mobile phone can be determined by using information about the base station of the current cell. The GSM 03.71 Standard defines a way for accessing location information in GSM based networks. It requires the network provider to operate a Mobile Location Center. This MLC collects cell information from the mobile switching center (MSC) currently responsible for the handset's base station and from the home location register (HLR) that stores subscription data and routing information for each handset. Clients that want to get location data send a request to the MLC. After the MLC has checked the HLR for the client's permission, it queries the handset's MSC for the location. Usually a client must actively query a user's current location, although the standard also specifies deferred responses that are sent when the user's location changes.

At the basic level, the MLC can determine the cell base station with the highest RSS indication for the user's handset. The MLC has access to the mobile phone operator's infrastructure. It is therefore possible to use more sophisticated location sensing mechanisms to get the location of a handset within a cell. The standard explicitly mentions TOA and timing advance based positioning mechanisms to be used by the provider. Because many base stations use antenna arrays, AOA is also feasible.

To date, cell phone locations can only be obtained by purchasing vendor-specific APIs. These are often limited to single operators and countries, and each location fix costs a fee. In most cases, the technical details are subject to nondisclosure agreements.

The Open Mobile Alliance Location Interoperability Forum (OMA LIF) focuses on the interoperability issues in the location-based services market. The vision of LIF is that location services are seamlessly integrated and available to all mobile users wherever they are. LIF has developed the Mobile Location Protocol (MLP) to standardize the interface between network operators and mobile application developers. MLP is based on well-known Internet technologies, like HTTP, SSL/TLS, and XML. Supporting this protocol is important, as it ensures the widest possible compatibility in the industry.

Cell Phone Location (Handset-Based)

The Mundo Cell phone Location System (Hartl, 2005) is based on software running on an individual user's cell phone rather than on a central server that may be queried about the location of a user. The software runs on smart phones based on Nokia's Series 60 or Microsoft's Pocket PC 2003 and monitors the cell information. Once the device enters a new network cell, it publishes the new cell information. For transmission, a small footprint UDP-based protocol is used, containing the relevant cell identifiers (mobile country code, mobile network code, location area code and cell-ID), the IMEI for identifying the phone and therefore the user, and a checksum. A proxy server on the Internet receives the data, transforms it into an XML/SOAP message containing the same information, and then dispatches it to the location-based service applications. In order to determine the location, the cell- and area-IDs have to be mapped to geographic coordinates using lookup tables.

In Germany, the operator O2 provides the Gauss-Krueger coordinates of the current base station in cell-broadcast messages. These coordinates can be directly converted into WGS84 geographic coordinates, without requiring any lookup tables.

Intel Place Lab

The Place Lab system (PlaceLab, 2007) by Intel Research estimates users' locations by means of fixed radio beacons, that is mostly WLAN access points. The basic idea is to use the MAC address of an access point as a unique ID and to store this ID together with the geographic location in a database. Users can later determine their location by scanning for nearby access points and querying the location database using the access point IDs.

Such location databases are usually created by war driving. War driving is the process of using a mobile computer equipped with WLAN and GPS and driving or walking through a neighborhood. The computer collects all beacons it receives from WLAN access points and stores the access point IDs along with the coordinates read out from the GPS receiver. Many people share the collected data sets on the Internet. At the time of writing, Wigle (Wigle, 2007) has an online database with more than 8.5 million entries. This enables new users to use the Place Lab software out-of-the-box as a positioning solution.

For privacy reasons, the location client does not send separate queries to the database server for each access point seen. Instead, it downloads a larger part of the database, for example for the whole city, and then determines the location locally. The Place Lab software can be downloaded for Windows, Linux, Mac OS/X, Pocket PC, and Series 60 phones. The source code is also publicly available, which allows integration into one's own software.

Ekahau

Ekahau (2007) is a commercial local positioning system based on WLAN and RSS fingerprinting. It does not require any special hardware. The required RSS map for the target area is created during the calibration process, which requires about 1 hour per 1200m^2. When the system is properly calibrated, it can achieve a positioning accuracy of about 1-3 meters. The system consists of Ekahau clients, the Ekahau manager, the Ekahau positioning engine and the Ekahau application framework.

The Ekahau manager is used for positioning model creation, maintenance, analysis, and live tracking on the floor map. This tool is also used during the calibration process, which involves collecting sample points every 3 to 5 meters.

The Ekahau client software must be installed on the computers to track. It is available for Windows and Pocket-PC based systems and relies on custom WLAN drivers. Ekahau provides a hardware compatibility list for supported devices and WLAN cards. The client collects the RSS indications for all access points in range and forwards this information to the positioning engine. Ekahau also offers stand-alone WLAN tags that can be used as people or asset tags.

The Ekahau positioning engine runs centrally on a server, receives the RSS data sets provided by clients and calculates clients' positions. Finally, the Ekahau application framework allows user applications to access position information.

Mundo WLAN Location Service

The Mundo WLAN Location Service (MWLS) is a research prototype and also based on RSS fingerprinting (Song, 2002). It does not require any special hardware. However, instead of measuring the RSS indications on the mobile terminal, the measurements are performed at multiple stationary receivers. Such receivers can either be Linux-based access points that also run the MWLS software or Linux computers acting as location sensors that only run the MWLS software, but do not provide network access. This scheme has a number of advantages.

First, any WLAN device able to send UDP packets can be tracked with the system. Since this can easily be done with almost any operating system and programming language, there are virtually no platform restrictions for clients. Mobile clients send broadcast UDP packets containing a serial number at regular intervals. The WLAN driver on the access point adds the RSSI and SNR values to the received packet and passes it to user space. A user space program forwards the RSS information to the location server, which calculates the clients' positions based on an interpolation algorithm.

Second, all RSS measurements are done on a per-packet basis, at the same time. This leads to a better accuracy when there are dynamic changes in the environment. In contrast, client-based solutions have to constantly scan for available access points in order to get multiple RSSI readings. Because each access point uses a different radio channel, the client has to permanently switch between channels. This degrades data throughput for all other applications using the WLAN interface at the same time. In addition, the signal-strength measurements are made at different times for different packets. MWLS measures the signal-strength values at the same time for exactly the same packet.

AeroScout

AeroScout (2007) is an advanced, infrastructure-based WLAN location system that is based on special access point hardware. It uses both RSSI and TDOA to determine location, depending on the environment and application. For TDOA installations, special AeroScout location receivers are required, for RSSI installations, the same receivers or existing Cisco access points can be used as readers. RSSI performs better in indoor walled environments (e.g., hospitals and distribution centers), while TDOA has advantages in unobstructed, indoor environments (e.g., manufacturing halls) and outdoor environments (e.g., shipping/trucking yards).

The AeroScout location receivers are equipped with special hardware to measure the time of arrival of standard 802.11b messages to the nanosecond. The measurements are forwarded to the AeroScout Engine, which determines clients' positions by multilateration. At least three location receivers are required for this algorithm. In TDOA mode, the system achieves an accuracy of about 1,5 m in open spaces and 6 m in tight indoor environments.

AeroScout also offers stand-alone location tags that can be tracked like any other WLAN device. In addition, tags can be triggered at short range (6,5 m) by an AeroScout Exciter, which allows the building of gate areas. Exciters send short messages to the tag which are then forwarded by the tag to the location receivers and thereby to the infrastructure.

Active Bat

The Active Bat (Ward, 1997) location system is a research prototype developed by AT&T. It uses ultrasound time-of-flight lateration to determine the accurate physical position of Active Bat tags. A central controller triggers a certain tag by sending a request over a short-range radio link. Each tag has a unique ID for addressing and recognition. In response to this request, the tag emits an ultrasonic pulse to a grid of ceiling-mounted receivers. At the same time the controller requests a pulse from the tag, it sends a reset signal to the ceiling sensors over a wired network. Each ceiling sensor measures the time interval between the reset signal and the arrival of the ultrasonic pulse. This time interval is directly proportional to the absolute distance between tag and receiver.

The sensors forward their time measurements to the central controller, which uses TOA lateration to calculate the tag's position. Because ultrasound pulses may be reflected by walls and objects in the room, the controller must try to eliminate all measurements that did not travel along the direct path from tag to sensor.

The system can locate tags to within 14 cm of their true position for 95% of the measurements (Ward, 1997). Active Bat relies on a large fixed-sensor infrastructure throughout the ceiling and is rather sensitive to the precise placement of sensors. Thus, scalability, ease of deployment, and cost are disadvantages of this system.

Cricket

Complementing the Active Bat system, Cricket (Priyantha, Chakraborty, & Balakrishnan 2000) uses ultrasound emitters in the infrastructure and receivers in the tags being located. Thus, the mobile tags have to perform their own lateration computations. Cricket also uses an RF channel for synchronization. In addition, the RF signal marks the time interval during which the receiver should consider the sounds it receives. In this way, a tag can consider ultrasound it hears after the end of this interval as a reflection and ignore it. The advantages of this system include location privacy and decentralized scalability. However, processing the ultrasound signals places a considerable computational burden on the mobile tags.

Infrared Badge Systems

Typical infrared badges emit their unique ID at fixed intervals. The signals are decoded in stationary mounted receivers. This simple principle only allows users to determine whether sender and receiver are within line-of-sight distance, or not. Depending on the requirements regarding area of coverage and resolution, potentially a large number of receivers have to be installed.

This principle can also be reversed, such that stationary mounted tags emit IDs that are received by mobile terminals. A commercial system offered by Eyeled (Eyeled, 2007) is based on strong, stationary emitters. The signals can be received with the IrDA interfaces of off-the-shelf PDAs. Because infrared badge systems are easy to build, numerous products and research prototypes exist.

Elpas

The Elpas EIRIS system (Visonic, 2007) is a flexible LPS that combines the usage of IR, RF (UHF), and LF (RF low frequency transponder)

Table 2. Possible interactions between Elpas components

Initiator	Relay	Receiver	Information
Tag/Badge		IR Reader	Tag T seen in room with reader R
Tag/Badge		RF Reader	Tag T seen in range of reader R (~25 m)
LF Exciter	Tag/Badge	IR Reader	Tag T is near place L (~3 m) and in room with reader R
LF Exciter	Tag/Badge	RF Reader	Tag T is near place L (~3 m) and in range of reader R (~25m)

signals. Visonic calls this "IRFID triple technology", which combines the advantages of each technology: the exact room location of IR, the wide range and constant communication of RF, and the tailored range sensitivity of LF.

The readers are connected to the server using the Local Operating Network (LON) bus, which is a well-known standard for building automation. Table 2 shows possible communication patterns between the different Elpas components and the location information obtained by these interactions.

Visonic and its partners offer complete LBS solutions for medical institutions (hospitals, nursing homes, mental homes), assisted living, industry, logistics, and administration. The EIRIS server provides a rule engine that can be configured to automatically trigger alarms (via SMS, email, custom client applications, etc.) or to control LON appliances (door openers, lights, etc.). As an application example, consider the BabyMatch package for pediatric wards. Mothers wear wrist tags and babies wear special baby tags, attached to the foot. To prevent mistakes and kidnapping, a mother taking the wrong baby triggers locking of exit doors and a nurse alarm. In addition, the unauthorized removal of tags can also trigger alarms. Figure 6 shows tags and readers of the Elpas system.

Figure 6. Elpas Hardware (reproduced by permission of Visonic Technologies)

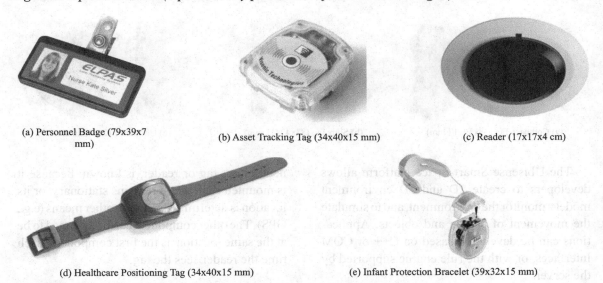

(a) Personnel Badge (79x39x7 mm)

(b) Asset Tracking Tag (34x40x15 mm)

(c) Reader (17x17x4 cm)

(d) Healthcare Positioning Tag (34x40x15 mm)

(e) Infant Protection Bracelet (39x32x15 mm)

Ubisense

Ubisense (Ubisense, 2007) is a precise location tracking system based on Ultra Wide Band (UWB) radio technology. This allows the system to handle multipath effects adequately, resulting in an order of magnitude better accuracy compared to systems based on a single frequency, like AeroScout. The Ubisense system comprises UbiTags carried by people or objects, stationary UbiSensors, and server software running on Linux or Windows servers. The Ubisense hardware is shown in Figure 7.

In addition to LAN connections, the UbiSensors require direct interconnections with timing cables. This allows the system to maintain a global clock per location cell. Because sensors are equipped with phased antenna arrays, they can also measure the angle-of-arrival. UbiTags are worn by people or attached to equipment and broadcast UWB pulses in regular intervals. The system now uses the DTOA and AOA scheme to calculate tag positions. Tag positions can be determined with an accuracy of about 15cm.

A sensor cell can be built out of one up to seven sensors. When only a single sensor is used,

an intersection plane must be defined. The sensor then measures two AOA angles (horizontal and vertical) and intersects it with this plane. The intersection point is reported as the tag's position. For example, a single sensor can be mounted on the ceiling and a horizontal intersection plane with a height of 1.5m above ground is defined, assuming that tags are usually worn at this height.

Starting with two sensors, 3D coordinates can be calculated based on AOA. At least three sensors are required for best operation of the system. Because tags have a directional antenna and the system virtually requires a direct line-of-sight between tags and sensors, cells must be built out of at least four sensors in practice. A single cell can cover up to 100m² and should contain no or only thin walls. Ubisense also supports larger cells, but at lower accuracies and tracking rates.

Ubisense combines TDOA and AOA to achieve precision and accuracy. The TDOA scheme allows a precise calculation of tag locations. However, multipath effects occasionally induce large errors into time measurements. Now, the AOA information enables an indication of the reliability of a position calculation.

Figure 7. Ubisense hardware (reproduced by permission of Ubisense)

(a) Compact Tag (38x39x17 mm)   (b) Slim Tag (83x42x11 mm)   (c) UbiSensor (20x13x6 cm)

The Ubisense Smart Space platform allows developers to create 2D and 3D environment models, monitor the environment, and to simulate the movement of people and objects. Applications can be developed based on C++ or COM interfaces, or with the rule engine supported by the server.

RFID

RFID technology can also be used to build location systems. The principle of function of such systems is very similar to that of infrared badge systems; only the transmission medium is different. When a tag is moved into close proximity of a reader, the reader is able to identify the tag and emits a notification. The location of one component, either tag or reader, is known, because it is mounted such that it remains stationary, or its location is determined by some other means (e.g., GPS). The other component can be assumed to be at the same location as the first component, each time the reader sees the tag.

A.R.T.

The A.R.T. system (ART, 2007) is an infrared optical tracking system with a high accuracy and low latency, designed mainly for motion capture and Augmented Reality (AR) applications. It measures the position and/or orientation of bodies. Tracking with position (3D coordinates) and orientation (3 independent angular coordinates) is also often called 6 degrees of freedom (6DOF) tracking.

Figure 8. A.R.T. hardware (reproduced by permission of A.R.T. GmbH)

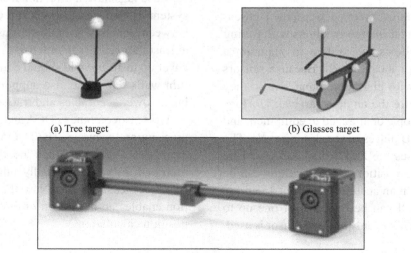

(a) Tree target   (b) Glasses target

(c) Cameras with IR flash

The system consists of the DTrack tracking software and two to sixteen cameras. The cameras are equipped with infrared filters and infrared flashes. Camera shutters and flashes operate globally synchronized. The objects to track carry passive markers reflecting IR light. 6DOF tracking requires the use of rigid bodies with multiple markers and well-known geometries. Figure 8 shows two different targets and a stereo camera.

At least two cameras are necessary to obtain sufficient AOA measurements to triangulate the marker location is space. More cameras can be used to reduce occlusions or to extend the cell size. A.R.T. reaches positioning accuracies of 0.4mm in a 3m x 3m cell.

Mundo IRIS

Mundo InfraRed Indoor Scout (Aitenbichler & Mühlhäuser, 2003) is an infrared optical tracking system. Tracked objects carry active tags that emit infrared signals, which are received by a stationary mounted stereo-camera. The system is based on cheap off-the-shelf PC components and USB or Fireware cameras. Beside the tags,

no specialized hardware is required. The system has two unique features.

First, the system has a large coverage, because the active tags can still be recognized from a distance of ~15m. Evaluation in a medium-sized lecture theater (130m²) yielded an accuracy of 16.67cm (RMS). With this accuracy, the system can distinguish between seats in a lecture theater.

Second, the signals sent by tags are modulated with their identifiers. This allows the distinguishing of tags with a single emitter, while almost any other system can only distinguish between tags by analyzing the geometry.

The drawbacks of infrared optical systems include that they require a direct line-of-sight between tags and cameras and that they must be shielded from sunlight.

Positioning System Summary

Table 3 summarizes the properties of the location systems presented in the previous sections. The column *technology* contains the underlying technology used for the communication and ranging links between infrastructure and mobile users/ob-

Table 3. Comparison of selected positioning systems

System	Technology	Positioning	Consolidation	Accuracy	Indoor/Outdoor
GPS	RF	TDOA	User	<6 m	outdoor
Cell phone	GSM	RSS, AOA	Infrastructure	50-300 m (E911)	both
Cell phone	GSM	RSS	User	~100 m (city)	both
Place Lab	WLAN	RSS	User	25-50 m	both
Ekahau	WLAN	RSS	User	<3 m	both
Mundo WLS	WLAN	RSS	Infrastructure	<3 m	both
AeroScout	WLAN	RSS, TDOA	Infrastructure	1.5-6 m	both
Active Bat	Ultrasound	TOA	Infrastructure	~14 cm	indoor
Cricket	Ultrasound	TOA	User	~15 cm	indoor
Elpas	IR, RF, LF	Proximity	N/A	1-50 m	both
Ubisense	UWB	TDOA, AOA	Infrastructure	~15 cm	indoor
RFID	RF	Proximity	N/A	0.1-3 m	both
A.R.T.	IR (passive)	AOA	Infrastructure	0.4 mm	indoor
IRIS	IR (active)	AOA	Infrastructure	~16 cm	indoor

jects. *Positioning* denotes the kind of sensor data used and the positioning method. *Consolidation* describes if the multiple sensor measurements are merged on the side of the infrastructure or on the side of the mobile user. The accuracy values are only rough estimations and strongly depend on the environment, such as radio cell sizes. Finally, *indoor/outdoor* indicates if the system is suitable for indoor use, outdoor use, or both.

LOCATION MODELS

A location tracking system, as described in the previous sections, allows the positions of people or objects to be determined in a representation that is specific to the system. Location models are now used to derive information that is more meaningful to applications, for example, location within a building, or location relative to other people or objects of interest from this system-specific position data.

Location Representation

Two basic classes of location representations can be distinguished: Locations can either be specified numerically by using coordinates, or symbolically by assigning names to locations.

The coordinates of a location are the components of a tuple of numbers used to describe a point in the plane or space. We further distinguish between local and global coordinate systems. For example, the GPS system uses the World Geodetic System 84 (WGS84), where coordinates are expressed as triples containing the geographic longitude, latitude, and the elevation above main sea level. Indoor tracking systems often provide 2D or 3D coordinates with respect to a local Cartesian reference system. Using geometric operations, we can calculate the distance between two points or determine if an area lies within another area. Hence, geometric coordinates already allow some reasoning about spatial proximity and containment.

Symbolic locations are specified in the form of abstract names, for example, identifier of the closest sensor, room number, street address, and so forth. In contrast to geometric coordinates, it is not possible to reason about distances or containment without additional knowledge about the relationship between symbolic locations. For example, this information can be provided by a world model.

Functions and Relations

With the help of the positioning algorithms described before, we are able to determine the position of people or objects in a representation that is specific to the location system. However, what is really desired at the application level is location within a building, or location relative to other people or objects of interest, whether moving or stationary. In many cases, a location model is a prerequisite for transforming the raw sensor data into a representation that is meaningful to applications.

A number of different location models will be presented in the following sections. These models have different properties and which model best suits an application depends on the queries required from the perspective of users and applications. In general, the following features are required from a location model:

- **Location function:** Determining the locations of mobile users or static objects is the most basic function. All models provide this information, but they differ in how location is represented.
- **Distance function:** This function provides a measure of the distance between two locations. A notion of distance is required by many location-based applications, for example consider a user that wants to find the nearest bus stop. If geometric coordinates are available, straight distances can simply be calculated using the Pythagoras's

theorem. However, in many cases, distance measures that take specific paths (road or railway network, etc.) into account are more useful in practice. To determine the distance between symbolic locations, the model must contain explicit definitions of distances.

- **Connected-to relation:** This relation describes the interconnections between neighboring locations and therefore how to get from one location to the next. Navigation applications require location models that allow them to find paths from one location to a different remote location. Paths may be defined by a transportation network (bus routes, etc.) and consist of several interconnected locations (bus stops).

- **Contained-in relation:** Topology is a mechanism for establishing spatial relationships between the user and her surroundings. This relation is required to query all objects located in a given area. If geometric coordinates are used, it can be easily calculated if an object is contained in a certain spatial area from defined geometry. For symbolic location, this relation has to be modeled explicitly between locations.

Geometric Location Models

A geometric location model describes locations by geometric figures. Many recent SQL server products (e.g., MySQL) support spatial extensions based on the OpenGIS Geometry Model. In this model, each geometric object is associated with a spatial reference system, which describes the coordinate space in which the object is defined, and belongs to some geometry class. All calculations are made assuming planar Euclidean geometry.

For example, a database table with the coordinates of three rooms can be constructed as follows (Figure 9):

```
CREATE TABLE room (name TEXT, poly POLYGON);
INSERT INTO room VALUES ('A101',
GeomFromText('POLYGON((0 0, 6 0, 6 4, 0 4, 0 0))'));
INSERT INTO room VALUES ('A102',
GeomFromText('POLYGON((6 0, 10 0, 10 4, 6 4, 6 0))'));
INSERT INTO room VALUES ('A103', GeomFromText('POLY
GON((10 0, 14 0, 14 4, 10 4, 10 0))'));
```

A second table contains the current locations of users:

```
CREATE TABLE user (name TEXT, position POINT);
INSERT INTO user VALUES ('john', GeomFromText('POINT(7
3)'));
```

Location: The location of a user can be determined by querying the user table.

```
SELECT AsText(position) FROM user
>> POINT(7 3)
```

Distance: The shortest distance between the user's position and any point of the geometry of room A103 can be determined with the following query.

```
SELECT Distance(poly, position) FROM room, user WHERE
room.name='A103';
>> 3.0
```

Connected-to: The rooms next to A102 can be determined using the Touches function.

```
SELECT b.name FROM room AS a, room AS b WHERE
a.name='A102' AND Touches(a.poly, b.poly);
>> A101
>> A103
```

However, we do not know if the rooms are directly connected to each other by doors. Thus, the connected-to relation has to be modeled explicitly.

Contained-in: The following query determines the room names for users' locations.

```
SELECT user.name, room.name FROM user, room WHERE
Contains(poly, position);
>> john, A102
```

While the topological relation contained-in can be derived from geometry, this is not possible for the connected-to relation. The calculated distances are the shortest distances between geometries and do not necessarily reflect the distance a user would have to travel.

Symbolic Location Models

Set-based model: In the set-based model, rooms that share certain properties are grouped into sets. At the highest level, the model starts with the set L that contains all possible locations. All other sets are subsets of L. As an example, consider the floor plan shown in Figure 9. All rooms in floor 1 and wing A of the building can be grouped into a set $L_{A1} = \{A101, A102, ..., A109\}$.

This model allows to determine overlapping and containment relations between sets. If $L_1 \cap L_2 \neq \varnothing$, then L_1 and L_2 overlap. If $L_1 \cap L_2 = L_1$, then L_1 is fully contained in L_2. Neighboring symbolic locations can also be modeled using sets, for example $L_C = \{A104, A105\}$ could express that the rooms A104 and A105 are directly connected by a door. When connected locations are described this way, it is also possible to derive paths for navigation applications. However, the huge number of resulting sets involves a high modeling effort.

Distances between locations can be set into relation by comparing the sizes of the smallest neighbor sets. For example, the distance between A105 and A104 is shorter than the distance between A105 and A101, because the smallest set that contains A105 and A104 is L_C, and the smallest set that contains A105 and A101 is L_{A1}, and $|L_C| < |L_{A1}|$. Beside this qualitative comparison, the set-based model does not permit the calculation of quantitative distances between locations.

Figure 9. Set-based location model

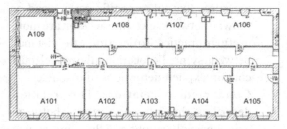

Hierarchical model: This model is an extension of the set-based model, where locations are ordered according to containment relations. A location l_1 is an ancestor of location l_2 (also written as $l_1 > l_2$), when l_2 is spatially contained in location l_1. If locations do not overlap, then the containment relations can be arranged into a tree. The lattice-based model is more general and allows overlapping locations.

For example, consider the building in Figure 10. The set of locations L consists of the building B, the floors F_i, the wings W_i, and several rooms R_i. Locations of the form F_iW_j denote an intersection of floor F_i with wing W_j. Distances can be compared by calculating the suprenum (least upper bound) of a set of locations. For example, the rooms R_1 and R_2 are considered to be closer to each other than the rooms R_2 and R_5, because R_1 and R_2 are located on the same floor and in the same wing, while R_2 and R_5 only share the same wing.

However, hierarchical models only describe containment and have no means for describing connections between locations. For example, there could be stairs connecting R_2 and R_5 directly.

Graph-based model: This model is based on a graph $G = (V, E)$, where the vertices V denote symbolic locations and the edges E denote connections between locations. An edge directly represents the *connected-to* relation and is added between two vertices, if a direct connection between the two locations exists. Thus, the model is suitable for nearest-neighbor queries and navigation applications. An example is shown in Figure 11.

Figure 10. Hierarchical lattice-based location model example (Becker, 2005)

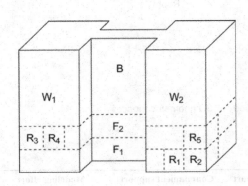

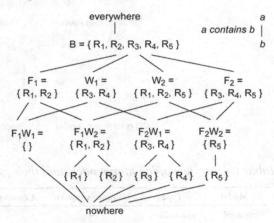

The distance between two locations can be calculated as the minimum number of hops between the two locations. To implement quantitative measures for distance, edges can be attributed with additional information, for example physical distance, or speed limit. A limitation of the graph model is that it cannot express *contained-in* relationships.

Combined models: The discussion above showed that the hierarchical model is well suited for describing spatial containment, while connections between locations cannot be described. In contrast, the graph-based model can describe connections well, but not containment. These two models can be combined to gain the benefits of both. The graph-based part describes the connections between locations, as shown before. The set-based part is used to describe containment, but only down to certain granularity, for example floors.

Figure 11. Graph-based model

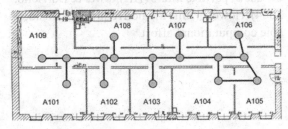

Hybrid Location Models

Hybrid location models combine symbolic and geometric representations. The basis of such a model can be a geometric model describing the extent of buildings using a global reference system, like WGS84. The structure of buildings is then described by means of a symbolic model that combines the hierarchical and graph-based approaches. If needed, detailed geometric descriptions for rooms can be added as vertex attributes in the symbolic model. Figure 12 shows an example for a multi-level hybrid location model.

The properties of different location models are summarized in Table 4. It should be noted that the overall modeling effort always depends on the amount of detail needed in the model. However, some models permit a straightforward implementation of a feature, while others require auxiliary constructions to achieve the same.

FURTHER RESEARCH DIRECTIONS

This chapter provided an introduction to positioning systems. We first described the different physical properties that can be measured with sensors and the basic principles to determine one's location from this sensor data. Next, the signal

Figure 12. Hybrid location model

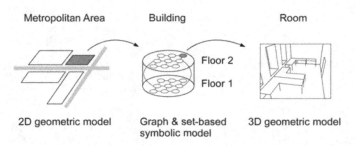

Table 4. Overview of location models and their properties

Model	Type	Distance support	Connected-to support	Containment support	Modeling effort
Set-based	symbolic	-	+	+	High
Hierarchical	symbolic	--	--	++	Low
Graph-based	symbolic	++	++	--	Low
Combined	symbolic	++	++	++	Medium
Geometric	geometric	+	-	++	High
Hybrid	both	++	++	++	High

propagation characteristics of electromagnetic waves were discussed. We then described 14 location systems as implementation examples and showed the connection to the theory presented beforehand. Finally, location models are used to derive information more meaningful to applications, for example, the location within a building, or the location relative to other people or objects of interest.

More information about the GPS system can be found in Kaplan (1996). The Book "Local Positioning Systems" (Kolodziej & Hjelm, 2006) contains a comprehensive collection of material on LPSs. For a description of more research prototypes, see Hightower and Borriello (2001). More details about location models are described in Becker (2005). Some particular areas where research is currently active and is likely to remain active in the near future are:

Elimination of multipath effects: For optimal accuracy, location sensors must be able to distinguish the signals that traveled on the direct path from navigation source to the user from indirect, reflected signals. This involves complex signal processing on the receiver side. Research topics include transmitter, receiver, and antenna (array) engineering for ultra wide bands (UWB) and signal processing algorithms.

Fusion: Because location systems have vastly different characteristics, it is unlikely that a single high-accuracy location system with ubiquitous coverage will become available in the near future. The availability of location systems will be uneven and thus the challenge will be to merge the information from multiple heterogeneous sources. In particular, it is difficult to fusion geometric and symbolic location data. A promising approach is the use of particle filters (Hightower & Borriello, 2004). However, this method requires a considerable computational effort.

REFERENCES

Aeroscout (2007). *Aeroscout: Enterprise visibility solutions*. Retrieved October 16, 2007, from http://www.aeroscout.com.

Aitenbichler, E., & Mühlhäuser, M. (2003). An IR local positioning system for smart items and devices. In *Proceedings of the IWSAWC03* (pp. 334–339). IEEE Computer Society.

ART (2007). *A.R.T. GmbH: Your expert for infrared optical tracking systems*. Retrieved October 16, 2007, from http://www.ar-tracking.de.

Awange, J. L., & Grafarend, E. W. (2002). Algebraic solution of GPS pseudo-ranging equations. *GPS Solutions, 5*(4), 20-32.

Bancroft, S. (1985). An algebraic solution of the GPS equations. *IEEE Transactions Aerospace and Electronic Systems, AES-21*(7), 56–59.

Becker, C., & Dürr, F. (2005). On location models for ubiquitous computing. *Personal and Ubiquitous Computing, 9*, 20–31.

Ekahau (2007). *Ekahau: Master your WiFi-network*. Retrieved October 16, 2007, from http://www.ekahau.com.

Eyeled (2007). *Eyeled: Mobile competence*. Retrieved October 16, 2007, from http://www.eyeled.de.

Hartl, A. (2005). A provider-independent, proactive service for location sensing in cellular networks. In *GTGKVS Fachgespräch*. Retrieved November 29, 2007 from http://www.wireless-earth.de/fg_lbs/meeting_2/meeting_2.html

Hightower, J., & Borriello, G. (2001). Location systems for ubiquitous computing. *Computer*, pages 57–66. IEEE Computer Society.

Hightower, J., & Borriello, G. (2004). Particle filters for location estimation in ubiquitous computing: A case study. UbiComp 2004: Ubiquitous Computing, pages 88–106.

Kaplan, E. (1996). *Understanding GPS: Principles and applications*. Artech House Publishers.

Kolodziej, K. W., & Hjelm, J. (2006). *Local positioning systems: LBS applications and services*. CRC Press.

PlaceLab (2007). *Place lab homepage*. Retrieved October 16, 2007, from http://www.placelab.org.

Priyantha, N. B., Chakraborty, A., & Balakrishnan, H. (2000). The cricket location-support system. In *Proceedings of the 6th Annual International Conference on Mobile Computing and Networking (MOBICOM 2000)* (pp. 32–43).

Song, Y. (2002). *In-house location tracking*. Unpublished master's thesis, Darmstadt University of Technology.

Ubisense (2007). *Ubisense: Precise real-time location*. Retrieved October 16, 2007, from http://www.ubisense.net.

Visonic (2007). *Visonic technologies: Elpas*. Retrieved October 16, 2007, from http://www.visonictech.com.

Ward, A., Jones, A., & Hopper, A. (1997). A new location technique for the active office. *IEEE Personnel Communications, 4*(5), 42–47.

Wigle (2007). *WiGLE: Wireless geographic logging engine*. Retrieved October 16, 2007, from http://www.wigle.net.

ADDITIONAL READING

Bahl, P., & Padmanabhan, V. N. (2000). RADAR: An in-building RF-based user location and tracking system. In *INFOCOM 2000*, pages 775–784.

Bahl, P., & Padmanabhan, V. N. (2001). *A software system for locating mobile users: Design, evaluation, and lessons* (Tech. Rep.) Microsoft Research.

Borriello, G., Chalmers, M., LaMarca, A., & Nixon, P. (2005). Delivering real-world ubiquitous location systems. *Communications of the ACM, 48*(3), 36–41.

Caffery, J. J., & Stüber, G. L. (1998). Overview of radiolocation in CDMA cellular systems. *IEEE Communications Magazine, 36*(4), pp. 38–45.

Cheng, Y-C., Chawathe, Y., LaMarca, A., & Krumm, J. (2005). Accuracy characterization for metropolitan-scale Wi-Fi localization. In *Proceedings of Mobisys 2005.*

Chen, M., Haehnel, D., Hightower, J., Sohn, T., LaMarca, A., Smith, I., Chmelev, D., Hughes, J., & Potter, F. (2006). Practical metropolitan-scale positioning for GSM phones. In *Proceedings of Ubicomp 2006.*

European Space Agency (2006). *The Galileo global navigation satellite system.* Retrieved October 16, 2007, from http://www.esa.int/esaNA/galileo.html.

Fishkin, K. P., Jiang, B., Philipose, M., & Roy, S. (2004). I sense a disturbance in the force: Unobtrusive detection of interactions with RFID-tagged objects. *Proceedings of Ubicomp 2004* (Vol. 3205), Springer.

Hightower, J., Brumitt, B., & Borriello, G. (2002). The location stack: A layered model for location in ubiquitous computing. In *Proceedings of the 4th IEEE Workshop on Mobile Computing Systems & Applications (WMCSA 2002)* (pp. 22–28).

Hightower, J., Consolvo, S., LaMarca, A., Smith, I., & Hughes, J. (2005). Learning and recognizing the places we go. In *Proceedings of Ubicomp 2005.*

Hightower, J., LaMarca, A., & Smith, I. (2006). Practical lessons from place lab. *IEEE Pervasive Computing, 5*(3).

LaMarca, A., Chawathe, Y., & Smith, I. (2004). Finding yourself: Experimental location technol-ogy relies on Wi-Fi and cellphone signals instead of orbiting satellites. *IEEE Spectrum 2004.*

LaMarca, A., Hightower, J., Smith, I., & Consolvo, S. (2005). Self-mapping in 802.11 location systems. In *Proceedings of Ubicomp 2005.*

LaMarca, A., Chawathe, Y., Consolvo, S., Hightower, J., Smith, I., Scott, J., Sohn, T., Howard, J., Hughes, J., Potter, F., Tabert, J., Powledge, P., Borriello, G., & Schilit, B. (2005). Place lab: Device positioning using radio beacons in the wild. In *Proceedings of Pervasive 2005.*

Letchner, J., Fox, D., & LaMarca, A. (2005). Large-scale localization from wireless signal strength. In *Proceedings of the National Conference on Artificial Intelligence (AAAI 2005).*

Minami, M., Fukuju, Y., Hirasawa, K., Yokoyama, S., Mizumachi, M., Morikawa, H., & Aoyama, T. (2004). DOLPHIN: A practical approach for implementing a fully distributed indoor ultrasonic positioning system. In *UbiComp 2004: Ubiquitous Computing.*

Otsason, V., Varshavsky, A., LaMarca, A., & da Lara, E. (2005). Accurate GSM indoor localization. In *Proceedings of Ubicomp 2005.*

Pahlavan, K., Li, X., & Mäkelä, J. P. (2002). Indoor geolocation science and technology. *IEEE Communications Magazine, 40*(2), 112–118.

Pfeifer, T., & Elias, D. (2003). Commercial hybrid IR/RF local positioning system. In *13. Fachtagung Kommunikation in Verteilten Systemen (KiVS 2003) Kurzbeiträge*, pages 119–127.

RF Technologies (2006). *PinPoint asset tracking solutions homepage.* Retrieved October 16, 2007, from http://www.rft.com/products/pinpoint

Raab, F., Blood, E., Steiner, O., & Jones, H. (1979). Magnetic position and orientation tracking systems. *IEEE Transactions on Aerospace and Electronics Systems, 15*(5), 709–717.

Smith, A., Balakrishnan, H., Goraczko, M., & Priyantha, N. B. (2004). Tracking moving devices with the cricket location system. In *Proceedings of the 2nd International Conference on Mobile Systems, Applications and Services (Mobisys 2004).*

Sohn, T., Varshavsky, A., LaMarca, A., Chen, M., Choudhury, T., Smith, I., Consolvo, S., Hightower, J., Griswold, W. G., & de Lara, E. (2006). Mobility detection using everyday GSM traces. In *Proceedings of Ubicomp 2006.*

Varshavsky, A., Chen, M., de Lara, E., Froehlich, J., Haehnel, D., Hightower, J., LaMarca, A., Potter, F., Sohn, T., Tang, K., & Smith, I. (2006). Are GSM phones THE solution for localization? In *Proceedings of the 7th IEEE Workshop on Mobile Computing Systems and Applications (HotMobile 2006).*

Want, R., Hopper, A., Falcão, V., & Gibbons, J. (1992). The active badge location system. *ACM Transactions on Information Systems* (TOIS), *10*(1), 91–102.

Chapter XIII
Adapting to the User

Matthias Jöst
European Media Laboratory GmbH, Germany

ABSTRACT

Adaptation is one of the key requirements to handle the increasing complexity in today's computing environments. This chapter focuses on the aspect of adaptation that puts the user into focus. In this context it introduces the different adaptation types possible for ubiquitous computing services like interaction, content, and presentation. To allow for an automatic adaptation it is important to get some means about the users. Basic requirements to model the users and approaches to personalize applications will be presented.

INTRODUCTION

In the near future... Imagine a businessman preparing for a trip to some western metropolis to meet a customer. As usually, he organizes his trip via the World Wide Web checking how to get to his destination, finding reasonable accommodation and investigating things to do in his free time. To keep himself occupied during his journey, he might listen to his music collection while surfing the mobile Internet and reading emails. At his destination, he checks in at the hotel and enters his room, the heating and ambient light is adjusted

to his preferences and in the morning, he expects to have a shower at his preferred temperature. At his customer's premises, the meeting room is well prepared for his presentation, his preferred hot drink is waiting for him and the business cards are automatically transferred between the participating businessmen.

This small scenario touches on many aspects of modern life, already in place or yet to come. For example, information acquisition via the World Wide Web, either stationary or mobile, interaction with intelligent infrastructures such as hotels or meeting rooms, and also IT supported interaction with others. In order to exploit the benefits of those services completely, the key requirement is adaptation to the user. But to allow for a reasonable adaptation, a deep understanding of the user by means of accounting for his preferences, capabilities and usage context is needed. This chapter introduces basic forms of adaptation followed by techniques to allow for inferences concerning the user's interests.

ADAPTING TO THE USER

When speaking about adaptation to the user one needs to focus on three main aspects of adaptation: Interaction, Content, and Presentation. In our traveling business man scenario interaction can be observed in various forms: *search for information via a desktop computer, listening to some music on the move or even enter the hotel room.* Content is the media/information and the means to interact with, either some Web pages or the music selection on a mobile device. Presentation defines how to inform the user about the outcome of a service usage, for example heating the shower in the morning or presenting only suitable travel connections according to the user's needs. It is obvious that all three forms of adaptation are highly connected and interweaved.

Interaction Adaptation

In the last few years, the high tech industry has started to learn that one of the most important features of all computerized services and devices is their interface to humans. This counts especially in ubiquitous computing scenarios, where those services often are not recognizable as such and where complexity of service arrangements reaches new levels. Think back to our hotel or meeting room example.

A basic concept to describe and cope with the complexity of information processing in this manner is the concept of communication

channels. Such a channel can be described as a directed temporal, virtual or physical link allowing for information exchange between different communicating entities. For example it can be the graphical user interface of a mobile device that notifies the user about the current battery status.

Different aspects need to be considered while establishing such a communication channel. Communication is not a one way process, it happens via various channels in parallel. Obviously the capacity of a sender or receiver to process information varies significantly, especially with respect to the actual context.

Furthermore, communication requires abstraction at different levels in order to process information chunks to a coherent view. The first step in this processing chain is information *fission*, which describes the decomposition of information into small chunks. It is than followed by information *fusion,* in which those chunks are combined to new pieces of information.

Along different communication channels, one can distinguish various interaction metaphors. In classical desktop computing, monomodal interaction via a graphical user interface with keyboard and pointing devices dominates. But in recent time, new interaction modalities or even combinations of modalities have gained momentum (Oviatt, 1996). This is on the one hand, due to the ubiquity of computing services, and on the other due to the progress in speech technologies and image recognition (see Chapter Intelligent User Interfaces). The latest prominent examples are pointing gestures for personal gaming consoles.

Modalities can be differentiated according to the activation mode, whether the user actively issues an interaction (e.g., via speech) or whether the system observes passively the user behavior (e.g., his mood based on the facial expression). Generally, multimodal interaction serves two main purposes: First, to allow for a more natural interaction with computerized services, and second, to disambiguate the given user input for complex tasks.

Interaction adaptation often follows a processing chain. First the amount of information that needs to be exchanged between the user and the system is defined. For this information the most suitable modality is selected in a second step. In case the system is not suited for multimodality, the modality for the interaction is chosen during the system design.

Content Adaptation

The adaptation of content can take multiple forms depending on the specific purpose of the system and depending on the user interface modalities. For graphical user interfaces and the presentation of content in graphical form factors such as display features (size, resolution, colors), the interaction method and general usage (for example indoor versus outdoor usage) matters.

Commonly, one can distinguish two different adaptation strategies: On the one hand to allow for adaptation within the general information content, and on the other hand, to enhance the information content with external information.

- **Additional ⇔ omitted information:** Additional information is given to the user in case he shows specific interest in a certain topic or he needs specific information for example, our businessman who wants to know the composer of a music track he is listening to on his journey. Such information could also be omitted if the businessman knows the composer already and the system is aware of this.
- **Individual recommendations and hints:** Those recommendations notify users about specific features and options of a service that might be currently relevant for them. This is often also used for product recommendations. Here specific characteristics of

products—in which the user is presumably interested—are highlighted. For example, while booking accommodation, additional information might be given, like the hotel having a fitness room (as the business man likes to do his daily workout).

In recent years various techniques have been developed to support content adaptation. The most common one is the realization of content variants via markup languages such as the eXtensible Markup Language—XML. Such markup languages allow for annotation of text elements with metadata, for example, indicating whether some information elements are optional or not.

Presentation Adaptation

In the past, presentation adaptation was only realized by means of hypertext adaptation on the World Wide Web in HTML Pages (Brusilovsky, 1996). New adaptation techniques were required as a result of the hypertext enrichment with multimedia items such as images, videos, sounds or even 3D animations (Rossi, Schwabe, Lucena, & Cowan, 1995). Since access to digital information is nowadays ubiquitous, presentation adaptation needs to answer several further questions:

- *Which medium is the most suitable one to present the content, according to the current user context?*
- *Does the chosen medium still follow the semantics of the original information? How can one preserve the original content during the adaptation process?*
- *How should the media be adapted to fit the current user context, for example, the screen size, or the respond to limited bandwidth?*

These questions focus more on the qualitative aspects of multimedia information, on semantics of the information and its correlation to the actual user context.

- **Media selection:** The basic step during the presentation adaptation is the selection of what media or media combination serves the users needs best, according to the current context. Mostly, the media chosen for a specific purpose is hard-coded into the system application logic. In order to allow for flexible media selection, the content needs to be semantically annotated to verify semantic equivalence of different content fragments.

- **Media adaptation:** Current hypermedia still targets two main human senses, sight and hearing. In recent years, most work on media adaptation has been done in the area of video streaming based on the upcoming Internet and mobile usage scenarios with their specific limitations in order to maintain the quality of service, such as bandwidth and hardware resources. These days', early prototypes also incorporate the olfactory sense and tangible user interfaces.

The foundation of meaningful service adaptation is understanding of the user and the user's needs. It is obvious that even current intelligent

services cannot cope with the complexity of human thinking and behavior. They need to rely on inferences that are made on the observable user behavior. In our example, on his last flight the businessman might have chosen to sit by the aisle. So an adaptive travel agency service might realize that he prefers sitting by the aisle. To draw such a conclusion, with the slight chance that it meets the user's needs, it is crucial to decide during the system design which data needs to be acquired.

MODELING THE USER

Knowledge about users is the key requirement for personalized adaptation. But as humans, their interests and their behavior are complex and manifold, it is crucial for the success of an adaptation process to incorporate some formal model about the users. This user model should structure the information that will be collected by the service about its users. Furthermore it should be open to incorporate new knowledge that is for example not gathered directly from the user but that is inferred from other users that have showed a similar behavior.

But to focus on the users solely is not enough, especially since this would not account for adaptation in ubiquitous computing scenarios. Here the classical desktop computing schema with a user sitting in front of a PC does not fit anymore. In fact the user is situated somewhere and experiences all sorts of influences from his current surrounding. For example, changing light conditions, noise levels, he might be in a hurry or surrounded by his family. All these factors influence his needs and interests and therefore should also be taken into account for an adaptation process (Jameson, 2001). The following figure represents an integration approach for combining a context model, knowledge representation and the user model.

Figure. 1. Dimensions of media adaptation

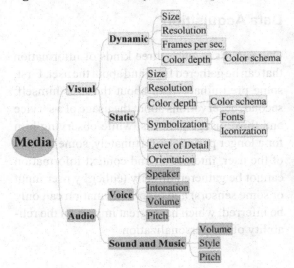

Figure. 2. Combined user and context-model (Zipf & Jöst, 2005)

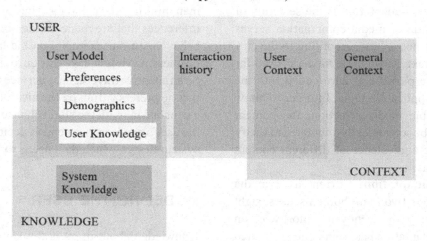

The system's representation of the user incorporates a user model. It describes the user with assumptions about his knowledge and preferences, the interaction history and a description of his current situation. For dealing with preference a distinction between interests and behavioral preferences is proposed. Interest preferences depict the user's interest in certain topics, for example buildings of a specific architectural style or a historical event. One can distinguish such interests as only of a short duration or as a general long-term interest in order to reflect the concept of interest shift during the use of the system. The interaction history comprises the different interactions between the user and the system either via natural language or a graphical user interface.

The user's context is part of the general situation. It is the attempt to describe the user's current situation with its various characteristics in the real world. Some of these occurrences can be gathered more or less directly through the use of external sensors such as the user's current position, whereas others can only be inferred through indirect indicators derived from the context model.

The third main component is a representation of the user's and the system's knowledge. The user knowledge provides references to information which had already been provided by the system in order to allow appropriate interaction and to refine the user preferences. The system knowledge should represent the system's overall knowledge about the world.

In order to provide personalized and user-tailored services, an adaptable/adaptive system requires a clear picture of the user. In our example the online travel agency needs to know which means of transportation the business man prefers, where he wants to sit or which price range he is willing to accept. But how can the necessary information be acquired?

Data Acquisition

One can distinguish three kinds of information that can be gathered from and about the user. First, some preliminary data about the user himself, second, observations about the usage of a service and third, usage patterns, while observing him for a longer period. Unfortunately, some aspects of the user, interaction and context information cannot be gathered directly (either by user input or some sensors) and other information can only be inferred, which has a great impact on the reliability of the personalization.

User Data

User data represents information which is directly related to a single user, for example origin, age, sex or interests. Quite often this data is provided explicitly by the user while asking him directly (e.g., during the service registration process). For this reason, it provides the background of every adaptation process. There are five categories of user data:

- **Demographic data:** Where does the user come from, how old is she/he? The demographic data covers specific common aspects that can be applied for all users in order to allow an initial grouping of them.
- **User knowledge:** The users' familiarity with the type of application and the information domain can be used to adapt a service. In our example it could refer to the fact that the user has been at his destination previously and he has already visited its most prominent sights.
- **User skills and capabilities:** What are his specific capabilities and does he potentially have some limitations such as, for example, physical constraints?
- **User interests and preferences:** What are the interests of the user concerning the application domain or information area? Does the user have preferences, for instance, as regards the interaction modalities?
- **User goals and plans**: Can the system infer the user's goals based on the interaction history or does the user specify his plan directly?

Interactions and Their Patterns

To allow for adaptation, personalized services need to observe the interaction with the user and—if possible—also with the situation he is in. This is due to the fact that users usually do not provide enough detailed information about themselves beforehand and their interests change due to situational factors. To cope with incomplete knowledge about their users, an adaptive system can employ different techniques to complete a picture of them:

- **Selective actions:** The term selective action refers to the choice of the user to exploit a service in a specific manner, for example, requesting information, listening to a song while sitting in the plane or adjusting the water temperature while having a shower. These selective actions allow for direct inference on potential interests or preferences of a user on the selected service/item. But to draw the direct conclusion that a user is really interested in or wants something can also be dangerous due to the fact an interaction with an adaptive service might have happened due to some random behavior.
- **Temporal usage behavior:** Temporal usage behavior is very ambiguous in terms of inferring positive or negative user interests in something. Even with new sensing technologies, it is often impossible to infer whether a user is really using a service. Is the business man really watching the TV which is switched on in his hotel room? Temporal usage behavior can, however, be used as negative evidence for services that are used only briefly.
- **Ratings:** Items of explicit user feedback, if given by the users, are the most valuable source of information regarding user interest because here the users explicitly rate a specific service action according to his preferences and interest. A prominent approach is to give ratings to some information items, which are basically the underlying concept of recommender systems. These mostly Web based applications attempt to offer information according to recommendations given by users with a similar profile. A major drawback of ratings is the fact that

often users do not want to rate or state their intentions.

The interaction data is not often used directly at an individual level, but rather as data to employ statistical inference techniques based on multiple users. In the following section, we will see some approaches to inferring user interests via statistical and machine learning approaches.

The user's interaction with computerized services is embedded in complex tasks and environments and often follows a specific pattern. In our example the business man might have his daily morning routine for example, watching the news on TV after using the bathroom but before having breakfast. Therefore it is desirable to enhance inference results and precision by employing additional information (Kobsa, Koenemann, & Pohl, 2001):

- **Usage frequency:** Usage frequency is surely the most obvious additional information that can be used for inference; for example, the fact that a user often returns to a specific Web site or listens to a song might serve as a strong indicator that he is interested in this site.
- **Context-action correlations:** The correlation of information demands with actions performed in parallel can be useful information for the personalization process, for example, a user is composing a business report and in order to do so he reads online news.
- **Action sequences:** Usually typical actions performed with computers tend to follow an action sequence that can be recorded, analyzed and predicted for the future, for example, a user reads his new mails every morning followed by a visit to some news portals.

INFERENCE TECHNIQUES FOR PERSONALIZATION

As previously mentioned, to facilitate adaptation and personalization services need to apply inference techniques. They are based on existing knowledge about the user, but they also try to fill gaps in this knowledge. Generally one can distinguish two types of inference: primary and secondary.

Primary inference considers observations gathered from the user's interaction directly. It tries to deduce potential preferences or plans from those observations. Here the system's inference capabilities are encoded directly upfront during system design. There are several ways to apply direct encoding in an adaptive system:

- **Acquisition rules:** In this method, rules are stored as predefined actions that an adaptive system should apply, once new information about the user is available due to another interaction. They are usually straightforward interpretation of the user interaction for example, *a user wants to perform a task x with the system, so he is currently not interested in information y that relates to task y.*
- **Plan recognition:** The aim of plan recognition is to identify the actual goal a user is aiming for by analyzing the necessary steps to achieve it based on his previous interactions. Systems that employ plans need to have a task model of potential actions that a user can perform, their combinations and sequences and the goals the system supports. Returning to our businessman, this could refer to the plan to book a business trip, so the usual sequences of steps is known already.
- **Stereotype matching:** Another very prominent method for transforming user data or interaction directly into a preference representation tries to sort actual users into manually predefined stereotypes. These

stereotypes comprise existing assumption about the interests, preferences or even goals a specific group of users might have. Typical examples are groupings according to age categories, cultural background or even profession. So for example, an IT consultant usually chooses a hotel type *x*, whereas a lawyer tends to choose hotel type *y*. The approach consists of three main elements: First the assumption about the users condensed into the stereotypes created by the system designer, second methods of how to associate a new user with these stereotypes automatically, and finally methods on how to reassign already known users to stereotypes after a period of time.

Secondary inference aims to infer user preferences not from direct observations of only one single user but rather by transferring knowledge gained from other users. It is also called indirect inference, and one can differentiate deductive from inductive approaches. Deduction means to reason from a specific case—that is thought to be valid—to a broader view, whereas induction is the reasoning process from a wide range of cases to the rationale behind them, taking in other words a bottom up or top-down approach. In both cases there is no direct link from assumptions to conclusions. In the following some deductive approaches are mentioned:

- **Logic-based inference:** The central concepts for logic-based reasoning in the context of personalization are assumptions and their formal representation. In general one can distinguish assumptions the user has about the real world and assumptions a system has about the real world and its user. A basic logical formalism is the propositional calculus. Simple proposition like as "*a business man is a Human*" are the basic entities —also called atoms—of this formalism. These atoms can be combined by logical connectives such as "like", "and" or "or to become more complex statements. Most systems that use this "propositional calculus" enhance its concept by graduated values such as numeric or symbolic values (Pohl, 1996). Recent approaches to formalizing logical concepts are ontologies. Ontology can be defined[1] as a branch of metaphysics concerned with the nature and relations of being or a particular theory about the nature of being or the kinds of existence. In the now increasingly common sense - ontologies try to model concepts and entities in the real world and their relationships between each other. So, for example, a hotel is a kind of a building as well as company premises. Both places can be visited by a businessman, but the main purpose of one place is to sleep and rest in and the other is to work.

- **Bayesian networks:** One of the more prominent approaches dealing with uncertainty is Bayesian networks also named Belief networks. These methods can be described as probabilistic graphical models, as they combine probability theory and graph theory. They span graph networks containing assumptions as nodes and their interdependencies as arcs between them. In the case of Bayesian Networks the graph networks are directed and allow for upward and downward propagation of probabilities. Microsoft Office Assistants (Horvitz, Breese, Heckerman, Hovel, & Rommelse, 1998) as a result of the *Lumiere* project is surely the most prominent example and is available in every day products.

- **Fuzzy logic:** Fuzzy logic provides a framework to cover the inherent disambiguities of real world information and to reason uncertainty. The term fuzzy sets and the derived term fuzzy logic were coined by Zadeh in 1965 (Zadeh, 1965). He describes a fuzzy subset "*A*" of greater class "*B*" by assigning each "*A*" a value "*b*" that represents its degree of membership in "*B*", see Figure 2. Despite of standard logic with discrete finite set, in fuzzy logic the degree of truth can take continuous values from zero to one. There are two main arguments to employ fuzzy logic for personalization in the area of recommender systems. First, users reason about themselves also in vague concepts and second the information that users might provide to such a system can be vague (Kobsa et al., 2001). The process of conducting fuzzy logic follows a three step procedure (Frias-Martinez, Magoulas, Chen, & Macredie, 2005):

1. **Fuzzifaction** of the input data.
2. **Conduction** of fuzzy reasoning based on the fuzzy information.
3. **Defuzzification** of the results into the final outcome.

The premises in inductive reasoning are based on observations. For personalization one can regard it as "*learning about the user*" (Kobsa et al., 2001). Typically the learning process follows a feature based approach. Depending on the application domain, the system designer tries to identify features of information objects or user actions that refer to interest, for example, in an online travel agency the features for travel booking might be duration, destination, price category, hotel

Figure 3. Fuzzy logic: Set A as part of a larger fuzzy set B

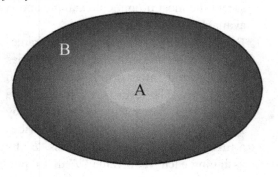

Figure. 4. Case-based reasoning cycle (modified after Aamondt & Plaza, 1994)

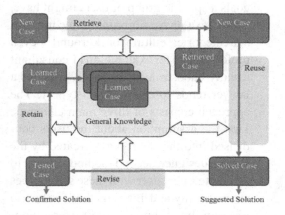

equipment or others. Whenever a user chooses to book a hotel these features are used to infer potential interests for other hotels.

Induction can be applied along two dimensions. First by comparing features chosen by a single user. This approach is called case-based reasoning. And second by inferring interest among different users—the so called clique-based approaches. According to Aamondt and Plaza (1994), a general case-based reasoning cycle may be described by the following four processes (see Figure 4):

1. **RETRIEVE** the most similar case or cases based on the distance metric of a feature vector.
2. **REUSE** the information and knowledge in that case to solve the problem.
3. **REVISE** the proposed solution.
4. **RETAIN** the parts of this experience likely to be useful for future problem solving.

In our example the adjusting of some temperatures might serve as an example. So is the adaptation of the room temperature, in the car, or for the shower the same and can one infer that the person has a specific well-being temperature? If so, when does this well-being temperature change? Kobsa (2001) describes the process of generating recommendation as follows: Finding similar users—select the most relevant ones—generate recommendation based on their profiles (see Figure 4).

The term Clique-based approaches was coined by Alspector, Kolcz, and Karunanithi (1997) and describes systems that aim at finding users who share similarities for example, interests, preferences, information needs or goals. Depending on the system purpose, users with such similarities are grouped into cliques. A major benefit of these cliques is that they allow for prediction for new users that are assigned to one of the cliques. One can regard these systems as stereotype matching approaches in which the stereotypes are not predefined. The following story might serve as an example. A new hotel guest is assigned by his demographics (age, sex, origin) to one specific clique. Based on this assignment, a system can suggest all hotel room settings like room temperature or light situation in a way that the majority of other users in this group have chosen. A prominent example is the *GroupLens* system that computes correlations between readers of Usenet newsgroups by comparing their ratings of articles (Konstan, Miller, Maltz, Herlocker, Gordon, & Riedl, 1997). Other examples regarding clique building based on Web navigation patterns can be found in Yan, Jacobsen, Garcia-Molina, and Dayal (1996) and Perkowitz and Etzioni (1998).

In the past years many algorithms and approaches from the domain of machine learning and artificial intelligence have been used to identify features that indicate user interest automatically:

- **Nearest-neighbor algorithm:** This approach as a prediction technique is among the oldest techniques used in area of data mining. Basically it ranks a set of known objects in terms of their distance from a new query object - q. The objects are represented as feature vectors and the measure of similarity is the computed distance in the n-dimensional vector space (Cost & Salzberg, 1993). Although nearest-neighbor algorithms are quite effective for large training data sets that hold not too much noisy data, they have some disadvantages: The major problem is that computation costs are quite high because the vector distance will not necessarily be suitable for finding intuitively similar examples, especially if irrelevant attributes are present.

- **Decision trees:** "*A decision tree takes as input an object or situation described by a set of properties, and outputs a yes/no decision. Decision trees therefore represent Boolean functions. Functions with a larger range of outputs can also be represented...*" (Norvig & Russel, 2003). Such a tree is composed of different types of nodes: intermediate nodes at which features or variables are tested during the decision process and leaf nodes that store and represent a final decision.

- **Genetic algorithms:** These algorithms—inspired by Darwin's concept of survival of the fittest—try to mimic the natural selection process. They are typically employed in the area of optimization and search. Starting point in this approach is a set of potential solutions to a problem, called population.

Figure 5. Clique-based filtering processes (Kobsa, 2001)

| Assign user to a clique e.g. according to his demographics, browsing behavior etc. | Select most similar user from this clique | Generate recommendation based on these selected users. |

Figure 6. Nearest neighbor: Cloud of features and their selection

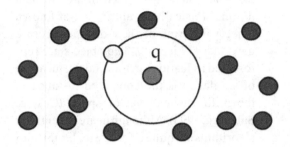

Figure 7. Decision tree

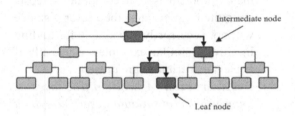

The population is combined and modified, resulting in a set of new solutions from which the ones closest to the optimum are selected. Another cycle starts. The fundamental element of this algorithm is the fitness function that characterizes the individual's utility via a numeric value. According to this score the individuals are selected for the next generation so that the best adapted one survives. Let us return to our example of the traveling businessman. Imagine him surfing the Internet on his mobile—as the display size is quite limited, an optimization process should try to select the best combination of news items coming from different Web sites to be displayed at once.

- **Neural networks:** Neural networks are also modeled on a corresponding concept in nature by means of imitating the construction of the human information processing unit, the brain. They are composed of single units—like neurons—that allow for multiple

Figure 8. Neural network including in and output vectors

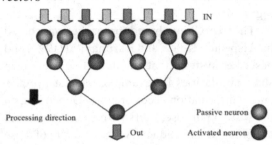

input streams that are then transformed to a single output stream. Usually a large amount of these units is employed in a highly-connected manner. Neural networks provide a unique benefit. They are able to discover patterns in unstructured data that are not observable by other means. One of the major drawbacks of neural networks is their need for training data and training time. So they are less capable of coping with dynamically changing information spaces. Furthermore, the outcome of the inference process is difficult to interpret due to the more or less hidden reasoning process within the network.

Depending on the type of service that should be tailored to the user not only a specific approach or algorithm is employed. Combinations of primary inference techniques by implementing explicit task knowledge and secondary inference techniques are often chosen to cope with unexpected user behavior.

CENTRALIZED, DISTRIBUTED AND ISOLATED PERSONALIZATION SERVICES

As described in the previous paragraphs, personalization is often about applying statistical methods to infer facts on users' interaction with some computerized service. These approaches

Figure 9. Personalization services models—modified after Heckmann (2005)

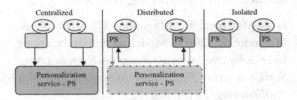

have proven to work well for standard desktop and especially Internet applications. But in ubiquitous computing scenarios users interact with various heterogeneous services that do not necessarily rely on a central infrastructure providing personalization services. It becomes evident that exchange of personalization information is necessary. In general, one can distinguish three kinds of situations a user might be in (see Figure 9).

In a centralized scenario he interacts directly with a centralized personalization service like the personalization of the travel agency. In the distributed scenario a user is accompanied by his own personalization service that allows for exchange with other users or—if available—a central repository, for example entering a meeting room. And finally the isolated scenario, in which no data exchange is possible. Nowadays data exchange is often done via dedicated XML-derivates. A prominent example for synchronization of personalization services is UserML—User Modeling Markup Language (Heckmann, 2005).

As personalization implies inferences based on observations, these inferences need to be synchronized. Either these inferences are transferred in a directed manner—from a source to a target personalization services or vice versa (upward ⇔ downward). Often one cannot distinguish between personalization services in source and target because both of them have gathered inferences independently of each other. In this case the inferences need to be mixed.

SUMMARY

Ubiquitous computing environments pose new challenges for personalization and adaptation approaches, because the classical desktop computing paradigm is often not applicable anymore. As personalization is based on machine learning techniques, it heavily relies on statistical analysis. One can differentiate deductive approaches that try to match user behavior to existing assumptions about his preferences from inductive approaches that aim to discover unknown aspects of the user and that try to cope with existing preference shifts. Inferences can be made along two main directions: first learning by cases and second learning by cliques.

Adaptation can follow a hierarchical ordering by means of adapting the content, the presentation and the user interaction methodologies. Given our example from the beginning, one can clearly see that the exchange of inference about a user between different personalization services is the key element for the success of personalization in ubiquitous computing environments. But this necessary exchange poses also great challenges to privacy considerations (see Chapter Trust and Accountability).

FUTURE RESEARCH DIRECTIONS

For further research, one can identify several promising tracks to follow. First of all, new machine learning approaches are needed that try to cope with the huge variety of data gained from sensors. These sensor observations on the user and his interaction with ubiquitous services must be transferred into reasonable predictions about the users' preferences and intentions. Ubiquitous services and applications have different capabilities and constraints—also regarding personalization and adaptation—for that reason means of sharing knowledge about the users are required. But that does not only refer to condensed knowledge, like user models, but also to deeper levels such as sensor data. So a user observation gained by one service must not necessarily be interesting for its personalization/adaptation capabilities, but it might be relevant for another service.

Along this line of incorporating more and more sensor knowledge and allowing the exchange of user models, privacy considerations must gain more and more momentum. This bright future of adaptive services everywhere could potentially turn into a nightmare as George Orwell describes in his famous novel "1984".

On the other side of the adaptation process, further research on new interaction methodologies and their interplay is needed. Recently speech interaction and pointing gestures have become more popular. But so far these approaches are mostly isolated. A real interplay between them is not yet there. Additionally multimodal interaction is so far only implemented for isolated services.

Further research on personalization and adaptation needs to be accompanied by studies on the social aspects of these technologies. The foundation for a better usability of existing and future services has been laid and even more exciting approaches are out there waiting to be developed.

REFERENCES

Aamodt, A., & Plaza, E. (1994). Case-based reasoning: Foundational issues, methodological variations, and system approaches. *Artificial Intelligence Communications, 7* (1), 39 - 59.

Alspector, J., Kolcz, A., & Karunanithi, N. (1997). Feature-based and clique-based user models for movie selection: A comparative study. *User Modeling and User-Adapted Interaction, 7*(4), 279-304.

Brusilovsky, P. (1996). Methods and techniques of adaptive hypermedia. *User Modeling and User-Adapted Interaction, 6*(2-3), 87-129.

Cost, S., & Salzberg, S. (1993). A weighted nearest neighbor algorithm for learning with symbolic features. *Machine Learning, 10*, 57-78.

Frias-Martinez, E., Magoulas, G., Chen S., & Macredie, R. (2005). Modeling human behavior *User-Adaptive Systems: Recent Advances Using Soft Computing Techniques, Expert Systems with Applications, 29* (2), 320–329.

Heckmann, D. (2005). Distributed user modeling for situated interaction, 35. GI Jahrestagung, Informatik 2005 - Workshop Situierung, Individualisierung und Personalisierung, ISBN 3-88579-396-2, Bonn, Germany, pp. 266-270

Horvitz, E., Breese, J., Heckerman, D., Hovel, D., & Rommelse, K. (1998). The Lumiere project: Bayesian user modeling for inferring the goals and needs of software users. In *Proceedings of the Fourteenth Conference on Uncertainty in Artificial Intelligence* (pp. 256-265), Madison, Wisconsin.

Jameson, A. (2001). Modeling both the context and the user. *Personal Technologies, 5*(1), 29-33.

Kobsa, A., Koenemann, J., & Pohl, W. (2001). Personalized hypermedia presentation techniques for improving online customer telationships.

Konstan, J. A., Miller, B. N., Maltz, D., Herlocker, J. L., Gordon, L. R., & Riedl, J. (1997). GroupLens: Applying collaborative filtering to usenet news. *Communications of the ACM, 40*(3), 77-87.

Norvig, P., & Russel, S. J. (2003). *Artificial intelligence: A modern approach* (2nd ed). Prentice Hall.

Oviatt, S. (1996). Multimodal interfaces for dynamic interactive maps. In *Proceedings of the Conference on Human Factors in Computing Systems*, (CHI '96) Vancouver, Canada.

Perkowitz, M., & Etzioni, O. (1998). Adaptive web sites: Automatically synthesizing web pages. In *Proceedings of Fifteenth National Conference on Artificial Intelligence*, Madison, Wisconsin.

Pohl, W. (1996). Learning about the user—user modeling and machine learning. In V. Moustakis & J. Herrmann, (Eds.), In *Proceedings of the ICML'96 Workshop Machine Learning meets Human-Computer Interaction.*

Rossi, G., Schwabe, D., Lucena, C. J. P., & Cowan, D. D., (1995). An object-oriented model for designing the human-computer interface of hypermedia applications. In *Proceedings of the International Workshop on Hypermedia Design (IWHD'95)*, Montpellier.

Yan, T., Jacobsen, M., Garcia-Molina, H., & Dayal, U. (1996). From user access patterns to dynamic hypertext linking. In *Proceedings of the 5th International World Wide Web Conference*, Paris, France.

Zadeh, L. (1965). Fuzzy sets. *Information and Control, 8*, 338-353

Zipf, A., & Jöst, M. (2005). Implementing adaptive mobile GI services based on ontologies - examples for pedestrian navigation support. *CEUS—Computers, Environment and Urban Systems—An International Journal. Special Issue on LBS and UbiGIS.* Elsevier: Pergamon Press.

ADDITIONAL READING

For further insights into the different topics of artificial intelligence have a look at the Association for the Advancement of Artificial Intelligence (AAAI) Web site: http://www.aaai.org

Bala, J., Huang, J., Vafaie, H., DeJong, K., & Wechsler, H. (1995). Hybrid learning using genetic algorithms and decision tress for pattern classification. In *Proceedings of the 14th International Joint Conference on Artificial Intelligence, IJCAI-95*, Montreal, Canada.

Bidel, S., Lemoine, L., & Piat, F. (2003). Statistical machine learning for tracking hypermedia user behavior. In *Proceedings of the 2nd workshop on machine learning, information retrieval and user modeling, 9th international conference in user modeling*, 56-65.

Boll, S., Klas, W., & Wanden, J. (1999). A cross-media adaptation strategy for multimedia presentation. In *Proceedings of the ACM Multimedia'99*, Orlando, Florida.

Bolt, R. A. (1980). Put-that-there. Voice and gesture at the graphics interface. *Computer Graphics, 14*(3), 262-270.

Boyle, C., & Encarnacion, A. O., (1994). Metadoc: An adaptive hypertext reading system. *User Modeling and User-Adapted Interaction, 4*(1), 1-19.

Cheyer, A., & Julia, L. (1995). Multimodal maps: An agent based approach. In *Proceedings of the International conference on Cooperative Multimodal Communication (CMC '95)* Eindhoven, The Netherlands.

Cohen, P. R., McGee, D., Oviatt, S., Pittman, J., Smith, I., Chen, L., & Clow, J. (1997). Quickset: Multimodal interaction for distributed applications. In *Proceedings of the Fifth ACM International Multimedia Conference*, New York.

Duarte, C., & Carriço, L. (2006). A conceptual framework for developing adaptive multimodal applications. In *Proceedings of the 11th international Conference on Intelligent User Interfaces—IUI*, Sydney, Australia.

Elting, C., Zwickel, J., & Malaka, R. (2002). What are multimodalities made of? - Modeling output in a multimodal dialogue system. In *Proceedings of the International Conference on Intelligent User Interfaces - IUI* , San Francisco, California.

Fausett, L. (1994). *Fundamentals of neural networks.* New York: Prentice-Hall.

Haykin, S. (1999). *Neural networks* (2nd ed). New York: Prentice Hall

Goren-Bar, D., Kuflik, T., Lev, D., & Shoval, P. (2001). Automatic personal categorization using artificial neural networks. In *Proceedings of the 8th International Conference on User Modeling 2001. Lecture notes in artificial intelligence* (2109), 188-198.

Jacko, J., & Sears, A. (2003) *The human-computer interaction handbook: Fundamentals, evolving technologies and emerging applications.* Mahwah, NJ: Lawrence Erlbaum Assoc.

Jameson, A. (1996). Numerical uncertainty management in user and student modeling: An overview of systems and issues. *User Modeling and User-Adapted Interaction, 5,* 193-251.

Kobsa, A. (1993). User modeling: Recent work, prospects and hazards. In M. Schneider Hufschmidt, T. Kühme, & U. Malinowski (Eds.), *Adaptive user interfaces: Principles and practice.*

Murphy (1998). *A brief introduction to graphical models and Bayesian networks.* Retrieved October 16, 2007, from http://www.cs.ubc.ca/~murphyk/Bayes/bnintro.html

Oviatt, S., Coulston, R., & Lunsford, R. (2004). When do we interact multimodally ? Cognitive load and multimodal communication patterns. In *Proceedings of the Sixth International Conference on Multimodal Interfaces -ICMI,* Pennsylvania.

Oviatt, S. L. (1999). Ten myths of multimodal interaction. *Communications of the ACM, 42*(11), 74-81.

Wahlster, W. (2004). SmartWeb: Mobile applications of the semantic web. In *Proceedings of Informatik 2004. Annual Conference of the German Association of Computer Science.*

ENDNOTES

[1]   According to Merriam Webster Online Dictionary—Found on 01/05/2006

[2]   http://www.amnh.org/exhibitions/darwin/ found on 01/18/2007

Section IV
Liability:
From IT Security to Liability

Max Mühlhäuser
Technische Universität Darmstadt, Germany

Andreas Heinemann
Technische Universität Darmstadt, Germany

GENERAL INTRODUCTION TO SECURITY AND LIABILITY

This part of the book covers liability in ubiquitous computing (UC). The term *liability* was deliberately chosen for two reasons. Firstly, due to the established understanding of common terms like *information assurance, dependability, accountability* and the like. Secondly, to provide a superseding term for **security for ubiquitous computing**, which—unlike traditional IT security—encompasses the following developments:

1. Absorption of security into information assurance, which itself is a more wide-ranging area within computer science.
2. Confluence of IT security with (everyday) real word security and liability issues
3. Tradeoffs between confidentiality and traceability.

The first observation is a general trend in computer science, whereas the second and third will experience rapidly increasing importance in ubiquitous computing specifically. Therefore, the first observation will be briefly addressed now while the others will be treated in distinct sections.

The reader should note that for each observation a sound definition is still missing and is being discussed intensely within the research community. Therefore, we must restrict ourselves to the following informal definition: *liability* means IT security for ubiquitous computing, including "absorption of security into information assurance," "confluence of IT security with real world security/liability," and reflection of the "confidentiality/traceability tradeoffs."

Before we discuss "absorption of security into information assurance" further, we very briefly address security in computer science.

Security in computer science pursues three "classical" goals (also called the *CIA triad*). In terms of data security, these goals are:

1. **Confidentiality:** Data should not be revealed to unauthorized[1] parties

2. **Integrity:** Data should not be altered by unauthorized parties

3. **Availability:** Data should not be made inaccessible by unauthorized parties

Besides data, these goals may concern executables, humans, identities, computer networks, and so forth. What exactly may be concerned is often determined by a concrete application.

Orthogonal to the goals above, a number of general security measures can be distinguished. These measures are achieved by more concrete security means (see the chapter "Security for Ubiquitous Computing"). A concrete means may serve several measures (and goals). The most common measures are:

1. **Concealment:** Ensures access denial for unauthorized parties (example means: encryption, access barriers).

2. **Authentication:** Ensures the correctness of claims – often of claimed identity (example means: digital signatures).

3. **Authorization:** Ensures the possession of rights, for example the right to read/write/ alter or execute a file.

4. **Non-Repudiation:** Ensures verifiability of elements of (non) actions—often the identity of the originator of an action or the details of an action.

5. **Anonymity** (contrary to **Non-Repudiation**): The identity of an originator of an action remains confidential/stays anonymous.

6. **Non-Observability** (contrary to **Non-Repudiation**): Execution of an action itself is not verifiable.

This list deliberately left pseudonymity, that is, the use of pseudonyms, aside. We regard the use of pseudonyms as a means that allow an entity to authenticate against a third party but to (some extent) stay anonymous.

Our first observation, **Absorption of Computer Security into Information Assurance**, as stated earlier, is a trend in computer science to broaden the view on security issues. Security in the *classical* sense looks into *intentional* (malicious) causes for malfunctions. Since unintentional causes may yield to similar effects and may be avoided with similar measures, it is reasonable to take *reliability, correctness,* and *safety* into consideration as well. Reliability aims to protect from failures, that is, an unintentional change in a component's behaviour. Correctness makes sure there is no design defect present and safety—being a fairly new goal—is a measure to protect against catastrophic effects and catastrophes as causes. Note that *classic* security together with reliability, correctness, and safety is traditionally subsumed under the term *dependability*.

In the context of risk management (i.e., protection measures for restoring a correct function after a malfunction occurs in correlation with the generated costs to deploy these measurements) dependability has been recently termed *information assurance*. In the context of ubiquitous computing, information assurance emphasizes the "CIA triad" together with authentication and non-repudiation. The reason for this is found in the other two observations, namely the confluence of computer security with real world security and a prevalent conflict between confidentiality and traceability. The next section discusses this in greater detail.

LIABILITY IN UBIQUITOUS COMPUTING

Confluence of Computer Security with Real World Security

Ubiquitous computing, in its final stage, will support virtually everything we do in our everyday life. This comes with an extensive penetration of computers and embedded systems in everyday objects. Smart spaces will be the norm. As a consequence, we will depend even more on computers than today. What we see is a confluence of computer security with real world security. Three key aspects must be considered:

a. Due to the exponential growth of both the number of computers involved in our actions and the frequency of independent security-related actions, there is a need for more scalable security than public key infrastructures (PKI) offer. PKI do not scale for two reasons. First, UC nodes vary a lot in respect of computing power and so forth. On nodes with poor resources, PKI-based solutions make use of a shorter key length that might be breakable by resource–rich nodes. Second, in order to check a certificate's validity, a node needs to ask the certificate issuer whether the certificate was revoked or not. This can't be done online and in real time for zillions of nodes, zillions of times per millisecond.

b. In UC settings, we carry out everyday actions supported by computers. Thus, computers have to comply with real-world liability issues in all kinds of contexts. In a business context, UC enabled transactions need to comply with warranty issues, guaranteed services, and guaranteed payments as familiar to the user. Further, compliance with legal regulations, for example, obedience of privacy protection laws, is required. Finally, user actions carried out in a UC world need to comply with access control issues as deployed in the real word, for example, access control to premises, buildings, rooms, appliances, or individual operations of appliances.

c. Another aspect emphasizes the confluence of computer security with real world security, namely the fact that computers will act on behalf of humans and they will interact with humans. Thus, computers have to reflect natural, *humane* concepts relevant for security, for example, *trust*, *reputation*, *recommendation* and the like. We regard trust as a key concept here and discuss trust in detail in the chapter "Trust and Accountability." Also, human-computer interaction (HCI) and *ease-of-use* become key issues, since computers need to convey security issues to humans and need to support them in taking security-related actions.

In Figure 1, points (a) through (c) are listed under "Confluence of comp. security and real-world security."

Tradeoffs Between Conflicting UC Goals

As computer security and real-world security merge, conflicting goals that are present in real life among different parties of a society (individuals, organizations, society as a whole) have to be balanced in UC as well. For one, an individual's right to have privacy has to be traded off against his responsibilities/obligations. As an example, think of *automated working hours recording* based on employee tracking. This might be stated in a contract between employee and employer and illustrates a typical privacy/responsibility trade-off (other terms might be: *conceal/reveal* trade-off, *freedom/control* trade-off, or *autonomy/compliance* trade-off).

We give two examples from the past, where conflicts have already popped up. With the first worldwide recognition of AIDS and the fear of a new epidemic, a public debate on how to deal with HIV patients' medical records arose. Should a patient's records remain private or should the doctor report his HIV patients? The conflicting interests of an individual and the society as a whole are obvious. As our second example, we state the procedure change in selling prepaid mobile phones. While initially it was possible to buy prepaid phones anonymously, today, one has to register with a certified ID for a purchase in many countries due to the intensive use in organized crime as a means of making anonymous phone calls.

Summarizing this paragraph, the liability challenge in UC with respect to conflicting goals is to provide means for adjusting an inevitable trade-off to respective cultural, ethical, and juridical settings—and to its evolution over time [see Langheinrich (2001) for a brief history on how the understanding of individual's privacy changed in the course of time]. In addition, a chosen trade-off has to be understandable by users, that is, its implications need to be conveyed to the user as clearly and simply as possible.

OVERVIEW OF FURTHER CHAPTERS

As *Figure 1* illustrates, we found it inappropriate to turn the key challenges described above one-to-one into book chapters. The reason is the evolutionary development of scientific methods and approaches, which applies to liability like to any other scientific field. This means that we have to look for sound existing research domains that we observe as converging sources for liability in UC. In this respect, we found the three most important fields to be as follows:

The next three chapters present these fields in greater detail. The chapter "Accounting and Billing, Guarantees and Contracts" presents accounting and billing as done by telecommunication companies. We address how contracts are settled electronically and how they are enforced. This includes a treatment on how far the above-mentioned privacy/responsibility trade-offs are supported today. By looking into guarantees and contracts, this chapter discusses how this area contributes to the confluence of computer security and real world security.

The chapter "Security for Ubiquitous Computing" covers security issues by distinguishing three typical UC settings, namely *mobile computing*, *ad hoc interaction*, and *smart spaces*. The discussion should make the reader aware of the broad and varied security challenges and risks present in different settings. The risks derive from the inherent characteristics present in UC settings and the challenges are introduced by typical UC resource and infrastructure limitations. Also, this chapter includes a brief introduction in computer security in general and—based on this knowledge—presents a number of selected measures for liability in UC in detail.

The chapter "Trust and Accountability" is split into two parts. The first part covers trust, a concept that is familiar to humans in real life and helps them to interact in the presence of uncertainty. It outlines how trust can help humans in a UC setting as well. The discussion focuses on trust modelling and the propagation of trust via recommendations. The second part shows how accountability can be enforced in the context of resource sharing in distributed systems. We place the focus on reputation and micropayment schemes.

A Precautionary Remark

One would wish to see a better coverage of liability in the remainder, but the topic is still in its infancy—appropriate means, models and concepts are just emerging. Especially the confluence of computer security with real-world security is pending since security for UC must first come up with appropriate and comprehensive solutions, before these can penetrate confluence. As a consequence, the even broader absorption of security in information assurance, as stated earlier, must be left out for the time being.

In order to recall our discussion on UC liability more easily, *Figure 1* breaks down liability and its coverage within this book in a visual manner.

We conclude this introduction by giving the reader pointers to literature that cover security in ubiquitous computing. The short list presents

Figure 1. Liability in UC and its coverage within this book

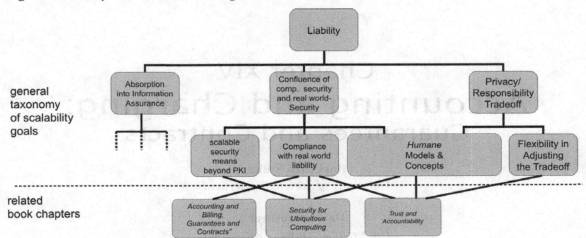

a selection of survey work with a focus on open/unsolved issues and challenges.

REFERENCES

Görlach, A., Heinemann, A., Terpstra, W.W., & Mühlhäuser, M. (2005). Location privacy. In A. Boukerche (Ed.), *Handbook of algorithms for wireless networking and mobile computing* (pp. 393-411). Chapman & Hall/CRC.

Haque, M., & Ahamed, S.I. (2006). Security in pervasive computing: Current status and open issues. *International Journal of Network Security*, 3(3), 203-214.

Langheinrich, M. (2001). Privacy by design - Principles of privacy-aware ubiquitous systems. In *Third International Conference on Ubiquitous Computing (UbiComp)* (pp. 273-291). Springer.

Ranganathan, K. (2004). Trustworthy pervasive computing: The hard security problems. In *PerCom Workshops* (pp. 117-121). IEEE Computer Society.

Stajano, F. (2002). *Security for ubiquitous computing.* John Wiley & Sons.

Stajano, F., & Crowcroft, J. (2003). The butt of the iceberg: Hidden security problems of ubiquitous systems. In T. Basten, M. Geilen, & de Groot, H. (Eds.), *Ambient intelligence: Impact on embedded system design* (pp. 91-101). Dordrecht, The Netherlands: Kluwer Academic Publishers.

ENDNOTE

[1]   It is obvious that this entails the question: Authorization is done by whom? By the sender, by the receiver, or by a third party?

Chapter XIV
Accounting and Charging:
Guarantees and Contracts

Burkhard Stiller
University of Zürich, Switzerland

David Hausheer
University of Zürich, Switzerland

Jan Gerke
University of Zürich, Switzerland

Peter Racz
University of Zürich, Switzerland

Cristian Morariu
University of Zürich, Switzerland

Martin Waldburger
University of Zürich, Switzerland

ABSTRACT

Charging for IP-based communications determines the overall term for metering or monitoring, accounting, pricing, charge calculation, and billing. These five actions are detailed in this chapter to provide a clear view on their interdependencies as well as their relations to distributed computing. Since an ubiquitous computing approach does require communication means between all entities involved, the provisioning of these communication channels is supported typically by commercial service providers—covering network, transport, and value-added services. Thus, the legal and contractual relationships between customers and providers as well as technological choices of protocols, mechanisms, and parameters define the area of interest here.

INTRODUCTION

Services being offered in a networking environment may range from traditional network access services through to value-added services provided by third party providers. The focus in this chapter has been placed on Internet and Internet Protocol (IP)-based services due to their great importance for basic communication as well as value-added services. In the case of ubiquitous computing, the areas of distributed communications as well as distributed computing merge to form an integrated approach in which those services mentioned provide an integrated portfolio to users and customers. As soon as these service providers and customers are identified, a contractual relation becomes necessary to formulate this contract in a legally enforceable manner. These contracts cover in general any type of service specification to be delivered from a provider to a customer. Specifications must be represented in an automatically interpretable manner in Service Level Agreements (SLAs) and may include computing cycles on a computing cluster, memory in storage area networks, value-added Web services representing business applications, network access, or Quality-of-Service (QoS) support, all of which showing a possible service guarantee level (if at all), numerical values for certain parameters to be monitored, and predefined delivery conditions. While SLAs for overall Information Technology (IT) services in a more traditional sense have been established for quite some time, SLAs in a communications and computing environment which can be interpreted without human interaction still face the problem of being hard to achieve.

The basis for these SLAs and their enforcement can be found in respective accounting mechanisms and protocols, which specify the set of essential operations and functions to be offered in a network. Note that accounting in this context addresses technical accounting questions, and it is not focused on financial accounting means. Since multiple providers may compete in a market-like situation in their service offerings, the need for such a technical service differentiation has to be complemented with suitable mechanisms which enable a service provider to account for these services and—optionally—their service usage. This type of accounting may serve a number of different purposes, such as network management supervision, determining resource bottlenecks in given topologies, or summarizing resource usage in view of subsequent charging. Typically, in a distributed computing environment all of these purposes are highly relevant, since a steady update and change of an existing networking infrastructure takes place, driven by networking equipment vendors, Internet Service Providers (ISP), and third party providers offering alternative value-added services.

Thus, a combination of traditionally pure technology-driven enhancements in network functionality with more recent economically controlled mechanism additions becomes essential for an operable, efficiently manageable, and future-proof communications and networking approach. The basics of each of these two fields, their application in a highly distributed environment, and a number of selected mechanisms will be laid out in this chapter.

Outline

This chapter on accounting and charging as well as guarantees and contracts has been structured into five main sections. While key terminology is defined first, the section "Technologies and Services" provides an overview of relevant technologies and services, which includes roles, accounting, and contracts. "Charging Approaches" extends this view into key charging, sometimes termed billing in public networks, covering basic charging principles, network and transport charging, and Web services and value-added service charging. Finally, "Future Research Directions" draws conclusions and offers a glimpse into major future issues and problems.

TERMINOLOGY

A clear and commonly used definition of key terms is essential. The list below outlines the basic terminology, which covers the most relevant terms related to accounting and charging of Internet services.

- **Account:** An *account* is defined as a repository which can be used to keep and aggregate accounting information, *for example*, the amount of data volume uploaded or downloaded or the number of CPU (Central Processing Unit) cycles used.
- **Accounting:** *Accounting* is the process of collection and aggregation of information on system activities as well as resource and service usage, stored in accounting records. Accounting has manifold purposes and accounting records can therefore serve as input for various subsequent processes, such as charging, network management, traffic management, traffic analysis, trend analysis, or capacity planning.
- **Accounting record:** *Accounting records* hold the accounting data collected by the accounting process.
- **Accountability:** *Accountability* is "the quality or state of being accountable" or the capacity "to account for one's actions" (Merriam-Webster Inc., 2005).
- **Auditing:** "*Auditing* is the verification of the correctness of a process with respect to service delivery. Auditing is done by independent (real-time) monitoring or examination of logged system data in order to test the correctness of operational procedures and detect breaches in security. Auditing of accounting data is the basis for after-

usage proof of consumed resources and customer charges." (Rensing, Karsten, & Stiller, 2002).

- **Billing:** *Billing* is the process of consolidating charging information on a per customer basis into a bill.
- **Charge:** *Charge* is the monetary value of a certain service usage and it is the result of the charge calculation for a particular service and user.
- **Charge calculation:** *Charge calculation* is the process to calculate the charge for a particular service usage based on the related accounting records and charging scheme. Charge calculation maps technical values into monetary units.
- **Charging:** *Charging* is used in this section as a synonym for charge calculation. In other more general cases it has been applied to the overall process described from the start of the metering process to the writing of the final bill.
- **Charging/Pricing scheme:** The *charging scheme*—sometimes termed pricing scheme as well—contains the charge calculation rules and prices for services, settled by pricing. The charging scheme is used during the charge calculation.
- **Charging record:** *Charging records* hold the charging data computed during the charge calculation process. Call Detail Records (CDR) determine an example of a dedicated charging record.
- **Customer:** *Customer* is an entity having a business relation with a provider.
- **Guarantee:** A *guarantee* determines a formal assurance that a physical product or an electronic service will be provided under predefined conditions or that it will meet a certain predefined specification.
- **IP flow:** An *IP Flow* is defined as a unidirectional sequence of packets with common characteristics between two endpoints. The common characteristics typically include

source and destination IP addresses, source and destination ports and IP protocol number.

- **Metering:** *Metering* is the process of observing user and system activities by gathering resource and service usage data on network components.

- **Pricing:** *Pricing* defines the method that a particular role (Application Service Provider, Internet Service Provider, or Telecommunication Service Provider) applies to determine the price for a particular service. This includes in a fully distributed approach the collection of information from local resources and/or other roles depending on the pricing strategy that is followed by the peer.

- **QoS:** *Quality-of-Service* (QoS) defines a certain level of performance and quality for all types of data communications, which is expressed in parameter sets according to the special standardization organization involved in the respective communication system's approach. QoS shall be measurable or, in more recent terms, it may determine the perceived QoS of a user in an objective manner.

- **Resource:** A *resource* is a "source of ... supply that can be drawn upon when needed" (Web WordNet 2.0, 2005).

- **Service:** A *service* defines a set of functions and capabilities offered by a provider to a customer. A *value-added service* is defined

as a service, which provides value due to extensions of a pure network access service, such as an IP access.

- **Service level agreement:** A *Service Level Agreement* constitutes a contract between an Internet Service Provider (ISP) or a third party service provider and a customer, which may be an ISP or a third party provider as well, to define legally binding service delivery specifications and to commit the ISP and the third party service provider to a required level of service, in case of network service to QoS specifications. The specifications within the Service Level Agreement can be interpreted automatically and require no human interpretation.

- **Session:** A *session* defines the use of a particular service or resource, for example, the download of a file or the use of some amount of computing power. A session always has two session partners, a provider and a consumer.

- **Tariff:** A *tariff* specifies how service usage needs to be accounted and charged for. It is represented by a specific *tariff formula* and a set of *tariff parameters* previously agreed upon between the service provider and the service consumer.

- **User:** *User* is an entity accessing and using a service.

As outlined in Kurtansky and Stiller (2005) the terminology for charging and accounting used

Table 1. Correlation of terminology in IP-based networks and 3G mobile networks (Kurtansky & Stiller, 2006)

IP-based Networks	3G Mobile Networks
Metering	Collecting charging information
Accounting	Charging
Accounting records	Charging Data Record
Charging options	Billing arrangements, Payment methods
Prepaid/postpaid charging	Pre-paid/post-paid billing
Charging mechanism	Charging mechanism
Billing and parts of charging	Rating (Parts of)
Inter-/Multi-Domain Charging/Billing	Accounting

in specifications for the Internet and for different mobile networks, addressing mainly Third Generation (3G) releases, looks different. Thus, Table 1 outlines in the left-hand column the terms used on the Internet and in the right-hand column 3rd Generation Partnership Project's (3GPP, 2005) vocabulary definitions (ETSI, 2005).

TECHNOLOGIES AND SERVICES

To be able to define interactions between providers and customers, a set of suitable roles and partners needs to be determined initially. Additionally, the underlying technology in terms of accounting for services is essential to understand how accounting works, which protocols are in use in the Internet, and which accounting models exist. Finally, the contractual side is discussed, combining the set of roles and relevant accounting parameters to ensure that legally binding Service Level Agreements can be constructed.

Roles and Partners

Considerations on contractual agreements, guarantees, accounting, and billing in ubiquitous computing imply services to be investigated which are offered commercially in a (potentially) fully competitive environment. This initial position determines the set of relevant roles and key players. Accordingly, this section develops the suitable role model for commercial service offerings.

The term *commercial* in this context means that service and resource usage need to be compensated. Compensation is often given by means of financial resources expressed in a widely used currency, turning the currency into a universal intermediary. Resource and service usage, is, however, also conceivable as being compensated by any kind of accepted value expressed by a currency that is accepted by contractual parties.

In ubiquitous computing, two distinct *service* (here in terms of an electronic product, thus, em-

bracing the respective economic notion) types are of relevance for commercial offerings. Pervasiveness requires communications infrastructure to be in place, so that the first service type accordingly embraces network access. On top of this network service, value-added services are offered, determining the second service type category.

Commercial service provisioning involves a wide range of functional steps besides the pure service provisioning phase. These steps comprise support mechanisms which are on the one hand required by legal determinations (including those that are mainly externally imposed, but also self-regulations) and which constitute on the other hand business-critical data. Figure 1 identifies these functional steps in the respective applicable sequential and parallel order as invoked upon a service request received.

Every service is provided and used, while it is provided by making use of resources. Accordingly, the base service provisioning role model consists of three general roles: a service provider, a service user, and a resource provider role, which each see instantiations specific to assumed circumstances. By inclusion of technical and business roles and structured based on the general value chain modeling approach (Porter, 1985), Figure 2 shows an example mapping of business roles to their corresponding value chain components.

Those functional steps as well as those business roles visualized in Figure 1 and Figure 2, respectively, need to be specified in further detail in order to match a specific real-world environment. Accordingly, the main challenges in concreting are determined as follows: Functional steps, such as auditing, need to be mapped to contractual agreements both, in terms of human and machine readable form (cf. the sections "Legal Contracts" and "Service Level Agreements"). Furthermore, these steps have to be technically implemented by underlying mechanisms. Regarding role models, increased complexity needs to be handled, as a role model is required to reflect those various characteristics of an actual cooperation taking place

Figure 1. Functional steps invoked upon service request

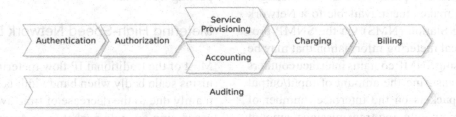

Figure 2. Example business role to value chain mapping

in a value network that potentially incorporates multiple legally independent and geographically dispersed organizations, probably even in a global context.

Metering

Metering is the process of capturing data related to network resource consumption, such as bandwidth, loss error rate, delay, or jitter. This data may further be used for accounting and charging purposes, Intrusion Detection Systems (IDS), or network planning. Metering data may generate inside an active network device (such as a switch or router) or passive nodes may be added on network links for monitoring all the traffic flowing through that link. The node on which the measurement process runs, acts as an *observation point*.

Depending on the final purpose, metered data may be captured with different granularities. The granularity required from the metering device impacts directly the computing requirements the metering device shall have. If an operator is only interested in the load of the links within its

network a few simple counters attached to each network link would be enough to achieve this task. If, however, the final goal is to feed this data into an IDS or to perform usage-based charging more advanced and computing intensive mechanisms are needed.

Protocols

Two of the most frequently used protocols for retrieving information from metering devices are SNMP (Simple Network Management Protocol) (Case, Fedor, Schoffstall, & Davin, 1990) and Netflow (Netflow Services and Applications, 2007).

SNMP is an IETF (Internet Engineering Task Force) defined protocol that allows the transmission of management information to/from a network device. These protocols enable network administrators to monitor and manage network performance, find problems within the network and plan for network growth. Each network device in a SNMP-managed network has a management agent that resides on that device. The management agent collects information from different counters and configuration parameters of the managed device and makes them available to a Network Monitoring Station (NMS) via the SNMP protocol. Typical metering information that may be retrieved using SNMP contains interface counters (e.g., for measuring the amount of input/output bytes and packets on the interface, number of errors for input/outgoing transmissions, amount of unicast/multicast packets, size of a routing table, device up-time). The Real-time Traffic Flow Measurement Architecture (RTFM) (Brownlee, 1999) and the Remote Management Information Base (RMON) (Waldbusser, 2006) use SNMP for transporting measured data.

Netflow is a protocol developed by Cisco Systems dedicated to collecting information about IP traffic. Similar protocols to Netflow have been implemented by other network vendors and embedded in their routers (cflowd used by Juniper Networks or NetStream developed by Huawei Technology). Netflow collects information about the network flows passing through a network device or a network link. A network flow may be defined in different ways, but the most typical and widely used definition is a unidirectional sequence of packets having the following IP header fields in common: *IP source, IP destination, IP protocol, source port, destination port.* The collected information for a network flow is used to create a flow record when the router detects that the flow has finished. A wide variety of information may be placed in a flow record, but the following is present in all flow records: source and destination IP address, source and destination port number, IP protocol number, number of bytes and packets in the flow. Additional information that may be included is: timestamps for first and last packet observed, Type of Service (ToS) value, TCP (Transmission Control Protocol) flags observed in the flow, input and output interface number, or source and destination Autonomous System (AS) number. The IETF standardizes the IP Flow Export (IPFIX) protocol (IP Flow Information Export, 2007) as the future protocol for transporting flow data.

Metering High-Speed Network Links

Most of the traditional IP flow metering mechanisms scale badly when bandwidth is increased, mainly due to the decrease of time available for processing a single packet (e.g., 4 nanoseconds for an Optical Carrier OC-192 link). Sampling mechanisms have been designed to reduce packet processing work while still achieving a high accuracy of the results (Estan & Varghese, 2002).

Distributed architectures for metering IP flows on high-speed links have been recently proposed in Duffield and Grossglauser (2001), Han, Kim, Ju, and Won-Ki Hong (2002), Kitatsuji and Yamazaki (2004) and Mao, Chen, Wang, and Zheng (2001). They aim at the distribution of the flow-processing task to multiple nodes. Another direction when talking about high-speed link measurements is development of dedicated hardware. Endace Systems (*DAG* Cards, 2007) developed hardware cards that are specialized for packet capturing. The European project SCAMPI (SCAMPI, 2007) investigated strategies for monitoring systems operating at 100 Gbps and beyond.

Open Issues and Research Challenges

Probably the most critical issue in network-related measurements today is metering high capacity links. The IETF working group PSAMP on Packet Sampling (Packet Sampling Working Group, 2007) is standardizing mechanisms for network elements to sample subsets of packets and to transport the sampled data. Another aspect dealt with within the IPFIX (IP Flow Information Export, 2007) working group is the standardization of a protocol for carrying flow records. Another interesting and still quite open field in network measurements is related to Intrusion Detection. Performing IP measurements at multiple places within an IP network and correlating these measurement results in order to obtain an overview on the overall network health determines an important topic to be investigated.

Accounting Principles

In order to be able to keep track of and charge for the provision and use of services and resources, the core function of an accounting mechanism is essential. Thus, the main goal of an accounting mechanism (in the following called *accounting scheme*) is to ensure *accountability* (Dingledine, Freedman, & Molnar, 2001) by providing functionality that enables keeping track of contribution and consumption of resources by service providers and users within a particular application. As such, accounting can serve as a basis for a charging mechanism (cf. the section "Charging Services") or be used as a non-monetary incentive to contribute resources and to punish selfish behavior like freeloading.

Vital accounting mechanisms are the processing of accounting events describing the amount of used resources, the application of respective tariffs, as well as the creation and maintenance of accounts to store and aggregate the accounting information and to keep track of the account balance. One of the main challenges of an accounting mechanism is clearly to bind the accounting information to a real identity or making re-entries of providers and users under a new identity costly and thus unattractive.

Accounting schemes may implement any specific type of accounting, from simple local or centralized accounting to more sophisticated remote or token-based accounting. Individual accounting schemes usually fulfill specific requirements with respect to efficiency, scalability, and economic flexibility, as well as security and trustworthiness, among which there is always a trade-off. An overview of the design space of accounting schemes is given in the following. To generalize the design options, the term *peer*

is used as an umbrella term to refer to any entity involved in a particular application. A peer may act as provider and user for several services at the same time.

Local Accounting

With this design option, peers keep accounting information locally, for example, based on receipts that are issued by the counterpart. Local accounting scales very well, however, it typically features bad security properties, as a peer may easily modify accounting information locally, for example, by forging receipts. Such a scheme would therefore only be suitable in trusted environments where security is not important, or for local uses. To increase the trustworthiness of local accounting, receipts could be signed by both transaction partners; however, fraud is still possible through collaboration between peers.

Examples for local accounting schemes are, for example, the Peer-to-peer (P2P) system BitTorrent's tit-for-tat mechanism (Cohen, 2003) or eMule's credit system (eMule, 2003). A related approach is SeAl (Ntarmos & Triantafillou, 2004), which creates digital receipts of every transaction and stores them locally. Another possibility to increase trustworthiness is to require peers to make their local accounting information public and auditable as proposed in Ngan, Wallach, and Druschel (2003).

Token-Based Accounting

Token-based accounting is similar to local accounting as it stores accounting information in tokens which are used by peers in exchange for the use of a service and can be aggregated locally. Tokens are different from receipts, as they are typically issued (and signed) by a trusted token issuer, for example, a bank or a quorum of peers (cf. Hausheer, Liebau, N., Mauthe, Steinmetz, & Stiller, 2003a; Hausheer, Liebau, Mauthe, Steinmetz, & Stiller, 2003b). Consequently, token-based accounting usually has a high level of trustworthiness.

The idea of this approach goes back to Chaum, who is regarded as the inventor of eCash, that is electronic payments (cf., for example, Chaum, 1982). One of the main drawbacks of token-based accounting is that tokens may be forged or spent twice like any other virtual currency. Thus, appropriate mechanisms have to be in place which take these problems into account. Double spenders may, for example, be punished by being exposed, as suggested by Chaum, Fiat, and Naor (1990).

An example for token-based accounting in P2P systems is Mojo Nation (Mojo Nation, 2002), where tokens are issued by a central bank. Other token-based mechanisms designed for P2P systems are, for example, Token Accounting (Liebau et al., 2005), PPay (Yang & Garcia-Molina, 2003) or the approach presented in Kamvar, Yang, & Garcia-Molina (2003). A related concept is the Digital Silk Road (Hardy & Tribble, 1993), which has been proposed in the context of agoric systems.

Remote Accounting

In contrast to local accounting, remote accounting is based on the idea that accounting information is held remotely on other peers. Remote peers are third party peers, which are typically different from the peers currently providing or using a particular service that needs to be accounted for. Using remote accounting, accounting information can be distributed and replicated over several peers, which, if designed appropriately, can increase the reliability and availability of the accounting data. In addition, greater credibility or trustworthiness can be achieved when many peers are involved in doing the accounting.

The concept of remote accounting is very general and covers several potential subtypes, such as central, hybrid, and distributed accounting. An overview of the possible variants is given in the following.

Central Accounting

This is the simplest form of remote accounting and is only mentioned for reasons of completeness. Using this type of accounting, accounting information is kept in a centralized place, that is on a central server. An example for an approach which is based on a central server (trusted third party) is proposed in Horne, Pinkas, and Sander (2001). Another central solution is GridBank (Barmouta & Buyya, 2003) which focuses on accounting for Grid services. Central accounting is simple to maintain and control and is thus usually highly trusted. However, such central elements represent a single point of failure and do not scale for a large number of peers.

Hybrid Accounting

Hybrid accounting features the simplicity of central accounting, while being more scalable with respect to the number of peers. In hybrid accounting a dedicated set of peers (so-called super-peers) are used to hold accounting information. Super-peers are typically peers which are highly trusted by a group of peers (clients) attached to them. If the size of such a group is limited, the hybrid approach scales quite well.

However, appropriate incentives need to be given to super-peers to provide the extra accounting efforts. For example, every peer may periodically pay a flat fee to its super-peer covering the costs for keeping and updating the accounting data. So far, the only accounting scheme which is partially based on a hybrid approach is the Token Accounting (Liebau et al., 2005). This approach uses several super-peers as a quorum of trustworthy peers to sign tokens.

Decentralized Accounting

Fully decentralized accounting seems to be most promising approach for distributed applications. It completely distributes the accounting load over all peers. As all peers are equally involved in doing the accounting the scheme scales very well and no payments are necessary to compensate for any accounting costs.

This approach is, for example, followed in Karma (Vishnumurthy, Chandrakumar, & Sirer, 2003), where the consumer sends an account update to the provider, which forwards it to its account holder (called bank). The provider's bank then sends the account update to the consumer's bank, in order to request permission to update the provider's account. If this is confirmed, both accounts are updated accordingly, and the two peers will be notified about the successful transaction so that the service transfer can start.

An important aspect of decentralized accounting is the redundancy of accounts. *Non-redundant* accounting describes the case where every account is held by only one peer, while *redundant* accounting refers to accounts being replicated over several peers. A non-redundant accounting approach supersedes the need for any synchronization between accounts; however, it has some severe drawbacks. If for any reason a particular peer goes offline, accounts held by that peer would temporarily not be accessible anymore. If a peer completely withdraws from the network, the corresponding accounting data would permanently be lost. In addition, a malicious peer could easily modify and misreport the balance of an account it is responsible for. The use of redundancy, that is the replication of accounts over several peers can increase the robustness of decentralized accounting.

PeerMint (Hausheer & Stiller, 2005) uses multiple remote peers to store and aggregate accounting information in a trustworthy and scalable way. It applies a structured P2P overlay network to map accounts onto a redundant set of peers and organize them in an efficient and scalable manner. Unlike Karma (Vishnumurthy et al., 2003) and similar work (cf. Agrawal, Brown, Ojha, & Savage, 2003; Ngan et al., 2003; Ntarmos & Triantafillou 2004), PeerMint uses session mediation peers to

maintain and aggregate session information about transactions between peers. This minimizes the possibilities for collusion among peers trying to increase their account balance without actually contributing resources. The scheme is secure in that it ensures the availability and integrity of the accounting data. However, it does not provide confidentiality or privacy, as every peer is, in principle, able to access the accounting data of any other peer.

Another decentralized accounting approach is described in Agrawal et al. (2003). Similar ideas are also pursued in the context of Grid computing (cf. Thigpen, Hacker, McGinnis, & Athey, 2002).

Open Issues and Future Problems

This section has provided an overview of different accounting principles existing today, covering the complete design space from local to remote accounting and from centralized to fully decentralized schemes, each with certain benefits and drawbacks and suitable for particular use cases. However, the use of Internet services in a ubiquitous manner will further increase. Correspondingly, scalability will become the major challenge that has to be addressed by future accounting mechanisms.

Thus, new accounting schemes have to be developed, which will be able to cope with the increased accounting load without compromising on the accuracy. As discussed above, fully decentralized accounting schemes are the most promising approach to store and aggregate accounting information in a scalable and accurate manner. However, in terms of efficiency decentralized accounting mechanisms still lag behind centralized schemes due to a quite high communication overhead. By further optimizing the communication of emerging fully decentralized accounting mechanisms, the efficiency of these schemes can be enhanced without reducing their scalability.

Accounting Protocols

Accounting protocols provide means to transfer accounting data on service and resource usage, enabling a commercial service provisioning. AAA (Authentication, Authorization, and Accounting) protocols enable additionally the communication for user authentication and authorization of service access and resource usage. In the following sections an overview of the most relevant protocols are provided.

RADIUS

The Remote Authentication Dial In User Service (RADIUS) protocol (Rigney, Willens, Rubens, & Simpson, 2000) was introduced to support user authentication in dial-up and terminal server access services, and it is the most widely used AAA protocol in IP networks. RADIUS is a client-server based protocol. Network components requiring AAA support, like a Network Access Server (NAS), operate as RADIUS clients. They request authentication and authorization from the RADIUS server and act according to the response of the server. RADIUS servers are responsible for authenticating the user, authorizing the service request, and informing the client about the result. Requests are forwarded in general based on realms, which are administrative domains users belong to. RADIUS servers can operate as a proxy, forwarding requests to another server if they cannot satisfy the request locally. In this case, the server acts as a client toward the other server. This allows a chain of servers with a more flexible configuration. Request forwarding is commonly used in roaming scenarios, where two or more administrative domains are involved in the service provisioning. RADIUS accounting (Rigney, 2000) extends the protocol with the support of accounting record transfer.

Diameter

The Diameter protocol (Calhoun, Loughney, Guttman, Zorn, & Arkko, 2003) considered as the next generation AAA protocol, is a flexible AAA protocol, consisting of the Diameter base protocol and various Diameter applications. The base protocol defines Diameter entities and specifies the message format together with common functionalities, including Diameter message transport, capability negotiation, error handling, and security functions. Diameter applications enable the flexible extension of the protocol, defining service-specific commands and attributes.

Diameter clients such as a NAS (Network Attached Storage) device are components performing access control and collecting accounting data. Diameter servers are responsible for authentication, authorization, and accounting in a particular realm. In contrast to RADIUS, Diameter allows also server-initiated messages, that is, any node can initiate a message. In that sense, Diameter is a peer-to-peer protocol. Thus, the server can, for example, explicitly instruct the access device to terminate the service of a certain user. Besides Diameter clients and servers, the protocol provides explicit support for agents which can be used to make message routing and message processing more flexible. A Diameter agent provides either relay, proxy, redirect, or translation services.

Accounting support in Diameter was considered from the design on and the base protocol includes basic accounting support. The accounting process is organized in sessions, where sessions provide the means to correlate accounting records belonging to the same service. Diameter supports start, stop, interim accounting records and as well as records for one-time events.

To provide reliable data transfer, Diameter runs over TCP or the Stream Control Transmission Protocol (SCTP). For fail-over purposes Diameter nodes maintain a connection with at least two peers per realm at the same time. Additionally, transport connections are explicitly monitored with watchdog messages to be able to react to failures. Messages are sent typically to the primary peer, but in case of fail-over they are sent to the secondary peer. Diameter explicitly defines the use of IPSec or Transport Layer Security (TLS), providing hop-by-hop security for secure communication between peers.

Similar to RADIUS, Diameter message attributes are coded in Attribute-Value-Pairs (AVP), enabling the transfer of any kinds of parameter in a common representation format. In RADIUS the number of possible attributes is limited to 255 due to the 1 byte long attribute type. In Diameter the AVP code is extended to 4 byte length to provide enough space for future attributes. Additionally, different flags are assigned to AVPs, indicating encryption, mandatory, and vendor-specific AVPs. Additionally, grouped AVPs, consisting of several other AVPs, are supported. Diameter enables the definition of new protocol commands and AVPs in a flexible manner, building Diameter extensions in the form of Diameter applications.

There are several Diameter applications extending the protocol with application specific attributes and messages. The network access server application (Calhoun, Zorn, Spence, & Mitton, 2005) provides the extension for network access services. It defines authentication, authorization, and accounting messages and attributes for network access environments. It derives several AVPs from RADIUS to provide interoperability. The Diameter Extensible Authentication Protocol (EAP) application (Eronen, Loughney, Guttman, Zorn, & Arkko, 2005) specifies Diameter messages and AVPs necessary to support EAP based authentication. The Diameter mobile IPv4 application (Calhoun, Johansson, Perkins, Hiller, & McCann, 2005) provides AAA functionality for mobile IPv4 services, combining mobile IPv4 components and the Diameter AAA infrastructure. The Diameter credit-control application (Hakala, Mattila, Koskinen, Stura, & Loughney, 2005) specifies an extension for real-time credit-control, required in prepaid scenarios.

IPDR

The Internet Protocol Detail Record Organization (IPDR.org, 2007) is an open consortium developing specifications for a common usage data representation and exchange format for IP-based services. The IPDR reference model (IPDR.org, 2004a) is divided into three layers. The *network and service element layer* includes the network and service elements required for the IP-based service provisioning. The *mediation layer* has an interface to the network and service element layer and to the business support system layer and it contains the components responsible for the collection of usage information. The *Business Support Systems (BSS) layer* provides business operation functions of a provider like customer care or billing. The BSS comprises all systems and functions that are required for the business processes of a commercial enterprise. The BSS also exchanges settlement data with foreign BSSs either directly or via a clearinghouse. The model does not define the physical deployment of these entities in a network environment.

To support a flexible and extensible service specific accounting data representation, IPDR defines the IPDR document (IPDR.org, 2004a, IPDR.org, 2004b, & IPDR.org, 2004c), which is a unified data scheme in Extensible Markup Language (XML) format. The IPDR document enables the integration of any kind of service specification. There are common document formats specified for some well-known services, for example, usage information for Voice-over-IP (VoIP) service is specified in IPDR.org (2004d). In order to make the IPDR document transmission more efficient, accounting data can also be represented in the XDR (eXternal Data Representation) format. The IPDR XDR format (IPDR.org, 2004b) is a compact, binary representation of IPDR XML documents.

Further Accounting Protocols

The Terminal Access Controller Access Control System (TACACS+) protocol (Finseth, 1993) is an AAA protocol developed by Cisco Systems. It supports reliable transport of AAA messages over TCP, which makes it resistant against packet loss. The protocol supports start, stop, and interim messages for accounting purposes. Regarding security the protocol provides hop-by-hop authentication, integrity protection, and message confidentiality.

The Simple Network Management Protocol (SNMP) (Case, Mundy, Partain, & Stewart, 2002) is widely deployed in intra-domain management applications. It can be used to collect accounting data typically by polling network equipment in regular intervals. It supports the transfer of accounting records in the form of SNMP Management Information Base (MIB). But SNMP-based accounting has limitations in terms of efficiency and latency. Additionally, SNMP has security deficiencies and problems in inter-domain deployment.

The Common Reliable Accounting for Network Element (CRANE) protocol (Zhang & Elkin, 2002) is another protocol to transfer accounting records. The protocol uses reliable transport protocols, that is TCP and SCTP, and application layer acknowledgments as well. A client can have several simultaneous connections to different servers, which enables fail-over in case of server failure. Security can be supported by IPSec (IP Security) and TLS. The accounting data transmission and representation format is based on templates, which can be negotiated between client and server. The use of templates enables an efficient and compact data transmission.

Next Steps in Accounting

Accounting protocols have been developed and used in IP networks for a long time. At the beginning the focus was on network access services within a single provider domain and accounting protocols supported mainly network access related parameters—like session duration, NAS identifier, NAS port—and IP traffic related parameters—like number of bytes, number of packets transferred. With the conversion of communication networks, IP has become the network technology for all kinds of networks. More complex IP-based service infrastructures are emerging, providing content and value-added services as well.

This results in the core requirement for service-oriented accounting and not only accounting for bits and bytes. Therefore, future accounting protocols should be able to transfer service-oriented accounting records and should provide a flexible accounting record format, since new services will appear frequently. Accounting record formats based on XML, for example, IPDR records, and the AVP format of the Diameter protocol fulfill this requirement. Additionally, the multi-domain aspect, like in Grid networks (cf. the section "Accounting Models"), becomes more important, since services are provided over several provider domains. Therefore, accounting protocols shall support inter-domain interactions.

Because of increasing network link speed and network traffic, a decentralized accounting approach and accounting record processing might become necessary, determining new challenges. Since mobility will further evolve in IP networks, accounting protocols should also become mobility-aware. Additionally, accounting protocols should support prepaid services (cf. the section "Charging Approaches") in the future, because of the high popularity of prepaid charging.

Accounting Models: AAA and A4C

The AAA Architecture (Authentication, Authorization, and Accounting) (De Laat, Gross, Gommans, Vollbrecht, & Spence, 2000) covers a highly effective approach to integrating authentication, authorization, and accounting into a common architecture. This has been extended to achieve the A4C Architecture, which additionally includes, besides traditional AAA functionality, Auditing and Charging functionality. An important aspect of commercial service provisioning is the interaction of A4C infrastructure of different service providers or network operators.

In detail, *Authentication* refers to verifying a user's identity. The authentication will allow later mapping of service usage information to individual users. Figure 3 shows an example of an authentication process. For the mobile terminal to use the access network, the NAS (Network Access Server) needs to know the identity of the user or the device that wants to attach to the network. Using an access link protocol (such as PANA (Protocol for Carrying Authentication for Network Access) (PANA Working Group, 2007) credentials may be encapsulated and sent to the AAA Server via NAS. Depending on the credentials given, the AAA Server may instruct the NAS to allow or deny user's access.

During the *authorization* process a user is allowed or denied access to the service he requested. Authorization typically relates to the service to be provided, so the IETF AAA architecture defines ASMs (Application Specific Modules) to be contacted for deciding whether a user will or will not be allowed to access a specific service.

Accounting is the process of collecting service usage information. This information usually generates during the metering process (see the section "Metering"). According to the AAA architecture the accounting information is sent by an accounting client to an AAA server. In mobile scenarios, multi-domain AAA communication is required. The IETF AAA architecture allows inter-domain AAA interactions by placing an AAA server in every administrative domain. Figure 4 shows an example of a multi-domain AAA communication. The *Mobile Node* which is a client of *Home ISP* may attach to the *Foreign ISP*'s network if a trust relationship exists between the two ISPs. Authentication, authorization and accounting

requests will be relayed by the foreign ISP's AAA server to the AAA server of the home ISP. Based on the existing trust relationship, the authentication and authorization performed by the home AAA server may be applicable in the foreign domain by the foreign AAA server. The foreign AAA server may also make local authorization decisions (e.g., even if the user would be authorized to use a certain amount of bandwidth in the home domain, while he is visiting the foreign domain he may have other bandwidth limitations).

The A4C approach determines an extension to the generic AAA architecture by incorporating SLA auditing as well as charging functions. This concept has been developed in several European projects such as Moby Dick (2007), Daidalos (2007), and Akogrimo (2007) as well as industry projects such as DAMMO (Eyermann, Racz, Schaefer, Stiller, & Walter, 2006).

Decentralized Accounting

As introduced in the section "Accounting Principles," decentralized accounting implements the idea of holding accounts on several remote, that is, third-party peers. Figure 5 defines the case of decentralized redundant accounting as used in PeerMint (Hausheer & Stiller, 2005). In this model two types of accounts are distinguished, *session accounts* and *peer accounts*. While session accounts are used to keep accounting information within a particular session, peer accounts aggregate information from several sessions, for example, the total amount of data volume uploaded and downloaded by a particular peer. Peer accounts may also be used to keep information about a peer's reputation or trustworthiness based on its behavior in the past, such as cheating or running a malicious attack.

Both session and peer accounts are held by several independent peers. For every session there is a corresponding *tariff*. Its main purpose is to specify how service usage needs to be accounted for. As such it is used to process *accounting events*

Figure 3. Authentication

Figure 4. Multi-domain AAA interaction

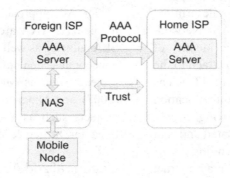

which are generated by the service instances running on both the provider and the consumer side of a session. It depends on the tariff applied when and by how much the balance of a particular session or peer account is updated. Based on the result of a tariff evaluation, a generic *balance update* is created and forwarded to a particular account. Note that the term balance update is used rather than *charge* to make clear that this does not necessarily imply a monetary payment.

Provider and consumer peers involved in a session send their balance updates to a redundant set of session mediation peers which are responsible for holding the session account for the current session (1). Each session mediation peer checks if the two peers agree and updates the session account accordingly. Whenever a session account triggers a peer account update, the mediation peers send a balance update to the peers holding the respective peer accounts (2).

The two phases may be repeated several times independently. To overcome Byzantine failures (Lamport, Shostak, & Pease, 1982), the resulting account balance is agreed upon using majority decisions. Only if the majority of mediation peers report the same balance update, the peer accounts will be updated. Whenever a peer goes offline or permanently withdraws from the P2P network a new peer takes over its task. The new peer (shown as dashed circle) obtains the current balance from the other account holders.

Grid Accounting

The latest Grid research focused primarily on the accountability of Grid services from a technical perspective and on a metalevel of Virtual Organizations (VO). VOs are seen as the appropriate organization model representing Grid infrastructures that allow for Grid service provisioning across administrative domains. There are many existing grid accounting models. The most prominent ones are APEL (Byrom, Walk, & Kant, 2005), DGAS (Anglano, Barale, Gaido, Guarise, Patania, Piro, Rosso, & Werbrouk, 2006), GASA (Barmouta & Buyya, 2003), GRASP (GRASP, 2006), GSAX (Beardsmore, Hartley, Hawkins, Laws, Magowan, & Twigg, 2002), MOGAS (Lim, Thuan Ho, Zhang, Sung Lee, & Soon Ong, 2005), and Nimrod/G (Barmouta, 2004). All those existing approaches either provide for mechanisms for handling resource usage records or offer a usage tracking service.

When considering commercial Grid services, however, economic and financial principles need to be respected in Grid accounting. This means, for instance, that actual costs have to be allocated to the resource usage of a service. Since VOs are based on the concept of resource virtualization, complexity in service provisioning is increased due to the inherent need for the management of heterogeneous systems and diverse resources located in different service domains. These facts demand a Grid accounting approach based on accountable units that reflect accepted accounting systematics, thus addressing the apparent gap of already existing accounting models. Accordingly, such accountable units are the key means for bridging the respective notions of financial and technical (Grid) accounting. They represent the relevant set of base building elements applicable to every Grid service. This means that every Grid service can be composed from these accountable units, whereas not all elements need to be used in a given service. They embrace four basic hardware functionalities, namely *processing*, *storage*, *transferring*, and *output*.

The accounting model introduced in Göhner, Waldburger, Gubler, Dreo Rodosek, and Stiller (2007) allows any service provider in a VO to calculate costs incurred when providing one specific service request. The model relies on two well-known accounting systems. On the one hand, it uses the Traditional Cost Accounting System (TCAS). In TCAS, cost elements originating from financial data are allocated in a first step to cost centers and in a second step to cost objects. This is where the presented accountable units come into play. With that, TCAS determines for the accountable units of a given service the corresponding cost rates. On the other hand, Activity Based Costing (ABC) (Kaplan & Bruns, 1987; Kaplan & Atkinson, 1998) is used. It is driven by the concept of activities. Cost objects are perceived to consume activities, whereas activities consume resources, which are seen as the cost driving event. These costs are assigned to cost objects not by the use of rough percentages (as is the case in TCAS) but rather by identified cause-and-effect relationships. Figure 6 gives an overview of the accounting system and illustrates the central role of its accountable units.

ABC is highly flexible in terms of configurability and applicability. Activities can be defined with the desired level of abstractions so that activities (composed from the basic accountable units) form in several rounds of abstraction the components of a complete IT product. Flexibility, however, not only holds a chance for fine-granular configuration of the accounting systematic but also for a risk of inefficiency. The process of accounting itself is costly itself. Thus, the most difficult task is to find the appropriate level of abstractions needed—in particular with respect to the number of accountable units used—in order to model Grid services with the help of the accounting model.

LEGAL CONTRACTS

Legal contracts are in their very essence promises that are given in exchange with a corresponding value. There are various types of contracts which differ in some fundamental aspects, such as the governing legal determinations to be compliant with. For instance, different contracts may require

Figure 5. Decentralized redundant accounting in PeerMint

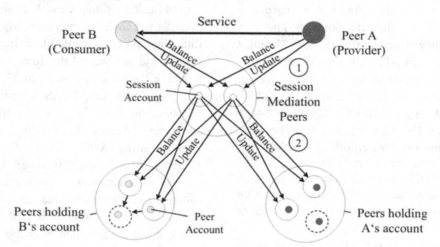

different levels of formality (oral or written form). Similarly, contracts under private law need to be differentiated from contracts under administrative law, since they are based on other principles, which leads to potentially conflicting assumptions. In the case of private law contracts, those basic principles embrace—in terms of a non-comprehensive list—the following rationales:

- *Good faith* (bona fides) assumes that contractual parties act honestly according to their respective knowledge. Good faith prevails for contracts under private law, whereas contracts under administrative law recognize the corresponding principle of legal certainty.

- *Pacta sunt servanda* means that contracts are legally binding. This results in the understanding of obligations that are incurred when concluding a contract. Accordingly, contracts typically involve procedures and remedies for the case that a contractual term was breached.

- Contracts need to be concluded *knowingly* (scienter) and *intentionally*. This means on one hand that contractual parties have to be aware of a contract, while on the other hand, contracts require consent from all involved parties, so that contracts are perceived as negotiated agreements.

- *Incompleteness*: Consent is not possible to be assumed for a given aspect if the respective contractual terms are uncertain or incomplete. This aspect is of high importance for automated contract negotiations without human interaction (cf. the section "Service Level Agreements").

Although the above-mentioned basic principles may appear obvious at first, they show some key consequences that are fundamental for civil law as such. A decision on whether an agreement in fact constitutes a contract respecting the full set of mandatory requirements is not always taken unambiguously. For instance, contractual law recognizes so-called quasi-contracts that are inconsistent to a certain extent with the principle of concluding a contract intentionally.

In contrast to the difficult task of finding an answer on whether an agreement can be termed contract, the process of contract conclusion is well defined. Figure 7 models the contract formation process in state diagram form for contracts that fall under United Nations law for the international trade of goods (UNCITRAL, 1980). The depicted automaton visualizes the different possibilities available for the so-called offerer (sender of a proposed agreement, called offer) and offeree (the receiver of an offer, an altered or a counter-offer, respectively) in order to consent to or dissent from a contract. It includes details on forming a contract, whereas it abstracts from the applicable specifics of contract termination.

Upon receipt of an offer, the offeree can either:

- Assent fully, which leads to an acceptance of the offer, rendering the offer a contract,

- Assent but alter it in non-material points, which leads to an acceptance of the slightly modified offer, automatically rendering the offer a contract under the new terms if the original offerer does not object,

- Dissent, which leads to rejection of the offer,

- Reply with a counter-offer which includes changes to the original offer that are of material nature, leading to final acceptance only if explicit consent with the counter-offer is received by the original offerer,

- Ignore the offer, which leads to rejection of the offer. For this reason, offers are equipped with a time frame in which they remain valid.

Material components in this type of contract are the respective terms on price, payment, quality and quantity of the goods, place and time of delivery, liability determinations, and settlement of disputes (UNCITRAL, 1980).

Figure 6. Grid accounting model overview (Gubler, 2006)

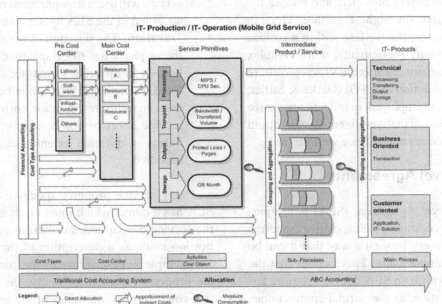

During contract negotiation, the user and the provider both aim to maximize their respective welfare. Thus, if the provider P offers a service S with tariff t(S) and cost c(S) to the user U with utility function u(S), the user attempts to alter the offer of S so that his welfare:

$$w(U) = u(S) - t(S) \qquad (1)$$

is maximized, while the provider attempts to make a counter offer with a service S which maximizes

$$w(P) = t(S) - c(S). \qquad (2)$$

It must be noted that these welfare functions do not take transaction costs into account, for example, the user's cost for waiting for an urgently required service or the provider's cost for reserving resources for the service which could be used otherwise are not taken into account. Transaction costs force user and provider to negotiate a compromise, instead of eternally exchanging altered offers and counter offers which maximize their respective welfare.

Furthermore, a user may negotiate the same service with different providers and choose the one offering him the highest welfare. Thus, in order to maximize the welfare within a service market with many participants, more complex pricing mechanisms, such as the Vickrey Welfare Procurement Auction (VETO) (Gerke & Stiller, 2005), have to be employed, in order to maximize the social welfare of the overall service market and to allocate services and service welfare fairly.

Service Level Agreements

A Service Level Agreement (SLA) is a representation of a contract which specifies the terms of service delivery in such a way that it can be interpreted automatically. This implies that the information within an SLA does not require human interpretation, as the normal contract does

(cf. the section "Legal Contracts"). The information within an SLA must enable service user and service provider to carry out their tasks during service usage and service delivery, respectively. Thus, every piece of information contained within an SLA belongs to one of two groups:

1. Information related to service delivery itself, that is, how it is delivered and used.
2. Information related to the accounting, charging for and payment of the service.

The information related to service delivery is listed in the following:

*   **Identities:** The service user and the service provider must be specified through unique identifiers.
*   **Service functionality:** The SLA must describe the functionality of the service, for example, that a video with a specific content is to be downloaded.
*   **Service parameters:** During contract negotiation, the service user and the service provider negotiate service parameters, for example, the bandwidth a video streaming service will use. These parameters have to be specified in the SLA by key/value pairs.
*   **Duration:** The duration of the service delivery phase has to be specified. This can happen in different forms, for example, a fixed start and end time, a fixed duration or even an unlimited duration with a possible service abort by either user or provider. Terms of duration extension can also be specified.

Every service property specified within an SLA has a name, which must be unique within the service description. Furthermore, its specification contains a description of the property, for example, a description of the functionality the property represents. Finally, the specification contains possible values of the property, as

Figure 7. State diagram of contract formation process for contracts governed by United Nations law for the international trade of goods (UNCITRAL, 1980)

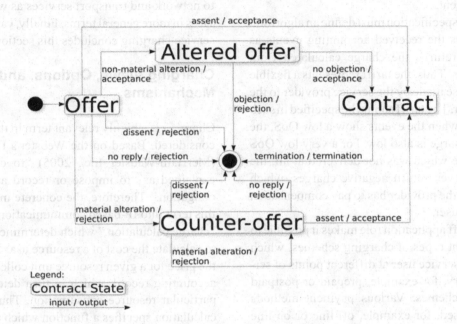

well as an explanation of what these values stand for. For some properties, the values do not have any meaning, which is then also specified in the explanation.

Furthermore, in order to enable accounting, charging, and paying for a service, the SLA has to specify the following five types of information not directly related to service delivery and usage:

1. It must specify what information about service usage is collected by the service-using instance and when it is sent to the provider.

2. The tariff must be specified which is used to calculate charges according to the information received about service usage. Various charging schemes can be employed, for example, a fixed amount has to be paid for the service usage or the amount is proportional to the time the service is used.

3. A rule must be specified which determines when the tariff is applied, that is, when the charge is calculated.

4. The method of payment must be specified, for example, bank transfer, credit card, or electronic online payment.

5. Reaction rules and actions can be specified which determine how a service provider reacts to the payment behavior of the service user, for example, the provider might stop the service delivery if the user does not pay.

Information about service usage is specified in so-called *accounting events*. For identification, every event has a name which must be unique within an SLA. The specification of every event must contain the specification of a condition when the event is sent. Furthermore, every event can contain numerous pieces of information about service usage at the time the event is sent. These pieces of information are called *properties*, as they are very similar to service properties. Analogously, their specification must also describe what they represent.

A tariff specification must define an algorithm which takes the received accounting events as input and returns the charge calculated from these events. Thus, the tariff represents a flexible QoS promise made by the service provider to the service user. The tariff should be specified in such a way that when the events show a low QoS, the returned charge is also low. For a very low QoS or a service which was not delivered at all, the tariff can even return negative charges, which means that the provider has to pay compensation fees to the user.

The tariff application role makes it possible to use different types of charging schemes, which charge the service user at different points of service delivery, for example, prepaid or postpaid charging schemes. Various payment methods could be used, for example, off-line or on-line methods. Finally, the specification of reaction rules and actions ensures that a service provider can properly respond to a service user which does not fulfill the SLA. To this end, an SLA, and especially reactions and compensation payments specified within this SLA, must be legally enforceable. Therefore the SLA must be signed by both user and provider. The process of creating and exchanging such a countersigned SLA between both user and provider is not trivial and can only be completely resolved with the help of a trusted third party. This, as well as the duration of validity of service offers and their enforceability, are discussed in Gerke (2006).

CHARGING APPROACHES

Based on the underlying functions of metering and accounting, the path for charging has been opened. While this chapter assumes to have pricing models in place—good overviews of IP-based pricing approaches can be found here—charging forms a major part, which is introduced through standards and recommendations. It is subsequently applied to network and transport services as well as services in more general terms. Finally, value-added service charging concludes this section.

Charging Views, Options, and Mechanisms

Charging is a highly relevant term in the domain considered. Based on the Webster's Dictionary (Merriam-Webster Inc., 2005) "to charge" is explained as "to impose or record a financial obligation." Therefore, the concrete mapping of this term into IP-based communications leads to "charge calculation," which determines the task to calculate the cost of a resource usage by using the price for a given resource unit collected in an accounting record, which in turn determines a particular resource consumption. Thus, charge calculation specifies a function which translates technical values that are also accounted for into monetary units. In turn, the monetary charging information is included in charging records which are utilized for billing purposes. Since prices typically are available for particular resources, the use of accounting records and such prices allow for a customer-specific charge calculation. In general, standards and research work tend to agree on a common understanding of tasks required for charging.

As outlined in Stiller (2003) the European Telecommunications Standardization Institute ETSI (ETSI, 1999) offers a charging definition as follows: "Charging is the determination of the charge units to be assigned to the service utilization (that is the usage of chargeable related elements)." Additionally, Karsten, Schmitt, Stiller, and Wolf (2000) define the full process: "Once these accounting records are collected and prices are determined in full pricing schemes on unit service, for example, encompassing different quality levels for services or service bundles, the data for an invoice need to be calculated. The process of this calculation is termed charge calculation, performing the application of prices of unit services onto accounted for records determining the resource consumption. Thus, the charging function transforms mathematically unequivocal technical parameter values into monetary units. These units need to be collected, if they appear at different locations in the given networking environment, and are stored in charging records. Of course, accounting as well as charging records determine a critical set of data which need to be secured to ensure its integrity when applied to calculate monetary values or when used to compute an invoice's total."

For ATM (Asynchronous Transfer Mode) services the charging process is also termed "rating and discounting process" (Songhurst, 1999) and it is "responsible for the charge calculation according to a specific pricing policy and using the collected usage data." Therefore, these charging mechanisms correlate the service usage and calculate the charge the customer is faced with after the completion of the service utilization. Finally, as outlined in TERMINOLOGY, the charging terminology used in specifications for different mobile networks is different (Kurtansky & Stiller, 2005).

As defined in the terminology section, the charge calculation step calculates the charge for a given service consumption based on accounting records and respective tariffs defined in the SLA. Thus, charge calculation mechanisms are used to implement two different charging options.

- The *prepaid charging option* defines a way in which customers have to be in possession of a certain amount of financial units—typically termed credits or credit points—prior to service usage. Periodical credit checks during service usage are performed and credits are deducted upon the service usage.
- In case of the *postpaid charging option* service charges are collected from the

provider's side for a certain period of time. They are debited to the user account after that period, typically by sending an invoice or charging a credit card.

The two charge calculation mechanisms in place differ as follows:

- The *on-line charging mechanism* determines the charge calculation process, which has to be performed in real-time. This implies that the underlying support functions besides the charge calculation—especially accounting and metering—have to be performed in real-time as well.
- In case of an *off-line charging mechanism* no fixed time constraints are defined. Thus, the processing time of the charge calculation may happen at any reasonable time after the service usage.

Additionally, hot billing defines a certain type of charging support, in which the final and last service usage needs to become available in real-time, such as for a phone bill during check out in a hotel. However, it is the operator's own definition of hot billing, such as short time or real-time or volume limits for Charge Detail Record (CDR) closure as well as priority (3GPP, 2005), which diversifies those actual mechanisms required in a given networking and service situation.

Thus, by discussing those two option and mechanism combinations in general, a prepaid on-line charging scheme (e.g., traditional phone card) is as useful as a postpaid off-line combination (e.g., traditional monthly phone bill), while a prepaid off-line charging scheme (e.g., the use of a credit card with a signature on the slip only) may be possible, but may imply risks, and a postpaid on-line charging scheme (performing an on-line account check, but not debiting the money) is possible, but inefficient and not useful.

Charging Components: Focus on Network and Transport

Charging may be applied to a number of different components within communications. Traditionally, as shown in Figure 8 the transport area in grey comprises the access, the connection, and usage-based components. On top of those, content charging may be in place. While any of these components may be considered as a general service being charged for—which is described in a dedicated form in the section "Charging Services" below—the content part has developed in the meantime into a more general value-added service charging, as discussed in the section "Charging Value-Added Services."

Focusing on the traditional transport, the number of packet-based approaches—mainly based on the Internet and IP—often term this component as network charging as well, since the packet determines the unit of interest and the respective layer in the Internet/Department of Defense Reference Model has been termed "Network Layer" as well. Thus, the access component enables a provider to charge for the physical access to a network, such as the ADSL (Asymmetric Digital Subscriber Line) cable or a WLAN (Wireless Local Area Network) access point.

Typically, the charge itself and the respective pricing model will be based on the physically available bandwidth or capacity this point of presence is able to offer to the user. Therefore, this component will be in many cases reflected in a flat fee, or a range of flat fees, depending on the physical layer characteristics.

However, a usage-based component can be found in many data communications. This determines a pre-defined, measurable parameter, which describes the resource usage of a customer on top of the physical access. For example, it may account for the time the user is accessing the network, where sending or receiving packets does not count in terms of volume. Just pure access will be accounted for, typically timed between

an authenticated login and a logout of a user at a Network Access Server or an access router. Furthermore, an accounting for volume may be possible, where the amount of bytes, packets, or cells will be metered and utilized to determine subsequent charges.

Of course, these components determine the potential for a charging scheme to be defined for a given technology. While a provider-centric and economic view may prefer all three components to be in place, a provider-centric and technology-driven view may not favor such a complex and costly approach. Therefore, a trade-off between these two contradicting goals needs to be found. Additionally, the customer has to be integrated in such a decision as well, if a charging approach may become acceptable in a market situation, mainly in the sense of offering services and charging options, which are incentive-compatible. Only a competitive price/quality ratio will enable providers to charge for their network services in a viable manner.

Charging Services

In order to charge for the use of services, several sub tasks have to be carried out: The process of measuring service usage (accounting), charging (applying the tariff specified within the SLA), and paying is depicted in Figure 9 and described in the following.

1. During the service delivery and usage, the service using instance repeatedly sends measurements of the service usage to the service user's charging module. These measurements consist of the service properties as observed up to this point of service usage.
2. The charging module forwards the received information, that is, the accounting record, about service usage to the service provider's charging module in an accounting event.
3. Steps 1 and 2 are repeated throughout the service usage phase. How often and when

exactly the measurements are made and sent, is specified in the SLA.

4. After the service delivery has been completed, the service provider's charging module applies the agreed upon tariff to the accounting events received and thus calculates the charge. It then sends a bill specifying this charge to the service user's charging module.

5. The service user's charging module has to ensure that the bill is paid. After the payment has been made, it sends a confirmation of payment back to the service provider's charging module.

Whenever an event describing service usage or service delivery is sent, it follows exactly the event's specification in the SLA, extended with a specification of the measurement values and the time the event is sent. Furthermore, in order to enable the identification of the corresponding SLA and to prevent replay attacks, the SLA identifier and a running sequence number are included in every event. Each event is signed by the service user, in order to make it impossible to refute the service usage afterwards. Thus, enforcing adherence to the SLA by both user and provider is restricted to the granularity of service usage events specified within the SLAs. Ultimately, discrepancies between user and provider can only be resolved through trusted third parties witnessing the service delivery. However, this approach

Figure 8. Components of charging

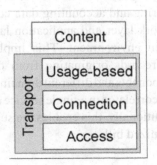

is often more expensive than the service charge itself, rendering it unusable. Rather, on the one hand, providers will stop service delivery or not even start service delivery to users they deem non-trusted, because of their past behavior. Such information can be gained through blacklists or reputation mechanisms. On the other hand, users may simply refuse payment for parts of service delivery which did not comply with the SLA. In turn, if they continuously do this without cause, they will end up being blacklisted or with a very low reputation.

Every bill a provider sends to a user contains the charge for service usage. Furthermore, in order to precisely identify the service which the user is being charged for, the bill contains the SLA. Finally, in order to enable the user to comprehend the charging process, the bill contains all events which were used within the tariff to calculate the charge.

The proof of payment message consists of the bill that was paid. Additionally, it can contain a declaration by the entity which handled the payment, for example, a bank that the payment was made. Charging and payment does not necessarily have to take place only after the service delivery. It could also take place before service delivery, that is, in a prepaid manner (Kurtansky & Stiller, 2006), or at intervals during the service delivery, for example, by making use of token payments such as described in Liebau et al. (2005). Still, which method is used for payment and when it takes place does not change the general interactions between the modules as described in this section, but only the order in which they occur.

Figure 10 illustrates how the five types of charging-relevant information contained within the SLA (cf. the section "Service Level Agreements") are used in the service charging process. The process is started within the charging module prior to the start of the actual service delivery. From this point on, it repeatedly checks whether the tariff application rule is fulfilled. When this is case, the tariff is used to calculate the charge for service usage, which is then used to charge the service user. The service user pays using the payment method specified in the SLA. Then, the reaction rules are applied to the behavior of the service user, resulting in actions such as a continuation of the service, a change of the service parameters or a stop of the service delivery. Finally, if the service is still running, the process returns to its beginning, that is, checks whether the tariff application rule is fulfilled.

It is important to note that the process described in this section focuses on the normal sequence of accounting, charging and paying when service user and service provider behave as they should. However, since money is involved, there is a strong incentive to cheat, for example, for the service user to fake measurements, in order to receive compensation payments for a correctly delivered service. Thus, additional mechanisms have to be provided to prevent such cheating or make it unprofitable. Such mechanisms are described in Gerke (2006) and include a complete discussion of possible attacks, as well as counter measures such as using witnesses or balancing expected revenues of service deliveries against expected losses.

Charging Value-Added Services

Value-added services (VAS) are usually referred to as non-core services, offering additional, higher-level application services to the user in contrast to the standard service offering. In the IP world VASs include services going beyond standard network access and data transport services. In the telecommunication world services beyond standard voice calls are usually termed as VASs. Value-added services include enhanced messaging, multimedia communication, audio and video streaming, gaming, and electronic content services. Although the charge calculation for value-added services is in general the same as discussed in the sections "Charging Components: Focus on Network and Transport" and "Charg-

ing Services," charging for value-added services might combine charges for related services into a single charging record.

Value-added services are offered either by the network provider itself or by third-party Value-added Service Providers (VASP). A VASP might be tightly coupled with the network provider using its network infrastructure or offer its service independent from the network provider. In the tightly coupled case, the VASP and network provider have a contractual agreement and the service is delivered over the network operated by the network provider. If VASP and network provider are independent, accounting and charge calculation are performed separately and the user receives separate bills from both providers.

The network provider usually has a special role in value-added service provisioning, since the service delivery is performed by its network infrastructure and users typically access a large number of VASPs over a limited number of network providers. If the VASP and network provider have a contractual agreement, accounting, charge calculation, and billing can be delegated partially or completely to the network provider. This tightly coupled case also allows providers to apply more sophisticated charging schemes for VASs, incorporating charges both for network usage and application usage. The user can access services from various VASPs without having a direct contractual relationship with each VASP and the network provider can prepare in this case a single, itemized bill for all accessed services.

The accounting infrastructure (cf. the section "Accounting Models: AAA and A4C") should enable metering and accounting data collection on the network layer and application layer in a multi-domain environment. This implies that accounting records originating from different service components and different domains should be able to be correlated in a single service delivery session. Additionally, this enables the support of a single, itemized bill.

Figure 9. Accounting, charging, and payment

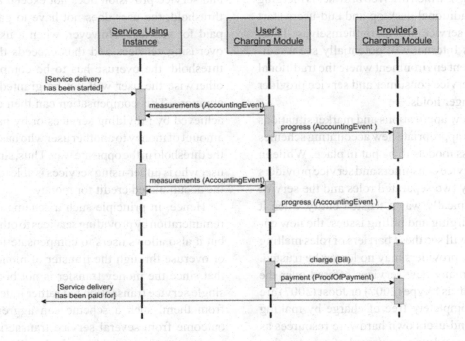

Since several entities, that is, user, network provider, VASP, are involved in the service consumption and delivery, as well as in the charge calculation process, security measures are essential for the accounting infrastructure. In particular the secure accounting record transfer between domains, providing data origin authentication, integrity, and confidentiality, the secure and trustworthy access of VASPs, and billing for VASs are of key importance.

FUTURE RESEARCH DIRECTIONS

The Internet as a common platform for various advanced services faces constant changes at the moment. Almost every month new services provided on top of the Internet are being introduced, from P2P file-sharing and Internet telephony to Grid computing services and IPTV (IP Television) applications. Moreover, the Internet is currently

Figure 10. Service charging process

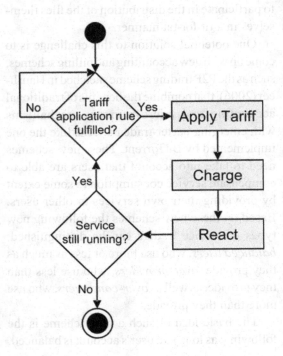

facing a new challenge that is commonly known as the Web 2.0, in which the Web browser is merging with the traditional desktop and end-users start to become service providers themselves. Thus, tomorrow's Internet will potentially see a radically different environment where the traditional notion of service consumer and service provider roles no longer holds.

These new applications and market situations will require appropriate new accounting schemes and business models to be put in place. While in the past, service consumers and service providers were clearly two separated roles and the service provider typically was a trusted entity when it came to charging and billing issues, the new environment will see these barriers of roles melting and the new providers may no longer be trusted. Moreover, many new services offered over the Internet such as Skype (2007) or Joost (2007) are provided completely free of charge by making use of the end-users own hardware resources as a distribution and management platform. Another example of this trend is BitTorrent which requires users who download files over this infrastructure to participate in the distribution of the files themselves in a tit-for-tat manner.

One potential solution to this challenge is to come up with new accounting and billing schemes, such as the P2P trading scheme sketched in Hausheer (2006), that combine the benefits of traditional accounting and micro-payment mechanisms with emerging barter-trade patterns like the one implemented by BitTorrent. These new schemes need to take into account that users are able to compensate service consumption to some extent by providing their own services to other users. Based on these new schemes the following new types of service traders can be distinguished: *balanced users*, who use more or less as much as they provide, *over-providers*, who use less than they provide, as well as *over-consumers*, who use more than they provide.

The basic idea of such a new scheme is the following: as long as a user's account is balanced,

that is the difference between service consumption and service provision does not exceed a certain threshold, the user does not have to pay or get paid for services. However, when a user starts overusing services and thus exceeds the given threshold, the overuse has to be compensated, otherwise the user will not be granted service anymore. This compensation can then either be achieved by providing services or by paying an amount of money to another user who has reached the threshold in the opposite way. Thus, similarly, a user who is under-using services is able to redeem the accumulated credit for money.

Hence, in principle such a scheme supports remuneration by providing services to other users, but it also allows users to compensate for under or overuse through the transfer of money. Note that since the money transfer is not bound to a single service transaction but rather independent from them, such a scheme can aggregate the outcome from several service transactions and remunerate them together, which will reduce the transaction costs.

The core requirement for new service-oriented accounting—going beyond the accounting for bits and bytes—is a future accounting protocol with the possibility to transfer service-oriented accounting records. Flexible accounting record formats forever changing and new services appearing frequently determine the second requirement. Thirdly, the multi-domain aspect, like in Grid networks (cf. the section "Accounting Models"), is becoming more and more important, since services are provided over several provider domains. Furthermore, accounting protocols should support prepaid services (cf. the section "Charging Approaches") in the future, because of the high popularity of prepaid charging in 3G type networks. Last but not least, the increasing network link speed and network traffic has to be tackled by a decentralized accounting approach and a distributed accounting record processing might become necessary.

Additionally, the negotiation of a Service Level Agreement (SLA) as well its parameters will make sense in some dedicated application cases. This negotiation shall be guided by purely economic incentives, such as the highest welfare achievable (cf. the section "Legal Contracts"). Therefore, the investigation of highly scalable, economically-driven, and technically feasible mechanisms determines an urgent need for suitable solutions in support of charging and accounting for guaranteed services and contracts.

Finally, since new service providers cannot necessarily be trusted anymore, new accounting and billing mechanisms have to take into account that users may act maliciously by providing false accounting records in order to increase their own benefit or simply to harm the system. Thus, new mechanisms like reputation schemes have to be developed and put into place which are able to keep track of a user's behavior in the past in order to possibly predict his trustworthiness in future transactions. Also, appropriate levels of redundancy need to be applied to compensate for the unreliability of individual traders and achieve a high robustness of such new schemes.

REFERENCES

3GPP (2005). *Technical specification group services and system aspects: CR 32215 PS domain charging;* 3GPP TSG-SA5 (Telecom Management), Tdoc S5-054463.

Agrawal, A., Brown, D., Ojha, A., & Savage, A. (2003). *Towards bucking free-riders: Distributed accounting and settlement in peer-to-peer networks.* Jacob School of Engineering Research Review, UCSD.

Akogrimo (2007). *EU IST project.* Retrieved October 16, 2007 2007, from http://www.akogrimo.org

Anglano, C., Barale, S., Gaido, L., Guarise, A., Patania, G., Piro, R., Rosso, F., & Werbrouk, A. (2006). *The distributed grid accounting system (DGAS).* Retrieved October 16, 2007, from http://www.to.infn.it/grid/accounting/main.html

Barmouta, A. (2004). *Authorization and accounting services for the world wide grid.* Unpublished master thesis, University of Western Australia.

Barmouta, A., & Buyya, R. (2003). GridBank: A grid accounting services architecture (GASA) for distributed systems sharing and integration. In *Proceedings of the 17th Annual International Parallel & Distributed Processing Symposium (IPDPS 2003) Workshop on Internet Computing and E-Commerce,* Nice, France.

Beardsmore, A., Hartley, K., Hawkins, S., Laws, S., Magowan, J., & Twigg, A. (2002). *GSAX grid service accounting extensions.* Retrieved October 16, 2007, from http://www.doc.ic.ac.uk/~sjn5/GGF/ggf-rus-gsax-01.pdf.

Brownlee, N. (1999). *RTFM: Applicability statement.* IETF, RFC 2721, October 1999.

Byrom, R., Walk, J., & Kant, D. (2005). *User guide for APEL - Accounting using PBS event logging.* Retrieved October 16, 2007, from http://hepunx.rl.ac.uk/edg/wp3/documentation/apel/apel-user-guide.pdf

Calhoun, P., Johansson, T., Perkins, C., Hiller, T., & McCann, P. (2005). *Diameter mobile IPv4 application.* IETF, RFC 4004, August 2005.

Calhoun, P., Loughney, J., Guttman, E., Zorn, G., & Arkko, G. (2003). *Diameter base protocol.* IETF, RFC 3588, September 2003.

Calhoun, P., Zorn, G., Spence, D., & Mitton, D. (2005). *Diameter network access server application.* IETF, RFC 4005, August 2005.

Case, J., Fedor, M., Schoffstall, M., & Davin, J. (1990). *A simple network management rotocol.* IETF, RFC 1157, May 1990.

Case, J., Mundy, R., Partain, D., & Stewart, B. (2002). *Introduction and applicability statements for internet-standard management framework.* IETF, RFC 3410, December 2002.

Chaum, D. (1982). Blind signatures for untraceable payments. *Advances in Cryptology: Crypto 1982* (pp. 199-203). New York: Plenum Press.

Chaum, D., Fiat, A., & Naor, M. (1990). Untraceable electronic cash. *Crypto 1988* (Vol. 403) (pp. 319-327). Springer Verlag.

Cohen, B. (2003). *Incentives build robustness in BitTorrent.* In *Proceedings of the Workshop on Economics of Peer-to-Peer Systems.* Berkeley, California.

DAG Cards (2007). Retrieved October 16, 2007, from http://www.endace.com/networkMCards.htm

Daidalos (2007). *EU IST Project.* Retrieved October 16, 2007, from http://www.ist-daidalos.org

De Laat, C., Gross, G., Gommans, L., Vollbrecht, J., & Spence, D. (2000). *Generic AAA architecture.* IETF, RFC 2903, August 2000.

Dingledine, R., Freedman, M., & Molnar, D. (2001). Accountability. *Peer-to-peer: Harnessing the power of disruptive technologies* (1st ed). O'Reilly & Associates.

Duffield, N. G., & Grossglauser, M. (2001). *Trajectory sampling for direct traffic observation.* *IEEE/ACM Transactions on Networking, 9*(3), 280-292.

eMule Project (2003). *eMule FAQ: Rating & score.* Retrieved October 16, 2007, from http://www.emule-project.net/faq/rating.htm.

Eronen, P., Hiller, T., & Zorn, G. (2005). *Diameter extensible authentication protocol (EAP) application.* IETF, RFC 4072, August 2005.

Estan, C., & Varghese, G. (2002). *New directions in traffic measurement and accounting.* UCSD technical report CS2002-0699, February 2002.

ETSI (1999). *Internet Protocol (IP) based Networks. Parameters and Mechanisms for Charging.* ETSI TR 101 734 V.1.1.1, Sophia Antipolis, France, September 1999.

ETSI (2005). *Digital cellular telecommunications system (Phase 2+). Vocabulary for 3GPP Specifications (3GPP TR 21.905 Ver. 6.10.0 Release 6),* ETSI TR 121 905 V6.10.0, 2005.

Eyermann, F., Racz, P., Schaefer, C., Stiller, B., & Walter, T. (2006). Diameter-based accounting management for wireless services. In *Proceedings of the IEEE Wireless Communications and Networking Conference 2006 (WCNC'06),* Las Vegas, Nevada.

Finseth, C. (1993). *An access control protocol, Sometimes Called TACACS.* IETF, RFC 1492, July 1993.

Gerke, J. (2006). *A Generic Peer-to-Peer Architecture for Internet Services;* Dissertation ETH No. 16673, ETH Zürich, Switzerland, 2006

Gerke, J., & Stiller, B. (2005). *VETO — Enabling a P2P-based market for composed services.* In *Proceedings of the IEEE 30th Local Computer Networks Conference (LCN'05),* Sydney, Australia.

Göhner, M., Waldburger, M., Gubler, F., Dreo Rodosek, G., & Stiller, B. (2007). An accounting model for dynamic virtual organizations. In *Proceedings of the Seventh IEEE International Symposium on Cluster Computing and the Grid (CCGrid 2007),* Rio de Janeiro, Brazil.

GRASP (2006). Retrieved October 16, 2007, from http://eu-grasp.net/english/default.htm

Gubler, F. (2006). *Accountable units for grid services in mobile dynamic virtual organizations.* IFI Diploma Thesis, University of Zürich.

Hakala, H., Mattila, L., Koskinen, J. P., Stura, M., & Loughney, J. (2005). *Diameter credit-control application.* IETF, RFC 4006, August 2005.

Han, S. H., Kim, M. S., Ju, H. T., & Won-Ki Hong, J. (2002). The architecture of NG-MON: A passive network monitoring system for high-speed IP networks. In *Proceedings of the 13th IFIP/IEEE International Workshop on Distributed Systems: Operations and Management* (pp 16-27). October 21-23, 2002.

Hardy, N., & Tribble, E. (1993). *The digital silk road*. Retrieved October 16, 2007, from http://www.agorics.com/agorics/dsr.html

Hausheer, D., Liebau, N., Mauthe, A., Steinmetz, R., & Stiller, B. (2003a). Token-based accounting and distributed pricing to introduce market mechanisms in a peer-to-peer file sharing scenario. In *Proceedings of the 3rd IEEE International Conference on Peer-to-Peer Computing*, Linköping, Sweden.

Hausheer, D., Liebau, N., Mauthe, A., Steinmetz, R., & Stiller, B. (2003b). *Towards a market managed peer-to-peer file sharing system using token-based accounting and distributed pricing*. TIK Report Nr. 179, ETH Zürich, TIK, August 2003.

Hausheer, D., & Stiller, B. (2005). PeerMint: Decentralized and secure accounting for peer-to-peer applications. In *Proceedings of the 2005 IFIP Networking Conference*, University of Waterloo, Waterloo Ontario Canada.

Hausheer, D. (2006). *PeerMart: Secured Decentralized Pricing and Accounting for Peer-to-Peer Systems*. Diss. ETH Zürich No. 16200, Shaker Verlag, ISBN 3-8322-4969-9, Aachen, Germany, March 2006.

Horne, B., Pinkas, B., & Sander, T. (2001). Escrow services and incentives in peer-to-peer networks. In *Proceedings of the Electronic Commerce (EC'01)*, Tampa, Florida.

IPDR.org (2004a). *Business solution requirements: Network data management-usage (NDM-U)*. Version 3.5.0.1, November 2004.

IPDR.org (2004b). *IPDR/XDR file encoding format*. Version 3.5.1, November 2004.

IPDR.org (2004c). *IPDR/XML file encoding format*. Version 3.5.0.1, November 2004.

IPDR.org (2004d). *Service specification – Voice over IP (VoIP)*. Version 3.5-A.0.1, November 2004.

IPDR.org (2007). *IPDR website*. Retrieved October 16, 2007, from http://www.ipdr.org

IP Flow Information Export (2007). *IETF*. Retrieved October 16, 2007, from http://www.ietf.org/html.charters/ipfix-charter.html

Joost (2007). Retrieved October 16, 2007, from http://www.joost.com

Kamvar, S., Yang, B., & Garcia-Molina, H. (2003). Addressing the non-cooperation problem in competitive P2P systems. In *Proceedings of the Workshop on Economics of Peer-to-Peer Systems*, Berkeley, California.

Kaplan, R. S., & Bruns, W. (1987). *Accounting and management: A field study perspective*. Harvard Business School Press.

Kaplan, R. S., & Atkinson, A. A. (1998). *Advanced management accounting* (3rd ed). Prentice Hall.

Karsten, M., Schmitt, J., Stiller, B., & Wolf, L. (2000). Charging for packet-switched network communications - Motivation and overview. *Computer Communications, 23*(3), 290-302.

Kitatsuji, Y., & Yamazaki, K. (2004). A distributed real-time tool for IP-flow measurement. *International Symposium on Applications and the Internet*, 2004 (pp. 91- 98).

Kurtansky, P., & Stiller, B. (2006). State of the art prepaid charging for IP services. In *Proceedings of the 4th International Conference on Wires/Wireless Internet Communications (WWIC 2006)*, Bern, Switzerland.

Kurtansky, P., & Stiller, B. (2005). Time interval-based prepaid charging of QoS-enabled IP services. In *Proceeding of the 1st International Workshop (WINE 2005)*, Hong Kong.

Lamport, L., Shostak, R., & Pease, M. (1982). The Byzantine generals problem. *ACM Transactions on Programming Languages and Systems, 4*, 382-401.

Liebau, N., Darlagiannis, V., Mauthe, A., & Steinmetz, R. (2005). *Token-based accounting for P2P-systems*. 14. Fachtagung Kommunikation in Verteilten Systemen 2005 (KiVS 05), February 2005.

Lim, D., Thuan Ho, Q., Zhang, J., Sung Lee, B., & Soon Ong, Y. (2005). MOGAS, A multiorganizational grid accounting system. *SCS International Journal of Information Technology, 11*(4), 84-103.

Mao, Y., Chen, K., Wang, D., & Zheng, W. (2001). *Cluster-based online monitoring system of web traffic*. In *Proceedings of the 3rd International Workshop on Web Information and Data Management*, Atlanta, Georgia.

Merriam-Webster, Inc. (2005). *Merriam-Webster online dictionary*. Retrieved October 17, 2007, from http://www.m-w.com

Moby Dick (2007). *EU IST Project*. Retrieved October 17, 2007, from http://www.ist-mobydick.org

Mojo Nation (2002). *Technical overview*. Retrieved October 17, 2007, from http://www.mojonation.net/docs/technical_overview.shtml.

NetFlow Services and Applications. (2007). *Cisco white paper*. Retrieved October 17, 2007, from http://www.cisco.com/warp/public/cc/pd/iosw/ioft/neflct/tech/napps_wp.htm

Ngan, T., Wallach, D., & Druschel, P. (2003). *Enforcing fair sharing of peer-to-peer resources*. In *Proceedings of the 2nd International Workshop on P2P Systems (IPTPS)*, Berkeley, California.

Ntarmos, N., & Triantafillou, P. (2004). SeAl: Managing accesses and data in peer-to-peer sharing networks. In *Proceedings of the Fourth International Conference on Peer-to-Peer Computing (P2P 2004)*, Zurich, Switzerland.

Packet Sampling Working Group (2007). *IETF*. Retrieved October 17, 2007, from http://www.ietf.org/html.charters/psamp-charter.html

PANA Working Group (2007). Retrieved October 17, 2007, from http://www.ietf.org/html.charters/pana-charter.html

Porter, M. E. (1985). *Competitive advantage: Creating and sustaining superior performance*. New York: Free Press.

Rensing, C., Karsten, M., & Stiller, B. (2002). *AAA: A survey and a policy-based architecture and framework. IEEE Network, 16*(6), 22-27.

Rigney, C. (2000). *RADIUS accounting*. IETF, RFC 2866, June 2000.

Rigney, C., Willens, S., Rubens, A., & Simpson, W. (2000). *Remote Authentication Dial In User Service (RADIUS)*. IETF, RFC 2865, June 2000.

SCAMPI (2007). *EU IST Project*. Retrieved October 17, 2007, from http://www.ist-scampi.org

Skype (2007). Retrieved October 17, 2007, from http://www.skype.com

Songhurst, D. (Ed.) (1999). *Charging communication networks: From theory to practice.*, Amsterdam, The Netherlands: Elsevier Publisher.

Stiller, B. (2003). A survey of charging internet services. In S. Aidarous & T. Pleyvak (Eds.), *Managing IP Networks*. IEEE Press & Wiley InterScience.

Thigpen, W., Hacker, T., McGinnis, L., & Athey, B. (2002). Distributed accounting on the grid. In *Proceedings of the 6th Joint Conference on Information Sciences* (pp. 1147-1150). 2002.

UNCITRAL (1980). United Nations Commission on International Trade Law. *United Nations* convention on contracts for the international sale of goods (CISG) (pp. 1-47). April 1980.

Vishnumurthy, V., Chandrakumar, S., & Sirer, E. G. (2003). KARMA: A secure economic framework for peer-to-peer resource. In *Proceedings of the Workshop on Economics of Peer-to-Peer Systems*, Berkeley, California.

Waldbusser, S. (2006). *Remote network monitoring management information base Version 2.* IETF, RFC 4502, May 2006.

Web WordNet 2.0 (2005). Retrieved October 17, 2007, from http://wordnet.princeton.edu/cgi-bin/webwn

Yang, B., & Garcia-Molina, H. (2003). *PPay:* Micropayments for peer-to-peer systems. In *Proceedings of the ACM Conference on Computer and Communications Security (CCS'03)*, Washington, DC.

Zhang, K., & Elkin, E. (2002). XACCT's common reliable accounting for network element (CRANE) protocol specification version 1.0. IETF, RFC 3423, November 2002.

ADDITIONAL READING

3GPP (2005), *Overall high level functionality and architecture impacts of flow based charging*, 3GPP TR 23.125 v6.5.0, 2005.

Aboba, B., Arkko, J., & Harrington, D. (2000). *Introduction to accounting management.* IETF RFC 2975, October 2000.

Bailey, J. P. (1997). The economics of internet interconnection agreements. In L. McKnight & J. P. Bailey (Eds.), *Internet economics* (pp 155-168). Cambridge, MA: MIT Press.

Bhushan, B., Tschichholz, Leray, E., & Donnelly, W. (2001). Federated accounting: Service charging and billing in a business-to-business environment. In *Proceedings of the IFIP/IEEE*

Integrated Management Symposium, Seattle, Washington.

Bubendorfer, K., & Komisarcczuk, P. (2006). *A position paper: Towards an utility computing and communications infrastructure.* Retrieved October 17, 2007, from http://www.mcs.vuw.ac.nz/~kris/publications/CIC.pdf

Carle, G., Smirnov, M., & Zseby, T. (1998). Charging and accounting architectures for IP multicast integrated services over ATM. In *Proceedings of the 4th International Symposium on Interworking (Interworking'98)*, Ottawa, Canada.

Estan, C., & Varghese, G. (2003). *New directions in traffic measurement and accounting: Focusing on the elephants, ignoring the mice.* ACM Transactions on Computer Systems, August 2003.

IETF (2006). *Next steps in signaling (NSIS).* Retrieved October 17, 2007, http://www.ietf.org/html.charters/nsis-charter

Kühne, J., Reimer, U., Schläger, M., Dressler, F., Fan, C., Fessl, A., Klenk, A., & Carle, G. (2005). Architecture for a service-oriented and convergent charging in 3G mobile networks and beyond. In *Proceedings of the 6th IEE Conference on 3G & Beyond (3G 2005)*, London, UK.

Koutsopoulou, M., Alonistioti, A., Gazis, E. & Kaloxylos, A. (2001). Adaptive charging accounting and billing system for the support of advanced business models for VAS provision in 3G systems. In *Proceedings of the IEEE Intl. Symposium on Personal Indoor and Mobile Radio Communication (PIMRC 2001)*, San Diego, California.

Koutsopoulou, M., Kaloxylos, A., Alonistioti, A., Merakos, L., & Kawamura, K. (2004). Charging, accounting and billing management schemes in mobile telecommunication networks and the internet. *IEEE Communications Surveys, 6*(1).

Lamanna, D., Skene, J., & Emmerich, W. (2003). SLAng: A language for defining service level agreements. In *Proceedings of the 9th IEEE Work-*

shop on *Future Trends of Distributed Computing Systems (FTDCS'03)*, San Juan, Puerto Rico.

Maniatis, S. I., Nikolouzou, E. G., & Venieris, I. S. (2004). End-to-end QoS specification issues in the converged all-IP wired and wireless environment. *Communications Magazine, IEEE, 42*(6), 80- 86.

Rigney, C., Willats, W., & Calhoun, P. (2000). *RADIUS extensions*. IETF, RFC 2869, June 2000

Ryan, C., Brazil, J., de Leastar, E., & Foghlú, M. (2002). Workbook approach to algorithm design and service accounting in a component

oriented environment. In *Proceedings of the IEEE Workshop on IP Operations and Management*, Dallas, Texas.

Schulzrinne, H., & Hancock, R. (in press). *GIMPS: General internet messaging protocol for signaling.* Internet-Draft.

Sprenkels, R., Parhonyi, R., Pras, A., van Beijnum, B.L., & De Goede, B. (2000). An architecture for reverse charging in the internet. In *Proceedings of the IEEE Workshop on IP-oriented Operations and Management (IPOM00)*, Craow, Poland.

APPENDIX

List of abbreviated terms

3GPP   3rd Generation Partnership Project

A4C   Authentication, Authorization, Accounting, Auditing, and Charging

AAA   Authentication, Authorization, and Accounting

ABC   Activity Based Costing

ADSL   Asymmetric Digital Subscriber Line

AS   Autonomous System

ASM   Application Specific Module

ATM   Asynchronous Transfer Mode

AVP   Attribute-Value-Pair

BSS   Business Support System

CDR   Call Detail Record

CPU   Central Processing Unit

CRANE   Common Reliable Accounting for Network Element

EAP   Extensible Authentication Protocol

ETSI   European Telecommunications Standardization Institute

IDS   Intrusion Detection System

IETF   Internet Engineering Task Force

IP   Internet Protocol

IPDR   Internet Protocol Detail Record

IPFIX   IP Flow Export

IPSec   IP Security

IPTV   IP Television

ISP   Internet Service Provider

IT   Information Technology

MD   Message Digest

MIB   Management Information Base

NAS   Network Access Server

NMS   Network Monitoring Station

OC   Optical Carrier

P2P   Peer-to-peer

PANA   Protocol for Carrying Authentication for Network Access

PSAMP Packet Sampling

QoS   Quality of Service

RADIUS Remote Authentication Dial In User Service

RTFM   Real-time Traffic Flow Measurement Architecture

RMON   Remote Management Information Base

SC   Service Consumer

SCTP   Stream Control Transmission Protocol

SE   Service Element

SLA   Service Level Agreement

SNMP   Simple Network Management Protocol

TACACS+ Terminal Access Controller Access Control System

TCAS   Traditional Cost Accounting System

TCP   Transmission Control Protocol

ToS   Type of Service

TLS   Transport Layer Security

UDP   User Datagram Protocol

VAS   Value-added Service

VASP   Value-added Service Provider

VETO   Vickrey Welfare Procurement Auction

VO   Virtual Organization

VoIP   Voice-over-IP

WLAN   Wireless Local Area Network

XDR   eXternal Data Representation

XML   Extensible Markup Language

Chapter XV
Security for Ubiquitous Computing

Tobias Straub
Fraunhofer Institute for Secure Information Technology, Germany

Andreas Heinemann
Technical University of Darmstadt, Germany

ABSTRACT

Taking typical ubiquitous computing settings as a starting point, this chapter motivates the need for security. The reader will learn what makes security challenging and what the risks predominant in ubiquitous computing are. The major part of this chapter is dedicated to the description of sample solutions in order to illustrate the wealth of protection mechanisms. A background in IT security is not required as this chapter is self-contained. A brief introduction to the subject is given as well as an overview of cryptographic tools.

INTRODUCTION

Mark Weiser's vision of ubiquitous computing (UC) raises many new security issues. Consider a situation where a large number of UC peers interact in a spontaneous and autonomous manner, without previously known communication partners and without a common security infrastructure. Such extreme conditions make it difficult to apply established security methods that have been tailored for "classical" information technology (IT). Virgil

Gligor emphasizes this by comparing the Internet cliché where "processing is free and physically protected, but communication is not" with the new cliché about UC where "neither processing nor communication is free and physically protected" (Gligor, 2005).

This chapter gives a systematic introduction into the field of security for UC. It is structured as follows: first (the section "Four UC Settings"), we illustrate the diversity of UC systems and applications in order to raise the reader's awareness of security questions. Our discussion focuses on four representative UC settings. For each of them, a characteristic application scenario is given. The diversity of the settings, for example, concerning presumed knowledge about components or system complexity, has direct implications for which mechanisms are appropriate to achieve a desired IT security objective.

The section "A Taxonomy of UC Security" starts with an introduction to basic terminology explaining the objectives of IT security as well as the threat model. UC security can be regarded from two different viewpoints: The special characteristics of UC may lead to known and new security risks, if not addressed appropriately. In addition, limitations concerning resources and infrastructure pose a number of challenges in order to achieve desired security objectives.

A compact overview of cryptographic tools suitable to enforce those objectives is given in the section "Overview of Cryptographic Tools". A brief explanation of cryptographic primitives like ciphers, hash functions, and signatures is provided for the nonspecialist reader. A discussion of the potential and limitations of cryptography in UC concludes the section.

After having learned the particularities and challenges of UC systems with respect to security, we look at sample solutions to mitigate these limitations. A selection of elaborated approaches for secure UC systems is given in the section "Sample Solutions". They tackle the issues of privacy and availability as well as the establishment of secure communication.

A brief summary and a list of references for further reading conclude this chapter.

FOUR UC SETTINGS

In order to pave the way for the development of a systematic view on UC characteristics and limitations in the section "A Taxonomy of UC Security", we sketch four representative settings.

Each setting exhibits one or more security-related properties. They are termed *mobile computing*, *ad hoc interaction*, *smart spaces*, and *real-time enterprises*.

Mobile Computing

Mobile computing supports *mobile* users with connectivity and access to services and backend systems while being on the move. A synonymous term is nomadic computing, emphasizing the goal of providing a working environment more or less equivalent to that of a desktop user. The widespread availability of cellular networks and 802.11 WiFi allows a field worker to connect to an arbitrary service on the Internet or to the company's backend at almost any place and at any time.

Mobile computing relies on a given infrastructure managed by a provider, for example, a cellular network company. This fact has implications for security: In order to access a service, a user needs to register with a provider. Thus, the user group is closed and the provider controls access to the infrastructure. In addition, users are not able to act in an anonymous manner.

Mobile devices can easily get lost, for example left behind in the proverbial taxi (see http://www.laptopical.com/laptops-lost-in-taxi.html). In case of theft, an attacker might be able to impersonate the legitimate device owner or learn her private data like business contacts or personal email. This physical threat is given whenever mobile devices are considered.

Scenario 1: The Mobile Salesman

While on the road, a salesman needs to regularly download up-to-date client reports from his company's databases. His laptop is equipped with several wireless communication interfaces which can be used to connect via different service providers depending on what kind of service/infrastructure is available.

At the client's office, there is a WiFi network the salesman can access. There are also some networked printers available for guests. However, it is unclear to what extent the infrastructure can be trusted.

This scenario raises three major issues: Firstly, the protection of communication (from the salesman's device to the company backend) over potentially insecure channels. Secondly, the secure storage of company internals on his laptop. Secure tunneling, VPNs (virtual private networks), and hard disk encryption are standard technologies in this field. The necessary cryptographic tools are explained in the section "Overview of Cryptographic Tools". However, the aspect of secure device association, discussed, for example, by Balfanz, Smetters, Stewart, and Wong (2002), is something new. Later in this chapter, we answer the following questions: Is there a way to securely send a confidential document over the air to a printer located in the office? Does it help if the salesman selects a printer close to him equipped with a secondary communication interface?

Ad Hoc Interaction

In contrast to mobile computing, the second setting does not rely on an infrastructure provider. Instead of that, UC devices build the infrastructure on their own by establishing temporary, wireless, and ad hoc communication links between them. On the application layer, they expose a spontaneous interaction behavior. A typical characteristic is the lack of a central instance allowing or restricting participation. *A priori*, there are no given or managed user groups; all devices are free to join. Plus, users and devices might act anonymously.

Here we illustrate a collaboration scenario based on spontaneous interaction. This type of communication is typical for *Opportunistic Networks* which are discussed in depth in the chapter "Opportunistic Networks".

Scenario 2: Passive Collaboration in Opportunistic Networks

In an Opportunistic Network, passers-by exchange information, for example digital advertisements (Straub & Heinemann, 2004), while being co-located. After an initial configuration, devices interact autonomously and without users' attention. Information dissemination is controlled by profiles stored on the users' devices. Such a profile expresses a user's interest in and knowledge about some pieces of information to share.

The particularities of ad hoc interaction pose numerous security challenges. On the one hand, devices do not already know each other when they start to communicate. On the other hand, personal data is kept on the devices and exchanged with strangers. As a consequence, privacy is inherently at risk if systems are not designed carefully.

Smart Spaces

Smart spaces, which form our third UC setting, emphasize user-friendliness and user empowerment as well as support for human interactions. Interaction within a smart space happens in an unobtrusive way. The use of contextual information (see chapter "Context Models and Context Awareness") plays also an important role here. Sometimes, it is assumed that users carry some type of digital identification and/or other devices with or on them.

Due to the sensing and tracking capabilities of a smart space, user privacy is at stake. Location privacy is an important field of UC research; an overview is given by Görlach, Heinemann, Terpstra, and Mühlhäuser (2005). In addition, due to the volatile nature of smart spaces, concepts like trust (see Chapter 15) and reputation play an important part in these kinds of applications. We take patient monitoring in a hospital as an example to illustrate a smart space.

Scenario 3: Patient Monitoring

In a hospital, all records of patients are digitally stored and maintained in a central database. Records are updated with the results of physical examinations or continuous monitoring. Husemann and Nidd (2005) describe a middleware capable of integrating a wide range of medical analyzers that have a common wireless interface. Consider a battery driven heartbeat monitor which is attached to the body and sends measurements to the database. The data can be used as well for a patient surveillance system that triggers an alarm in case of an anomaly.

This scenario raises a number of security issues: for new patients the heartbeat monitor has to be unambiguously and securely associated with their record. The data from the monitor needs to go to the right record, communication needs to be protected, and the correctness of the data must be assured. In addition, after a patient leaves the hospital, the heartbeat monitor needs to be detached from the digital record for reuse. The resurrecting duckling (Stajano & Anderson, 1999) security policy framework helps in this setting. It is described in the section "Sample Solutions".

Real-Time Enterprises

Real-time enterprises, which are defined in the preface of this book, are an effort to leverage UC technology and methods within enterprises. A driving force behind these efforts is the goal of having immediate access to comprehensive and up-to-date information about processes and procedures within an enterprise. This allows management to react very flexibly to variances in the market and to increase customer support and satisfaction. For example, an enterprise with detailed real-time information on all production steps, including delivery statuses of subcontractors, can provide a customer with very accurate information on when an order will be delivered.

Scenario 4: RFID-Based Warehouse Management

Radio frequency identification (RFID) offers a variety of opportunities in tracking goods (see e.g., Fleisch & Mattern, 2005). Suppose all goods stocked at a warehouse are tagged with an RFID transponder. With the corresponding readers integrated into storage racks, the process of stocktaking can be completely automated and inventory information is available in real-time.

The use of RFID allows for more efficient stocking, product locating, and product theft protection, to name a few. The deployment of tags and readers within a company gives rise to security questions, for instance, those of industrial espionage. A competitor, equipped with a mobile RFID reader, might be able to derive useful information about a company, by reading their product tags. RFID tags should also be looked at from a privacy point of view as they—under certain conditions—may allow the surveillance and tracking of humans.

RFID privacy is currently also a hot topic in the context of machine-readable travel documents. Privacy is discussed with respect to biometric data like photos and fingerprints stored on the chip. Another question is whether ID cards can be used to create movement profiles of their holder. The reader is referred to Knospe and Pohl (2004) for an overview of RFID security. We come back to this issue in the section "Sample Solutions".

A TAXONOMY OF UC SECURITY

The beginning of this section provides a compact introduction to IT security by explaining the common objectives and the threats to them. We then formulate two views on UC security issues.

In section "First View: UC Characteristics and Associated Risks," we explain which and how typical characteristics of UC lead to well-known, but also new risks that demand appropriate countermeasures. UC limitations concerning resources and deployed infrastructures are in focus of the second view in the section "Second View: UC Limitations and Associated Challenges". These limitations give rise to security challenges that require novel methods, some of which are presented in the section "Sample Solutions".

Basic Terminology and Objectives of IT Security

Security of IT systems is usually discussed in the following way: First, *assets* (and their respective value) are identified. The notion of assets covers data as well as hardware. With respect to our four scenarios, data that has to be protected, for instance, comprises:

- Confidential documents (Scenario 1),
- An individual's habits and preferences (Scenario 2),
- Medical information (Scenario 3),
- The stock list at a warehouse (Scenario 4).

When speaking of the protection of data, we mean that particular attributes are preserved. In the information security community the mnemonics CIA or CIAA are often used to refer to the following fundamental *protection objectives*:

- **Confidentiality (C):** Refers to the aim of keeping pieces of information secret from unauthorized access.
- **Integrity (I):** Is the requirement that data is safe from changes, be it either accidentally or deliberately.
- **Authenticity (A):** Concerns itself with the genuineness of messages or the identity of entities in a networked system.

These objectives can be achieved by cryptography as we will see below. In this respect, the next objective is different as it typically requires noncryptographic efforts as well.

- **Availability (A):** Means the provisioning of a system's services to its users in a reliable way.

An attacker may try to prevent legitimate use in a so-called *denial-of-service* (DoS) attack. Demanding a large portion of (computational and/or network) resources is a strategy to slow down the system. Another flavor of DoS is the blocking of communication links between legitimate parties. Designing a UC system for redundancy and diversity is a standard way towards achieving availability (see e.g., Vogt, 2005). This can be done, for instance, by using peer-to-peer networks, the replication of information, or distributed computing facilities. Intrusion-detection systems, which are a common protection technology for computer systems in an organization, are starting to attract attention in the UC community (Robinson, 2005). Bahl, Chandra, Padhye, Ravindranath, Singh, Wolman (2006) describe a system to fight DoS attacks on corporate wireless networks and to detect malicious mobile devices.

Threat Modeling

Having discussed basic terminology and objectives, we now turn to a common abstract network model to describe security threats: Two parties exchange messages over a *channel* to which an *attacker* has access, too. This notion captures any kind of attackers (computer systems, individuals, organizations) and is independent of the data transport medium itself. There is no need to differentiate between the transmission and the storage of data as the latter can be seen as a special case of the model.

We follow the security community's convention in using the names Alice and Bob for the legitimate actors (instead of simply numbering them serially) and in calling the attacker Mallory ("malicious"). Mallory may *change* data Alice sends to Bob, may *generate* her own messages under the name of another person, or simply *eavesdrop* on their connection. An attack of the latter kind is called *passive* while the other two are called *active*. A passive attacker can compromise confidentiality at best, but an active one—who is also called *man-in-the-middle* (MITM)—targets at all CIAA goals. Acting as a MITM, Mallory sits in between the communication link, making Alice believe she is Bob and spoofs Bob into believing she is Alice.

Attacks are typically directed toward more than one of the before-mentioned security objectives. For instance, Mallory may launch a DoS attack in order to paralyze the system's defense mechanisms.

The *risk* that a system may become compromised is proportional to both its *vulnerabilities* and the *threats* acting upon it. Risks have to be identified and rated in the light of the corresponding assets' value. Threat perception can be very subjective: While one individual cares about data emitted by her UC device, which might be linked back to her, another does not. Furthermore, not all objectives are equally important in practice. For instance, a bank primarily has a vital interest in keeping its account data's integrity, but a research lab emphasizes confidentiality. The choice of algorithms and security also takes into consideration the (assumed) attacker's strategy and resources, especially computational power.

First View: UC Characteristics and Associated Risks

In order to put the UC vision to work, most scenarios, including the ones described in the last section, rely on wireless communication between nodes. Communication might happen in an *ad hoc* manner as illustrated in the ad hoc interac-

tion setting; other applications might ask for a wireless *multi-hop* communication (see sensor networks in the chapter "Wireless and Mobile Communication"). Wireless communication makes eavesdropping very easy as radio signal are usually emitted in all directions. They can be received by anyone in the senders' vicinity without her noticing it. MITM attacks are feasible in the case of multi-hop wireless communication and they do not even require the attacker to be physically close to the victim. In addition, wireless ad hoc communication bears the risk of impersonation, that is, an attacker might be able to steal a peer's credential by eavesdropping and use it to access a certain service.

The pervasive nature of UC introduces even more risks. Sensor nodes or RFID tags for example, are physically exposed, unmanaged, and unsupervised. This bears the risks of device and/or data theft as well as device manipulation. As a consequence, access to the data stored on the device must be carefully protected in order to prevent identity theft (Eckert, 2005). The Black-Berry PDA for instance is a centrally manageable system that supports a remote "kill" command to erase data on a stolen device (Greiner, 2006).

UC devices are often battery-powered, which allows for a DoS attack called *sleep deprivation torture* (Stajano & Anderson, 1999): By constantly sending requests to a device, an attacker can quickly drain its battery, thus rendering the device useless. Last but not least, the UC settings offer the capability of tracing objects or humans. This feature is useful in many UC applications like the real-time enterprise setting, but may violate user's privacy. Networked sensors, for instance, may gather a good deal of personal information that can be used to build user profiles.

The characteristics in UC and their corresponding risks are summarized in Table 1. In the section "Overview of Cryptographic Tools" we cover appropriate countermeasures.

Table 1. First view: Characteristics and risks

characteristics		risks
communication	wireless	eavesdropping
	ad hoc	impersonation
	multi-hop	man-in-the-middle attacks
pervasive nature	physical exposure	device/data theft, manipulation
	battery-powered	sleep deprivation torture
	traceability	privacy violation

Second View: UC Limitations and Associated Challenges

Our second view on UC security concerns resource and infrastructure limitations of UC and their corresponding challenges. The functionality provided by UC devices varies widely and is limited by a number of parameters. These include device capabilities—concerning, for example, memory capacity, energy supply, CPU power, and the user interface—or connectivity which is characterized among others by network coverage, bandwidth, environmental conditions (like shielding or speed in case of moving devices).

Since a UC device can be less powerful that a desktop computer, it is important to use appropriate, that is, lightweight, security mechanisms. Otherwise, wasting memory and energy resources would achieve the exact opposite effect of keeping the system safe. Observe that a slow CPU might

take significant time to carry out sophisticated cryptographic operations which may negatively affect the user experience. User interface capabilities may also limit the choice of appropriate methods, too: For example, a mobile device with a *voice only* user interface such as described by Aitenbichler, Kangasharju, and Mühlhäuser (2004), demands different authentication methods to a device that comes with a keyboard. At the bottom end, very small and feeblish UC devices like passive RFID chips are found. These devices do not even come with a user interface at all. A limited user interface makes it difficult to establish what is called a *trusted path*. This is a mechanism to ensure that users can assert that they are interacting with a genuine system or program instead of one controlled by an attacker (for instance when asked for a password).

The absence of a centralized authority is typical for UC systems like the ad hoc interaction setting presented in section "Ad Hoc Interaction". This

Table 2. Second view: Limitations and challenges

Limitations		Challenges
Infrastructure	lack of centralized authority	entity authentication, policy decision
Resource	limited CPU power, few/no memory, limited power supply	algorithm implementation, protocol design
	user interface limitations	trusted path

makes it hard to build an infrastructure where UC peers can authenticate each other in order to communicate securely. Another consequence is the lack of common support for trust and policy decision. The following chapter discusses appropriate countermeasures for this issue. Alternative methods for entity authentication based on out-of-band communication schemes are the subject of section "Out-of-Band Channels".

The limitations corresponding to UC security and their induced challenges are summarized in Table 2. Selected methods that address these challenges are discussed in section "Sample Solutions".

OVERVIEW OF CRYPTOGRAPHIC TOOLS

This section provides a compact overview of cryptographic tools which are suitable to enforce the security objectives introduced in the section "A Taxonomy of UC Security". It serves as a basis for the following discussion of the solutions addressing UC characteristics and challenges. Cryptographic *primitives*, namely symmetric and public key cryptosystems, hash functions, and authentication schemes, are the building blocks of more complex techniques and protocols. We also introduce some general rules of cryptography and reason about security parameters. At the end of this section we turn to the potentials and limitations of cryptography in a UC setting. Readers with previous knowledge in the area of cryptography may directly proceed to section "Potential and Limitations of Cryptography in UC."

Symmetric Cryptosystems

Messages can be *encrypted* to prevent disclosure of their content and ensure confidentiality. Encryption is a transformation that renders *plaintext*, that is, the original message in its readable form, into *ciphertext* which is unintelligible to an outsider.

The reverse transformation is called *decryption*. In order to give Alice and Bob a competitive edge, there must be some information Mallory does not have. The encryption and decryption function of all modern *cryptosystems* (or *ciphers*) are parameterized by *keys*. A key is a short fixed-length piece of data (while the plaintext may be of arbitrary length). It has to be kept secret from Mallory as only the correct key allows successful decryption of the ciphertext.

As early as the 19th century, cryptographer Kerckhoff claimed the following important law: A cryptosystem's strength should not be based on the assumption that its algorithm is kept secret, but only on the attacker's uncertainty regarding the key. An elementary security requirement is the fact that it should be unfeasible for Mallory to simply try out all possible keys by a *brute-force* attack. This imposes a lower bound on the cardinality of the set of all possible keys and demands that keys be generated randomly.

The distinction whether the same key is used for encryption and decryption or not may seem marginal at first sight, but is in fact crucial. *Symmetric* cryptosystems require two or more communication partners to know the same *shared key*. Modern symmetric cryptosystems use keys of bitlength 112, 168 (3DES) or 128, 192, 256 (AES). As a rule of thumb, keys shorter than 80 bits should be used with great care. A good place to look up reliable key lengths based on cryptographic analysis is the Web site http://www.keylength.com.

On this occasion, we exhibit a problem common to all symmetric ciphers: The use of shared keys implies a secure *key distribution* step before the actual communication takes place. Key distribution is often a problem as it needs *out-of-band* mechanisms, that is, an additional communication channel not accessible to the attacker. We will come back to this issue in the context of UC in the section "Out-of-Band Channels". Another downside of shared keys is that the risk grows proportional to the number of group members.

If one device falls into Mallory's hands, she will be able to read all messages of the group. A real-world example for the use of shared keys is 802.11 WEP ("Wired Equivalent Privacy", see for example Eckert, 2006).

Asymmetric Cryptosystems and PKI

The key distribution problem can be avoided by using *asymmetric cryptosystems*, which are synonymously called *public key cryptosystems*. In this case, encryption and decryption use different keys, such that these functions can be effectively separated. The respective keys are denoted *public key* and *private key*. Such a *key pair* has to satisfy certain mathematical conditions depending on the particular cryptosystem. Bob solely has to keep his private key secret, but can make the corresponding public key available to Alice or everybody else in the world—including Mallory—as it is infeasible to compute the private key from the public key. Public key encryption is thus an example of a so-called *one-way function* since the ciphertext can be computed efficiently, while inversion is infeasible. More specifically, public key encryption falls into the category of one-way functions with *trapdoor* as knowledge of the private key allows the inversion of the mapping. We will see below that asymmetry is an important pillar of modern cryptography.

The *RSA* cryptosystem, named after R. Rivest, A. Shamir, and L. Adleman (1978), is the most prominent example of an asymmetric cryptosystem. Typical key lengths are 1024, 2048, or 4096 bit. Its security is based on the presumed intractability of the factorization of large composite numbers. The *ElGamal* cryptosystem in contrast is based on the problem of computing discrete logarithms in finite cyclic groups (a typical group size is 2^{160} or 2^{230}). A standard construction for ElGamal is to use a subgroup of the multiplicative group of $\mathbb{Z}/\mathbb{Z}p$, where p is a prime (typically 1024 or 2048 bits in length). *Elliptic curves* (EC) over finite fields can also serve as a mathematical struc-

ture for ElGamal encryption (see e.g., Hankerson, Menezes, and Vanstone, 2004) for an introduction to EC cryptography).

Observe that public key cryptography alleviates the problem *of confidential* secret key distribution for the price of *authentic* public key distribution in the following way: Alice who wants to send a private message to Bob needs to have his genuine public key K_B. If Mallory manages to foist her key K_M on Alice, the message would be encrypted for her and not for Bob. *Digital certificates* are a common solution to this problem. A certificate is a statement linking a public key to an identity (e.g., a user's name, a device address, or a pseudonym). In order to prevent certificates from being forged they are digitally signed (see the following section for an explanation of digital signatures). Certificates form the basis of a so-called *public key infrastructure* (PKI), an environment where the authenticity of public keys is assured.

Hash Functions

In order to ensure data integrity, some kind of redundancy has to be added to the payload. A *modification detection code* (MDC) is a *hash algorithm*, that is, a function that compresses bitstrings of arbitrary finite length to bitstrings of fixed length. State-of-the-art algorithms like RIPEMD-160 (Dobbertin, Bosselaers, & Preneel, 1996) or SHA-1 (Eastlake & Jones, 2001) produce outputs with a length of 160 bit, which should be considered the lower bound due to security reasons. To be useful for integrity protection, a hash function has to be *2nd preimage resistant*: Given an input x that hashes to $h(x)$, an attacker must not be able to find a value $y \neq x$ such that $h(y) = h(x)$. Such a pair of different inputs that result in the same hash value is called a *collision*. Collisions always exist due to the pigeon-hole principle since the co-domain is finite while the domain is infinite. Cryptographic hash functions must be *collision-resistant*, that is, finding concrete collisions must be computationally infeasible. This allows us to protect data x of arbitrary length against modifications by storing $h(x)$, a small piece of information, in a safe place. A widespread application of this mechanism is integrity-protected software distribution via download mirror sites on the Internet. Flipping a single bit in x results in a hash value that differs in about half of the bits from $h(x)$ if h is one of the common hash functions.

Message authentication codes (MACs) are hash functions that are additionally parameterized with a secret key. Assume that Alice and Bob share a key k, which for instance has been established in a key exchange scheme as explained below. Alice adds a MAC $h_k(x)$ to her message x to Bob. From the pair $(x, h_k(x))$ Bob can tell that the message came from her since it is infeasible for Mallory to create a pair $(y, h_k(y))$ without knowing k. Remember that a MDC does not have this property, since Mallory may change x to y and compute the (unkeyed) hash function $h(y)$. MACs in turn not only provide *data origin authentication*, but also integrity as Bob could detect a modification $x' \neq x$ because the received $h_k(x)$ would not match the value $h_k(x')$ he computed himself. Each MDC h can be extended to a MAC in the following way: On input x, compute $h(k \| p_1 \| h(k \| p_2 \| x))$ where k is the key, p_1, p_2 are constant padding strings, and $\|$ denotes concatenation. This generic construction is called *HMAC* (hash-based MAC), see Krawczyk, Bellare, and Canetti, 1997 for implementation and security details.

Digital Signatures

MACs are useful for guaranteeing the authenticity of a communication link. However, they do not provide a transferable proof of authorship: As the parties at both ends of the channel share knowledge of the key, a "MACed" message $(x, h_k(x))$ could originate from either of them. As a matter of fact, a third party cannot deduce its author. Transferable proofs of authorship are required to model digital workflows, for example orders in electronic commerce that must be verifiable by multiple parties (possibly including a judge in order to arbitrate in a dispute). *Digital signature* schemes are a means to provide such evidence. They are also implemented with public key cryptography. Signature verification is a one-way function with trapdoor, referring to the ability to create signatures.

The RSA signature scheme is based on the same mathematics as the RSA cryptosystem. Signing corresponds to decryption while verification corresponds to encryption. *Digital Signature Algorithm* (DSA) and its EC-based variant EC-DSA are alternative schemes which are not yet as prevalent as RSA. EC-DSA is more efficiently computable than RSA and uses shorter keys for comparable strength.

Signatures are, in fact, computed over the hash value $h(x)$, not the message x itself. One reason is the reduction of computational costs associated with public key cryptography. Secondly, the one-way property of the hash function prevents so-called existential forgery of signatures (see e.g., Buchmann, 2004). However, h must be collision-resistant as in the case where $h(x) = h(x')$, a signature of x is always a signature of x', too.

Messages that comprise declarations of intent should be legally binding for the originator. On the one hand, this implies that the originator commits himself to the content in a way that he cannot deny his intent later. On the other hand, no one other than the legitimate person should be able to make a commitment in his name. This property is called *non-repudiation*. Non-repudiation can be achieved with the help of dedicated hardware, for example a smartcard or TPM (Trusted Platform Module, see e.g., Eckert, 2006) chip that keeps the signing key under the sole control of its owner.

Observe that *deniability*, the opposite of non-repudiation, may indeed be a desirable security goal sometimes, for instance in order to cope with censorship in UC networks. In such a setting, MACing should be preferred to signing of messages.

Hybrid Encryption and Key Exchange

In practice, asymmetric and symmetric cryptosystems are combined in *hybrid encryption* in the following way: Symmetric cryptosystems typically have a much higher throughput compared to public key systems with a comparable security level. Therefore Alice first encrypts the plaintext with a symmetric cryptosystem using a random, ephemeral *session* or *transaction key*. Then she transmits the symmetric key to Bob in a confidential way by encrypting it with his public key (if the message has multiple recipients, they all obtain the same ciphertext accompanied by the same symmetric key encrypted with their individual public key). The mechanism of distributing key material is called *key exchange*. The term *key agreement* is often used synonymously, but may sometimes emphasize the fact that both parties contribute to the generation of the key. The *Diffie-Hellman* (DH) protocol is the most famous interactive key exchange scheme. It allows two parties linked by an authentic, but not necessarily private, channel to agree on a common secret—which seems counter-intuitive at first sight. Note that unauthenticated DH is inherently prone to MITM attacks. Authenticated DH can be implemented by having each party digitally sign its protocol messages. The mathematics and security properties of DH are closely related to the ElGamal cryptosystem.

An authentic key agreement protocol like the DH scheme allows parties to achieve *forward secrecy*, that is, to limit the possible impact of a broken key: If a long-term signing key falls into Mallory's hand, this does not leak the plaintext of past communications Mallory may have recorded. On the other hand, a broken ephemeral symmetric key only affects the particular messages encrypted with it. Forward secrecy allows the parties to use relatively short symmetric keys provided they are changed frequently. When this trade-off is made in a UC scenario, the cost reduction for symmetric encryption due to smaller key sizes has to be balanced against the overhead for key exchange.

Potential and Limitations of Cryptography in UC

Having outlined the general tools of cryptography, we conclude this section by a discussion of computational costs. Since energy consumption is a serious issue in UC, we direct the reader's attention to Table 3. These figures are the outcomes of experiments with a 206 MHz Compaq iPAQ H3670 described by Potlapally, Ravi, Raghunathan, and Jha (2003). The table shows the setup and current costs for the families of algorithms we explained above. Observe that the costs of hashing and symmetric encryption are given in μJ, whereas mJ is the unit for digital signatures.

Due to its output size of only 128-bit, we included the hash function MD5 for comparison although its use is no longer recommended. The figures for the AES algorithm refer to the standard operation mode CBC (see e.g., Buchmann, 2004). AES is a so-called iterative block cipher. Its computation is organized in multiple rounds implementing the same subroutines, but with different round keys. The round keys are derived from the actual (128, 192, or 256 bit) key. This process is called key scheduling.

The table shows the signature algorithms RSA, DSA, and EC-DSA with their respective security parameters. These three combinations are considered of having comparable strength. While the costs for the respective setup do not differ too much, the costs for signing and signature verification vary significantly. Obviously, EC-DSA is a better choice than DSA as each operation is cheaper. However, the choice between RSA and EC-DSA is determined by the expected number of operations of the UC system. If the number of signature verifications compared to signature generations dominates, the RSA signature scheme is clearly favorable compared to EC-DSA.

However, concerning key exchange, EC-DH definitely outperforms standard DH (where computations are done in $\mathbb{Z}/\mathbb{Z}\,p$) with the same security level. In order to achieve roughly the same costs as EC-DH, DH keys must be restricted to 512 bits in length.

We have not mentioned asymmetric encryption so far. Since the same mathematical formula is used for the RSA cryptosystem and the RSA signature scheme, the corresponding numbers can be looked up in the table. This shows that in some UC situations with constrained devices, asymmetric cryptosystems may quickly become impractical while symmetric encryption is cheaper by magnitudes. Contemporary public key algorithms are not very well suited for the capabilities and needs of UC (Buchmann, May, & Vollmer, 2006). A back-of-the-envelope calculation shows that a pocket PC's battery with a 1500 mAh capacity and a 5V voltage would have lost 20% of its charge after 5000 executions of a DH protocol or 10000 RSA signatures.

These facts illustrate that it is worthwhile to precisely analyze the security demands of a UC system since choices on the cryptographic layer directly affect energy consumption. A comprehensive examination of energy costs is provided by Seys (2006). Lightweight UC cryptography has also been the subject of recent research activities, for example, by the ECRYPT Network of Excellence in Cryptology (http://www.ecrypt. eu.org). This issue will surely gain even more momentum with the deployment of RFID tags for industrial applications as we already sketched in Scenario 4.

Lightweight cryptography has several aspects. On the one hand, it comprises the design choice of algorithms and efficient engineering to implement them in hard- and software. On the other hand, it requires a re-assessment of the threat model by assuming a less powerful opponent and ruling out some particular attacks which are considered less likely. This may imply that weaker security mechanisms, like weak authentication (discussed

Table 3. Energy costs

Algorithms	Setup Costs	Current Costs		
Hash Functions		**Hashing (µJ/Byte)**		
MD5		0.59		
SHA-1		0.75		
HMAC		1.16		
Symmetric Encryption	**Key Scheduling (µJ)**	**Encryption (µJ/Byte)**		
AES (128 bit)	7.83	1.62		
AES (192 bit)	7.87	2.08		
AES (256 bit)	9.92	2.29		
Digital Signatures	**Key Generation (mJ)**	**Sign (mJ)**	**Verify (mJ)**	
RSA (1024 bit)	270.13	546.5	15.97	
DSA (1024 bit)	293.20	313.6	338.02	
EC-DSA (1024 bit)	226.65	134.2	196.23	
Key Agreement	**Key Generation (mJ)**	**Key Exchange (mJ)**		
DH (1024 bit)	875.96	1046.5		
EC-DH (163 bit)	276.70	163.5		
DH (512 bit)	202.56	159.6		

next), or lower security parameters are acceptable for low-value transactions (cf. the discussion of forward secrecy).

Cryptography offers a wealth of ideas that can be applied to UC: For instance, traditional protocols can be enhanced to provide privacy protection using mechanisms like the private authentication scheme explained below. We also point out that threshold cryptography (see for example, Gemmell (1997) for an introduction) is a valuable tool for UC that merits further study. For instance, it can be used in sensor networks that are prone to so-called *Byzantine* faults, that is, there is a risk that devices fall into the attacker's hands and then act incorrectly. Provided that the number of such "Byzantine" nodes is lower than an adjustable bound, the attacker learns nothing about a secret (e.g., a common key for signing responses) shared among the nodes. Interestingly, this statement holds in an unconditional sense, that is, for an adversary with unlimited computational power.

SAMPLE SOLUTIONS

In this section five example solutions for secure UC systems are described. References to the literature and UC applications as well as links to our scenarios are given in the text.

At first, we present two strategies of privacy-enhancing technologies: the technical concept of anonymity and a policy-driven approach. While anonymity is favorable from a privacy perspective, it nevertheless leads to new threats as malicious parties may benefit from it, too. One such threat is the so-called *Sybil* attack which is discussed in the section "Fighting Sybil and DoS Attacks". We explain the technique of proof-of-work as a countermeasure which can also be used as a defense against DoS. A typical situation in UC is the lack of *a priori* trust relations among the participants. In order to cope with such a setting, a secure communication channel has to be bootstrapped

somehow. The section "Bootstrapping Secure Communication" treats this aspect from a theoretical point of view. Above all, the *resurrecting duckling security policy model* is explained here. The following section gives several real-world examples for out-of-band channels used to set up secure UC communication. Finally we touch on the hot topic of RFID security and discuss in particular privacy concerns and protection mechanisms of electronic travel documents.

We deliberately omitted reputation systems from the set of examples, as this topic is the subject of the following chapter. Trusted Computing is also an interesting direction of current UC research, but would go beyond the scope of this chapter. We refer the interested reader to the work of Hohl and Zugenmaier (2005).

Privacy-Enhancing Technologies

A large number of UC environments rely on sensing and tracking technologies of users and devices in order to carry out their tasks. For example, in order to provide location-based services, a user's position has to be determined beforehand. But even without a given UC service in place, the fact that most communication takes place over a wireless link opens the door for attacks based on *traffic analysis*. All communication patterns that can be successfully linked to a human jeopardize a user's privacy. In this sense, the notion of confidentiality has to be extended to *message source confidentiality* and/or *message destination confidentiality*. This property of hiding the fact that particular communication relationships exist at all is also called sender or recipient *anonymity*, respectively. Anonymity is significantly more difficult to achieve than message content confidentiality, as it requires careful design of communication protocols. Examples in the Internet setting include mix networks (Chaum, 1981), onion routing (see http://tor.eff.org for a popular implementation), or anonymous re-mailers. Those protocols however cannot be directly adapted to the UC world, since they typically make assumptions about connectivity and resources. A first step in this direction is the idea of "Mist Routing" (Al-Muhtadi, Campbell, Kapadia, Mickunas, & Yi, 2002). "Mix Zones" are a variant of the concept of mix networks to locations (see Beresford & Stajano, 2004).

As mentioned before, anonymity is of particular interest in UC when it comes to achieving location privacy, that is, to prevent people bearing devices emitting radio signals from being tracked without noticing it. We discuss two different strategies to preserve a user's privacy. First, a number of technical means are presented in order to blur data that could later be used to identify a person/subject. Second, the policy-based approach to achieve user privacy as proposed by Langheinrich (2002).

Blurring Data

Gruteser and Grunwald (2003) propose a middleware-based approach to blur location information from clients before passing the location information onwards to a location based service provider. They assume that clients communicate their position as very precise location information to a location server. Position is determined on the client itself, for example, via GPS or by the wireless service provider through signal triangulation. Location-based service providers access location information through the location server (see Figure 1).

A client specifies that he wants to be indistinguishable from at least $k - 1$ other clients within a given area and time frame. In other words, the clients want to stay k-anonymous. To reach k-anonymity, their algorithm, an adaptive form of a quadtree-based algorithm, adjusts the resolution of location information along spatial and temporal dimensions in order to meet the specified anonymity constraints, say k.

Providing anonymity requires careful system design as identification may happen on each network layer (Avoine & Oechslin, 2005). As a practical consequence, user-controlled pseudonyms on the application layer are pretty useless if the devices itself can be re-identified. This is the case when static IP or Media Access Control addresses are used. A proposal for temporary addresses for anonymity on the data link layer is made in Orava, Haverinen, and Honkanen (2002). UC environments like scenario 2 are particularly suitable for addresses that are picked at random, since the number of devices that are connected to each other at the same time is by magnitudes smaller than in an Internet setting. This guarantees, with a high probability, that device addresses do not coincide.

Private Authentication

The following example illustrates how cryptographic protocols can be modified to provide location privacy on the application layer. In typical schemes for mutual authentication like the one used in TLS/SSL (Dierks & Rescorla, 2006), the parties reveal their identity during the handshake. As a consequence, Mallory may pretend to be a legitimate party and start a handshake in order to see who is in her vicinity. She may also eavesdrop while Alice and Bob are authenticating each other and learn about their communication relation. *Private authentication* tackles this prob-

Figure 1. Anonymizing middleware for location-based services

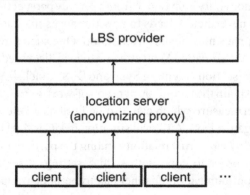

lem. The approach of Abadi (2002) allows Alice to prove her identity to some self-chosen set S of peers in order to establish a private and mutually authenticated channel. Entities outside of S cannot detect Alice's presence while entities inside S do not learn more than their own membership. Without loss of generalization, we restrict ourselves to the case where Bob is the only member of S. If the set S contains more than one element, Alice simply goes through parallel executions of the protocol for each element. In order to start a communication with Bob, Alice broadcasts the plaintext "hello" accompanied with

$$c := \mathrm{Enc}_{K_B}(\text{"hello"} \parallel K_A \parallel \mathrm{Sig}_{K_A^{-1}}(K_A \parallel K_B \parallel K \parallel t)).$$

(1)

Here K_B is Bob's public key used for encryption, (K_A, K_A^{-1}) denotes her own key pair, K a session key, and t is a timestamp. As Bob is the only entity who knows the private key K_B^{-1}, he is able to extract from c the sender's identity (which is unforgeable due to the digital signature). Assuming that Alice is on his whitelist of peers, he answers with a message protected by K. Bob's presence in turn cannot be detected provided that the cryptosystem is which-key concealing (i.e., K_B cannot be deduced from c) and Bob ensures t's recency. Otherwise Mallory could mount a replay attack by sending c and checking whether there is a corresponding answer. Abadi (2002) also describes a second protocol without timestamps at the price of additional communication rounds. This variant might be useful in cases where one cannot assume synchronized clocks.

A Policy-Based Mechanism

Langheinrich (2002) proposes *pawS*, a system that provides users with a privacy *enabling* technology. This approach is based on the Platform for Privacy Preferences Project (P3P, see http://www.w3.org/TR/P3P/), a framework which enables the encoding of privacy policies into machine-readable XML. Making use of a trusted device, the so-called *privacy assistant (PA)*, the user negotiates his privacy preferences with the UC environment. For this purpose, the PA is able to detect a *privacy beacon* upon entering a UC environment, for example, a smart space. The privacy beacon announces the available services, for example, a printer, or a video camera, with a reference to their data collection capabilities and policies. The PA in turn contacts the user's personal privacy proxy located on the Internet, which contacts the corresponding service proxies at their advertised addresses (through the privacy beacon) and asks for the *privacy policies* of the services located in the smart space. These privacy policies are compared to the user's privacy preferences and a result may be to decline usage of a tracking service, which will result in disabling a video camera. Further, the work of Langheinrich (2001) includes four design principles for UC environments, the main ideas of which we sum up as follows:

- **Notice:** Since future UC environments will be ideally suited for unnoticed operation, monitoring and tracking, the author proposes some kind of announcement mechanism that allows users to notice the data collection capabilities in their environment. This announcement mechanism should be standardized and agreed on.
- **Choice and consent:** To preserve privacy, a future UC system should offer users the choice of allowing or denying any kind of data collection. A system should respect this choice and operate only on user consent. Since a user will not always explicitly express her will, her choice and the derived consent should be expressed in machine-readable policies
- **Proximity and locality:** Locality information for collected data should be used by the system to enforce access restriction. This restriction may be based on the location of a

user who wants to use the data, for example, a user is able to record an audio stream at a meeting while attending, but not from the opposite side of the world (proximity). Also the audio stream should not be disseminated through the network (locality). This idea is also present in location-limited channels and location-based authentication (see below).

- **Access and recourse:** A system should give users easy access to collected personal information (e.g., using a standardized interface). Also, they should be informed about any usage of their data. Thus, abuse would be noticed.

Following these principles, Langheinrich's goal is to allow people and systems which *want* to respect a user's privacy to behave in such a way. This should help in building a lasting relationship based on mutual trust and respect. However his goal is not to try to provide perfect protection for personal information that is hardly achievable anyway.

Fighting Sybil and DoS Attacks

As mentioned in the section "First View: UC Characteristics and Associated Risks", DoS may be a serious attack in UC. In a world of widely-deployed pervasive computing devices, a phenomenon comparable to unsolicited email as we experience it today in the Internet setting would be disastrous. In this section we describe a mechanism that can be use as a remedy for DoS attacks and for so-called *Sybil attacks* as well (see Levine, Shields, and Margolin (2006) for an overview). The latter are an inherent threat to *recommender or reputation systems*, which are the subject of the following chapter. The term Sybil stems from the name of a schizophrenic literary character that has a total of 16 personalities. Analogously, an attacker takes part in a recommender system under multiple identities in order to manipulate the trustworthiness rating of

nodes. DoS and Sybil attacks have some similar characteristics which is why they are jointly dealt with in this section.

In a setting where UC nodes can be identified in a reliable way, the risks for both attacks are quite low. Clearly, a necessary condition for a Sybil attack is a node's ability to remain anonymous. In the DoS case, illegitimate messages can be filtered out by so-called *whitelists* and *blacklists* containing accepted and non-accepted entities, respectively. Filtering in its turn can be done on each network layer provided the sender can be (re-)identified. The earlier the filtering is done, the better, as this saves processing time: For instance, if data can already be discarded based on the sender's IP address, this is easier than first decrypting the payload and verifying a signature or MAC.

However, there are situations where identifying information is not reliable or not available at all. Remember that we even argued that sender anonymity is in fact a desirable feature from a privacy point of view. As a consequence, this means that DoS or Sybil attacks cannot be prevented completely. In order to make them at least more difficult, the system must ensure that sending requests or creating a new identity respectively requires some effort.

Proof-of-Work

So-called *proof-of-work* (PoW) techniques treat the computational resources of each user of a resource or service as valuable. To prevent arbitrarily high usage of a common resource by a single user, each user has to prove that she has made some effort, that is, spent computing resources, before she is allowed to use the service. This helps to prevent for example, users from sending millions of spam emails, or from mounting denial of service attacks.

The idea of PoW is to require the sender of a message or service request to provide the answer to a computational challenge along with the actual message. If the verification of the proof fails, the recipient discards the whole request without further processing. Obviously, the costs of creating such a proof must be some order of magnitude higher than for system setup and proof verification. A challenge in a PoW scheme may either be generated by the recipient or calculated based on implicit parameters that cannot be controlled by the sender (in order to prevent the re-usage of a proof). The second variant is very well suited for UC as no infrastructure or multi-round communication is required.

In the following example we sketch a mechanism that is similar to the one applied by Hashcash (Back, 1997). Here, the challenge is time-dependent. The proof of work consists of partially inverting a one-way hash function h by brute-force search. The sender of a message has to find a solution X to the following equation:

$$h_\ell(\text{id} \parallel t \parallel X) = \underbrace{0 \ldots 0}_{\ell\text{-times}} \quad (2)$$

Here, *id* is the recipient's identifier (e.g., a pseudonym), t is a time stamp and h_t is the output of h shortened to the leading ℓ bits. The tuple (id,t,X) is sent along with the payload. The following checks are made at the receiver's side: At first, she checks whether *id* is her own ID and whether the message is suitably recent, that is, t differs less than a predefined clock skew bound of s seconds from her local time. Furthermore the above condition must hold. In order to prevent a PoW from being reused, (t,X) can be checked for freshness against a database that caches previous values for s seconds.

The sender has to try out 2^ℓ possibilities for X on average, until a solution is found. This implies that the sender has to invoke the hash function 2^ℓ as many times as the recipient. The complexity for the sender grows exponentially in ℓ. Depending on the performance of the devices in use, ℓ should be adjusted in a range of, say, 10–20 in practice.

We will revert to the concept of PoW in the following chapter in the context of micropayment schemes.

Bootstrapping Secure Communication

Consider the situation where two UC devices want to establish a secure communication channel between each other in the presence of an adversary. Here *secure* may have the meaning of confidentiality and/or authenticity. As confidentiality is achieved by encryption, the parties have to secretly agree on a shared key or exchange their public encryption keys in an authentic way—depending on whether they use a symmetric or asymmetric cryptosystem. The requirements for authenticity are quite similar: a MAC key has to remain secret as well and the public key for the verification of a digital signature has to be authentic.

The *bootstrapping* of a secure channel thus boils down to either initially obtaining some information in a confidential or authentic way. Observe that, by using public key cryptography, an authentic communication relation can be enhanced to an encrypted one. If there is no (common) central authority like a certification authority or a key distribution center the devices have a trust relation with, they have to resort to direct exchange of cryptographic information via so-called *out-of-band* communication. This is a well-known concept which is applied, for instance, in the context of secret key distribution by messengers or the verification of public key fingerprints on the phone.

Out-of-band communication requires a secondary link, typically with some technical limitations, but with the huge advantage of being safe from attacks. Such limitations, that make this secondary channel unattractive for general data transfer, include bandwidth, signal strength, error rate, latency, and so forth. What is typically considered a downside simultaneously reduces the risk of attacks on this channel. Balfanz, Smetters,

Stewart, and Wong (2002) use the term of *location-limited channels* and emphasize that humans can be in control of the communication links. These authors assume an authentic out-of-band communication channel while the resurrecting duckling security policy model by Stajano and Anderson (1999) requires a confidential one. Stajano and Anderson use a confidential channel in order to securely pair mobile devices for a certain period of time; they use the term *secure transient association*. We will discuss their model in greater detail now.

Secure transient association addresses the problem of device authentication in the absence of a central and always available authority, for example a public key infrastructure. Devices authenticate each other and agree upon a shared key by physical contact. For a user, physical contact has the advantage that it is simple to understand and it is clear which devices are involved in the paring. The two devices take different roles:

- A slave (or duckling) obeys a master
- A master (or mother duck) controls a slave

Initially the slave is in state *imprintable*. As soon as a master has sent a key to the slave—this process is called imprinting—via a physical contact, the slave follows commands only given by the master who owns the key. The slave is now in the state *imprinted*.

The association can be broken in three ways. First, the master sends a special *kill* command to the slave. The slave will reset itself into the initial state *imprintable*. Second, after a predefined time interval has gone by, the slave kills itself. And third, after the completion of a certain transaction, the slave will reset itself to *imprintable*.

The two states of a slave and its transition are depicted in Figure 2. Note that the slave needs to be constructed in a tamper resistant manner. This guarantees that it is uneconomical for an attacker to attack by artificially causing a slave to die, that is, to force a slave into state *imprintable*. Otherwise, this would allow an attacker to imprint the slave using its own key and gain control over the slave. We quote Stajano's four formal principles that make up the resurrecting duckling security policy (Stajano, 2002):

1. **Two state principle:** The entity that the policy protects, called the duckling, can be in one of two states: imprintable or imprinted. In the imprintable state, anyone can take it over. In the imprinted state, it only obeys its mother duck.

2. **Imprinting principle:** The transition from imprintable to imprinted, known as imprinting, happens when a principal, from then on known as the mother duck, sends an imprinting key to the duckling. This must be done using a channel whose confidentiality and integrity are adequately protected. As part of the transaction, the mother duck must also create an appropriate backup of the imprinting key.

Figure 2. Two states of a slave (duckling)

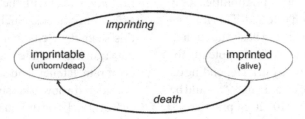

3. **Death principle:** The transition from imprinted to imprintable is known as death. It may occur under a very specific circumstance, defined by the particular variant of the resurrecting duckling policy model that one has chosen. Allowable circumstances, each corresponding to a different variant of the policy, include

   o   Death by order of the mother duck.

   o   Death by old age after a predefined time interval.

   o   Death on completion of a specific transaction.

4. **Assassination principle:** The duckling must be constructed in such a way that it will be uneconomical for an attacker to assassinate it, that is, to cause the duckling's death artificially in circumstances other than the one prescribed by the Death principle of the policy.

An appropriate key backup of the imprinting key is necessary in order to keep control of the slave in case the master is broken. Coming back to the patient monitoring scenario from the section "Four UC Settings", the resurrecting duckling security policy works for secure transient pairing of a heartbeat monitor with a patient's record. Here, the record takes the role of the master and the heartbeat monitor the role of the slave. Being at first in an *imprintable* state, as soon as the heartbeat monitor is attached to the patient, it is also imprinted by the patient's record. Being imprinted, only the master is able to read the heartbeat and store it in the record. As soon as the patient is fully recovered and leaves the hospital, the patient's record sends a kill command to the heartbeat monitor. The pairing is broken and the monitor is available for another patient.

Out-of-Band Channels

Many communication technologies are found in the UC world that are suitable for cryptographic out-of-band transmission. We now give a non-exhaustive list of examples that have been already used in practice. Usually switching to a secondary channel requires some human intervention, but may also be triggered automatically by an appropriate protocol command on the primary channel. McCune, Perrig, and Reiter (2005) provide a comparison of different out-of-band channels with respect to their security, convenience, and hardware requirements.

- *Infrared light* is used in IrDA interfaces for data transmission. It requires a direct line of sight and distances of 1 meter or less between the communicating parties. The salesman from the first scenario may use IrDA to establish a secure connection to a printer by exchanging a short-lived symmetric session key for the next print job or alternatively go through a pre-authentication protocol based on public key cryptography (like in Balfanz, Smetters, Stewart, & Wong (2002)). The idea of an IrDA-based "magic wand" that can be used to point to a device for establishing a secure connection is described by Spahic, Kreutzer, Kähmer, and Chandratilleke (2005).

- Dynamically generated *2D barcodes* can encode about 50-100 bits of information. They are suitable for modern mobile phones, which have high-resolution displays and built-in cameras. Claycomb and Shin (2006) have recently shown how to use colorized barcodes to exchange a public key fingerprint with an application to secure communications with ATMs. The authentication of an 802.11 access point using a sticker with a barcode on its casing is described in McCune, Perrig, and Reiter (2005).

- Devices that have a speaker and a microphone could use *audio* to transfer a fingerprint modulated on a piece of music. While the diffusion of the signal is larger than in the case of infrared, the presence of a second audio sender can be detected by a human. This technology is also suitable for *location-based authentication* of devices. An example is a café rewarding customers with media downloads by distributing access keys for the service via music played inside the building (Coulouris, Dollimore, & Kindberg, 2005).

- Buhan, Doumen, Hartel, and Veldhuis (2006) propose a user-friendly, two-party key agreement protocol that takes as an input *biometric data* of the device owners obtained via a grip pattern sensor. A downside of this approach, however, is the fact that biometric templates are static information and become useless once they fall into an opponent's hands.

- Capkun and Cagalj (2006) apply *ultrasonic* to measure the distance and spatial direction of UC communication partners. Their concept of *integrity regions* forces the attacker to be physically close to the targets. When devices are operated by humans and the maximum distance is appropriately short, say 1 meter or less, the presence of a man-in-the-middle can be ruled out. Mayrhofer and Gellersen (2007) show how to transmit short messages over ultrasound in such a way that only a recipient at an expected distance from the sender can decode the signal.

- UC devices that do not support any of the above mechanisms, but have at least a *user interface,* can let the user enter a sequence of numbers by hand. Bluetooth applies an algorithm called "pairing" that allows two devices to agree on a common secret key derived from a random value (transmitted in the clear) and a static PIN (typically only a few characters long) that has to be known to each device.

- Even a simple user interface consisting, for instance, of an LED and a pushbutton is enough to transmit *1 bit* of information telling the device that it is now safe to exchange

public keys via the primary channel. This may happen when the devices are connected in an environment that is considered safe, for example at the user's home.

The last example is an application of *weak authentication* as described by Arkko and Nikander (2002). According to the temporal separation principle, at a certain point in time the parties consider safe they exchange a key via the primary channel—without further protection, that is unauthenticated and in plaintext. Provided that no attacker is present in this phase, a long-term secure communication channel can be set up. The weak authentication mechanism completely defeats passive attacks (by exchanging public keys in an authentic fashion). It also raises the bar for active attacks, since a man in the middle who engaged during key agreement has to intercept and re-encrypt each subsequent message in order to remain undetected. A similar mechanism is used in the Secure Shell (SSH) protocol.

RFID Security from EPC to E-Passport

In this section the security of RFID systems is discussed, mainly by means of two examples: tags with a 96 bit *Electronic Product Code* (EPC) are used for the lifecycle management of commercial goods as described in Scenario 4. Such tags are at the lower end of the scale since they offer very limited functionality. At the other extreme, tags embedded in modern identity cards or *e-passports* (electronic passports) support state-of-the art cryptographic algorithms.

The threat of abusive tracking of UC systems in general and RFID tags in particular has already been mentioned. Basically, tracking is what EPC tags are built for: Unlike barcodes, they do not simply indicate the manufacturer and product type, but a serial number that is distinct for each object. As access control and reader authentication is only an option in the EPC standards (see http://www.epcglobalinc.org), tags are inherently prone to *skimming*. That means that unauthorized parties reasonably close may read the chip without its owner noticing it. In the case of EPC tags that operate at a frequency of around 900 MHz, the specified reading range is 3 meters or more. E-passports use so-called *proximity tags* operating at a frequency of 13.56 MHz and a reading range of at most 15 cm. Note that fraudulent RFID readers do not necessarily adhere to standards and may therefore exceed reading ranges significantly (see e.g., Kirschenbaum & Wool, 2006).

Countermeasures Against Skimming and Tracking

EPC tags illustrate a common limitation of most RFID chips: Their identifier is defined during the production process and cannot be changed afterwards. This allows a tagged object to be misused for tracking a person it is linked to. In the discussion of anonymity in the section "Privacy-Enhancing Technologies", we have already seen that identification is a problem affecting all network layers. RFID systems are no different in that respect as tracking may in theory happen on the application, the data link, or the physical layer. Consider, for instance, tags used in access control systems like the Hitag, Legic, or Mifare series. In order to prevent cloning and replay attacks, such tags may encrypt their communication on the application level. While this hides personal information of their owner, the tags themselves can be easily traced using their static data link layer ID.

In the EPC system, there is at least a basic, yet very effective privacy protection mechanism: A reader may send a tag the so-called "kill" command rendering it irreversibly inoperable. In order to prevent DoS attacks, the kill command requires authentication via a secret 32-bit number. The METRO group's vision of an RFID-based store (see http://www.future-store.org) already encompasses a dedicated device behind the cash desk to kill tags. However, this comes at the price of excluding the tag ID from being used by the consumer at her home or for the purpose of recycling.

There a several non-destructive countermeasures against skimming and tracking, for a comparison see for example, Weis, Sarma, Rivest, and Engels (2003) or Juels, Rivest, and Szydlo (2003). For instance, RFID chips in identity cards can be shielded in a Faraday cage made of metal foil which is integrated in a wallet. "Clipped tags" (Karjoth & Moskowitz, 2005) provide a user-friendly way to deactivate a tag by manually separating chip and antenna. Such a method provides immediate visual feedback about the tag's state. Instead of completely deactivating the tag, the antenna may be transformed in a way that reduces reading range considerably. *Blocker tags* (Juels et al., 2003) are devices that fool readers by simulating a pile of tags in order to prevent them to single out and communicate with a single one. As the EPC addressing scheme is hierarchical, a blocker tag may restrict the range of IDs selectively.

E-Passport Security Measures

Compared to EPC tags, the tags embedded in e-passports contain information that is much more sensitive. The specifications (ICAO, 2004a, 2004b) for "machine readable travel documents" provided by the International Civil Aviation Organization (ICAO), a United Nations body, govern the storage of personal and especially biometric data on the chip. Mandatory pieces of information include name, date of birth, nationality, and a digitized portrait photograph. While the standard defines iris scans and fingerprints as optional features, the member states of the European Union have agreed on including fingerprints in passports issued to their citizens (European Union, 2006).

As a baseline security mechanism, all e-passports have to implement "passive authentication". This means that the data stored on the chip is digitally signed by the issuing nation. The signature algorithm may be one of RSA, DSA, or EC-DSA. While passive authentication prevents modifications of the chip, it does not help against chip cloning; only the optional feature "active authentication" does. Here, the chip is given a key pair the public key of which is included in the signed data set. During a challenge-response protocol, the chip proves possession of the private key and therefore its authenticity to the reader. While other chip data can be read and cloned, the private key is not disclosed similarly to a smartcard.

The ICAO specifications offer "Basic Access Control" (BAC) as an optional protection against eavesdropping, skimming, and tracking. When implemented on the chip, a reader is required to authenticate before being able to read non-sensitive data, that is, any information except fingerprints (and iris scans if present) which require additional authentication. EU e-passports implement BAC while US e-passports do not. This opens the door for "American-sniffing bombs" or even personalized RFID-enabled bombs (Juels, Molnar, & Wagner, 2005). The design of the BAC mechanism is guided by the idea that a passport has to be handed over to border control personnel, that is, physical access to the document is a prerequisite to reading the RFID chip. In order to start the communication, a reader must pass a challenge-response protocol with the chip. In this protocol, the reader has to implicitly prove that it knows two cryptographic keys derived from the passport number, the bearer's date of birth, and the expiration date. These parameters are part of the so-called "Machine Readable Zone" (MRZ) which is why an e-passport has to be swiped through an optical reader first. The keys derived from the MRZ are used for 3DES encryption and integrity protection respectively. Note that, although the 3DES encryption uses a 112-bit key, the entropy obtained from the MRZ is much lower. The number of possible values can be at most 2^{56} in theory, but practical figures

may be significantly lower: The feasibility of a brute-force attack on Dutch e-passports, which provide encryption strength of around 35 bit due to their predictable serial numbers, is described by Smith (2006). Note that even strong encryption does not prevent tracking by parties that have read the MRZ once, as the derived keys are static.

Another challenge-response scheme is used to protect the fingerprints on the chip. In this protocol, the chip authenticates the reader in order to decide whether to disclose the fingerprint or not. This mechanism involves national authorities that issue certificates to border control organization of foreign countries upon condition that fingerprints are treated in accordance with data security and protection legislation. These organizations in turn issue certificates to individual readers. A detailed description of the infrastructures used for issuing certificates to passport manufacturers and to readers respectively is given by Straub, Hartl, and Ruppert (2006).

RESEARCH OUTLOOK

This chapter gave an overview of the field of UC security taking into account UC characteristics and limitations. By means of representative settings, ranging from mobile work to RFID-based real-time enterprises, common security challenges were exhibited. At the heart of the chapter was the presentation of a bunch of concrete solutions to such challenges. This list is not claimed to be exhaustive, but it is an initial step toward a taxonomy. The solutions stand *pars pro toto* for UC security, as they are generic and scalable enough to be adaptable to a large number of scenarios.

Social acceptance of UC technology strongly depends on the security of UC systems. On the one hand, the growing use of UC in everyday life must not lead to security breaches as demonstrated, for instance, in a recent attack on RFID-enabled credit cards (Heydt-Benjamin et al., 2007). It is also a safe bet that conflicts of interest will again occur between privacy and law enforcement as we have already seen in the aftermath of 9/11, for example, concerning the traceability capabilities of UC. We hope that this chapter motivates the reader to delve deeper into the subject and refer to the following textbooks:

- IT security in general: Eckert (2006), Stallings (2006),
- Focus on cryptographic aspects: Buchmann (2004), Stallings (2005); Menezes, Oorschot, and Vanstone (1996),
- UC security in particular: Stajano (2002),
- RFID: Finkenzeller (2003).

Among the promising areas of UC security research we could not discuss in detail here are UC and its relation to Grid Computing (Storz, Friday, & Davies, 2003) and relay attacks on RFID systems (Kfir & Wool, 2005; Hancke 2006).

REFERENCES

Abadi, M. (2002). Private authentication. In *Proceedings of the Workshop on Privacy-Enhancing Technologies (PET)*.

Aitenbichler, E., Kangasharju, J., & Mühlhäuser, M. (2004). Talking assistant: A smart digital identity for ubiquitous computing. *Advances in pervasive Computing* (pp. 279–284). Austrian Computer Society (OCG).

Al-Muhtadi, J., Campbell, R., Kapadia, A., Mickunas, M., & Yi, S. (2002). Routing through the mist: Privacy preserving communication in ubiquitous computing environments. In *Proceedings of IEEE International Conference of Distributed Computing Systems (ICDCS)* (pp. 65–74).

Arkko, J., & Nikander, P. (2002). Weak authentication: How to authenticate unknown principals without trusted parties. In *Proceedings of the IWSP: International Workshop on Security Protocols*.

Avoine, G., & Oechslin, P. (2005). RFID traceability: A multilayer problem. In A. S. Patrick & M. Yung (Eds.), *Financial cryptography and data security, 9th International Conference, FC 2005, Roseau, The Commonwealth of Dominica, February 28 - March 3, 2005, Revised Papers* (Vol. 3570, pp. 125-140). Springer.

Back, A. (1997). *Hashcash*. Retrieved October 17, 2007, http://www.cypherspace.org/~adam/hashcash/.

Bahl, P., Chandra, R., Padhye, J., Ravindranath, L., Singh, M., Wolman, A., Zill, B. (2006). Enhancing the security of corporate Wi-Fi networks using DAIR. In *Proceedings of the MobiSys 2006: Proceedings of the 4th international conference on Mobile systems, applications and services* (pp. 1–14). New York.

Balfanz, D., Smetters, D., Stewart, P., & Wong, H. (2002). *Talking to strangers: Authentication in adhoc wireless networks*. In *Proceedings of the Symposium on Network and Distributed Systems Security (NDSS '02)*, San Diego, California.

Beresford, A. R., & Stajano, F. (2004, March). Mix zones: User privacy in location-aware services. In *Proceedings of the IEEE International Workshop on Pervasive Computing and Communication Security (PerSec)*.

Buchmann, J. (2004). *Introduction to cryptography*. Springer.

Buchmann, J., May, A., & Vollmer, U. (2006). Perspectives for cryptographic long-term security. *Comm. ACM, 49*(9), 50–55.

Buhan, I. R., Doumen, J. M., Hartel, P. H., & Veldhuis, R. N. J. (2006, June). *Feeling is believing: A location limited channel based on grip pattern biometrics and cryptanalysis* (Tech. Rep. No. TR-CTIT-06-29). Retrieved October 17, 2007, from http://eprints.eemcs.utwente.nl/5694/.

Capkun, S., & Cagalj, M. (2006). Integrity regions: Authentication through presence in wireless networks. In *Proceedings of the WiSe '06: Proceedings of the 5th ACM workshop on Wireless security* (pp. 1–10), New York.

Chaum, D. (1981). Untraceable electronic mail, return addresses, and digital pseudonyms. *Commun. ACM, 24*(2), 84–88.

Claycomb, W. R., & Shin, D. (2006). Secure real world interaction using mobile devices. In *Proceedings of the PERMID / Pervasive 2006.*

Coulouris, G., Dollimore, J., & Kindberg, T. (2005). *Distributed systems: Concepts and design.* Addison-Wesley Longman.

Dierks, T., & Rescorla, E. (2006). *The transport layer security (TLS) Protocol Version 1.1.* RFC 4346.

Dobbertin, H., Bosselaers, A., & Preneel, B. (1996). RIPEMD-160, A strengthened version of RIPEMD. In *Proceedings of the Fast Software Encryption* (pp. 71–82). Springer LNCS 1039.

Eastlake, D., & Jones, P. (2001). *US Secure hash algorithm 1 (SHA1).* RFC 3174.

Eckert, C. (2005). Security issues of mobile devices. In *Proceedings of the Security in Pervasive Computing, Second International Conference, SPC 2005* (Vol. 3450). Boppard: Springer.

Eckert, C. (2006). *IT-Sicherheit. Konzepte – Verfahren: Protokolle.* Oldenbourg.

European Union (2006). *EU passport specification, Working document (28/06/2006)* (Tech. R ep.).

Fleisch, E., & Mattern, F. (2005). *Das Internet der Dinge: Ubiquitous Computing und RFID in der Praxis.* Springer.

Gemmell, P. S. (1997). An introduction to threshold cryptography. *RSA Laboratories' CryptoBytes, 2*(3), 7–12.

Gligor, V. (2005). *Cryptolite: How lite can secure crypto get?* Information Security Summer School.

Görlach, A., Heinemann, A., Terpstra, W. W., & Mühlhäuser, M. (2005). Location privacy. In A. Boukerche (Ed.), *Handbook of algorithms for wireless networking and mobile computing* (pp. 393–411). Chapman & Hall/CRC.

Greiner, L. (2006). The urge to converge. *netWorker, 10*(2), 26–30.

Gruteser, M., & Grunwald, D. (2003). Anonymous usage of location-based services through spatial and temporal cloaking. In *Proceedings of the First International Conference on Mobile Systems, Applications, and Services (MobiSys)* (pp. 31–42). USENIX.

Hankerson, D., Menezes, A. J., & Vanstone, S. (2004). *Guide to elliptic curve cryptography.* Springer-Verlag.

Heydt-Benjamin, T. S., Bailey, D. V., Fu, K., Juels, A., & O'Hare, T. (2007). Vulnerabilities in first-generation RFID-enabled credit cards. *Financial Cryptography.*

Hohl, A., & Zugenmaier, A. (2005). Safeguarding personal data using trusted computing in pervasive computing. *Privacy, Security and Trust within the Context of Pervasive Computing* (pp. 147–155). Springer.

Husemann, D., & Nidd, M. (2005). Pervasive patient monitoring – Take two at bedtime. *ERCIM News*, 70–71.

ICAO (2004a). *Development of a logical data structure: LDS for optional capacity expansion technologies, Revision 1.7* (Tech. Rep.). Retrieved October 17, 2007, from http://www.icao.int/mrtd/.

ICAO. (2004b). *PKI for Machine Readable Travel Documents offering ICC Read-Only Access, Version 1.1* (Tech. Rep.). Retrieved October 17, 2007, from http://www.icao.int/mrtd/.

Juels, A., Molnar, D., & Wagner, D. (2005, September). Security and privacy issues in e-passports.

In *Proceedings of the Conference on Security and Privacy for Emerging Areas in Communication Networks: SecureComm,* Athens, Greece.

Juels, A., Rivest, R., & Szydlo, M. (2003, October). The blocker tag: Selective blocking of RFID tags for consumer privacy. In V. Atluri (Ed.), *Conference on computer and communications security: ACM CCS* (pp. 103–111). Washington, DC.

Karjoth, G., & Moskowitz, P. A. (2005). Disabling RFID tags with visible confirmation: Clipped tags are silenced. In *Proceedings of the WPES '05: Proceedings of the 2005 ACM Workshop on Privacy in the Electronic Society* (pp. 27–30). New York.

Kirschenbaum, I., & Wool, A. (2006). How to build a low-cost, extended-range RFID skimmer. In *Proceedings of the USENIX Security Symposium* (pp. 43–57).

Knospe, H., & Pohl, H. (2004, November–December). RFID security. *Information Security Technical Report, 9*(4), 39–50.

Krawczyk, H., Bellare, M., & Canetti, R. (1997). *HMAC: Keyed-hashing for message authentication.* RFC 2104.

Langheinrich, M. (2001). Privacy by design—Principles of privacy-aware ubiquitous systems. In G. D. Abowd, B. Brumitt, & S. A. Shafer (Eds.), *Ubicomp* (Vol. 2201, p. 273-291). Springer.

Langheinrich, M. (2002). A privacy awareness system for ubiquitous computing environments. In G. Borriello & L. E. Holmquist (Eds.), *Ubicomp* (Vol. 2498, pp. 237–245). Springer.

Levine, B. N., Shields, C., & Margolin, N. B. (2006, October). *A survey of solutions to the sybil attack* (Tech. Rep. No. 2006-052). Amherst, MA: University of Massachusetts Amherst.

Mayrhofer, R., & Gellersen, H. (in press). On the security of ultrasound as out-of-band channel. In *Proceedings of the IPDPS 2007: International Parallel and Distributed Processing Symposium.* IEEE Computer Society Press.

McCune, J. M., Perrig, A., & Reiter, M. K. (2005). Seeing-is-believing: Using camera phones for human-verifiable authentication. In *Proceedings of the IEEE symposium on security and privacy* (pp. 110–124). IEEE Computer Society.

Menezes, A., Oorschot, P. C. van, & Vanstone, S. A. (1996). *Handbook of applied cryptography.* CRC Press.

Orava, P., Haverinen, H., & Honkanen, J.-P. (2002). *Temporary MAC addresses for anonymity.*

Potlapally, N. R., Ravi, S., Raghunathan, A., & Jha, N. K. (2003). Analyzing the energy consumption of security protocols. In *Proceedings of the ISPLED—03* (pp. 30–35).

Rivest, R. L., Shamir, A., & Adleman, L. (1978). A method for obtaining digital signatures and public-key cryptosystems. *Commun. ACM, 21*(2), 120–126.

Robinson, P. (2005). An application-led approach for security research in ubicomp (position paper). In *Proceedings of the Ubiapp Workshop, Pervasive 2005.*

Seys, S. (2006). *Cryptographic algorithms and protocols for security and privacy in ad hoc networks.* Unpublished doctoral dissertation, Katholieke Universiteit Leuven.

Smith, R. W. (2006). *E-passport hack demonstrated on Dutch TV.* Retrieved October 17, 2007, from, http://www.heise.de/english/newsticker/news/69197.

Spahic, A., Kreutzer, M., Kähmer, M., & Chandratilleke, S. (2005). Pre-authentication using infrared. *Privacy, Security and Trust within the Context of Pervasive Computing* (Vol. 780, pp. 105–112).

Stajano, F. (2002). *Security for ubiquitous computing.* John Wiley & Sons.

Stajano, F., & Anderson, R. J. (1999). The resurrecting duckling: Security issues for ad-hoc wireless networks. In *Proceedings of the Security Protocols, 7th International Workshop, Cambridge, UK, April 19-21, 1999, Proceedings* (p. 172-194).

Stallings, W. (2005). *Cryptography and network security*. Prentice Hall.

Stallings, W. (2006). *Network security essentials*. Prentice Hall.

Straub, T., Hartl, M., & Ruppert, M. (2006). Digitale Reisepässe in Deutschland - Prozesse und Sicherheitsinfrastruktur. In *Proc. Sicherheit 2006* (p. 233-243).

Straub, T., & Heinemann, A. (2004). An anonymous bonus point system for mobile commerce based on word-of-mouth recommendation. In L. M. Liebrock (Ed.), *Applied computing 2004. Proceedings of the 2004 ACM Symposium on Applied Computing* (pp. 766–773), New York: ACM Press.

Vogt, H. (2005). Small worlds and the security of ubiquitous computing. In *Proceedings of the WOWMOM '05: Proceedings of the First International IEEE WoWMoM Workshop on Trust, Security and Privacy for Ubiquitous Computing* (pp. 593-597), Washington, DC.

Weis, S. A., Sarma, S. E., Rivest, R. L., & Engels, D. W. (2003). Security and privacy aspects of low-cost radio frequency identification systems. In *Proceedings of the Security in Pervasive Computing* (p. 201-212).

ADDITIONAL READING

Eckert, C. (2006). *IT-Sicherheit. Konzepte: Verfahren: Protokolle*. Oldenbourg.

Finkenzeller, K. (2003). *RFID handbook: Fundamentals and applications in contactless smart cards and identification*. John Wiley & Sons.

Hancke, G. P. (2006). Practical attacks on proximity identification systems (Short Paper). In *Proceedings of the 2006 IEEE Symposium on Security and Privacy*, 328-333.

Kfir, Z., & Wool, A. (2005). Picking virtual pockets using relay attacks on contactless smartcard systems. In *Proceedings of the 1st Intl. Conf. on Security and Privacy for Emerging Areas in Communication Networks* (p. 47-58). IEEE.

Stajano, F. (2002). *Security for ubiquitous computing*. John Wiley & Sons.

Stallings, W. (2006). *Network security essentials*. Prentice Hall.

Storz, O., Friday, A., & Davies, N. (2003). Towards "ubiquitous" ubiquitous computing: An alliance with the "grid". In *Proceedings of the System Support for Ubiquitous Computing Workshop (UbiComp Workshop 2003)*.

Chapter XVI
Trust and Accountability

Sebastian Ries
Technical University of Darmstadt, Germany

ABSTRACT

Ubiquitous computing implies that literally any activity in everyday life can be assisted or accompanied by networked computers. Therefore, the concepts of everyday social life must be carefully reflected on when developing applications for ubiquitous computing. The present chapter focuses on the concepts of trust and accountability. First, both concepts are introduced with their everyday semantics. Second, we explain why trust is relevant for ubiquitous computing, and introduce the main issues for dealing with trust in computer science. Third, we show how accountability can be achieved in distributed systems using reputation and micropayment mechanisms. In both sections, we provide a short overview of the state-of-the-art and give detailed examples for a deeper understanding. Finally, we provide a research outlook, again arguing for the integration of these concepts into future ubiquitous computing applications.

INTRODUCTION

Introduction of the Social Concepts of Trust and Accountability

Trust and accountability are two well-known concepts in everyday life. In real life, trust can serve as the basis for decisions subject to risk and uncertainty, and accountability helps to prevent misuse of common or shared goods. For the introduction of the common meaning of both concepts we refer to the Merriam-Webster Online Dictionary (Merriam-Webster, 2006):

For the definition of **trust** we find among others the following: trust is the "assured reliance on the character, ability, strength, or truth of someone or something," and the "dependence on something future or contingent" (Merriam-Webster, 2006).

Merriam-Webster Online Dictionary defines **accountability** as "the quality or state of being accountable; especially: an obligation or willingness to accept responsibility or to account for one's actions" (Merriam-Webster, 2006).

Relation to Ubiquitous Computing

In Bhargava, Lilien, Rosenthal, and Winslet (2004), Bhargava et al. point out that "trust [...] is pervasive in social systems" and that "socially based paradigms will play a big role in pervasive-computing environments." We believe that the concepts of trust and accountability, which are well-known from real-life experiences, are important and promising enablers for ubiquitous computing.

According to Weiser's vision (Weiser & Brown, 1997), ubiquitous computing will become a *calm technology* with many invisible computers, sometimes called smart devices. Due to the human-centric approach of ubiquitous computing, smart environments are expected to *support the users in everyday tasks and to provide personalized services*, for example, timekeeping or ordering food when the fridge is empty, respecting the user's habits. The devices in such a smart environment will be *heterogeneous* regarding their support for communication channels, storage, user interfaces, and power supply. Therefore, smart devices are expected to complement each other by using the potential of the devices available in the environment. Furthermore, there will not be a well-known infrastructure, which is hosted by only a few service providers. Instead, many users' and providers' smart devices—which can be known or unknown—will share their capabilities with other devices. Therefore, arbitrary devices can act as providers and consumers of information or services, which leads to *highly dynamic collaboration*.

Since ubiquitous computing aims to support users in everyday tasks, applications like the "intelligent fridge," may have legal or financial implications. Therefore, the confidence of users in the capabilities of these applications is an important factor for their acceptance. In the case of trust-aided applications, we believe that the user has to be able to control and to adjust the parameters, which are a basis for decisions in an easy and accessible way. There is the need for helpful user interfaces, which, for example, allow a user to adjust the parameters for trust, to define trust management policies, and to get a survey of their own reputation values or micropayments that have been made.

As ubiquitous computing enforces the interaction of many devices, the user will sometimes not know which devices are interacting in each task. Thus, it is especially important that the user is able to configure which devices are trusted for which contexts and tasks. In addition to trust, accountability can help to enforce responsible usage of shared resources in smart environments, and delimit a possible exploitation of entities participating in those environments.

Lessons to Learn

In the second section, we first explain the notions and properties of trust, and show the prerequisites for successfully transferring it to ubiquitous computing. Furthermore, we introduce the main components for the integration of trust into applications and give a short survey of the state-of-the-art. For a deeper understanding of trust modeling, we present examples of two trust models before we come to the conclusion of the section.

The third section starts with an introduction of the concept of accountability. We subsequently show how reputation and micropayment systems can be used to enforce accountability. For both approaches we provide a classification and a short survey of the state-of-the-art. Finally, we present the conclusion for this chapter.

TRUST

In ubiquitous computing, as in real life, trust can serve as a basis for risky engagements in the presence of uncertainty. It is an interesting challenge to evaluate the trustworthiness of the devices that surround users in ubiquitous computing envi-

Figure 1. Areas with applications of trust

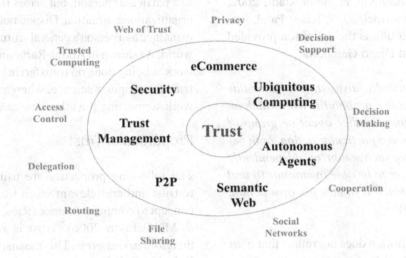

ronments. If we are able to identify trustworthy devices, we can interact with them, and use their capabilities and services. Thus, we can profit from the potential of ubiquitous computing, and avoid disappointments. There are a growing number of computer scientists from different research areas working on very different aspects of trust or trustworthiness in different application areas (see Figure 1 for areas of application). In this chapter we focus on approaches that are based on social trust.

Introduction of (Social) Trust for Computer Scientists

Trust is a well-known concept in everyday life, which simplifies many complex processes. Some processes are enabled by trust, since they would not be operable otherwise. On the one hand, trust in our social environment allows us to delegate tasks and decisions to an appropriate person. On the other hand, trust facilitates an efficient rating of information presented by a trusted party.

There is much work on trust, not only in computer science—the seminal work in this area has been carried out by Marsh (1994)—but also in other academic fields, for example, sociology, economics. In general, trust is connected to the presence of a notion of uncertainty, and trust depends on the expected risk associated with an engagement (McKnight & Chervany, 1996; Gambetta, 2000; Marsh, 1994; Jøsang, Ismail, & Boyd, 2007; Grandison & Sloman, 2000; Cahill et al., 2003).

Definitions of Trust

Although trust is a well-known concept in everyday life and despite the fact that there is a set of properties of trust (see below), on which most researchers agree, it is hard to define trust. Apart from the definition in the Merriam-Webster Online Dictionary stated in the introduction, there are a couple of definitions provided by several academic areas with different focuses and goals (Marsh, 1994; Abdul-Rahman, 2004). A definition, which is shared or at least adopted by many researchers

(Jøsang et al., 2007; Abdul-Rahman & Hailes, 2000; Mui, Mohtashemi, & Halberstadt, 2002; Kinateder & Rothermel, 2003; Teacy, Patel, Jennings, & Luck, 2006), is the definition provided by the sociologist Diego Gambetta:

trust (or, symmetrically, distrust) is a particular level of the subjective probability with which an agent assesses that another agent or group of agents will perform a particular action, both before he can monitor such action (or independently of his capacity ever to be able to monitor it) and in a context in which it affects his own action. (Gambetta, 2000)

Since this definition does not reflect that trust is closely related to risk, we would also like to provide the following definition (Ries, Kangasharju, & Mühlhäuser, 2007):

Trust is the well-founded willingness for risky engagements.

Categories of Trust

According to McKnight & Chervany (1996) there are three principle categories of trust: *interpersonal* (or *personal*) trust, *structural* (or *impersonal*) trust, and *dispositional* trust. Interpersonal trust describes trust between people or groups. It is closely related to the experiences which people had with each other. Structural trust is not bound to a particular person, but arises from a social or organizational situation. Dispositional trust can be explained as a person's general attitude towards the world. As shown in Abdul-Rahman (2004), much work is being done on transferring interpersonal trust to computer science, whereas there is little work supporting the other two categories.

Properties of Trust

The following properties are usually assigned to trust and are relevant when transferring this concept to computer science (Ries, Kangasharju, & Mühlhäuser, 2006). Trust is *subjective* and therefore *asymmetric*. This means, if Alice trusts Bob, then Bob does not necessarily have the same trust in Alice. Furthermore, it is *context dependent. Obviously, there is a difference in trusting someone with respect to health care or online banking.* Since trust can increase with positive experience and decrease with negative experience or due to the absence of experience over time, trust has a *dynamic* aspect. This also makes it clear that trust is *non-monotonic* and that there are *several levels of trust.* A sensitive aspect is the transitivity of trust. Assuming Alice trusts Bob and Bob trusts Charlie, what can be said about Alice's trust in Charlie? Marsh (1994) points out that trust is non-transitive. At least, it does not seem to be intuitive that trust can transitively be

Figure 2. Main influence factors on trust-based decisions

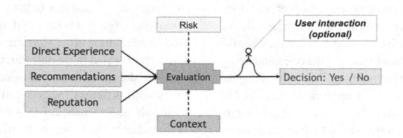

passed over arbitrarily long chains. Nonetheless, we consider trust to be *recommendable*, since recommendations are an important issue for trust establishment. Usually trust is modeled as being based on a combination of the following building blocks: direct experience, recommendations and reputation information.

Figure 2 shows the main issues that have to be considered for the evaluation of trust as a basis for decision making, derived from the properties of trust and second definition. Besides the building blocks of trust, the main influence factors for trust evaluation are the context and risk of the engagement. The person on the arrow between the evaluation and the decision expresses that the users should be able to interact with the system if they want to, or if necessary.

Main Aspects when Dealing with Trust in Ubiquitous Computing

Prerequisites

As introduced, trust is closely related to an expectation about the future behavior of an entity based on past experience. Past experience can be personal or direct experience, experience collected by others, which are passed on as recommendations, or experiences aggregated in the reputation of an entity. This enforces that entities can be recognized, if there have been past encounters, and that past behavior allows a prediction of future behavior.

Recognition

Identification and authentication are well-known problems in computer science. In managed domains, authentication is done based on a public key infrastructure (see Chapter on 'Security for Ubiquitous Computing'). Aware that public key infrastructures are barely applicable for ubiquitous computing and that identity does not necessarily convey information about the future behavior of

an entity, Seigneur et al. describe "A Peer Entity Recognition" scheme (APER) (Seigneur, Farrell, Jensen, Gray, & Chen, 2003). The focus in APER is not on determining the real-world identity of an entity (whatever this might be), but its aim instead is to recognize an entity as a trustworthy collaborator. The principle idea is that an entity can use arbitrary identifiers. As long as an entity re-uses the same identifier, other entities can link their experiences with this entity using this identifier, and build up a history with past experience. If an entity is searching for new interaction partners and recognizes some entities by their identifiers, it can make assumptions about the trustworthiness of these entities based on past experience.

As Seigneur et al. point out, it is likely for ubiquitous computing that users are represented by artificial intelligence agents, which act on behalf of their owner. Since those agents are only a piece of software, which can almost be arbitrary programs, the question arises of whether it is reasonable to assume that software agents have continuous behavior, which will allow the prediction of future behavior based on past experience.

Even if we assume that those predictions about the behavior of software agents are plausible, we have to consider attacks of malware and viruses on these agents. This means that parts of the functionality of an agent could be corrupted or replaced without the knowledge of the user.

Trusted Computing: Basis of Trust

So far we have dealt with recognition as a basis upon which to establish trust between agents or devices. But the previous paragraph raises the question of why the user should trust in her devices and the software (agents) running on these devices, especially if faced with the threats of malware and viruses. Actually, the user wants her devices to be a basis for trust, so that she can assume that at least her devices behave as expected.

This is one of the issues addressed by the Trusted Computing Group (TCG) (TCG, 2006).

The TCG is a not-for-profit organization formed to develop, define, and promote open standards for hardware-enabled trusted computing and security platforms (TCG, 2006). The predecessor of the TCG was the Trusted Computing Platform Alliance (TCPA), which was founded in 1999 by Compaq, HP, IBM, Intel and Microsoft. A central element of the TCG specification is the trusted platform module (TPM). The TPM is a tamper-proof micro-controller, which has a physical binding to the other physical parts of the platform, for example, to the motherboard of a PC. A trusted platform should at least have these basic features (TCG, 2004):

- **Protected capabilities:** A set of commands with the exclusive access to shielded locations, for example, memory, where it is safe to operate on sensitive data.
- **Integrity measurement:** The process of obtaining and storing the platform characteristics that affect the integrity (trustworthiness) of a platform, for example, hardware and software configuration.
- **Integrity reporting:** The process of attesting to the contents of the integrity storage.

The TPM provides these features. The TCG defines the *roots of trust* as "components that must be trusted because misbehavior might not be detected" (TCG, 2004). If the user trusts in the functionality of the TPM, it can serve as a basis to protect the hardware and software configuration against manipulation. More technically speaking, trusted computing involves the following four concepts (Burmester & Mulholland, 2006):

- **Memory curtaining:** Preventing applications (including the operating system) from accessing or changing sensitive information, for example, cryptographic keys, in the memory.
- **Secure input and output:** Ensuring a secure data transfer between the user interfaces and the computational device (see "trusted path" in the chapter on "Security in Ubiquitous Computing").
- **Sealed storage:** Allowing for confidential data to be stored safely.
- **(Remote) attestation:** Allowing for the attestation of the configuration of the local platform or of a remote platform.

Although trusted computing (TC) is a promising approach to restraining the spread of viruses and malware, there are also critics. The main criticism does not focus on the concept of TC itself, but on the possible applications of TC for digital rights management (DRM). According to critiques (Anderson, 2003), remote attestation can be used to allow the provider of DRM protected content to ensure that this content can only be used on platforms that respect the DRM. Consequently, this would constrain the users in the decision of which software to use on their platforms.

Other projects and initiatives that have to be mentioned in this context are the security initiative by Microsoft, "Next-Generation Secure Computing Base" (NGSCB) (Microsoft Corporation, 2006), aiming on a trustworthy computing environment, and the Open Trusted Computing (OpenTC) consortium [Open Trusted Computing (OpenTC), 2006], which is a project focusing on defining and implementing an open trusted computing framework. Both projects build their work on top of the TCG architecture.

Integration of Trust into Applications

As stated above, the goal is to utilize the concept of trust as a basis for engagements in complex and dynamic environments subject to uncertainty and risk. Figure 3 shows a typical problem. In this example agent A wants to interact with agent U. A does not have any direct experience of U (i.e., U is unknown to A, either completely or just in this particular context), but A knows three (at least partially) trusted agents T_1, T_2, and T_3, who

Figure 3. Trust based on recommendation chains

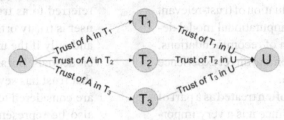

can pass their opinion about the trustworthiness of *U* as a recommendation to *A*.

To cope with the challenges of unstructured environments and dynamically changing interaction partners, applications using trust as basis for (semi-) autonomous decisions have to deal with the following aspects:

They have to keep track of the available devices; collect information regarding direct experience with other devices and collect recommendations and reputation information. Thus, the applications are able to adapt to changes in the environment and to update user preferences for acquainted devices. Since trust is subjective, this allows automated, but personalized, decision-making. Depending on the calculated trust and the estimated risk of an engagement, the applications can ask for user interaction or autonomously come to a decision. Thus, the user can be disburdened from constantly being asked to attend to routine decisions. Derived from Cahill et al. (2003), Grandison and Sloman (2001), and Ries, Kangasharju, and Mühlhäuser (2007), three main components

can be identified, which are necessary to enable applications to reason about trust and to enable (semi-)autonomous, trust-aided decision making (see Figure 4).

- *Trust management* focuses on the collection and filtering of evidence. Therefore, it is necessary to monitor the devices that are available and to collect evidence from those devices. Furthermore, it is necessary to filter the collected evidence and recommendations based on policies to achieve a certain level of attack-resistance. Other aspects of trust management are the evaluation of the context and the risk associated with an engagement.

- *Trust modeling* provides the representational and computational models of trust. Since the users need to be able to set up, control and adjust the trust model, there is the need for a user interface that can be used intuitively. Furthermore, there is the necessity for an interface, which is suitable for software agents

Figure 4. Main components for the integration of trust in applications

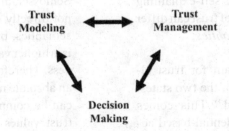

allowing automated integration feedback, and autonomous evaluation of trust-relevant information. The computational model defines the aggregation of recommendations, reputation information and direct experience into a single opinion.

- *Decision-making* is often treated as a part of trust management. Since it is a very important aspect, and users probably will judge the performance of a trust-based system based on the quality of its decisions, we mention it separately. Decision-making has to consider the collected and calculated information about trust as well as the information about the expected risk. Although we would like to automate the decision process as far as possible, there must be a facility for user interaction to support the user in getting used to this new process of decision-making, and to be able to interact with the system in critical cases.

State-of-the-Art

Having introduced the main components that are necessary for the use of trust in applications, we now give a short summary of the state-of-the-art regarding each component separately (Ries et al., 2006). Table 1 at the end of this section gives a short overview of different approaches.

Trust Modeling

The main issues of **trust modeling** are the representation and the computation of trust. In general, trust models represent trust as numbers and in few cases as a set of more or less self-explaining labels. Thus, the representation of trust can differ in *domain, dimension*, and *semantics*:

- **Domain:** A *binary* domain for trust allows only the expression of the two states: "trusted" and "untrusted." This comes close to certificate or credential-based ac-

cess control approaches (sometimes also referred to as trust management), where a user is trustworthy and access is granted if and only if the user presents the necessary credentials. But since most researchers agree that trust has several levels, binary models are considered to be insufficient. Trust can also be represented using more than two *discrete* values. This can be done either by using labels or by using a set of natural numbers. The advantage of this approach is that trust values can be easily assigned and understood by human users (Jøsang et al., 2007; Golbeck, 2005). *Continuous* representations of trust are supported by well-known mathematical theories depending on the semantics of the trust values.

- **Dimension:** The **dimension** of trust values can be either one or multi-dimensional. In *one-dimensional* approaches this value usually describes the degree of trust the user or an agent assigns to another one, possibly bound to a specific context. *Multi-dimensional* approaches allow the introduction of additional parameters, for example, a notion of uncertainty.

- **Semantics**: The **semantics** of trust values can be in the following set: rating, ranking, probability, belief, fuzzy value. As *rating* we interpret values that are directly linked with a trust-related semantics, for example, on a scale of natural numbers in the interval *[1,4]*, *1* can be linked to "very untrusted," ..., and *4* to "very trusted." In contrast, the trust values which are computed in *ranking*-based models, for example, in Kamvar, Schlosser, and Garcia-Molina (2003), are not directly associated with a meaningful semantics, but only in a relative way, that is, a higher value means greater trustworthiness. Therefore, it is only possible to assign an absolute meaning to a value if this value can be compared to a large enough set of trust values of other users. Furthermore, trust can be modeled as *probability*. In this case, the trust value expresses the probability that an agent will behave as expected. The details of *belief* are explained together with "subjective logic." For a trust model based on *fuzzy values*, we refer to ReGreT (Sabater & Sierra, 2002; Sabater, 2003). This model uses trust values in the range of real numbers in *[-1,1]*. Overlapping subintervals are mapped by membership functions to fuzzy set values, like "very good," which implicitly introduce semantics to the trust values. In contrast to probabilistic models, trust is formally not treated as the subjective probability that an agent will behave as expected in the next encounter, but the interpretation of a fuzzy value like "very good" is instead left up to the user or agent. Since fuzzy values are allowed to overlap, this also introduces a notion of fuzziness, that is, an agent can be, for example, "good" and "very good" at the same time to a certain degree.

Trust Management

In Blaze, Feigenbaum, Ioannidis, and Keromytis (1999) and Blaze, Feigenbaum, and Lacy (1996), **trust management** is defined as "a unified approach to specifying and interpreting security policies, credentials and relationships that allow direct authorization of security-critical actions." This definition describes what can be considered to be a traditional approach of trust management, where trust management is mainly treated as policy-based access control, and trust is only treated implicitly and in a rather static manner (Cahill et al., 2003; Grandison, 2003). Well-known examples of this approach are presented in Blaze et al. (1996) and Blaze, Feigenbaum, and Keromytis (1998). A main drawback of both systems is that they treat trust as monotonic, that is, additional credentials can only increase granted permissions. More recent approaches to trust management give stronger weight to the dynamic aspect of trust,

the collection and re-evaluation of trust-relevant evidence, and evaluation of risk (Cahill et al., 2003; Grandison, 2003). Such trust management approaches allow the definition of statements (rules or policies), which allow us to derive how much trust one should place in another entity depending on its specific purpose. In particular, rules can allow for the delegation of a trust decision, for example, entity *A* only trusts entity *C* if *B* trusts *C*.

Decision-Making

Since **decision-making** is an important aspect it is treated separately, although it can also be treated as a part of trust management. As motivated above, a trust-based decision is context dependent and is based on the calculated "trustworthiness" of the interaction partner and the expected risk of the engagement. Up to the point of decision-making, information about trust and risk can be managed in arbitrarily representational structures. The task of decision-making is to resolve all information provided in order to reach a decision, whether to trust and join the engagement or not. In the case of binary trust representation, for example, based on certificates, engagement is supported if the necessary credentials have been collected. In other cases, where, for example, decision-making is threshold-based (Marsh, 1994; Cahill et al., 2003), that is, the threshold for trust required to take part in an engagement in general increases with the risk associated with this engagement.

The presence of uncertainty and contradicting evidence complicates decision-making. A possible solution could be to integrate the user into a decision-making process providing a preliminary decision and asking for commitment. Although this can lead to higher acceptance of trust-aided technology by the user, it takes away the benefit of automation, and will not comply with the principles of a calm technology.

Table 1. Classification of different approaches dealing with trust (Ries et al., 2006)

	Trust modeling			Trust management	Decision making
	Domain	Dimension	Semantics		
Marsh (1994)	cont. in [-1,1]	1 (situational trust)	rating	– (but risk evaluation)	threshold-based
TidalTrust (Golbeck, 2005)	disc. in [1, 10]	1 (rating)	rating	global policy (no risk evaluation)	–
Abdul-Rahman & Hailes (2000)	disc. labels	1 (trust value)	rating	–	–
SECURE Project (Cahill et al., 2003; Carbone et al., 2003)	disc. in [0,∞]	2 (evidence based)	probability	local policies (incl. risk evaluation)	threshold-based
	cont. in [0, 1]	3 (belief, disbelief, uncertainty)	belief		
Subjective Logic (Jøsang, 2001)	disc. in [0,∞]	2 (evidence based)	probability	not directly part of SL	not directly part of SL
	cont. in [0, 1]	3 (belief, disbelief, uncertainty)	belief		
ReGreT (Sabater & Sierra, 2002; Sabater, 2003)	fuzzy values	2 (trust, confidence)	fuzzy values	local policies (fuzzy rules)	–

Examples of Trust Models

TidalTrust

Golbeck (2005) provides a trust model, which is based on 10 discrete trust values defined by the FOAF trust module (FOAF trust module, 2006) in the interval of natural numbers from [1,10]. Golbeck claims that humans are better at rating on a discrete scale than on a continuous one, for example, in the real numbers of [0,1]. She furthermore states that the 10 discrete trust values should be sufficient to approximate continuous trust values.

The trust model is evaluated in a social network called FilmTrust (Golbeck & Hendler, 2006) with about 400 users. In this network, the users can rate movies. Furthermore, they can rate friends in the sense of "[...] if the person were to have rented a movie to watch, how likely it is that you would want to see that film" (Golbeck, 2005).

A recursive trust or rating propagation allows inference of the rating of movies by the recommendations provided by friends. For a source node s in a set of nodes S, the rating r_{sm} inferred by s for the movie m is defined as:

$$r_{sm} = \frac{\sum_{i \in S} t_{si} \cdot r_{im}}{\sum_{i \in S} t_{si}}, \qquad (1)$$

where intermediate nodes are described by i, t_{si} describes the trust of s in i, and r_{im} is the rating of movie m assigned by i. To prevent arbitrarily long recommendation chains, the maximal chain length or recursion depth can be limited. Based on the assumption that the opinions of the most trusted friends are those most similar to the opinion of the source node, it is also possible to restrict the set of considered ratings to those provided by the most trusted friends.

Example

Let us assume A's trust in T_1, T_2, and T_3 is $t_{AT_1} = 9, t_{AT_2} = 8, t_{AT_3} = 1$, and the rating of T_1, T_2, and T_3 for U is $r_{T_1U} = 8, r_{T_2U} = 9, r_{T_3U} = 2$ (based on Figure 3).

The rating of A for U is calculated as:

$$
\begin{aligned}
r_{AU} &= \frac{t_{AT_1} \cdot r_{T_1U} + t_{AT_2} \cdot r_{T_2U} + t_{AT_3} \cdot r_{T_3U}}{t_{AT_1} + t_{AT_2} + t_{AT_3}} \qquad (2) \\
&= \frac{9 \cdot 8 + 8 \cdot 9 + 1 \cdot 2}{9 + 8 + 1} \\
&= \frac{146}{18} = 8.11\ldots
\end{aligned}
$$

In this example we see that the final rating r_{AU} is mainly influenced by the ratings of A's more trusted friends. Although T_3 provides a very bad rating for the movie, this rating has only little influence, since T_3 gains only little trust from A.

Although recommendation propagation is simple, the evaluation in Golbeck (2005) shows that it produces a relatively high accuracy, that is, the ratings based on recommendation are close to the real ratings of the user.

This approach does not deal with uncertainty or confidence of trust values. The model does not allow users to provide an opinion about how confident they are that their rating of a movie or their trust in a friend is assigned correctly.

This leads to the following problem. If there is only a single path from the source node to the sink, the rating calculated by the source will be the rating of the node directly adjacent to the sink, because the weights (t_{si}) are used for multiplication and division in each recursive step. It is not possible to express that the calculated rating is more or less uncertain. If it were possible to express the confidence of a trust value, the confidence of a trust value could be increased, if it is calculated based on multiple paths with similar ratings. This approach does not deal with any form of risk or decision-making.

Subjective Logic

"Subjective logic" (Jøsang, 2001) allows agents to calculate trust based on the number of positive and negative experiences in the past and it allows the update of trust values after new experiences have been made. This is especially interesting for ubiquitous computing, since it allows for an easy integration of feedback to re-evaluate trust after an engagement. The TidalTrust model does not address this aspect of iterative update of trust values.

"Subjective logic" combines the elements of Bayesian probability theory with belief theory. The Bayesian approach allows the modeling of trust based on evidence. The mapping to belief theory allows expression of trust in a representation that attempts to model a human notion of belief.

In "subjective logic," the *Bayesian approach* is used to calculate the *a posteriori* probability of binary events based on *a priori* collected evidence using beta probability density functions (*pdf*). For the sake of simplicity we do not explain the concept of atomicity, which is introduced by Jøsang to also use his model for non-binary events.

The beta probability density function f of a probability variable p can be described using the two parameters α, β as (Γ denotes the gamma function):

$$f(p \mid \alpha, \beta) = \frac{\Gamma(\alpha + \beta)}{\Gamma(\alpha)\Gamma(\beta)} p^{\alpha-1}(1-p)^{\beta-1}, \quad (3)$$

By defining $\alpha = r + 1$ and $\beta = s + 1$, it is possible to relate the *pdf* directly to the a priori collected evidence, where r and s represent the number of positive and negative pieces of evidence respectively. Providing a rationale for this choice of the parameters is beyond the scope of this chapter, but can be found in textbooks on statistics.

The mean $E(p)$ of a beta distribution $Beta(\alpha, \beta)$, is the expectation value of the distribution. It is given as:

$$E(p) = mean(\alpha, \beta) = \frac{\alpha}{\alpha + \beta} = \frac{r+1}{r+s+2}. \quad (4)$$

The mode $t = mode(\alpha, \beta)$ of the corresponding beta distribution is given as:

$$t = mode(\alpha, \beta) = \frac{\alpha - 1}{\alpha + \beta - 2} = \frac{r}{r+s}. \quad (5)$$

In this model, trust is represented by opinions which can be used to express the subjective probability that an agent will behave as expected in the next encounter. It is possible to express an agent's opinion about the trustworthiness of another agent. The opinion of agent A about the trustworthiness of agent B is denoted as o_B^A. Furthermore, an opinion about the truth of arbitrary propositions can be expressed. The opinion of agent A about the truth of the proposition x is denoted as o_x^A.

The advantage of this approach is that opinions can be easily be derived from the evidence collected. If an agent A has collected 10 pieces of evidence which support the assertion that agent B is trustworthy and 2 pieces of evidence

stating the opposite, the opinion of A o_B^A can be described using the parameters r and s as $(10,2)^{rs}$, or using the parameters α and β as $(11,3)^{\alpha\beta}$ (the superscripts here just help to distinguish both representations according to the parameters used). The corresponding *pdf* is shown in Figure 5. For decision-making, one can use the mean of the corresponding *pdf* along with a function defining the utility of the interaction of concern (Jøsang, 1999b). If agent A decides on an engagement with agent B, then A can update her opinion about B based on the behavior of B in this engagement. In the case of a positive experience, the updated opinion would be $o_B^A = (11,2)^{rs}$, in the case of a negative experience the opinion would evaluate to $o_B^A = (10,3)^{rs}$.

Furthermore, this approach attempts to model a human notion of belief, based on the *belief theory* as introduced in Jøsang (2001). In belief theory, an opinion can be expressed as a triple (b,d,u), where b represents belief, d represents disbelief, and u represents uncertainty about the trust of a statement. The three parameters are interrelated by the equation $b + d + u = 1$. Jøsang provides a mapping between the Bayesian approach and the belief approach by defining the following equations:

Figure 5. Probability density functions

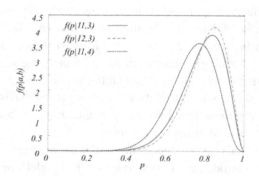

$$b = \frac{r}{r+s+2}$$

$$d = \frac{s}{r+s+2} \qquad \text{where } u \neq 0. \qquad (6)$$

$$u = \frac{2}{r+s+2}$$

Furthermore, he defines operators for combining (consensus) and recommending (discounting) opinions. The model also supports operators for propositional conjunction, disjunction and negation, which we will not explain for the sake of convenience.

The combination of two opinions about the same proposition x, e.g., $o_x^A = (r_x^A, s_x^A)^{rs}$ and $o_x^B = (r_x^B, s_x^B)^{rs}$ into single opinion $o_x^{A,B}$ is carried out by adding the evidence: $o_x^{A,B} := o_x^A \oplus o_x^B = (r_x^A + r_x^B, s_x^A + s_x^B)^{rs}$. This corresponds to the opinion of an agent, which makes the observations of A and B. Therefore, the evidence of A and B needs to be independent. The order in the consensus can be arbitrary, since the operator is commutative and associative.

The discounting operator is used to process recommendations. Let A's opinion about the trustworthiness of B be described by $o_B^A = (b_B^A, d_B^A, u_B^A)$ and the opinion of B about x is $o_x^B = (b_x^B, d_x^B, u_x^B)$. The opinion $o_x^{AB} := o_B^A \otimes o_x^B = (b_x^{AB}, d_x^{AB}, u_x^{AB}, a_x^{AB})$ of A about x, based on the recommendation of B, can be calculated as:

$$b_x^{AB} = b_B^A b_x^B,$$
$$d_x^{AB} = b_B^A d_x^B, \qquad (7)$$
$$u_x^{AB} = d_B^A + u_B^A + b_B^A u_x^B.$$

In Jøsang (1999a), it is shown how "subjective logic" can be used to model trust in the binding between the keys and their owners in public key infrastructures. Other papers introduce how to use "subjective logic" for trust-based decision-mak-

ing in electronic commerce (Jøsang, 1999b) and how the approach can be integrated into policy-based trust management (Jøsang, Gollmann, & Au, 2006).

Example

Let's assume the opinions of A about the trustworthiness of T_1, T_2, and T_3 (see Figure 3) are $o_{T_1}^A = (0.9, 0, 0.1)$, $o_{T_2}^A = (0.8, 0.1, 0.1)$, $o_{T_3}^A = (0.2, 0.2, 0.6)$, that is, two very trusted users, and one more or less unknown. Using the mapping defined in *Equation 6*, the opinion $o_{T_1}^A$ is equal to an opinion based on 18 positive and 0 negative experiences, that is, $o_{T_2}^A = (18, 0)^{rs}$.

Furthermore, the opinions of T_1, T_2, and T_3 about U are given as $o_U^{T_1} = (0.8, 0.1, 0.1)$, $o_U^{T_2} = (0.9, 0, 0.1)$ and $o_U^{T_3} = (0.1, 0.8, 0.1)$, that is, two rather good ratings, and one is very bad.

Using *Equation 7*, the discounting of the recommendations of T_1, T_2, and T_3 evaluates to:

$$
\begin{aligned}
o_U^{AT_1} &= (0.72, 0.09, 0.19) \\
o_U^{AT_2} &= (0.72, 0, 0.28) \qquad (8) \\
o_U^{AT_3} &= (0.02, 0.16, 0.82)
\end{aligned}
$$

The first two opinions maintain high values for belief, since the value of uncertainty dominates the opinion of A about T_3, the opinion $o_U^{AT_3}$ has an even larger component of uncertainty.

To aggregate these three opinions into a single one, we have to use the consensus operator. Since we provided the equation for the consensus operator only for evidence-based representation, we need to translate the representations of all opinions to the evidence space using Equation 6. Applying the consensus operator to the three opinions, that is, adding the positive and negative pieces of evidence, and transforming the result back to the belief representation, the final opinion $o_U^{AT_1, AT_2, AT_3}$ evaluates to:

$$o_U^{AT_1, AT_2} = o_U^{AT_1} \oplus o_U^{AT_2}$$
$$= (0.8119, 0.06046, 0.12764)$$
$$o_U^{AT_1, AT_2, AT_3} = o_U^{AT_1} \oplus o_U^{AT_2} \oplus o_U^{AT_3} = o_U^{AT_1, AT_2} \oplus o_U^{AT_3}$$
$$= (0.7928, 0.08304, 0.12416)$$

$$(9)$$

When combining two opinions with a dominating belief component, the belief in the resulting opinion increases and uncertainty decreases (see $o_U^{AT_1, AT_2}$). When combining an opinion with dominating belief and the one with dominating uncertainty, the opinion with high uncertainty has only little influence on the resulting opinion.

Challenges

Having explained the concept of trust and ways to model trust in detail, we summarize the main challenges and problems in dealing with trust.

A great challenge, as in almost all ubiquitous computing applications, is the collection and evaluation of context related data, since context dependence is one of the main properties of trust. It is not only important who the partner in an engagement is, but also the type of the engagement, for example, file sharing, online banking, selling of cars, or health care. Furthermore, we can expect that also context information, such as location or time constraints (see the chapter on "Context Models and Context Awareness"), may influence a trust-based decision. The transfer of trust between similar contexts is also an interesting area of research.

Another main challenge is dealing with malicious users trying to manipulate the trust models. Typical approaches are to attack the systems by providing misleading recommendations, that is, false accusations or false praise. If an attacker does not only use a single identity for this attack, but uses an arbitrarily high number of fictitious identities giving misleading evidence, the potential of a successful attack increases, since most trust models assume that the collected pieces

of evidence are independent. This special type of attack is well known as "Sybil attack" (Douceur, 2002) or "ballot (box) stuffing" (Schlosser, Voss, & Brückner, 2006; Jøsang et al., 2007).

Furthermore, trust is closely linked to uncertainty and risk. Thus, trust-based decisions may sometimes be misleading, and lead to a certain kind of damage, such as loss of time or money. Therefore, trust models should fulfill a set of criteria (Dingledine, Freedman, & Molnar, 2000; Jøsang et al., 2007): to ensure that the overall performance of trust is positive, the computational models need to be *robust to attacks*. Since trust in agents is based on evidence collected in the past, it will not be possible to prevent all kinds of attacks, but trust models become more reliable if the costs for attacks are reasonably high. Furthermore, the collected *evidence has to be weighted over time*. More recent experience needs to be given higher weighting to better reflect an agent's current behavior. In addition, trust models should also be *smooth*, that is, new evidence should only have a limited impact on trustworthiness.

Moreover, the user interfaces employed to assign trust values and to represent the current state of the system should be able to *present the information in an intuitive way*. This requirement is especially valid for trust models based on continuous domains, since humans are better at working with discrete scales and verbal statements (Golbeck, 2005; Jøsang et al., 2007).

Challenges in trust management are the estimation of the risk of an engagement, and the collection of independent evidence, since independence is a basic assumption of many trust models.

ACCOUNTABILITY

In the previous section we showed that trust could serve as a basis for risky engagements. The concept of accountability can complement the idea of trust, since it can help to establish responsible behavior concerning the usage of common resources. While trust helps the individual to deal with the risk and uncertainty of engagements, accountability focuses on the protection of interests of the collective and the usage of its resources.

Accountability in Computer Science

The Committee on National Security Systems (CNSS) defines accountability for information systems (IS) and for communications security (COMSEC) [Committee on National Security Systems (CNSS), 2003]:

- **IS:** Process of tracing IS activities to a responsible source.
- **COMSEC:** Principle that an individual is entrusted to safeguard and control equipment, keying material, and information and is answerable to proper authority for the loss or misuse of that equipment or information.

Both definitions, as well as the definition by the Merriam-Webster Online Dictionary provided in the introduction, point out that accountability enforces the responsibility of the individual to prevent misuse. This is especially important, since individual rational behavior may lead to misuse of common resources.

Individual Rationality vs. Collective Welfare

As Feldman and Chuang (2005) point out, there is a economic tension between individual rationality and collective welfare. File-sharing networks, like KaZaA (KaZaA, 2006a) or Gnutella (2006), as well as file-storing networks like Free Haven (Free Haven, 2006) are based on the idea that their users share their local resources, for example, files or disk space, with the community. But evaluations have shown that many peers, if possible, try to avoid sharing their own resources. For example, in file-sharing networks users try to avoid uploading files, since this uses up their bandwidth without them having a direct benefit. This is called *freeriding*. Freeriding works only as long as there are enough other users who are interested in the welfare of the community and provide their resources. In Adar and Huberman (2000), it is shown that 70% of Gnutella users do not share files. In a file storing network like Free Haven (Free Haven, 2006), it is even more the case that users need to be reliable and behave as expected by the system, since the Free Haven users store the data of other users. Another well-known problem, addressing misuse of a shared source, is the sending of e-mail spam. Since e-mail accounts and sending e-mails are often available for free, spammers try to misuse, or overuse, this medium for sending unsolicited messages in great mass.

How to Enforce Accountability

But how can a responsible usage of shared resources by individuals be enforced? Dingledine et al. (2000) state that accountability is a concept to handle resource allocation in collaborative systems.

According to Dingledine et al. (2000), accountability can be achieved in two ways. The first way is to select favored users, who are allowed to use a certain resource, and the second one is to restrict access to the shared resources, for example by quantity of available disk space.

The concept of *selection favored users* can be technically supported by trust systems and reputation systems. Since the idea is that the whole community determines which users should be favored, and not a single user, we focus on reputation systems for this aspect.

The concept of *restricting access* can be technically supported by micropayments. The basic idea is that the user has to pay for access to or usage of a shared resource by expending another resource, which is commonly assumed to be scarce. This can be real money as well as other resources, for example, artificial currencies or CPU cycles.

Reputation Systems

Reputation systems, sometimes also called rating systems, are based on the assumption that good reputation is desirable. If users behave as good users are expected to behave, their reputation improves. For other users these ratings can be used to select service providers based on their reputation. The threshold for cooperation increases with the potential risk.

Reputation and Trust

The idea of trust systems is very similar to reputation systems. Reputation systems collect evidence related to the user's behavior and provide ratings to other users. Reputation systems are widely used in online communities, for example, the eBay feedback forum (eBay Inc., 2006) or the Amazon review scheme (Amazon, 2006), whereas trust systems have their foundations in the security area, for example, PGP (Zimmermann, 1994), Policy-Maker (Blaze et al., 1996). The main difference between trust and reputation systems according to Jøsang et al. (2007) is that trust systems deal with the subjective trust values between entities, whereas reputation systems calculate one system-wide reputation score per entity.

Sabater and Sierra (2005) point out that reputation is one of the elements upon which one can build trust. It is especially useful in cases in which direct experience is rare. Yet it is not possible to give a strict rule for differentiation, since there is mixed usage of both terms in current research work.

Prerequisites: Incentives, Long Term Pseudonyms

As stated above, reputation systems are based on the assumption that good reputation is desirable.

This leads to the consequence that reputation systems only work well with long term pseudonyms. In the case of anonymous users, it is not possible to build up any reputation at all, since reputation cannot be linked to an entity. In the case of short-term pseudonyms, there is only a minimal incentive for building a good reputation, since reputation disappears on adoption of a new pseudonym.

It is not a trivial problem to establish an online community with long-term pseudonyms. On the one hand, if new pseudonyms are easy to receive and are assigned a neutral score, it is easy for freeriders or betrayers to misuse a pseudonym until it has a bad reputation. Then, instead of being blemished with a bad reputation preventing others from interacting with them, they come back with a new pseudonym. On the other hand, if it is "very expensive" to get a new pseudonym, or if new pseudonyms have an outstanding bad reputation, this will prevent new potential members from joining the community.

Example: eBay Feedback Forum

The most well-known rating system is probably the eBay (eBay Inc., 2006) feedback forum. After each transaction buyer and seller can give each other a rating, stating if they were satisfied with the transaction. The effect of the feedback forum is twofold. On the one hand it helps to establish accountability. For sellers, a high number of good transactions leads to a high feedback score, or reputation. Studies by Resnick, Zeckhauser, Swanson, and Lookwood (2006) have shown that a high feedback score is awarded, since well established sellers with a high reputation rating can achieve higher prices than new sellers with a low reputation rating. Thus, the feedback score helps to achieve accountable behavior of the sellers. On the other hand, it helps to establish trust between the buyer and the seller. For buyers, the reputation of the seller is an important piece of information needed for estimating the risk of a transaction.

The basic idea of the reputation model in eBay is very simple. Buyers and sellers are allowed to rate each other after each transaction. This feedback can either be positive (+1), neutral (0) or negative (-1), and can contain some additional free text information. Each user profile shows a feedback score as the total sum of feedback provided, and the percentage of positive feedback in relation to the total feedback. The domain of the score is unbound in [-∞,∞]. This lack of normalization can lead to very misleading interpretations, since 100 positive and 0 negative ratings end in the same total score as 300 positive and 200 negative ratings. The percentage of positive values helps to overcome this problem. The interpretation of the percentage alone can again be misleading. Only if both values are used together is a reasonable interpretation possible. Both representations, the score and the percentage of positive ratings, have the character of a relative ranking. Their semantics means *more is better*, whereas the value alone says little.

Finally the decision whether a score of, for instance 80 and 99% positive ratings is trustworthy, or if another seller with a score of 5,000 and 84% positive ratings is to be preferred, is left up to the user.

Classification of Reputation Systems

Schlosser et al. (2006) provide a classification of reputation systems based on their computational model. They developed a formal model to describe computational aspects of reputation models (reputation metrics) and identified the following classes:

- **Accumulative systems** calculate the reputation of an agent as the sum of all provided ratings. An example for this is the total score in the eBay feedback forum. The disadvantages of this approach have already been discussed above.

- **Average systems** calculate the reputation as the average of ratings, which an agent has received. This corresponds, for instance, with the percentage of positive ratings in the eBay feedback forum.

- **Blurred systems** calculate the reputation of an agent as the weighted sum of all ratings. The weight depends on the age of a rating, that is, older ratings receive a lower weight.

- **OnlyLast systems** determine the reputation of an agent as the most recent rating. Although these systems seem to be very simple, the simulation had shown that they provided a reasonable level of attack-resistance.

- **EigenTrust systems** calculate the reputation of an agent depending on the ratings, as well as on the reputation of the raters. An interesting property of these systems is that each agent calculates the reputation of the other agents locally based on its own rating and the weighted ratings of the surrounding agents. If all agents adhere to the protocol, the locally stored reputation information of all agents will converge. Thus, all agents have the same reputation value for any agent. For more details see Kamvar et al. (2003).

- **Adaptive systems** calculate the reputation of an agent depending on its current reputation. For example, a single positive rating has a higher impact on the reputation of an agent with a low reputation than on the reputation of an agent with a high reputation.

- **Beta systems** calculate the reputation of an agent based on beta distributions, as introduced with the Bayesian approach above, using positive and negative experiences as input.

Summary

Reputation systems can be used to achieve accountability, if good reputation is accepted as incentive for responsible behavior. The typical attacks on reputation systems are very similar to the attacks of trust systems, that is, false accusation, false praise, and Sybil attack.

In addition to the computational aspects, there are a set of other aspects, which are important for the usability and attack-resistance of a reputation system, as discussed in Schlosser et al. (2006) and Feldman and Chuang (2005), for example, the incentives to provide ratings, the location for the storage of the reputation values, and the reputation of newcomers. For a more detailed survey of different reputation systems we recommend Jøsang et al. (2007), Sabater and Sierra (2005), and Schlosser et al. (2006).

Micropayment Systems

The Concept of Micropayments

In contrast to reputation systems, which reward users who contribute to the welfare of the community with a good reputation, the idea of micropayment systems is that the users have to pay for access to a resource or a service. In general, usage is kept quite cheap for typical users, but high enough to prevent individuals from arbitrarily high (mis-)usage of a resource. The payments and the value of a single service are kept rather small, which helps to limit the risk for the user or the provider of a resource. If the user is not satisfied with the service, or the provider is not satisfied with the payment, both can decide not to continue with the interaction, without losing too much.

The effect of micropayments on accountability is twofold. First, typical users will reduce their usage of the common resource to a reasonable level, since they have to pay for it. Thus, mircopayments help to achieve accountable behavior of typical users. Second, users who want to exploit the community by arbitrarily high usage of the common resource have to pay for it. Thus it is no longer possible to exploit the community. The payment can be done with any kind of scarce resource.

In this section, we focus on micropayments, which can be used as a counter measure to the resource allocation problem, and help to prevent freeriding, and denial-of-service (DoS) attacks (see the chapter on "Security for Ubiquitous Computing"). Therefore, we focus on very small micropayments (in the magnitude of 1 cent or smaller) and on non-monetary approaches.

Classification of Micropayments

Dingledine et al. (2000) propose the differentiation in *fungible* and *non-fungible* micropayments. Based on Dingledine et al. (2000) and Microsoft Corporation (2006), we provide the following classification (Table 2).

Fungible Micropayments

Fungible micropayments have some intrinsic or redeemable value, that is, the recipient can use fungible micropayments to pay others.

Monetary Micropayments

Monetary micropayments are very small payments, for example, one cent or less per payment, in contrast to macropayment schemes, such as eCash (Chaum, Fiat, & Naor, 1988; Chaum, 1992). These micropayments can be charged per download for a Web page or file. Since the payments are very small, these schemes need to be very efficient, that is, the transaction costs for the payments have to be lower than the payment itself. Due to these requirements these approaches are lightweight in the sense that misuse, for example, cheating the system of a few cents, is reasonably hard, but not impossible (Rivest & Shamir, 1997). Typically, these approaches need central brokers (Efstathiou & Polyzos, 2004), which are required to be trusted by users and providers, here often called vendors, to access the accounts of the users and vendors and to exchange the payments. Since the idea of central brokers is incompatible with

Table 2. Classification of micropayments

fungible micropayments	monetary approaches	PayWord and MicroMint (Rivest & Shamir, 1997)
		Millicent (Glassman, Manasse, Abadi, Gauthier, & Sobalvarro, 1995)
		PPay (Yang & Garcia-Molina, 2003)
	non-monetary approaches	P2PWNC (Efstathiou & Polyzos, 2003; Efstathiou & Polyzos, 2004; Efstathiou & Polyzos, 2005)
		KARMA (Vishnumurthy, Chandrakumar, & Sirer, 2003)
non-fungible micropayments	proof-of-work based on CPU cycles	Dwork & Naor, 1992
		Back, 2002
		Juels & Brainard, 1999
		Jakobsson & Juels, 1999
	proof-of-work based on memory	Dwork, Goldberg, & Naor, 2003
		Abadi, Burrows, Manasse, & Wobber, 2005

the idea of equal peers in P2P networks, these approaches are rather rare in P2P. Also, when transferring micropayments to ubiquitous computing scenarios, a central broker might become a problem in unmanaged environments.

Example: PayWord

The approaches described by Rivest and Shamir (1997) (PayWord and MircoMint) were designed to charge users for the download of web pages, for example, 1 cent per page, with reasonable effort. Both approaches are based on public key infrastructures and collision-resistant one-way hash functions (for details, see the chapter on "Security for Ubiquitous Computing").

To introduce this type of micropayment, we briefly present the PayWord scheme: PayWord assumes a few nationwide brokers who authorize

the users to make micropayments to the vendors. There is a long-term relationship between users and brokers, and vendors and brokers. The relationships between users and vendors are short-lived.

Before the user U interacts with a new vendor V, for example, the user wants to download a Web page requiring payment, U calculates a set of $n + 1$ values $w_0, ..., w_n$, called "paywords." The paywords are calculated in reverse order. The last payword w_n is chosen randomly, the others are calculated recursively. It holds that:

$$w_i = h(w_{i+1}) \tag{10}$$

where h is a well-known hash function, for example, MD5 or SHA-1.

Before the first interaction, the user U sends her certificate and the value w_0 as "commitment," to the vendor V. The value w_0 is the initial value for this chain of paywords, and not a payment itself. As first payment U additionally sends w_1. The vendor checks if Equation 10 holds, and if true, V accepts the payment and delivers the Web page. In further interactions, U only sends only (w_i, i) to V as i-th payment, which can again be verified using Equation 10.

At the end of the day, V sends the last payment (w_i, l) received by a user and the corresponding commitment w_0 to the broker. B charges U's account with l cents and pays them to V, that is, each payword is worth 1 cent. For further details, and possible attacks see Rivest and Shamir (1997) and O'Mahony, Pierce, Tewari, and Peirce (1997).

Yang and Garcia-Molina (2003) showed that in approaches like PayWord, MicroMint, and Millicent (Glassman et al., 1995; O'Mahony et al., 1997), the central brokers can become a bottleneck, since their work load is $O(n)$, where n denotes the number of payments. If a broker in PayWord receives a payment, she has to use l-times the hash function h, to verify $w_0 = h^i(w_i)$. Additionally, the Millicent approach has the disadvantage that the broker needs to be online whenever a user wishes to interact with a new vendor (Rivest & Shamir, 1997). To overcome these problems, Yang and Garcia-Molina (2003) presented PPay, which requires the involvement of the broker when peers open or close accounts, and in exceptional cases. Furthermore, they reduce the workload of the broker by making the coins *transferable*, that is, the coins can be reused by the receiver for paying for another service.

Non-Monetary Micropayments

Non-monetary micro-payments introduce artificial currencies to allow payment in exchange for a service. Since there is no involvement of real money, the risk of misuse is limited. Thus, it is easier to design systems that do not need a central trusted broker to handle the exchange of payment. Therefore, this type of micropayment is more common in P2P networks.

Simple approaches are implemented in the file sharing networks KaZaA (KaZaA, 2006a) or eMule (eMule, 2006b) (Liebau, Darlagiannis, Heckmann, & Mauthe, 2005). The KaZaA approach (KaZaA, 2006b) is very similar to the reputation approaches described in this chapter. There is only one value per user, which describes the past behavior of a user towards the community. This value is calculated as the ratio between uploads and downloads. The higher this value is, the higher the download speed. The approach allows cheating very easily, since each client stores information about itself locally (Liebau et al., 2005), without any elaborate security mechanisms. The approach chosen by eMule (eMule, 2006a) allows users to only profit locally from past behavior, that is, if A uploads files to B, A can get a better position in the download list of B, but not in the download list of another client.

More elaborate approaches are presented, for example, by Efstathiou and Polyzos (2003, 2004, 2005) and by Vishnumurthy et al. (2003). Those approaches introduce artificial currencies, sometimes referred to as receipts or tokens.

Since the tokens do not have any intrinsic value per se, the system needs to be designed in such a way that tokens are a scarce resource.

In the approach chosen by Efstathiou et al., this is done in such a way that at least the issuer of a token can be forced to return an adequate service when she is presented with one of her tokens. If this holds, tokens become a scarce resource, since the users will issue a token only in return for a service, which is appropriate to the service which they are expected to deliver in return for a presented token.

To make those approaches more flexible, the currency needs to be *transferable*, that is, user A can reuse the payments received from user B to pay user C. When the payments become transferable, the problem of storing the tokens becomes nontrivial, since attackers might try to *forge* tokens, or to spend one token twice (*double spending*).

The approach of Vishnumurthy (2003) introduces an artificial currency, called Karma. The users of the system are able to pay with Karma for services. The system relies on the idea that there is a substantial proportion of honest users in the P2P network, who enforce the correct accounting of payments by replicating the accounts of each user on different peers.

Example: P2PWNC

The P2P Wireless Network Confederation (P2PWNC) (Efstathiou & Polyzos, 2003; Efstathiou & Polyzos, 2004; Efstathiou & Polyzos, 2005) uses a token-based micro-payment system, which is based on *non-simultaneous n-way exchanges*. The idea of P2PWNC is that the participants in P2PWNC provide each other with access to their WLAN hotspots.

If user B is allowed to access the hotspot of A, B issues a signed receipt, which states that B owes a favor to A, that is, B was granted access by A, and passes it to A.

If A wants to access B's hotspot at a later point of time, B will only grant access to A if A can show a receipt stating that B owes a favor to A (two-way exchange).

To make the scheme more flexible, A can also present a chain of receipts, from which B can learn that she owes something to A by transitivity. For example, A shows two receipts to B. One receipt which states that B owes something to C, and the other one stating that C owes something to A. Thus, B can learn from these two receipts that she owes something to A (three-way exchange).

To achieve security the system uses a self-managed public key infrastructure, which allows certificates to be introduced to sign receipts and prevents forgery of tokens. The scheme also allows prevention of double spending (Efstathiou & Polyzos, 2005).

Non-Fungible Micropayments

Non-fungible micropayments, in general, do not have an intrinsic value. Instead the user of a resource has to prove that she has done some work, for example, solved a computational problem, before she is granted access. This type of micropayment is well known as **proof-of-work** (PoW). It has already been discussed in the previous chapter with Hashcash (Back, 2002) as an example. Another proposal, which also uses CPU cycles as scarce resource, is due to Dwork and Naor (2002).

PoW challenges developed more recently (Dwork et al., 2003; Abadi, Burrows, Manasse, & Wobber, 2005) treat not the CPU cycles but the time for *memory accesses as a scarce resource*. The reason is that memory latency is more equal between high-end and low-end computers (or even PDAs) than the CPU speed. Therefore, the basic idea of these approaches is the same as for CPU cycle-based approaches, but the solution of the challenge especially includes operations with a great number of memory accesses.

Reusing PoW

Jakobsson and Juels (1999) provide a PoW concept based on the well-known idea of a bread pudding. A bread pudding is a dish that reuses stale bread. The authors show that the provider of a service (verifier of the PoW) can take advantage of the PoWs performed by its clients. They provide a protocol, which allows the reuse of the result of PoW to mint coins for the MicroMint scheme presented in Rivest and Shamir (1997).

Summary

There is a huge variety in the field of micropayments. The general idea of making users pay for the resources used prevents the exploitation of those who are willing to share their resources. The advantage of micropayment systems that are based on real money clearly is that the provider of the resource knows exactly the worth of the payment. Furthermore, those systems can, at least theoretically, be built on short-term identities or anonymity. The need for a central broker and the great effort required to grant an acceptable level of security to make users accept those systems seem to be a major drawback. A few approaches to establishing micropayments commercially came up at the end of the 1990s, such as Millicent (Glassman et al., 1995) (developed by Digital Equipment Corporation (DEC) and later acquired by Compaq Inc.) (Stalder & Clement, 1999), but were not successful.

The barrier for the acceptance of non-monetary approaches seems not to be as high as for monetary ones. Such approaches have therefore been implemented, for example, in P2P file sharing networks. Since there is no need for a central broker, those systems are also more similar to the nature of distributed networks. Nonetheless, in those schemes there is the need for at least short-term pseudonyms since it is necessary to link the entities to their accounts.

The main drawback of the PoW approach is the huge variety of hardware. High-end systems have a big advantage over low-end systems, and for computational devices in ubiquitous computing this gap becomes even wider.

RESEARCH OUTLOOK

So far we have introduced the concepts of trust and accountability, presented the state-of-the-art in the fields of trust, reputation and micropayments, and provided examples for deeper insights.

Now we would like to give a brief outlook for future research challenges. We believe that both concepts are enablers for ubiquitous computing, since they can be milestones on the way to a seamless integration of ubiquitous computing in the real life. As stated in Garlan, Siewiorek, Smailagic, and Steenkiste (2002): "Increasingly, the bottleneck in computing is not its disk capacity, processor speed, or communication bandwidth, but rather the limited resource of human attention." Therefore, autonomous collaboration is one of the key features of ubiquitous computing.

The modeling of trust and reputation are still in a pioneering phase (Jøsang et al., 2007); there is still a lot of work to be done until trust-aided applications will become widespread. As addressed above, the main challenges are still robust computational models for trust and the transfer of trust between similar contexts, to extend the applicability of this approach.

The concepts of micropayments still have to be transferred to ubiquitous computing. While monetary micropayments usually rely on an infrastructure and a central broker, the drawback of proof-of-work obviously is in the different computational resources of ubiquitous computing devices.

When those concepts mature, their use in applications will depend greatly on their acceptance by users. Therefore, it is a major issue not only to model concepts of everyday life, but to present them in a way that is appropriate for everyday usage.

REFERENCES

Abadi, M., Burrows, M., Manasse, M., & Wobber, T. (2005). Moderately hard, memory-bound functions. *ACM Transactions on Internet Technology, 5*(2), 299–327.

Abdul-Rahman, A. (2004). *A framework for decentralised trust reasoning.* Unpublished doctoral dissertation, University College London.

Abdul-Rahman, A., & Hailes, S. (2000). Supporting trust in virtual communities. In *Proceedings of the 33rd Hawaii International Conference on System Sciences* (Vol. 6, p. 6007).

Adar, E., & Huberman, B.A. (2000). Free riding on gnutella. *First Monday, 5*(10).

Amazon.com. (2006). *Amazon Web site.* Retrieved December 2006 from www.amazon.com.

Anderson, R. (2003). *'Trusted computing' frequently asked questions (Version 1.1).* Retrieved December 2006 from http://www.cl.cam.ac.uk/~rja14/tcpa-faq.html.

Back, A. (2002). *Hashcash - a denial of service counter-measure* (Tech. Rep.).

Bhargava, B., Lilien, L., Rosenthal, A., & Winslet, M. (2004). Pervasive trust. *IEEE Intelligent Systems, 19*(5), 74–88.

Blaze, M., Feigenbaum, J., Ioannidis, J., & Keromytis, A.D. (1999). Secure Internet programming: Security issues for mobile and distributed objects. In J. Vitek & C. Jensen (Eds.), *Secure Internet programming: Security issues for mobile and distributed objects* (pp. 185–210). Springer-Verlag.

Blaze, M., Feigenbaum, J., & Keromytis, A.D. (1998). Keynote: Trust management for public-key infrastructures. In *Security Protocols: 6th International Workshop, Cambridge, UK* (LNCS 1550, pp. 59-63).

Blaze, M., Feigenbaum, J., & Lacy, J. (1996). Decentralized trust management. In *SP '96: Proceedings of the 1996 IEEE Symposium on Security and Privacy* (p. 164). Washington, DC: IEEE Computer Society.

Burmester, M., & Mulholland, J. (2006). The advent of trusted computing: Implications for digital forensics. In *SAC '06: Proceedings of the 2006 ACM Symposium on Applied Computing* (pp. 283–287). New York, NY: ACM Press.

Cahill, V., Gray, E., Seigneur, J.M., Jensen, C., Chen, Y., Shand, B., Dimmock, N., Twigg, A., Bacon, J., English, C., Wagealla, W., Terzis, S., Nixon, P., Serugendo, G., Bryce, C., Carbone, M., Krukow, K., & Nielsen, M. (2003). Using trust for secure collaboration in uncertain environments. *IEEE Pervasive Computing, 2/3,* 52-61.

Carbone, M., Nielsen, M., & Sassone, V. (2003). A formal model for trust in dynamic networks. In A.

Cerone & P. Lindsay (Eds.), *Proceedings of IEEE International Conference on Software Engineering and Formal Methods (pp. 54-63).* Brisbane, Australia: IEEE Computer Society.

Chaum, D. (1992). Achieving electronic privacy. *Scientific American, 267*(2), 96-101.

Chaum, D., Fiat, A., & Naor, M. (1988). Untraceable electronic cash. In *CRYPTO '88: Proceedings on Advances in Cryptology* (pp. 319–327). New York, NY: Springer-Verlag.

Committee on National Security Systems (CNSS). (May 2003). *National information assurance glossary (cnssi-4009) (rev. ed.).* Retrieved December 2006 from http://www.cnss.gov/Assets/pdf/cnssi_4009.pdf.

Dingledine, R., Freedman, M.J., & Molnar, D. (2000). Accountability measures for peer-to-peer systems. In A. Oram (Ed.), *Peer-to-peer: Harnessing the power of disruptive technologies* (pp. 271-340). O'Reilly.

Douceur, J.R. (2002). The Sybil attack. In *IPTPS '01: Revised Papers from the First International Workshop on Peer-to-Peer Systems* (LNCS 2429, pp. 251–260). London, UK: Springer-Verlag.

Dwork, C., Goldberg, A., & Naor, M. (2003). On memory-bound functions for fighting spam. In *Advances in Cryptology - CRYPTO 2003, 23rd Annual International Cryptology Conference* (LNCS 2729, pp. 426-444). Springer.

Dwork, C., & Naor, M. (1992). Pricing via processing or combating junk mail. In *CRYPTO '92: Proceedings of the 12th Annual International Cryptology Conference on Advances in Cryptology* (pp. 139–147). London, UK: Springer-Verlag.

eBay Inc. (2006). *eBay homepage.* Retrieved from www.eBay.com.

Efstathiou, E., & Polyzos, G. (2004). *Fully self-organized fair peering of wireless hot-*

spots (Tech. Rep.). Athens University of Economics and Business, MMLAB.

Efstathiou, E., & Polyzos, G. (2003). A peer-to-peer approach to wireless LAN roaming. In *WMASH '03: Proceedings of the 1st ACM International Workshop on Wireless Mobile Applications and Services on WLAN Hotspots* (pp. 10–18). New York, NY: ACM Press.

Efstathiou, E., & Polyzos, G. (2005). A self-managed scheme for free citywide Wi-Fi. In *WOWMOM '05: Proceedings of the First International IEEE WoWMoM Workshop on Autonomic Communications and Computing (ACC'05)* (pp. 502–506). Washington, DC: IEEE Computer Society.

eMule. (2006a). *eMule credit system*. Retrieved December 2006 from http://www.emule-project.net/home/perl/help.cgi?l=1&rm=show_topic&topic_id=134.

eMule. (2006b). *eMule Web site*. Retrieved December 2006 from www.eMule-project.net. Feldman, M., & Chuang, J. (2005). Overcoming free-riding behavior in peer-to-peer systems. *SIGecom Exch., 5*(4), 41–50.

Foaf trust module. (2006). Retrieved December 2006 from http://trust.mindswap.org/ont/trust.owl.

Free Haven. (2006). *Free Haven Web site*. Retrieved December 2006 from www.freehaven.net.

Gambetta, D. (2000). Can we trust trust? In D. Gambetta (Ed.), *Trust: Making and breaking cooperative relations (electronic edition)* (pp. 213-237).

Garlan, D., Siewiorek, D., Smailagic, A., & Steenkiste, P. (2002). Project Aura: Toward distraction-free pervasive computing. *Pervasive Computing, 1*(2), 22-31.

Glassman, S., Manasse, M., Abadi, M., Gauthier, P., & Sobalvarro, P. (1995). The Millicent protocol for inexpensive electronic commerce. In *Proceedings of the 4th WWW Conference, Boston, MA* (pp. 603-618).

Gnutella. (2006). *Gnutella Web site*. Retrieved December 2006 from www.gnutella.com

Golbeck, J. (2005). *Computing and applying trust in Web-based social networks*. Unpublished doctoral dissertation, University of Maryland, College Park.

Golbeck, J., & Hendler, J. (2006). Filmtrust: Movie recommendations using trust in Web-based social networks. In *Proceedings of the Consumer Communications and Networking Conference*.

Grandison, T. (2003). *Trust management for Internet applications*. Unpublished doctoral dissertation, Imperial College London.

Grandison, T., & Sloman, M. (2000). A survey of trust in Internet applications. *IEEE Communications Surveys and Tutorials, 3*(4).

Jakobsson, M., & Juels, A. (1999). Proofs of work and bread pudding protocols. In *CMS '99: Proceedings of the IFIP TC6/TC11 Joint Working Conference on Secure Information Networks* (pp. 258–272). Deventer, The Netherlands: Kluwer, B.V.

Jøsang, A. (1999a). An algebra for assessing trust in certification chains. In *Proceedings of the Network and Distributed System Security Symposium*. San Diego, CA: The Internet Society.

Jøsang, A. (1999b). Trust-based decision making for electronic transactions. In L. Yngström & T. Svensson (Eds.), *Proceedings of the Fourth Nordic Workshop on Secure IT Systems,* Stockholm, Sweden *(NORDSEC'99)*..

Jøsang, A. (2001). A logic for uncertain probabilities. *International Journal of Uncertainty, Fuzziness and Knowledge-Based Systems, 9*(3), 279-212.

Jøsang, A., Gollmann, D., & Au, R. (2006). A method for access authorisation through delegation networks. In R. Safavi-Naini, C. Steketee, & W. Susilo (Eds.), *Fourth Australasian Information Security Workshop (Network Security) (AISW 2006)* (Vol. 54, p. 165-174). Hobart, Australia: ACS.

Jøsang, A., Ismail, R., & Boyd, C. (2007). A survey of trust and reputation systems for online service provision. *Decision Support Systems, 43(2), 618-644.*

Juels, A., & Brainard, J.G. (1999). Client puzzles: A cryptographic countermeasure against connection depletion attacks. In *Proceedings of the Network and Distributed System Security Symposium (pp. 151-165).* The Internet Society.

Kamvar, S.D., Schlosser, M.T., & Garcia-Molina, H. (2003). The Eigentrust algorithm for reputation management in p2p networks. In *Proceedings of the 12th International Conference on World Wide Web* (pp. 640-651). New York: ACM Press.

KaZaA. (2006a). *KaZaA Web site.* Retrieved December 2006 from www.kazaa.com

KaZaA. (2006b). *Participation level.* Retrieved December 2006 from http://www.kazaa.com/us/help/glossary/participation_ratio.htm

Kinateder, M., & Rothermel, K. (2003). Architecture and algorithms for a distributed reputation system. In P. Nixon & S. Terzis (Eds.), *Proceedings of the First International Conference on Trust Management,* Crete, Greece (LNCS 2692, pp. 1-16). Springer-Verlag.

Liebau, N., Darlagiannis, V., Heckmann, O., & Mauthe, A. (2005). Accounting in Peer-to-Peer-Systems. In R. Steinmetz & K. Wehrle (Eds.), *Peer-to-peer systems and applications.* (Vol. 3485, pp. 547-566). Springer.

Marsh, S. (1994). *Formalising trust as a computational concept.* Unpublished doctoral dissertation, University of Stirling.

McKnight, D.H., & Chervany, N.L. (1996). *The meanings of trust* (Tech. Rep.). Management Information Systems Research Center, University of Minnesota.

Merriam-Webster, I. (2006). *Merriam-Webster online dictionary.* Retrieved December 2006 from www.m-w.com. Microsoft Corporation. (2006). *Next-generation secure computing base (NGSCB).* Retrieved December 2006 from http://www.microsoft.com/ngscb

Microsoft Corporation. (2006). *The penny black project.* Retrieved December 2006 from http://research.microsoft.com/research/sv/PennyBlack/

Mui, L., Mohtashemi, M., & Halberstadt, A. (2002). A computational model of trust and reputation for e-businesses. In *Proceedings of the 35th Annual Hawaii International Conference on System Sciences (HICSS'02)* (Vol. 7, p. 188). Washington, DC: IEEE Computer Society.

O'Mahony, D., Pierce, M., Tewari, H., & Peirce, M. (1997). *Electronic payment systems.* Norwood, MA: Artech House, Inc.

Open Trusted Computing (OpenTC). (2006). *Open trusted computing Web site.* Retrieved December 2006 from http://www.opentc.net.

Resnick, P., Zeckhauser, R., Swanson, J., & Lockwood, K. (2006). The value of reputation on ebay: A controlled experiment. *Experimental Economics, 9(2), 79-101.*

Ries, S., Kangasharju, J., & Mühlhäuser, M. (2006). A classification of trust systems. In R. Meersman, Z. Tari, & P. Herrero (Eds.), *On the Move to Meaningful Internet Systems 2006: OTM Workshops,* Montpellier, France (LNCS 4276, pp. 894-903). Berlin: Springer.

Ries, S., Kangasharju, J., & Mühlhäuser, M. (2007). Modeling trust for users and agents in ubiquitous computing. In *Proceedings of Kommunikation in Verteilten Systemen,* KiVS'07.

Rivest, R.L., & Shamir, A. (1997). Payword and Micromint: Two simple micropayment schemes. In *Proceedings of the International Workshop on Security Protocols* (pp. 69-87). London: Springer-Verlag.

Sabater, J. (2003). *Trust and reputation for agent societies.* Unpublished doctoral dissertation, Institut d'Investigacion en Intelligencia Artificial, Spain.

Sabater, J., & Sierra, C. (2002). Reputation and social network analysis in multi-agent systems. In *Proceedings of the 1st International Joint Conference on Autonomous Agents and Multiagent Systems* (pp. 475-482). New York: ACM Press.

Sabater, J., & Sierra, C. (2005). Review on computational trust and reputation models. *Artificial Intelligence Review, 24*(1), 33-60.

Schlosser, A., Voss, M., & Brückner, L. (2006). On the simulation of global reputation systems. *Journal of Artificial Societies and Social Simulation, 9*(1).

Seigneur, J.-M., Farrell, S., Jensen, C.D., Gray, E., & Chen, Y. (2003). End-to-end trust starts with recognition. In *First International Conference on Security in Pervasive Computing* (LNCS 2802, pp. 130-142). Springer.

Stalder, F., & Clement, A. (1999). *Electronic cash: Technologies and issues* (Tech. Rep.). Research Report for Industry Canada. Information Policy Research Program (IPRP), Faculty of InformationStudies, University of Toronto.

TCG. (2006). *Trusted Computing Group (TCG).* Retrieved December 2006 from www.trustedcomputinggroup.org

TCG. (2004). *TCG architecture overview.* Retrieved December 2006 from https://www.trustedcomputinggroup.org/specs/IWG/TCG_1_0_Architecture_Overview.pdf

Teacy, W.T., Patel, J., Jennings, N.R., & Luck, M. (2006). TRAVOS: Trust and reputation in the context of inaccurate information sources. *Autonomous Agents and Multi-Agent Systems, 12*(2), 183-198.

Vishnumurthy, V., Chandrakumar, S., & Sirer, E.G. (2003). KARMA: A secure economic framework for P2P resource sharing. In *Proceedings of Workshop on the Economics of Peer-to-Peer Systems.*

Weiser, M., & Brown, J.S. (1997). The coming age of calm technology. In *Beyond calculation: The next 50 years of computing* (pp. 75-85). Copernicus.

Yang, B., & Garcia-Molina, H. (2003). PPay: Micropayments for peer-to-peer systems. In S. Jajodia, V. Atluri, & T. Jaeger (Eds.), *Proceedings of the 10th ACM Conference on Computer and Communications Security* (pp. 300-310). ACM.

Zimmermann, P. (1994). *PGP user's guide.* MIT Press.

ADDITIONAL READING

Aberer, K., & Despotovic, Z. (2001). Managing trust in a peer-2-peer information system. In *CIKM '01: Proceedings of the Tenth International Conference on Information and Knowledge Management* (pp. 310-317). New York: ACM Press.

Axelrod, R.M. (1984). *The evolution of cooperation.* Basic Books.

Buchegger, S., & Le Boudec, J.-Y. (2004). A robust reputation system for peer-to-peer and mobile ad-hoc networks. In *Proceedings of P2PEcon2004, Harvard University,* Cambridge, MA.

Dasgupta, P. (2000). Trust as a commodity? In D. Gambetta (Ed.), *Trust: Making and breaking cooperative relations* (pp. 49-72).

Dingledine, R., Freedman, M.J., & Molnar, D. (2000, November). Accountability measures for peer-to-peer systems. In A. Oram (Ed.), *Peer-to-peer: Harnessing the power of disruptive technologies* (pp. 271-340). O'Reilly.

Grandison, T., & Sloman, M. (2000). A survey of trust in Internet applications. *IEEE Communications Surveys and Tutorials, 3*(4).

Grandison, T., & Sloman, M. (2003). Trust management tools for Internet applications. In Proceedings of the First International Conference of Trust Management, *iTrust* 2003, Crete, Greece (LNCS 2692, pp. 91-107). Springer.

Hardin, G. (1968, December). The tragedy of the commons. *Science, 162*(3859), 1243-1248.

Jøsang, A., Ismail, R., & Boyd, C. (2007). A survey of trust and reputation systems for online service provision. *Decision Support Systems, 43*(2), 618-644.

Kinateder, M., Baschny, E., & Rothermel, K. (2005, May). Towards a generic trust model. In *Proceedings of the Third International Conference on Trust Management: iTrust'05;* Rocquencourt, France (pp. 177-192). Springer-Verlag.

Krukow, K., & Twigg, A. (2005). Distributed approximation of fixed-points in trust structures. In *Proceedings of the 25th IEEE International Conference on Distributed Computing Systems (ICDCS'05)* (pp. 805-814). Washington, DC: IEEE Computer Society.

Langheinrich, M. (2003, October). *When trust does not compute – the role of trust in ubiquitous computing.* Workshop on Privacy at Ubicomp 2003, Seattle, Washington.

Levien, R., & Aiken, A. (1998). Attack-resistant trust metrics for public key certification. In *Proceedings of the Seventh USENIX Security Symposium* (Vol. 7, p. 18). Berkeley, CA: USENIX Association.

Lipton, R.J., & Ostrovsky, R. (1998). Micropayments via efficient coin-flipping. In *FC '98: Proceedings of the Second International Conference on Financial Cryptography* (LNCS 1465, pp. 1-15). London: Springer-Verlag.

Luhmann, N. (1979). *Trust and power.* Wiley.

Nixon, P., Wagealla, W., English, C., & Terzis, S. (2004). Security, privacy, and trust issues in smart environments. In D. Cook & S. Das (Eds.), *Smart environments: Technology, protocols and applications* (pp. 249-270). Wiley.

Resnick, P., Kuwabara, K., Zeckhauser, R., & Friedman, E. (2000, December). Reputation systems. *Communications of the ACM, 43*(12), 45-48.

Sabater, J., & Sierra, C. (2005, September). Review on computational trust and reputation models. *Artificial Intelligence Review, 24*(1), 33-60.

Schneider, F.B. (Ed.). (1998). *Trust in cyberspace.* Washington, DC: National Academy Press.

Staab, S., Bhargava, B., Lilien, L., Rosenthal, A., Winslett, M., Sloman, M., et al. (2004). The pudding of trust. *IEEE Intelligent Systems, 19*(5), 74-88.

Wrona, K., & Mähönen, P. (2004). Cooperative and cognitive networks with reputation and trust. *China Telecommunications Journal, 1*(1), 64-75.

Yu, B., & Singh, M. (2001). Towards a probabilistic model of distributed reputation management. In *Proceedings of the 4th Workshop on Deception, Fraud and Trust in Agent Societies,* Montreal, Canada (pp. 125-137).

Section V
Ease–of–Use:
Natural and Multimodal Interaction

Iryna Gurevych
Darmstadt University of Technology, Germany

Max Mühlhäuser
Darmstadt University of Technology, Germany

WHAT IS MULTIMODAL INTERACTION?

Multimodality is the property of ubiquitous computing systems, which supports user interactions with the system involving multiple ways of interacting with the system (also called modalities). Examples of multimodality are voice combined with gesture, handwriting together with typing, audio-visual speech, and so forth. It should be noted that a modality is not equal to the notion of a human sense. It includes the method of interaction based on some human sense and some common engineering platform of a user interface. Often, a pragmatic definition of multimodality is adopted, whereby it is defined as a combination of at least two human senses on the input or the output side, for example, audio-visual output. The main motivation behind designing multimodal ubiquitous computing systems is to improve their accessibility on the input side and their usability on the output side.

Generally speaking, natural and multimodal interaction means great diversity in human computer interaction. It can mean different things to different groups of users in different situations, for example, portable access to multimedia communication, news and entertainment services with the convenience of speech for text entry from everywhere. In mobile contexts, such as in a car, it can mean an integrated dashboard system offering hands-free navigation, entertainment, news, and communications applications. In homes, this is the remote control of the home entertainment center's integrated multimedia player or recorder for television, radio, music, video and games in a living room. Finally, in the office the user can choose how to interact with the computer, for example, using a pen, keyboard, or spoken commands.

WHY IS MULTIMODAL INTERACTION IMPORTANT?

Ubiquitous computing systems usually require *advanced human-computer interaction.* There exist several driving forces central to the design of such systems: (i) making the interaction between users and systems *as natural as possible*, (ii) constraints arising from the *context of usage*, such as limited attention, eyes/hands busy, and (iii) constraints arising from the *devices*, such as cell phones being mouth & ear centric. Therefore, the user should be offered the option of communicating with ubiquitous computing systems using a choice of different *channels of communication.* A channel of communication is *a pathway mediating information* between the user and the system. On the input side, it can involve the user's voice, or a set of input devices such as a keypad, keyboard, mouse or stylus. On the output side, the user can listen to spoken prompts and audio, or to view information on graphical displays.

Improving accessibility means that different groups of users with different abilities can interact with ubiquitous computing systems, which otherwise would not be possible. For example, the technical complexity of devices can be hidden behind a voice (natural language) interface. Thus a user can talk to a ubiquitous computing device, such as a cell phone, in order to use a specific function unfamiliar to her, for example, "can I send a text message now?," rather than use other modalities to find out how to carry out the desired action. Another aspect of improved accessibility is to enable disabled users or users in mobile contexts to use ubiquitous computing systems, which otherwise would not be possible. Special properties of the environment, such as noise or darkness, or particular factors of the workplace, such as thick gloves, may require multimodality for the system to be usable.

On the output side, multimodality can substantially improve the usability of ubiquitous computing systems. For example, the presentation of information can be adapted to the context and the situation of the user, such as her location (in the car, in the kitchen, or in the office), or temporal constraints (during the daytime or at night).

HOW TO CREATE "MULTIMODAL APPLICATIONS?"

In the following, we present some examples of input and output to multimodal systems. As an example framework for developing multimodal applications, the W3C Multimodal Interaction Framework is introduced. Thereafter, we illustrate the information flow in a multimodal application using a sample user-system interaction.

Multimodal ubiquitous computing systems allow the user to provide input in more than one modality and receive output in more than one modality. There exist different classifications of multimodal applications. For example, the input can be classified as sequential, simultaneous, or composite. Sequential input is generated using a single channel of communication, though this channel of communication can change over time. Simultaneous input is generated using several channels of communication at the same time. They are analyzed separately by subsequent processes, such as interpretation. Finally, composite input also uses several channels of communication simultaneously. However, they are treated as a single, composite input in the process of interpretation. In this case, inputs resulting from single modalities are combined using a special fusion component. This component typically utilizes a set of formally encoded constraints or is supported by some reasoning implemented within the dialogue manager.

The output generated by the system can take various forms and can be classified according to communication channels, such as hands/eyes or mouth/ear interaction. In particular, the output can involve:

- audio, including spoken prompts resulting from natural language generation and text-to-speech technologies, or synthesized audio;
- video, for example, XHTML or SVG markup rendered on displays;
- animated agents, that is, multimedia output where an artificial agent is involved whose lip movements are synchronized to render audio information.

For example, SMIL 2.0, Synchronized Multimedia Integration Language (http://www.w3.org/TR/SMIL2/) allows the creation of interactive multimedia presentations. It describes the temporal behaviour of a multimedia presentation; associates hyperlinks with media objects, and specifies the layout of the presentation on a screen.

Figure 1 represents major components of a multimodal system according to the W3C Multimodal Interaction Framework (http://www.w3.org/TR/mmi-framework/). It should be noted that the Multimodal Interaction Framework is not an architecture, since it represents a level of abstraction above it. The framework does not specify how components are allocated to hardware devices and how the communication between them is realized.

Each component encompasses a set of specific functions. The information required by components and the data flowing between them is represented using markup languages, such as EMMA, Extensible MultiModal Annotation Language (http://www.w3.org/TR/emma/). EMMA has been designed to support exchanges of information between multimodal components. *Figure 1* involves input and output channels of communication widely used today and can be extended to include additional modes of communication in the future, as soon as they become available.

The interaction between the user and the system can be separated into different processing steps. Typically, the user's input has to be recorded and recognized by the respective recognition component. For example, speech recognition is the technology employed to convert the acoustic signal into an orthographic representation. In the next step, the interpretation is carried out. During this process, the information collected during the recognition process is translated to an

Figure 1. Major components of a multimodal system

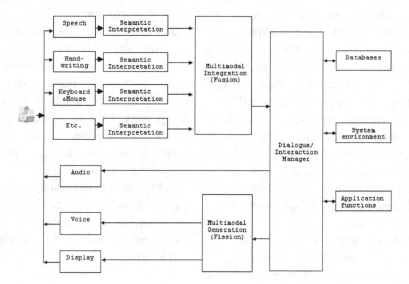

internal semantic representation, for example, by a language understanding component.

Multimodal fusion and fission represents a higher level of quality in the design of multimodal user interfaces. If multiple channels of communication have been employed, the results of their analysis are combined by a multimodal fusion component and are passed to the dialogue manager. The dialogue manager decides on the system's next action, for example, mapping the semantic representation of the input to a database query, and passes the results to a presentation-planning component. A multimodal fission component decides on distributing the output to multiple output channels of communication, if this is appropriate in a given situation, and output is passed to respective generation components, for example, to the text-to-speech component. Then the output of the system is rendered to the user using the chosen modalities in the most appropriate manner.

The interaction between the user and the system can be conceptualized as a series of turns, or a dialogue, managed by a dialogue manager. The dialogue can be based either on natural language or direct manipulation, corresponding to the so-called conversational or model world metaphor. Turn-taking is an important property of the dialogue. In each turn, the user's input is collected, processed to recognize the user's intention, compute a response and present an answer. All these steps are done while considering the context, internal and external knowledge sources. The dialogue manager can employ special algorithms to disambiguate the user's input, deal with uncertainties in the output of the recognition components, and initiate sub-dialogues.

Generally, the dialogues can be classified as directed (either by users, or by the system), mixed-initiative, or natural, that is, free-flow dialogues. Sometimes dialogue managers have a complex structure with multiple distributed components situated at various points of the network, includ-

ing local clients. In such a case, an event-based mechanism can be utilized for communication between distributed components.

To illustrate one possible use of multimodality in a ubiquitous computing system, let us consider a simple example. While driving in the car, the user points to a position on a displayed map and says, "How do I get there?" The system responds by asking the user, "Do you want driving instructions to the central railway station in Darmstadt?" The user confirms this. Consequently, the system computes a route from the user's current position to the railway station in Darmstadt and presents driving instructions on a graphical display and as voice. In *Table 1*, we summarize the actions of the system's components necessary to carry out this dialogue.

BEST PRACTICES TO CREATE NATURAL INTERFACES

When a new interaction technology is introduced, inexperienced developers can design annoying user interfaces. If multiple input and output modalities are combined in a chaotic manner, they can easily become loud, confusing, and annoying and result in poor user performance and dissatisfaction. In order to develop usable and well-accepted multimodal interfaces for ubiquitous computing systems, it is important to consider and follow a set of guidelines, so-called *best practices*. W3C suggests organizing the guidelines into four main principles of user interface design:

1. Satisfy real-world constraints
2. Communicate clearly, concisely, and consistently with users
3. Help users recover quickly and efficiently from errors
4. Make users comfortable

Table 1.

Party/Component	Input	Result
User	points to a position on a map using her finger and utters "How do I get there?"	Tactile and voice input
Speech recognition	maps the acoustic signal to an orthographic representation	A sequence of words "How do I get there?"
Recognition of pen strokes	Maps the tactile input to x-y coordinates of the position that the user has pointed to on a map	x-y coordinates
Language interpretation	Converts the recognized utterance "How do I get there?" into semantic representation	<request-driving-instructions; source-location; target-location>
Pointing interpretation	Converts the recognized x-y coordinates of the position that the user selected into semantic representation, computes railway station in Darmstadt as the most probable target location corresponding to x-y coordinates	<target-location; railway-station-Darmstadt>
Integration component	Integrates semantic representations from language and pointing interpretation components, the word "there" is resolved to the <railway-station-Darmstadt >	<request-driving-instructions; source-location; railway-station-Darmstadt>
Dialogue manager	Requests the user's current position	GPS-request
GPS	Determines the user's current position	x-y coordinates
Dialogue manager	Integrated the user's current position into semantic representation and asks the user for confirmation	<request-driving-instructions; x-y coordinates; railway-station-Darmstadt>
User	Confirms the correct interpretation by uttering "Yes"	Confirmation recognized
Dialogue manager	Converts the semantic representation to a database request, submits the request to the component for computing a route, receives the response and sends it to the presentation component	Semantic representation of the requested route <x-y coordinates; railway-station-Darmstadt>
Presentation component	Determines voice and graphical display as channels of communication available in a given situation and sends the semantic representation to the language and graphical generation components	Semantic representation of the route split to audio and graphical output
Language generation component	Converts the internal representation of the route to a string and uses text-to-speech to present driving instructions	Audio output
Graphical generation component	Converts the internal representation of the route to visual graphics for the user to see and presents driving instructions	Graphical output

A detailed discussion of common sense suggestions for developing multimodal user interfaces can be found in a W3C document (http://www.w3.org/TR/mmi-suggestions/) and in the chapter *on Multimodal and Federated Interaction* of the present book.

RESEARCH AND DEVELOPMENT PROJECTS

In the past, several large research and development projects have been conducted in the area of multimodal interaction. The EU project *COMIC* (http://www.dfki.de/pas/f2w.cgi?iuip/comic-g) aimed at defining generic cognitive models for multimodal interaction. The theoretical motivation behind that is the hypothesis that multimodal human-computer interaction should be modelled after general cognitive models of multimodal interaction between human partners. The approach and research results of the COMIC project were implemented in a system for planning bathrooms featuring a multimodal interface to be used even by untrained users. Channels of communication in COMIC are speech, together with prosodic information, pen input on a display ranging from simple pointing gestures and referencing objects to drawing sketches of the bathroom and handwriting input.

The *SmartKom* project (http://www.smartkom.org/) is another large-scale German project aimed at developing user adaptive and self-explanatory interfaces. In particular, it features the smooth integration and coordinated semantic processing of mutually enhancing input, the robust processing of possibly unspecified, ambiguous or partially incorrect input, context sensitive interpretation of dialogic interaction on the basis of dynamic discourse, output and user models, the adaptive generation of coordinated, multi-modal presentations, the semi or fully automatic completion of delegated tasks through the integration of information services, the intuitive appearance of the interface as a personalized presentation agent, extensive and intuitive help and explanatory functions in dialogue context as well as numerous meta-communicative functions, and the adaptive control of dialogues via user and situation adapted interaction styles. The main difference to the above mentioned COMIC is that the interaction is cooperative, that is, the parties aim at the same goal, whereas the interaction in COMIC is non-cooperative, that is, the parties aim at different goals (the user wants to buy her dream bathroom at a low price, while the system tries to find arguments and suggest more expensive options).

The *EMBASSI* project (http://www.embassi.de) developed an approach to provide users with disabilities with multimodal and personalized access to public information systems. Since such users often have severe problems in operating public terminal systems, a system was built where persons with the disabilities, such as blindness, motor or language-impairment, can operate various terminal systems such as bank terminals, ticket machines or shopping terminals using customized impairment-dependent personal mobile control devices with individual user interface layouts. The content is transmitted wirelessly to the users' personal devices and is displayed using the visual, tactile, or auditory channel of communication. The users' input can be entered via keyboards, speech, or buttons according to the user's personal profile.

In the project *DynAMITE* (http://www.dynamite-project.org), a software framework was developed, which enables intelligent multimodal interaction with distributed network devices within dynamically changing ensembles. For example, coming into a meeting, the mobile device detects all available DynAMITE devices and sets up a spontaneous device ensemble. The interaction and presentation capabilities are coordinated with the additional abilities of other available devices. For example, if a video projector is to be used, the light will be dimmed synchronously. This can be achieved since all devices form an ensemble and cooperate dynamically according to a shared goal and the strategy planned according to it.

STRUCTURE OF PART "NATURAL AND MULTIMODAL INTERACTION"

The part "Natural and Multimodal Interaction" is structured in the following way. The chapter "Mobile Speech Recognition" gives an overview about the main architectures to enable speech recognition on embedded devices, including their characteristic features and properties. The chapter "Mouth and Ear Interaction" gives an overview of the challenges that have to be mastered in ubiquitous computing while working with audio, which is not easy to handle as a medium. The chapter "Advanced Hands and Eyes Interaction" focuses on ambient display interfaces in ubiquitous computing environments in their full range from large projection displays to tiny mobile phone screens and the respective channels of communication with them, such as gestures, space mouse, or sensing user input. The chapter "Intelligent User Interfaces" will explain what makes a human-computer interface intelligent. It presents the main concepts and algorithms for implementing intelligent user interfaces. In the chapter "Multimodal and Federated Interaction," the main attention is devoted to the possibilities of combining different modalities as well as the exploration of the conditions to select a certain kind of multimodality as reasonable for the user. Furthermore, the chapter "Multimodal Software Engineering" concentrates on the issues of software engineering related to the creation of multimodal interfaces for a range of ubiquitous end devices. Finally, the chapter "Ambient Learning and Cooperative Interaction" concludes the extensive discussion of human-centric issues in ubiquitous computing by showing how intelligent environments composed of multiple federated devices can support the easiness and the natural way of human-computer interaction.

SUGGESTED FURTHER READINGS

A lot of useful information about multimodality can be found on the Web pages of the W3C Multimodal Interaction Activity (http://www.w3.org/2002/mmi/). The Multimodal Interaction Working Group was launched in 2002. The Working Group's initial focus was on use cases and requirements. This led to the publication of the W3C Multimodal Interaction Framework, and in turn to work on extensible multi-modal annotations (EMMA), and InkML, an XML language for ink traces. The Working Group has also worked on integration of composite multimodal input, dynamic adaptation to device configurations, modality component interfaces, and current approaches to dialogue management. The Working Group has given rise to a further W3C Working Group on Device Independence (http://www.w3.org/2001/di/), which focuses on access to unified Web from any device in any context by anyone. W3C Working Groups seek to issue recommendations that can be implemented on a royalty-free basis.

More theoretical works in the area of natural and multimodal interfaces can be found in the article by Oviatt (2003) and Popesku and Burdea (2002).

REFERENCES

Oviatt, S. (2003). Multimodal interfaces. In J. Jacko & A. Sears (Eds.), *The human-computer interaction handbook: Fundamentals, evolving technologies and emerging applications* (pp. 286-304). Mahwah, NJ: Lawrence Erlbaum.

Popescu, V., & Burdea, G. (2002). Multimodal interaction modeling. In K.M. Stanney (Ed.), *Handbook of virtual environments*. Mahwah, NJ: Lawrence Erlbaum Assoc.

Chapter XVII
Mobile Speech Recognition

Dirk Schnelle
Technische Universität Darmstadt, Germany

ABSTRACT

This chapter gives an overview of the main architectures for enabling speech recognition on embedded devices. Starting with a short overview of speech recognition, an overview of the main challenges for the use on embedded devices is given. Each of the architectures has its own characteristic problems and features. This chapter gives a solid basis for the selection of an architecture that is most appropriate for the current business case in enterprise applications.

OVERVIEW

Voice-based interaction is a common requirement for ubiquitous computing (UC). However, the idea of having speech recognition on wearable devices is not simply copying the recognizer to such a device and running it. The limitations of the device, especially computational power and memory, pose strong limitations that cannot be handled by desktop size speech recognizers. This chapter gives a brief overview of the different architectures employed to support speech recognition on wearable devices. A background in speech recognition technology is helpful in order to understand them better, but is not required. At some points you will be provided with pointers to the literature to achieve a better understand-

ing. A detailed understanding of the available architectures is needed to select the appropriate architecture for the enterprise, if it wants to support audio-based applications for mobile workers. The selection process has to consider the available resources, such as servers, wireless network, the software that has already been bought in order to save the investment, and to be able to justify the decision to invest more money in required infrastructure.

Most of the figures use UML 2.0 as a means of communicating architectural descriptions. The diagrams are easy to read, even if the reader is not familiar with this modeling language. The UML specification can be obtained from the Object Management Group (OMG, 2006).

Figure 1. Speech recognition

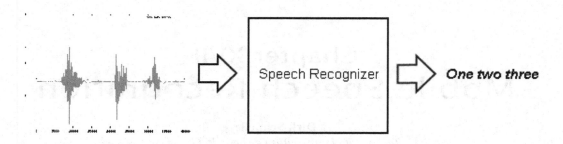

Figure 2. General architecture of a speech recognizer

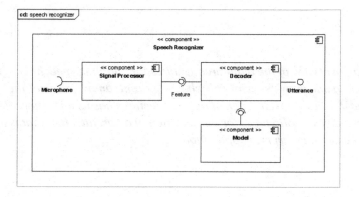

A speech recognizer has the task of transcribing spoken language into a text (see Figure 1). The input is the *speech signal,* the human voice that is recorded, for example, with a microphone. The textual output, in this case *"one two three,"* is called an *utterance.*

The architecture of a speech recognizer has not changed over the past decades. It is illustrated in Figure 2 based on Jelinek (2001).

It comprises the main components of recognizers as they are used today, regardless of the technology used. They are available as pure software solutions or implemented in hardware to gain speed. In the following sections we focus only on the main components involved. Some recognizers may use additional components or components that are slightly different. However, the architectures presented show the main functionalities of each of them and discuss the main challenges that have to be faced when applied to mobile devices.

The *signal processor* generates real valued vectors σ_i from a speech signal, obtained from a microphone. They are also called feature vectors. Currently, most speech recognizers use at least 13 features in each vector. We will have a closer look at them in the section "Evaluation of Sphinx 3.5." Normally computation of the features happens at regular intervals, that is, every 10msec., where the feature vectors are passed to the *decoder* to convert it into the utterance. The *decoder* uses the *model* for decoding. In the simplest case, the *model* contains a set of prototypes ρ_j, which are of the same kind as σ_i. Then, the *decoder* finds the ρ_i closest to σ_i for a given distance function d

$$a_i = \min_{j=1}^{k} d(\sigma_i, \rho_j) \qquad (1)$$

a_i is the acoustic symbol for σ_i, which is emitted to the rest of the recognizer for further processing.

For **word-based speech recognizers** these acoustic symbols are the single words. For the example shown in Figure 1, this would be the concatenation of $\{a_1=one, a_2=two, a_3=three\}$.

A **phoneme-based speech recognizer** would output a concatenation of phonemes for each word. Phonemes are small sound units. The word *this* comprises the following phonemes $\{a_2=TH, a_2=I, a_2=is, a_2=S\}$. Obviously this output requires some post processing to obtain an output comparable to word-based recognizers that can be used by an application.

The benefit of phoneme-based speech recognizers is that they are generally more accurate, since they reduce the decoding problem to small sound units, and that they are more flexible and can handle a larger vocabulary more easily. Remember the first attempts in writing, starting from symbols for each word over symbols for each syllable to the letters that we find today.

This chapter is organized as follows: the section "Speech Recognition on Embedded Devices" gives an overview about the limitations of embedded devices to address speech recognition functionality. Then the two main architectures to work around these limitations are presented, which will be discussed in the two following sections in more detail. The section "Parameters of Speech Recognizers in UC" names some aspects that

are needed to rate the solutions presented in the section "Service Dependent Speech Recognition" and the section "Device Inherent Speech Recognition." The section "Future research directions" concludes this chapter with a summary and an overview of the required computational resources on the device and the server for the architectures discussed.

SPEECH RECOGNITION ON EMBEDDED DEVICES

Speech recognition is computationally expensive. Advances in computing power made speech recognition possible on off-the-shelf desktop PCs beginning in the early 1990s. Mobile devices do not have that computing power and speech recognizers do not run in real time. There are even more limitations, which will be discussed later in this section. Moore's law states that memory size and computational performance increase by a factor of two every 18 months.

Frostad (2003) writes:

"Most of what is written on speech is focused on server based speech processing. But there is another speech technology out there that's powerful enough to sit on a stamp-sized microchip. It's called "embedded speech." Advances in computing power gave server side speech the power boost it needed in the early 90s. Now that same rocket fuel is launching embedded speech into the limelight."

Although computing power is increasing on these smaller computers, making it possible to run a small recognizer, performance is still not efficient enough to enable speech recognizers off-the-shelf on such devices. The attempt to use speech recognition on a mobile device, such as a computer of PDA size or a mobile phone, encounters the same problems that were faced on desktop PCs years ago and which have been solved by the growth of computing power. The following section gives an overview of these limitations.

Limitations of Embedded Devices

The development of all applications, especially speech recognition applications for embedded devices has to tackle several problems, which arise as a result of the computational limitations and hardware resources on the device. These limitations are:

- **Memory:** Storage Capacity on embedded devices, such as a PDA or a cell phone, is very limited. This makes it impossible to have large *models*.
- **Computational Power:** Although the computational power of embedded devices has grown continuously over the last few years, it is still far from that what is available on desktop size PCs. The *signal processor* and the *decoder* perform computationally intense tasks.
- **Power Consumption:** Battery lifetime is a scarce resource on embedded devices. The device will stop working if the battery is empty. Since speech recognition is computationally intensive, processing consumes a lot of energy.
- **Floating Point:** Most processors for PDAs, like the Strong ARM or XScale processor, do not support floating-point arithmetic. It has to be emulated by fixed-point arithmetic, which is much slower than direct support. The value vectors σ_i are real valued and most state-of-the-art recognizers work with statistical methods. Thus, support of floating point arithmetic is essential and emulation results in loss of speed. Moreover, this may lead to a loss of precision. Especially signal processing is a critical task, since the quality of the output has a direct impact on the preserved information. Jelinek (2001) states

that "Bad processing means loss of information: There is less of it to extract."

In the following the approaches to work around these limitations will be discussed. A short overview of the technology used is given to understand how they cope with the challenges of embedded devices.

Main Architectures for Speech Recognition on Embedded Devices

Progress in speech recognition has made it possible to have it on embedded devices. Cohen (2004) states that, "Although we did not know in the 1990s all of the tricks we know today, we can use 1990s-like computing resources ... to good advantage to compute a task which would have been difficult in 1990, but is simpler today because of our technical advancements." However, the limitations of mobile devices that were mentioned in the previous section still pose a lot of challenges. There have been several attempts to deal with them and enable speech recognition on embedded devices. An overview of these approaches is given in the following sections. We concentrate on the most common approaches that can be divided into two main categories:

- Service dependent speech recognition, Figure 3(a)
- Device inherent speech recognition, Figure 3(b)

The main difference between these two architectures is the node where the *speech recognizer* component is deployed. Architectures for service dependent speech recognition will be introduced in the section "Service Dependent Speech Recognition" and those for device inherent speech recognition in the section "Device Inherent Speech Recognition."

Zaykovskiy (2006) proposed another categorization. He distinguishes:

Figure 3. Deployment of voice enabled service usage with mobile devices

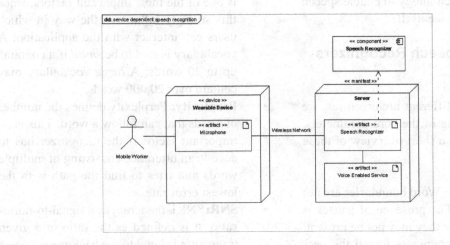

(a) Service dependent speech recognition

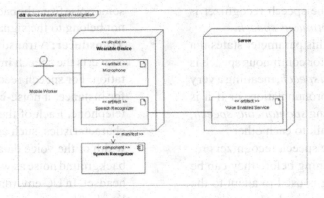

(b) Device inherent speech recognition

- Client,
- Client-server, and
- Server-based architectures.

The main reason for his differentiation is the location of the *signal Processor* and the *decoder*. In the service-oriented view of ubiquitous computing it makes more sense to emphasize the ability to have speech recognition as a network service or as an independent functionality of the

device itself. This is a fundamental fact in smart environments, where services can be inaccessible while the user is on the move. Bailey (2004) requires that "there need to be clear boundaries between the functionality of the device, and the functionality of the network." The technological orientation of these approaches confirms this differentiation. Whereas service dependent speech recognition deal with APIs for remote access to a speech recognizer, device inherent speech recognition uses the techniques of desktop size speech recognition technology to enable speech recognition on the device itself.

Parameters of Speech Recognizers in UC

In order to rate the different architectures, we need an understanding of the core parameters. This section will give a short overview of these parameters.

- **Speaking Mode:** Word boundaries are not easy to detect. The presence of pauses is not enough, since they may not be present. Early speech recognizers forced the user to pause after each word. This is called *isolated word* recognition. If there are no such constraints, the speech recognizer is able to process *continuous speech*.

- **Speaking Style:** This parameter states if a speech recognizer for continuous speech is able to process *read speech*, meaning a very precise and clear pronunciation, or if it is capable of processing *spontaneous speech*, as used when we talk to each other.

- **Enrollment:** Some speech recognizers require an initial training before they can be used. This training is used to adapt to the speaker in order to achieve higher accuracy. These recognizers are called *speaker dependent*. This concept is often used on desktop PCs, but is also possible in UC, where the device is personalized. The opposite case is *speaker independent* speech recognizers that are trained to work with multiple speakers. Thus they have a lower accuracy. This concept is used, for example, in telephony applications. There are only a few scenarios that really require speaker independence with embedded devices. For these applications, speaker-independent systems do not have an advantage over speaker-dependent systems, but can benefit from a better accuracy.

- **Vocabulary:** The size of the vocabulary is one of the most important factors, since this strongly influences the way in which users can interact with the application. A vocabulary is said to be *small* if it contains up to 20 words. A *large* vocabulary may contain over 20,000 words.

- **Perplexity:** Perplexity defines the number of words that can follow a word. This is an important factor if the recognizer has to decode an utterance consisting of multiple words and tries to find the path with the lowest error rate.

- **SNR:** SNR is the acronym of signal-to-noise-ratio. It is defined as the ratio of a given transmitted signal to the background noise of the transmission medium. This typically happens where the microphone also captures some noise from the background, which does not belong to the signal to decode.

- **Transducer:** A transducer is the device that converts the speech into a digital representation. For speech recognition this may be, for instance, a noise-cancelling headset or telephone. Each of them features different characteristics, such as the available bandwidth of the voice data or the ability to cut background noise as with a noise cancelling headset. In UC environments noise-cancelling headsets are typically used.

In a UC world there are some additional parameters depending on the location, where recognition takes place. These parameters, as presented in Bailey (2004) are:

- **Network Dependency:** One major aspect is the dependency on a network resource. A recognizer located on the device will not need any network to be operated, while a recognizer streaming raw audio data to a server (see the section "Audio Streaming") will not work without a network. Apart from the technical aspect, the user expects the device to work and may not be able to distinguish between a non-functional recognizer and missing network connectivity if the device is "broken."

- **Network Bandwidth:** Available network bandwidth is a scarce resource. Architectures performing recognition on the device have a more compact representation of the data that has to be transmitted than those architectures streaming pure audio data.
- **Transmission Degradation:** With the need to transmit data from the mobile device to a server, the problem of transmission degradation arises. Failures, loss of packets or corrupted packets while transmitting the data means a loss of information. If the raw audio is transmitted to a server, recognition accuracy goes down.
- **Server Load:** In a multi-user scenario it is important that the application scales with an increasing number of users.
- **Integration and Maintenance:** Embedded devices are hard to maintain, especially if parts of the functionality are implemented in hardware. A server, on the other hand, is easy to access and bug fixes are available for all clients at once. This issue goes in a similar

direction to the discussion of centralized server architectures versus rich clients.

- **Responsiveness:** A must for speech recognition is that the result is available in real time. This means that the result of the recognition process must be available as fast as possible.

In the following sections the different architectures will be characterized according to these parameters.

SERVICE DEPENDENT SPEECH RECOGNITION

The architectures presented in this section have in common that they require network connectivity to work.

Audio Streaming

An immediate idea to solve the performance bottleneck on embedded devices is not to perform the recognition process on the device itself. A general model of the recognizer, shown in Figure 4, uses the audio recording capabilities of the

Figure 4. Architecture of an audio streaming speech recognizer

embedded device as a microphone replacement to record the raw audio as the input for the *signal processor*.

The audio is streamed over the wireless network, for example, Wi-Fi or Bluetooth, to the *signal processor* on a server. This allows the use of a full-featured recognizer with a large vocabulary running on the server. A disadvantage of this solution is that a stable wireless network connection is required. Another disadvantage is a possibly very large amount of data streamed over the network. Since recognition is not performed on the embedded device, we have all the benefits of a desktop-size speech recognizer at the cost of high network traffic.

MRCP

Since server side speech recognition is mainly an immediate idea, developers tend to implement this architecture on their own using a proprietary protocol, which makes it unusable with other applications that do not know anything about that proprietary protocol. In addition, real time issues are generally not considered which can result in

misrecognition. A standard for server side speech recognition that has been adopted by industry is MRCP. MRCP is an acronym for **m**edia **r**esource **c**ontrol **p**rotocol. It was jointly developed by Cisco Systems, Nuance Communications and Speechworks and was published by the IETF as an RFC (Shanmugham, 2006).

MRCP is designed as an API to enable clients control media processing resources over a network to provide a standard for audio streaming. Media processing resources can be speech recognizers, text-to-speech engines, fax, signal detectors and more. This allows for a use in distributed environments, for example, a small device that accesses a recognizer on the network.

The specification is based on RTSP in Schulzrinne (1998), the **r**eal **t**ime **s**treaming **p**rotocol, as a MIME-type the **M**ultipurpose **I**nternet **M**ail **E**xtension. MIME is used to support, for example, no-text attachments in e-mail messages. RTSP defines requests, responses, and events needed to control the media processing resources. The protocol itself is text based. Mechanisms for the reliable exchange of binary data are left to protocols like SIP, the **S**ession **I**nitiation **P**rotocol,

Figure 5. Simplified view on MRCP requests for ASR and TTS

(a) MRCP ASR request

(b) MRCP TTS request

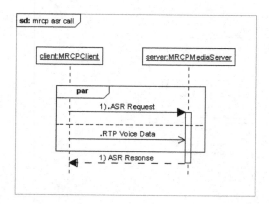

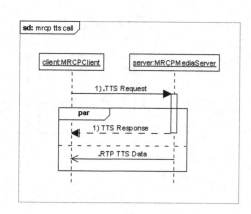

or RTSP. SIP enables control of sessions such as Internet telephone calls.

A media server that can be accessed by RTSP mechanisms controls all resources, in this case, recognizer and synthesizer.

Figure 5 shows a simplified view on the messages that are exchanged in an **a**utomatic **s**peech **r**ecognition (ASR) request and a **t**ext-**t**o-**s**peech (TTS) request.

In an *ASR request*, the MRCP client initiates the request and delivers the voice data via RTP in parallel. The recognition process is executed on the *MRCP Media Server* and the result of the recognition is delivered to the client as the *ASR Response*.

In a *TTS request*, the MRCP client initiates the request. The *MRCP Media Server* answers with a *TTS response* and delivers the synthesized voice data via RTP in parallel.

Figure 6. Architecture of a distributed speech recognizer

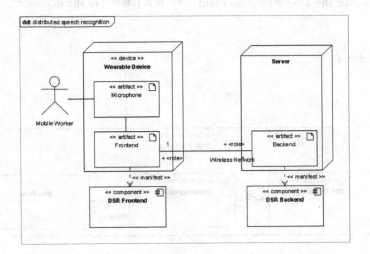

Figure 7. DSR front-end

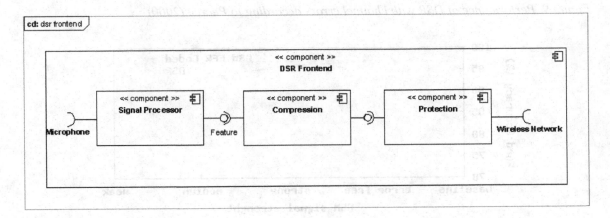

Distributed Speech Recognition

Another possibility to enable speech recognition on mobile devices uses an architectural compromise. Since full-featured recognizers are hard to implement on embedded devices and streaming of raw audio data produces too much network traffic, ETSI, the European Telecommunication Standard Institute, introduced a solution to perform parts of the recognition process on the device and the rest is handled on a server. This architecture is called *Distributed Speech Recognition* (DSR). Pearce (2000) named the component, which is deployed on the device the *DSR Front-end* and

the component deployed on the server the *DSR Backend*. This concept is shown in Figure 6.

An obvious point for such splitting is the separation of *signal processor* and *decoder*. Instead of sending all the audio over the network, the feature vectors ρ_i are computed on the embedded device and sent to the *decoder* on a server. In order to reduce the amount of data and to ensure a secure transmission, the data is compressed and a CRC value is added. The architecture of the DSR Front-end is shown in Figure 7.

The DSR Backend, shown in Figure 8, checks the CRC value and decompresses the data before it is passed to the *decoder*.

Figure 8. DSR backend

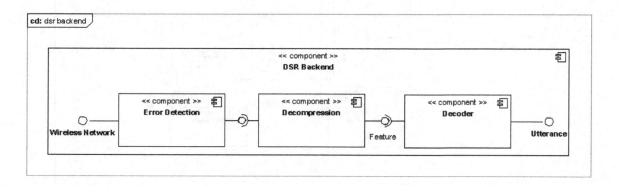

Figure 9. Performance of DSR with channel errors according to Pearce (2000)

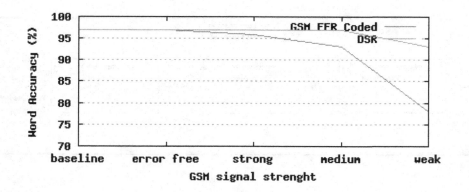

In this way, the computational capabilities of the device are used for the tasks of the *signal processor* in the *DSR Front-end*, whereas the *decoder* and the *model* reside on the server in the *DSR Backend*. The architecture is a result of discussion between multiple companies, that is, Nokia and Motorola in the Aurora project. The data exchange of DSR Frontend and DSR Backend is standardized by ETSI. This specification includes the features used, CRC check and their compression. Compared to pure audio streaming, the transmitted data is reduced without much loss of information. This also means that the error rates in transmission are reduced. As a positive

consequence, DSR also works with lower signal strength, as shown in Figure 9.

The experiment was conducted in the Aurora project and is described in more detail in Pearce (2000). The figure shows the recognition performance of DSR compared to a mobile speech channel. The measurement proves that recognition still works with lower signal quality. A great advantage of this technology over streaming solutions like audio streaming or MRCP is the reduced network traffic. Like MRCP it defines a standard, but with less acceptance. Speech recognition can be used in various environments, as long as they are compliant to the DSR standard. Unlike MRCP it relies on computation on the device, decreasing its chances of being established in a company's network in contrast to a pure protocol. Again, the recognition has all the features of a desktop size recognizer.

As a negative point, the set of feature vectors is a compromise. This also means that other or additional features used in specific recognizers cannot be transmitted using this technology.

ETSI promises a better use of available resources and better transmission. The following section gives some insight into the computational requirements.

Evaluation of Sphinx 3.5

Sphinx is an open source speech recognizer from Carnegie Mellon University. It was DARPA funded and was used in many research projects in speech recognition.

Figure 10. Profile information of Sphinx 3.5 phases according to Mathew (2002)

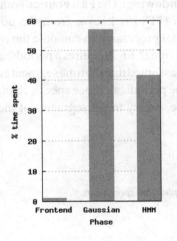

Figure 11. Front-end processing

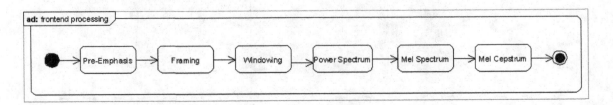

The anatomy of Sphinx can be divided into three phases:

1. Front-end processing,
2. Gaussian probability estimation, and
3. Hidden Markov evaluation.

The Gaussian phase and the HMM phase are part of the *decoder*. A closer look at it is given in the section "Hidden Markov Models." Mathew (2002) gives an overview of the time that Sphinx 3.5 spends on each phase (see Figure 10).

Obviously, the front-end processing constitutes the smallest part of the computation to be performed. This shows that this is an ideal candidate to be performed by smaller devices, as it is done with DSR. Consequently, Mathew et al. (2000) consider it to be not worthy of further investigation, stopping their analysis at this point. They focus more on the optimization of the latter two phases.

Front-end processing usually comprises the computational steps shown in Figure 11.

The following paragraphs show how these steps are handled in Sphinx. A more general view can be found in the literature, for example, in Schukat-Talamazzini (1995).

Processing starts with a speech signal, as captured, for example, from a microphone. An example of such a speech signal is shown as the input to the speech recognizer in . The transformation into a digital representation, also called *quantization*, means also a loss of information, but this can not be avoided.

*   **Pre-Emphasis:** In this step the quantized signal is filtered. This step becomes necessary from the observation that the signal is weaker in higher frequencies, which can be solved using a digital high-pass filter. Figure 12 shows an example of the speech signal and the effect of this filtering step.
*   **Framing:** The input signal is divided into overlapping frames of N samples. The frame shift interval, that is, the difference between the starting points of consecutive frames, is M samples.
*   **Windowing:** The Fast Fourier Transformation (FFT) is known from the domain of signal processing to compute the spectrum of a signal. FFT requires a periodical signal, it is assumed that the time segment continues to be periodical. Since speech changes over time, we try to get segments of the signal,

Figure 12. Pre-emphasis of the speech signal

(a) Quantized speech signal

(b) Pre-emphasized speech signal

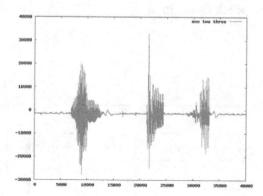

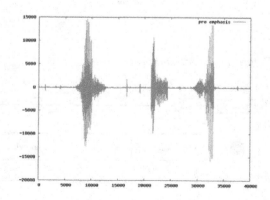

Figure 13. Framing

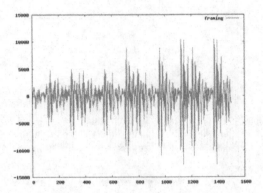

Figure 14. Windowing

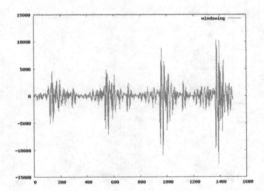

Figure 15. Power spectrum

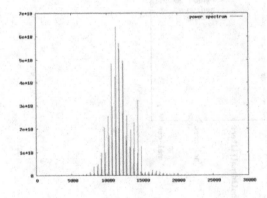

where it can be considered to be constant. These time segments last from 5-30 ms. An example for such a windowing function is the *Hamming Window*. The following figure shows four such time segments of the utterance. It is noticeable that the signal is smoothed to the borders of the time segments.

- **Power Spectrum:** For speech recognition, the discrete case of the FFT, the **d**iscrete **f**ourier **t**ransformation (DFT) is used. The output of the DFT usually consists of a power of 2 of complex numbers. The power spectrum is computed by the squared magnitude

Figure 16. Mel filter

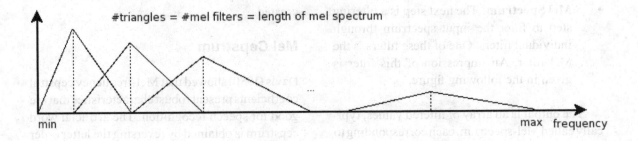

#triangles = #mel filters = length of mel spectrum

Figure 17. Mel-Spectrum

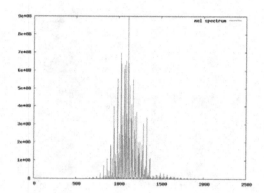

Figure 18. Mel cepstrum

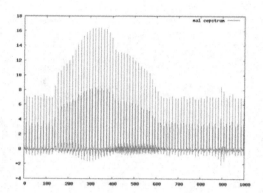

Figure 19. Profile information of sphinx 3.5 front-end

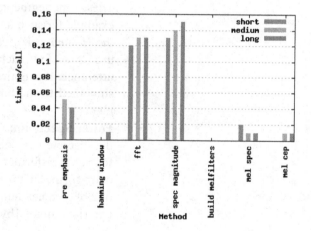

of these complex numbers. The following figure shows the power spectrum for the word *one* of the utterances.

- **Mel Spectrum:** The next step is a filtering step to filter the input spectrum through individual filters. One of these filters is the Mel filter. An impression of this filter is given in the following figure.

The output is an array of filtered values, typically called Mel-spectrum, each corresponding to

the result of filtering the input spectrum through an individual filter. Therefore, the length of the output array is equal to the number of filters created.

Mel Cepstrum

Davis (1980) showed that Mel-frequency cepstral coefficients present robust characteristics that are good for speech recognition. The artificial word cepstrum is obtained by reversing the letter order in the spectrum to emphasize that this is an inverse transformation. These cepstral coefficients are computed via a discrete cosine transform.

Sphinx uses 16-bit raw audio data as input and produces 13 cepstral parameters as output for each time segment. In order to determine the execution time consumption by individual parts of Sphinx, we used a profiling tool to get detailed information on functions and routines on a Sparc processor-based platform. The profiling was done with three audio files of different lengths as input:

- Short (2.05 sec),
- Medium (6.02 sec), and
- Long (30.04 sec).

The profiling result is shown in Figure 19.

Obviously, the computation of the power spectrum, which comprises the methods fft and spec magnitude, consumes most of the time. Both are part of the power spectrum computation. Tuning this method can speed up the computation a great deal. Alternatively, it can be replaced by a hardware solution, such as a **d**igital **s**ignal **p**rocessor (DSP). This issue will also be addressed in the section "Hardware-Based Speech Recognition."

The process becomes more complicated if the device does not support floating-point operations. Junqua (2001) mentions, "While most automatic speech recognition systems for PC use are based on floating-point algorithms, most of the processors used in embedded systems are fixed-point processors. With fixed-point processors there is only a finite amount of arithmetic precision available, causing an inevitable deviation from the original design." A study by Delaney (2002) showed that for Sphinx 2 a StrongARM simulator spent over 90% of the time on the floating-point emulation. These results can be transferred to Sphinx 3.5, since they use the same code base for front-end processing.

A way in which to solve these issues is to substitute floating-point arithmetic by fixed-point arithmetic. This is done using scaled integers to perform basic math functions. The scaling factor, that is, the location of the decimal point, must be known in advance and requires careful decision. For adding two numbers, the number n of bits after the decimal point must line up. A multiplication of two numbers yields a number with $2n$ bits after the decimal point.

Unfortunately, this also means a loss of information and the risk of overflowing the register size of 32 bits. This is especially important for the computation of the power spectrum and the Mel-spectrum. Delaney (2002) suggests changing the computation for the Mel-spectrum using a square root to compute the Mel coefficients. It is guaranteed that the square root results in small values, which means that the result of multiplication is small. They also suggest storing the Mel coefficients in a lookup table to avoid the computationally complex calculations of the square root. An experiment conducted in Huggins (2005) showed that feature extraction on a Sharp Zaurus had a 2.7-fold gain in speed using this method. The loss in precision for the result in computing the Mel Cepstrum increased from 9.73% to 10.06%.

DEVICE INHERENT SPEECH RECOGNITION

In contrast to the architectures described above, those described in this section are handled on the device only, without the need for a server or service from the network. These architectures are also often referred to as *software-only* and *embedded* architectures (Eagle, 1999; Frostad, 2003). Embedded architectures require the existence of a dedicated DSP. They reside as hardware-based speech recognition, since the term *embedded* is totally overloaded with the meanings of a DSP, an embedded device or embedded into an application. So this architecture does not deal only with software-based architectures, but also include partial or full support with hardware.

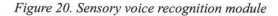

Figure 20. Sensory voice recognition module

Hardware-Based Speech Recognition

Some manufacturers offer designated chips for mobile devices. An example of such a chip is shown in Figure 20.

The technology that is used in these chips differs. All software-based speech technologies for device inherent speech recognition, as described in the following sections, can be found implemented as a port to a DSP. It is even possible to replace just certain parts of the recognizer, that is, the FFT computation for the feature extraction in DSR, with a hardware solution. The main advantage is that a hardware-based solution does not have the runtime problems of software-based approaches, since the hardware is designed to address this specific problem. This is gained at the cost of less flexibility. The range of hardware implementations is as broad as the underlying technology. It starts from a fixed vocabulary used in toys through dynamic time warping, the technology used in most mobile phones, up to programmable DSPs like the sensory chip shown in.

Advantages and drawbacks of these solutions are not discussed in this section, since they are inherited from the technology used. Benefits and drawbacks of the architectures are discussed in the corresponding sections.

Dynamic Type Warping

One of the earliest approaches of enabling speech recognition is the dynamic time warping (DTW). The architecture is shown in Figure 21.

Figure 21. Dynamic time warping

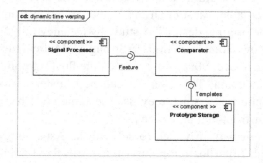

The *signal processor* is responsible for the feature analysis of the raw speech signal. The computational steps are the same as the front-end processing of DSR (see). An output of the feature analysis component is a feature vector of a test utterance $\sigma = (\sigma_1,..., \sigma_n)^T$ which is compared in the *comparator*, which replaces the *decoder*, with all reference feature vectors $\rho_i = (\rho_{i,1},..., \rho_{i,m})^T$ stored in the *prototype* storage, replacing the *model* of the utterances ρ_i in the set of trained utterances with the help of a distance function $d(\sigma_i, \rho_j)$ that was already mentioned in the section "Overview." Usually the prototypes are gained in a single recording. The features of this recording are computed, stored in the *prototype storage* and associated with the output. If the distance of the currently spoken word to the template is too big $d(\sigma_i, \rho_j) > \mu$, it is likely that no prototype matches the utterance. In this case, the comparator rejects the input.

The problem of calculating the distance from σ_i to ρ_j with the help of a distance function $d(\sigma_i, \rho_j)$ consists of two parts:

1. Definition of a distance function to calculate the distance of two related feature vectors
2. Definition of a time warping function to define a relationship between the elements of σ_i and ρ_j

Multiple distance functions exist and are used. For a Gaussian distribution, Mahalanobis distance is used. Since this is complex and we do not have many computational resources on the device, Euclidean distance is more common. This requires that the features be normalized to unity variance.

The problem with a pairwise distance calculation is that it is unlikely that the lengths of the template and of the input are the same, that is, the length of the *o* in *word* may vary. DTW uses dynamic programming to find an optimal match between two sequences of feature vectors allowing for stretching and compression of sections [see Sakoe (1990)]. The template word having the least distance is taken as a correct match, if its value is smaller than a predetermined threshold value μ.

The technique of comparison with a template word makes this an ideal candidate for isolated word recognition with a small vocabulary, but unsuitable for continuous speech. Since the templates are generally taken in a single recording, DTW is also speaker dependent with little computational effort. The computational requirements are slightly higher than those for DSR, see the section "Distributed Speech Recognition," but lower than those for hidden Markov models (see next section), or artificial neural networks, see the section "Artificial Neural Networks."

Figure 22. Architecture of a HMM-based recognizer

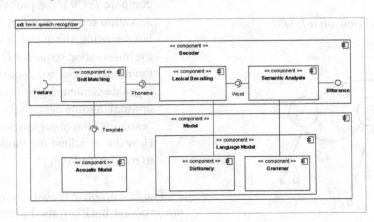

Hidden Markov Models

Most modern speech recognizers are based on hidden Markov models (HMM). An overview of the architecture of a HMM based recognizer is shown in Figure 22, which is in fact a phoneme-based recognizer.

It is also possible to use HMM-based recognition for word-based models. In this case, the architecture is slightly different, as Schukat-Talamazzini (1995) points out. More about the basics of Markov chains and their use can be obtained from the literature, for example, Rabiner (1989). Although this approach is very old, it is still the most successful approach for speech recognition.

Instead of using the computed features as a seed for the states, most recognizers use vector quantization (VQ) to reduce the data rate. Since speech recognition deals with a continuous signal, a certain amount of data arrives periodically. This is called the *data rate*. Since HMM decoding is time consuming, a lower data rate promises real time performance. Furthermore, the storage size is reduced, since only the codebook is stored instead of the cepstral parameters. A *codebook* stores the mapping of the feature vectors as they are computed from the speech signal to a discrete label. Thus the codebook is a discrete representation of the continuous speech data.

Figure 23. Schematic view on a HMM

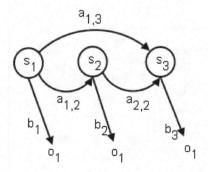

Unit Matching

HMMs are the core of the *unit matching* component. They are described as a tuple $\lambda = (S, A, B, \pi, V)$ with

- $S = \{s_1,..., s_n\}$ representing a set of states,
- $A = \{a_{i,j}\}$ representing a matrix of transition probabilities, where $a_{i,j}$ denotes the probability $p(s_j, s_i)$ for the transition from state s_i to s_j,
- $B = \{b_1,..., b_n\}$ representing a set of output probabilities, where $b_i(x)$ denotes the probability $q(x|s_i)$ to observe x in state s_i and
- O as a set of observations, which means the domain of b_i.

A schematic view on a HMM is given in the following figure.

The probability of observing an output sequence $O = O_1 O_2 ... O_r$ is given by

$$P(O = O_1 O_2 ... O_r) = \sum_{\{s_1, s_2, ... s_T\}} \prod_{i=1}^{T} p(s_i \mid s_{i-1}) q(x_i \mid s_{i-1})$$

(2)

Rabiner (1989) raises three basic questions that are to be solved for speech recognition with HMMs.

1. Given the observation sequence $O = O_1 O_2 ... O_r$ and a model λ, how do we efficiently compute $P(O|\lambda)$, the probability of the observation sequence, given the model?
2. For decoding, the question to solve is, given the observation sequence $O = O_1 O_2 ... O_r$ and the model λ how we choose a corresponding state sequence $Q = q_1, q_2, ... q_T$, which is optimal in some meaningful sense (i.e., best "explains" the observations)?
3. How do we adjust the model parameters λ to maximize $P(O|\lambda)$?

The first problem is also known as the *evaluation problem*, but it can also be treated as a *scoring problem*. In that case, the solution to this problem allows us to choose the model that best explains the observations.

The third problem tries to optimize the model parameters to describe a given observation sequence as well as possible. This optimization can be used to *train* the model. Training means to adapt the model parameters to observed training data.

The most important one for speech recognition is the second problem, since it tries to find the *correct* state sequence.

A well-known approach to this is the Viterbi algorithm, based on dynamic programming (DP) to find the most likely sequence of hidden states. A more detailed description, related to speech recognition, can be found in the literature, for example, Rabiner (1989) and Jelinek (2001). The Viterbi algorithm tries to find the best score, which means the highest probability, along a single path at time *t*, also known as *trellis*.

Computational Optimization

The Viterbi algorithm is computationally intensive, especially for larger vocabularies. It requires roughly $|A_u|$ multiplications and additions, where $|A_u|$ is the number of transitions in the model (Bahl, 1993). In order not to search the entire Viterbi trellis, the number of branch-out search candidates can be limited using beam-search, as Lowerre (1976) points out.

The idea is to eliminate all states from the trellis that have a probability above a certain threshold, which depends on the maximum probability of the states at this stage. This reduces the number of states without affecting the values, if the threshold is appropriately chosen.

Novak et al. (2003) suggest an even more aggressive pruning with their two-pass strategy. Instead of using the probabilities directly, they convert them to probabilities based on their rank. Thus, the probability space is bounded and the

values of the best and worst state output probabilities remain the same for each time frame. Instead of computing the output probabilities, they simply take a single value from the tail of the ranked probability distribution. This is based on the approach described in Bahl et al. (1993) where the authors claim a speedup by a factor of 100.

There are many more attempts to simplify the computational effort of Viterbi search. Most of them try to replace multiplications by additions, which are faster to compute (Ming, 2003). Usually these attempts increase speed at the cost of accuracy and/or memory demands.

Lexical Decoding and Semantic Analysis

The result of the unit matching is a scoring for the different recognition hypotheses. The next two steps help to determine the word chain with the highest probability with respect to the constraints imposed by the language model. For word-based recognition with HMMs, the recognition process is finished at this point.

In the *lexical decoding* phase those paths are eliminated that do not have an existing word in the dictionary. In an alternative approach, using a so-called *statistical grammar*, the sequences are reduced a couple of phonemes in a row, for example, trigrams. The output of the latter case is a list of trigrams, ordered according to their probability. This is not suitable for isolated word recognition. The next step is *syntactic analysis*, where those paths are eliminated that do not match an allowed sequence of words from the dictionary.

These steps do not require intensive computation except for fast memory access to the dictionary and the grammar. Again, smaller vocabularies offer a faster result and require less memory.

The word or utterance with the highest probability in the remaining list of possible utterances is taken as the recognition output.

HMM-based recognition is computationally intensive, but shows good results in isolated word recognition as well as continuous speech. If the HMM is trained well, it is also a suitable technology for speaker independent recognition.

Artificial Neural Networks

Artificial neural networks (ANN) is a method in computer science that is derived from the way the human brain works. The goal is to create a system that is able to learn and that can be used for pattern classification. More detailed information about ANN is given in the chapter "Socionics & Bionics: Learning from 'The Born.'" The use of ANN for classification and their use in speech recognition can be found in the literature, for example, Cholet (1999).

Expectations were very high when ANNs were discovered as a means for speech recognition. Modelling of speech recognition by artificial neural networks doesn't require *a priori* knowledge of the speech process and this technique quickly became an attractive alternative to HMM (Amrouche, 2006).

Neural nets tend to be better than HMMs for picking out discrete words, but they require extensive training up front [see Kumagai (2002)].

An output of an artificial neuron (see the chapter *"Socionics & Bionics: Learning from 'The Born'"*) in multi-layer perceptron (MLP) networks is computed via

$$f_z = \sum_{i=1}^{n} w_i x_i \tag{3}$$

There is nearly no optimization to reduce the large amount of calculations that have to be done to compute the output of a complex multilayer perceptron. The good point is that there are only additions and multiplications. The bad point is that there are too many of them, which makes it unusable on devices with a lower CPU frequency.

A way out of this dilemma is the use of proprietary hardware, as used in hardware-based speech recognition, consult the section "Hardware-Based Speech Recognition".

Nowadays ANNs play a minor role in continuous speech recognition, but are still used in hybrid architectures with HMM-based recognition. In contrast to HMMs, which try to achieve their goal based on statistical and probability models, ANNs deal with classification. They are able to classify a given pattern into phonemes, but are not ideal for the processing of continuous speech. This means that neural networks are used as a replacement for various pieces of a HMM-based recognizer. This is more a philosophical difference with little relevance to use in embedded environments.

As an example of such a network, we look at the multilayer perceptron developed by Bourlard (1992). This network has nine 26-dimensional feature vectors to compute 61 phonemes with 500-4000 neurons in a hidden layer. It allows computing the a posteriori probability $p(q_k|x_i)$. The Viterbi algorithm requires $p(x_i|q_k)$, which can be guessed using the Bayes theorems via

$$p(x_i \mid q_k) = \frac{p(q_k \mid o_T) p(o_T)}{p(q_k)} \tag{4}$$

where $p(o_T)$ can be treated as a constant for all classes and $p(q_k)$ is the frequency distribution of all phonemes, which is known in advance.

FUTURE RESEARCH DIRECTIONS

This chapter gave an overview of the challenges of implementing speech recognition on mobile devices. None of the architectures is ideal in all aspects. Most researchers in speech recognition hope that embedded devices will become powerful enough to have enough performance running off-the-shelf speech recognizers on embedded devices. However, this attitude does not solve the problems that users have if they want to use speech recognition today.

Currently, there are two main approaches to enabling speech recognition on future mobile devices. The first one is followed by hardware engineers who are trying to improve the performance of embedded devices. The development of better hardware will not be able to solve all the challenges in a short time, but will at least address some of them. One aspect is the lack of support for floating point arithmetic, which is also present for rendering of graphical interfaces. Others, like limited memory capacity, will persist. Evolution in recognition performance currently entails a shorter battery life. This is where research in the domain of electrical engineering is required. An alternative is presented by streaming technologies like MRCP that are increasingly used, for example, on mobile phones. Here, standards are needed that allow the distribution of mass data over a wireless connection, or better reduce the traffic.

The second approach is research in speech recognition, looking for tricks to enable speech recognition on these devices with limited capabilities. Advancements in recognition technology are needed too to overcome the challenges. The current approaches have the drawback that they are accompanied by a loss of precision. Here we need better strategies.

The first steps have been taken, but more work is needed to make the vision of voice input on embedded devices come true.

SUMMARY

There are multiple architectures and technologies for implementing speech recognition on mobile devices. They can be divided into *service dependent speech recognition* and *device inherent speech recognition*. Service dependent architectures require a service running on the network to move the computational burden from the client. These architectures offer the same potential as desktop speech recognition at the cost of environmental dependencies. Speech recognition on the device is independent of services running on the network, but pose high computational effort to the mobile device.

This is also the main reason why the speech recognition parameters of service dependent speech recognition cannot be determined exactly. They depend on the technology used on the server side, resulting in full network dependency and high server load. The values of the additional parameters for UC are generally worse than those for device inherent speech recognition.

The required network bandwidth is better for DSR than for the streaming architectures, since it aims at reducing the transmitted data. As a consequence, transmission degradation and server load is slightly better.

HMM and ANN based recognizers offer the greatest flexibility and have the best scores for the parameters of speech recognition systems. This

Figure 24. Distribution of computational resources

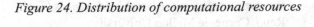

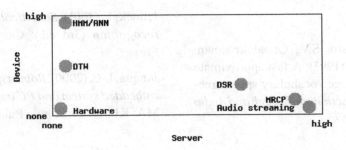

is the main reason why service dependent speech recognition performs better in that area.

The transducer is in all cases a noise-canceling microphone. Thus SNR is not a crucial factor.

Implemented on the device, these technologies require too many resources to achieve the same performance as their counterparts on the server. This results in smaller vocabularies, smaller models and lower perplexity. They have generally a lower recognition rate than server implementations. In addition, implementations may not have real time capabilities, resulting in a low scoring for responsiveness. The decisive factor is the use of computational resources.

Figure 24 gives a graphical representation of how the type of architecture influences the distributed use of computational resources on the device and on the server.

Hardware-based speech recognition seems to be an appropriate candidate to enable speech recognition on mobile devices, but its rigidity makes it impossible to address multiple application scenarios. Thus it has the worst value for integration and maintenance. DTW requires fewer resources on the device than HMM or ANN, but is highly speaker dependent. It requires enrollment, and supports only isolated word-based recognition, which makes it unusable for certain scenarios.

This analysis can serve as a decision criterion for the architecture to implement or to use. None of the architectures is ideal in all contexts. Especially server dependent architectures require a higher invest, hampering their use in enterprise applications.

REFERENCES

Bahl, L.R., Genneraro, S.V., Gopalakrishnan, P.S., & Mercer, R.L. (1993). A fast approximate acoustic match for large vocabulary speech recognition. *IEEE Transactions on Speech and Audio Processing, 1*(1), 59-67.

Bailey, A. (2004). *Challenges and opportunities for interaction on mobile devices* (Tech. Rep.). Canon Research Centre Europe Ltd.

Bourlard, H., Morgan, N., Wooters, C., & Renals, S. (1992). CDNN: A Context Dependent Neural Network for Continuous Speech Recognition. In *Proceedings of IEEE International Conference on Acoustics, Speech and Signal Processing* (Vol. 2, pp. 349-352).

Chollet, G. (Ed.). (1999). *Speech processing, recognition and artificial neural networks*. Berlin: Springer.

Cohen, J. (2004). Is embedded speech recognition disruptive technology? *Information Quarterly, 3*(5), 14–16.

Delaney, B., Jayant, N., Hans, M., Simunic, T., & Acquaviva, A. (2002). A low-power, fixed-point, front-end feature extraction for a distributed speech recognition system. In *Proceedings of the IEEE International Conference on Acoustics, Speech and Signal Processing* (Vol. 1, pp. 793-796).

Eagle, G. (1999, June/July). Software-only vs. embedded: Which architecture is best for you? *Speech Technology Magazine*.

Frostad, K. (2003, April). The state of embedded speech. *Speech Technology Magazine*.

Huggins-Daines, D., Kumar, M., Chan, A., Black, A., Ravishankar, M., & Rudnicky, A. (2005). *Pocketsphinx: A free, real-time continuous speech recognition system for hand-held devices* (Tech. Rep.). Carnegie Mellon University.

Jelinek, F. (2001). *Statistical methods for speech recognition* (3rd ed.). Cambridge, MA: MIT Press.

Junqua, J.-C. (2000). *Robust speech recognition in embedded system and PC applications*. Norwell, MA: Kluwer Academic Publishers.

Kumagai, J. (2002, September 9). Talk to the machine. *IEEE Spectrum Online.*

Lowerre, B. (1976). *The HARPY speech recognition system.* Unpublished doctoral dissertation, Dept. of Computer Science, Carnegie-Mellon University, Pittsburgh, PA, USA.

Mathew, B.K., Davis, A., & Fang, Z. (2002, November 11). *A Gaussian probability accelerator for SHINX 3* (Tech. Rep. No. UUCS-03-02). Salt Lake City, UT: University of Utah.

Ming, L.Y. (2003). *An optimization framework for fixed-point digital signal processing.* Unpublished master's thesis, The Chinese University of Hong Kong.

Novak, M., Hampl, R., Krbec, P., Bergl, V., & Sedivy, J. (2003). Two-pass search strategy for large list recognition on embedded speech recognition platforms. In *Proceedings of the 2003 IEEE International Conference on Acoustics, Speech, and Signal Processing* (Vol. 1, pp. 200–203).

Pearce, D. (2000a, May 5). *Enabling new speech driven series for mobile devices: An overview of the ETSI standard activities for distributed speech recognition front-ends* (Tech. Rep.). Motorola Labs.

Pearce, D. (2000b, May 5). Enabling new speech driven services for mobile devices: An overview of the ETSI standard activities for distributed speech recognition front-ends. *AVIOS 2000: The Speech Applications Conference,* San Jose, CA, USA.

Rabiner, L.R. (1989, February 2). A tutorial on hidden Markov models and selected applications in speech recognition. *Proceedings of the IEEE, 77*(2), 257–286.

Rabiner, L.R. (1997). Applications of speech recognition to the area of telecommunications. In *Proceedings of the IEEE Workshop on Automatic Speech Recognition and Understanding* (pp. 501-510).

Rabiner, L.R., & Juang, B.-H. (1993). *Fundamentals of speech recognition.* Prentice Hall PTR.

Sakoe, H., & Chiba, S. (1990). Dynamic programming algorithm optimization for spoken word recognition. A.Waibel & K.-F. Lee (Eds.), *Readings in speech recognition* (pp. 159–165). Morgan Kaufmann Publishers, Inc.

Schukat-Talamazzini, E.G.(1995). *Automatische spracherkennung.*

Schulzrinne, H., Rao, A., & Lanphier, R. (1998, April 4). *Real time streaming protocol.* Retrieved May 19, 2006, from http://www.rfc-archive. org/getrfc.php?rfc=2326. Shanmugham, S., Monaco, P., & Eberman, B. (2006, April 4). *A media resource control protocol (MRCP).* Retrieved from http://www.rfc-archive.org/getrfc. php?rfc=4463.

Zaykobskiy, D. (2006). Survey of the speech recognition techniques for mobile devices. In *Proceedings of the 11th International Conference on Speech and Computer,* St. Petersburg, Russia.

ADDITIONAL READING

Amrouche, A., & Rouvaen, J. M. (2006). Efficient system for speech recognition using general regression neural network. *International Journal of Intelligent Technology, 1*(2), 183–189.

Burke, D. (2007). *Speech processing for IP networks: Media resource control protocol (MRCP).* Wiley & Sons.

Chollet, G., DiBenedetto, G., Esposito, A., & Benedetto, G.D. (1999). *Speech processing, recognition and artificial neural networks.* Springer.

Chugh, J., & Jagannathan, V. (2002). Voice-Enabling Enterprise Applications. In *Proceedings of the 11th IEEE International Workshops on Enabling Technologies* (pp. 188–189). Washington, DC: IEEE Computer Society.

Digital speech: Coding for low bit rate communication systems. (1994). John Wiley & Sons, Ltd.

Dynkin, E.B. (2006). *Theory of Markov processes.* Dover Publications.

IEEE (Ed.). (1999). *Speech coding for telecommunications 1999 IEEE workshop.* IEEE Press.

Held, G. (2002). *Voice and data internetworking. Voice over IP gateways.* McGraw-Hill Professional.

Jurafsky, D., & Martin, J. H. (2000). *Speech and language processing: An introduction to natural language processing, computational linguistics and speech recognition.* New Jersey: Prentice Hall.

Jurafsky, D., & Martin, J.H. (2003). *Speech and language processing: An introduction to natural language processing, computational linguistics and speech recognition.* Prentice Hall.

Kahrs, M., & Brandenburg, K. (Eds.). (1998). *Applications of digital signal processing to audio and acoustics.* Springer-Verlag.

Loizou, P.C. (2007). *Speech enhancement: Theory and practice.* Taylor & Francis Ltd.

Manning, C., & Schütze, H. (1999). *Foundations of statistical natural language processing.* Cambridge, MA: MIT Press.

Minker, W., & Bennacef, S. (2004). *Speech and human-machine dialog.* Springer US.

Nakagawa, S., Okada, M., & Kawahara, T. (Eds.). (2005). *Spoken language systems.* IOS Press.

Niemann, H. (1990). *Pattern analysis and understanding.* Springer-Verlag.

Novak, M., Hampl, R., Krbec, P., Bergl, V., & Sedivy, J. (2003). Two-pass search strategy for large list recognition on embedded speech recognition platforms. *Proceedings of the IEEE International Conference on Acoustics, Speech and Signal Processing* (Vol. 1, pp. 200–203).

Oppenheim, A.V., Schafer, R.W., & Buck, J.R. (1999). *Discrete-time signal processing.* Prentice Hall.

Sieworik, D.P. (2001, September 9). *Mobile access to information: Wearable and context aware computers* (Tech. Rep.). Carnegie Mellon University.

Waibel, A., & Lee, K.-F. (Eds.). (1990). *Readings in speech recognition.* Morgan Kaufmann Publishers, Inc.

Wang, Y., Li, J., & Stoica, P. (2005). *Spectral analysis of signals: The missing data case.* Morgan & Claypool Publishers.

William R.G., & Mammen, E.W. (1975). *The art of speaking made simple.* London: Doubleday.

Chapter XVIII
Mouth and Ear Interaction

Dirk Schnelle
Technische Universität Darmstadt, Germany

ABSTRACT

This chapter gives an overview of the challenges that have to be mastered while working with audio. The vision of ubiquitous computing involves challenges for the future workplace. Tasks to be performed by workers are becoming more and more complex, which leads to an ever-increasing need to deliver information to workers. This can be information from a manual or instructions on how to proceed with the current task. Workers typically have their hands busy and use of a mouse or a keyboard will force them to stop working. Mouth and ear interaction can be performed without focusing attention on the device. But audio is also a medium that is not easy to handle. This chapter provides an understanding of why audio-based interfaces are difficult to handle and you will also be provided with some pointers as to how these challenges can be mastered to improve the quality of applications involving mouth & ear interaction.

MOTIVATION

Ubiquitous computing allows the delivery of information to the worker while she is engaged in her task. The mobile worker typically wears a small computer and the information is transmitted from a server to this wearable computer. Since workers typically have their hands busy while performing their tasks, the use of hands and eyes devices, that is, mouse and keyboard, will force them to interrupt working. Use of the acoustic channel does not have this limitation. Audio can be used to deliver information to the worker and to enable her to interact with the system using voice commands. In addition, the acoustic channel is still functional under extreme cases, for example, darkness and limited freedom of movement. A headset requires only limited space. Moreover the acoustic channel can be used in addition to other modalities, like conventional screens and buttons.

A drawback of voice is that it becomes unusable in noisy environments. Noise coming from the environment may cause the speech recognizer to detect unwanted commands and makes it harder for the user to listen to the system's output. In this case, graphical interfaces are preferable.

Nevertheless, in many cases the use of audio has some advantages to be used exclusively or in addition to other interfaces in smart environments. Melvyn Hunt (1992) stated that: "Reports and theses in speech recognition often begin with a cliché, namely that speech is the most natural way for human beings to communicate with each other."

This statement of Hunt is still true and the question arises why we see so little use of voice interfaces in today's human-computer interaction. Speech is certainly one of the most important means of communication for humans. It has been used from the beginning of mankind to transfer customs and knowledge from one generation to the next. Although new communication technologies have been developed throughout history, speech remains a very efficient way of communication. But is this also true for the computer as the counterpart?

Hunt's statement expresses implicitly the common expectation that a computer can be treated similarly to a human, leading to the vision of the patient listening homunculus in a computer's shape: as a result, less pretentious but more realistic and helpful applications were of low interest for academic research. This vision requires that computers have the active and passive communicative competence of a human, a theory that is supported by Schukat-Talamazzini (1995). It is also a message of Shneiderman (1986), who states that although the recognition rate is increasingly accurate for dictation systems, adoption outside the disabled user community has been slow compared to visual interfaces. In the past years, the area of natural language processing made a lot of progress in research towards this vision, but we are still a big step behind. Amy Neustein (2001) states that this "…does not seem far fetched when we consider how the field of linguistics, with its

wide spectrum of methods to study interactive speech, provides the building blocks for spoken language systems that simulate human dialog."

But she has to admit that this progress is only a necessary first step toward an open collaborative relationship between computational linguists and conversation analysts. As a consequence, this leads to more interactive conversational interfaces. But we will need more of this collaboration. Today the use of the computer as a patient listening homunculus remains a vision. Otherwise the big advantage of audio, being more natural, would have displaced the ubiquitous graphical user interface. In fact, banking companies, who offer both Web-based customer self-service and telephony-based self-service, are observing a trend in favor of the graphically oriented medium.

Nevertheless, the use of voice-based user interfaces seem to be promising as an alternative to graphical interfaces, or to be used in addition in the shape of multimodal interfaces. Imagine a warehouse picker who needs to pick different items from different shelves. The worker's hands are busy, calling for the use of voice interaction, and the high mobility of the worker makes carrying additional equipment impractical.

This chapter is organized as follows: the section "Dialog Strategies" describes the main differences between voice-based interfaces and graphical interfaces and introduces the four main concepts for voice-based interaction. In order to use voice as an input medium the definition of grammars is required. Grammars are a fundamental concept to define the valid input of a speech recognizer. The section "Domain Specific Development" introduces current approaches to using them in more than a single context. The section "Mouth & Ear interaction in Smart Environments" describes the concept of a browser for smart environments with a focus on mouth & ear interaction. The concept is similar to a Web browser, using a minimal command-set for interaction. Besides the main problems of browsing, the development of mouth and ear applications faces several challenges, which are different to applications for hands and eyes devices. These challenges are discussed in the section "Challenges with Audio." The section "Ways to Master these Challenges" provides some pointers to master these challenges, before the section "Future Research Directions" concludes this chapter.

DIALOG STRATEGIES

Interaction with voice-based user interfaces is different from interaction with graphical user interfaces. This section names the four main concepts of mouth and ear interaction based on the major requirements for mouth and ear interaction. These requirements become clearer with the story of Ali Baba and the Forty Thieves.

Ali Baba discovered the secret words that opened the thieves' cave. His brother-in-law, Kasim, forced him to reveal the secret. Kasim then went to the cave. When he reached the entrance of the cavern, he uttered the words, "Open sesame!" The door immediately opened, and when he was in, closed on him. In examining the cave he was greatly astonished to find much more riches than he had expected from Ali Baba's relation. He quickly loaded at the door of the cavern as many bags of gold as his ten mules could carry, but his thoughts were now so full of great riches he should possess, that he could not think of the necessary words to make the door open. Instead of "Open sesame!" he said "Open barley!" and was amazed that the door remained shut. He named several sorts of grain, but still the door would not open. Kasim never expected such an incident, and was so alarmed at the danger he was in that the more he endeavored to remember the word sesame the more his memory was confused, and he had as much forgotten it as if he had never heard it mentioned. Kasim never got out. The thieves returned, cut off Kasim's head and quartered his body.

Designers of voice-based user interfaces can learn from this old story. Fortunately most users will not get their heads cut off if they fail to remember how to interact with the system. However, interaction with a system must be:

- Easy to learn
- Easy to remember
- Natural

Besides these lessons that we can learn from the story that it is also important for the speech recognizer that the commands are *acoustically different* in order to reduce recognition errors.

To be honest, the lessons to learn from this example can also be transferred to the world of graphical user interfaces, where the user has to enter a password to access an application, but VUI designers have to face this issue with *each* step in the dialog. We will discuss this in more detail in the section "Challenges with Audio."

There are four main approaches, also know as **dialog strategy**, to using voice as an input medium:

Command and Control

In command and control environments the application can handle a voice command menu that contains voice commands. This can be used to enable the user to control the computer without the need for a mouse or keyboard. It also means that the user has to learn a special vocabulary. In general such a special vocabulary has to be developed for each application. Thus, this approach of developing special command sets does not scale. As a consequence companies and researchers started to find multi-purpose command sets for several tasks to be solved with voice interfaces. Some command sets exist, like the ones from ETSI (2000), satisfying all of the above-mentioned requirements, for example a set of commands to control an audio player.

Menu Hierarchy

If the user has to provide data that can be gathered through a selection process and the options to be presented to the user are interrelated in a hierarchy, or can be made to appear that way, the application can prompt her with a set of options from which she may choose one.

Form-Based

This is the simplest and most common type. Form items are executed exactly once in sequential order to collect data from the user as if she was filling out a form. The computer directs the conversation, prompting the user for the next field to be filled.

Mixed Initiative

In mixed initiative dialogs, both the computer and the human direct the conversation. The user can speak freely. Input items are set and the corresponding actions are taken in response. This dialog strategy requires natural language understanding (NLU) capabilities, confronting us again with the vision of the computer as a conversational counterpart.

In command and control environments, the user is the active part, controlling the computer by voice. This is why it is also called *user initiative*.

Applications that we find today are mostly of the kind of menu hierarchy and form-based, or a combination of both. In these environments, the computer directs the dialog, while the user can only react. These dialog strategies are also called *system initiative*.

Some applications using *mixed initiative* exist, but since this requires a higher programming effort (having a direct relation to the money being paid for development) they are not very common. However, this dialog strategy is the one most likely

to be accepted by users. This is also the one that is the closest to the vision of the homunculus.

All of these dialog strategies are relevant for smart environments, serving as a source of context data. Especially mixed initiative dialogs can benefit from contextual data. Imagine a visitor to a museum, standing in front of an exhibit. If she wants to get more information about it, she can simply ask, "what is this?" The unspecified term *this* can be filled from the knowledge about the contextual environment. This is explored in the chapter "Multimodal & Federated Interaction."

In this chapter you will come across two fundamental terms to name user interfaces using the audio channel as their primary communication channel. These are:

Definition: Voice user interfaces (VUI)s are user interfaces using speech input through a speech recognizer and speech output through speech synthesis.

and

Definition: Audio user interfaces (AUI)s are an extension to VUIs, allowing also the use of sound as a means to communicate with the user.

In the past few years, the term VUI has become more dominant and is also used to talk about AUIs. The definition is made for historical reasons and is used, for example, in Barras (1997). In the rest of this chapter, we follow this trend and use the term VUI in the sense of the definition of AUI.

DOMAIN SPECIFIC DEVELOPMENT

Most applications are not stand-alone applications, but have to be integrated into a certain business context and infrastructure. Currently most applications that are developed for voice are manually adapted to the domain in a lengthy development phase. Development is data and labor intensive and requires heavy involvement by experts who meticulously craft the vocabulary, grammar and semantics for the specific domain. Examples are telephone banking or ticket reservation applications.

There are some approaches to reduce costs for the development. One intuitive approach is the use of *speech contexts*. Speech contexts are modular solutions for handling a specific task in the dialog. An example is the definition of widgets for time and date to enter the data for a recurring appointment.. This also leads to complex GUIs for a visual manipulation of the dialog. An example is GenieBuilder from VoiceGenie. It features a drag-and-drop graphical environment for the rapid creation of advanced voice applications using configurable and reusable VoiceXML modules.

VoiceXML is a programming language in XML for voice-based applications and is standardized by the W3C (VoiceXML, 2004). Since the language is in XML format, it is well suited for use by code generators for device independent user interface generators. VoiceXML is ideal for developing system initiative dialogs via a direct support of menu hierarchy through the *menu* tag and form-based through the *field* tag in combination with the *form* tag. Mixed initiative dialogs are supported at a basic level. Multiple grammars can be used (*active*) at the same time. It is possible to speak to any active grammar, thus filling the correspondent fields, but it lacks NLU capabilities.

Another promising approach is *Speech Graffiti,* the Universal Speech Interface (USI) project (USI, 2006), a project managed by Carnegie Mellon University, trying to transfer the idea of look

Figure 1. Palm Graffiti text entry

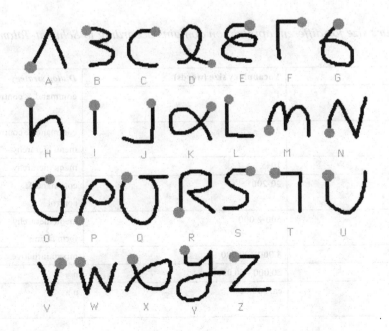

& feel from the world of graphical user interfaces to audio-based user interfaces.

Until now, no universal interface has yet been proposed for humans to communicate effectively, efficiently and effortlessly with machines via speech. The use of unconstrained NLU severely challenges recognition accuracy. It overburdens the computational resources and/or available bandwidth and fails to communicate to the user the limitations of the application.

Interactive voice response (IVR) systems are located in telephony environments and use carefully crafted hierarchical menus which are navigated using touch tones or short, spoken phrases, typically loathed by users due to their inefficiency, rigidity, incompleteness and high cognitive demands. USI assumes that this prevents them from being deployed more widely. They argue that these two interaction styles are extremes along a continuum. The optimal style for human-machine speech communication arguably lies somewhere in between. An interaction is needed that is more structured than natural language and yet more flexible than simple hierarchical menus. Speech Graffiti tries to establish a means of interaction that transfers the idea of Palm's Graffiti for mobile text entry. As shown in Figure 1, the allowed entry for hand writing recognition is optimized in favor of a good recognition result after a short learning phase, where the user has to adapt to the computer.

Speech Graffiti introduces another reduced command set that can be used after a short training phase. They identified several contexts besides a core of eight commands. The commands are not self-contained. If the user wants to ask for details about something that was mentioned in the system output, she may use words that are not part of the command set.

It becomes clearer with the help of an example from a cinema reservation system.

System: ...movie is Titanic ... theatre is the Manor ...
User: What are the show times?

Table 1. Vocabulary size for different application domains according to Schukat-Talamazzini (1995)

Domain	Vocabulary size (words)	Dialog strategy
Alarm system (alarm command)	1	command & control
menu selection (Yes/No)	2	command & control menu hierarchy
Digits	10+x	menu hierarchy
Control	20-200	command & control
Information Dialog	500-2,000	menu hierarchy form filling
Daily talk	8,000 - 20,000	mixed initiative
Dictation	20,000 - 50,000	n/a
German (no foreign words)	ca. 300,000	n/a

The phrase *"what are"* is standardized in USI, but the concretization *"show times"* is domain specific. This is a drawback with respect to an enclosed command set and a tribute to a more convenient interface.

The application domain has also a strong impact on the size of the vocabulary. The typical size of the vocabulary for different application domains is listed in Table 1.

MOUTH AND EAR INTERACTION IN SMART ENVIRONMENTS

This section will show some examples of existing applications for mobile workers featuring mouth and ear interaction. The concept of an audio browser is discussed in detail for STAIRS, a project in the Telecooperation Group at the Technische Universität Darmstadt. This example is used to show a possible architecture to use mouth and ear interaction in a smart environment. Afterwards

some enterprise size applications are presented, before a short perspective for the use of such systems in industry is given.

STAIRS

Overview

STAIRS is a system that enables workers who cannot use traditional hands and eyes devices to access information and is completely built upon mouth and ear interaction. STAIRS is an acronym for **S**tructured **A**udio **I**nformation **R**etrieval **S**ystem. Its focus is to deliver audio information through a headset using voice commands for interaction and navigation. It uses the **T**alking **A**ssistant (TA) headset also developed at the Telecooperation Group as a prototype for the future audio interaction device. An overview of the TA is given in Aitenbichler (2001).

The headset features audio input/output capabilities, a wireless networking connection, an

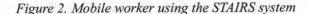

Figure 2. Mobile worker using the STAIRS system

427

infrared-based local positioning system, and it has a CPU for local processing. Using the wireless networking and audio input/output capabilities, it can deliver audio information to the worker everywhere in the workplace. It also captures voice commands from the worker and feeds them through a voice recognition system and translates them into navigation commands.

The Talking Assistant can also act as a source of location context, thanks to its positioning system. This allows the information delivered to the worker to be restricted to cover only information relevant to the context of the worker.

The worker shown in Figure 2 is wearing the TA in a car repair scenario. The positioning system informs the back-end system about the worker's current location. Based on this context information and the list of repairs to be performed, it is possible to provide more guidance to the worker. Besides the functionality as a checklist for the repairs, it is also possible to browse manuals, for example, asking for the part number for a screw that is needed. The worker can also add custom voice notes, for example, about material that was used to perform the repair.

Realization of STAIRS

This section describes the key features of STAIRS:

- audio output,
- use of context information, and
- the command set used.

These features are common to all applications in that context. The solution presented can be transferred to other realizations.

Audio Output

Graphical documents offer many possibilities to structure the contents by means of headlines, different fonts and many others. This structure helps the user to stay oriented and allows for easy and fast access to the desired information. The structural meta-information gets lost while reading the document aloud.

Frankie James (1998) considered structured audio in her doctoral thesis. Structured audio information needs to contain additional audio cues to tell the listener what kind of information, for example, heading, link, is currently being delivered in addition to the natural language generated by a **text-to-speech** engine (TTS engine). Sound can be used in three ways.

- **Background sounds** can help the user to stay oriented, if the same sound is always used to give a sense of unity to the steps a user is performing. These auditory indicators serve as a binding for related steps to the current task. In that way, users can distinguish whether the current point belongs to the ongoing activity or if the latest action implied a change of activity.

- **Auditory icons** or **earcons** are pre-recorded or synthesized sounds that occur between word boundaries to indicate the structure to

Figure 3. Example of an auditory icon to indicate a hyperlink

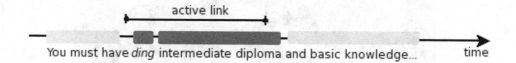

the user or as a means of signaling. Figure 3 shows an example of an auditory icon to mark the appearance of a hyperlink. Here, the sound *ding* is used to mark the start of a hyperlink. Other elements of structuring a document can be represented in the same manner.

- **Different speakers** are an alternative to auditory icons and earcons for structuring a document.

Use of Context Information

Location is the most important context information that is used in STAIRS. Location can be used in two ways:

- **Absolute Positioning:** The coordinates, for example, room coordinates, of the user are tracked by a location system. A world model reflects the artifacts of the real environment and is used to determine those artifacts that the user can see, or which are near by.
- **Relative Positioning:** Several tags are placed in the environment as representatives for artifacts of the real world and the user is equipped with a tag reader, or vice versa. Then the location of the user can be determined, if the reader *sees* the tag.

Figure 4 illustrates the absolute positioning case. Artifacts of the world layer are the starting point for browsing in the document layer.

Figure 4. Mapping of documents to artifacts of the real world

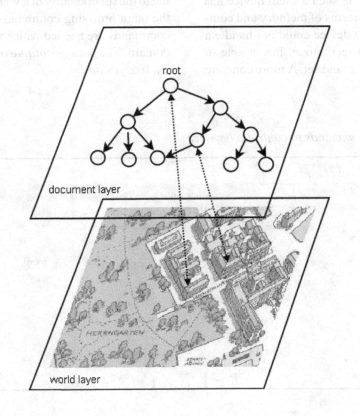

The worker can move in a physical (world layer) and electronic (document layer) location using the command set. In addition it is also possible to link documents other than the root document, which is the starting point of browsing to artifacts of the world layer. This can be exploited, for example to direct the user to artifacts that are described in the document.

The Command Set

As mentioned in the section "Domain Specific Development," a domain specific command set is needed to capture the user input, since GUI-based browsers need only a few commands for control, as shown in Figure 5. The browsing concept of STAIRS adopts this concept for VUI.

In addition to these commands, a location-based system is used to determine the location of the user and the object she is looking at.

Due to the nature of an embedded device, a recognizer that runs on such a small device has strong limitations in terms of memory and computing power. Such a device could not handle a fully-fledged speech recognizer, but is able to handle our small command set. A more concrete

discussion can be found in the chapter "Mobile Speech Recognition." A further advantage of a small command set is that it is simple and easy to learn.

A survey was made to find a command set that satisfied the needs for the audio browser. This survey was not representative of the whole population of users. However, one of the goals with the survey was to find out how closely the answers would correspond to the words proposed by ETSI. ETSI standardized several command sets for different domains in telephony-based environments. Table 2 shows those domains that are of potential interest for navigating in audio-based information.

The users answering the survey were unaware of the ETSI words. In addition, ETSI does not provide words for all the scenarios needed in this project, thus requiring us to use the words from the survey.

The command set is shown in Table 3, according to the functionality of a Web browser. Besides the main browsing commands, some additional commands are needed which relate to the audio domain, like *pause/continue* or a selection facility, like *yes/no*.

Figure 5. Required commands to control a browser

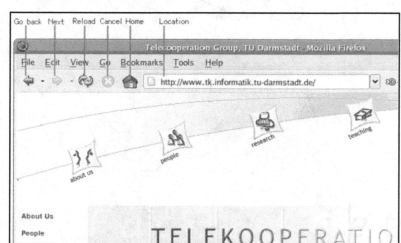

Table 2. ETSI command sets for selected domains

Domain	Function	Command
Context independent	List commands and/or functions	*Options*
	Terminate service	*Goodbye*
	Go to top level of service	*Main menu*
	Enter idle mode	*Standby*
	Transfer to human operator	*Operator*
	Go back to previous node or menu	*Go Back*
Context dependent	Help	*Help*
	Read prompt again	*Repeat*
	Confirm operation	*Yes*
	Reject operation	*No*
	Cancel current operation	*Stop*
Media control	Play a recording	*Play*
	Stop temporarily	*Pause*
	Resume interrupted playback	*Continue, Play*
	Stop playing a recording	*Stop*
	Move forward faster than play	*Fast Forward*
	Move backward	*Rewind*
Browsable list for navigation	Go to next item	*Next*
	Go to previous item	*Previous*
	Provide more information about selected item	*Details*

Table 3. The minimal command set

Function	Web browser	Command
Provide information about current item	Click on hyperlink	*Details*
Cancel current operation	Cancel	*Stop*
Read prompt again	Reload	*Repeat*
Go to next node or item	Next button	*Next*
Go to previous node or item	Go back button	*Go back*
Go to top level of service	Home	*Start*
Go to last node or item	n/a	*Last*
Confirm operation	n/a	*No*
Reject operation	n/a	*No*
Help	n/a	*Help*
Stop temporarily	n/a	*Pause*
Resume interrupted playback	n/a	*Continue*

FURTHER EXAMPLES

In the following we show some examples of existing applications. The examples show that the use of audio interfaces to support mobile workers is more than a vision and is already being used by industry. The advantages of such systems for the enterprise will be summarized below in the section "Perspective for the Enterprise."

Pick by Voice

Mouth and ear interacting systems can be used in pick-by-voice scenarios, where workers need to pick different items from different shelves. Their hands are busy performing their tasks. The location context can be used to determine the optimal route between two picks and to give guidance to the picker using audio instruction. This is important for new employees to learn the route. In addition, the picker does not need to think about the inventory list, thus reducing a cause of error. There are already several implementations for such systems. One example is lekkerland from topsystem Systemhaus GmbH.

This system uses a communication based on existing infrastructure, which is WiFi (IEEE 802.11b) data exchange with the voice-over-IP (VoIP) application H.323 standard telephoning in a wireless LAN. The system needs a short training of the required key words. This is necessary to adjust the speech system exactly to the individual picker. As a positive side effect, the pickers learn how to interact with the system. The picking process is as follows:

1. The pickers are directed to go to a particular location using voice-based information and earcons. Earcons are used to indicate that the picker is on the wrong route.
2. Once the picker arrives at the shelf she confirms the position by naming a check number that is attached to the storage shelf location.
3. The system names the amount of merchandise to remove from the shelf.
4. The picker confirms the actual removal.
5. The system removes the merchandise from the inventory list.
6. Finally the picker is directed to advance to the next picking location.

In this example, the contextual information is used as in STAIRS. The location context is explicitly confirmed by the picker by reading the check number. The audio output is not structured, because it is not needed. This system uses domain specific vocabulary, which has to be learned.

Xybernaut

Another example of a wearable that can be used in training@work scenarios is Xybernauts MA V. Its output capabilities comprise a standard, full-color VGA or SVGA desktop resolution, flat-panel displays and head mounted displays with binocular or monocular viewing and integrated microphone and earphones. As input devices, it can be equipped with a featherweight, 60-key, wrist-worn QWERTY keyboard, standard third-party USB keyboards and input devices. Moreover it features integrated speech recognition. It can receive still images or stream audio and video in real time.

This system is an industrial size replacement of the Talking Assistant.

Museum Guide

Another scenario in which the headset can be used is a museum guide. Currently most museums offer their visitors the possibility to borrow audio guides. The visitor can use it to get detailed explanations about exhibits. This is traditionally the first application for ubiquitous and pervasive computing research.

An example for such a museum guide is guide-PORT from Sennheiser. Their design goal was to be simple for visitors to use and also easy for exhibitors to operate. It is fully battery powered and requires a WLAN. It communicates through wireless with *identifier units* placed near selected exhibits. The parameters of the identifier units can be configured using a standard infrared-capable PDA. guidePORT receivers are triggered to play audio streams associated with the exhibit.

This application uses location information like in the picking example. It does not support voice input but uses buttons instead. The audio output is not structured, which could be seen as a good improvement to the system.

Perspective for the Enterprise

A positive effect of such systems is that workers can learn their tasks while they are actually performing them. This is an important factor for the enterprise. This is also addressed in the chapter "Ambient Learning."

Currently many industries are attempting to shorten their product life cycles and to bring products to the market faster. Unfortunately, the speed up of production is often hampered because workers need to be trained to follow the new procedures. This is often achieved by a supervisor giving instructions to the new worker on how to accomplish the current task. The headset has the potential to replace the supervisor, thus saving money. The information is delivered from the information base directly to the worker. It is also possible to tailor the information to be relevant to the task she is currently learning. More information concerning a particular task can be delivered instantly on demand. As a result the learning time is shortened, while the quality improves with the worker's experience. Other advantages are fewer errors, since the worker is actively guided by the system and more reliable data.

CHALLENGES WITH AUDIO

VUIs are particularly difficult to build due to their transient and invisible nature. Unlike visual interfaces, once the commands and actions have been communicated to the user, they "are not there anymore." Another particular aspect of VUI is that the interaction with the user interface is not only affected by the objective limitations of a voice channel, but human factors play a decisive role: auditive and orientation capabilities, attention, clarity, diction, speed, and ambient noise (noise coming from the environment).

These aspects can be grouped into two categories named below. Each of them will be explained in more detail in the following subsections.

Technical Challenges
- Speech Recognition Performance
- Speech Synthesis Quality
- Recognition: Flexibility vs. Accuracy

Audio Inherent Challenges
- One-dimensionality
- Transience
- Invisibility
- Asymmetry

It can be assumed that the technical problems can be solved as technical progress is being made. Especially the item's speech recognition performance and speech synthesis quality can be easily solved by using more accurate, typically commercial products. In command-and-control interfaces the flexibility vs. accuracy issue is not applicable. The problems inherent to audio will be impossible to solve completely, but it is important to know them and to find workarounds.

Technical Challenges

Speech Recognition Performance

Speech is not recognized with an accuracy of 100%. Even humans are not able to do that. There will always be some uncertainty in the recognized input, which has to be handled somehow. This is different from the experience of developers of graphical user interfaces, where keyboard and mouse input are recognized without any doubts.

From a naive perspective, an utterance is simply a sequence of words. Words, again, can be regarded as a sequence of phonemes (small minimal sound units), but this impression is wrong. We will discuss this in the following list:

- **Continuous:** In contrast to our assumption that speech is only a sequence of phonemes, sound is continuous. This means, that there are, in general, no discontinuities, making it easy to detect boundaries of words, syllables or phonemes. A safe detection of boundaries between two phrases is only possible if the speaker makes a pause to separate them. This is expressed by Figure 6a.
- **Flexible:** The same sentence can be spoken in many different ways (Figure 6e, Figure 6f)). This makes it difficult to find prototypes that are needed to recognize the phonemes. Causes are
  - **Inherent to the audio input channel:** Type and position of the microphone, echoes of the room, and quantization error (Figure 6g) and
  - **Acoustic problems:** Voices of other persons [cocktail party effect (Figure 6h)] or noise from the environment.
- **Complex:** Speech recognition requires a lot of computational power and memory. The main causes for this is the data rate of speech input (there are typically 8,000-20,000 samples per second) and the amount of possibilities in building sentences. For K words it is (mathematically) possible to create K^L different word sequences with length L. For recognition it is necessary to store the corresponding models or prototypes, thus requiring a large amount of storage. In addition they are also responsible for the amount of comparisons in the decoding phase.
- **Ambiguous:** In general, there is no strong relationship between the sentence and its acoustic representation. Different words or sentences can possibly be spoken in the same manner. These ambiguities have different aspects:
  - **Homophony,** for example, *had* and *hat*
  - **Word boundary,** for example, *I scream* and *Ice cream*
  - **Syntactic,** for example, *He saw the man with the telescope*
  - **Semantic,** for example, *"12 p.m."* and *"midnight"*

The last aspect is also addressed in the section "Flexibility vs. Accuracy."

These aspects increase the difficulty of decoding, that is, understanding what was said. Humans additionally use domain knowledge and situational awareness among others for decoding. Used in ubiquitous environments, the limited computational resources on wearable devices pose additional challenges to the recognizer. These are mainly memory (needed to store the models), computational power (speech recognition is computationally intense), and power consumption (battery lifetime is a scarce resource). Additionally most processors used in wearable devices, like the XScale processor, which is currently the standard processor used in PDAs, do no support floating point operations. Since speech recognition technology is based on statistical methods this increases the problem of having too little computational power.

Figure 6. Difficulties with speech recognition according to Schukat-Talamazzini (1995)

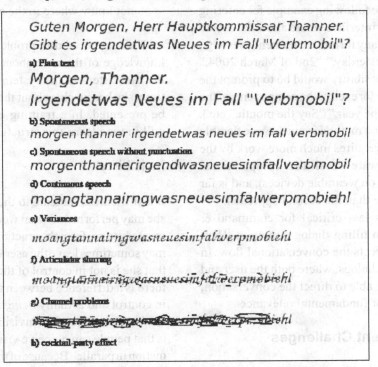

As a consequence, the recognizer on such wearable devices is less accurate than speech recognizers for desktop size computers. There are only a few commercial speech recognizers available that can deal with these limitations. If the computational limits are too low, the only way to support speech recognition is to use lower level technologies, like a simple pattern matching or to use distributed speech recognition.

Speech Synthesis Quality

The quality of modern text-to-speech engines is still low, although a great deal of progress has been made in speech synthesis during the past years. In general, people prefer to listen to pre-recorded audio because it sounds more natural. However, for this to work, the data to be delivered has to be known in advance and recorded as audio, which

consumes additional memory. The effort required to get pre-recorded audio is high and cost intensive. To achieve good quality, a professional speaker is needed and a studio environment to make the recording. For dynamic documents, where the content depends on the user's actions, text-to-speech may be the only feasible solution. As a trade-off it is possible to record only audio snippets and paste them together as needed. A professional speaker is able to produce voice with a similar pitch. Humans are very sensitive in listening and hear this difference in the pitch.

Flexibility vs. Accuracy

Speech can have many faces for the same issue and natural language user interfaces must serve many of them. This has a direct impact on recognition accuracy. To illustrate this trade-off between flexibility of the interface and its accuracy, consider the following example for entering a date. A flexible interface would allow the user to speak the date in any format the user chooses (e.g., "March 2nd," "yesterday," "2nd of March 2004," etc.). Another possibility would be to prompt the user individually for each of the components of the date (e.g., "Say the year," "Say the month," etc.). Obviously, the first method is much more flexible for the user, but requires much more work by the recognition software (recall that computational power is limited on wearable devices), and is far more error-prone than the second approach.

This issue is less critical for command & control and form filling dialog strategies. Here the computer directs the conversational flow. In mixed initiative dialogs, where both the user and the computer are able to direct the conversation, this problem is of fundamental relevance.

Device Inherent Challenges

One-Dimensionality

The eye is active whereas the ear is passive; that is, the ear cannot actively browse a set of recordings in the same way as the eye can scan a screen of text and figures. It has to wait until the information is available, and once received, it is not there anymore.

Transience

Listening is controlled by the short-term memory. Listening to long utterances has the effect that users forget most of the information that was given at the beginning. This means that speech is not an ideal medium for delivering large amounts of data.

Transience has also the effect that users of VUIs often have the problem of staying oriented. They describe a phenomenon that is called the *lost in space* problem, which is also known in Web-based applications.

Definition: A user gets *lost in space* if she does not know where in the application she is.

The extent of this problem depends on the knowledge of the user about the application. If the user listens to the system output for the first time, she has no clue about the structure that will be presented. In a training environment, users will in time learn this structure.

Invisibility

It is difficult to indicate to the user what actions she may perform and what words and phrases she must say to perform these actions. This invisibility may sometimes leave the user with the impression that she is not in control of the system. Note that there is a difference between the *feeling of being* in control and actually *being* in control.

An advantage of the invisible nature of speech is that people can perceive visual and aural information in parallel. Because of this property, speech is ideal for delivery of information without forcing the user to switch context, since she may listen to the information while continuing with her work. Consider the scenario when you come home and listen to the voice messages on your telephone-answering machine. It is possible to listen to the recorded messages while doing something else, such as preparing dinner.

Asymmetry

Asymmetry means that people can speak faster than they type, but can listen much more slowly than they can read. This has a direct influence on the amount of audio data and the information being delivered. This property is extremely useful in the cases where we have the facility of using additional displays to supplement the basic audio interface. We can use the displays for delivering information, which is unsuitable for audio due to its length, and focus on using the audio device for interaction and delivering short pieces of information. This is explored in the chapter "Multimodal & Federated Interaction."

Additional Challenges for UC

The ubiquitous computing environment poses additional challenges to the voice user interface. Users calling voice applications or using them in a desktop environment have the ability to look for a quiet place while they are using the interface in order to avoid as much ambient noise as possible. This, for instance, is something that cannot be influenced by the system designer. Users on the move in contrast cannot act in this way. They have to use the voice interface in the place they are currently in. This has a direct impact on the performance of the speech recognizer, and conversely the user's ability to perceive all the auditory output of the system. In addition to the challenges named in the previous sections, designers of voice-based applications in UC environments have to master the following challenges:

Conversation

If the user is speaking to another person, or if a person that passes by addresses the user by saying something, the recognizer has no way of distinguishing these utterances to other persons from commands used to control the system. In contrast to noisy environments, which are part of the speech recognition performance challenge, the risk of unwanted triggering of the recognizer is higher, since the user may use words that are valid input but have the same source.

Privacy

Being on the move, other persons may be around the user while she is interacting with the system. Both audio input and output should be hidden from these people. In practice, this is a problem that is impossible to solve. The only workaround is to not deliver critical or confidential information via mouth and ear devices.

Service Availability

While the user is walking around, some services may not be available, or even cease to be available while they are being used. The user has to be informed about the service she may use in a certain moment. Changing grammars depending on the current context, the commands with which the user interacts with the system may vary. The user has to be notified of this change and about the commands she may use to control the system.

WAYS TO MASTER THESE CHALLENGES

Individual solutions exist to work around these challenges. The famous book by Barras (1997) about the use of audio in the context of navigating in a 3D visualization of geological structures names several of them. He explains the use of *audio signaling*, *auditory icons*, and *earcons* in a field that Frankie James (1998) called *structured audio* in her Ph.D., which has been used in STAIRS (see the section "STAIRS"). This section names several strategies for mastering the challenges that were described in the section "Challenges with Audio." Starting with the most important challenge is the mastering of recognition errors using error handling and error prevention strategies, the section "Lost in Space" names ways of limiting the lost in space problem, and the section "General Solutions" names general ways of mastering these challenges using guidelines and patterns.

Error Handling

In contrast to visual user interfaces, speech recognition as an input medium is still error prone. It is even more severe because it is not enough to think about input errors by the human, but also about errors in recognizing the user's input. Consequences of recognition errors are severe, because it is possible for them to destroy the user's mental model. Junqua (2000) states that "the cost of an error is application dependent, and so is the error correction technology used. Errors have serious consequences because they can destroy the user's mental model."

Users tend to build their own model of how things work. Performing the wrong actions because of recognition errors may confuse the users.

Errors can be reduced by improving the technology but they cannot be totally eliminated. Consequently, an application that uses speech recognition should account for error handling. This increases the lost in space problem, see above, and the feeling of not being in control. We will be able to detect an error only if a word is recognized that is not allowed in the current context. Possible causes are

- An out-of-vocabulary word
- A word that cannot be used in this context
- Recognition error
- Background noise
- Incorrect pronunciation (e.g., non-native speaker)

Note that in all of these cases we know that an error has occurred, but do not know the source. Asking the user to repeat the command once may help us to solve problems with recognition errors, incorrect pronunciation, or noise. However, if the error persists, it is likely that the user is trying to use a wrong command. In this case we should prompt the user again with an indication that the command is not appropriate in the current situation.

Junqua (2000) suggests the following ways of dealing with a detected error:

- Do nothing and let the user find and correct the error
- Prevent the user from continuing
- Complain and warn the user using a feedback mechanism
- Correct it automatically without user intervention
- Initiate a procedure to correct the error with the user's help through

Unfortunately, all of the above-mentioned strategies, especially the first one, have the drawback that users refrain from working with the application because dialogs become too long and they do not want to confirm everything. A better solution is to prevent errors.

Error Prevention

In most of the cases it is not possible to detect an error. In turn, it is more important to find solutions to prevent evaluation of unwanted commands. To reduce the probability of misrecognized words we have to

- Limit background noise and
- Allow the user to turn off the input device.

In these cases a high-performance speech recognizer would mostly help. Overcoming the challenge of making speech recognition systems robust in noisy acoustic environments is classified as a fundamental challenge. It has been one of the most popular problems addressed by both academic and industrial researchers in speech recognition and is still unsolved.

The presence of noise is even more severe if the user is on the move. Moreover, if the user is in a room with bad acoustics, the echo has an additional negative impact on the recognition result. For the mobile user, these problems are nearly impossible to avoid, triggering the recognizer to cause unwanted behavior.

Noise canceling headsets and noise robust microphones, like a neck microphone, are a good way to reduce this problem. It is always good practice to turn off the recognizer if it is likely that it is not needed. This saves the battery and does not trigger the recognizer if it is not required. The recognizer can be turned on upon request by the user (*push-to-talk*) or triggered by a certain context.

Noisy environments and *talking* cause the simple idea that it should be possible to enable or disable the recognizer. Since audio is invisible, the user has also to be notified about the current state of the recognizer. If the recognizer can be activated by triggers coming from the environment, it must indicate this state change to the user. One possibility to achieve this is the use of auditory icons.

This problem will become less severe as technical progress is made and recognition performance improves.

Most of the problems can be solved by evaluating context information. Context information can be combined with the output of the recognizer to find the user's goal. It can also be used to tailor the information that is already present by the context. The chapter "Multimodal & Federated Interaction" provides more pointers to this topic.

Lost in Space

The lost in space problem is more dominant in VUI than any other modality. Barras (1997) names the following strategies for handling the lost in space problem:

- **Calling** is when someone calls to you from somewhere and you can head in that direction to find them.
- **Telling** is when someone sitting next to you gives you directions, as in driving a car.
- **Landmarks** is when you hear a familiar sound, such as the clock chiming in the

village and you can use it to orient yourself and work out where to head.

These techniques can be used to help the user stay oriented. To provide a mechanism for calling, an additional keyword is required that can be used to name the current path upon request. Landmarks can be implemented as structured audio, for example, a background sound as was introduced in the section "Audio Output."

General Solutions

In a more general approach, there are several guidelines around describing, for example, the use of a persona to achieve a common *look and feel* of the application. Guidelines try to capture design knowledge in small rules. Below is a list of guidelines "Top 10 VUI No-No's" that is listed on http://www.angel.com/services/vui-design/vui-nonos.jsp as an example for such guidelines. It is not necessary to understand them all, since they serve only as examples for guidelines.

1. Don't use open ended prompts
2. Make sure that you don't have endless loops
3. Don't use text-to-speech unless you have to
4. Don't mix voice and text-to-speech
5. Don't put into your prompt something that your grammar can't handle
6. Don't repeat the same prompt over and over again
7. Don't force callers to listen to long prompts
8. Don't switch modes on the caller
9. Don't go quiet for more than 3 seconds
10. Don't listen for short words

Although they appear very clear and precise at first sight, guidelines have several disadvantages. The guidelines mentioned are used to explain these disadvantages by example.

- **Guidelines are often too simplistic or too abstract:** Guideline 7 suggests avoiding long prompts, but it is unspecified when a prompt is too long and what to do if long prompts cannot be avoided, as in a brokerage application.
- **Guidelines often have authority issues concerning their validity:** Guideline 10 suggests not listening for short words. It remains unclear when a word is too short.
- **Guidelines can be conflicting:** Guidelines 3 and 4 are in conflict with each other. It is not clear what to do if an application is allowed to use TTS to deliver dynamic content if it uses pre-recorded voice in all prompts.
- **Guidelines can be difficult to select:** As pointed out above it is difficult to know when to apply Guideline 3 and when to apply Guideline 4.
- **Guidelines can be difficult to interpret:** Guideline 8 cannot be interpreted without explanations.

As a consequence of these disadvantages, the HCI community is starting to convert their existing guidelines into patterns. Patterns define the context and problem explicitly and the solution is provided along with a rationale. For patterns it is important that a solution is provided for a problem in a certain context, because the solution may not make sense in other contexts. Another important factor is that the solution is a proven solution. Consequently, compared to guidelines, patterns contain more complex design knowledge and often several guidelines are integrated in one pattern.

A first approach for voice user interface design using patterns was described by Schnelle (2007). His pattern language is shown in Figure 7. A pattern language's patterns usually relate to each other and form a network of patterns. If a community agrees upon this network, it is possible to speak of a *pattern language*. The language comprises several patterns that address the challenges named in the section "Challenges with Audio."

Escalating Detail is an approach for handling recognition errors, but also transience and invisibility. The main idea is to use different error handlers for different types of errors. A counter is used for the occurrences and levels of the affected type in a row. Different prompts are used to increase the amount of help provided at each level. The higher levels may also offer alternative approaches, for example, a form-based data entry for a date versus free-form input to enter the required data. Within these repetitions the initial prompt can be reused to provide information about the input possibilities. In cases of a timeout (the user did not say anything) or in case of a reject (the utterance could not be mapped to the grammar) this can help to provide sophisticated guidance to the user.

Information spreading is an approach for handling one-dimensionality if large amounts of data have to be delivered. Here the idea is to group the information to be delivered into several sub-nodes. Groups can consist of information items that meet certain criteria or are limited by their number. In the latter case they have to be sorted in an order that is obvious to the user. A command or a timeout after each information sub-node can be used to proceed with the next sub-node. This requires additional commands to allow navigation back and forth, and to handle the case that users realize that the information of interest cannot be in the current sub-node, but may appear in a previous sub-node or a sub-node to come next.

These examples show possible ways of mastering the challenges with audio.

FUTURE RESEARCH DIRECTIONS

The challenges brought about by audio are still not solved completely. Most designers of multi-

Figure 7. VUI pattern language

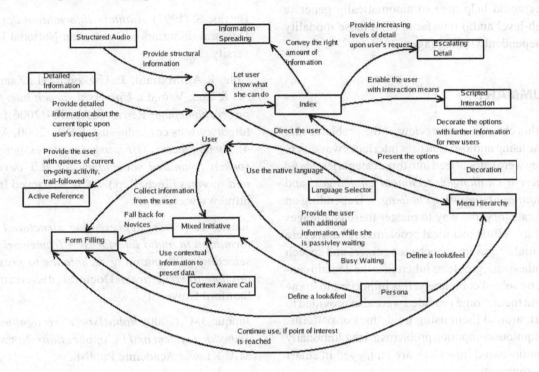

modal applications are not even aware of these challenges. The current approaches to solving these challenges use guidelines and patterns. It turned out that patterns are a better approach to solving these challenges than guidelines. However, only the first necessary steps have been made in the direction of patterns. It is important to continue mining of patterns for the audio domain and expand it to multimodal applications. In order to be accepted by the community it is also important to support developers in applying the patterns. This can be achieved, for example, by tools that are available online to be accessible to a wide community. Here it is important to look for techniques that allow for easy access to patterns of a similar context.

Some challenges, like speech recognition performance or speech synthesis quality are less critical for higher quality speech recognizers. The technology is still not perfect, and probably will never achieve an accuracy of 100%. As pointed out above, even humans are not able to do this. Besides an improvement of the pure recognition technology, we need more research in developing better strategies to use context information in addition to the pure recognition process. This is where interdisciplinary work between researchers in speech recognition technology, artificial intelligence, and ubiquitous computing is needed.

Most multimodal applications use code generators to address the different modalities supported. Code generators use a modality independent description of the UI, like XForms, and generate the interface to use at run-time. Most researchers focus on graphical user interfaces and have pure quality VUIs. Since patterns are structured, they could help here to automatically generate high-level audio interfaces from these modality independent UI languages.

SUMMARY

In this chapter, an overview of the problems that arise using audio-based user interfaces was given. They were categorized into three categories: *audio inherent challenges, technical challenges,* and *ubiquitous computing challenges.* Depending on the category, the way to master these challenges differs. While technical problems are less severe for higher quality speech recognizers and speech synthesizers, problems inherent to the domain cannot be solved completely. It is important to know about them. Some provided were also provided to work around them using guidelines or patterns. Ubiquitous computing problems arise additionally if audio-based interfaces are employed in smart environments.

The challenges can be mastered using guidelines or HCI patterns. Patterns are superior to guidelines, since they offer proven solutions for a given context.

The lessons learned from the use of pure audio-based interfaces can also serve as solid background information that can also be used in multimodal user interfaces. Humans are visually oriented and some problems that users have with audio-based interfaces do not exist in graphical interfaces. However, multimodal interfaces combine at least both types. In order to develop high quality interfaces, developers must also be aware of the specific problems using audio.

REFERENCES

Aitenbichler, E., & Mühlhäuser, M. (2002). *The talking assistant headset: A novel terminal for ubiquitous computing* (Tech. Rep. No. TK-02/02). Telecooperation Group, Department of Computer Science, Darmstadt University of Technology.

Barras, S. (1997). *Auditory information design.* Doctoral dissertation, Australian National University.

Cole, R.A., Mariani, J., Uszkoreit, H., Zaenen, A., & Zue, V. (n.d.). *Universal speech interface project homepage.* Retrieved April 24, 2006, from http://www.cs.cmu.edu/~usi. ETSI. (2000, April 4). *Human factors (HF); user interfaces; generic spoken command vocabulary for ICT devices and services* (Tech. Rep.). ETSI. Retrieved from http://www.etsi.org.

James, F. (1998). *Representing structured information in audio interfaces: A framework for selecting audio marking techniques to present document structures.* Doctoral dissertation, Stanford University.

Junqua, J.-C. (2000). *Robust speech recognition in embedded system and PC applications.* Norwell, MA: Kluwer Academic Publishers.

Neustein, A. (2001, October 10). The Linguistics of a Non-Fictional HAL. *ej Talk.* Retrieved from http://www.ejtalk.com/Top/Tech/Opinion/Non-Hal.html.

Schukat-Talamazzini, E.G. (1995). *Automatische Spracherkennung.* Braunschweig/Wiesbaden: Vieweg Verlag.

Shneiderman, B. (1986). *Designing the user interface: Strategies for effective human-computer interaction.* Boston, MA: Addison-Wesley Longman Publishing Co., Inc.

VoiceXML. (2004, March 3). Retrieved August 28, 2006, from http://www.w3.org/TR/voicexml20/.

ADDITIONAL READING

Alexander, C. (1979). *The timeless way of building.* Oxford University Press.

Alexander, C., Ishikawa, S., & Silverstein, M. (1977). *A pattern language: Towns, buildings, constructions*. UK: Oxford University Press.

Arons, B. (1991). Hyperspeech: Navigating in speech-only hypermedia. In *Proceedings of the Third Annual ACM Conference on Hypertext,* San Antonio, Texas (p. 133-146). New York: ACM Press.

Bailey, A. (2004). *Challenges and opportunities for interaction on mobile devices* (Tech. Rep.). Canon Research Centre Europe Ltd.

Borchers, J. (2001). *A pattern approach to interaction design*. John Wiley & Sons, Inc.

Bürgy, C. (2002). *An interaction constraints model for mobile and wearable computer-aided engineering systems in industrial applications*. Unpublished doctoral dissertation, Carnegie Mellon University, Pittsburgh, Pennsylvania, USA.

Cohen, M.H., Giangola, J.P., & Balogh, J. (2004). *Voice user interface design*. Boston, MA: Addison-Wesley.

Deng, L., & Huang, X. (2004). Challenges in adopting speech recognition. *Communications of the ACM, 47*(1), 69–75.

Dey, A. K. (2000). *Providing architectural support for building context-aware applications*. Unpublished doctoral dissertation, Georgia Institute of Technology.

Dix, A., Abowd, G., Beale, R., & Finlay, J. (1998). *Human-computer interaction*. Europe: Prentice Hall.

Duggan, B. (2002). *Revenue opportunities in the voice enabled Web* (Tech. Rep.). Kevin St. Dublin 8, Ireland: School of Computing, Dublin Institute of Technology.

Falk, D.R., & Carlson, H. (1995). *Multimedia in higher education: A practical guide to new tools for interactive teaching and learning*. Medford: Information Today.

Fraser, N.M., & Gilbert, G.N. (1991). Simulating speech systems. *Computer Speech and Language,*

5, 81-99. Gross, T., & Specht, M. (2001). Awareness in context-aware information systems. In *Proceedings of Mensch & Computer 2001* (pp. 173–181).

Gunderson, J., & Mendelson, R. (1997). Usability of World Wide Web browsers by persons with visual impairments. In *Proceedings of the RESNA Annual* Conference, Pittsburgh, PA (pp. 330-332).

Hearst, M.A. (1999, September 9). Mixed-initiative interaction. *IEEE Intelligent Systems*, 14–16.

Jeffcoate, J. (1995). *Multimedia in practice: Technology and applications*. New York, London, Toronto, Sydney, Tokyo, Singapore: Prentice Hall.

Jelinek, F. (2001). *Statistical methods for speech recognition* (3rd Ed.). Cambridge, MA: MIT Press.

Jurafsky, D., & Martin, J.H. (2000). *Speech and language processing – an introduction to natural language processing, computational linguistics and speech recognition*. New Jersey: Prentice Hall.

Kumagai, J. (2002, September 9). Talk to the machine. *IEEE Spectrum Online*.

Mahemoff, M.J., & Johnston, L.J. (1998). Principles for a Usability-Oriented Pattern Language. In *Proceedings of the 1998 Australian Computer Human Interaction Conference OZCHI'98,* Adelaide, Australia (pp. 132-139). Los Alamitos.

Manning, C., & Schütze, H. (1999). *Foundations of statistical natural language processing*. Cambridge, MA: MIT Press.

Miller, G.A. (1956). The magical number seven, plus or minus two: Some limits on our capacity for processing information. *Psychological Review, 63*, 81-97.

Muller, M.J., & Daniel, J.E. (1990). Toward a definition of voice documents. In *Proceedings of the ACM SIGOIS and IEEE CS TC-OA Confer-*

ence on Office Information Systems, Cambridge, Massachusetts (p. 174 - 183). New York: ACM Press.

Newell, A. (1990). *Unified theories of cognition.* Harvard University Press.

Nielsen, J. (n.d.). *Ten usability heuristics.* Retrieved April 13, 2006, from http://www.useit.com/papers/heuristic/heuristic_list.html.

Norman, D.A. (1988). *The design of everyday things.* Morgan Kaufman Publishers Inc.

Norman, K.(1991). *The Psychology of Menu Selection: Designing Cognitive Control at the Human/Computer Interface.* Norwood, NJ: Ablex.

Olsen, D.(1992). *User Interface Management Systems: Models and Algorithms.* Morgan Kaufmann Publishers Inc.

Rabiner, L.R. (1989, February 2). A tutorial on hidden Markov Models and selected applications in speech recognition. In *Proceedings of the IEEE, 77,* 257–286.

Rabiner, L.R. (1997). Applications of speech recognition to the area of telecommunications. In *Proceedings of the 1997 IEEE Workshop on Automatic Speech Recognition and Understanding* (pp. 501-510).

Rabiner, L.R., & Juang, B.-H. (1993). *Fundamentals of speech recognition.* Prentice Hall PTR.

Ramakrishnan, I.V., Stent, A., & Yang, G. (2004). Hearsay: Enabling audio browsing on hypertext content. In *Proceedings of the 13th Conference on World Wide Web* (pp. 80–89). New York: ACM Press.

Raman, T.V. (1998). *Audio system for technical readings* (Vol. 1410). Berlin, Heidelberg, London: Springer Verlag.

Chapter XIX
Advanced Hands and Eyes Interaction

Michael Weber
Ulm University, Germany

Marc Hermann
Ulm University, Germany

ABSTRACT

This chapter gives an overview of the broad range of interaction techniques for use in ubiquitous computing. It gives a short introduction to the fundamentals of human-computer interaction and the traditional user interfaces, surveys multi-scale output devices, gives a general idea of hands and eyes input, specializes them by merging the virtual and real world, and introduces attention and affection for enhancing the interaction with computers and especially with disappearing computers. The human-computer interaction techniques surveyed here help support Weiser's idea of ubiquitous computing (1991) and calm technology (Weiser & Brown, 1996) and result in more natural interaction techniques than in use of purely graphical user interfaces. This chapter will thus first introduce the basic principles in human-computer interaction from a cognitive perspective, but aimed at computer scientists. The human-computer interaction cycle brings us to a discussion of input and output devices and their characteristics being used within this cycle. The interrelation of the physical and virtual world as we see it in ubiquitous computing has its predecessors in the domain of virtual and augmented realities where specific hands and eyes interaction techniques and technologies have been developed. The next step will be attentive and affective user interfaces and the use of tangible objects being manipulated directly without using dedicated I/O devices.

INTRODUCTION AND BASIC PRINCIPLES

One of the major principles in the interaction of a human with the real world is the combined use of the human vision system with our motor system (this is true for most animals as well). While visually sensing our environment, we are able to control our movements and our haptic action, such as touching and grasping things, thus interacting with the environment using our hands. The principles of hand-eye coordination have been studied intensively by human biologists and by psychologists (Anderson, 2004).

In the area of human-computer interaction, hand and eye coordination dominates most of our current use of contemporary computers. We mainly utilize a visual display where interaction elements are visualized, and we operate on these user interfaces with a keyboard to enter text and other symbols. We typically use a mouse as a pointing device allowing us to place the interaction focus onto one specific position on the display and to click on, and thus activate, the interaction element at this position.

In order to analyze existing user interfaces, to construct more efficient ones, and also to investigate human performance in senso-motoric systems Card, Moran, and Newell (1983) describe a simplified model of the human as an information processor (Figure 1). This model served the three authors as the foundation of their GOMS model to predict human performance (GOMS = goals, operators, methods, selection rules).

Concerning hands and eyes interaction using a computer, the model works as follows: At first, we see a specific visual output on a display using our eyes (the ears are left out intentionally in this chapter). Our perceptual processor senses the respective input as physical light and color stimuli. Inside our cognitive system we offer as a part of our short-term memory a store for visual impressions (besides one for auditive input). The content in the short-term visual memory is interpreted by the cognitive processor to decide on whether the impression should be stored for longer (for potential later use) and to decide how to react to the impression with our motor system. If we, for instance, see a car approaching us, the cognitive processor would decide to tell the mo-

Figure 1. Card, Moran and Newell's model human processor (Card, Moran, & Newell, 1983)

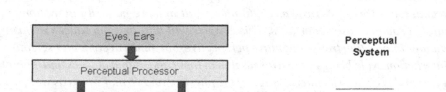

tor system to get off the road. When interacting with a computer, the cognitive processor would, for instance, decide to instruct the motor system to move the mouse with the right hand until the corresponding mouse pointer is located inside the button area we saw first. Hand and eye interaction are very close-knit in our overall cognitive system. Most of the actions we perform with our hands are controlled by the eyes to verify that the hands are doing what they are supposed to do.

Through empirical studies, it is possible to quantify the capacities of the cognitive system and to measure the durations taken by the various parts of our perceptual, cognitive and motor system. It takes 100 ms to bridge the gap between the perceptual system and the short-term memory. Another 170 ms are required to interpret the impression in the visual cortex. Again 230 ms are required to inform the motor system and to move the hand (cf. Figure 2). It seems obvious that moving the hand along various distances takes different lengths of time. Performance measures for pointing or grasping tasks are especially required to fully model human hands and eyes interaction including these motor skills.

Fitts (1954) observed humans in pointing tasks with varying movement distances. He empirically studied how long users need to move a pointer over a distance D in one dimension somewhere into a specific area S. Figure 3 illustrates the experiment.

The observations showed improved performance when either D decreases or S increases. The experimental results could be formulated as a linear function for the movement time MT (1) where the logarithmic term denotes the so-called *index of difficulty*, I_d (2) based on the distance D and the area size S.

$$MT = a + b \cdot \log_2 \frac{2D}{S} \qquad (1)$$

$$I_d \equiv \log_2 \frac{2D}{S} \qquad (2)$$

The parameters a and b are experimentally derived values of human performance. These values themselves are dependent on the task (e.g., positioning versus dragging) and on the input device (e.g., mouse versus trackpad).

Since it is not trivial to acquire one's own results for the parameters a and b, Jef Raskin (2000) gave a rule of thumb for mouse positioning: a=50, b=150.

Fitts' Law holds for one-dimensional tasks only, but computer displays are two-dimensional. For circular or square areas approximations are

Figure 2. Performance of human processor

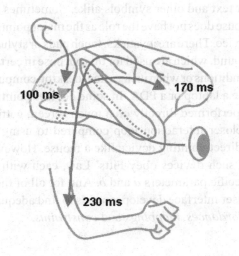

Figure 3. Analysis of the movement of a hand to a target

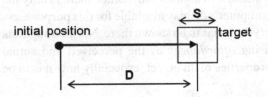

straightforward, for rectangular shapes however there are various extensions of the law (MacKenzie et al., 1992). The best fit of these showed the *smaller of model*, which takes the minimum of height and width as *S* in Fitts' Law and proceeds accordingly.

Human Interaction Cycle

Having the basic psychological and motor principles at hand, we can embed these findings in a more coarse human interaction cycle. Don Norman (1988) described this cycle comprising seven phases in a process and action-oriented view aimed at human-computer interaction tasks. There are seven stages of action:

1. Forming the goal
2. Forming the intention
3. Specifying an action
4. Executing an action
5. Perceiving the state of the world
6. Interpreting the state of the world
7. Evaluating the outcome

As one can easily conclude, for computer usage stage 4 is mostly performed using a mouse today, while stages 5 to 7 rely on the visual feedback given on the computer's display. Especially in window-based user interfaces, we rely on this hand-eye coordination to directly manipulate the objects on the screen. And we expect to experience a *What You See Is What You Get* behavior of the interactive system.

Besides the visual output on the screen, we heavily use (existing) knowledge in our head to form goals and intentions. Required knowledge, which is not present in our head, has to be given somehow in another way. Since there is only the computer's display available for this purpose, everything has to be shown there. Norman suggests using *affordances* as the perceived and actual properties of an object, especially how it is to be used. A well-designed button, for instance, has the *affordance* of being pressable. When using an interaction device to control the object, there should be a natural *mapping* between the controls and the behavior being activated by using the control. In the button example, a label could indicate the function behind the button and a changed color the selection of the button's function. Thus the *mapping* allows a user to intuitively observe his operations. The third concept introduced by Don Norman is called *constraint*. *Constraints* restrict an object from being operated in an unintended way. A button, for instance, does not allow a user to select and drag it on the screen, a function that a window system usually would support. Every time *affordances*, *mappings* and *constraints* are badly designed, users have difficulties to seamlessly perform the seven stages of action. Norman calls this the *gulf of evaluation*, since very often users are not able to evaluate the outcome of the system as regards what they intended and expected from the system.

Traditional Desktop Computer Interaction

All the above principles are applied in today's traditional desktop computer interaction featuring mouse and screen interaction. A specific role is given to the keyboard as the major input device for text and other symbols alike. Sometimes the mouse does not have the role as the major pointing device. There are joysticks, touch pads or styluses around, which are used for this purpose in certain conditions or when using a non-desktop computer like a laptop or a PDA. In some devices pointing is performed directly on a touch screen, getting a closer interaction loop compared to using an indirect pointing device like a mouse. However, all such devices obey Fitts' Law, each with its specific parameters *a* and *b*. And for all of them a user interface developer needs to find adequate *affordances*, *mappings* and *constraints*.

Towards Ubiquity

The current trends in computer technology follow the vision of ubiquitous computing in that more and more specific devices are being used by people. The desktop computer is still around, but many users are beginning to prefer laptops even for office work at their desk. Additionally, personal digital assistants (PDA) or smart phones are used for specific tasks. Such devices take over entertainment functionality like music playing as well. Together with this striving towards smaller and thus portable devices falls the intention of people to have computing power and their relevant data everywhere and all the time at hand. We see on the one hand a diversification of devices, and on the other hand a convergence of functionality. Enhanced mobility, flexibility and context and situation dependence is common to all these scenarios. Projecting this development onto future hand and eye interaction, we conclude that the strict correlation between the one display and the one corresponding pointing device will no longer be true.

In ubiquitous computing everything tends to happen in real life space. So the user is in his physical 3-D world while interacting with the ubiquitous computing system. Users move, they are at various locations; they use different equipment and many devices. A decoupling of the tight correlation between a screen and its I/O device(s) is mandatory. In many cases the standard monitors of the devices might not be adequate for the tasks to be performed. Similarly, the mouse and the keyboard cannot be the predominant input devices any more. New interaction metaphors are required, which may even lead to new devices and device types. And there will be new user interface software technologies required to construct interactive ubiquitous computing systems. Voice input will play an important role in such user interfaces (see the chapter "Mobile Speech Recognition" and the chapter "Mouth and Ear Interaction" for this issue).

When users are mobile and move around, they will not (always) be able to use desktop screens anymore. Currently mobile users will use a "mobile" screen on their laptop or PDA. There will also be a need for ambient screens having larger resolution than earlier ones, which can be used while moving towards them (see the next section "Multiscale Output").

Context and situation (see the part "Adaptability" of this book) heavily influence the selection of the appropriate interaction devices and the appropriate interaction metaphors. Sensor information augments the interaction loop between the human and the computer. The gulf of evaluation might be bridged by the enhanced information base the computer now has to react to. However, the computer's behavior might also widen this gulf when user interface developers do not respect relevant usability criteria and fail on affordances, mappings and constraints.

From these fundamental considerations, we can infer that in ubiquitous computing we see a shift from explicit interaction towards more and more implicit interaction. Interfaces will adapt to context of use and situation and they will adapt to a more natural interaction. Robert J.K. Jacob (2006) coined the term reality-based interaction and reality-based interfaces to express this new direction in human-computer interaction.

In the remainder of this chapter we will discuss various approaches and technologies that will help to achieve advanced hands and eyes interaction in the ubiquitous computing domain.

MULTISCALE OUTPUT: LARGE DISPLAYS AND SMALL DISPLAYS

Visual displays are the way computer systems present information to the user through the human visual system. We can find several relevant criteria, which characterize displays for the case of ubiquitous computing. After looking at these characteristics we will have a look at different display device types such as:

- monitors;
- projective displays;
- surround-screen displays;
- head-mounted displays;
- virtual retina displays;
- handheld displays;
- haptic displays, and
- auditory displays.

For an in-depth discussion on displays, especially for 3-D environments, refer to Bowman et al. (2005).

Visual Display Characteristics

In order to classify visual displays, their characteristic features are being elaborated. We can distinguish the various display types by their:

- field of regard and their field of view,
- their spatial resolution,
- light transfer, and
- display mobility.

Field of Regard and Field of View

The field of regard denotes the visual angle for which a display surrounds the user. The field of view, however, is the angle that can be seen by the user at one instance in time. A seamless surround projection screen (see the subsection "Visual Display Device Types," and "Surround-Screen Displays"), for instance, might have a horizontal field of regard of 360 degrees, while the horizontal field of view is only 120 degrees when a user looks straight ahead. For flat 2-D displays the field of view heavily depends on the distance of the user to the display. For example, using a PDA's screen close-up, a user might have a larger field of view than watching video on a far away large size television set. Figure 4 illustrates the two notions field of regard and field of view.

Spatial Resolution

Spatial resolution of displays is usually measured in dots per inch (dpi) and thus it is a function of pixel size. The perceived resolution depends on the number of pixels, the screen size, and the viewing distance. It is interpreted as a high resolution

Figure 4. Field of regard and field of view with: (a) large surround screen and (b) desktop screen

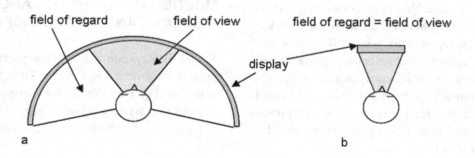

when the individual pixels are not distinguishable. Thus a PDA with many dpi may show a higher perceived resolution compared to a large screen where a user is standing close to it.

Light Transfer

In ubiquitous computing scenarios users are often mobile and use wall screens. When these are front projections the user's body may get in the way and throw shadows on the displayed information. Rear projection displays do not have this drawback, but there still may be obstacles between the user and the displayed information. Head-mounted displays never obstruct the view of their user. The technology of projection displays and head-mounted displays are covered in more detail in the subsection on display types.

Display Mobility

We can distinguish between mobile and stationary displays in ubiquitous computing. Stationary displays range from desktop monitors to wall screens and to 360-degree projection rooms for CAVE systems (CAVE = cave automatic virtual environment, see the subsection "Visual Display Device Types," and "Surround-Screen Displays"). More traditional mobile screens are attached to laptops, but they are not very usable while a user is walking around, even if, at least, she can take the screen with her. Usable in a truly mobile context are tablet PCs, PDAs, or smart phones, where one hand remains free to interact with the device, while the other prevents it from dropping. Entirely hands-free displays have to be attached to the body. In this category we see head-mounted displays or virtual retinal displays, both being covered in more detail in the subsection on display types.

Visual Display Device Types

In ubiquitous computing, we see the entire range of display devices. Besides the visual displays, haptic and auditive output devices augment the facilities of some applications. First, we will consider visual displays.

Monitors

Conventional monitors are commonly used also in ubiquitous computing applications. Depending on their size and position in the application, monitors show a different field of regard and field of view. Monitors are by their nature 2-D display devices. Anyhow, 3-D scenes may also be rendered on such a conventional monitor using geometric 3-D to 2-D projection. To get a more immersive impression, stereoscopic displays show a different image to each eye and use additional hardware like stereo glasses to convey the 3-D impression. Due to their power source and weight, monitors are stationary.

Projective Displays

Video projectors can be used to display visual output on larger areas than monitors can do. Having similar or even lower resolution than monitors only, the field of regard and field of view can be extended depending on the viewer's distance. However, spatial resolution is rather limited as pixels are physically large. We distinguish between front and rear projection (see Figure 5). Front projection places projectors on the same side of the screen as the viewer; rear projectors are placed behind the screen. With the latter technology, viewers cannot cast shadows on the display. Projective displays are stationary, but first miniature projection displays for mobile devices have been announced (www.microvision.com).

Figure 5. (a) front projection display; (b) rear projection display

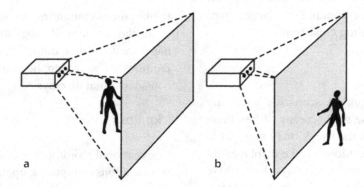

a   b

Surround-Screen Displays

Surround-screen displays use three or more projection-based screens that surround the user. Mostly the screens are rear projected, so users do not cast shadows on the visualization (Figure 6). Rear projection however takes a large amount of space and is mostly not viable for a floor display, that is, pictures are also visualized on the floor.

The first surround-screen was called the CAVE, cave automatic virtual environment, (Cruz-Neira et al., 1993) and coined the terminology for all types of displays where users are placed inside the device itself. Surround-screen displays feature a large field of regard and also a large field of view. They give a truly immersive perception. Such displays are stationary.

Figure 6. Surround-screen display

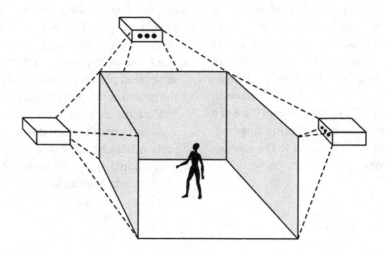

In ubiquitous computing users are usually mobile and may not always be happy to use stationary displays only. They may have a great need for mobile displays in order to perform their tasks. We will discuss such displays in the following.

Head-Mounted Displays

A head-mounted display (HMD) is a portable device attached to the viewer's head. HMDs being worn like a pair of glasses instead of utilizing helmet-like installations are also called head-worn displays. Monoscopic HMDs provide a display for a single eye, while stereoscopic HMDs support three-dimensional visualization through a small display for each of the two eyes. The first

head-mounted display was reported by Ivan Sutherland (1968).

Depending on the technology, three types of HMDs can be distinguished. The first type blocks out the real world entirely (Figure 7a). Users view a fully virtual environment. The second type has a camera attached to the HMD, which captures the real world scene in the viewing direction of the user. This video stream can be superimposed onto the virtual scene visible in the HMD. Such devices are also called video see-through HMDs (Figure 7b). Using such devices, the user's vision is restricted by the quality of the video. Furthermore the field of view is limited to the size of the display. The third type is the optical see-through display (Figure 7c), which superim-

Figure 7. Three types of head-mounted displays: (a) fully virtual, (b) video see-through, (c) optical see-through

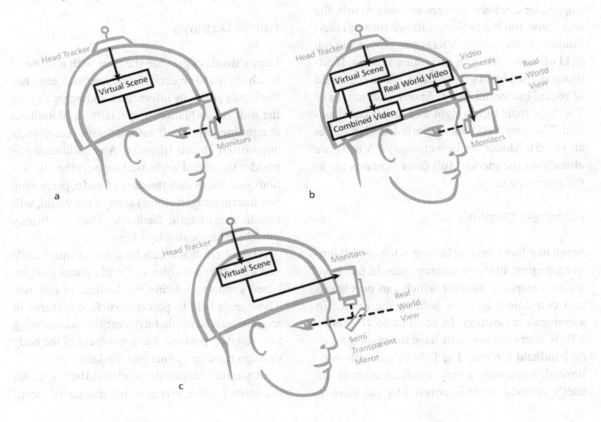

poses the virtual image over the real scene. Such displays use semi-transparent mirrors allowing the user to see through them and to display the computer-generated images as well. Thus the field of view of the real scene is less restricted than with video see-through devices and users do not lose peripheral vision entirely. It depends on the application which type of head-mounted device is preferable. Head-mounted displays are intensively used in augmented reality and virtual reality application (see the section "Integration of Physical and Virtual World").

Virtual Retinal Displays

Virtual retinal displays (VRD), sometimes also called light scanning displays, project intensity-modulated light beams directly onto the retina. Depending on the intensity of these laser beams VRDs can produce fully immersive impressions of the projected images and also see-through impressions, where viewers are able to mix the real scene and the projected image through their human vision system. VRDs can provide a high field of view with high-resolution images. If additionally the head gets tracked, also a high field of regard can be achieved. Another advantage of VRDs is their lightweight and small construction. The first VRD was reported by Tidwell et al. (1995). Monochrome versions of VRDs are already on the market, full color versions are at the prototype stage.

Handheld Displays

Small handheld devices having a display fall into this category. PDAs or smart phones in fact have a small graphics monitor which can be viewed at a convenient location holding the device in a convenient position. In contrast to HMDs or VRDs, users intentionally have to put their focus on handheld screens. The field of regard is very limited, since only a very small fraction of the user's viewing angle is covered by the display.

Furthermore the field of view is restricted to the small screen size. However, handheld displays are embedded into a fully functional computing device. Therefore we have a device offering also input capabilities like push buttons and scroll wheels, or we can use the display as a touch screen for direct manipulation.

Recently handheld devices have entered augmented reality applications. A small camera attached to the device allows display of the real scene on the handheld display. This scene can then be augmented with virtual objects. Such application of handheld devices is an alternative to video see-through HMDs. While HMDs are single-user devices, a handheld display can be viewed by several users. However the degree of immersion is rather low and at least one hand is required to carry the device. Furthermore the second hand will be required to perform the input tasks. Another drawback could be the limited computing power and memory capacity of small devices.

Haptic Displays

Haptic displays provide the user with a sense of touch of virtual objects. Haptic feedback enriches the hands and eyes interaction and helps closing the gulf of evaluation. Especially in ubiquitous computing users will interact with real objects and virtual objects likewise. Any additional cue besides the visual sense will support the interaction cycle. Especially the stages 5 and 6, perceiving and interpreting the (new) state of the world, will benefit from haptic feedback. Thus we briefly introduce haptic displays here.

Haptic feedback can be divided into tactile and kinesthetic feedback. Tactile refers to skin-based excitations being mechanical or thermal. These cues help to perceive surface textures or temperature. Kinesthetic refers to the forces being perceived by position and movement of the body through muscles, joints and tendons.

An optimal haptic display would have to cover the entire body. Current tactile displays concentrate on hands such as data gloves with inflatable bladders or small vibrators. Current kinesthetic displays are force-feedback devices either being ground-referenced or body-referenced. A more detailed discussion of haptic displays and haptic rendering can be found in Sherman et al. (2003).

Auditory Displays

Hearing is the third most important sense of humans. Especially our ability to use 3-D sound as localization means gives auditory displays a major role in ubiquitous computing interaction. Compared to visual and haptic cues, sound is the only sense that has a 360-degree field of regard. Thus 3-D auditory displays can be used to augment hands and eyes interaction to draw a user's attention to events outside the current field of view. 3-D audio is supported by all contemporary sound cards for PCs and thus a simple and low-cost extension to the stationary display types or to in-room ubiquitous computing scenarios. Shilling et al. (2002) give a detailed overview of auditory displays.

Peripheral Displays

As we can see from the name, peripheral displays are placed in the surroundings of the user. Peripheral displays are designed to reduce the information overload of other displays by placing information into the periphery of the human perception. Thus the displays are not in the field of view of the user, as long as the user does not focus on them. Especially scales where the exact values are less important than the degree of change are good candidates for being presented by peripheral displays. We will have a closer look at peripheral displays in the section "Attention," subsection "Peripheral Awareness."

Table 1 summarizes the output devices being considered in ubiquitous computing applications and their characteristic attributes.

INPUT DEVICES AND CHARACTERISTICS

After having discussed devices for the "eye" part of hands and eyes interaction in ubiquitous com-

Table 1. Output device types

Output Devices	Attributes
Monitors	stationary, high resolution
projective displays	stationary, limited spatial resolution
surround-screen displays	stationary, large field of regard and field of view
head-mounted displays	Portable a) Fully virtual view: field of view restricted to virtual environment b) Video see-through: vision restricted by quality of video c) Optical see-through: field of view and peripheral vision not much restricted
haptic displays	perceive surface textures or temperature, wearable
auditory displays	360° field of regard with 3-D sound
peripheral displays	perceivable without being in the field of view

puting we treat relevant input devices and types of interaction related to them. In general, interaction techniques and input devices are separate topics, since interactions of the same type can be performed using different types of input devices. Pointing as an interaction technique can, for instance, be done using a standard 2-D mouse or by tracking the user's eye movement as in a view pointer (Feiner et al., 1997). Elaborate discussions on input devices can be found in Sherman et al. (2003) or Bowman et al. (2005). As in the display section we will look at characteristics first and consider the device types afterwards.

Input Device Characteristics

In order to classify input devices, their characteristic features are elaborated. We can distinguish the various input device types by their:

- degree of freedom;
- whether they deliver discrete input values or a continuous stream of values, and
- whether input is actively produced by the user or passively gathered.

Degree of Freedom

The degree of freedom (DOF) specifies how many independent parameters are provided by an input device. A conventional mouse, for instance, delivers an x and y value, and is thus a 2-DOF device. Tracking devices for 3-D applications typically capture three position values and three orientation values and are thus 6-DOF devices.

Discrete vs. Continuous Input

Input devices can be characterized by the frequency with which they provide data values and the triggering of when this happens. Discrete input devices deliver a single data value mostly only when the user performs some action with the device. An example is clicking on a mouse button. Continuous input devices provide the application with a continuous stream of data values mostly without specific user action. A tracking device continuously delivering position and orientation information is an example of such a device.

Active vs. Passive Input

Active input devices require the user to actively operate the input device. Only then will the device deliver data values, these being a single discrete value or a continuous stream. Passive input devices deliver their captured data values all the time. A head-tracking device, for instance, might report its position and orientation values also when its user does not move at all.

Input Device Types

Most of the input devices we use in traditional computing are also being used in ubiquitous computing. In the following we will discuss those and also input devices from the 3-D domain usable here.

Keyboards

The traditional input devices are keyboard and 2-D mouse. The keyboard is a discrete, active input device offering a number of keys. In ubiquitous computing scenarios keyboards are often required to enter alphanumerical characters. In order to make them portable, small wrist- or arm-worn keyboards may be used, or they even may be projected on a surface with the typing being recognized through computer vision algorithms.

2-D Mice and Pointing Devices

Two-dimensional mice are the standard point-and-click device in WIMP interfaces (WIMP = windows, icons, menus, and pointers). They have a continuous component delivering a relative position in 2-D space and buttons as discrete components. A drawback of the 2-D mouse in ubiquitous computing is its dependence on a 2-D surface to be operated upon. This can be relieved by trackballs, which can be held in free space while turning the ball with a finger.

Other desktop input devices in this category are joysticks. Besides continuous 2-D location actively provided by operating the levers of the device, joysticks have a couple of buttons and switches for specific purposes.

With the advent of handheld computers pen-based input became popular. A stylus is used as an input device operated directly on the screen. A stylus can be used in desktop scenarios as well as in mobile scenarios, since it is a lightweight component, which can be used on any type of touch sensitive screen whether it is on a PDA or a wall-sized screen.

Tracking Devices

In many ubiquitous computing applications it is required to know what the user's or a physical object's location is. The position might be required of the entire user, or we might only be interested in the position and orientation of her hand for instance. Mostly this information is provided continuously and in a passive way.

The task of tracking a user's or object's position is achieved by motion trackers. Motion trackers are characterized by their range, latency, accuracy and jitter (see also the section "Augmented Reality" of this chapter). Some technologies are available for motion tracking including magnetic, mechanical, acoustic, inertial, optical, and hybrid tracking.

Sometimes it is important to get the position and orientation of a user's hand and fingers. Data gloves are input devices that provide such information. Bend-sensing gloves detect hand postures or gestures through a set of sensors embedded into the glove. Such data gloves can, for instance, be used to detect pointing or grasping interactions. Circular gestures could be interpreted as selecting an object. Flicking the fingers could be throwing an object away. Pinch gloves detect the touching of two fingers by conductive material. Grabbing gestures can be mapped to the various combinations of finger touches. For more information on gesture detection see the section "Gesture Interaction."

3-D Mice

A mixture between the standard 2-D mouse and the possibilities of hand tracking are 3-D mice. Such devices are motion-tracked and feature a specific set of buttons, knobs and wheels. The first such mouse was a handheld device called the "bat" by Ware and Jessome (1988). In the meanwhile smaller and more convenient 3-D mice have been constructed which can be worn like a ring on the finger. A small trackball can be operated with the thumb and some buttons allow for discrete active user input.

Table 2. Input device types

Input device	Attributes
Keyboards	discrete, active
2-D mice and pointers	discrete and continuous components
tracking devices	position and orientation detection
3-D mice	hybrid of 2-D mice and tracking devices

Another category of 3-D mice do not use motion tracking to get their own position and orientation, but offer the user levers or rods to actively enter 6 degrees of freedom (Fröhlich et al., 2000).

Table 2 summarizes the input devices being considered in ubiquitous computing applications and their characteristic attributes.

INTEGRATION OF PHYSICAL AND VIRTUAL WORLD

One major characteristic of interaction in ubiquitous computing is the integration and merging of the physical world represented by real-life objects and the virtual world represented by computer-generated visualizations or computer output in general.

Milgram and Kishino (1994) conceived the range of possible mixtures as the virtuality continuum (Figure 8). At the one end (on the left of the figure) there are real environments consisting only of real objects, at the other extreme there are purely virtual environments. Depending on the extent of virtuality, Milgram and Kishino distinguish between augmented reality and augmented virtuality and call this span mixed reality (MR).

The most straightforward way to view mixed reality is by overlaying virtual and real objects in one single display; for instance, by overlaying virtual objects into a live video stream. Visual MR user interfaces differ in the degree of immersion they offer:

1. Monitor-based displays are non-immersive. They are usually called Window-on-the-World displays and were the first displays used in the virtuality continuum.
2. Head-mounted displays significantly extend the field of regard of the first class. Since they are worn on the head, users are free to move and get an immersive feeling of the virtual environment.
3. Head-mounted displays with see-through capability allow the superimposition of virtual objects directly over real world scenes.
4. Head-mounted displays that use additional video input capturing the real scene in front of the user enable overlaying virtual objects with the real objects in the video.
5. A completely graphic display environment where the user is inside the realm of the display, like in surround-scene displays.

In ubiquitous computing, when users take advantage of various and embedded devices all of the above user interfaces could be used depending on context and situation. Additionally, users will be willing to use a broad range of input devices in order to interact with the system. This observation is driven by the fact that in ubiquitous computing the user is inside the system and

Figure 8. The virtuality continuum (cf., Milgram & Kishino, 1994)

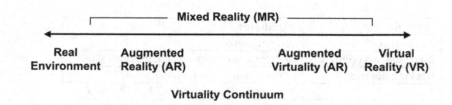

not looking into the system through a window. Ubiquitous computing thus is close to the left edge of Milgram and Kishino's taxonomy. As we will see in the next subsection, "Augmented Reality," as a domain heavily featuring hands and eye interaction, is a step towards true ubiquitous and pervasive technologies.

Augmented Reality

Ronald T. Azuma (1997) defines augmented reality as combining real and virtual, as being interactive in real time, and as being registered in 3-D, that is, virtual objects are registered in the real world. The combination of real and virtual objects is realized by appropriate display technology. Interactivity is provided by specific input devices. Registration requires tracking.

Tracking

Initially virtual and real world coexist independent of each other. The coordinate systems of both worlds have to be related to correlate them. For instance, we need the position of the user. When using head-mounted devices the position of the eyes and the head's orientation are required to compute the correct superimposition. This is called head tracking. Tracking of position and orientation of real objects that can be moved in the scene is called object tracking. A user can be seen as being an object as well.

The various tracking techniques can be characterized according to some criteria, which can also be used to review suitable tracking for different applications in ubiquitous computing.

Refresh Rate and Latency

A sufficiently high refresh rate and low latency are important for a credible superimposition of coordinates. Human perception requires a rate of 25 frames per second to view a continuous movement. If the tracking is slower, virtual and real objects will drift and shake. Correlation will be imprecise with high latencies.

Accuracy

Depending on the application, different resolutions of tracking samples are required. In a surgical application resolution needs to be in the millimeter or micron range, whereas in a mobile entertainment AR system with PDAs this could be in a centimeter range or even more.

Reliability

When the tracking data shows wide variation over time, object positions tend to jump. Especially accumulated errors can destroy the entire coordinate correlation.

Degree of Freedom

The number of dimensions covered by the tracking method is called *degree of freedom* (DOF). If position and orientation are sampled in a 3-dimensional space, the tracking method has six degrees of freedom, which will be required in many ubiquitous computing applications.

Multi-Object Capability

Multi-object and multi-user applications often use a single tracking system being able to track several objects and persons at once. Such systems are typically installed in equipped rooms used as a virtual environment.

Portability

Mobile tracking capability is an important issue in ubiquitous computing applications. For such purposes the tracking system needs to be limited in size and weight. Other significant aspects are energy consumption and the distance range of the sensors applied. Furthermore, environmental conditions have to be considered such as light conditions, magnetic fields, occlusions and so forth.

From Mobile Augmented Reality Towards Ubiquitous Computing

Making augmented reality systems mobile and portable is a further step towards ubiquitous computing applications with intensive hands and eyes interaction. Application scenarios range from pedestrian navigation support (Mahler et al., 2007) to game applications (Wagner et al., 2005). All scenarios have in common that the input and output devices shall be small and lightweight. Often PDAs are used to substitute computers in a backpack and using head-mounted displays as in the first such system, the Touring Machine (Feiner et al, 1997), where a user could stroll through a city, wearing a head mounted device superimposing textual information on buildings of interest.

In the future we will see developments sewing the computing power, keyboards and other active input devices into the fabric of our clothes. Whether many users will wear these devices or even wear a head-mounted display voluntarily is doubtful.

It is much more viable that users will utilize small devices like PDAs or smart phones and augment them by surrounding equipment shared in a room or environment as Mark Weiser (1991) predicted. With this, the close interaction loop using a dedicated set of input and output devices will open up. The attention focus has to broaden; the field of regard spans our entire surroundings and covers several modalities.

ATTENTION

By adding the real world to the scope of human-computer interaction, the bridge between virtual information and the user can be drawn much more easily. People are familiar with real objects, since they started to discover the world as young children. In the previous section we have come to know the different ranges of mixed reality, and we have already had a closer look at the field of augmented reality. The area discussed now is even closer to pure reality than AR. Adapting knowledge from the fields of psychology; the interaction between human and computer in the future will probably be far more appealing.

Attention Detection

When interacting with someone or something, we draw our attention to this person or object. It stands to reason that if you have to figure out whether a person is paying attention to you or not, you simply can check where he or she is looking. In addition to methods used in augmented reality, where the user wears devices like head-mounted cameras for the detection of head and eye orientation, several computer vision-based methods were invented for this issue. They automatically analyze captured images or frame sequences to

Figure 9. A camera with Infrared LEDs arranged in two rings around the lens (cf., Morimoto et al., 2000) allows quick detection of multiple pairs of eyes

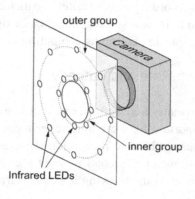

find out where the person or persons on the images are looking at.

A typical approach is to first find out the position of head and eyes. Theis et al. (2002) detect the user's face by clustering the skin colored areas in a captured image and then use a corner detection algorithm to match the typical eye position in the face. This approach works fine if a user is very near to the capturing camera (approx. 60cm).

Morimoto et al. (2000) presented a method where they use multiple light sources around a camera (Figure 9). This method allows fast detection of more than one person in a distance of up to five meters. Two sets of infrared LEDs (light emitting diodes) are mounted on the camera. One set is placed directly around the lens so the angle of the emitted light is approximately at the same axis as the camera. When activating these illuminators, the captured image shows a red eye effect (or bright eyes within black and white pictures, see Figure 10a). The radius of the other set's circle depends on several aspects of the camera, for example, what lens is used. The resulting images show black eyes at the same place where the bright eyes were in the image captured while the inner LEDs flashed (Figure 10b). If one image is subtracted from the other, all eye positions on the image are detected.

Morimoto et al. empirically assigned a radius of 45mm for the outer group of LEDs and 7.5mm

for the inner group. One group is synchronized with the odd frames of the captured film, the other with the even frames. The groups and the camera are concentric, providing one position of the corneal reflection in both images (see Figure 5). With this reflection being near the middle of the pupils, the focus of the user's attention is in direction of the camera and other devices nearby. This method was used in various projects like those of Vertegaal and his group (2006). Their "Eye Contact Sensor" represents an eye-tracking device, implementing the features of Morimoto's eye detection to build attentive user interfaces.

Attention-Awareness

An interface with knowledge of the user's focus can easily use this context information to allow automatic adaptation of program activities, for example, to direct the attention to something.

Reingold et al. (2003) developed a gaze-contingent display (GCD) where only the region in the focus of the user's attention has full resolution of the source image (Figure 11). This method allows a smaller image size, influencing transmission time of image data. Reingold et al. used this technique to transfer movies. The high-resolution region changes with the gaze of the user, so she can view details wherever she wants.

Figure 10. The red eye effect (a) and the black eye effect (b) images are subtracted to find the eyes in the captured images (cf., Morimoto et al., 2000). The position of the corneal reflection within the pupil reveals the gaze direction.

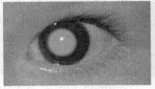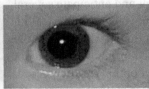

a   b

Figure 11. Gaze-contingent display: Details of the photo are shown only where the focus of the user's attention lies. All other information is rendered in lower resolution with a blur effect. (Photo: Marc Hermann)

Barth et al. (2006) use a red dot to guide eye movements to special areas in the field of view. Imagine you are driving a car. Outside it is raining and you fail to see a pedestrian crossing the street. But luckily, your car has a device that detects the pedestrian's movement. Your attention is guided by a small red dot to the area inside the field of view where the pedestrian is walking. You merely saw the red dot, but you now are aware of the pedestrian and step on the brake. Such applications guiding a user's attention can be used in ubiquitous systems to lead the attention to real objects or even to virtual objects, if complemented by a head-mounted display to superimpose these virtual objects. Barth et al. go one step further by measuring eye movement and anticipate several options where the eye movement will go. With this information, one option is chosen and the chance of that is increased by showing a red dot for a short time. The other options are decreased, for example, by blurring or movement removal.

Peripheral Awareness

Due to the information overload a user is confronted with nowadays, researchers are trying to reduce the cognitive load by changing the presentation of information. Psychologists found out that a mass of information can easily be hidden from our mind unless we pay attention to it, for example, the sound of a waterfall nearby or the motor sound of our car when driving. Peripheral awareness of the information does not require the focus of our attention, but we are able to recognize it by easily "switching" to our auditory sense. For example, if the sound of our car engine changes in an unfamiliar way, we pay attention to it. Adapting this knowledge to the field of human-computer interaction, several information systems have been developed over the last decades to be used in ubiquitous computing scenarios. Pousman et al. (2006) present a classification of the three most common terms. We illustrate them by giving examples in automobile scenarios.

Notification System

The prevailing term for ubiquitous information systems is notification systems. This term is used when information is delivered in a multitasking scenario and on multiple output devices. The attention of the user can equally be focused on the retrieval of information in the user's primary task (current main job) or her secondary task (minor businesses). In the driving example this means that the primary task is driving the car, the major attention of the driver is focused on the road and the road users, but she also observes her speedometer for speed control, hears traffic news on the radio, and so forth.

Peripheral Display

When the design purpose of the system was to present the information in the secondary task, we can refer to it as a peripheral display. Not all notification systems are peripheral displays, but nearly all peripheral displays are notification systems. In our example, this could be the following. The fuel tank display in the car gives the driver information on how much fuel she has. This can be transferred into information on how far she is able to drive. When the fuel tank is close to being empty, most cars have an additional display, for example, a red fuel station symbol to warn the driver. Many peripheral displays have these warning systems, which try to switch the focus of the user to the secondary task.

Ambient Display

The last term, ambient display, is a subclass of peripheral displays. When information is minimized to a few intuitive states and the system fits into the environment by aesthetic design, a peripheral display becomes an ambient display. Coming to the driving scenario again, we can roughly define the turn signal as an ambient display. The automobile industry tries to fit the indicators into the whole car design. There are four states of the display: blinkers off, left light blinking, right light blinking and both lights blinking. The states are quite intuitive except maybe the fourth one.

AFFECTION

In his book, "Emotional Design," Don Norman (2004) gives a favorable opinion on factoring emotions into the design process. He posits "three different levels of the brain: the automatic, prewired layer, called the visceral level; the part that contains the brain processes that control everyday behavior, known as the behavioral level; and the contemplative part of the brain, or the reflective level" (p. 21).

These three levels work together, building the complexity of emotions, moods, traits and personality of a person. If these thoughts flow into the design process of user interfaces, the results will be affective and appealing interfaces.

Norman maps the three levels to characteristics that can be applied to user interfaces as well as products. The visceral level can be supported by appealing appearance. This includes not only the visual appearance, but also appearance of sound, haptics, taste, and so forth.

If we want a behavioral design, we have to make the user interface effective. The user should not be annoyed by it, but instead enjoy using it. The more effectively the interface can be used, the more the behavioral level is satisfied.

For the reflective level, the interface has a major attraction if the user has a personal relationship to it; for example, the interface evokes memories with positive associations in her. Or to use the interface seems to be a challenge, which she is able to master. It is quite obvious that the combination of these characteristics remains difficult for the designer to apply to one interface (or product).

Tangible Interaction

As we already mentioned, in everyday life people interact with real physical objects. In tangible interaction, digital information is represented with real objects, supporting the ability of direct physical manipulation and usage of this information in ubiquitous computing systems, where mouse and keyboard are not at hand. The usage of real objects therefore especially supports behavioral design (and in many cases also visceral design).

Durell Bishop, who designed the *Marble Answering Machine* (MAM) (Crampton-Smith, 1995), was a pioneer in creating a *Tangible User Interface* (TUI). The MAM is a telephone answering machine presenting new forms of user interaction techniques: every phone call message is associated with a marble (see *Figure 12*), which then is collected in a panel. If you want to hear a message, you simply take one marble out of the panel and put it into a recess on the machine. The marble is recognized and the associated message replayed. In the same way that you can put the marbles onto an augmented phone, implying an automatic callback, several other functions like storage are possible, too. The haptic interaction process simplifies the functions of the answering machine, making the messages graspable. The easy-to-use interface demonstrates the potential of associating digital information with physical objects.

A tangible user interface represents digital information with a physical, graspable object in the real world. Manipulation of the object has a direct effect on the digital representation according to the application. The goal of TUI design is to have highly intuitive interfaces. TUIs adapt public *affordances* and *constraints* from everyday life, assuring that we are familiar with the usage of new interfaces. If the TUI supports good *mappings* of the manipulation technique with the effect it has on the digital representation, a new user should be able to instantly work with the device without further instructions. Similar efforts were made in GUI research by Don Norman (1988) (see the section "Introduction and Basic Principles" of this chapter).

Figure 12. Bishop's Marble Answering Machine (cf., Crampton-Smith, 1995): The drawing shows the main system. The user can easily perceive that three messages were recorded by the answering machine, as there are three marbles in the panel.

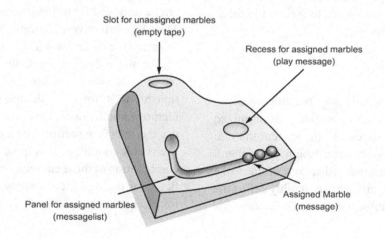

Fishkin (2004) gives a universal description of TUI with the following sequence (p.348):

1. "Some input event occurs. This input event is typically a physical manipulation performed by a user with their hands on some 'everyday physical object,' such as tilting, shaking, squeezing, pushing, or, most often, moving. Later, we will remove the 'typically' qualifier.
2. A computer system senses this input event, and alters its state.
3. The system provides feedback. This output event is via a change in the physical nature of some object—it alters its display surface, grows, shrinks, makes a sound, gives haptic feedback, etc."

A synonym for tangible user interfaces is the older term *graspable user interface*, but GUI also stands for graphical user interface. However the term TUI is also potentially ambiguous, standing for a text user interface. Other not so popular terms are *physical user interface*, *embodied interface*, and *extreme interface*.

Several toolkits were built by researchers for fast prototyping of tangible user interfaces, for example, Papier-Mâché (Klemmer et al, 2004). Input is realized by camera, scanner and RFID reader, making it possible to use any object for interacting with the computer. Output is restricted to acoustic or on-screen output, but for basic tests it is satisfactory. Papier-Mâché is an open-source Java toolkit, working with three event types:

- **phobAdded**: Whenever a new object is detected by the input source (camera, scanner or RFID reader), a phobAdded event is generated.
- **phobUpdated**: If the position, size or other attributes of the object change, the phobUpdated event notifies this change.
- **phobRemoved**: If the input source loses contact with the object (the object is out of sight or range), a phobRemoved event is evoked.

The events are equal for all input sources except their attributes. The RFID reader can only determine the ID of the tag, whereas the camera or scanner also can detect the exact position, size, orientation, bounding box, main color, and a reference to the image frame where the object was found. These events can be interpreted by any application, making prototyping of tangible interfaces fast and efficient.

Gesture Interaction

When people communicate, their main information channel is voice. A second channel is body language. The way we stand or sit, look at each other, our facial expression, and the hand gestures we use tells others about our emotions. Researchers already have discussed the use of gestures for input by using various tracking methods. See the section "Tracking" for some tracking methods also usable for gesture recognition and, for example, The Gesture Pendant (Starner et al., 2000). We have here a quick spot on techniques where no physical device is needed by the user. Fails et al. (2002) project operating controls onto surfaces like armchair, desk, or wall. They call these controls light widgets. The controls can be used by simply moving a hand over the widget and performing a gesture. Two cameras are needed for the gesture to be recognized correctly. One video image would not suffice to detect the distance from hand to widget, as skin-detection is used for detecting the hand. Von Hardenberg et al. (2001) developed a real-time finger-finding and hand-posture recognition algorithm, which allows free-hand input in a broad range. Ståhl et al. (2003) discuss using gestures for affective input.

They analyzed movement theories and the body language of actors. They built their model on three dimensions of movement and emotions:

- **Shape**: The body movement in horizontal, vertical and sagittal directions creates shapes.
- **Effort**: The effort is a four-dimensional space with the axes time, space, weight and flow, representing dynamics of the movement.
- **Valence**: Valence represents the degree of pleasure of the movement. Ståhl et al. use pressing the fist to indicate pleasure. Less pressure means more pleasure.

Ståhl et al. demonstrate in an example scenario that using these dimensions allows better learning of gestures. Additionally, the computer can better determine the emotional state of the user and respond accordingly.

SUMMARY

For ubiquitous computing systems, new human-computer interaction techniques have had to be invented. In this chapter we first reflected on the basics in hands and eyes interaction we know from pre-ubiquitous computing, where a typical user has one desktop computer with mouse and keyboard and a monitor. We then listed types and characteristics of output and input devices that go beyond the desktop metaphor. They build the bridge to collaborative and ubiquitous computing systems, but they are only the first step towards calm technology as being devised by Mark Weiser. We also gave a short overview of some new interaction techniques involving attention and affection. Research in this field of human-computer interaction has gathered momentum in the last decade, and there will be much new to see and to touch in the future.

FUTURE RESEARCH DIRECTIONS

Nowadays, and even more in future UC environments, attention is a fundamental element to be considered in the design process of user interfaces. With the information overflow still growing, it is hard to direct the user's attention to where the designer of a system intended to have it. We explored how the computer can identify the focus of the user's attention and how attention can be guided to a specific point. We also spotted how the perception of a user can be unburdened by usage of peripheral displays, which allow her to better concentrate on the primary task of work.

Especially the last issue is important in a time where people communicate by e-mail, SMS or online chat. The workflow is permanently interrupted by notifications of messages (mobile phone or e-mail) or friends going online (e.g., AIM, ICQ, Jabber). By introducing calm technology, interruptions can be minimized, and the user is less distracted (Weiser et al., 1996).

But like so many new technologies, these useful techniques hold perceivable risks: the more the computer can analyze the user and his behavior, the more she can be directly influenced by the wishes of designers or developers of such systems. The advertising industry, for example, has successfully managed to use every new technology for their purpose. Hopefully there will always be an option to switch off (as we know from television or Java popups). Affective interfaces promote Weiser's vision of ubiquitous computing and calm technology. The interfaces of the future will be more intuitive and fun to use, appealing, useful and will not disturb the user in his main task.

REFERENCES

Anderson, J.R. (2004). *Cognitive psychology and its implications* (6th ed.). Palgrave Macmillan.

Azuma, R.T. (1997). A survey of augmented reality. *Presence: Teleoperators and Virtual Environments*, 6, 355-385.

Barth, E., Dorr, M., Böhme, M., Gegenfurtner, K.R., & Martinetz, T. (2006). Guiding eye movements for better communication and augmented vision. In *Perception and Interactive Technologies* (LNAI 4021, pp. 1-8). Springer

Bowman, D.A., Kruiff, E., LaViola, Jr., J.J., & Poupyrev, I. (2005). *3D user interfaces – theory and practice*. Addison-Wesley, Boston.

Card, S.K., Moran, T.P., & Newell, A. (1983). *The psychology of human-computer interaction*. Lawrence Erlbaum Associates.

Crampton-Smith, G. (1995). The hand that rocks the cradle. *ID Magazine*, 60–65.

Cruz-Neira, C., Sandin, D., & Defanti, T. (1993). Surround screen projection-based virtual reality. In *Proceedings of the 20th Annual Conference on Computer Graphics and Interactive Techniques* (pp. 135-142). New York: ACM Press

Fails, J.A., & Olsen, Jr., D. (2002). Light widgets: Interacting in every-day spaces. In *IUI '02: Proceedings of the 7th International Conference on Intelligent User Interfaces* (pp. 63-69). ACM Press.

Feiner, S., MacIntyre, B., Höllerer, T., & Webster, A. (1997). A touring machine: Prototyping 3D mobile augmented reality systems for exploring the urban environment. In *Proceedings of the First International Symposium on Wearable Computers* (pp. 74-81). IEEE Press.

Fishkin, K.P. (2004). A taxonomy for and analysis of tangible interfaces. *Personal Ubiquitous Computing*, 8, 347-358.

Fitts, P.M. (1954). The information capacity of the human motor system in controlling the amplitude of movement. *Journal of Experimental Psychology*, 47, 381-391

Fröhlich, B., & Plate, J. (2000). The Cubic Mouse: A new device for three-dimensional input. In *Proceedings of the ACM Conference on Human Factors in Computing Systems*, CHI '2000 (pp. 526-531). ACM Press.

Jacob, R.J.K. (2006). What is the next generation of human-computer interaction? In *Conference on Human Factors in Computing Systems*, CHI '06 (pp. 1707-1710). New York: ACM Press.

Klemmer, S.R., Li, J., Lin, J., & Landay, J.A. (2004). Papier-Mâché: Toolkit support for tangible input. In *CHI '04: Proceedings of the SIGCHI Conference on Human Factors in Computing Systems* (pp. 399-406). ACM Press.

MacKenzie, I.S., & Buxton, W. (1992). Extending Fitts' law to two-dimensional tasks. In *Proceedings of the ACM Conference on Human Factors in Computing Systems*, CHI'92 (pp. 219-226). New York: ACM Press.

Mahler, T., Reuff, M., & Weber, M. (2007). Pedestrian navigation system implications on visualization. In *Proceedings of the 12th International Conference on Human-Computer Interaction*, HCII '07 (LNCS 4555).

Milgram, P., & Kishino, F. (1994). A taxonomy of mixed reality visual displays. In *IECE Transactions on Information and Systems*, 1321-1329.

Morimoto, C.H., Koons, D., Amir, A., & Flickner, M. (2000). Pupil detection and tracking using multiple light sources. *Image and Vision Computing*, 18, 331-335.

Norman, D.A. (1988). *The psychology of everyday things*. New York: Basic Books.

Norman, D.A. (2004). *Emotional design*. New York: Basic Books.

Pousman, Z., & Stasko, J. (2006). A taxonomy of ambient information systems: Four patterns of design. In *AVI '06: Proceedings of the Working*

Conference on Advanced Visual Interfaces (pp. 67-74). New York: ACM Press.

Raskin, J. (2000). The humane interface. Boston: Addison-Wesley.

Reingold, E.M., Loschky, L.C., McConkie, G.W., & Stampe, D.M. (2003). Gaze-contingent multi-resolutional displays: An integrative review. *Human Factors, 45*(2), 307-328.

Sherman, B., & Craig, A. (2003). *Understanding virtual reality*. Morgan Kauffman Publishers.

Shilling, R., & Shinn-Cunningham, B. (2002). Virtual auditory displays. In K. Stanney (Ed.), *Handbook of Virtual Environments: Design, Implementation, and Applications* (pp. 65-92). Lawrence Erlbaum Associates.

Ståhl, A., Höök, K., & Fagerberg, P. (2003). Designing gestures for affective input: An analysis of shape, effort and valence. In *Proceedings of the 2nd International Conference on Mobile and Ubiquitous Multimedia*. ACM Press.

Starner, T., Auxier, J., & Ashbrook D. (2000). The Gesture Pendant: A self-illuminating, wearable, infrared computer vision system for home automation control and medical monitoring. In *The Fourth International Symposium on Wearable Computers*, Atlanta GA (pp. 87-94). IEEE Computer Society Press.

Sutherland, I. (1968). A head-mounted three dimensional display. In *Proceedings of the Fall Joint Computer Conference* (pp. 757-764).

Theis, C., & Hustadt, K. (2002). Detecting the gaze direction for a man machine interface. In *Proceedings of the 11th IEEE International Workshop ROMAN* (pp. 536-541).

Tidwell, M., Johnston, R., Melville, D., & Furness, T. (1995). The virtual retina display: A retinal scanning imaging system. In *Proceedings of Virtual Reality World '95* (pp. 325-333).

Vertegaal, R., Shell, J.S., Chen, D., & Mamuji, A. (2006). Designing for augmented attention: Towards a framework for attentive user interfaces. *Computers in Human Behavior, 22*(4), 771–789.

Von Hardenberg, C., & Bérard, F. (2001). Bare-hand human-computer interaction. In *PUI '01: Proceedings of the 2001 Workshop on Perceptive User Interfaces* (pp. 1-8). ACM Press.

Wagner, D., Pintaric, T., Ledermann, F., & Schmalstieg, D. (2005). Towards massively multi-user augmented reality on handheld devices. In *Third International Conference on Pervasive Computing* (LNCS 3468, pp. 208-219). Springer.

Ware, C., & Jessome, D. (1988). Using the Bart: A six-dimensional mouse for object placement. In *Proceedings of Graphics Interface '88* (pp. 119-124).

Weiser, M. (1991). The computer for the twenty first century. *Scientific American, 265*(3), 94–104.

Weiser, M., & Brown, J.S. (1996). Designing calm technology. *Powergrid Journal, 1*(1).

Welford, A.T. (1960). The measurement of sensory-motor performance: Survey and reappraisal of twelve years' progress. *Ergonomics, 3*, 189-230.

ADDITIONAL READING

Abowd, G.D., Mynatt, E.D., & Rodden, T. (2002). The human experience [of ubiquitous computing]. *Pervasive Computing, 1*(1), 48-57.

Baudisch, P., DeCarlo, D., Duchowski, A.T., & Geisler, W.S. (2003). Focusing on the essential: considering attention in display design. *Communications of the ACM, 46*(3), 60–66.

Dix, A., Finlay, J., Abowd, G., & Beale, R. (1997). *Human-computer interaction*. Prentice-Hall, Inc.

Dourish, P. (2001). Where the action is: The foundations of embodied interaction. MIT Press.

Duchowski, A.T. (2003). Eye tracking methodology: Theory and practice. New York: Springer-Verlag.

Hourizi, R., & Johnson, P. (2004). Designing to support awareness: A predictive, composite model. In *CHI '04: Proceedings of the SIGCHI Conference on Human Factors in Computing Systems* (pp. 159-166). ACM Press.

Ishii, H., & Ullmer, B. (1997). Tangible bits: Towards seamless interfaces between people, bits and atoms. In *CHI '97: Proceedings of the SIGCHI Conference on Human Factors in Computing Systems* (pp. 234-241). ACM Press.

Matthews, T., Dey, A.K., Mankoff, J., Carter, S., & Rattenbury, T. (2004). A toolkit for managing user attention in peripheral displays. In *UIST '04: Proceedings of the 17th Annual ACM Symposium on User Interface Software and Technology* (pp. 247–256). New York: ACM Press.

McCrickard, D.S., & Chewar, C.M. (2003) Attuning notification design to user goals and attention costs. *Communications of the ACM, 46*(3), 67–72. Myers, B.A. (1998) A brief history of human-computer interaction technology. *Interactions, 5*(2), 44-54. ACM Press.

Raffle, H.S., Parkes, A.J., & Ishii, H. (2004). Topobo: A constructive assembly system with kinetic memory. In *CHI '04: Proceedings of the SIGCHI Conference on Human Factors in Computing Systems* (pp. 647-654). ACM Press.

Sandor, C., & Klinker, G. (2005). A rapid prototyping software infrastructure for user interfaces in ubiquitous augmented reality. *Personal Ubiquitous Computing, 9*(3), 169-185.

Sebe, N., Lew, M.S., & Huang, T.S. (2004). *The state-of-the-art in human-computer interaction* (LNCS 3058, pp. 1-6). Springer.

Shaer, O., Leland, N., Calvillo-Gamez, E.H., & Jacob, R.J.K. (2004). The TAC paradigm: Specifying tangible user interfaces. *Personal Ubiquitous Computing, 8*(5), 359–369.

Shneiderman, B., & Plaisant, C. (2004). *Designing the user interface: Strategies for effective human-computer interaction*. Addison-Wesley.

Ullmer, B. (2002). *Tangible interfaces for manipulation aggregates of digital information*. Ph.D. dissertation, Massachusetts Institute of Technology.

Wang, J. (2003). Human-computer interaction research and practice in China. *Interactions, 10*, 88-96.

Want, R., Fishkin, K.P., Gujar, A., & Harrison, B.L. (1999). Bridging physical and virtual worlds with electronic tags. In *CHI '99: Proceedings of the SIGCHI Conference on Human Factors in Computing Systems* (pp. 370-377). ACM Press.

Wisneski, C., Ishii, H., Dahley, A., Gorbet, M.G., Brave, S., Ullmer, B., & Yarin, P. (1998). Ambient displays: Turning architectural space into an interface between people and digital information. In *CoBuild '98: Proceedings of the First International Workshop on Cooperative Buildings, Integrating Information, Organization, and Architecture* (pp. 22-32). Springer.

Zhai, S. (2003). What's in the eyes for attentive input? *Communications of the ACM, 46*(3), 34-39.

Chapter XX
Intelligent User Interfaces for Ubiquitous Computing

Rainer Malaka
Bremen University, Bremen

ABSTRACT

Designing user interfaces for ubiquitous computing applications is a challenging task. In this chapter we discuss how to build intelligent interfaces. The foundations are usability criteria that are valid for all computer products. There are a number of established methods for the design process that can help to meet these goals. In particular participatory and iterative so-called human centered approaches are important for interfaces in ubiquitous computing. The question on how to make interfaces more intelligent is not trivial and there are multiple approaches to enhance either the intelligence of the system or that of the user. Novel interface approaches follow the idea of embodied interaction and put particular emphasis on the situated use of a system and the mental models humans develop in their real-world environment.

User interfaces for computational devices can be challenging for both their users and their designers. Even such *simple* things as VCRs or TV sets feature interfaces that many people find too difficult to understand. Reviews and tests of consumer electronic devices very often rank bad usability even higher than technical aspects and the originally intended main function of the devices or features. Moreover, for most modern appliances there is not much technical difference in their core functions. For instance TV sets differ less in quality of display and sound and more in the way the user interacts with the device. This already shows why user interface design is crucial for any successful product. However, we want to extend the question of user interface design in two directions: the user interface should become more intelligent and adaptive and we want more suitable interfaces for ubiquitous computing scenarios.

The first aspect seems to be clear at first sight: intelligent user interfaces are just what we want and nobody will neglect the need for smart, clever, and intelligent technology. But it becomes more difficult if we strip away the buzzwords and dig a bit deeper into the question of what an intelligent user interface actually should do and how it would differ from an ordinary interface. Would the standard interface then be a stupid one?

The second aspect introduces a new level of complexity: an interface is by definition a clear boundary between two entities. A user interface resides between human and machine; other interfaces mediate, for instance, between networks and computers. In ubiquitous computing we have the problem that there might not be a clear boundary any more. Computers are no longer visible and, in the end, they can disappear from the user's conscious perception. We will, therefore, face the challenge of building an interface for something that is rather shapeless.

In the following, we will go into more detail through these questions and will introduce some general approaches for designing user interfaces. We will see that we can learn from good interface design for other—classical—devices, and that we can apply many of those user interface design principles for ubiquitous computing as well. A central aspect will be the design process that helps to find the right sequence of steps in building a good user interface. After discussing these general aspects of user interface design, we will focus on the specific needs for ubiquitous computing scenarios and finally on how to build intelligent user interfaces—or to be less euphemistic: to avoid stupid interfaces.

BUILDING GOOD USER INTERFACES

The design of a good user interface is an art, which has been ignored for a long time in the information and communication technology (ICT) business. Many software developers just implemented whatever they found useful for themselves and assumed it would also be ben-

eficial for the respective users. However, most users are not software developers and their way of interacting with technology is very different. Sometimes, the result is technology that is highly functional and useful for a small group of people, namely the developers of the system, and highly inefficient, frustrating or even unusable for most other people. Some of the highlights of this dilemma can be found in the communication with the user when something goes wrong: An error message notifying the user: "an error occurred, code 127" might be of some use for the developer and help in his efforts in debugging the system, but a user will hardly be able to understand what went wrong.

Today usability plays a much bigger role and many systems (including computer systems) are now designed with more care for easy and safe usage. On the one hand this is due to legal constraints demanding accessibility, but also due to the fact that many systems do not differ so much in their technical details and vendors have to diversify their products solely in terms of their "look and feel." We now have a wealth of methods, tools, and guidelines, which all help to develop a good user interface (Dix et al., 1998; Mayhew, 1999). However, there is not one single recipe whose application guarantees 100% success. The essence of usability engineering is to work iteratively in order to achieve the goal of better usability. Let us briefly go through these steps and summarize some of the most important issues of usability engineering. For more detailed information, a number of textbooks and research articles can be consulted (Dix et al., 1998; Nielsen, 1993; Shneiderman, 1997).

The first question of usability engineering is the question of what goals we actually want to achieve. The typical list of usability goals contains at least the following five (ISO 9241, 2006):

- **Safety and Security:** Good design should not harm users or other people affected by the use of a product. It should also help to avoid errors made by humans in using the system.

- **Effectiveness:** A good user interface supports a user in solving a task effectively, that is, all aspects of a task can be actually handled.
- **Efficiency and Functionality:** A well-designed and usable system should allow for quick and timely work.
- **Joy and Fun:** How enjoyable is it to work (or play) with the system? Is it fun or is it a pain to interact with it?
- **Ease of Learning and Memorizing:** How fast can new users interact with the system and will they remember what they learned?

This list, of course, is not exhaustive and not all aspects can be fulfilled to the same (high) degree, which is to say that there are classic trade-offs. Some aspects, therefore, might even be in conflict with others and it is important to identify such conflicts and to decide which aspect to optimize and to what extent. For instance, when designing an interactive game, joy and fun might be more important and effectiveness is less important. In contrast, a system for firemen has to be more efficient and can be less fun. Another typical trade-off exists between the need for efficient work and for training. One solution can be to provide two modes: an expert mode and a novice mode.

As a general rule, all efforts and goals of usability should be measurable in quantitative or qualitative ways. And since most usability criteria depend on the actual use of a system, there is a need to involve users in the design process. Of course, many human factors have been studied and psychologists have theories about how people can perceive information and how they can—in principle—react. But, in order to actually find out if the goals are met, one must try things out with actual users. And the more unknown your application terrain is, the more involvement of

users is required, which is of particular importance for ubiquitous computing because there is not yet a large set of experience, studies, and guidelines at hand.

The design process that involves users has been named *human-centered design* (ISO 13407, 1999). Its principle is to develop an application iteratively with evaluations in every cycle. Human-centered design also is regarded as the best approach when design goals are hard to formalize in technical terms.

There have been multiple approaches for system design processes that involve the users. Their roots are in the participatory design idea from Scandinavia that involves workers in the definition and design of their working environment (Olson & Blake, 1981). In contrast to the classical waterfall model in systems engineering (Royce, 1970) that segments the design process into a linear order of clearly separable steps, these models iterate and involve users and evaluations in each cycle. A number of models have been proposed replacing the waterfall scheme by cycles or stars, that is, the design process is open and decisions can be revised depending on user feedback during development (Gould et al., 1991; Hartson & Hix, 1989; Hix & Hartson, 1993). Since many usability goals are not well defined and cannot be formally defined beforehand, these models allow for a continuous evolution of the usability of the system (Figure 1).

The design steps in these models are the following:

- **Definition of the Context:** As a first step, designers should consider the context of their envisioned product. This includes defining the way the system will be used, if it will be used for life-critical or fun purposes, and in home or in office environments, as well as the market situation. The latter is important because it tells something about expectations of users and about who is going to buy the

Figure 1. Star model for user-centered design (Hartson & Hix, 1989)

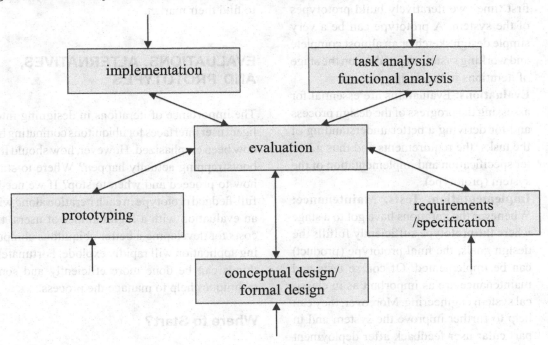

product. In general, not only the target users are involved in deciding about the success (i.e., sales) of a product. Decisions can be made by managers of the users and they can influence third parties such as the customers or clients of the users.

- **Description of the Users:** Based on the context definition, each group of directly or indirectly affected users must be carefully analyzed. Their physical and cognitive abilities and their cultural and social background may affect the way they interact with the system. Special needs may play a role. Accessibility has become important for IT systems and is demanded by many legal constraints, in particular in working environments.

- **Task Analysis:** Multiple techniques help to derive a rather formal description of the task users want to solve from informal interviews and observations. Most importantly, designers should find out how users actually solve their task currently (not how they think they do it) and how they make use of tools at hand, how they communicate and how their context influences the course of activities.

- **Requirements/Specification:** This step would have been the first step of the classical software development process. For user-centered design, it is now based on a better understanding of the users, their context and their tasks. Moreover, the specifications can be changed in each iteration, when a better understanding of the system could be gained through evaluations.

- **Conceptual Design/Formal Design:** The requirements and specifications are translated into system components.

- **Prototyping:** Instead of "doing it right the first time" we iteratively build prototypes of the system. A prototype can be a very simple design sketch or an almost complete and working system depending on the stage of iterations in the design process.
- **Evaluations:** Evaluations are essential for assessing the progress of the design process and for deriving a better understanding of the tasks, the requirements and thus a better specification and implementation of the system (prototype).
- **Implementation, Tests, Maintenance:** Whenever the iterations have got to a stage where the prototype sufficiently fulfills the design goals, the final prototype (product) can be implemented. Of course tests and maintenance are as important as in classical system engineering. Moreover, they can help to further improve the system and in particular user feedback after deployment can be used for defining new development cycles.

These design steps are the building blocks for good user interface design. They are very generic and they are valid for basically every interactive system. Iterative development, however, is inevitable for the design of human-computer interaction in ubiquitous computing as we enter a domain of interactive systems, where we cannot derive system requirements from interaction goals without user involvement. This is mainly due to the fact that interaction in ubiquitous computing aims at intuitively usable pervasive IT systems that assist users in their real-world endeavors. Without taking these aspects into account, these systems are subject to failure. Many ubiquitous computing prototypes are completely technology-driven. Their developers focus on smart new gadgets, networks and infrastructure but they do not focus their design efforts on their users. Just for the sake of plausibility, some usage scenarios and users are added to the design. Such systems

will not leave the research labs and they will fail to find their market.

EVALUATIONS, ALTERNATIVES, AND PROTOTYPES

The importance of iterations in designing intelligent user interfaces for ubiquitous computing has now been emphasized. However, how should that bootstrapping actually happen? Where to start, how to proceed and when to stop? If we need a full-fledged prototype in each iteration along with an evaluation with a high number of users, the costs for developing a better ubiquitous computing application will rapidly explode. Fortunately, things can be done more efficiently and some techniques help to manage the process.

Where to Start?

In order to get a first impression of how to build a system that actually meets the usability goals, for example, being an understandable and enjoyable assistant for some user task, we do not need any system but can make up a fake system without bothering with how to build a real one. A number of methods can be used (Dix et al., 1998; Shneiderman, 1997):

Design Sketches

Instead of actually building something that looks like a real system, users or usability experts can evaluate early design ideas. First sketches on paper or on a blackboard can already give an impression of the designer's ideas, and feedback can already help to avoid basic mistakes. Moreover, the discussion can facilitate the mutual understanding of the users' world and the prospective system.

Wizard of Oz Experiments

If, however, the users should already get an impression of how the interaction with the system might look, a system can also be simulated. A human operator remote controls all functions of the environment and the test users are told they are already interacting with the system. This technique has been proven to be extremely fruitful for systems that need data on the interaction in advance. For instance for systems that are language controlled, Wizard of Oz experiments can be used to collect utterances and language patterns that help to build speech recognizers and grammars for the real system.

Mock-Ups

A mock-up is a model of the system that already exposes the "look and feel" but does not yet include real functionality of the intended system. Early mock-ups for graphical interfaces can, for instance, consist of a PowerPoint walkthrough through a system or some Web sites emulating a system.

Prototypes

In contrast to the mock-up, the prototypes include actual functionalities of the target system. They may iteratively evolve to the final system.

Since many applications for ubiquitous computing scenarios are embedded into real-world tasks and many of them are also affected by or affect other objects in the users' surroundings, Wizard of Oz experiments are a cheap and very beneficial first step in system design. They can help to understand how people would interact in an environment that is enhanced by ubiquitous computing technology. Moreover, the designers get data that help to design interaction with the system. For most cases of more natural interaction such as speech or gesture, such data is necessary anyway because the recognizers need training data.

How to Proceed?

Evaluation is the core of the above-mentioned "star-model." Depending on the maturity of the design, the budget and the nature of the system, a great variety of evaluation techniques can be used. Evaluation methods can be classified according to the following dimensions:

- **Qualitative vs. Quantitative Methods:** In qualitative methods, feedback in form of comments, impressions and subjective ratings is collected in interviews or questionnaires. Quantitative methods measure parameters such as error rates, task completion times or movements of users in order to estimate the quality and efficiency of an interface.

- **Studies in the Field or in the Lab:** Field studies are conducted under realistic conditions where the systems are actually used, for example, in the office or home of the users. They usually need more effort than studies in the lab under simulated conditions, but they yield more realistic results.

- **User Tests or Expert Evaluations:** User studies involve real test users. They are more expensive than expert evaluations where a few experts judge the system by their experience on user behavior and the application domain. There are many well-known techniques for both—such as cognitive walkthrough, discount evaluation, thinking aloud—and in some cases even combinations may be useful.

- **System State (Sketch, Mock-Up, Prototype, ...):** As discussed above, in early evaluations, a system does not necessarily have to be fully functional but can rather be a sketch or a mock-up.

It is beyond the scope of this chapter to go into all details of evaluation techniques. We will focus rather on the most important aspects for ubiquitous computing interfaces.

Even though evaluation is crucial for the design of good interfaces, it should be noted that evaluation techniques do not solve all problems and can even be misleading. One of the main problems of evaluations is that they are always limited snapshot observations restricted in the time of usage and the complexity of the context. This is important to note, in particular, for ubiquitous computing systems interfaces. Take, for instance, the famous ubiquitous computing scenario of an intelligent refrigerator that keeps track of its contents and can alert a user when she is running out of milk. In an evaluation setting one could look at users while they are at home or while they are in a supermarket and one could measure how they react to notifications of the system. A questionnaire reveals if the users like the system and would like to buy it when it comes on to the market. In a realistic setting, a study would observe some 10 to 20 users each over a time span of one to two hours of interaction. All would be in the same representative supermarket and in some model kitchen. The results would be definitely interesting and the study would even go beyond many other evaluations of similar systems. However, it is too limited for multiple reasons:

- **No Long-Term Observation:** Since users would interact with such a ubiquitous computing system not only for a few hours but rather over months or years, the short interaction of a novice user does not reveal much about the user's future interaction.
- **Limited Frame of Context:** In order to gain comparable results, all users are set to the same or a similar context. In everyday situations, however, contexts may differ a great deal and users show a much higher degree of variation in their behavior.
- **Additional Tasks, People, and Devices:** As with most ubiquitous computing applications, users may not be focused on

just one task but may be doing many other things concurrently. They could have other devices with them or be interacting with their colleagues or family members.

These limitations of evaluation results make some of them questionable. However, by using a good and careful evaluation design, some aspects can be counterbalanced. Moreover, keeping the limitations in mind may help to focus on the right questions and avoid overstating the results. And finally: even when evaluations only shed limited light on the usability of a system, this is much better than working in complete darkness without evaluations.

As a rule of thumb, it should be noted that evaluations for ubiquitous computing interfaces should be made as realistic as possible. Thus field studies would be better than lab conditions. Moreover, the designers should have a clear understanding of what they want to achieve with their system in order to know what they want to prove using evaluations.

When to Stop?

The development cycle should not be an endless loop. In general, the (re-)design-prototype-evaluation cycle can go on forever leading to a continuous increase of usability. In practice, either the number of cycles is fixed beforehand or certain measures define when the loop has to be stopped and the final design is achieved. Typically these measures would quantify the usability goals listed at the beginning of this chapter. Such a goal could be "95% of the test users rate the system as very convenient" or "the task completion rate within 30 minutes is 98%." In some cases the stop-criterion is not bound to usability but to other measures such as "we are out of budget" or "the deadline is next week."

SPECIFIC CHALLENGES OF USER INTERFACES FOR UBIQUITOUS COMPUTING

So far we have learned about how to design a good user interface. The principles we discussed are rather generic and they apply—of course—for designing intelligent user interfaces for ubiquitous computing, but they are also valid for other user interfaces such as Web interfaces or interfaces of desktop applications. The general process of human-centered design could even be applied to non-IT products such as cars, coffee machines and other objects of our daily life. It is a matter of fact that we have got to such a generic process. On the one hand, good usability is a property that is generic and the design process is fairly similar in multiple domains. On the other hand, ubiquitous computing is about integrating things into the objects of our normal life. Thus usability has, owing to the very nature of ubiquitous computing, got something to do with the usability of everyday things.

Since the early days of ubiquitous computing, usability has been in its focus. Mark Weiser's idea of ubiquitous computing encompasses "invisible" interfaces that are so naturally usable that they literally become invisible for the user's conscious perception (Weiser 1999a, b). This notion goes back to the German philosophers Georg Gadamer and Martin Heidegger, who call such interaction with things that we use without conscious awareness things that are "ready-to-hand" or at our "horizon." In this phenomenologist view, the meaning of the things is actually derived from our interaction with them. Such a view on interactive artifacts has become popular in ubiquitous computing and is closely related to the notion of embodiment (Dourish, 2001). This is a fundamental shift from the classical positivist approach in computer science, that is, modeling the real world in simplistic formal computer programs, to an embodied approach that takes the user in the real world into account. This is

relevant for ubiquitous computing for multiple reasons. On the one hand, ubiquitous computing applications are to be used in complex real-world settings and their meaning (for the user) will, in fact, only evolve in the course of action. Additionally, if things should become natural extensions of our physical abilities, they must be designed such that they do not need conscious interference from their users.

Given this notion of being "invisible" we can see that this does not necessarily mean "not there," but rather present without conscious interaction. The most basic examples for such physical objects are our body parts. We do not have to think consciously about what we do with our arms, but we just do the things we want. When we leave our house, we do not have to remember: "let's take the arm with us, we might need it today." It is there and ready for immediate use. When we throw a ball, we just throw it and we do not think and plan how to make our hand grasp the ball and our arm swing around in order to accelerate the ball. In this sense, our arm is invisible but also very present. Thus if we speak of ubiquitous computing interfaces that are "invisible" or computers that are "disappearing," we actually speak of things that are present and "ready-to-hand." However, the artifacts we interact with might not be consciously realized as computers.

A good example of such a "ubiquitous" technology is present in our homes already: electrical light. Whenever we enter a room that is dark, we just find a switch with our hands next to the door and the light goes on. Without thinking we turn on the light. We do not think of cables that conduct electrons. We do not have to consider how the light bulb works or how they generate electricity at the power plant.

We have a very simplistic model of how the thing works and it is internalized to such a degree that we do not have to think about it when we enter a room. These "mental models" of how things work play an important role in designing good user interfaces as well as in designing other everyday things (Norman, 1998). Donald Norman emphasizes that a good design is about providing good mappings (Figure 2):

- The design model must be mapped to the system image.
- Users must be able to map their understanding (mental model) to the system.
- The system must allow the user to map its image to the user's model.

The question is now: how can a system image support the appropriate user's mental model? The answer—with our notion of embodiment in mind—must bring the meaning of things into the things themselves and thus a user can derive the meaning of something from the interaction with it or from its mere appearance that may signal some properties indicating how to use it. Such properties have been named affordances (Norman, 1998). The idea of affordances is to bring knowledge into the world instead of having it in mind. Many highly usable things that surround

us just let us know by their physical appearance how we can use them. A chair for instance does not need a label or instructions on how to sit on it. We just see and know it is a chair and we know what to do with it.

Similarly, affordances have been defined as virtual affordances for computer interfaces and many metaphors on our computer screens signal functionalities, for example, mouse pointers and scrollbars. With the advent of ubiquitous computing, the term affordance becomes again more literally a property attached to the physical properties of things. Many ubiquitous computing objects include tactile interfaces or smart objects with physical and not just virtual properties.

There are a number of consequences arising from this perspective of embodied interaction for ubiquitous computing:

- **Support Mental Models:** Humans use mental models to understand and to predict how things react to their actions. The system

Figure 2. Mappings of design model, mental model and system images (Norman, 1998)

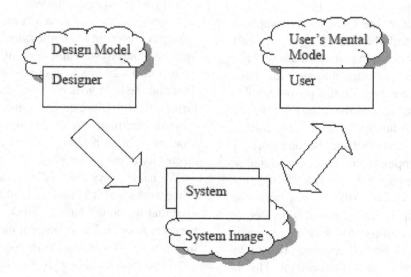

image should support such mental models and make it easy to understand it.

- **Respect Cognitive Economy:** Humans re-use their mental models. If there are well-established mental models for similar things, then they can be a good basis for an easy understanding of a new artifact.

- **Make Things Visible and Transparent:** In order to understand the state of an object it should be obvious what is going on. For instance, a container can indicate if it is loaded or not.

- **Design for Errors:** Mappings between the user's model and the system sometimes fail. Most "human errors" are, in fact, mapping errors. Therefore, systems must assist users in finding a solution for their task even if something has gone wrong. There are a number of techniques for doing so, for example, allowing undo-actions or sanity checks on user inputs.

- **Internal and External Consistency:** Things within an application should work consistently. For instance, pushing a red button always means, "stop." External consistency refers to expectations users may have from usage of other applications. If we add some ubiquitous computing technology to a cup and turn it into a smart cup, a user will still expect the cup to work as a cup.

With these guidelines and the general design process considerations we are already well prepared for building very good interfaces for ubiquitous computing applications. However, there are a number of further practical considerations and human factors that play a role for ubiquitous computing user interfaces. Some of these issues are related to the very nature of these applications being "ubiquitous" and some are more related to technical problems in mobile and ubiquitous scenarios. We will briefly highlight some of these aspects. Due to the broad spectrum of possible applications, we cannot go into details of all possible factors.

Human Factors for Ubiquitous Computing

In classical human-computer interaction, we have a well-defined setting. In ubiquitous computing, we do not know where the users are, what tasks they are doing currently, which other persons may be around. This makes it very hard to account for some human factors that can greatly influence the interaction. Depending on time, concurrent tasks, and so forth, the user's cognitive load, stress level, patience, and mood may vary extremely. Thus an interface can, in one situation, be well suited and in another situation the user is either bored or overloaded.

Another problem lies in spatial and temporal constraints. In many ubiquitous computing applications, location and time play a crucial role. Users need the right information at the right time and place. In a system that helps a user to navigate her vehicle through a city, the information "turn right" only makes sense at a very well defined point in space and time. An information delay is not acceptable. Even though space and time are the most prominent context factors in systems today, other context factors may also play a big role (cf., the chapter "Context Models and Context Awareness"). An interface can adapt to such context factors and take into account what is going on. In particular, the user might not have the focus of attention on the system but rather might be busy doing something else. But not only user-driven activities can distract the user; other people and events are not the exception but the normal case in many ubiquitous computing scenarios. This has a huge effect on the interface and dialog design. While in desktop applications, the designer can assume that the user is looking at the screen and a system message is (in most cases) likely to be read by the user, in ubiquitous computing we must reckon with many signals from the system being ignored by the user.

The interfaces can try to take the users' tasks into account and thus adapt their strategy to reach the user's attention. For example, when the user is driving a car, the system might interact in a different way than when the user is in a business meeting. However, when the system is literally ubiquitous, the number of tasks and situations the user might be in can be endless and it is not feasible to model each and every situation. The system interface might then instead be adaptable to a few distinct modes of interaction.

Who is in Charge?

As we mention adaptation and adaptivity, we get to a point where the system behaves differently in different situations. This can be a perfect thing and can significantly increase the ease of use. A mobile phone, for instance, that automatically adapts to the environment and stays silent in a business meeting, but rings in other situations is rather practical. However, the trade-off is a reduced predictability and, as discussed above, many usability goals can be in conflict with each other. The developers and (hopefully) the users have to decide which goal is more important. It is important to know about these conflicts and to decide explicitly how to deal with them.

Typically, usability goals in ubiquitous computing that come into conflict with others are:

- **Controllability:** Is it the system or the user who controls the situation?
- **Support of Mental Models:** How can a user still understand a very complex system?
- **Predictability:** Humans want to be able to predict the outcome of their actions. If a system is too adaptive and autonomous, users get lost.
- **Transparency:** If the system adapts to all sort of context factors, its state becomes less transparent.

- **Learn Ability:** A system that learns and behaves differently in new situations can be hard to understand.

The designers have to decide to what degree they want to achieve which level in each of these dimensions and how other aspects such as autonomy or adaptivity may affect them. In general, there are no rules or guidelines that can give clear directions. While in many other IT domains, such as Web systems, some established standards may set the stage and good guidelines exist, the designer of a ubiquitous computing system will have to derive his own solution on the basis of the goals he wants to achieve. The only way to prove that the solution actually fits these goals, are, in turn, evaluations. Therefore, a user-centered design approach is the only way to design ubiquitous computing systems that incorporate good user interfaces.

INTELLIGENT AND DUMB INTERFACES FOR UBIQUITOUS COMPUTING

In the last part of this chapter we want to focus on intelligent user interfaces. The term "intelligent user interface" has been debated for a while and it is not so clear what it means and if at all intelligent interfaces are something beneficial. But even the term intelligence is not well defined and has been used (or misused) in multiple ways. Before going into technical details we should, thus, first discuss what the term means and then see some techniques that are used for realizing them. We will finish with a discussion on how much intelligence a good interface actually needs.

What is an Intelligent User Interface?

So far we have presented a number of techniques for building good interfaces. We also saw how the view of embodied interaction can be used as a paradigm for ubiquitous computing. In general, a technical solution can be called "intelligent" for two reasons: (1) there is some built-in intelligent computation that solves some otherwise unsolvable problem; (2) using the system, a user can solve an otherwise unsolvable problem, even though the system itself does not actually do anything intelligent. Suppose that calculating the logarithm of a number is a hard problem for a human, then a calculator is a good example for case (1) and an abacus would be an example for (2). The calculator solves the problem for the human and the abacus empowers the user to solve the problem on her own.

The classical approach of artificial intelligence (AI) is a rationalist one. According to this approach, a system should model the knowledge that human experts have and thus emulate human intelligence. In this sense, the "intelligence" moves from the user to the system (Figure 3a, 3b). This approach is valid for many cases, for example, if expert knowledge is rare and non-experts should

also be able to work with a system. As discussed above, the embodied interaction view would rather try to make the interaction more intelligent (Figure 3c). This fits too many new trends in AI where embodied intelligence is viewed as a property that emerges from the interaction of an intelligent agent with the environment. In this view, even simple and lightweight agents can perform intelligent behavior without full reflective and conscious knowledge of the world. With respect to this definition, all of the above-mentioned material already describes how to build an intelligent interface. Because the processes for designing human-centered systems are just the right techniques for designing intelligent interactive systems, we already defined to a great extent how to build intelligent user interfaces.

Instead of leaving all the intelligence to the system, the user or the interaction, we can also try to get the best of all worlds and combine these techniques into a cooperative system, where both the system and the user cooperate with their

Figure 3. Multiple views on intelligent user interfaces

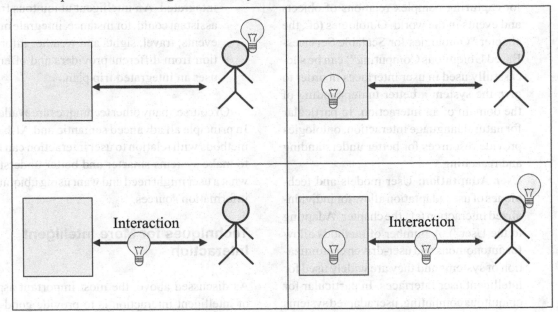

knowledge on solving some tasks supported by intelligent interaction techniques (Figure 3d).

As discussed above, we can make the system more intelligent by enhancing the system, the interaction or the user. Intelligent user interface techniques exist for all three aspects. We will briefly list the key methods. Some details on them can be found in other chapters of this volume.

Techniques for Enhancing the System's Intelligence

A huge number of AI techniques can be used to put more knowledge and reasoning into the system. Besides state-of-the-art IT methods such as databases, expert systems, heuristic search and planning, a number of more recent developments have attracted a good deal of interest by researchers and practitioners in the field:

- **World Knowledge and Ontologies:** Semantic technologies and formal models of world knowledge have had a great renaissance in the last couple of years. In context of the Semantic Web efforts, ontologies have been established as a standard method for capturing complex relations of objects and events in the world. Ontologies (cf., the chapter "Ontologies for Scalable Services-Based Ubiquitous Computing") can be successfully used in user interfaces in order to give the system a better understanding of the domain of an interaction. In particular for natural language interaction, ontologies provide resources for better understanding and reasoning.
- **User Adaptation:** User models and techniques of user adaptation allow for individualized interaction (cf., the chapter "Adapting to the User"). A number of methods allow for autonomous and user-driven customization of systems and they are widely used for intelligent user interfaces. In particular for ubiquitous computing, user adapted systems

play a big role since these systems often have to support a great variety of use cases where a single standardized interface is not appropriate.

- **Context Adaptation:** Context plays a crucial role for ubiquitous computing (cf., the chapter "Context Models and Context Awareness"). As discussed already, context-dependent user interfaces can greatly enhance the usability of these systems. However, context can also be challenging because it can depend on a huge number of parameters and it is hard to formalize the meaning of contexts and to learn the relations between them autonomously.
- **Service Federation:** Integrating a variety of services and providing a single interface can be a significant step towards intelligent user interfaces. If users do not have to interact with all sorts of services separately, but can use a single portal, they can work much more efficiently with less cognitive load. However, service integration can be a hard problem, in particular when multiple services have to be integrated semantically that had not originally been designed to be integrated. An intelligent ubiquitous travel assistant could, for instance, integrate maps, events, travel, sights and weather information from different providers and offer the user an integrated trip plan.

Of course, many other techniques are available. In principle all advanced semantic and AI-based methods with relation to user interaction can help to make systems smarter and better understand what a user might need and want using ubiquitous information sources.

Techniques for More Intelligent Interaction

As discussed above, the most important aspect of intelligent interaction is to provide good and working mappings of the user's models of the world and the system's model. These mappings depend highly on the semiotics, that is, the meaning and perception of the signs and signals established between user and the system. These can be both actively communicated codes in form of a language but also passive features of the artifact that signal the user affordances. Both aspects can be supported through intelligent methods that aim at more natural interaction such that the interaction takes place based on the premise of human communication rather than machine languages.

- **Multimodal Interaction:** Multimodal techniques make use of the human ability to combine multiple input and output modalities for a semantically rich, robust and efficient communication. In many ubiquitous computing systems, language, gestures, graphics, and text are combined to multimodal systems (cf., the chapters "Multimodal and Federated Interaction" and "Multimodal Software Engineering"). Multimodality is on the one hand more natural, and, on the other hand, it also allows for more flexible adaptation in different usage situations.

- **Cross-media Adaptation:** Ubiquitous computing systems often use a number of different media, devices and channels for communicating with the user. A user can, in one situation, carry a PDA with a tiny display and, in another situation, interact with a wall-sized display in public or even use no display but just earphones. Intelligent interaction can support media transcoding that presents content on different media adapted to the situation.

- **Direct Interaction:** Humans are very good at multimodal communication, but for many tasks we are even better using direct interaction. It is, for instance, much easier to drive a car using a steering wheel than to tell the car to which degree it should steer to the left or to the right. For many activities, direct interaction is superior to other forms of human-computer interaction.

- **Embodied Conversational Agents:** Since humans are used to communicating with humans (and not with machines), anthropomorphic interfaces presenting animated characters can in some circumstances be very useful. In particular in entertainment systems, so-called avatars have become quite popular. However, there is also some debate about these interfaces and some people dislike this form of interaction.

Again, the list of techniques could be much longer. Here we just highlight some of the most important trends in the field. More ideas have been proposed and there will be more to come.

Techniques for Amplifying the User's Intelligence

In principle, we can try to build better interface techniques, but we will not be able to change the user's intelligence—leaving aside e-learning and tutorial systems that might explicitly have teaching or training purposes. But even if we do not affect the user's intelligence, we can still do a lot about her chances to make use of it. In the scientific community there has been a controversy about the goal of intelligent user interfaces over the last couple of years on where to put how much intelligence (Figure 3). And even though it might be counterintuitive, an intelligent interface can sometimes be the one that leaves the intelligence on the part of the user rather than putting it into the system (Figure 3a, 3b). In the debate about these approaches, the slogan "intelligence amplification (IA) instead of artificial intelligence (AI)" was coined. The idea is that a really intelligent interface leaves intelligent decisions to the user and does not take away all intelligent work from the user by modeling it in the system. The question is: how can the system support users in acting intelligently? The answers have been given already when we discussed usability goals: A system that is easy to learn, where users have control and understand what is going on, and where mental models are applicable is more likely to let people act intelligently. In contrast, a system that only leaves minor steps to the user, that does not provide information about its states and how it got there and for which the users do not have appropriate mental models will in the long run bore its users and decrease their creativity and enthusiasm.

It should be noted that both type of systems can be packed with AI and be extremely smart or very dumb things. It is more the kind of interaction design that facilitates human intelligence or not.

HOW MUCH INTELLIGENCE?

Intelligent user interfaces for ubiquitous computing will be a necessary thing in the future. However, there are multiple competing views and philosophies. In general, three things could be intelligent: the user, the system or the way in which they interact. Most researchers focus on enhancing the system's intelligence and the assumption is that this will lead to a better usability. This is often the case but not always. A different approach is to say that users are the most intelligent agents and their intelligence should be enhanced rather than replaced by artificial intelligence (IA instead of AI). In practice, however, we should do all together in order to make the interaction as easy and efficient as possible. But each decision should be made carefully keeping in mind that the overall goal of an intelligent user interface still should be defined by the usability goals. And like with all good things "less is sometimes more" and some simple things often are more enjoyable and easier to understand than highly complex and automated devices.

CONCLUSION

This chapter introduced aspects of designing user interfaces for ubiquitous computing in general and intelligent interfaces in particular. The basics for building intelligent interfaces are techniques for building good interfaces. Consequently, we first presented an up-to-date introduction to methods of human-centered design. A central aspect of this technique is to iteratively design systems with repeated evaluations and user feedback. This approach is especially important for ubiquitous computing systems, since they lack clear guidelines and decades of experience; and thus iterations are crucial in order to approach the desired design goals.

Obviously, many of these basic techniques are also valid for many other systems. However, ubiquitous computing introduces some more specific issues, such as a high variety of contexts, the lack of single dedicated interface devices and—by its very nature—ubiquitous interaction at any time and location. Therefore, ubiquitous computing interfaces must place even more emphasis on good mappings to mental models and provide good affordances. The view of embodied interaction gives us a good theoretical idea of the way we should think of and model interaction in such systems.

With these prerequisites, designers can build very good interfaces and can take many usability aspects into consideration. However, so far the "intelligence" of the interfaces has not been discussed. We did that in the last part of the chapter and presented a modern and sometimes controversial view on intelligent user interfaces. There are different paradigms that may contradict each other. The main question can be formulated as: "AI or IA—artificial intelligence or intelligent amplification?" We discussed these design philosophies and presented some ideas on how to combine the best of both worlds. We also presented a number of current trends in the field that can be found in modern ubiquitous computing systems.

FUTURE RESEARCH DIRECTIONS

As the field of ubiquitous computing matures, its user interface techniques will also undergo an evolutionary process and some best practices will be established, making things much easier. We currently see this happening for Web applications where developers can choose from established interaction techniques that are well known to the users and guarantee efficient interaction.

However, ubiquitous computing might never reach that point since the ambition to support users in every situation at every time and place, which is the final goal of it, requires such rich interfaces that have to cope with the complexity of the users' entire life. This might be good news for researchers in the field because they will stay busy searching for better and more intelligent interfaces.

The main challenges for future research will lie in the problem of extensibility and scalability of intelligent user interfaces. How could a system that has been designed for a user A in situation S be extended to support thousands of users in a hundred different situations?

REFERENCES

Dix, A., Finley, J., Abowd, G., & Beale, R. (1998). *Human-computer interaction*. Upper Saddle River, NJ: Prentice-Hall.

Dourish, P. (2001): *Where the action is: The foundations of embodied interaction*. Cambridge, MA: MIT Press.

Gould, J.D., Boies, S.J., & Lewis, C. (1991). Making usable, useful, productivity-enhancing computer applications. *Communications of the ACM, 34*(1), 74–85.

Hartson, H.R., & Hix, D. (1989). Toward empirically derived methodologies and tools for human–computer interface development. *International Journal of Man-Machine Studies, 31*(4), 477–494.

Hix, D., & Hartson, H.R. (1993). *Developing user interfaces: Ensuring usability through product and process*. New York: John Wiley and Sons.

International Organization of Standardization. (1999). *Human-centred design processes for interactive systems*. ISO 13407. International Organization for Standardization.

International Organization of Standardization. (2006). *Ergonomics of human-system interaction*. ISO 9241. International Organization of Standardization.

Mayhew, D.J. (1999). *The usability engineering lifecycle*. Burlington, MA: Morgan Kaufmann.

Nielsen, J. (1993). *Usability engineering*. Boston, MA: Academic Press.

Norman, D.A. (1998): *The design of everyday things*. Cambridge, MA: MIT Press.

Olson, M.H., & Blake, I. (1981). *User involvement in system design: An empirical test of alternative approaches*. New York: Stern School of Business.

Royce, W.W. (1970). Managing the development of large software systems: Concepts and techniques. *Technical Papers of Western Electronic Show and Convention (WesCon)*, Los Angeles, CA, USA.

Shneiderman, B. (1997). *Designing the user interface: Strategies for effective human-computer interaction*. Boston, MA: Addison Wesley.

Weiser, M. (1999a). The computer for the 21st century. *ACM SIGMOBILE Mobile Computing and Communications Review, 3*(3), 3-11. Special issue dedicated to Mark Weiser.

Weiser, M. (1999b). Some computer science issues in ubiquitous computing. *ACM SIGMOBILE Mobile Computing and Communications Review, 3*(3), 12-21. Special issue dedicated to Mark Weiser.

ADDITIONAL READING

Cooper, A., & Reimann, R.M., (2003). *About Face 2.0: The essentials of interaction design.* New York: John Wiley.

Dautenhahn, K. (1996). Embodied cognition in animals and artifacts. In *Embodied Action and Cognition: Papers from the AAAI 1996 Fall Symposium,* Boston, MA (pp. 27-32).

Hornecker, E., & Buur, J. (2006). Getting a grip on tangible interaction: A framework on physical space and social interaction. In *Proceedings of the SIGCHI Conference on Human Factors in Computing Systems* (pp. 437-446). New York: ACM Press.

Preece, J., Rogers, Y., & Sharp, H. (2002). *Interactive design.* New York: John Wiley.

Sharkey, N., & Zeimke, T. (2000). Life, mind and robots: The ins and outs of embodied cognition. In S. Wermter & R. Sun (Eds.), *Symbolic and neural net hybrids.* Cambridge, MA: MIT Press.

Winograd, T., & Flores, F. (1987). *Understanding computers and cognition: A new foundation for design.* Boston, MA: Addison Wesley.

Chapter XXI
Multimodal and Federated Interaction

Frankie James
SAP Research, USA

Rama Gurram
SAP Research, USA

ABSTRACT

This chapter introduces the concepts of multimodal and federated interaction. Because multimodality means, simply, the combination of multiple modalities (or types of input and output), the authors first introduce some of the various modalities available for computer interaction. The chapter then discusses how multimodality can be used both in desktop and mobile computing environments. The goal of the chapter is to familiarize scholars and researchers with the range of topics covered under the heading "multimodality" and suggest new areas of research around the combination of modalities, as well as the combination of mobile and stationary computing devices to improve usability.

THE BASICS OF MULTIMODALITY

As was discussed in the introduction to "Liability," interaction with a computer (or computer-based device) can take place using a variety of different forms or modalities. On the input side, information can be transferred from a human operator to the computer via keyboards, keypads, touch screens, mice, joysticks, spoken language, or even gesture and motion sensors. Information can be output through visual displays (large and small), audio displays (including spoken text and non-speech sounds; see also "Mobile Speech Recognition"), and tactile displays (such as Braille or raised-line displays), as well as more exotic forms, such as force-feedback (haptic) joysticks and mice, and olfactory ("aroma-based") displays.

Each of the input and output channels mentioned above have their own benefits and limitations. For example, large visual displays are able to present a great deal of information at the same time, which users can quickly scan to find the data that is relevant to their current needs. However, visual displays are not appropriate for blind users, and they are also inappropriate for mobile users who are not able to stand or sit in one place to read the display (or carry it with them while traveling).

The purpose of this chapter is to discuss the concepts of *multimodal* interaction, where two or more modalities (such as vision or audio) are combined. Multimodal interaction is frequently used to compensate for limitations in one interaction modality by providing a second one. For example, the limited visual display capabilities of a mobile device can be augmented by providing audio output, or speech input can be provided to a user with limited typing ability to increase data entry speed. Multiple modalities can also be combined within a single input (or output) to increase efficiency; a seminal example here is the combination of a spoken action command (e.g., "color this red") with mouse or touch-screen selection of the object to be acted upon. There are, of course, many other reasons for using multimodality, which will be discussed later in this chapter.

We will begin in this introduction with a discussion of the different forms of multimodality, as well as the different purposes to which multimodal interactions can be applied. In the next two sections, we address the use of multimodality for desktop applications and on mobile devices, where the reasons and methods for using multimodality can be quite different. We then discuss the concept of device federation, where multiple devices (each with their own available modalities) can be combined within a single interaction. Finally, we conclude with the chapter summary.

DIFFERENT FORMS

The basic definition of multimodality is the use of more than one modality within a single interface. The availability of both keyboard and voice input is one of the most common examples of multimodality, as is the use of both visual (text or graphical) and audio output. Most of the five classical human senses (sight, hearing, touch, smell, and taste) can be used for both the input and output sides. Each sense allows a broad range of possibilities.

Table 1 gives a brief list of the types of input and output that are associated with the senses.

The most common use of the sense of sight is in the visual presentation (output) of information on small and large displays. Sight can also be used for input: eye tracking can be used for selection or to gauge interest in a particular area of a screen, and retinal scanning can be used to identify the user.

Input options based on the sense of hearing include speech, for entering text or giving commands, speaker identification (to identify or authenticate the user), and even humming (Ghias et al., 1995). Audio output can be used for presenting written text (using text-to-speech), recorded audio files, document and interface structures, and sonifications of graph data [see the chapter "Mobile Speech Recognition" and James (1998) for an overview]. Speech input and audio-based output are useful in a variety of contexts, including mobile and vehicle-based scenarios, as well as accessibility.

The sense of touch is already commonly found in computer inputs today, through the use of keyboards, pointing devices, and touch screens. In addition to detecting simply that a key, button, or screen area has been clicked or touched, more advanced devices (such as game controllers and track pads) can also detect the amount of pressure exerted by the user. Handwriting and gesture are

Table 1. Human senses and associated input and output types

Sense	Input Types	Output Types
Sight	Eye tracking Retinal scan	Visual displays (small and large) of graphics and text
Hearing	Speech Speaker identification Humming	Text-to-speech Recorded audio Auditory icons and earcons Sonification
Touch/Gesture	Keyboard Mouse/pointing device Handwriting Gesture and motion Pressure sensing Heat sensing Fingerprint recognition	Tactile display Braille display Haptic/force feedback display
Smell	Chemical odor-detecting sensors	Olfactory output
Taste	(currently none)	Gustatory output

also gaining in popularity within certain contexts, along with the use of fingerprints for user identification. In the near future, we can expect to see heat and motion-sensing inputs, possibly for tracking people and objects. Tactile and haptic displays are also used for output, especially to make computers accessible to disabled users. Tactile displays include Braille and raised-line displays, which can be felt with the fingertips or hands to recognize shapes and text. Haptic displays use force feedback, generally to the hands and fingers, to present textures and boundaries that represent elements within the user interaction.

Smell and taste have spawned the creation of some new output possibilities, including the intriguing, if somewhat irreverent, Edible Bits (Maynes-Aminzade, 2005) gustatory display. The applicability of these senses to human-computer interaction, however, appears to be limited to specialized applications and artistic contexts.

Multimodal applications differ in which modalities and techniques they choose to combine,

as well as in the *ways* that the modalities are used together. Some applications use modalities in a redundant way, so that input can be given in any of the available modalities, and the same output is rendered simultaneously in multiple modalities. Other applications use the modalities to complement one another, combining multiple inputs or outputs to produce a single command or piece of output (also called *multimodal fusion*). The choice of whether to use redundant or complementary modalities is dependent on the goals, context of use, and target user group for the application. Examples and use cases for both of these methods are described below.

DIFFERENT PURPOSES

Applications are designed to use multimodal interactions for a wide variety of reasons. Having several modalities available can allow designers to create applications that are easier or more

Table 2. Purposes for using multimodality

Type of Multimodality	Purpose
Complementary Modalities (*Multimodal Fusion*)	o natural interaction; good mapping to task o avoid "clutter"/overload (output) o disambiguation (input) – *non-mobile*
Replacement Modalities	o natural interaction; good mapping to task o reduce screen clutter o compensate for limited input (or output) capabilities – *mobile*
Redundant Modalities	o accessibility o improve efficiency o compensate for hands- or eyes-busy tasks – *mobile* o compensate for environment – *mobile*

natural to use, or that can be used by more users within more contexts. Table 2 shows the different purposes of using multimodality, categorized by the way the modalities are combined in the interaction. In many cases, the purposes are valid both for mobile and non-mobile (i.e., desktop) devices; in other cases, there is special value in using multimodality for specific device categories.

The most common usage of complementary modalities (or multimodal fusion) is to attempt to make the interaction more natural, where modalities are chosen that are the best fit to different parts of the task. For example, pointing and other gestures are appropriate for selection, while voice may be more efficient for entering text. Complementary modalities can also be used to spread the input or output across different modalities, reducing the load on any one channel. One example here is on the output side, where the most important or urgent information is presented in audio while supporting information is presented visually. The benefit is that the user can get both the key and supporting information simultaneously by listening to the audio and attending to the visuals at the same time.

Replacement modalities, as the name implies, replace one modality for another. Replacement can produce a more natural interaction, when, for example, keyboard entry of a password is replaced by speaker identification in a system that already allows voice input. On a mobile device, replacement can also be used to compensate for the limited capabilities of the device—long portions of text output are difficult to read and scroll through on a small screen, and may be easier to comprehend using an audio presentation.

Redundant modalities provide users with the ability to choose from different interaction options. By allowing both voice and keyboard input, for example, an application is more accessible to users who can't type well or who have a physical disability. Redundant output, presented both visually and auditorially, can benefit not only users with visual disabilities, but also users performing tasks requiring their visual attention to be focused elsewhere (for example, while driving). The remainder of this chapter presents these purposes in more detail within the context of example applications and research prototypes.

MULTIMODALITY ON THE DESKTOP

Because desktop computers are still the primary computing environment for most users, we begin our discussion of multimodality on this platform. People frequently see multimodality as unnecessary or even inadvisable on desktop computers—"I don't want to talk to my computer, or have it talk back to me, in my office…someone might hear some of my private information!" This section will show that there are many cases where the uses of multimodal input or output (even speech and audio) are indeed very useful tools for desktop interaction.

In desktop settings, there are several uses of multimodality:

1. To make the interaction more natural, by mapping information to be input or output to the most appropriate modality;
2. To provide better and more usable security;
3. To increase accessibility for disabled users.

This section discusses each of these uses, and concludes with the presentation of an area of possible research around the use of multimodal output in desktop computing.

Using Multimodality to Make Interaction More Natural

Standard desktop systems use keyboard and mouse for input, with visual displays and some (limited) audio output. For many interactions, these tools and modalities are appropriate; for example, selecting an icon on a desktop or some text in a document is straightforward using a mouse or other pointing device. However, other interactions involving pointing devices require far more effort on the part of the user, when the mapping requires users to search long menus or complicated tool bars for desired commands (for example, when specifying the attributes of a shape or icon placed on a canvas). Keyboards, while useful for entering text into a document, are not as useful for issuing commands or entering

passwords, where arcane syntax and structures must be remembered. By providing more input modalities to a desktop computer user, interactions can be optimized to be more natural, and may also reduce the amount of visual clutter on the display.

Speech is perhaps the most commonly available input modality after keyboards and pointing devices (although as Oviatt [1999] points out, it should by no means be considered the primary information carrying modality within a multimodal system). Speech recognition systems use *grammars* to define the commands or phrases that can be accepted by the system. Speech recognition grammars can range from types found in standard computer theory (regular grammars, context-free grammars) to statistical grammars (e.g., *n-gram* grammars, where the system uses the preceding $n-1$ words spoken by the user to help identify the nth word).

Replacement Modalities

Within the desktop context, speech input can be used to make an interaction more natural and also more visually appealing, by eliminating the need to display complicated tool bars and menus. A striking example of this is the CommandTalk system, which enabled users to create, control, and modify battlefield missions and control the map display of the ModSAF battlefield system using spoken language and mouse input (Moore et al., 1997). Through the addition of the CommandTalk speech interface, the researchers were able to reduce the screen clutter of ModSAF, eliminating almost all of the tool bars that had previously been required for specifying details of checkpoints and ordinances, controlling the display, and specifying mission movements.

The architecture of CommandTalk included many natural language processing components to create an intuitive command language. The speech recognition grammar was designed to allow the same commands and object referents as would be used in a human-to-human interaction. Complications regarding the resolution of noun phrases ("the M1 platoon") to specific units shown on the display, and the mapping of predicates to interface actions ("move," which can map to one of two different commands depending on the type of platoon to be moved) were handled automatically and made transparent to the user. By designing the grammar using a corpus of sample human-to-human dialogues, the interaction is made extremely natural for users who already understand the domain, and the system can be used without much initial training.

In CommandTalk, the spoken language interface provides an alternative means of input. CommandTalk also changed the visual display of the underlying application, although this is not strictly necessary when creating a multimodal version of an existing application. The available input modality, speech, was in this case used as a *replacement* modality. Replacing one modality with another should, however, be done with caution. The spoken language input for CommandTalk was designed to be natural for expert users in the domain, based on sample dialogues. Non-expert users who are unfamiliar with the domain will require some time to learn the command structure that is used for the task. Toolbars and buttons can act as visible reminders of the available commands—these reminders allow users (especially non-experts) to build up their understanding of the domain using *recognition* memory. Removing the visible reminders forces users to rely on *recall* memory (Lodding, 1982). In multimodal systems designed for non-expert users, it may be more appropriate in many cases to add a new modality without removing the old; in this case, the speech input would have been a redundant modality.

Complementary Modalities

Input modalities can also be used in a complementary way, where the inputs from several modalities are fused to produce a single input command. This is commonly known as *multimodal fusion*. Multimodal fusion allows users to mix and match modalities as they choose, and the system attempts to find a coherent meaning for the set of inputs. For example, when speech and gesture input are combined, spoken commands can be used to specify actions, while mouse or pen gestures specify the objects or action details. This can be much more efficient or more usable than using the mouse to both select the object and the command, since the two parts can be done simultaneously and because the user does not have to search the visual menus or tool bars for the command. Combining voice and a pointing device is also more natural than using voice alone, since object selection and many other tasks (such as resizing and moving) can be tedious and error-prone to accomplish using voice alone (see, for example, the Voice-Enabled Portal project, described later) (Grasso et al., 1998; Tyfa & Howes, 2000).

Many multimodal fusion systems focus on the use of speech with other modalities. One of the first systems to combine voice and gesture was the "Put-That-There" system (Bolt, 1980). The system focused on the basic concept of combining voice and gesture into what Bolt called a "concerted, natural user modality." The system allowed users to place shapes on a large screen display, when seated facing the screen. Gesture sensors were used to determine the placement of the shape, while speech commands gave additional information, including the type of shape, color, and size. The gestures disambiguated *deictic* references (references whose interpretation is relative to the context of the utterance) in the spoken commands, such as "that" and "there."[a] As Oviatt (1999) points out, deictic commands tend to dominate multimodal input, since they are also widely used in human-to-human communication.

The combination of speech with gestures has most commonly been demonstrated in map-related tasks. Koons et al. (1993) describe a system that integrates speech, gesture, and eye gaze input to query objects on a map. Their focus is on the interpretation of multimodal commands from the three modalities, using reasoning to combine the modalities and determine the objects and actions requested. The Multimodal Maps application designed by Adam Cheyer and Luc Julia (Cheyer & Julia, 1998) is another example of a system that fuses gesture and voice inputs to produce a natural, less error-prone application (their paper is also a good reference to other publications related to multimodal fusion). The application is a travel planning tool that shows locations of interest on a map display. Users can ask questions using either modality, or both in combination. For example, users can give the spoken command "show restaurants within one mile of this hotel," specifying the hotel by circling it on the map.

Multimodal commands involving speech can be formed and used in a variety of ways, and systems built to understand them have to be able to handle these differences. For example, while some commands may be formed by actions that co-occur, such as a circling gesture or pointing action that occurs simultaneously with the speech, many commands that should be combined are temporally separated: the gesture or pointing action may occur either before or after the spoken command. It is extremely important to properly associate the actions, since the information given in the spoken command may be impossible to fully interpret without the gesture, and vice versa. Standard algorithms pay attention to the temporal ordering of actions in various modalities, evaluating whether two actions are related based on how long the "gap" is between the actions, whether the individual actions themselves can be well-formed commands, and other criteria. Even systems that are designed with multimodal fusion in mind must be able to support unimodal commands (independent gestures or speech), since users typically intermix unimodal and multimodal commands (Oviatt, 1999).

Multimodality and Security

Computer security and usability often find themselves in conflict. For example, computer security suggests that user passwords should contain digits, non-alphanumeric characters, be more than six characters long, and not listed in a standard dictionary. Usability findings suggest that passwords that conform to these rules will be difficult to remember, causing users to compromise security by writing the passwords down for future reference. New modalities, in the form of biometrics and other techniques, may provide a solution to this problem.

Biometric identification systems include speaker identification, fingerprint recognition, and retinal scanning. These systems rely on obtaining a unique identifier for a user that is based on *who the user is*. In addition to reducing the need for users to remember an arcane security code, biometric identification can make a system easier to use by combining the identification task with other interaction tasks. For example, voice identification could theoretically be done while the user is giving a voice interaction command. The user experience is that the extra identification step is being "skipped," when in fact it is being processed in the background.

Because current biometric identification systems are not 100% accurate, identifiers based on *what the user knows* (similar to passwords) will likely continue to be part of computer security. Multimodal techniques in this category include picture recognition tasks, where users must identify a familiar picture from among a set of unfamiliar ones (Weinshall & Kirkpatrick, 2004). Other applications are beginning to emerge within the picture recognition space, such as the SiteKey feature of the Bank of America website,[b] where users select a picture to be displayed after they have logged in to online banking. The display of the user-selected picture reassures users that the pages and information they are viewing have indeed come from the bank. Interestingly, decades-old research (Bakst, 1988) suggests that the best computer security will require a combination of who the user is, what the user knows, and *something the user carries* (for example, a keycard). By definition, a system that includes all of these would have to be multimodal.

Multimodality and Accessibility

New, often redundant, modalities can be added to an application to simply provide an alternative means to enter or receive information. One of the major reasons for doing this is to support the goal of *accessibility*, where computer systems are made to be usable by people with disabilities. By providing speech input capabilities, for example, users with physical disabilities that affect their ability to type or handle a pointing device can have access to the same applications that non-disabled users do. Similarly, audio (both speech and non-speech) output can be provided in addition to a visual screen to make an application or system accessible to blind users.

Accessible applications can be created in several ways, depending on when in the design process the issue is considered and the function of the application. Table 3 gives an overview of approaches that can be taken to make an application accessible, and lists benefits and drawbacks for each approach.

If accessibility is considered early in the process and a design is created that incorporates multiple input and output options to support a wide range of users, this is an example of *universal design*.[d] Although there is some argument about whether it is in fact possible to create a design that is universally usable (Mace, 1998), especially given the difference between input modes and the kinds of information that they can most easily express (Oviatt, 1999), universal design is frequently applied to systems that are to be used in a public context. Legislation regarding equal accessibility to information (such as the Americans with Disabilities Act and Section 508 of the Rehabilitation Act in the United States) encourage the designers of kiosks, automated teller machines (ATMs), and other public computing sources to take this approach.

Table 3. Approaches to accessibility

Approach Taken	Example	Benefits	Drawbacks
Create new app.	*Kiosk using "universal design"*	o accessible to all user groups o avoid "traps" by considering accessibility early	o requires design planning for all potential user groups o must be started at initial design phase
Create app. targeted to a group of disabled users	*Audio-based Web browser for blind/visually-impaired users*	o increase accessibility of existing content o no changes required to existing app.	o new app. may not be accessible to all o collaboration hard for disabled/non-disabled users
Add new modality to existing app.	*Mac OS X VoiceOver*[e]	o increase accessibility of existing content	o requires original manufacturer to decide to make product change
Create "helper" app.	*Screen readers, Voice-Enabled Portal*	o original application unchanged	o need access to underlying app.

Some applications are designed early on to be accessible, but with a focus on a specific group of users. For example, several commercial systems and research projects [such as pwWebSpeak[e], ASTeR (Raman, 1993), and AHA (James, 1998)] have addressed the issue of giving blind users better access to WWW-based content, taking different approaches to presenting structured documents in audio. One of the interesting things about this area of research is that the underlying WWW documents are not altered, but are instead interpreted differently by the new application to achieve accessibility.

Accessibility can also be added to products later on, as in the case of voice-enabled portal. The voice-enabled portal (VEP) [originally called "Voice over Workplace" in James & Roelands (2002)] is another example of a speech interface that was developed as a redundant means of input for an application, in this case a business portal. The system was designed to support physically disabled users by adding speech capabilities to multiple applications within a portal, without requiring those applications to be changed. To do this, the VEP interface supported navigation and basic text entry based on the application's syntax. Users selected items by speaking their names or by referring to elements by their type (e.g., "text box"). A major problem for this system was in disambiguating commands that could refer to multiple targets: if there are four text boxes on the screen, to which one does the command "text box" refer? Because the main goal was to provide access for physically disabled users, the solution chosen uses voice input exclusively: VEP used a predefined prioritization scheme to prioritize targets based on their location on the screen, choosing the target with the highest priority. If more than one target had equally high priorities, VEP numbered the targets using semi-transparent icons and required the user to specify the desired one.

Screen readers are another type of application where accessibility is added *after* an application has already been designed and built. Screen readers give blind users access to graphical interfaces using audio feedback and text-to-speech systems to read back text on menus, within open documents, and related to icons. These systems typically use access "hooks" provided by the applications and the operating system to find text, icons, and other graphical elements. For physically disabled users, third-party speech recognition systems (as well as those offered by the operating systems vendors themselves) also use the "hooks" to generate command grammars that allow users to control applications as well as enter text.

Accessibility and design for users with disabilities may seem like a specialized area of work, with a relatively small target population. However, as pointed out in Perry et al. (1997) and other sources, users can be *handicapped*, or unable to accomplish a task, merely because of the circumstances in which they try to perform it. So-called *temporary disabilities*, such as the inability of a user to direct his visual attention to a computer monitor, can be mitigated through the use of alternative modalities.

Multimodal Output and Transferring Tasks between Modalities

Much of this section has focused on the use of multimodal *input* in desktop settings. Multimodal *output* can also be used in desktop computing, especially for accessibility, as in the example of screen readers for blind users. Another potential use for multimodal output in a desktop setting is related to computing tasks that may be continued in a *non*-desktop setting, such as reading and reviewing documents while mobile.

Imagine the case where a sales representative is in her office reviewing her previous interactions with a client whom she will be visiting later that day. She reads through meeting minutes, e-mails, and other text-based documents to refresh her understanding of the situation. At the meeting that afternoon, the client says something that reminds the sales representative of a note in one of the documents she read, so she wants to go back to the document to get more details. Because the sales representative is out of her office, she is only carrying a mobile device, which does not have a large enough screen to display the document. The device is, however, capable of presenting the information via an audio interface. Will an audio review of information that had been previously only viewed visually be as helpful as a reminder as would a visual glance?

The intriguing question rising from this and similar scenarios is based on the concept of source memory (Johnson et al., 1993), or the memory of the qualities of the information presented (e.g., was it spoken or read, who said it, was it new information, etc.). If information is presented in one modality, but then must be retrieved using a different modality, does this affect the user's success rate, efficiency, and other retrieval factors? If research shows the answer to be yes, it may turn out to be beneficial to support additional output modalities (e.g., speech and audio) in a desktop computing environment. Information can initially be presented in several modalities simultaneously, so that later review or search in any of the modalities is made easier.

MULTIMODALITY FOR MOBILE DEVICES

Increasingly, computer usage is moving from desktop-based systems towards mobile devices, including personal digital assistants (PDAs) and mobile smart phones. New business and consumer applications for mobile devices are being created on an almost daily basis, to provide services and information to mobile users. However, the design of mobile applications presents many challenges from the standpoint of usability.

Mobile devices are limited by their very nature in terms of the user experience they can provide. In order to remain portable, mobile devices are constrained to a small form factor, which means that their input and output devices are also small. Tiny keypads and touch screens make input a challenge, especially when the user is walking or moving through the world. Small output screens are difficult to read and cannot present much information at one time. This section describes how multimodal input and output support can enhance the usability of mobile devices.

Input Modalities for Mobile Devices

Mobile devices come in several varieties, two of the most common being PDAs and mobile phones. The default input for these two device groups differs: mobile phones typically use a keypad (usually a 12-button telephone keypad, with perhaps a few additional function buttons), whereas PDAs (especially consumer-based models) as well as certain smart phones (for example, the Palm-based Handspring series) typically rely on handwriting input on a pressure-sensitive screen or small keyboards. It is interesting to note that although phones were originally designed to facilitate voice communication, interaction with mobile phone devices for tasks other than talking to another person (e.g., messaging, changing settings, and dialing) still rely heavily on non-speech input and output.

The small keypads used by most mobile phones make it difficult for the user to efficiently enter text and perform other input functions. Telephone keypad mappings requiring multi-tap or predictive text entry can be error-prone and add additional steps to the user interaction. QWERTY[f] keyboards on mobile devices are so small that the buttons can be difficult to accurately select. Initial attempts to mitigate these problems were taken by the device manufacturers themselves: PDA designers offered external keyboards that could be attached to the devices. The problem with this solution, as well as related research into keyboards that can be projected on a tabletop, is that keyboards are difficult (if not impossible) to use while standing, walking, or moving. If the user is forced to sit and remain stationary to use the keyboard, it defeats much of the purpose of the mobile device.

Keyboard alternatives have been proposed for mobile and wearable device input. These include a variety of gesture-sensing devices, such as the FingeRing device (Fukumoto & Tonomura, 1997), which senses chord-style typing using a set of wearable rings. Chord typing is based on particular combinations of fingers tapped on a surface simultaneously; for example, tapping a combination (or "chord") of index, middle, and ring finger describes a single letter of input. FingeRing allows users to tap chords on any surface, including a leg or arm, making it more useful while walking or moving. Other chord keyboards, such as the Twiddler^g, are small hand-held devices with strategically placed keys that can be selected in groups to form the chords. The limitations of chording, though, are a small input alphabet (for FingeRing: five fingers, with two positions each per chord, yields only 32 different chords) and a fairly high cost of learning effort.

On the PDA side, handwriting recognition via stylus has been available since the early days of the Apple Newton. Unfortunately, problems with the quality of the recognition using this system were at least partially responsible for the device's demise. More recently, the Graffiti system offered with Palm devices has seen better success, with its stroke-based (rather than word-based) recognition. Although Graffiti (or, rather, the underlying Unistrokes alphabet) was specifically *designed* to minimize recognition errors, Shneiderman (2002) also attributes the success of Graffiti to the ability of users to more easily see the locality and cause of errors than with word-based recognition.

Stylus input, then, seems to be a fairly good input modality for small devices. However, styli, as well as the small keyboards found on Blackberry-style devices, face limitations in many mobile settings. These include situations where the user's hands are busy or encumbered by gloves, or where the user's eyes are busy. Both the stroke-based recognition used by Graffiti and small keyboards can be a bit slow and rather cumbersome for entering large amounts of text. Other modalities, such as voice, can alleviate some of these problems.

Voice input is a common and well-accepted alternative to stylus or keypad input for mobile devices. ("A Conversation with Jordan Cohen," 2006) Mobile phones are especially well adapted to voice input, given that they already contain a microphone to support the telephony functions of the device. Voice input can free up the user's hands to perform the other functions necessary when mobile, such as carrying packages, opening doors, steering a car, or wearing gloves. Of course, voice input has its limitations in a mobile context, as well. In extremely noisy environments, recognition quality can deteriorate to the point that voice is unusable. Quieter environments may also be problematic for voice input, when it is inappropriate to talk or when it would be undesirable to be overheard. Technologically speaking, speech recognition via mobile phone often has a higher error rate than desktop-based recognition, both due to potential background noise and the quality of the device's microphone. And, limitations in device memory can force speech recognition grammars to be quite small, which impacts usability.

Another way to improve user input to a mobile device is to eliminate or reduce the need for the input. With new capabilities to determine the location of mobile phones, such as global positioning systems (GPS) and cell towers, mobile devices can automatically gather information that would otherwise require human input. For example, if a user conducts a search for restaurants, he is likely to want to find a restaurant close by. With an application that is not context-aware, the search query needed for this task will be something like "restaurant Palo Alto." If the device is able to detect the user's location, the query from the user would only have to be "restaurant," and the application could use the device's location to filter the results.

Context-awareness can be used in even more clever ways, as well. The MICA (Multimodal Interaction in Context-Adaptive Systems) project used context awareness to sense actions by the user that could be used as inputs (Lorenz et al., 2005). The warehouse-based prototype designed in the MICA project can sense when the user was passing an item that needed to be picked from a shelf and placed on the user's trolley, and indicate this to the user. In addition, the system was able to recognize when the user was looking for, but unable to find, an object on a shelf and provide guidance to the exact location.

Finally, mobile device input can be augmented using technologies that sense movements (e.g., tilting or lateral motion) of the device itself (Hinckley et al., 2005). For example, a phone can detect when it has been picked up and placed by the user's ear to automatically activate the speaker. Or, a device can detect that it has been tilted, to scroll down on a menu. Such interactions can be achieved by augmenting the device with rotational and gyroscopic sensors, or by new techniques that make use of mobile phone cameras (Wang & Canny, 2006).

Output Modalities for Mobile Devices

The small screens available on mobile devices are not really adequate to display all of the complex information that is requested by mobile users, such as maps, directions, and documents. The most common way of addressing this is through the use of audio output to augment the small-screen display. For example, many navigation systems show a small portion of a map view on the phone screen, with turn-by-turn directions presented using voice. This type of interaction also benefits mobile users by allowing them to focus more of their visual attention on locomotion tasks, such as walking and driving, which are common when using mobile devices. The next section goes into

more detail on the use of audio output in divided attention scenarios.

Mobile devices can also make use of haptic feedback as an output modality. The canonical example here is a vibration alert on a mobile phone. These alerts do not require either visual or auditory attention, making them useful in very noisy or very quiet environments while the user is mobile. Haptic feedback can be used in mobile applications, such as navigation, to support the movement-based input described above (e.g., tilting and rotation). Haptic output can provide the user with more feedback and control during tilting input, for example, by providing some level of resistance to help the user's actions stay in sync with the action taken on the visual display (Oakley & O'Modhrain, 2005). More experimental uses of haptics include the expression of presence by a remote participant to enhance social interaction [for example, Rovers & van Essen (2004) and Teh et al. (2006), where hand-holding, petting, or hugging by the remote participant is expressed to the user through vibration on the local device].

Designing for Divided Attention

As mentioned above, mobile devices are used in many contexts where the user is unable to devote his or her full attention to the mobile device interface. These contexts include device interaction while walking or driving: situations where the mobile device task is secondary, and the task of locomotion or navigation through the world is primary. The user's attention must be divided between the primary and secondary task, and the mobile device interaction must be sensitive to the fact that it is secondary. This means that the interaction must be designed to be usable without requiring undue amounts of attention, and must be especially sensitive to the modalities used to avoid overloading any of the sensory channels.

Multimodality can be used effectively in divided attention situations, most frequently by providing information input and output capabilities on channels that are not as important to the primary task. For example, visual attention requirements can be reduced by providing redundant output using the audio channel. This also reduces the need for the user to be in close physical proximity with the device, since audio can be heard over a greater distance than small visual displays can be used. Prototypes for warehouse picking have been designed in this way: the MICA system, for example, provides redundant visual and audio information so that the worker can move away from the visual display on the warehouse trolley to retrieve an item from the shelf, while still receiving information about the item to retrieve (Lorenz et al., 2005).

An important caveat, however, is that simply changing modality does not always produce an interaction that can be used effectively in divided-attention scenarios, especially vehicle-based scenarios. A study on speech-based interaction in a driving context showed that menu navigation produced competition for attentional resources with the spatial aspects of navigating the vehicle (Lee et al., 2001). The central processing theory of attention suggests that this is because *central* resources are being overloaded, even if none of the individual modalities are (Moray, 1999). Therefore, divided-attention interactions should also be careful about the sheer amount of information that is to be presented, perhaps by adapting to the current driving situation based on information about traffic conditions, driver stress, and so forth.

Finally, investigations of vehicle interfaces have shown that the *style* of information presentation has a strong impact on driving ability. Lee et al. (1999) found that drivers responded differently, in terms of response time and action taken, depending on several factors. These factors included not only modality, but also display location and message style (e.g., whether the system advised of a situation or gave explicit instructions for action). Other studies have also shown that the phrasing of messages, as well as the emotions expressed

by the voice used for output, have an impact on driving performance and attention (Jonsson et al., 2004; Jonsson et al., 2005). Voice *gender* can also make a difference, especially for certain tasks such as navigation and feedback on driving performance (Nass & Braves, 2005).

DEVICE FEDERATION

An emerging area of research in human-computer interaction involves the combination of small, portable devices with ambient computing and interaction resources in the user's environment. This concept, which is cropping up in industrial and academic research projects at various locations, is an attempt to balance the dual problems of portability and usability through a new model for mobile interaction, which we will call here *device federation*.

The idea of device federation is to augment small, portable devices such as smart phones (called *personal devices*) with ambient computing resources, such as large displays, printers, computers, PDAs, and keyboards. The personal device can be used to establish the user's identity (see the discussion above related to improving security by combining *something the user carries* with what the user knows and who the user is), run applications, or connect to back-end databases and servers, while ambient resources are leveraged to provide usable input and output. Conversely, personal devices can be connected to external sensors that have minimal or no user interfaces of their own, allowing the user to view or manipulate data that would otherwise be hidden within the environment.

Device federation is a broad concept, which covers a wide range of federation types. An obvious example is federating large displays with small mobile devices. Other types include federating sensors and other resources with limited human interaction capabilities with mobile devices, federating portable user devices with audio output, and federating portable input devices with ambient computers to provide accessibility.

Ad Hoc Wireless Federation

Device federation promises the ability to augment the large amount of computing resources found in today's portable devices using the ambient devices found nearly everywhere in the Western world. More and more offices, coffee shops, airports, and other locations contain large displays, speakers, and keyboards that could be used to make up for the limited input and output capabilities of mobile devices. Within the context of business usage, goals include allowing users to federate keyboards or other input devices with a personal mobile device to enhance input, or allowing voice input through a mobile device to be recognized and sent to a federated large-screen display.

It is already possible today to connect input and output devices to mobile phones and PDAs. USB and other wired connections provide a standard interface for keyboards, mice, displays, and other devices to connect to personal devices in a fairly seamless manner. However, wired connections require device proximity, which can be problematic for some use cases, such as connecting a mobile phone to a large-screen display. It would be preferable to be able to connect to the display from anywhere in the room, without having to be right next to it. In addition, some phones may not have standard wired connection points and instead use proprietary ports and connectors. Therefore, device federation holds *wireless* connectivity as one of its main goals.

The second main goal of device federation is to allow *ad hoc* connectivity. Many common wireless standards, such as Bluetooth, use handshaking and pairing protocols that are far too cumbersome to be of value when a personal device is to be connected to a particular ambient resource only once or twice in its lifetime. These protocols are also not very user-friendly, especially for inexperienced users.

One concern regarding ad hoc wireless federation is, of course, security. Devices that can easily connect and disconnect can also be easily compromised. Unfriendly devices could be used to snoop on data connections, or to grab computing resources. However, the need for security must be balanced with usability, so that the benefits of federation are not compromised.

Input and Output Federation

One of the most basic scenarios for device federation is display federation. Mobile devices often have screens that are too small to adequately display information, especially if the information involves complicated visualizations, graphics, or large quantities of text. Output federation can solve this problem by connecting with a nearby display to present the information. Additionally, input mechanisms to large screen displays have been investigated by many research groups [see Bezerianos & Balakrishnan (2005) for a recent example]. Federation offers another alternative, by allowing input through a mobile device to control a large-screen display.

The implementation of display federation is not as future reaching as it may seem. Intel's Ubiquity project is currently prototyping a device called the "Personal Server," which could be used for this purpose. The personal server is "a small lightweight computer with high-density data storage capability."[h] The primary purpose of the device is to store data and provide computing power that can be leveraged by other devices (such as a laptop, desktop, or projection displays) using a local wireless connection (Want et al., 2002). In fact, some of the original incarnations of the Personal Server have included *no* direct input and output capabilities: the very use of this device depends on display federation (as well as federation to input devices). WinCuts from Microsoft Research allows users to push shared areas of live screen content to other machines, which are controlled locally (Tan et al., 2004).

PdaReach by June Fabrics[i] displays the contents of a PDA screen on a computer connected via the PDA synchronization cable.

What remains to be investigated are usage scenarios and design for display federation. For example, should *all* content automatically be routed to a federated large display, or should users explicitly control the portions of the output to be displayed? Such considerations likely depend on the applications involved, the security or privacy of the environment, and other factors.

The federation of input devices would allow users to federate the input devices of their choice with other resources. Users could, for example, federate a speech input device to a computer, thereby allowing multimodal input to the computer's applications. This would not only be beneficial to mobile users, but was also proposed more than ten years ago as a solution to the accessibility problem (Perry et al., 1997). The basic idea was to provide users with a portable device that exactly met their needs in terms of input capabilities: low-mobility users could use single-switch or voice entry, blind users could use Braille entry devices, and so forth. This would be an example of creating a "helper application" to support disabled users (as discussed earlier in this chapter): the new element here is that the helper application would not need to reside on the same computer as the original application.

The Apple iPod is also a good example of input federation. The iPod is portable and allows self-contained functionality, but its input and output functionality increase when federated with other devices such as computers and car stereos. Federation with car stereos is especially interesting in regards to the distribution of I/O: some products federate the iPod to a car stereo's *speakers*, handling input via the iPod itself, while others use the car's output *and* input. User satisfaction with the different products can provide insight into federation for other consumer or business applications.

Because flexible connection and disconnection is a goal for device federation, it is possible that users may want to federate (or de-federate) within the course of performing a task. This again raises the possibility of using redundant outputs to facilitate task transfer, as described above.

Data Source Federation

Data sources, in the form of sensors, RFID tags, and other "smart items" are becoming more prevalent in today's environment. Sensors and tags can be used to track objects and provide real-time information. Federated devices can provide new opportunities to access these nearly invisible information sources by federating them with other devices (such as PDAs or laptop computers) that can display their state, or even modify their behavior.

Federating with data sources can also be used in ubiquitous computing environments to provide support for context-aware applications. Knowing what data sources are currently in proximity to the user's personal device can give a good sense of location, and data such as noise level, temperature, and other environmental factors can be used to modify the interaction. For example, if the noise level reported by nearby sensors is very high, a mobile device can make the decision to present information using the visual and haptic channels, rather than using audio.

Research projects that investigate software updates for embedded and networked devices point the way for data source federation. The OSGi Alliance is creating an open service delivery and management platform so that "software components can be installed, updated, or removed on the fly without having to disrupt the operation of the device."[j] Similarly, Sun Labs is researching "Small Programmable Object Technology," or Sun SPOT[k], which allows running Java programs to be moved between sensors. The flexibility inherent in these projects opens the possibility of federating devices to access data from nearby sensors or tags.

In data source federation, it is important to investigate the process of connecting and disconnecting devices. This topic of course also arises in input and output federation scenarios, but the sheer volume of sensors and tags available within a local area increases the magnitude of the problem. If the system requires users to search for nearby devices and explicitly grant pairing rights, selecting a few sensors (or a nearby display) from a list of thousands of possible devices becomes overwhelming. On the other hand, totally automatic pairing with thousands of nearby devices will generally be undesirable, as the user is unlikely to *want* to interact with all of them and may be uncomfortable not knowing which devices are connecting at any given time.

SOCIAL IMPACT OF VOICE TECHNOLOGIES

A discussion of multimodality would be incomplete without paying some consideration to the social impact of voice technologies. As mentioned earlier in the chapter, speech is one of the most common input technologies after keyboards and pointing devices. However, communicating with computer devices using speech raises many issues regarding how people respond to technologies that engage in this very "human" activity. The "Media Equation," as it was coined by Reeves & Nass, can be summarized by the idea that people treat interactions with computers and other media the same way that they treat interactions in real life (Reeves & Nass, 1996). Among other things, users react to and expect the same social phenomena in human-computer communication as in human-human communication, including following the rules of politeness and interpersonal difference. Nass & Braves (2005) extend these findings to state that humans are "Wired for Speech," and have

even stronger expectations about how systems that can speak or listen should behave.

In this section, we will reflect on one fundamental issue related to multimodal interactions that is implied by this work: the mismatch of modalities between input and output (James, 1998). When a device (or desktop application, for that matter) provides voice output, but does not allow voice input, this puts the user in a subordinate position to the computer, and may make the user feel out of control. As Brenda Laurel puts it:

"We...tend to expect symmetry between the input and output modalities of a system; that is, we expect that they are operating in the same sensory universe as the rest of the representation. If a computer talks to us, we want to be able to talk back, and vice versa.... In most systems, our side of the I/O equation is severely impoverished. The system can present images, sounds, movements, words, and possibly even speech, but we must act inside a straitjacket of menu items and mouse clicks. No wonder we often feel that computers are always in control—the system is holding all the cards! Working toward symmetry in input and output channels in human-computer activities can vastly improve our experience of engagement and agency." (Laurel, 1993)

Control is not the only issue. Mismatching modality can also be perceived as impoliteness. The polite response to a letter is another letter; answering a letter with a phone call is less polite. Computer systems that require an input in a different modality than the modality used for output, according to Reeves & Nass (1996), force the user to make an impolite response.

Due to the factors discussed above, care should be taken when adding a modality to make sure that it is available both for input and output, if it is technically possible to do so. There is, however, every possibility that new generations of computer users who have been exposed to interfaces with modality mismatches since birth may not have the same control and politeness responses [changes in politeness behavior related to technology use have been shown to some extent in relation to mobile phones, for example (Ling, 2004)]. Although computer interfaces evolve at a much faster pace than humans, people who grow up using multimodal interfaces that may not conform to human-human social interaction standards may adapt their reactions to the computers and be more accepting of seemingly impolite behavior.

SUMMARY

This chapter has described some of the basic principles of multimodality. We began with a description of some of the ways that the human senses can be used to interact with a computer, and discussed the idea that modalities can be used *redundantly*, where more than one modality is used to either present or gather the same information, or *complementarily*, where information from more than one modality must be combined to produce the whole input or output message. Each of these methods can be used for either desktop or mobile interactions, although generally for different reasons.

Multimodal interfaces to desktop computers strive to provide natural mappings between the information to be input or output and the modality used. This more frequently leads to interfaces that use complementary modalities, or multimodal fusion. Desktop applications also use multimodality to support users with disabilities or to provide more usable security. Another interesting research area for multimodality is around the use of redundant output modalities to support users who move from desktop to mobile computers during the course of an interaction.

Mobile applications use multimodality to improve the input and output capabilities of the devices. Because mobile devices must be small to be portable, they often have very small visual displays and keypads. Voice and audio are obvious choices here, and have been used widely. Finally, because mobile devices are often used in contexts where the user is carrying out another (more primary) task, such as walking or driving, it is important to design interfaces that do not require too much of the user's attention or overload any of the senses.

Next, we described an emerging area of human-computer interaction that seeks to combine the portability of mobile devices with the interaction capabilities of larger ambient devices, called device federation. Input and output federation can, and have already begun to, be used to support mobile users with both business and consumer applications. Federation with data sources, such as sensors and RFID tags, could also benefit business users and support context-awareness.

The final section of this chapter discussed an important consideration when using voice interactions, namely, the social implications. Based on continuing research from sociology, it is clear that people treat media in many of the same ways that they treat other people, and have many of the same expectations. This is especially true for voice-based systems, so care must be taken when using voice input and output.

FUTURE RESEARCH DIRECTIONS

The importance of multimodal interaction design will continue to increase as users move more and more towards interaction with mobile devices, and away from traditional desktop computing environments. Increasing wireless connectivity is shifting users toward an "always-on, always-available" mentality that will be supported by newer and better mobile devices.

The widespread use of mobile devices will require a focus on supporting work that is done within the context of other activities. This work has already begun to some extent, but there are open questions around the types of tasks users choose to engage in while busy doing other things and how to manage interruptions within an interaction. For example, in the vehicle context, it will be important to understand what kinds of tasks are of interest to users, and then create interfaces that will help users complete them safely and without creating an undue mental burden. Even without considering interruptions, it will be important to investigate the confirmation of actions taken by users whose attention is divided between interaction with a mobile device and interaction with the rest of the world.

The federated device concept discussed in this chapter certainly falls under the area of future research. Initial projects have shown that it should be possible to (wirelessly and seamlessly) interconnect mobile and ambient devices; what remains to be seen is how the interactions with device federations should be structured. What information should be shown on a personal display, as opposed to a public display? Should the personal device be used for input to a device federation, and if so, how should it operate? Will the personal device act as a remote control, or will users respond to it simply as one component of the larger system? These and other questions are important to understand as the world moves toward ubiquitous computing environments.

Finally, this chapter listed a wide range of modalities available for human-computer interactions. Some of these modalities are already part of many computer systems, such as voice and audio, while others are less widely used. Haptics and other modalities could be valuable additions to new interaction designs, but more research is required to understand where they would be most appropriate for everyday use.

REFERENCES

Bakst, S. (1988). The future in security methods. *The Office, 108*(19-20).

Bezerianos, A., & Balakrishnan, R. (2005). *The vacuum: Facilitating the Manipulation of Distant Objects* In *Proceedings of the SIGCHI Conference on Human Factors in Computing Systems*, Portland, OR (pp. 361-370). New York: ACM Press.

Bolt, R.A. (1980). *"Put-that-there:" Voice and gesture at the graphics interface.* In *Proceedings of the Seventh Annual Conference on Computer Graphics and Interactive Techniques* (pp. 262-270). New York: ACM Press.

Cheyer, A., & Julia, L. (1998). Multimodal maps: An agent-based approach. In H. Bunt, R.-J. Beun, & T. Borghuis (Eds.), *Multimodal human-computer communication* (pp. 111-121). Springer.

A conversation with Jordan Cohen. (2006, July/August). *ACM Queue,* pp. 14-23.

Fukumoto, M., & Tonomura, Y. (1997). *"Body coupled FingeRing": Wireless wearable keyboard.* In *Proceedings of the SIGCHI Conference on Human Factors in Computing Systems*, Atlanta, GA (pp. 147-154). New York: ACM Press.

Ghias, A., Logan, J., Chamberlin, D., & Smith, B.C. (1995). *Query by Humming: Musical Information Retrieval in an Audio Database.* In *Proceedings of the Third ACM International Conference on Multimedia*, San Francisco, CA (pp. 231-236). New York: ACM Press.

Grasso, M.A., Ebert, D.S., & Finin, T.W. (1998). The integrality of speech in multimodal interfaces. *ACM Transactions on Computer-Human Interaction, 5*(4), 303-325.

Hinckley, K., Pierce, J., Horvitz, E., & Sinclair, M. (2005). Foreground and background interaction with sensor-enhanced mobile devices. *ACM Transactions on Computer-Human Interaction, 12*(1), 31-52.

James, F. (1998). *Representing structured information in audio interfaces: A framework for selecting audio marking techniques to represent document structure*. Unpublished Ph.D. Dissertation, Stanford University, Stanford, CA.

James, F., & Roelands, J. (2002). *Voice over Workplace (Vowp): Voice Navigation in a Complex Business Gui*. In V.L. Hanson & J.A. Jacko (Eds.), *Proceedings of the ACM Conference on Assistive Technologies*, ASSETS 2002, Edinburgh, Scotland (pp. 197-204).

Johnson, M.K., Hashtroudi, S., & Lindsay, D.S. (1993). Source monitoring. *Psychological Bulletin, 114*(1), 3-28.

Jonsson, I.-M., Nass, C., Endo, J., Reaves, B., Harris, H., Ta, J.L., et al. (2004). *Don't blame me, I am only the driver: Impact of blame attribution on attitudes and attention to driving task*. In *CHI '04 Extended Abstracts on Human Factors in Computing Systems*, Vienna, Austria (pp. 1219-122). New York: ACM Press.

Jonsson, I.-M., Zajicek, M., Harris, H., & Nass, C. (2005). *Thank You, I Did Not See That: In-Car Speech Based Information Systems for Older Adults*. In *CHI '05 Extended Abstracts on Human Factors in Computing Systems*, Portland, OR (pp. 1953-1956). New York: ACM Press.

Koons, D.B., Sparrell, C.J., & Thorisson, K.R. (1993). Integrating simultaneous input from speech, gaze, and hand gestures. In M. Maybury (Ed.), *Intelligent multimedia interfaces* (pp. 257-276). Menlo Park, CA: MIT Press.

Laurel, B. (1993). *Computers as theatre* (2nd ed.). Reading, MA: Addison-Wesley Publishing Company.

Lee, J.D., Caven, B., Haake, S., & Brown, T.L. (2001). Speech-based interaction with in-vehicle computers: The effect of speech-based e-mail on drivers' attention to the roadway. *Human Factors, 43*, 631-640.

Lee, J.D., Gore, B.F., & Campbell, J.L. (1999). Display alternatives for in-vehicle warning and sign information: Message style, location, and modality. *Transportation Human Factors, 1*(4), 347-375.

Ling, R. (2004). *The mobile connection: The cell phone's impact on society*. San Francisco, CA: Morgan Kaufmann.

Lodding, K.N. (1982). Iconics: A visual man-machine interface. In *Proceedings of the Third Annual Conference and Exhibition of the National Computer Graphics Association, Inc.* (Vol. 1, pp. 221-233). Lorenz, A., Zimmermann, A., & Eisenhauer, M. (2005). *Towards natural interaction by approaching objects*. Paper presented at ABIS 2005, Saarbrücken.

Mace, R. L. (1998). *A perspective on universal design*. Paper presented at Designing for the 21st Century: An International Conference on Universal Design.

Maynes-Aminzade, D. (2005). *Edible bits: Seamless interfaces between people, data and food*. Paper presented at Conference on Human Factors in Computing Systems, Portland, OR.

Moore, R.C., Dowding, J., Bratt, H., Gawron, J.M., Gorfu, Y., & Cheyer, A. (1997). *Commandtalk: A Spoken-Language Interface for Battlefield Simulations*. In *Proceedings of the Fifth Conference on Applied Natural Language Processing* (pp. 1-7). San Francisco: Morgan Kaufmann Publishers Inc.

Moray, N. (1999). Commentary on Goodman, Tijerina, Bents, and Wierwille, "Using cellular telephones in vehicles: Safe or unsafe". *Transportation Human Factors, 1*(1), 43-46.

Nass, C., & Braves, S. (2005). *Wired for speech: How voice activates and advances the human-computer relationship*. Cambridge, MA: MIT Press.

Oakley, I., & O'Modhrain, S. (2005). Tilt to scroll: Evaluating a motion based vibrotactile mobile interface. In *Proceedings of the First*

Joint Eurohaptics Conference and Symposium on Haptic Interfaces for Virtual Environment and Teleoperator Systems (pp. 40-49). IEEE.

Oviatt, S.L. (1999). Ten myths of multimodal interaction. *Communications of the ACM, 42*(11), 74-81.

Perry, J., Macken, E., Scott, N., & McKinley, J.L. (1997). Disability, inability and cyberspace. In B. Friedman (Ed.), *Human values and the design of computer technology* (Number 72 Ed., pp. 65-89). Stanford, CA: CSLI Publications.

Raman, T.V. (1993). *Audio system for technical readings*. Unpublished Ph.D. Thesis, Cornell University, Ithaca, NY.

Reeves, B., & Nass, C. (1996). *The media equation: How people treat computers, television and new media like real people and places*. New York: Cambridge University Press.

Rovers, A.F., & van Essen, H.A. (2004). *HIM: A framework for haptic instant messaging*. In *CHI '04 Extended Abstracts on Human Factors in Computing Systems*, Vienna, Austria (pp. 1313-1316). New York: ACM Press.

Shneiderman, B. (2002). *Leonardo's laptop: Human needs and the new computing technologies*. Cambridge, MA: MIT Press.

Tan, D.S., Meyers, B., & Czerwinski, M. (2004). *Wincuts: Manipulating Arbitrary Window Regions for More Effective Use of Screen Space*. In *CHI '04 Extended Abstracts on Human Factors in Computing Systems*, Vienna, Austria (pp. 1525-1528). New York: ACM Press.

Teh, K.S., Lee, S.P., & Cheok, A.D. (2006). *Poultry.Internet: A Remote Human-Pet Interaction System*. In *CHI '06 Extended Abstracts on Human Factors in Computing Systems*, Montreal, Quebec, Canada (pp. 251-254). New York: ACM Press.

Tyfa, D.A., & Howes, M. (2000). Speech recognition for command entry in multimodal interaction. *International Journal of Human-Computer Studies, 52*, 637-667.

Wang, J., & Canny, J. (2006). *Tinymotion: Camera Phone Based Interaction Methods*. In *CHI '06 Extended Abstracts on Human Factors in Computing Systems*, Montreal, Quebec, Canada (pp. 339-344). New York: ACM Press.

Want, R., Pering, T., Borriello, G., & Farkas, K. (2002). Disappearing hardware. *IEEE Pervasive Computing, 1*(1), 36-47.

Weinshall, D., & Kirkpatrick, S. (2004). *Passwords You'll Never Forget, but Can't Recall*. In *CHI '04 Extended Abstracts on Human Factors in Computing Systems*, Vienna, Austria (pp. 1399-1402). New York: ACM Press.

ADDITIONAL READING

Arons, B. (1991). *Hyperspeech: Navigating in Speech-Only Hypermedia*. In *Proceedings of the Third Annual ACM Conference on Hypertext*, San Antonio, TX (pp. 133-146). New York: ACM Press.

Blattner, M.M. (1992). *Metawidgets: Towards a theory of multimodal interface design*. In *Proceedings of the Sixteenth Annual International Computer Software and Applications Conference*, Chicago, IL (pp. 115-120). IEEE Press.

Bly, S. (1982). Presenting information in sound. In *Human factors in computer systems* (pp. 371-375). Gaithersburg, MD.

Buxton, W.A.S. (1994). The three mirrors of interaction: A holistic approach to user interfaces. In L.W. MacDonald & J. Vince (Eds.), *Interacting with virtual environments*. New York: Wiley.

Edwards, W.K., Mynatt, E.D., & Stockton, K. (1994). *Providing access to graphical user interfaces—not graphical screens*. In *Proceedings of*

ASSETS '94: The First Annual ACM Conference on Assistive Technologies, Marina del Rey, CA (pp. 47-54). New York: ACM Press.

Flowers, J.H., Buhman, D.C., & Turnage, K.D. (1996). Data sonification from the desktop: Should sound be part of standard data analysis software?. *ACM Transactions on Applied Perception*, *2*(4), 467-472.

Gaver, W.W. (1990). The Sonicfinder: An interface that uses auditory icons. In E.P. Glinert (Ed.), *Visual programming environments: Applications and issues* (pp. 561-581). Los Alamitos, CA: IEEE Computer Society Press.

Gilman, A.S., Vanderheiden, G., & Zimmermann, G. (2000). *Universal design and the grid*. Paper presented at Grid Forum 5.

Gong, L. (2003). Multimodal interactions on mobile devices and users' behavioral and attitudinal preferences. In C. Stephanidis (Ed.), *Universal Access in HCI: Inclusive Design in the Information Society* (pp. 1402-1406). Mahwah, NJ: Lawrence Erlbaum Associates.

Oviatt, S.L. (1996). User-centered design of spoken language and multimodal interfaces. *IEEE Multimedia, 3*(4), 26-35.

Smith, A., Dunaway, J., Demasco, P., & Peischl, D. (1996). *Multimodal Input for Computer Access and Augmentative Communication*. In *Proceedings of the 2nd Annual ACM Conference on Assistive Technologies*, Vancouver, BC (pp. 80-85). New York: ACM Press.

Wise, G.B., & Glinert, E.P. (1995). *Metawidgets for multimodal applications*. In *Proceedings of the RESNA '95 Conference*, Vancouver, Canada (pp. 455-457). Washington, DC: RESNA Press.

ENDNOTES

[a] Deictic references can also include reference to times, such as "now" or "later" and people (such as "you" or "me").

[b] http://www.bankofamerica.com/privacy/index.cfm?template=privacysecur_olb

[c] http://www.apple.com/macosx/features/voiceover/

[d] See http://trace.wisc.edu/world/gen_ud.html for a general discussion of the concept of universal design.

[e] http://www.soundlinks.com/pwgen.htm

[f] QWERTY is the name for a standard U.S. keyboard layout, and comes from the first six letter keys in the top row starting from the left. See Wikipedia for a more detailed explanation (http://en.wikipedia.org/wiki/QWERTY).

[g] http://www.handykey.com/site/twiddler2.html

[h] http://www.intel.com/research/exploratory/personal_server.htm

[i] http://www.junefabrics.com/index.php

[j] http://www.osgi.org/

[k] http://research.sun.com/projects/dashboard.php?id=145

Chapter XXII
Multimodal Software Engineering

Andreas Hartl
Technische Universität Darmstadt, Germany

ABSTRACT

Ubiquitous computing with its multitude of devices certainly makes it necessary to supplant the desk-top metaphor of graphical user interfaces by other kinds of user interfaces. Applications must adapt themselves to many modalities: they must support a wide variety of devices and interaction languages. Software engineering methods and tools also need to embrace this change so that developers can build usable adaptive applications more easily. This chapter will present three different software engineering approaches that address this challenge: extensions to Web-based approaches, abstract user interface definitions that add a level of abstraction to the user interface definition, and model-based approaches that extend model-based application development to integrate user interface issues as well.

INTRODUCTION

Ubiquitous computing (UC) makes computing power available in a lot more devices than just PCs. Consequently, the currently prevailing methods of human-computer interaction will come under heavy pressure from other ones. The desktop metaphor introduced with the Xerox Alto and popularized by the Apple Macintosh is already being challenged by Web applications that use other ways to organize their content—usually such applications are centered around the idea of a page instead the desktop.

The Idea of Multimodality

Most prevalent forms of human-computer interaction focus on graphics and written text for interaction between users and computers. For everyday users, such user interfaces are much easier to use than their command line-based predecessors. Yet they are not necessarily the best way for human-computer interaction: the evolution of user interfaces continues and multimodal user interfaces are a promising concept for the future.

The term *multimodal* was first used by Bolt (1980) in his paper "Put-that-there." With multimodal user interfaces, users interact with the system using several independent means of interaction. "Put-that-there" used graphical output and speech and gesture input and eye tracking. Colloquially speaking, one could define multimodality as "multimedia the computer understands." Nigay and Coutaz (1995) provide a more formal definition; to them, a modality is a *coupling of an interaction language L with a physical device d: <d, L>*. The formal definition of a physical device is that of *an artifact of the system that acquires or delivers information. An interaction language is a language used by the user or the system to exchange information. A language defines the set of all possible well-formed expressions [...]*.

We will use this definition of a modality throughout this chapter.

Windows, Icons, Menus, and Pointing Devices and Beyond

The first devices that challenged the personal computer's dominance as the most used tool for accessing and processing information were cellular phones and personal digital assistants like the Palm or the Blackberry. As means of interaction with their users, these small devices continue to use the established graphical interaction techniques based on windows, icons, menus, and pointing devices, albeit slightly modified. Application developers know how to build user interfaces with such techniques, which makes it easy to adapt similar techniques also for mobile devices. Yet the widening range of possible target devices will probably change the user interface from slightly modified desktop interfaces to something new for several reasons:

- Graphical user interfaces implicitly define some constraints on the devices that are using them: they require a decently sized display, and a way to move the pointer, two things that may not be available on a very small device.

- By their very definition, graphical user interfaces focus on graphical output and input, often neglecting other possible means of interaction. Hence, users can only interact with such an interface if they are not too distracted and if their hands and eyes are free to use it.

- Interaction metaphors that work well for desktop-based graphical user interfaces may not be adequate for UC devices. Other forms of interaction may be better suited for ubiquitous computing devices. Satyanarayanan (2005) gives Apple's iPod as an example, whose "success in displacing older portable music devices shows the power of combining the right device functionality with a good form factor and user interface."

Most applications apply a closed-world approach where every property of the system is known beforehand. For example, applications know the minimum screen size they can expect, and input and output features available to them. This makes it possible to tailor the user interface well to specific devices, and ideally makes an application easier to use. The drawback of this approach is that the application cannot adapt its user interface beyond the closed world it lives in, even if that would make sense; for example, it cannot use a newly found large screen for displaying complex data but stays restricted to the small screen of the portable device it was developed for.

As the number of devices that want to communicate with their users increases, the closed-world approach becomes less and less feasible for each of them. The most pressing issue is of course that users expect such devices simply to work, without complex personalization beforehand. For this reason, applications must adopt an open-world approach where they interoperate with each other.

There is a windfall benefit to this open-world approach that applications must implement: with easier interoperability and cross-device user interfaces, applications not only become more powerful, but they may also be more usable. As an *emergent property*, applications that work on interconnected devices automatically implement multimodal interaction. For example, one part of the interface may be rendered by a device that used speech-based interaction, whereas another part of the interface may be rendered on a touch-screen display.

Innovations made in other areas of UC are likely to promote open-world applications:

1. Communication infrastructures that make it possible to exchange user interface events easily between devices (cf., the chapter "Event-Based and Publish/Subscribe Communication");
2. Services running on different devices that are able to find each other (cf., the chapter "Service Discovery").
3. Context-sensing devices, which may find other components that may be used for presenting the user interface (cf., the chapter "Context Models and Context Awareness").

Changes in the infrastructures, however, are not enough. Multimodal applications also present new challenges to application developers who need to adopt new development tools, new concepts, and new software development methodologies.

Web-based applications soon had to support multiple modalities, which is why they are currently the most widespread kind of multimodal applications. In order to be successful and to at-

tract as many users as possible, Web applications usually have to present their content on a wide range of devices with different browsers, different capabilities and different constraints. This chapter will start with the software engineering approaches implemented by Web applications. However, Web-based applications have some shortcomings when it comes to more complex tasks. For these tasks, so-called *rich applications* are more feasible. Rich applications have much more fine-grained control over the user interface of the device; they do not require a browser or something similar to render their user interface. It is the goal of the abstract user interfaces and model-based user interfaces mentioned later in the chapter to make such applications also adaptive and multimodal by defining higher-level abstractions for user interface specifications to them.

WEB-CENTRIC APPROACHES

Whereas desktop applications usually run in an extremely predicable environment that only rarely differs significantly from the developer's system, developers of Web applications soon faced the problem that they had to deliver their content to a multitude of targets. Leaving aside the standardization problems that emerged during the late-1990s browser wars, people soon wanted to access information from the Web on non-desktop-PC devices such as cellular phones.

The first product to successfully bring Web content to such resource-constrained devices was NTT DoCoMo's iMode launched in 1999 (Barnes & Huff, 2003). Soon after its introduction, the provider-proprietary iMode was followed by the open WAP standard initiated by Ericsson (Erlandson & Ocklind, 1998). Both approaches define their own markup language for portable devices. Later, markup languages for other modalities followed as well, for example VoiceXML (McGlashan et al., 2004) and SMIL (Bulterman et al., 2005). Developers can use such markup languages either stand-alone or in combination with each other, where a document consists of several modules for each modality and some additional code that glues together the modules by synchronizing the data between them. A prominent example for the combination of languages is the X+V profile proposed by Axelsson, Cross, Lie, McCobb, Raman, and Wilson (2001) which combines graphical interaction using XHTML and speech interaction using VoiceXML.

Whenever a new markup language comes into play, a representation of the existing content must be represented in this new language. One way to do that is by *transcoding* existing Web applications from an old source markup language into the new target language (cf., Bharadvaj, Joshi, & Auephanwiriyakul, 1998). Another option is to change the source representation of the Web application: instead of using a markup language like HTML, which makes several implicit assumptions about the browser's ability (e.g., that it can view two dimensional entities such as tables), the Web application may use an extensible markup language (XML)-based higher-level representation. Depending on the target modality, *stylesheets* (see below) then define how the higher representation gets represented.

Transcoding

In computer science, the term *transcoding* originally was used to refer to conversions between digital media file formats—for example, saving a video originally packed with MPEG4 in the MPEG2 format. In a broader sense, transcoding is a way to automatically convert data available in one source format to a given target format. Source and target format may be different or two manifestations of the same source format, but with different properties—for example, images may be transcoded into a lower resolution.

When applied to user interfaces, transcoding refers to the conversion of user interfaces from one representation format to another. The most widely used representation format for user interfaces is HTML, a format that many transcoding approaches focus on. Other reasons that make the HTML markup language a good choice for transcoding is that it is stateless, it is an easily readable plain text format and it already has some *structural elements*. Structural elements make transcoding easier, because they describe how a document is organized logically (e.g., by chapter, with an introduction and table of contents, etc.), instead of only presentational properties (e.g., font size and thickness). The formal definition by Chisholm, Vanderheiden, and Jacobs (2001) specifies that an element *"[...] that specifies document structure is called a structural element"* (p. 50).

Both media and user interface transcoding typically are *lossy* and skip or ignore some parts of the original content. User interface transcoding may even apply media transcoding techniques to adapt embedded multimedia data to the target environment, for example, by resizing images of the Web pages.

Compared to other ways for creating multimodal applications, transcoding requires little or no changes with existing Web pages. As a downside, the usability of the resulting user interface may vary widely.

User interface transcoding may be done on the device itself, in the network, or on both locations. Examples for device-based transcoding are Web browsers for handheld devices, such as Opera and WebKit, which have an *optimized view* feature for Web pages. Network-based transcoding uses software that acts as proxy server between the original page source and the target device. The proxy server first fetches the original page and then applies a set of transcoding rules on that page. The resulting transcoded page then is sent to the target device. An example for a network-based transcoding proxy server is IBM's *WebSphere Transcoding Publisher* (2006).

Both approaches have specific advantages and disadvantages:

- Device-based transcoding rules may be extremely well tailored to the specific device, taking the precise device metrics into account. This may result in better usability. On the other hand, the rules have to work with almost every possible Web page the users may want to access, so device-based transcoding usually employ extremely general-purpose heuristics. In some extreme cases this may result in unusable target pages. On the device, transcoding requires additional computing power and memory, which may result in slow user response and higher battery usage. Device-based transcoding is easier to turn off than network-based transcoding. Some transcoding techniques – for example, re-compressing images with a higher compression ratio, giving faster download speed – are impossible for device-based transcoders.

- Transcoding proxies do not consume memory and computing power on the device itself, which may be a scarce resource. Because of the resources available on proxy servers, their rules may be more numerous and more complex. Also, one proxy can transcode pages for more than one device, making the process more efficient. Server-based approaches usually are extensible and make it possible to implement new rules on demand, so they can support new device classes or provide special-purpose rules for pages that otherwise would result in unusable transcoding results. Being a centralized resource, the proxy can become a single point of failure for the devices that rely on them. On heavy network load, the proxy is a bottleneck that slows down system response times and leads to a less pleasing user experience. Proxy-based transcoding approaches are more difficult to turn off; an unusable page may therefore become inaccessible. Proxies also have the ability to log and store each page retrieved, which may cause data protection and privacy issues.

Device-Based Transcoding

Device-based transcoding techniques are often used if source and target use the same markup language. In this case, the interaction language of the target stays the same, and the physical device changes. This makes the transcoding process simpler: it has to identify page elements that are difficult to realize on the target device and replaces them by semantically equivalent, but more usable elements. For example, browsers may re-layout Web pages that use tables for layout – a common, albeit deprecated layout technique that requires users to scroll horizontally if the horizontal resolution of the target device is less than the minimum width of the table. By removing the table, while preserving its content on the Web page, the free-flow algorithm of the Web browser can place the table elements underneath each other. Other transformation rules may resize images or render text with a smaller font.

Figure 1 shows how a device may combine these rules to alter a Web page for a smaller screen.

Users of device-based transcoding often may choose to turn the transcoding feature off. This is useful for pages where transcoding leads to results that are less usable than their unmodified counterparts. This option is possible if the device browser can display all features of an original page. Turning device-based transcoding on and off does not affect network load, because the source is already present on the device.

From the software engineering perspective, device-based transcoding requires little to no changes in the development process of Web-based applications. Developers can use existing, deployed, and evaluated software engineering methodologies like Rational Unified Process. Especially lightweight, agile methodologies [cf.,

Figure 1. Normal Web page (left) vs. rendering on a smaller screen (right)

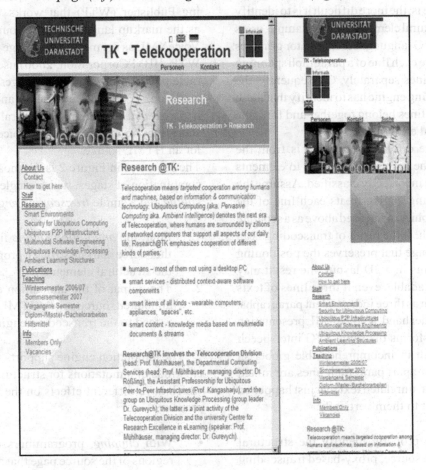

Ge, Paige, Polack, Chivers & Brooke (2006)], which may already be common in real-time enterprises, are well suited for developing Web applications to be used with device-based transcoding. Existing Web development tools may be used without change.

Network-Based Transcoding

If source and target are separate languages rather than just instances of the same markup language, proxy-based transcoding techniques are predominant. In such a case, the transcoding rules try to convert the *structure* of a document from the source into the target language.

Also, if the target language is different from the source language, it is unnecessary to fetch the source at the device, as the device is unable to present the unmodified source.

It is therefore vital to the transcoding engine that the transcoding rules identify the structural elements of the source correctly. Depending on the source language, this may be more or less difficult. Apart from the transformation rules, two factors are relevant for the quality of the transformation process:

- The more presentation-centric the source language is, the more difficult it is to identify the structural elements. As an example, users of the SVG language for 2D vector graphics may place each line of a paragraph spanning several lines separately. Consequently, the transcoding engine has to identify that these separate lines belong together and form the structural element *paragraph*.
- The more different the target is from the source, the more sensitive it is to elements that were incorrectly classified. Assume the transcoding engine treats each line of the SVG graphics mentioned above as a separate paragraph. If the result of transcoding is an HTML page that preserves the positioning of elements in a 2D layout, the result may still be readable, even if three lines of texts are shown as three independent paragraphs. On the other hand, a VoiceXML presentation that transforms the same SVG into speech may result in incomprehensible gibberish if the torn-apart paragraph lines are mixed with other, unrelated text that just happened to be next to them vertically.

In order to properly identify the structural elements of the source, proxy-based transcoding engines often make this identification-process configurable. The example in Figure 2 shows the architecture of IBM's WebSphere Transcoding Publisher (WTP) that works with HTML as the markup language of the source and with VoiceXML as the markup language of the target. WTP (IBM Corporation, 2006) uses a configurable pipeline of transcoding stages. Each stage works on a given source language and transcodes it to a given target language. Several transcoding stages may be chained, giving a VoiceXML target for an HTML source.

The sequence in Figure 2 is the most basic combination of stages, with a single *annotation engine* and a single *transcoding engine*:

1. First, the *annotation engine* first modifies the source markup so that it properly reflects the structural elements.
2. The output of the annotation engine is an annotated source page's HTML, which then is feed to the transcoding engine.

The annotation engine supports three different kinds of annotations for structural elements, which have different effects on the transcoding process:

- With *clipping*, programmers can specify regions of the source page that are optional. The annotation engine will then cut away these regions. A common application of

Figure 2. The WebSphere Transcoding Publisher

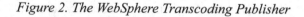

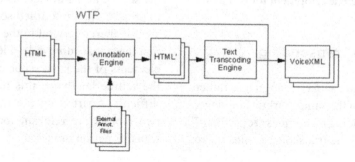

clipping is to remove navigational elements from the source, since they are common for Web pages.

- The *content replacement* annotation is quite similar to clipping. Instead of skipping a whole region, content replacement defines alternative content for that region. A possible use for content replacement is to replace a long text by its summary and providing a "more" link for users who want to get the entire text.
- The *form simplification* annotation is useful if the target interaction language is tedious to interact with, for example, speech interaction. Form simplification can define default values for form fields or skip human-computer interaction and supply default values from other sources. Also, form simplification may replace free-form text entry with a list of common possible values, thus simplifying the interaction task.

The decision of which annotation to use can depend on various parameters: target device, network, or user. This makes it possible to tailor the transcoding very specifically to a target, if necessary, but this comes at a price: each target must contain one or more annotations. Therefore, the finer-grained the transcoding process works, the more annotations need to be developed, deployed, and supported. It is up to the transcoding proxy's maintainer to balance the tradeoff between easy support and fine-grained control over the transcoding results.

Control over the transcoding process is not limited to the maintainers of the proxy, however. Developers may integrate annotations into the source pages as well. Web browsers ignore the annotations, also the proxy's annotation engine leaves them untouched, but the transcoding engine uses the annotations coming from the original source document as well as the ones added by the annotation engine.

Compared to device-based transcoding technologies, network-based transcoding requires more changes: one must set up and maintain the proxy server. Annotation rules must be selected and tested. This effort also comes with additional flexibility that makes it possible to support different interaction languages as well. Just like the device-based transcoding technologies, it does not require changes in the development methodologies and tools used. Unlike with device-based transcoding, however, developers have the power to improve the user experience for the software incrementally by improving annotation rules or by adding annotations to the source language. This favors agile development processes, as it fits well with the idea of frequently delivered working software that gets evaluated on-site. By making annotations possible, developers can fine-tune pages that otherwise would fail to get transcoded correctly. Being optional, the annotations do not complicate pages that can be transcoded easily.

In general, both device-based and network-based transcoding techniques maintain compatibility with the existing Web design process. This means that existing products don't have to be re-developed, thus saving money.

Higher-Level Representation with Stylesheet Transformation

With transcoding, enterprises can avoid the—perhaps costly—re-implementation of their existing Web applications. In the case of network-based transitions, they can gradually add new rules to the server, or annotations to the Web applications' output to optimize the result of the transcoding process. However, transcoding must identify the semantic meaning of the page elements, a tedious and error-prone task. Transcoding is therefore limited to simple transformation rules like clipping, content replacement, and form simplification.

While these simple transcoding rules may lead to a user interface with sufficient usability, a user interface specially designed for the target modality is often better (Kaikkonen & Roto, 2003).

Most Web applications are a front-end to a more-or-less complicated database. It is the responsibility of the application to present this database content in a way that makes sense to the user. The application usually does so by querying the database and filling out HTML templates.

Stylesheets try to make use of this fact by applying the following train of thought: If one replaces the rather low level HTML by an intermediate representation using some higher-level language, it is then possible to transform this representation into an application that is tailored to a specific modality. By adding other stylesheets, the applications can support more modalities. The World Wide Web Consortium (W3C) sees this approach as the one that would one day give birth to the *Semantic Web* (cf., the chapter "Ontologies for Scalable Services-Based Ubiquitous Computing"), because the higher-level XML language features gives detailed information about the semantics of the data, whereas the stylesheets provide the user interface. The W3C does not mandate a specific higher-level language

Figure 3. Sample code for an interface in high-level XML

```
<?xml version="1.0"?>
<interface xml:lang="en_US">
 <label for="tel">Call number</label>
 <input id="tel" type="phone"/>

 <label for="type">with</label>
 <select id="type">
   <item>Land line</item>
   <item>Cell phone</item>
 </select>

</interface>
```

to developers as it expects it to be domain-specific. Often, the stylesheet-based approach is combined with modern databases' capability to produce XML views of their tables.

The W3C's language of choice for transforming XML documents is XSLT (Clark, 1999), which itself is an XML based language. Usually, the target languages are also selected from the rich assets of the W3C, for example, XHTML for traditional browsers, VoiceXML for voice-based applications, and SVG+SMIL for multimedia presentations. It is, however, also possible to use other, non-XML output languages, like Flash, PDF, or PostScript. This makes it possible to address other devices that do not support XML-based languages.

Figure 4 depicts the data flow for stylesheet-based applications. It is quite similar to the network-based transcoding process in Figure 5, but uses the higher-level XML instead of HTML as an intermediate language. The XSL processor parses the declarative XSL stylesheet and uses its transformation rules to convert the source representation into the target representation. For more complex transformations, it is also possible to use several passes through the processor, with stylesheets providing a more detailed result in each pass.

For specifying the transformations, the XSL language provides so-called templates. Developers use XPath (Clark & DeRose, 1999) expressions to specify which part of the source XML tree is affected by the template. The processor searches the stylesheet for the template of the root element, that is, the XML element that surrounds all other elements of the source, and applies it. Templates may output arbitrary text, invoke XSLT functions to define and retrieve variables, fetch other parts of the source document or other documents, check conditions, or recursively pass control on to the XSL processor again, which then searches for templates matching XML elements below the level of the current one.

Figure 4. Sample data flow for XSL/stylesheet-based applications

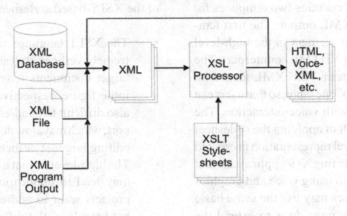

Figure 5. XSLT stylesheet for the input *element of the higher-level description in Figure 4 with XHTML and VoiceXML*

```
<?xml version="1.0" encoding="utf-8"?>
<xsl:stylesheet xmlns:xsl="http://www.w3.org/1999/XSL/Transform" xmlns:vxml="http://www.w3.org/2001/vxml"
xmlns:xhtml="http://www.w3.org/1999/xhtml" version="1.0" exclude-result-prefixes="xhtml">

 <xsl:template match="input" mode="xhtml">
  <xhtml:input name="{@id}" id="{@id}" ev:event="focus" ev:handler="#voice_{@id}" class="text" />
 </xsl:template>

<xsl:template match="input" mode="vxml">
 <vxml:form id="voice_{@id}">
  <vxml:field name="{@id}">
   <xsl:variable select="@id" name="id" />
   <xsl:variable select="../label[@for=$id]" name="text" />
   <xsl:if test="$text">
    <vxml:prompt>
     <xsl:value-of select="$text" />
    </vxml:prompt>
   </xsl:if>
   <vxml:grammar src="builtin:grammar/{@type}" />
  </vxml:field>
  <vxml:catch event="help nomatch noinput">Please input a telephone number.</vxml:catch>
  <vxml:filled>
   <vxml:assign name="var_{@id}" expr="{@id}" />
  </vxml:filled>
 </vxml:form>
</xsl:template>
</xsl:stylesheet>
```

The sample code in Figure 5 shows a simple XSLT stylesheet that contains two templates for XHTML and VoiceXML output. The first template converts an input element in the high-level representation into its XHTML counterpart. The second template creates a VoiceXML form with voice prompt and telephone input, so that users can access the interface with voice interaction. The figure shows the result of applying the stylesheet to the sample high-level representation presented in the figure. For supporting X+V applications that a user can interact with using voice and graphics simultaneously, authors may use the same basic template set. All they must do is to extend the stylesheet to also contain templates for *glue code* that synchronizes the XHTML and the VoiceXML document.

Stylesheets are more flexible than the transcoding-based approach because they work on the higher-level representation, which may contain metadata that is not available anymore in a lower level. Consequently, the stylesheets' transformations can do more than the transcoding counterparts: they are not restricted to clipping and form simplification, but can re-order items, provide specialized input items based on the data type of the form data, or can combine multiple source documents into one output.

The example also demonstrates the weaknesses of the XSLT-based stylesheet approach:

- The XSLT language tends to produce extremely verbose stylesheets even for small target documents (compare the code size in the figure, respectively). XML files are also difficult to hand-edit without tool support, which may slow down developers when editing larger stylesheets.

- The high-level format is not specified, which may lead to duplication of efforts if two projects want to address the same target, but have (slightly) different high-level formats.

- Although XSLT is rather powerful when it comes to XML transformations, it does not provide standard frameworks for many design patterns. This may lead to code duplication and all its attendant problems, such as bugs needing to be fixed in more than one place or poorly tested code.

The stylesheet-based approach also requires existing applications to be rewritten or at least modified heavily to produce the high-level representation instead of HTML. For the development process of the stylesheets, methodologies need

Figure 6. The result of the stylesheet for XHTML (left) and VoiceXML (right)

<input name="tel" id="tel" ev:event="focus" ev: handler="#voice_tel" class="text" />	<vxml:form id="voice_tel"> <vxml:field name="tel"> <vxml:prompt>Call number</vxml:prompt> <vxml:grammar src="builtin:grammar/phone" /> </vxml:field> <vxml:catch event="help nomatch noinput">Please input a telephone number.</vxml:catch> <vxml:filled> <vxml:assign name="var_tel" expr="tel" /> </vxml:filled> </vxml:form>

to be adapted for identifying important items in the source data and selecting the higher-level representation.

ABSTRACT USER INTERFACES

Although Web-centric approaches currently are the most widespread ones for developing multimodal applications, they have certain drawbacks:

- Although technologies like Asynchronous XML and JavaScript (AJAX) have made the Web more responsive, Web applications are still mostly centered on the idea of a "form." This scales well and keeps network load low but is a concept that does not fit well for many applications.
- There is no standardized high-level format for interface descriptions. Transcoding approaches therefore use low-level formats like HTML, whereas stylesheets user non-standardized high-level formats that do not promote software reuse between projects.
- The logic for adapting the interface to a modality is either a black box transcoding engine or developers need to write it manually using stylesheets.

Obviously, one of the drawbacks of the Web-centric approaches is that they lack a common foundation that is based on a higher level than HTML. This is the very problem *abstract user interfaces* (AUIs) try to fix.

AUIs take the concepts of traditional graphical user interfaces (GUI) one step further: although graphical, developers of GUI applications only rarely deal with each pixel separately, but instead use *widgets* as basic building blocks. The word "widget" itself may come from a combination of the words "window" and "gadget," and has been used since the 1980s to refer to the controls of a

graphical user interface, like text input boxes, or menus.

GUI widgets are available on exactly one platform and modality. As such, they are even less flexible than Web-centric approaches, because developers need to re-implement all user interface parts of their application if they want to run it on another platform. Web applications, on the other hand, run on any graphical user interface that provides a Web browser. AUIs create a similar platform-agnostic view for widgets. AUI-widgets define *abstract concepts* (hence the name) a user can perceive, enter, and modify. They aim at capturing the *intent* of an interaction. How the AUI represents these concepts to the user is the responsibility of a *mapping process*. In a sense, abstract user interfaces are a standardized way of representing higher-level concepts like they also are used in the stylesheet-based approach.

AUI widgets provide the presentation information of a user interface in an abstract form that is independent from the target device and the interaction language. The AUI widgets are interoperable regardless of the target modality.

Similar to the stylesheet-based approach and unlike the transition-based ones, the user interface applications cannot be gradually converted from a conventional one into one that is based on abstract user interfaces. The reason for this is that the developers must explicitly represent all items of the user interface using abstract widgets.

The mapping process converts AUIs at runtime into device specific *concrete user interfaces* (CUI) on demand, taking into account the context of use. The CUI may be a traditional graphical user interface, or a GUI for mobile devices that uses gestures as interaction language or a voice-based user interface. Just like in the transcoding-based approaches presented above, applications automatically support new devices and modalities that developers were not aware of at design time just by modifying the mapping process.

Requirements of Abstract User Interfaces

The usability of the CUI depends on the quality of the abstract representation: AUI widgets must be flexible enough to support the kind of input that an application requires while the application developers must make good use of the features offered by the AUI. An AUI must contain widgets that at least explicitly represent the following interactions between users and computers:

- Information presented to users
- Commands users may invoke
- Program variables users can manipulate

The resulting user interface may have higher quality if the description of the abstract user interface also contains dependency information between several widgets. Nichols, Myers, Harris, Rosenfeld, Shriver, Higgins, and Hughes (2002) show that information about the dependency between widgets may improve usability. A well-known example for such dependency information is user interface items that are unavailable to the user currently and therefore "grayed out;" for example, a user cannot copy an item into the clipboard unless she has selected one. In traditional applications, this dependency information is hard coded: the application observes its current state and enables or disables the command. If the abstract user interface contains dependency information, then the mapping process can identify states that never occur simultaneously and optimize the concrete user interface accordingly. Also, dependency analysis makes user input less ambiguous and easier to interpret, because unavailable commands and variables can be disregarded by the system.

Just like their GUI counterparts, some AUI widgets may be *containers* for other widgets. This establishes a hierarchy of widgets, which makes it easier for users to find functions they are searching for. Hierarchies improve usability especially for interaction languages that cannot offer a detailed overview to the user, such as voice interaction. When seen from the adaptation side, the explicit information that results from this hierarchy makes it easier to determine whether CUI widgets are placed close together or further apart.

An important observation of Nichols et al. (2002) is that developers must provide sufficient text *labels* for their controls. Having labels is important for conventional user interfaces too: user interface guidelines for traditional GUIs as well as the Web accessibility guidelines also point out the importance of labels for application accessibility. In AUIs labels are especially important because the system can present text labels with all interaction languages, be they graphical, voice-based, or tactile. Labels serve an important need of the applications' users: they clarify the meaning of other interface elements, which otherwise may be difficult to discover.

The mapping process from the AUI to the CUI for abstract user interfaces is easier in well-defined environments. In well-defined environments, the mapping between AUI and CUI widgets is much more predictable for the application developers, whereas in a more flexible environment the implicit assumptions of the developers must be made explicit. The reason for poorly performing mapping processes that produce less-than-usable concrete user interfaces from an abstract definition lies in the creative task user interface designers fulfill in traditional user interfaces. Developers provide semantic knowledge about the task to be completed and code it into the user interface. They also integrate conventions from other applications and from real world entities into the application. For example, a telephony application for a keyboardless PDA with touch-screen usually resembles the familiar 4×3 arrangement of conventional telephone keypads. For good usability of the CUI, the mapping process has to employ strategies for at least the most common cases, which is easier in a well-defined environment.

Examples of Abstract User Interfaces

The Pebbles project at the Carnegie Mellon University in Pittsburgh (Lucas & Myers, 2002) uses AUIs for their personal universal controller software that turns personal digital assistants (PDAs) into remote controls for appliances. Devices that want to make use of the universal controller define an abstract user interface for their capabilities using an XML file. The AUI definition contains the type of interaction variables and dependency information for a higher quality concrete user interface. Figure 6 shows the concrete user interface built for a home stereo system that has a volume control and several output modes, like tuner and CD.

For creating a graphical user interface out of the AUI, the mapping process uses a decision tree. Pebbles uses the rules defined by de Baar, Foley, and Mullet (1992) for determining the concrete user interface widget in the tree. They take into account the type of the variable a user can control, whether users can modify it, the range of legal input values, and other information. In a second step, the mapping process uses grouping and dependency information in the AUI definition to infer the panel structure of concrete user interface and to group CUI items belonging together accordingly.

Figure 7. Pebbles user interface for a home stereo; left: tuner ouput; right: CD output

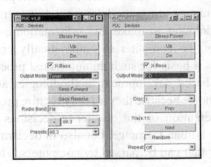

For voice user interfaces, the mapping process is slightly different: It differentiates between query and control actions, both of which are sorted into different categories. If a user performs a query action, this will result in voice output of all variables in a group, both read-only and read-write. Control actions on the other hand restrict usage to variables that can be written to.

An example that manages to build an abstract user interface out of the widgets of an existing graphical user interfaces is the WAHID toolkit of Jabarin and Graham (2003). It operates in an extremely narrow field of abstractness—only scrollbars and menus are altered depending on the output device: for large screen devices, scrollbars and pull-down menus are replaced by better-usable counterparts. The paper also clearly shows the limits of such an approach: the underlying framework that WAHID is based upon makes many implicit assumptions about the presentation of its concrete widgets. An extensive part of the paper deals with the problems of turning them into abstract widgets that overcome the restrictions posed by these assumptions.

One production-quality example for abstract user interfaces is JavaServer Faces (JSF) (Burns & Kitain, 2006) that use *tag libraries* for specifying the abstract user interface. Tag libraries are not restricted to user interface elements. Conceptually, they are Java components that developers can access using XML entities. Tag libraries responsible for the user interface of JSF-based applications create and modify live Java objects. The Java objects then are converted into their markup language representations using *Renderers*. All Renderers that belong to the same target platform/markup are grouped together in a RenderKit. The JSF specification defines one *core tag library* of abstract user interface elements, containing tags like selectItems for selecting one item out of a list of items. It is the decision of the Renderer to choose what concrete representation this tag has, which could be a list, a set of radio buttons or a list of links.

Developers may influence this automatic mapping using lower level tag libraries that are specific to a target platform, thus using losing the abstractness of the user interface. Another way is to refine the role of an abstract user interface element with *facets*. A facet simply extends the abstract element by a role name. The RenderKit may use this role information in order to create a different concrete user interface element, if necessary. For example, a table may have multiple columns, one of which has the facet "header." An HTML RenderKit may choose to use this information and render such a column using th tags instead of td tags. Unsupported facets may be ignored.

XForms (Boyer, Landwehr, Merrick, Raman, Dubinko, & Klotz, 2006) is an XML-based, modularized forms module factored out of HTML. Unlike HTML, it separates the presentation of a form from its model. Also the presentation controls work on a higher level and are explicitly designed for multiple device support. For example, XForms features a select1 tag for selecting an element that supersedes both the select tag HTML uses for lists and its input type="radio" for radio buttons. Figure 8 shows an XForms user interface for editing hierarchical bookmarks. The example is taken from Boyer et al. (2006), Appendix G.2, and rendered with Firefox.

Figure 8. Sample XForms user interface

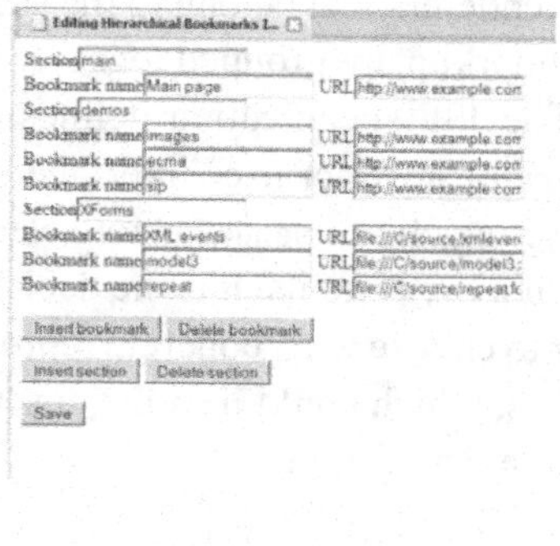

Developers can increase the usability of their applications by providing single elements with *appearance hints*. If hints are not present, an XForms user agent may freely choose any user interface component that is suitable for rendering the XForms element. The standard specifies the three default appearance hints, *full*, *compact*, and *minimal* that specify the screen real estate to be used by a control. The user agent should make any effort to accommodate this hint and to optimize real estate for the element. It is possible to define additional hints in separate namespaces. Any meaning may be associated with additional hints. User agents are not required to understand additional hints; they may ignore unknown or unsupported hint values.

MODEL-BASED USER INTERFACES

Abstract user interfaces are a promising way to create applications that support multiple modalities. AUIs require a great deal of explicit information about the user interface components in order to parameterize the mapping process: the more concepts the mapping process can take into account, the better the resulting concrete user interface can be. Fortunately, this information is available already: during the design of an application, its developers have decided about data types, dependencies, features, and so forth. Depending on the software development methodology, these decisions are documented more or less formally in the software specification.

Model-based user interface development augments existing model-based development methodologies to make this information available for the computer to automatically create UIs. As a basis for such an automated process, model-based development methodologies are a good choice because they already require project documentation of the developer decisions not only in human language, but also in declarative models that can be parsed by computers. These models are usually expressed using the Unified Modeling Language (UML).

Most of the model elements a system needs to create user interfaces are already available in some of the components the system model consists of, but the connections between these components may be defined only informally. For the system, these connections must be defined formally and the system must be able to parse them. For example, the domain model of the application needs to be mapped to the information the application presents to the end-users, and the model components users can manipulate.

The challenge that arises when integrating user interfaces into the conventional model-based development is that existing models are very much centered on the system development side, leaving aspects of the user interface aside. Puerta and Eisenstein (1999) identify a *level-of-abstraction mismatch,* which limits the usefulness of models. Application modelers must bridge this mismatch. A comprehensive user interface model is composed of *domain elements, user tasks, users, presentation items,* and *dialog structures.* Other approaches use very similar concepts, but name them differently. Calvary, Coutaz, and Thevenin (2001) for example model their user interface using *concepts, tasks, platforms, environment,* and *interactors:*

- The *domain model* or *concepts model* defines the objects users can access and manipulate. It is an extension of the *data model* used in the conventional model-based development, but also explicitly defines the relationships between objects of the domain.
- The *task model* describes the tasks users can accomplish using the application. Task models are hierarchical, with sub-tasks that need to be accomplished as well. Task models contain also ordering relationships between tasks and conditions.
- The *presentation model* can be split into two sub-models, which are *platform model*

and the *environment model.* It defines which representation the application can use for its concepts and tasks on given target devices (platform) and under which conditions (environment) the application is designed to run.

- The *dialog model* or *interactors model* describes the way in which application and users interact with each other. This model maps elements of the other models onto widgets. Although the widgets created as an outcome of the dialog model may be concrete widgets already, tailored to the target device, most model-based user interfaces use AUI widgets instead. Based on the large amount of computer-readable data, they can automatically specify the explicit information required by AUIs (see above), which in turn may help to improve usability of the generated user interface. Calvary et al. call the feature by whose means an application can adapt its user interface depending on changes to the context of use, while staying usable, *plasticity.*

Not only the models themselves, but also the mappings between these models are an important part of the application definition. Application developers must provide mappings between: tasks and dialogs, tasks and representations, domain and representations, task and user, and task and domain (Puerta & Eisenstein 1999).

Concurrent Task Trees as Task Modeling Method

The task model acts as a hub for other model components because it hosts most of the connections to other models. Standard UML does not provide a notation for task specification and must be extended to do so. Currently, the most prominent way to represent the task model is using *Concurrent Task Trees* (CTTs) developed by Paternò, Mancini, and Meniconi (1997). CTTs contain tasks and sub-tasks in a tree structure where tasks are represented by icons, depending on the task type they represent:

- *User tasks* are performed by the application users entirely for themselves. During user tasks, users respond to the environment they currently live in, and do not interact with the system directly. An example for a user task may be reading a list of currently available chat partners in an instant message application and selecting one of them.
- *Interaction tasks* are tasks where the human and the computer interact with each other, that is, the human invokes a command or modifies a program variable. An example for an interaction task may be a user entering a message for a chat partner.
- *Application tasks* are performed by the application itself. While application tasks may present information to the user, they rely on information supplied by the system. An example for an application task may be a messaging application receiving a message from the network and popping up a message window.
- *Abstract tasks* are all tasks that are more complex than the previous ones and are composed by other tasks.

Two tasks T1 and T2 may have a temporal dependency between each other, indicated by *operators* that are applied to task entries on the same hierarchy level. The operators connect two tasks and add a symbol to it:

- *Interleaving*: T1 ||| T2 where both tasks can be performed in any order
- *Synchronization*: T1 |[]| T2 both tasks need to synchronize with each other at given points so that they can exchange information
- *Enabling*: T1 >> T2 where T1 activates T2 and then terminates

- *Enabling with information passing*: T1 []>> T2 similar to *enabling*, except that T1 also passes some additional information to T2
- *Deactivation*: T1 [> T2 deactivates T1 if some action in T2 occurs
- *Iteration*: T1 * the task can be done an arbitrary number of times
- *Finite iteration*: T1 (n) the task will be done at most *n* times
- *Optional*: [T1] the task may or may not be executed
- *Recursion*: T1 Tasks can include themselves by having a child node that has the same name as the task node

When generating the user interface, these operators will determine whether task items are split up into several sequential items, or made available simultaneously. The system uses its knowledge about enabling and deactivation of tasks from the CTT to present only the user interface items that make sense at a given time.

Concurrent Task Trees are relatively verbose; they may become large and difficult to read quickly

Figure 9. Example Concurrent Task Tree modeling the process of making coffee

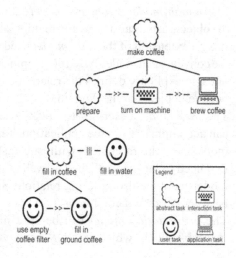

for more complex tasks with many subtasks on the same hierarchy level. The operators work only between nodes on the same hierarchy level. For modeling complex enabling/deactivation hierarchies, developers must include artificial pseudo-elements, which may also obstruct reading. The readability problem may be addressed by adding modularity-features to the CTT notation; the complexity-problem needs more comprehensive extensions of the notation.

Examples for Model-Based User Interfaces

The THERESA system developed by Mori, Paternò, and Santoro (2003) at ISTI-CNR is a model-based tool that generates the user interface from a high level task model of the application and a model of the target platforms. After specification, the models get transformed first into an abstract user interface and then into the final user interface. The transitions used by THERESA may be specified by the application developer, giving her one possibility to influence the user interface generated. Abstract user interface components can be composed from one another, with *operators* defining their relationship. User interface designers may intervene in the reification process by defining the appearance of a specific operator on a given target platform.

The CAMELEON reference framework (Calvary, Coutaz, & Thevenin, 2001) and its ARTStudio tool use a three-stage process to convert its models into abstract user interfaces, concrete user interfaces, and final user interfaces. Models are defined using UML and Concurrent Task Trees, the user interfaces "comets," short for *context moldable widgets* (Calvary, Coutaz, Dâassi, Balme, & Demeure, 2004), which have an interface that gives developers the possibility to influence the reification process at each stage of reification by referencing the context of use.

CAMELEON differentiates between open-adaptiveness and close-adaptiveness. Close-adap-

tive comets are polymorphic, that is some parts of them can have different reifications on the concrete user interface level. The polymorphism provides possible alternatives if the context of use changes. The user of a polymorphic comet has to manually select the reification of it, giving both full control as well as full responsibility for the final result. Open-adaptive comets are also polymorphic. In addition, they contain sensing and adaptation logic which makes them self-adaptive: they switch their reification automatically upon changes of the context, freeing developers from deciding which reification to use as well as from control.

USIXML, the User Interface Extensible Markup Language developed by Limbourg, Vanderdonckt, Michotte, Bouillon, and López-Jaquero (2004) is another model-based user interface tool that uses graph transformation in order to create a final user interface from the models. The same USIXML markup language is used in all layers from model definition down to the concrete user interface, which makes it easy to augment the higher-level models with information for reification. With *interModelMappings* it is also possible to link between model elements that belong to different models.

FUTURE RESEARCH DIRECTIONS

The abstract user interface and the model-based user interface approach presented in this chapter are not mutually exclusive, but supplement each other: model-based tools produce abstract user interfaces which later are turned into concrete user interfaces once the target modalities have been specified. Unfortunately, the way in which abstract user interfaces are specified has not yet been standardized. This means that each model-based approach also contains its own AUI technology. Standardized AUI markup languages would make it possible to advance AUI and model-based approaches separately and to combine the best implementations with each other easily. A first step towards standardized AUI concepts may be the multimodal interaction framework of the W3C. Its Extensible Multimodal Annotation Language (EMMA) is a standardized language for describing user input. The framework does not yet contain a similar language for describing the contents of the multimodal user interface itself, so additional efforts for creating a standardized AUI markup language seem necessary.

The Concurrent Task Tree meta-model extension to UML has been proven successful by Paternò and Santoro (2002) for developing multimodal user interfaces such as museum tour guides. The CTT concept does, however, have some shortcomings when it comes to brevity and modularity, which means that more complex task models may be difficult to design and modify. Further research towards meta-models that work well for complex tasks with lots of items, devices, and human users without letting the model designer lose focus seems necessary. Also, other models of the design language must be extended to include formally specify items that are of concern for user interfaces.

Visual user interface editors, popularized by Visual Basic and Hypercard, have fostered the success of GUIs by making the user interface programming a WYSIWIG task itself. Tools that provide similar easy access to multimodal user interfaces for non-specialists are still missing. Given the nature of multimodal user interfaces that adapt themselves to a given modality, such tools are likely to be different from their drawing program inspired GUI counterparts, so not only the tools themselves, but also the usage concepts for them must be developed. Most likely, a tool for designing multimodal user interfaces would be multimodal itself, thus reducing switches in media. Because of the open-world approach of multimodal user interfaces, it is also highly likely that rapid user interface tools for multimodal user interfaces will have to deploy new programming concepts, such as example-based programming, where the programmer gives examples for concrete realizations of a user interface and the tools try to deduce the abstract concepts behind them.

Most efforts on multimodal user interfaces focus on the integration of several graphical interaction languages and natural language. The benefit of combining these interaction languages is easy to understand, as it mimics the voice and gesture-based interaction between humans. While this is a powerful combination, other interaction languages should not be forgotten. It should be equally possible to add support for other concepts. These may be concepts that build upon existing ones, like zoomable user interfaces that extend the traditional GUI interaction language and which are well suited for browsing large collections of data that can be laid out two-dimensionally. It may also be interaction languages that are extremely different from the other existing languages, like tangible user interfaces that solidify user interfaces quite literally by making them real-world objects a user can look, feel, and interact with. Integration of such interaction languages not only would serve the multimodal applications that can use other interaction languages, but could also lead to a better understanding of the basic elements of the user interface and therefore in return make the software engineering concepts for creating multimodal user interfaces easier to understand and more powerful.

ACKNOWLEDGMENT

The author would like to express special gratitude to Dr. Guido Rößling for his valuable comments and corrections to the original manuscript.

REFERENCES

Axelsson, J., Cross, C., Lie, H.W., McCobb, G., Raman, T.V., & Wilson, L. (Eds.) (2001, December 21) XHTML+Voice Profile 1.0. *W3C Note.* Retrieved August 22, 2006, from http://www.w3.org/TR/2001/NOTE-xhtml+voice-20011221.

Barnes, S.J., & Huff, S.L. (2003). Rising sun: iMode and the wireless Internet. *Communications of the ACM, 46*(11), 78-84.

Bharadvaj, H., Joshi, A., & Auephanwiriyakul, S. (1998). An active transcoding proxy to support mobile Web access. In *Proceedings of the 17th IEEE Symposium on Reliable Distributed Systems* (p. 118). Washington, DC: IEEE Computer Society.

Bolt, R.A. (1980). "Put-that-there:" Voice and gesture at the graphics interface. In *Proceedings of the 7th Annual Conference on Computer Graphics and Interactive Techniques, SIGGRAPH '80* (pp. 262-270). New York: ACM Press.

Boyer, J.M., Landwehr, D., Merrick, R., Raman, T.V., Dubinko, M., & Klotz, L.L., Jr. (Eds.) (2006, March 14). XForms 1.0 (2nd Ed.). *W3C Recommendation.* Retrieved January 12, 2007 from http://www.w3.org/TR/2006/REC-xforms-20060314/.

Bulterman, D., Grassel, G., Jansen, J., Koivisto, A., Layada, N., Michel, T., Mullender, S., & Zucker, D. (Eds.). (2005, December 13). Synchronized Multimedia Integration Language (SMIL 2.1). *W3C Recommendation.* Retrieved August 22, 2006, from http://www.w3.org/TR/2005/REC-SMIL2-20051213/.

Burns, E., & Kitain, R. (Eds.) (2006). *Java Server Faces Specification Version 1.2 – Proposed Final Draft 2.* Retrieved January 12, 2007 from http://jcp.org/en/jsr/detail?id=252.

Calvary, G., Coutaz, J., & Thevenin, D. (2001). A unifying reference framework for the development of plastic user interfaces. In *Engineering for Human-Computer Interaction: 8th IFIP International Conference, EHCI 2001* (pp. 173-192). Berlin, Heidelberg: Springer-Verlag.

Calvary, G., Coutaz, J., Dâassi, O., Balme, L., & Demeure, A. (2004). Towards a new generation of widgets for supporting software plasticity: The "Comet." In *Engineering Human Computer Interaction and Interactive Systems: Joint Working Conferences EHCI-DSVIS 2004* (pp. 306-326). Berlin, Heidelberg: Springer-Verlag.

Clark, J. (Ed.) (1999, November 19). XSL Transformations (XSLT) Version 1.0. *W3C Recommendation.* Retrieved August 22, 2006, from http://www.w3.org/TR/1999/REC-xslt-19991116.

Clark, J., & DeRose, S. (Eds.) (1999, November 16). XML Path Language (XPath) Version 1.0. *W3C Recommendation.* Retrieved August 22, 2006, from http://www.w3.org/TR/1999/REC-xpath-19991116.

Chisholm, W., Vanderheiden, G., & Jacobs, I. (2001). Web content accessibility guidelines 1.0. *ACM Interactions, 8*(4), 35-54.

de Baar, D., Foley, J.D., & Mullet, K.E. (1992). Coupling application design and user interface design. In *Proceedings of the SIGCHI conference on Human factors in computing systems* (pp. 259-266). New York: ACM Press.

Erlandson, C., & Ocklind, P. (1998). WAP - The wireless application protocol. *Ericsson Review 2*(4), 150-153.

Ge, X., Paige, R.F., Polack, F.A., Chivers, H., & Brooke, P.J. (2006). Agile development of secure Web applications. In *Proceedings of the 6th International Conference on Web Engineering, ICWE '06* (pp. 305-312).. New York: ACM Press.

IBM Corporation. (2006). *IBM WebSphere Transcoding Publisher Version 4.0 Developer's Guide.* Retrieved December 4, 2006, from ftp://ftp.software.ibm.com/software/webserver/transcoding/brochures/tpdgmst.pdf.

Jabarin, B., & Graham, T.C.N. (2003). Architectures for widget-level plasticity. In *Interactive Systems. Design, Specification, and Verification:*

10th International Workshop (pp. 124-138). Berlin, Heidelberg: Springer-Verlag.

Limbourg, Q., Vanderdonckt, J., Michotte, B., Bouillon, L., & López-Jaquero, V. (2004). USIXML: A language supporting multi-path development of user interfaces. In *Engineering Human Computer Interaction and Interactive Systems: Joint Working Conferences EHCI-DSVIS* (pp. 200-221). Berlin, Heidelberg: Springer-Verlag.

Lucas, P., & Myers, B. (2002). *Personal Universal Controller (PUC)*. Presentation held to the Pittsburgh Digital Greenhouse, February 13, 2002. Retrieved February 6, 2007, from http://www.cs.cmu.edu/~pebbles/papers/PUC_PDG_02-13-02.ppt.

Kaikkonen, A., & Roto, V. (2003). Navigating in a mobile XHTML application. In *Proceedings of the SIGCHI Conference on Human Factors in Computing Systems, CHI '03* (pp. 329-336). New York: ACM Press.

McGlashan, S., Burnett, D.C., Carter, J., Danielsen, P., Ferrans, J., Hunt, A., Lucas, B., Porter, B., Rehor, K., & Tryphonas, S. (Eds.). (2004, March 16). Voice Extensible Markup Language (VoiceXML) Version 2.0. *W3C Recommendation*. Retrieved August 22, 2006, from http://www.w3.org/TR/2004/REC-voicexml20-20040316/.

Mori, G., Paternò, F., & Santoro, C. (2003). Tool support for designing nomadic applications. In *IUI '03: 8th International Conference on Intelligent User Interfaces* (pp. 141-148). New York: ACM Press.

Nichols, J., Myers, B., Harris, T.K., Rosenfeld, R., Shriver, S., Higgins, M., & Hughes, J. (2002). Requirements for automatically generating multi-modal interfaces for complex appliances. In *Proceedings of the Fourth IEEE International Conference on Multimodal Interfaces* (pp. 377-382).

Nigay, L., & Coutaz, J. (1993). A Design Space for Multimodal Systems: Concurrent Processing and Data Fusion. In *Proceedings of the SIGCHI Conference on Human Factors in Computing Systems, CHI '93* (pp. 172-178). New York: ACM Press.

Paternò, F., Mancini, C., & Meniconi, S. (1997). ConcurTaskTrees: A diagrammatic notation for specifying task models. In *INTERACT '97: Human-Computer Interaction: Proceedings of the Seventh TC13 Conference* (pp. 362-369). Chapman & Hall.

Paternò, F., & Santoro, C. (2002). One model, many interfaces. In *Proceedings of the Fourth International Conference on Computer-Aided Design of User Interfaces* (pp. 143-154). Kluwer Academics Publishers.

Puerta, A., & Eisenstein, J. (1999). Towards a general computational framework for model-based interface development systems. *Knowledge-Based Systems, 12*(8), 433-442.

Satyanarayanan, M. (2005). Swiss Army knife or wallet? *IEEE Pervasive Computing, 4*(2), 2-3.

ADDITIONAL READING

Baggia, P., Carter, J., Dahl, D.A., McCobb, G., & Raggett, D. (2007, April): *EMMA: Extensible MultiModal Annotation Markup Language* (W3C Working Draft 9). Retrieved May 10, 2007, from http://www.w3.org/TR/2007/WD-emma-20070409/.

Bishop, J. (2006): Multi-platform user interface construction: A challenge for software engineering-in-the-small. In L. Osterweil, H.D. Rombach, & M.L. Soffa (Eds.), *28th International Conference on Software Engineering (ICSE 2006)*, Shanghai, China (pp. 751-760). New York: ACM Press.

Calvary, G., Coutaz, J., Thevenin, D., Limbourg, Q., Bouillon, L., & Vanderdonckt, J. (2003). A Unifying Reference Framework for multi-target user interfaces. *Interacting with Computers, 15*(3), 289-308.

Deng, L. (2006). *Dynamic speech models - Theory, algorithm, and application,* LaPorte, CO: Morgan & Claypool Publishers.

Dutotit, T., Nigay, L., & Schnaider, M. (2006). Multimodal human-computer interfaces. *Signal Processing* (Introduction to a special section on multimodal human-computer interfaces), *86*(12), 3515-3517.

Gogate, L., Walker-Andrews, A., & Bahrick, L. (2001). The intersensory origins of word comprehension: An ecological-dynamic systems view. *Developmental Science, 4*(1), 1-18.

Herzog, G., Ndiaye, A., Merten, S., Kirchmann, H., Becker, T., & Poller, P. (2004). Large-scale software integration for spoken language and multimodal dialog systems. *Natural Language Engineering, 10*(3/4), 283–305.

Iivari, N. (2006). "Representing the User" in software development--a cultural analysis of usability work in the product development context. *Interacting with Computers, 18*(4), 635-664.

Lewis, M., & Havil-Jones, J.M. (2000). *Handbook of emotions.* New York: Guilford.

Luyten, K., Van Laerhoven, T., Coninx, K., & Van Reeth, F. (2003). Runtime transformations for modal independent user interface migration. *Interacting with Computers, 15*(3), 329-347.

Kaiser, E.C. (2005). Multimodal new vocabulary recognition through speech and handwriting in a whiteboard scheduling application. In *Proceedings of the 10th International Conference on Intelligent User Interfaces,* San Diego, California (pp. 51-58). New York: ACM Press.

van Kuppevelt, J., Dybkjaer, L., & Bernsen, N.O. (2006). *Advances in natural multimodal dialogue systems (text, speech and language technology).* Berlin, Heidelberg: Springer Verlag.

Obrenovic, Z., & Starcevic, D. (2004): Modeling multimodal human-computer interaction. *Computer 37*(9), 65-72.

Pantic, M., & Rothkrantz, L.J. (2003). Toward an affect-sensitive multimodal human computer interaction. *Proceedings of the IEEE, 91*(9), 1370- 1390.

Paternò, F. (1999). *Model-based design and evaluation of interactive applications.* Berlin: Springer Verlag.

Renals, S., & Bengio, S. (2006). *Machine Learning for Multimodal Interaction, Second International Workshop, MLMI 2005,* Edinburgh, U.K.(LNCS 3869). Springer.

Rosson, B., & Carroll, J.M. (2001). *Usability engineering: Scenario-based development of human-computer interaction.* Morgan Kaufmann.

Savidis, A., & Stephanidis, C. (2004). Unified user interface development: The software engineering of universally accessible interactions. *Universal Access in the Information Society, 3*(3/4), 165-193.

Chapter XXIII
Ambient Learning

Fernando Lyardet
Technische Universität Darmstadt, Germany

ABSTRACT

The vision where living and working spaces adapt to people is becoming a reality thanks to the increased embedding of computing power into everyday objects. Ambient learning focuses on the way people adopt technology in their everyday life and how technology adapts to the environment. Ambient learning is a new area in ubiquitous computing (UC) about the different learning processes that occur between people and smart technology environments. This chapter is organized as follows. First, we provide a definition of what ambient learning is, and its relevance to ubiquitous computing. Next, we present the learning concepts behind ambient learning and a detailed example of training a user. Then we examine in detail the technological building blocks behind the smart products supporting their ability to learn from each other and assemble or "compose" their functionality.

INTRODUCTION

As smart technology becomes ubiquitous, we must keep in mind that both humans and technology are in a process of constant evolution. We must foresee a process in which technology and humans cooperatively increase and adapt their knowledge about one another.

This process has three technology related facets:

1. Technology must learn from—and adapt to—its users.
2. Users must learn from—and about—technology.
3. Technology must learn from—and adapt to—other technology.

Accordingly, we define ambient learning as the learning issues and activities of ubiquitous computing: ambient learning is the evolution of mutual knowledge among technology components and humans in the course of their cooperation, with the aim of improving the level of cooperative achievements.

Obviously, this definition requires autonomous, communication-enabled and "smart" technology components, and is therefore bound to ubiquitous computing, unthinkable in the preceding eras of technology. We will call such components *smart products*.

In this chapter, we will only be able to—roughly—lead the way towards a first level of ambient learning, with rather modest learning goals, centered on operational features and workflows of technology and relatively simple user needs and plans. This first step can be called "ambient instruction:" technology and users instruct each other. It is our belief that scientific maturity of this first step is required as a prerequisite for next steps towards more ambitious educational or pedagogical goals, where technology and users truly educate one another.

Other definitions of ambient learning have recently emerged in the literature. Most often, they can be rephrased as mobile learning; corresponding projects emphasize the adaptation of learning material and learning processes to the learning context, that is, the situation in which a user learns. However, the situation is usually considered to be unrelated to the learning content itself (e.g., learning while riding the bus as opposed to learning about riding a bus). Admittedly, these projects are not as restricted in terms of educational ambitions as we are (yet). In the future, we expect a convergence of these conflicting notions of ambient learning:

- Ambient learning as sometimes defined in the literature—better called mobile learning—will gradually move from "context-aware learning" to "in-situ learning."
- Ambient learning as we address it in the present chapter—which may even be called ambient instruction—will gradually

move towards more ambitious educational goals.

The first of the three facets of ambient learning as mentioned in the beginning is already covered in the chapter "Adapting to the User" in this book. We will therefore concentrate on the other two facets, rephrasing them as follows:

- "Technology teaches users" (see point 2 above): it is important to foster the development of smart products that explain themselves and their usage to their users. In this way, the products should dynamically adapt to the level of knowledge acquired by their users – in addition to adapting to the context of use, user preferences, and to other parameters as already discussed in the chapter "Service Discovery."
- "Technology teaches technology" in the UC vision, assemblies of smart products (smart environments, if you wish) are not blueprinted and carefully configured from scratch. Users and smart products come and go rather arbitrarily, without a need for explicit configuration. Beyond the service discovery mechanisms described in the chapter "A Focus on Location Context" of this book, we need ways for "accidentally" grouped entities (users, objects) to make sense of their being grouped together. They must be able to understand one another beyond syntax and beyond pre-established common semantics, and to collectively develop and carry out plans towards common higher-level goals.

UBIQUITOUS COMPUTING AND LEARNING

Modern life poses new challenges to people, since changes and technologies are being introduced with increasing speed in our lives and jobs. Therefore, we must learn more things through our entire working life to remain useful and competitive.

In this context, traditional learning has some important disadvantages:

- It concentrates all the learning into one period of life, when learners may not be mature enough, ready or just don't care.
- It assumes that what is learned today will be available when needed many years later.
- It ignores the powerful social impact of communities of practice, social discussion, and cooperation.

Our ability to learn new things is also a bottleneck for introducing new exciting technologies and services. It is too difficult to remember, for instance, what the new word processing software can do or understand all the functions of our TV remote control.

Technology vendors that acknowledge the need to make their products more accessible also find themselves in what is known as the complexity paradox: easier to use interfaces mean less complexity (fewer buttons, controls and options). On the other hand, in order to introduce new functionality, technology vendors need to increase again the number of buttons, options and controls.

The development and availability of ubiquitous computing technologies helped to shape a vision that would overcome these problems, because technology could be smoothly integrated in the living spaces of people, making interaction more meaningful, productive and engaging. This vision of technology-enabled environments is known as smart environments. Although in this vision technology is now embedded and "invisible" in the surroundings, this does not mean there is no user interface. The user interface arises as a result of the human-centered smart interaction and composition of services and devices (see also the chapter "Intelligent User Interfaces").

In order to achieve this goal, technology should become intelligent enough to reveal itself (become self-explanatory) on a need-to-know basis, freeing users from lengthy and sometimes difficult to read manuals. Simple examples are assisting users in setting up a software or device, providing assistance to use it also in combination with other unanticipated devices and services that could be available, adapting their behavior to the user's feedback and usage patterns. Such behavioral flexibility is based on enriching technology with learning capabilities:

1. Learning about other devices and services available in the surroundings (as described in the chapter "Service Discovery");
2. Learning about other technologies' capabilities to establish meaningful interactions and actively seek to free users from cumbersome procedures such as installing drivers, patching cables or changing file formats;
3. Learning about the user's skills, habits and preferences.

The goal is to achieve the continuous assistance and adaptation of technology-enabled environments and allow people take advantage of new services and technologies while gradually increasing their knowledge and awareness. We know today that we do not learn only at school or when we consciously decide to do so, but rather, we learn all the time. This vision is a departure from the traditional educational view, where most of the learning was understood to take place during a particular period of life, assuming that knowledge and skills would be effectively acquired and remain valid for the rest of our lives.

Ambient learning is a new direction enabled by ubiquitous computing: the ability to support learning in ubiquitous human situations, and it is different in that the learning process is embedded within the activities of the person. However, the most profound impact of all these new possibilities is the gradual understanding that we learn all the time and in different ways throughout our entire lives in any activity we engage in regardless of the occasion, time or place.

LEARNING THEORIES SUPPORTING AMBIENT LEARNING

Learning theories study the processes involved when people learn. They take into account different views of the learner and define what *learning* is in human terms. They are important because they provide a framework of thinking that help us define and understand what kind of learning experience we seek to create and organize for other people. There are many learning theories and it is not uncommon that they contradict each other in part or completely. However, some of them, such as *constructivism*, *behaviorism*, *experiential* and *social learning,* are among the most established in the field.

Learning happens all the time, and thanks to advances in technology, it has become something that can happen anywhere. This growth from the classroom led to a scenario in which, in spite of the widespread adoption of computer-based training (CBT) or Web-based training technologies (WBT), the acquisition of new skills and competencies strongly relies on the *formal learning* approach, which happens in structured learning events (as it was in the classroom). Although necessary and valuable, formal learning leaves substantial gaps between the training and the actual capability of a person to apply the knowledge acquired in the real world. Such skill mismatches are later covered through "a process of learning that takes place in everyday experience, often at subconscious levels" (Marsick & Watkins, 1997). The process is known as *informal learning*, and has the particular characteristic of being driven by the individual rather than the organization, "regardless of the formality [or] informality of the goals and objectives toward which the learning is directed" (Stamps, 1998).

Further classification available in the literature also distinguishes another dimension of the learning experience, where intentional denotes the active involvement and decision of the individual to engage in a learning activity. By contrast, the term incidental is mainly used to describe situations where individuals learn things during their everyday activities and they have not intended or expected to. This kind of learning is often related to *implicit learning*, where the learner acquires knowledge, but, although he or she is able to apply what he or she has learnt, the learner is not able to explain why or how he knows that. The problem with implicit learning is that it is *very* difficult to anticipate, detect, reproduce or measure due to the unexpected nature of the event. In some cases, it is unclear whether skills acquired over the course of several events (e.g., riding a bike) can be understood as implicit learning examples, whether or not the subject is able to articulate how she performs a given action. Therefore, very slow advances have been achieved in this area where experiments are often reduced to the learning of implicit rules in character sequences.

Other theories consider scenarios of varying degrees of attention, where knowledge is acquired through a number of interactions or experiences that shape this knowledge over time. This is the case of the *experiential learning* model that focuses on the role that experience plays in the learning process. It is different from other theories that focus on the acquisition, recall and manipulation of symbols, or theories that deny any role of consciousness and subjective experience in the learning process.

The approach taken by experiential learning is of particular interest for ambient learning, because, if we consider learning as a process that occurs over time, then we can expect that a person's knowledge will begin with a very vague idea following some basic instructions and therefore we can expect different interpretations of a problem or concept. However, as exposure to functionality and consistent explanations continue, our hypothesis is that those models should converge to a correct view and a growing understanding of the nature and purpose of the particular technology.

The way ambient learning provides user assistance follows a prominent idea in the 1990s of providing just-in-time-learning, that is, providing the switching of smallest e-learning units on the job as a function of knowledge gaps, which revealed themselves in the context of a vocational setting of tasks. The restrictions on office workstations and problems with the close coupling between work and the learning process limited its success.

In the meantime, with the new revolution of ubiquitous computing technologies, the coupling of the physical, working sphere and IT systems begins. In this revolution, real time enterprises blend the physical world (production processes and goods, logistics, etc.) and the digital world. All coworkers, whether in the field service or at the assembly line, are connected through mobile terminals together with context sensors.

Through this expanded instrumentation, a new quality of integration of work and learning processes becomes possible.

IT STARTS WITH THE PRIMITIVES

Consider the car manufacturing industry. The introduction of new equipment and building procedures implies the need to train workers to follow the new procedures associated with new car production needs. Through ambient learning, the workers can access information that is relevant to their current task. Furthermore, using sensor-based information, the system knows the user's position, direction of gaze, and is aware of the process the user is performing.

Ambient learning support can provide the relevant information to the worker to allow continuing the task (e.g., tighten left screw, turn lever

90 degrees clockwise). The term *primitive* refers to the educational-didactic requirement, since only simple instructions are conveyed during training and at the beginning only a simple learner model will be used.

After training, the online coupling between the physical and digital world makes situational learning possible. Details of performing co-workers are detected automatically via sensors, and training materials are always available to reinforce steps that are complex and/or imply security concerns.

Several other scenarios would similarly benefit from this functionality, such as supporting people in their homes and offices. For instance, in order to perform simple, everyday tasks such as displaying a presentation on a desired display, help the user solve a problem, setting up a device or finding ways to use the available technology.

Continuous Trainings

After initial guidance, and through system tracking, people continue receiving assistance when required or accepted by the user (we consider both reactive and proactive interaction). Over time the training and continuous support, although always available, ceases its intervention. We will explore the technology and an example of user assistance to perform a non-trivial maintenance task later in this chapter.

ENABLING AMBIENT INTELLIGENCE AND LEARNING

The technological building blocks of ambient intelligence vision are the increasing embedding of computing power, and new communication technologies that bind increasing numbers of micro-controllers and sensors. The application software infrastructure that connects these building blocks depends on knowledge about people, their preferences and activities, as well as what technology is available and what services can be of use to the people.

The first approaches in developing such integrated environments made use of knowledge that was highly customized and, in most cases, implicitly available.

Designers embedded within their software what data and relationships about people and services would be available to determine what a user could do, and which adaptation techniques could be applied in a given scenario. This embedding of data and relationships includes application-oriented context-aware systems that make opportunistic use of information and activity detection. This information is also used as context for system adaptation and user interaction as well as generic sentient computing infrastructures that collect and provide information (Arts, 2004).

Examples of such systems and infrastructures are consumer-oriented locations, for example, office (Barton et al., 2002; Cooperstock et al., 1997) and home (Brumitt et al., 2002; Kidd et al., 1999; Munguia et al., 2004). Other systems also took into account the activities of their occupants (Barton et al., 2002; Fox et al., 2006; Franklin et al., 2001), and the interaction between users and their mobile devices (Lukowicz et al., 2004; Schmidt et al., 1999; Starner et al., 1998). Unfortunately, only a few of these projects have been taken to a higher scale, such as the Cooltown initiative (Barton et al., 2002).

There are two major problems with this top-down approach:

1. In real life there are too many scenarios to be modeled one by one
2. The scenarios, people and technology change over time

The notorious absence of large-scale settings is strongly influenced by the complexity and effort required to build them. The examples we mentioned have been carefully designed top-down at drawing boards. However, future ambient intelligent infrastructures must be able to configure themselves and grow from the available, purposeful objects (be it software applications or consumer appliances) in order to become effective in the real world (Encarnaçao et al., 2005).

The notion of smarter objects aware of their situation has been increasingly explored in business scenarios for tracking (Fano et al., 2002; Siegemund et al., 2003), with enhanced sensing and perception to autonomously monitor their physical integrity (Decker et al., 2004) or to avoid dangerous physical proximity. The increasing computer power and network capabilities embedded allow ad hoc interactions using P2P techniques to gather and disseminate information (Heinemann et al., 2003). However, many of these artifacts are based on the event-condition-action (ECA) principle (Terada et al., 2004). These smarter objects, even with increasing embedding complexities, are still far from becoming everyday objects people use outside industrial environments, in their homes and offices.

A more suitable approach focuses on the federation of devices where ad hoc device assemblies are created in order to combine both hardware input and output capabilities. These devices would be embedded with explicit knowledge to leverage reasoning capabilities supported either internally or externally. We call this new generation of devices *smart products*.

In the following sections we will present in detail what these smart products are, and we'll dive deeper into the concepts required for their construction. We will start with basic concepts used in the first smart objects such as ECA rules, finite state machines and processes. Afterwards, we will describe some practical artificial intelligence techniques required to create assemblies of devices that work together composing their behavior in non-trivial ways.

SMART PRODUCTS

As we are now surrounded by small computers controlling our tools and appliances, we would like them to connect and work together more easily anticipating our needs, and adapting to us.

We want to build smarter devices that are aware of themselves, and that are able to learn about their surroundings and their users. These smarter devices—called *smart products*—should be able to explain themselves to the user, understanding when they should provide what assistance according to the user's needs. Smart products are a new generation of connected devices and services that adapt to the current situation. Therefore, devices would rely more on their own capability to learn, adapt and provide a better service, instead of the user's learning ability.

We define *smartness* as the ability of an object to adapt and combine its behavior according to the situation in which it operates. The term *situation* is the set of possible things that are happening and conditions that exist at a particular time and place.

Nowadays, there is already a range of devices with varying degrees of embedded knowledge. For instance, hard drives can check their own health and predict when they will fail, personal training assistants adjust the pace according to the user's pulse, or smart phones that can be voice controlled with PDA features. There are also interesting examples in the business area, such as asset tracking, accountability or enhanced sensing and perception for monitoring the physical integrity of goods, and detection of hazardous physical proximity (Bornhövd et al., 2005).

Definition. Smart products (SP) are real-world objects, devices or software services bundled with knowledge about themselves and their capabilities, enabling new ways of interacting with humans and the environment autonomously.

Smart products have a set of properties that makes them unique:

- *Self-Explanatory:* Smart products reveal their own purpose and functionality to the users and other smart products. Besides being *intelligible* to users, Smart Products must also be *intelligent*, to interpret user's actions and provide a rationality of their own.
- *Self-Organizing:* They provide the ability to combine with other federated smart products to provide meaningful, value added functionality.
- *Extensible*: An important part of a smart product's functionality requires some kind of communication capability. Communications allow the SP to be extended and supported locally or by third-party subscriptions.
- *Self-Sustainable:* Smart products should be able to work in a self-supported or infra-structure mode.

These characteristics turn smart products into the future building blocks of ambient intelligence. As such, smart products organize their knowledge into different layers according to the level of abstraction they address: device capabilities, functionality, integrity, user services, and connectivity. In *Figure 1*, we present a conceptual reference architecture showing this separation of concerns to allow the integration of different vendors providing their own technology. Such a scenario is particularly critical at the device level, since changes to embedded systems must be kept to a minimum to keep their cost viable.

Adopting a service-oriented architecture (SOA) (see chapters "Ubiquitous Services and Business Processes" and "Service Discovery") approach allows devices to be extended in their functionality and user adaptation capabilities with minimal embedded infrastructure requirements. Extensions to a smart product may involve external hardware, software, or both. The first layer is the Smart Product Device Layer. In embedded systems, this is where the runtime operating software or firmware lies. The processing power available at this level operates the actuators, sensors, I/O, and the user interface (typically LCD displays, status LEDs and buttons). The knowledge embedded in this layer defines a set of valid events, states, and a set of ECA rules that govern the transitions between states. These rules determine the functionality of the device, implement current smart behavior, and ensure the operating conditions required to preserve the hardware integrity and safe operation.

The *User Model* provides information about the user that operates the device. Using other information sources and sensors from the infrastructure, the User Model module can recognize a person and related data such as preferences.

The *Embedding* bridges the physical world with software, enabling self-explanatory functionality. It decorates the processes described by the embodiment for adaptation using the information provided by the *User Model*.

The *Embodiment* externalizes the knowledge of what a device consists of, what its parts are and their interrelationship. This knowledge also specifies the processes controlling the functionality; for instance, the process of making a coffee or a more complex one: descaling a coffee machine.

The *Controller* that sometimes resides within the embedded device coordinates processes bridging the physical world behavior and software-based functionality.

The second layer is the Smart Product Layer, which consists of four main parts.

When no external contextual information about the user is available, this module gathers the user input and compares it to user expertise patterns to better match user level to device functionality and assistance. The Embedding gathers the information from the User Model and determines the actual steps and explanations required for a user to perform a task.

THE DEVICE LAYER

Adding electronics to control devices, tools and appliances has been common practice for almost two decades now. With every new generation, these controllers provide an increasing functionality in the form of assistance, information, customization, or other services. However, it is the addition of communications capabilities that changes the perspectives of what such systems can

Figure 1. Smart product conceptual architecture

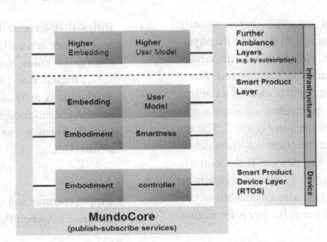

do. They can now gather information from other sensors, devices and computers on the network, or enable user-oriented customization and operations through short-range communication.

The lower layers of the smart products' conceptual architecture refer to the particular kind of system software that controls the device operation, processes information from the underlying hardware sensors and performs the appropriate action. This basic operation layer defines the device's physical functionality, operational margins, valid states, user-safety safeguards and device integrity. In the following sections, we explore how to define the basic behavior of such a device.

Simple, Automatic Behavior: Events, Rules and Conditions

Definition: *Simple Behaviors* are one-step functions that would normally be triggered with a button. These interactions should be natural to users. This should even be true if people are using a product for the first time. The product should behave just as the user intuitively expects. Such interactions are implemented by monitoring the user's actions with suitable sensors and typically do not involve graphical or voice-based user interfaces. An example for a simple interaction is that the user puts her coffee mug under the coffee dispenser and automatically gets her favorite type of coffee.

This is the kind of behavior that is usually embedded within the smart product, be it a physical device or software. However, it is important to note that when we talk about physical devices, we must remember the basic notion of a control system, which reacts according its inputs and produces an output as shown in *Figure 2*. The set of reactions encoded in the control system determines the behavior of the device. If the outputs are determined automatically upon the inputs or events of the system, it is called a combinatorial system. If the system requires further information

Figure 2. A basic control system with inputs, outputs and state machine

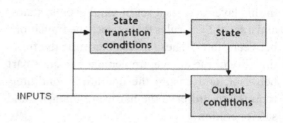

about the sequence in which the input took place to determine the appropriate output, the system is said to be sequential. In this context, we call the logic that determines the system behavior a state machine, and the history of inputs becomes the state of the control system.

Definition: An *event* is something that happens at a point in time. Specifying an event therefore involves providing a description of a particular situation that is to be monitored. Events are often multivalued, and the kind of information included is arbitrary and depends on the source or generator of the event.

Another important factor is the ability to specify rules to determine which changes, actions (and, as we'll see later, also which state transitions) should take place. There are two kinds of rules:

- Rules that have only a condition and an action part are called *condition-action* or *production* rules, that is: if *condition* $(C_1, C_2, ..., C_K)$ then *action* $(A_1, A_2, A_3, ..., A_m)$.
- Rules that consist of three parts are known as ECA (event-condition-action) rules. They have the form: *event* $(E_1, E_2, E_3, ..., E_n)$ if *condition* $(C_1, C_2, ..., C_K)$ then *action* $(A_1, A_2, A_3, ..., A_m)$.

A simple comparison can help us understand the difference between the two kinds of rules:

1. Production rules are triggered because of the occurrence of a specific event, while ECA rules are triggered when the system reaches a specific state that is periodically checked.
2. The triggering of the rule in the second case depends solely on the state of the database, rather than on the occurrence of external events.
3. Several ECA rules with different conditions can be declared to have the same event part, whereas for a CA rule a specific condition can trigger only one rule.

A simple procedure for ECA rule execution is as follows:

```
boolean Exec (Rule, Granularity, Evaluation, Priority)
{ exec= true
        match1=false
        while ( exec )
            { if ( notempty ( input eventqueue ) )
                { event1 = choose event ( input
                event queue )
                while ( not matched or end of
ECArules )
                        match1= match ( event1,
        ECArule )
        i f (match1 ) { if ( ruleconditon) do ruleaction ( )
                exec=false ;
                }
        }
    }
}
```

However, for more complex systems with hundreds or thousands of ECA rules, we need a better approach rather than checking all the rules every time an event occurs. A good example is the RETE algorithm (Forgy, 1990). This algorithm optimizes the process of rule evaluation with different heuristics to determine the minimal subset of rules to be evaluated at any particular

time. This is the case of expert systems in artificial intelligence or rule engines such as JESS (http://www.jess.org).

An interesting example of an ECA-based approach for ubiquitous computing systems is called the Ubiquitous Chip (Terada et al., 2004). This system uses very simple, programmable and wireless units that together are able to bring a sense of smart behavior to an environment through easy to deploy objects that provide non-trivial levels of automatism. For instance, when the door opens, the ubiquitous chip turns on the light and the air-conditioner in cooperation with other ubiquitous chips embedded in the room. Some of the rules are:

1. Detect the door opening and sets a one-minute timer.
2. Sound the buzzer when the timer fires.
3. If the door is closed within one minute resets the timer.
4. Request the door to unlock.

Finite State Machines

When the behavior we want to implement is more complex, such as reacting in different ways to the

Figure 3. An example of a "smart room" built with the Ubiquitous Chip

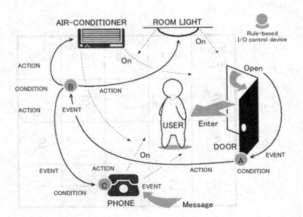

same event according to the present operational status, we need to structure what events and actions are valid at any particular moment.

This is important to ensure a correct operation and, when developing devices, to ensure their physical integrity (e.g., avoid interrupting an operation that could damage the device or make it hazardous to the user).

A mechanism to control the flow of operations and reactions according to the events received is a finite state machine (FSM).

Definition: A *finite state machine* defines a set of valid states in which the device may operate, a set of valid transitions between the valid states, and what actions should be executed under which conditions following the events received to trigger a transition from one state to the other. There are different variations of state machines, according to the particular kind of applications. In our case, the two more relevant types are the Mealy model, where the output takes into account both the current state and the event, and the Moore model, where the output depends solely on the state. A more formal definition of these two types of FSM is the following:

1. Σ is a non-empty set of events (also known as input alphabet)

2. S is a non-empty set of states

3. s_0 is an element of S, an arbitrary initial state

4. δ is a state transition function

5. Γ is the set of final states, a (possibly empty) subset of S

6. w is the output function. In the case of a Mealy model FSM that takes both states and events into account then ($w: S \times \Sigma \to \Gamma$), while in the Moore model FSM that takes only the state into account, the δ would be: ($w : S \to \Gamma$)

Processes: Implementing Complex Behavior

Definition: Complex behavior refers to multi-step procedures that require the user to have product-specific knowledge. Such interactions involve graphical or voice-based user interfaces and the system guides the user during these interactions. An example is descaling the coffee machine, which requires the user to perform several manual steps.

By *long running processes* we mean actions that can be arbitrarily fast followed by long wait periods.

Figure 4. An example of a state machine for a coffee machine, showing the corresponding transition table

Input State	w01	w00	b00	p00
S_1	S_3	–	S_2	–
S_2	S_3	–	–	S_1
S_3	S_3	S_1	–	–

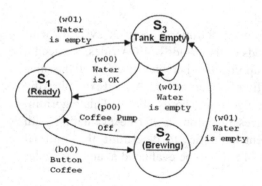

In Java (or any other general-purpose programming language) there is no native notion of a persistent wait state. Hence it is difficult to express the overall process in a language such as Java. The solution is to use a workflow language in which one can express processes. The process has a state machine nature. It can express the overall, long-running process.

Complex behavior involves the realization and sometimes coordination between different atomic actions. A first approach to model such behavior is using state machines. For simple, sequence-oriented behavior, state machines map perfectly onto processes. However, more complex, real-life processes can have multiple concurrent paths of execution, whereas a traditional state machine can only have one. Instead, we can use workflows.

Definition: Workflow is the automation of a business process, in whole or part, during which documents, information or tasks are passed from one participant to another for action, according to a set of procedural rules.

In the example below, the high-level application logic is implemented as a workflow description. This allows us to design the user interactions in a model-driven way.

In Figure 5, we see a partial definition of a complex operation modeled with workflow for descaling a coffee machine. This definition is used in the Smart Saeco Project (see Aitenbichler et al., 2007) to guide the user through all the steps of the process.

BUILDING AMBIENT INTELLIGENCE

Symmetric Intelligence

The first generation of smart products involves knowledge about the world, rules, sensors and a standard inference engine. This infrastructure allows tiny objects to infer consequences within their context using first-order logic statements and knowledge facts to reach a conclusion. Examples of this kind of intelligence are the collaborative business items (CoBIS) (Kubach, 2004), where smart items are able to figure out wrong groupings or concentrations of dangerous materials. In this kind of scheme, all participants have the same amount of knowledge and inference capabilities. Their value is the ability to deduce within the conditions of local, sensed context, which makes them very practical and easy to deploy.

Another project known as Cooperative Artifacts (Strohbach et al., 2004) takes a similar approach. The authors embed knowledge facts

Figure 5. An example of a standard workflow definition

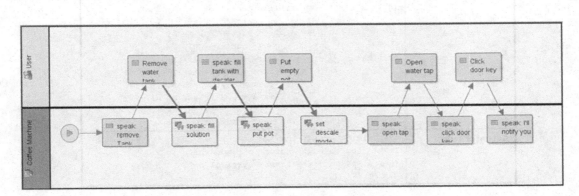

and rules using an embeddable version of Prolog in order to achieve goods that are sentient about their own location, proximity to others and are able to estimate the potential hazards. In Figure 6 we can see how a simple knowledge base built out of facts and simple rules provide a first level of self-organizing, and self-sustainable, functionality.

Limitations of Symmetric Intelligence

The problems of this approach are the same as those of distributed systems: achieving higher sophistication quickly requires more complex algorithms that in turn are harder to debug and maintain.

Asymmetric Intelligence

Asymmetric intelligence assumes different, more specialized entities for different tasks that eventually must cooperatively achieve or provide functionality. This vision is closer to what actually happens in the real world. Today, the introduction of technology in an environment in the form of network communications, sensors, devices and computers deploys a number of services that go increasingly beyond what meets the eye. Furthermore, the scenario of having the required technology available, but not being able to use it, is not uncommon. Even simple variations in the use or combination of means for simple purposes usually require intensive user knowledge and intervention

Figure 6. An example of a symmetric intelligence knowledge specification using Prolog from Strohbach et al. (2004). The example models smart tanks, to avoid dangerous proximity of hazardous goods.

Domain knowledge	`reactive(<chemical>,<chemical>)`
	`content(me,<chemical>)`
	`mass(me,<number>)`
	`critical_mass(<chemical>,<number>)`
	`critical_time(<chemical>,<time>)`

Observational knowledge	`proximity(<container>,<container>)` `location(<container>,<in/out>,<time>)`

Inference rules	`(R1) hazard_unapproved:- content(me, CH),`
	`                           critical_time(CH, T1),`
	`                           location(me, out, T2),`
	`                           T1 < T2.`
	`(R2) hazard_incompatible:- content(me, CH1),`
	`                           proximity(me, C),`
	`                           content(C, CH2),`
	`                           reactive(CH1, CH2).`
	`(R3) hazard_critical_mass:- content(me, CH),`
	`                           cond_sum(M1,(proximity(me,C),`
	`                           content(C,CH), mass(C,M1)),S),`
	`                           mass(me, M2), sum(S, M2, SUM)`
	`                           critical_mass(CH, MASS),`
	`                           MASS < SUM.`

Actuator rules	`(R4) alert_hazard:- hazard_unapproved`
	`(R5) alert_hazard:- hazard_incompatible`
	`(R6) alert_hazard:- hazard_critical_mass`

to decide what functionality can be combined and how in order to achieve a simple goal.

A goal denotes "what" the user wants. An example of a simple user goal could be showing a presentation stored on the user's mobile phone or laptop on a given display.

A knowledgeable user would upload the presentation to make it accessible to the presentation software available on a particular machine and display the slides in the desired place. To successfully accomplish this, the user must identify the available means (discover the functionality), figure out how they could be combined (compose), and determine the order in which they should be taken (make a plan) to successfully achieve what he wants (the goal).

Ideally as a smart response, the environment would figure out how to accomplish a given goal given the current available capabilities. In this way, it is up to the environment to determine "how" to realize the user's wish. This separation—between what the user wants from how to do it—allows the user to be freed from having to have the specific knowledge about the underlying technology available and how to apply it to the particular situation at hand.

Each available functionality that can be programmatically accessed is called a "service." Services are any functional program that produces

corresponding output with appropriate input, and every available device can provide one or more services $S_1, S_2, \cdots, S_n$, which can be defined as a service set $\{S_1, S_2, \cdots, S_n\}$. In the chapter "Service Discovery," services and their semantic description are described in detail.

For the sake of simplicity, we define a simple service S as a tuple $\langle$ ID, I, O, F, C $\rangle$, where:

- ID is the unique identification of service S
- I is the input pattern of service; any input i that matches I can be used as input of S
- O is the output pattern of service S; any output o that matches O can be used as an output of S
- F is the function that service S provides. An input i can be converted to o by F
- C is the cost for performing service S.

Service Composition

Service composition refers to the technique of combining an arbitrary number of these services into a more meaningful, richer service to meet the changing requirements of users.

We can view a complex and dynamic task as the composition of several basic sub-tasks, which can be completed by the cooperation of several simpler services.

Figure 7. Assemblies of smart products combine their functionality to better adapt to user's needs

These compositions can happen in either *reactive* or *proactive* manner:

Reactive composition refers to the process of creating compound services on demand. This kind of composition takes place only when there is a request from a user for such functionality. An example of a reactive composition could be the initial example of a user who wants to display a presentation in a given place. These compositions are mostly generated automatically, taking into account the current context and available services.

Proactive composition refers to the off-line composition of available services to form new services. Thus, these types of composed services are usually stable and constantly running in resource-rich environments. Examples of proactive compositions are business processes. Pro-active compositions are usually determined either manually or interactively through mixed-initiative tools such as SAP's Guided Procedures Framework.

The process of service composition can be further refined in two main aspects, *synthesis* and *orchestration*. Synthesis refers to the actual creation of a plan on how to achieve a desired behavior by combining the abilities of multiple services. In contrast, orchestration refers to coordinating the control and data flow among the various components when executing a plan.

A Notation for Service Composition

In a dynamic ad hoc environment, there are n mobile nodes, each of which has a unique identification id_1 to id_n. Every node id_m ($1 \leq m \leq n$) has p_m services from S_{m1} to S_m, p_m, and id_m only has knowledge (the services provided by node) of itself and nodes within k-hops range. Now, some node id_s (the user's PDA for instance), which we call the task initiator, starts a task $t \langle tid, I(i), O \rangle$ where *tid* is the unique identification of t, i is the input of t that matches pattern I, and O is the output pattern which can be acquired when t is completed. Determine the flow to complete task

t under the following restriction and then finish the task.

Definition: Two services, $S_1 = \langle ID_1, I_1, O_1, F_1, C_1 \rangle$, $S_2 = \langle ID_2, I_2, O_2, F_2, C_2 \rangle$, are range neighbors, and o_1 is an output of S_1. If the whole or part of o_1 can be used as the *(partial)* input of S_2, we say that S_1 and S_2 can be completely composed, and the direction of the composition is from S_1 to S_2. It can be denoted as $S_1 \rightarrow S_2$, or $i_1 S_1 o_1 1 S_2 o_2$ in detail, where o_2 is the output of S_2 that takes o_1 as input.

Reactive Composition Approaches

In this section, we will study how the composition of what service is realized. The first approaches to service composition appeared some decades ago in the area of artificial intelligence (AI), aiming to solve problems with robotic manufacturing processes. This type of problem created a whole area of study known as automatic planning and scheduling. Although in smart environments we have software services instead of robots in an assembly line, most of the basic concepts originally envisioned are very much in use today.

Automatic Planning and Scheduling

Planning and scheduling is an area of artificial intelligence (AI). Planning algorithms seek to produce a *plan*. A plan is a specification of what action sequences should be performed by the available services and devices in order to achieve the desired goal, within given constraints.

The generation of such a plan can be influenced by different planning generation techniques, strategies or heuristics that a planning system may implement in order to improve the calculation efficiency. Once a plan to accomplish a goal is found, it is forwarded to other intelligent agents and robots that consume this information to perform the steps determined by the plan.

The ability to create a plan before it is executed allows the introduction of several analysis techniques in order to evaluate how good the found

Figure 8. Overview of services available in a given SP assembly

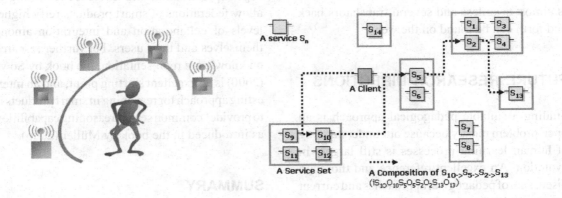

solution is. It also allows the system to compare such a solution against other alternatives or determine whether the impact of the solution strategy can meet other less rigorous criteria such as user acceptance. Furthermore, separation is necessary since the planning algorithm depends on the assumption that can be made in the particular domain. For instance, it could be assumed that the conditions in which the system will operate are deterministic or if it is more likely to operate in a highly dynamic, probabilistic environment.

In order to introduce the basic concepts, we will assume that knowledge about the environment is available, complete, and that it will remain without changes during the whole planning process (deterministic approach). There are three important pieces of information that a planning system needs as input:

1. A description of the world with all the facts and possible actions that can take place.
2. The starting point, also know as "initial state."
3. The desired "goal" or specification of how the planner knows that it has succeeded.

The requirement of describing the world is to clearly define the physics of the domain, formally defining the causal laws of the operations, its requirements and the effects they produce the world in case they are executed. Different domain theories proposed different, purely logic-based formalisms. Another popular approach is the one adopted in the area of AI known as *STRIPS* (Stanford Research Institute Problem Solver). In STRIPS, a planning problem can be defined as a five-tuple $\langle S, S_0, G, A, \Gamma \rangle$, where S is the set of all possible states in the world, $S_0 \boxtimes S$ is the initial state of the world, A the set of actions the planner can perform in attempting to change one state to another state in the world, and the translation relation $\Gamma \boxtimes S \times A \times S$ defines the precondition and effects for the execution of each action.

Several extensions like ADL (Action Description Language) were added to the original STRIPS definition in order to support more expressiveness, such as universal quantifiers, context dependent effects, negation and disjunction. Finally a new standard known as PDDL (Planning Domain Definition Language) was defined for the domain. Other definitions appear with the increased use of Web services. One such definition was DAML-S, known today as OWL-S, a service Web Ontology Language. OWL-S is a close descendant of PDDL, so that the translation of the definitions is almost seamless and several translators back and forth can be found on the web.

FUTURE RESEARCH DIRECTIONS

Finding a suitable pedagogical approach is an open problem mostly because our understanding of human learning processes is still largely in evolution. An excellent reference and thorough discussion of pedagogical approaches and current trends can be found in Reigeluth (1999).

The research area in smart products is very active and further directions will focus on the areas of mixed initiative planning systems to integrate user interaction. For an introduction and good pointers on planning systems see the book of *Artificial Intelligence* of Russell and Norvig (2002). The research on context awareness as well as service discovery and composition will also benefit smart products (see the chapter "Service Discovery" for further references on these topics).

Finally, other very important areas are knowledge representation and inference/reasoning to allow federations of smart products reify higher levels of collaboration and integration among themselves and their users. For further research on knowledge representation, the book by Sowa (2000) is an excellent starting point, and an interesting approach for reasoning in smart products is to provide "common sense" reasoning capabilities, as introduced in the book by Müller (2006).

SUMMARY

This chapter gave an introduction to how ambient learning is the key to create environments that will become intelligent through dense technological instrumentation. Ambient learning has two clearly identifiable areas: assistance to the user and learning capabilities embedded into technology, since both benefit from each other. The ambient learning chapter describes the different learning processes between users and technology, and how agentive behavior will be achieved by

Figure 9. An example of a PDDL-like world description, the operators, a proposed goal and the plan produced by a planner.

providing learning capabilities and mechanisms to support both the technology and the people that benefit from it.

Despite the current availability of technology, there is a notorious absence of large-scale settings, and this fact reveals complexity and effort required today for building such intelligent living and working spaces. Smart products shape the vision of intelligent infrastructures that are able to configure themselves and grow from the available, purposeful objects (be it software services or consumer appliances) in order to become effective in the real world. As building blocks of the future ambient intelligence settings, we described in this chapter the smart product concept in detail, as well as what learning and adaptation capabilities they bring.

Finally, different examples of intelligent behavior were shown as well as basic concepts involved in the construction of smart products.

REFERENCES

Aarts, E. (2004). Ambient intelligence: A multimedia perspective. *IEEE Multimedia, 11*(1), 12–19.

Addlesee, M., Curwen, R., Hodges, S., Newman, P., Steggles, A., & Hopper, A. (2001). Implementing a sentient computing system. *IEEE Computer, 34*(8), 50–56.

Aitenbichler, E., Lyardet, F., Austaller, G., Kangasharju, J., & Mühlhäuser, M. (2007). *Engineering intuitive and self-explanatory smart products*. In *Proceedings of the 22nd Annual ACM Symposium on Applied Computing* (pp. 1632-1637). New York: ACM Press.

Barton J., & Kindberg, T. (2002). The Cooltown Project. Retrieved November 14th, 2006, from http://www.cooltown.hp.com.

Bornhövd, C., Lin, T., Haller, S., & Schaper, J. (2005). Integrating smart items with business processes - an experience report. In *Proceedings of the 38th Hawaii International Conference on System Sciences* (p. 227c).

Brumitt B., Meyers B., Krumm J.,. Kern, A., & Shafer, S.A. (2000). Easyliving: Technologies for Intelligent Environments. In *Proceedings of the 1st International Symposium on Handheld and Ubiquitous Computing* (HUC'99) (pp. 12–27).

Cooperstock, J.R., Fels, S.S., Buxton, W., & Smith, K.C. (1997). Reactive environments. *Communications of the ACM, 40*(9), 65–73.

Decker, C., Beigl, M., Krohn, A., Robinson, P., & Kubach, U. (2004). eSeal - a system for enhanced electronic assertion of authenticity and integrity. In *Pervasive Computing* (LNCS 3301, pp. 254–268). IEEE Computer Society.

Encarnaçao, J.L., & Kirste, T. (2005). Ambient intelligence: Towards smart appliance ensembles. In *From integrated publication and information systems to virtual information and knowledge environments* (pp. 261–270). Springer.

Fano, A.A., & Gershman, A. (2002). The future of business services in the age of ubiquitous computing. *Communications of the ACM, 45*(12), 83–87.

Fox, A., & Winograd, T. (2006). *Stanford interactive workspaces-iWork* (project Web site). Retrieved November 14th, 2006, from http://iwork.stanford.edu/.

Franklin, D., & Hammond, K. (2001). The intelligent classroom: Providing competent assistance. In *AGENTS '01: Proceedings of the Fifth International Conference on Autonomous Agents* (pp. 161–168). New York: ACM Press.

Forgy, C.L. (1990). Rete: A fast algorithm for the many pattern/many object pattern match problem. In P.G. Raeth (Ed.), *Expert systems: A software methodology for modern applications* (pp. 324-341). IEEE Computer Society Reprint Collection. Los Alamitos, CA: IEEE Computer Society Press.

Heinemann, A., Kangasharju, J., Lyardet, F., & Mühlhäuser, M. (2003a). Ad hoc collaboration and information services using information clouds. In T. Braun, N. Golmie, & J. Schiller (Eds.), *Proceedings of the 3rd Workshop on Applications and Services in Wireless Networks,* Bern, Switzerland (ASWN 2003) (pp. 233–242). Institute of Computer Science and Applied Mathematics, University of Bern.

Kidd, C.D., Orr, R., Abowd, G.D., Atkeson, C.G., Essa, I.A., MacIntyre, B., Mynatt, E.D., Starner, T., & Newstetter, W. (1999). The aware home: A living laboratory for ubiquitous computing research. In *CoBuild '99: Proceedings of the Second International Workshop on Cooperative Buildings, Integrating Information, Organization, and Architecture* (pp. 191–198). London, U.K.: Springer-Verlag.

Kubach, U., Decker, C., & Douglas, K. (2004). Collaborative control and coordination of hazardous chemicals. In *Proceedings of the 2nd International Conference on Embedded Networked Sensor Systems*, Baltimore, MD (pp. 309-309). New York: ACM Press.

Lukowicz, P., Ward, J.A., Junker, H., Stäger, M., Tröster, G., Atrash, A., & Starner, T. (2004). *Recognizing workshop activity using body worn microphones and accelerometers.* In *Proceedings of the 2nd International Conference on Pervasive Computing* (pp. 18–32). IEEE Computer Society.

Marsick, V.J., & Watkins, K.E. (1997). Lessons from incidental and informal learning. In J. Burgoyne & M. Reynolds (Eds.), *Management learning: Integrating perspectives in theory and practice.* Thousand Oaks, CA: Sage.

Munguia Tapia, E., Intille, S.S., & Larson, K. (2004). Activity recognition in the home using simple and ubiquitous sensors. In *Proceedings of the Second International Conference on Per-*

vasive Computing, Vienna, Austria (LNCS 3001, pp. 158-175).

Schmidt, A., & Laerhoven, K.V. (2001). How to build smart appliances. *IEEE Personal Communications*, pp. 66–71.

Schmidt, A., Asante Aidoo, K., Takaluoma, A., Tuomela, U., Van Laerhoven, K., & Van de Velde, W. (1999). Advanced interaction in context. In *Proceedings of the 1st International Symposium on Handheld and Ubiquitous Computing* (HUC'99) (pp. 89–101). London, UK: Springer-Verlag.

Siegemund, F., & Flörkemeier, C. (2003). Interaction in Pervasive Computing Settings Using Bluetooth-Enabled Active Tags and Passive RFID Technology Together with Mobile Phones. In *Proceedings of the First IEEE international Conference on Pervasive Computing and Communications.* (p. 378). Washington, DC: IEEE Computer Society.

Sowa, J. (2000). *Knowledge representation: Logical, philosophical, and computational foundations.* Pacific Grove, CA: Brooks Cole Publishing Co.

Stamps, D. (1998). Learning ecologies. *Training, 35*(1), 32-38.

Starner, T., Schiele, B., & Pentland, A. (1998). Visual contextual awareness in wearable computing. In *Second International Symposium on Wearable Computers. Digest of Papers* (pp. 50–57).

Strohbach, M., Gellersen, H.W., Kortuem, G., & Kray, C. (2004). Cooperative artefacts: Assessing real world situations with embedded technology. In *Proceedings of Ubicomp 2004* (pp. 250-267). Springer Verlag.

Terada, T., Tsukamoto, M., Hayakawa, K., Yoshihisa, T., Kishino, Y., Kashitani, A., & Nishio, S. (2004). *Ubiquitous chip: A rule based i/o control device for ubiquitous computing. Pervasive*

Computing. (LNCS 3001, pp. 238–253). Springer Verlag.

ADDITIONAL READING

Müller, E. (2006). *Commonsense reasoning.* San Francisco, CA: Morgan Kaufmann.

Reigeluth, C. (1999). *Instructional-design theories and models: A new paradigm of instructional theory* (Vols. 1 & 2). Lawrence Erlbaum Associates.

Russell, S., & Norvig, P. (2002). *Artificial intelligence: A modern approach* (2nd Ed.). Prentice Hall.

Sowa, J. (2000). *Knowledge representation: Logical, philosophical, and computational foundations.* Pacific Grove, CA: Brooks Cole Publishing Co.

Section V
Pilots and Trends at SAP–Research

Chapter XXIV
CoBIs:
Collaborative Business Items

Patrik Spieß
SAP Research, Germany

Jens Müller
SAP Research, Germany

ABSTRACT

This chapter describes example use cases for ubiquitous computing technology in a corporate environment that have been evaluated as prototypes under realistic conditions. The main example reduces risk in the handling of hazardous substances by detecting potentially dangerous storage situations and raising alarms if certain rules are violated. We specify the requirements, implementation decisions, and lessons learned from evaluation. It is shown that ubiquitous computing in a shop floor, warehouse, or retail environment can drastically improve real-world business processes, making them safer and more efficient.

BACKGROUND

Currently every year, despite enormous preventive effort, a significant number of employees in the chemical, oil, and gas industry become seriously injured or die due to accidents at production or storage sites (Fewtrell & Hirst, 1998). Technology can help to minimize the risk of such tragic events that also cost companies and society a great deal of money. Increasing the safety of employees is a fundamental ethical value and part of corporate social responsibility (CSR), a concept more and more demanded from companies that contributes to their (accounting) goodwill.

The research project *Collaborative Business Items,* or CoBIs, made real-world items smarter by attaching wireless sensor nodes to them. These nodes communicate in a peer-to-peer fashion, collaboratively executing business logic and interacting with back-end enterprise systems. An enterprise software back-end and the network of ubiquitous sensors together formed ubiquitous applications. Using this technology, the project looked into the promising application scenario of making business processes that involve hazardous goods safer and more efficient. The project, partly funded by the European Union, brought together corporate end-users like BP[a] and Infineon[b] with SAP as a provider of enterprise software solutions as well as leading experts in research on ubiquitous hardware and software.

The project focuses on one central scenario: *supervision of hazardous goods*. Using the tools and expertise generated by working on this scenario, we also looked into *safe entry into confined vessels* and *real-time inventory and RFID reader coordination*.

APPLICATION SCENARIO

Focus Scenario: Supervision of Hazardous Goods

Hazardous goods must be stored safely in order to prevent accidents. Appropriate storage conditions are expressed by regulations imposed by governments and companies. Companies are obliged to comply with these regulations, which set the minimum standard in an industry. Most companies, however, voluntarily commit to standards that go beyond legal requirements. Storage regulations include rules like these:

1. For a given substance, only a maximum amount may be stored in the same storage location.

Figure 1. Architecture overview of integration middleware

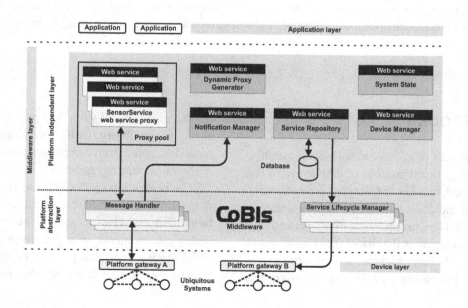

2. Some combinations of substances must not be stored in the same location.
3. At some locations, substances may only be stored for a limited amount of time.
4. Certain substances may only be stored in special, enclosed locations.
5. Most substances must be kept in a tolerable range of environmental conditions such as temperature, humidity, light level, or pressure and must be disposed after a certain expiration date.

Examples of substances subject to rule 1 are flammable, explosive, or radioactive substances. Exceeding a maximum storage amount can lead to accidents like the one in the Dutch city Enschede in May 2000, where a fire in a fireworks company killed more than twenty people, injured almost a thousand others, and destroyed almost five hundred apartments.

Inflammable and oxidizing substances are a good example of an incompatible pair of substances according to rule 2. To give another example of what can happen if such rules are not followed, take the accident that happened in February 2004 in Iran, where a freight train was loaded with gasoline (inflammable) and fertilizer (oxidizing). While these substances are not very hazardous on their own, when they were mixed after the train derailed, a huge detonation occurred and fire destroyed five villages.

Rule 3 applies, for example, to the temporary storage areas within warehouses, where incoming goods are stored before they are brought to their final storage place. Accordingly, a similar place may exist for outbound products. It should be detected if a container is stored for too long in one of these areas.

Rule 4 applies to radioactive material, for instance, which must be stored in an enclosed room that shields radiation.

To prevent a substance from decomposition because of exposure to inappropriate environmental conditions or protracted storage, rule 5

can be applied. This kind of monitoring could also be used for perishable goods in the food industry. Earlier systems for enforcing storage rules for hazardous goods used, for example, RFID technology (Williams, 2004). Those solutions are limited, because RFID tags are only scanned at defined transition points like warehouse gates. This procedure implies that business logic (rule checking) is executed in a central system, which causes scalability issues and prevents rule checking when no infrastructure is available.

In contrast, the ubiquitous system developed in CoBIs can detect, log, and signal the breach of any of the aforementioned rules autonomously, for example, during transport by train or truck, without needing an online connection to a back-end system.

Safe Entry into Confined Vessels

Another cause of accidents in the chemical industry is the entry of a worker into a hazardous area without the necessary equipment or training. To give an example, it is common practice to flood a chemical reactor with nitrogen prior to manual cleaning, inspection, or maintenance in order to minimize the risk of explosion. If a worker enters the reactor without wearing the correct breathing apparatus, she will instantly become unconscious and may die of asphyxiation. To prevent this, access is denied unless all of the following rules are fulfilled:

1. The worker has attended the appropriate training course and is certified to perform the task;
2. Equipment that is required for the task is present;
3. The minimum number of persons required to fulfil the task are collaborating.

This can be achieved by identifying the person trying to enter the confined vessel, the equipment she is carrying, and by crosschecking identification data with back-end data about the employee, the task, and the equipment.

Real-Time Inventory and RFID Reader Coordination

Analyzing and understanding the data collected by RFID readers and integrating it into business processes is still a challenge for today's software. In this scenario, Infineon combines RFID and sensor networks. The system treats RFID readers merely as complex identity sensors attached to an I/O interface of a sensor node.

The current generation of so-called *smart shelves* can identify products located on them.

They are used, for example, in warehouses or retail stores. Product identification is achieved by tagging each product with an RFID label that contains an individual ID or an ID of the product type. RFID readers built into the shelf read the product tags located on each shelf. Those systems do not include any infrastructure to turn RFID readings into rich events that make sense within a business process.

The so-called *smarter RFID shelves* developed in CoBIs feature a combination of wireless sensor nodes with RFID readers, leading to a wireless processing network for tag data. It provides increased scalability, because it reduces the amount of data to be processed centrally in the

Figure 2. SAP WebDynpro GUI Screen showing events ware and scenarios

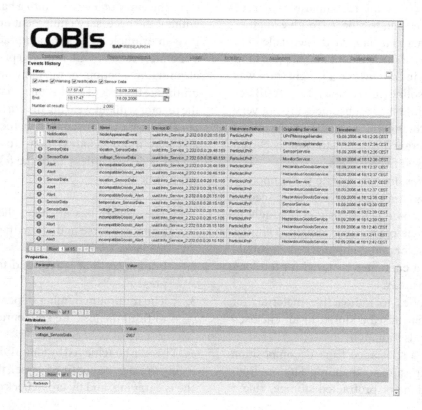

Figure 3. Chemical containers equipped with particle sensor nodes

back-end business applications and pushes filtering, smoothing, aggregation, and enrichment to the very network edge where the data is created. The nodes are also used to prevent simultaneous readings by neighbouring shelves, which would cause interference and bad quality of readings. Additionally, if the sensor nodes are equipped with a location system, they can determine the current position of a mobile smarter shelf that can be included in business events.

ARCHITECTURE/DESIGN

One of the goals of CoBIs was to create a generic middleware for the integration of smart items with business applications that supports a wide range of scenarios by including and integrating a multitude of heterogeneous hardware platforms. This middleware should support real-world items that are made smart by technologies ranging from simple, passive RFID tags via wireless sensor/actor nodes to full-fledged industrial PCs. Our approach was

to analyze the requirements of the aforementioned application scenarios in order to design hardware and software that supports their operation, and to make the system easily extensible to support other hardware and scenarios.

The middleware developed by SAP integrates ubiquitous installations into enterprise software. The prototype requires ubiquitous systems to offer their functionality as a set of services (such as Web services or UPnP[c] services). This requirement will probably remain valid in a future commercial solution offered by SAP. To allow their ubiquitous platforms to interact seamlessly with an SAP installation, hardware and solution providers are advised to offer a service-oriented abstraction for their systems. This will increase the odds that a company running SAP will prefer their ubiquitous platform as opposed to others, which do not offer such an abstraction.

The concept of a service in CoBIs is similar to the concepts behind Web services. A service is defined by its interface (like the interface of a class in an object-oriented programming language). The interface of a service consists of a set of *actions* and *event messages.*

The actions (operations) have a fixed signature comprising invocation and return parameters. A service instance is a concrete instance of a service that has a unique address. *Service invocations* are invocations of service actions on a concrete service instance (comparable to remote procedure/method calls). They can be synchronous (blocking), that is, the execution of the service client is suspended until the result of an error message is returned. In the case of an asynchronous invocation, the service client provides a callback address to which the result is delivered as soon as it is available.

Service instances also can create asynchronous event messages. These events are distributed using a publish/subscribe paradigm. When an event occurs, the event message is created with certain attributes. Event consumers can subscribe to certain types of events based on a combination of attributes.

Figure 1 shows an architectural overview of the prototypical middleware. Components on a grey background represent the part of the integration middleware developed by SAP. Both the platform-dependent part of the middleware and the device layer are parts provided by hardware manufacturers or solution providers. On top, business applications and the management application are shown that consume the functionality of the ubiquitous systems through the middleware. The components shown in the diagram only interact through service invocations and asynchronous events.

A *platform gateway* presents all services offered by one underlying ubiquitous system. It allows the invocation of their actions, forwards events, and offers functionality to deploy new services. It converts event messages from a platform-specific format to a generic format and conversely converts generic service invocation messages into platform-specific ones. By connecting to more than one platform gateways (of one or more types), the system can simultaneously communicate with several ubiquitous systems (of one ore more types).

Message handlers forward events to the *notification manager* and route service invocations to the correct *platform gateway.* The notification manager offers a publish/subscribe system for events where any interested middleware component or application can subscribe to any type of event. For each service presented by the platform gateway (e.g., as a UPnP service) the *dynamic proxy generator* component creates a Web service proxy that is added to the proxy pool. These service proxies can be easily accessed by back-end business applications. An application can also query a *system state* component that monitors all dynamic information regarding the attached networks, for example, which devices are currently connected, what services they are running and how much memory and CPU, and so forth are available. A *device manager* handles the registration of devices, and stores static, device-related information in a persistent device registry where information about a device can be obtained regardless of whether it is currently connected or not.

The *service repository* contains a database of service executables and corresponding service descriptions. Each service description contains human-readable documentation, interface, technical requirements of the respective service (e.g., on which platform it can run), as well as dependencies on other services. Using the *management application* a user can deploy new services over-the-air (i.e., reprogram the nodes through the wireless channel) and get system state information such as the quality of links between nodes or current sensor values. The installation, removal, starting, and stopping of service instances on nodes is done by a platform-dependent service lifecycle manager. We also looked into automatic service deployment using current system state and service requirements to automatically install or remove service instances on appropriate nodes.

IMPLEMENTATION

The platform-independent layer of the CoBIs architecture has been implemented using standard technologies like Web services, Java Enterprise Edition (Java EE) on SAP Web Application Server and Java Messaging Service (JMS). The persistence model of Java EE is database-agnostic, so that any database system can be used with our implementation.

For the graphical user interface, we chose SAP WebDynpro, the standard tool within SAP to generate browser-based application interfaces. *Figure 2* shows an example screen displaying events and detailed event data generated by wireless sensor nodes.

EVALUATION

To evaluate the solution created in CoBIs, several lab trials and on-site pilot application trials took place. In July 2006, the system was installed at a BP production site in Kingston upon Hull in the United Kingdom. Figure 3 shows some of more than twenty chemical containers equipped with wireless nodes featuring temperature sensors and a cellular location system. These were used together with our integration middleware to track containers of several types of oil under real-world conditions. The nodes had a bright red LED indicator to inform workers of storage rule violations.

The storage rules were maintained in the SAP application *Environment Health & Safety* and each time the rules parameters were changed in the application, the services on the sensor nodes were reconfigured using the new values. The sensor node hardware, so called *Particles* provided by the TecO research group at the University of Karlsruhe, had to be equipped with a waterproof housing to meet the safety rules of the production site.

The nodes collaboratively checked rules 1, 2, 3, and 5. The trial period was one month. The first two weeks were needed to set up the system and perform some tests. In these tests, storage rules were voluntarily broken to test the reliability of alerting. In another test case, previously not configured nodes were attached to drums and the services on the nodes were configured with the correct data about the drums. After the test period, the installation was left for two weeks of unattended operation during which extensive data logging was performed.

During both set-up and operation phase, we were facing some challenges. The following points describe some of them along with advice on how to avoid them:

1. Unreliability of the wireless channels: both the nodes' wireless communication from and to the gateway as well as a WLAN link we used failed from time to time. The failures were not frequent but of long duration. A system should be able to tolerate such failures.
2. Bugs in embedded software and middleware: every project partner implemented their part of the software on their own and only minimal integration testing was done beforehand. Extensive testing should be done, including early integration tests with the complete system.
3. Complexity of the system that included embedded software, local middleware, and both a remote and a local management application: Assemble documentation of all standard components used; produce documentation of your own components, and document all interactions between your and your partner's components.
4. Security regulations for a chemical production plant are stringent. Every piece of hardware had to be certified. Protective, water-resistant packaging of hardware is required.

During operation, battery efficiency proved to be crucial. We tested several configurations of node software. There was an expected trade-off between reactivity (time to detect rule breaks) and battery lifetime. At a reactivity of one second, a battery lifetime of one week could be achieved, but when we introduced a duty cycle resulting in a reactivity of 10 seconds, the battery lasted longer than the trial period. We expect it to be two or three months.

CONCLUSION

The CoBIs project developed hardware and software that enhances real-world business processes with ubiquitous technology. The use of technology makes these processes safer and more effective. Back-end business software can get a more detailed and timelier view of the real world. The hardware and especially the software designed in CoBIs were engineered to be re-usable in many other scenarios. The middleware is extensible, offering a plug-in model for new hardware platforms. It abstracts from details of the underlying hardware platform, offering the platform's functionality through Web services, a paradigm independent form operating systems or programming languages. More about CoBIs and its results can be found at http://www.cobis-online.de/.

REFERENCES

Fewtrell, P., & Hirst, I.L. (1998, April). A review of high-cost chemical/petrochemical accidents since Flixborough 1974. *Loss Prevention Bulletin, 140.*

Williams, L. (2004, Dec). *NASA Dryden Flight Research Center deploys advanced hazardous material management program with oracle sensor technology.* Press Release.

ENDNOTES

[a]   http://www.bp.com/
[b]   http://www.infineon.com/
[c]   Universal Plug and Play

Chapter XXV
PROMISE:
Product Lifecycle Management and Information Tracking Using Smart Embedded Systems

Jürgen Anke
SAP Research CEC Dresden, Germany

Bernhard Wolf
SAP Research CEC Dresden, Germany

Gregor Hackenbroich
SAP Research CEC Dresden, Germany

Hong-Hai Do
SAP Research CEC Dresden, Germany

Mario Neugebauer
SAP Research CEC Dresden, Germany

Anja Klein
SAP Research CEC Dresden, Germany

ABSTRACT

Product lifecycle management (PLM) processes can be greatly improved and extended if more information on the product and its use is available during the various lifecycle phases. The PROMISE project aims to close the information loop by employing product embedded information devices (PEIDs) in products. In this chapter, we present the goals and application scenarios of the project with special focus on the middleware that enables the communication between PEIDs and enterprise applications. Furthermore, we give details of the design and implementation of the middleware as well as the role of Universal Plug and Play (UPnP) as device-level protocol.

INTRODUCTION

The PROMISE project (PROMISE Consortium, 2006) aims at improving business processes of product lifecycle management (PLM) by using the information loop across the various stages in a product's lifecycle, from beginning-of-life (design, production) to middle-of-life (use, maintenance) and end-of-life (recycling, disposal). The technological approach of the project is to use smart networked devices that are embedded into products to gather data on the product's status, properties, and working environment. The data is then made available to back-end systems to perform data analysis for decision support. Moreover, the information acquired is exchanged between the various interested parties, for example, manufacturer, customers, service and recycling companies.

The vision of closing the information loop for PLM has attracted the interest of a number of large companies, like *Infineon* (Germany), *Bombardier Transportation* (France), *Fiat/Iveco* (Italy), and *Caterpillar* (France/USA), in addition to SAP, to take part in the project. This emphasizes the relevance of the idea and also the commitment of industry in realizing it. In particular, *Infineon* is developing the hardware for PEIDs (product embedded information devices) to be installed in physical products.

PROJECT GOALS

The goals of PROMISE fall into the categories of technical, business, and research goals:

Technical Goals

- **Product Embedded Information Devices (PEIDs):** Suitable PEIDs have to be developed which turn products into smart items. PEIDs will provide data about the product to external applications. Using PEIDs will enable automatic data acquisition of high accuracy, which is less error-prone and more efficient than manual collection and entry of the data.

- **Integration of PEIDs with Backend Systems:** To enable the communication between PEIDs and backend applications, a middleware providing abstraction from device-level protocols and data transformation is required.

- **Product Data and Knowledge Management (PDKM):** Product-related data from PEIDs, field databases, and other sources have to be integrated to allow for sophisticated data analysis.

- **Decision Support:** Data from the PDKM has to be analyzed to transform the data into actionable knowledge for PLM decision support.

- **Cross-Company Information Flows**: A major hurdle for today's PLM applications is the inaccessibility of product-related data in other organizations. To overcome this, methods and software that allow sharing of data, information and knowledge among certified actors of the system have to be developed.

Business Goals

- **Enable New Business Models:** Using technology developed in PROMISE, new business models, for example in the areas of product service and recycling, will be developed to increase the economic impact of results from applied research.

- **Improve Existing Business Processes:** Business processes related to PLM will be improved and extended, for example, by achieving lower operational cost, better quality and safety, reduction of errors, and better informed decisions.

Research Goals

- **Generic PLM Models:** The consolidated requirements of many PLM application scenarios are to be integrated into domain-specific and generic models of PLM information flow and PLM workflow.

- **Information and Knowledge Management Methodologies:** To turn the collected product data into useful knowledge for decision support, methods and concepts for information enrichment and transformation of information into knowledge have to be developed.

INNOVATIONS IN PLM BUSINESS PROCESSES

In the following, three application scenarios are presented to show how PROMISE technology can be applied to a PLM business process in beginning-of-life (BOL), middle-of-life (MOL), and end-of-life (EOL).

Improved Product Design: Bombardier (BOL)

Bombardier is a provider of rail equipment and servicing. Based on a component platform, Bombardier designs and produces a large number (over 400) of different locomotives. Applying the PROMISE idea, Bombardier aims at closing the information loop between the experience in service (field data) and the knowledge needed in order to develop improved locomotives for specific criteria, such as design for reliability, availability & maintainability/life cycle costs, product safety, environment, and so forth. For these purposes, field data is recorded on the locomotives and transferred to a field database using GSM (Global System for Mobile Communication). The data is then analyzed for information on the

performance of components compared to their expected behavior. Based on that, the engineers can evaluate the suitability of their designs and improve them accordingly.

Flexible Maintenance Planning: Fiat (MOL)

Fiat focuses on predictive maintenance of trucks. To improve the effectiveness of fleet management, FIAT seeks new ways to better understand the product usage and the mission profile of Iveco commercial vehicles. The objective is to provide customers with flexible maintenance planning, which is based on the actual degradation of vehicle components instead of fixed intervals. With this approach, costly breakdowns are avoided, while preventing the replacement of parts that are still in good condition. The correct timing for maintenance is determined by measuring the wear-out of selected critical components with sensors that are integrated into the vehicle. Furthermore, the mission profiles of trucks are determined in order to predict the wear-out for components depending on the respective mission profile. For each truck, the output of the decision support system is a calendar containing the time and the type of planned interventions. The maintenance crew is provided with a consolidated view on all interventions of the fleet.

Effective Recycling: Caterpillar (EOL)

Caterpillar is a manufacturer of construction and mining equipment. Using PROMISE technology, Caterpillar aims to support decommissioning of heavy-load machinery at the end of its life. More specifically, the value of the vehicle's components has to be evaluated to identify those that can be reused. Previously, end of life decision-making was based on inspection in order to determine whether a component could be remanufactured.

Now, a PEID monitors the product's status and systematically collects data during the machine's operation. Using a smart item middleware, this data can be accessed from the PEID and stored in a database. When the machine is decommissioned, the data associated with the built-in parts is retrieved from the databases and serves as input to a decision support system (DSS), where it is combined with data on economic demand. Thus, the appropriate handling of the various components is determined, for example, deciding whether to dispose of, recycle, reuse or remanufacture components in order to increase the re-use of components.

TECHNICAL SOLUTION OVERVIEW

Overall PROMISE Architecture

The technical solution of PROMISE consists of different layers, which are consolidated into the overall PROMISE architecture (see Figure 1).

Business processes from various application areas are supported by applications for decision support and product data and knowledge management (PDKM). These applications access PEID data through a middleware, which provides functionality for reading and writing of PEID data, as well as notifications on data updates, and PEID management. On the PEID level, mechanisms for detection of devices and invocation of services are offered.

Brief Overview of the PROMISE Middleware

A key part of the PROMISE architecture is the middleware, which was co-developed by SAP. Its purpose is to connect PEIDs with backend applications to facilitate data exchange between them (see Figure 2). One of the main challenges in the design of the middleware was to support mobility of products. As products can be mobile (e.g., trucks, locomotives), they might not be permanently connected to the network. To handle this,

Figure 1. PROMISE architecture

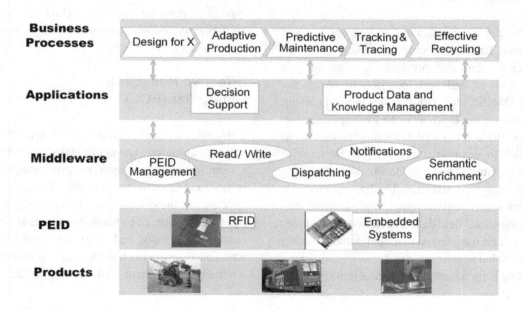

Figure 2. Logical components of the PROMISE middleware

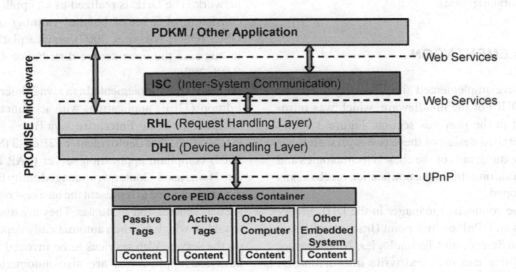

the communication between backend applications has to be asynchronous. Furthermore, the presence of devices has to be detected automatically in order to trigger the execution of pending requests.

The middleware is divided into three logical layers, which are described here briefly:

- **Device Handling Layer:** The DHL provides mechanisms for device discovery and invocation of services on the PEID to access data. In the PROMISE middleware, this was achieved by using Universal Plug and Play (UPnP Forum, 2006). All PEIDs implement a unified UPnP interface called "Core PAC" (Core PEID Access Container). When a PEID is detected, the DHL connects to it and sends a notification to upper layers of the middleware. Additionally, it translates incoming requests into UPnP services invocations to read or write PEID data.
- **Request Handling Layer:** The RHL provides Web services to interface with back-end applications, which can place requests

for PEID data at the RHL. If the required PEID is currently connected, the request is directly forwarded to the DHL. Otherwise, it is buffered until a connection notification is received from the DHL, which triggers the forwarding of the request. In a large-scale deployment, a RHL node can be connected to multiple DHL nodes, which can be installed in different physical locations to provide PEID connectivity.
- **Inter-System Communication:** To provide cross-organizational communication, the ISC was developed. It is an optional part of the middleware stack for scenarios where external parties are to access PEID data. In these scenarios, each organization has at least one Inter-System Communication (ISC) node installed, which then connects to other ISC nodes in a peer-to-peer fashion. Back-end applications place their request at an ISC node, which then forwards the request to the correct RHL, PDKM or third-party system. Companies can thus gather

product-related information from other organizations.

IMPLEMENTATION

We have implemented the lower layers (RHL and DHL) of the middleware, which was introduced in the previous section. Figure 3 shows the detailed design of these two layers. Here we give some details of the chosen technologies and elaborate on some of the notification mechanisms developed.

The connection manager in the DHL implements an UPnP control point (Institute of Information Science and Technologies, 2006; Konno, 2006) that can read and write information on PEIDs once they have been discovered in the network. The DHL is realized as an application consisting of a set of bundles running on an OSGi (OSGi Alliance, 2007) service platform, in our case the open source distribution Oscar (Hall, 2006).

The RHL is implemented as a Java 2 Enterprise Edition (J2EE) application, with its functional components being Enterprise Java Beans (EJB) (SUN, 2006). For deployment, a J2EE 1.3 (SUN, 2002) compliant application server (SAP Help, 2007) was used. Container-managed entity beans are implemented to represent the business objects such as targetIds and infoItemIds. They are mapped to tables, which are then automatically deployed on the server. Web services to be invoked from back-end applications are also automatically

Figure 3. Detailed design of RHL and DHL layers

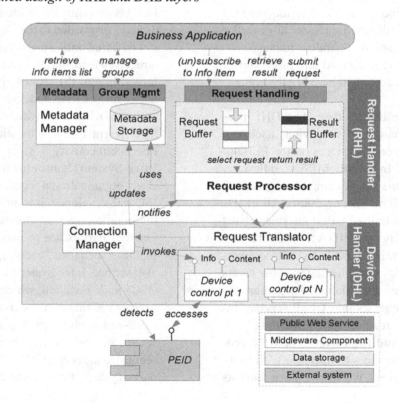

generated from the beans. A timing service was required for the management of subscriptions to RHL requests. To compensate for the lack of an EJB Timer service in J2EE 1.3, the Open Symphony Quartz (Open Symphony, 2006) was used as a powerful library for scheduling.

Communication between RHL and DHL is established using Java Messaging Service (JMS), which provides reliable asynchronous messaging. The JMS Provider manages three queues to exchange messages between the two layers. A request queue and a response queue are dedicated to receiving requests from the back-end applications via the RHL and the corresponding responses from the DHL respectively. A third queue is used for the delivery of notification messages for PEIDs discovered as well as metadata about those PEIDs.

For the processing of messages on the DHL, a JMS MessageListener is implemented to listen on the request queue for incoming requests. To enable the DHL to retrieve the factories required for JMS communication, a J2EE client library (Opgenorth, 2005) has been included as an application bundle. On the RHL, the request processor contains message-driven beans (MDB), listening on the response queue and notification queue to process the messages, which are received on it.

When a device is discovered by the connection manager and permitted to connect by the device manager, a JMS notification message with the PEID and respective metadata is sent to the notification queue. The dedicated MDB within the request processor then performs the necessary processing to check for pending requests for that PEID. If there are requests buffered, they are sent via the request queue to the DHL as JMS messages. After performing the required operation (read/write), the result for each request is then sent back via the response queue to the RHL. The result messages are handled by the above-mentioned MDB, which places the results in a buffer to be retrieved by the back-end applications through a Web service interface. Incoming requests are forwarded to the request queue until the RHL is notified of the disconnection of the PEID.

When a back-end application has placed a subscription on the request handler, a trigger is created with a subscription interval and the subscription is then scheduled as a Quartz job. Whenever the RHL is notified of the disconnection of a PEID, all the subscriptions on that PEID are paused. When the PEID connects again, all the subscriptions placed on it are resumed. Whenever it is activated, the scheduled job sends a request according to the given interval, which is then handled as described above.

BENEFITS AND LIMITATIONS

The system presented allows back-end systems to acquire data from product embedded information systems, which can then be used to support business decisions. Using UPnP as standard technology for detection and invocation of services as well as a common data access scheme ("InfoItems" and their IDs), an abstraction from concrete products can be achieved. Thus, the middleware enables reading and writing of PEID data for a large number of heterogeneous products.

One of the major drawbacks is that all products not only have to be UPnP compatible, but also implement the UPnP interface which was defined in the PROMISE project. It remains to be seen to what extent this interface is used in real-world applications. However, our middleware architecture is designed with abstraction as a major goal. Therefore it is also possible to support other protocols and interfaces by implementing a designated DHL instance for it. Such an extension would not affect back-end applications and the RHL. Additionally, we have not yet conducted a thorough analysis of performance and scalability for the middleware.

SUMMARY

The PROMISE project shows how smart embedded systems can be employed for future generations of product lifecycle management applications. Real-world application scenarios not only give a proof-of-concept, but also show the variety of different business problems that can be addressed with the help of PROMISE technology. Transparency about product data and its exchange across company boundaries are the main drivers for these new capabilities. However, it also highlights the importance of standards for product identification, detection and data exchange. These standards have not only to be suitable for a technical problem, but also accepted in the industry to enable interoperability.

REFERENCES

Hall, R. S. (2006). *Oscar: An OSGi framework implementation*. Retrieved September 5, 2006, from http://oscar.objectweb.org

Institute of Information Science and Technologies (ISTI) Pisa. (n.d.). *Domoware*. Retrieved November 22, 2006, from http://domoware.isti.cnr.it/

Konno, S. (n.d.). *CyberLink for Java*. Retrieved December 10, 2006, from http://www.cybergarage.org/net/upnp/java/index.html

Open Symphony. (n.d.). *Quartz Enterprise Job Scheduler Homepage*. Retrieved December 2, 2006, from http://www.opensymphony.com/quartz/

Opgenorth, J. (2005, October). SAP J2EE Migration Guide. *SAP Developer Network (SDN)*.

OSGi Alliance. (n.d.). *Open Services Gateway Initiative*. Retrieved January 21, 2007, from http://www.osgi.org

PROMISE Consortium. (n.d.). *Product lifecycle management and information tracking using smart embedded systems*. Project Web site. Retrieved January 3, 2007, from http://www.promise.no/

SAP Help. (n.d.). Architecture of the SAP Web Application Server. Retrieved January 21, 2007, from http://help.sap.com/saphelp_nw04/helpdata/en/84/54953fc405330ee10000000a114084/content.htm

SUN. (2002). Java 2 Platform, Enterprise Edition (J2EE) 1.3. Retrieved January 29, 2007, from http://java.sun.com/j2ee/1.3/index.jsp

SUN. (2005). Enterprise JavaBeans Technology. Retrieved October 20, 2006, from http://www.java.sun.com/products/ejb/

UPnP Forum. (n.d.). Retrieved September 14, 2006, from http://www.upnp.org

Chapter XXVI
Real−Time Location Tracking Mashup for Enterprise

Louenas Hamdi
SAP Labs Canada, Canada

Rama Gurram
SAP Research, USA

Samir Raiyani
Dolcera Inc., USA

ABSTRACT

Real-time location applications are mainly desktop based and costly for development and maintenance. In this project we worked on a Web service based architecture for monitoring and driving real-time analysis of fire truck missions. We used Web 2.0 technologies on the client side and SAP NetWeaver enterprise service oriented platform on the server side.

INTRODUCTION

Cities and communities have large vehicle fleets for emergency services. These fleets, which are centrally dispatched, need to be deployed efficiently and dispatchers need to know the current location of the vehicles.

Automatic vehicle location (AVL) technology from a number of different vendors has been in use for many years. Our group has designed and implemented a new AVL system from the ground up, with the goal of taking advantage of technologies that are currently gaining popularity in the enterprise, namely, online maps, real-time GPS location tracking, and service-oriented architectures (SOA).

Our prototype uses a service-oriented architecture and Ajax-style user interface technology. Ajax technology is not ideally suited for applications that require real-time updates. For Ajax technology to be widely adopted for applications involving real-time data updates, a server-side push mechanism is needed.

AUTOMATIC VEHICLE LOCATION (AVL)

Automatic vehicle location (AVL) technology has been in use for many years. Devices that obtain location information using the global positioning system (GPS) are installed inside vehicles. These devices are connected to a desktop software application over wireless radio communication networks. Desktop AVL applications are easy to use but expensive to maintain because of their monolithic or thick client implementation. Moreover, the data collected by these applications cannot be easily accessed or analyzed, because the applications usually are not integrated with other enterprise applications such as financial management systems.

NEW TECHNOLOGIES

To address the problems mentioned above, we have designed and implemented a new enterprise-scale AVL system from the ground up. Our goal was to take advantage of the following three technologies that are currently gaining popularity in the enterprise:

1. **Online Maps:** Interactive online maps from Google, ESRI, Yahoo! and Microsoft are very popular. They can now be embedded in Web applications or enterprise portals, usually via a Javascript Application Programming Interface (API). They provide "flicker-free" zooming and panning functionality inside a Web browser. Location information can thus be made easily accessible through a Web browser side-by-side with other enterprise data.

2. **Real-Time GPS Location:** With inexpensive GPS devices, accurate real-time location data collection has become relatively easy.

3. **Service-Oriented Architecture:** Enterprise and geographic information is now available through Web services. This information can be used to create a variety of mashups – applications that combine disparate data from multiple sources into a single application running inside a Web browser.

Besides these, we incorporated two other technologies:

1. **VoIP:** Voice-over-IP technology can be used to reduce communication costs and to integrate voice communication with the workflow inside the dispatch center.

2. **High-Speed Wireless Network Connectivity** such as WiFi, WiMax, and third generation cellular networks (3G): Increased wireless communication bandwidth makes it possible for vehicles to communicate rich information (such as location information) more frequently and using more standardized protocols, such as eXtensible Markup Language (XML) or Simple Object Access Protocol (SOAP).

However, bringing all these technologies together poses many challenges for system integration, usability and reliability.

SYSTEM ARCHITECTURE

The AVL application uses a service-oriented architecture and a mashup structure (Figure 1). The two main services used are:

1. **Real-Time Data Management Service:** This service is used to receive, filter and aggregate real-time location information, and make it available for viewing and analysis

purposes. This service runs on an enterprise application server (SAP NetWeaver).

2. **Maps Service:** Mapping services are provided by companies such as ESRI, Google and Yahoo!. These include map visualization services and services such as geocoding and reverse geocoding (obtaining the latitude and longitude from a street address and vice versa).

The AVL mashup application is built on the SAP NetWeaver platform using the SAP Enterprise Portal development environment. In the AVL application, information from the real-time data management service and mapping service is superimposed on an online interactive map rendered by ESRI, Google, Yahoo! or Microsoft running inside an SAP Enterprise Portal.

APPLICATION FLOW

A GPS device located inside the tracked vehicle sends the vehicle location GPS data to SAP's

real-time data management service over the WiFi network. The real-time data management service filters the location data and pushes it to the SAP Portal server. The SAP Portal server makes this data available to the Web browser.

When the location data gets to the browser, it is "mashed up" with the geographical data provided by ESRI or Google and the vehicle's physical location is shown on the map. This mashup is accomplished using the Javascript API provided by the map service providers. With the help of Asynchronous Javascript and XML (Ajax), as the vehicle travels its location is continuously updated on the map in a flicker-free manner without having to refresh the browser screen.

The dispatcher who is monitoring the vehicle is able to open a contextual menu and call the driver of the vehicle by using Skype or a similar VoIP client running on their computer.

Figure 1. AVL application architecture

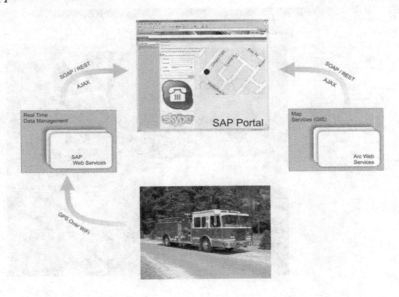

APPLICATION FEATURES AND SCREENSHOTS

The AVL application has been primarily designed for the vehicle dispatcher and the fleet manager. It has the following features:

- For the vehicle dispatcher (Figure 2):

  1. Select vehicles to monitor
  2. Display and update incidents such as fires
  3. Update vehicle location and status in real time
  4. Connect dispatcher to vehicle crew using a Voice-over-IP (VoIP) connection

- For the fleet manager (Figure 3):

  1. Analyze vehicle response time by integrating location data with vehicle dispatch data

  2. Compare vehicle response time with ideal travel time
  3. Feed incident and personnel information to enterprise time management system

In this view, that is, the Dispatcher View, one can search for vehicles and as a result get a list of fire trucks. When the user selects a truck ID, the system displays instantaneously that truck's current position on an online geographical map. If the user clicks on the fire truck icon a contextual menu appears. The user can see the driver's name, the ID and the name of the vehicle and can call the driver using an integrated IP telephony system such as Skype. The user can also send a partially filled text message to the driver.

In this view, that is, the Analysis View, the user can select a truck and display its route corresponding to a chosen period of time. The system retrieves all the historical locations of that truck and clusters them in a reasonable set of icons to

Figure 2. Dispatcher view

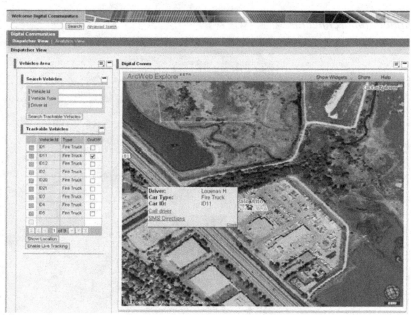

be displayed on the online map on the right-hand side of the picture. The green bullets indicate that the truck was in motion at that location and the red bullets indicate the truck has stopped for some time. If the user clicks on the red bullet the system displays the amount of time spent at that position. The system offers a feature to check whether the path taken was optimal. In this picture the dashed line shows the optimum route to go from the green flag to the black and white flag. On the left-hand side the system outputs the actual time and turn-by-turn directions compared to those of the optimal path.

LESSONS LEARNED

Our goal in this project was to build a service-oriented AVL application for real-time GPS data using online mapping technology. We are currently testing this application with the City of Palo Alto and its fleet of fire trucks. While we have successfully implemented a service-oriented architecture for the real-time data in the AVL application, the online mapping technology has posed several challenges. This section lists the main problems we have faced during the implementation of the prototype.

Map Data and APIs

Most public sector organizations have their own map data with city landmarks and assets marked accurately. Uploading custom map data is not supported by all mapping services providers. Also, there is no standardization for the APIs provided by the various mapping service providers. Mapping service providers are just introducing commercial licensing models for their mapping functionality. Currently, their usage models are expensive for AVL types of applications, since they charge on a per Web service call basis (ESRI, Microsoft). There are no quality of service (QoS) guarantees from mapping service providers either.

Figure 3. Analytics view

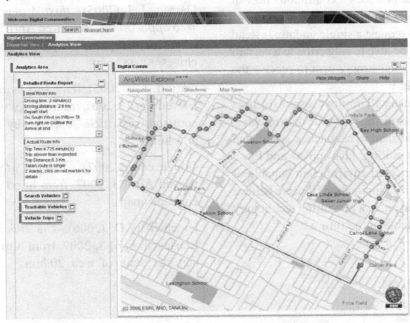

JavaScript

Currently, mashups are built using Javascript running inside the browser. Debugging Javascript is difficult and time-consuming due to the lack of quality debugging tools. The Javascript map APIs from most mapping service providers are fairly limited. Most of these tools do not provide advanced functions like geofencing (drawing a virtual box on a map to identify all the assets inside a particular area on a map, for example) yet.

Ajax

Ajax, when used to update information in a Web page, is basically a polling method. Some Ajax-based Web applications use an asynchronous-polling paradigm, which is polling with a variable cycle.

When it comes to real-time applications, to really implement the time-sensitivity requirement and keep the promise of scalability at the same time, a change in paradigm from synchronous or partially asynchronous to asynchronous is needed. We need a push or streaming system with a mechanism that provides a continuous flow of data from the server to the client, without the client needing to request a single update. Instead the client should be able to subscribe to a certain type of data and then simply wait to receive the updates in real time.

Server-side push will improve responsiveness for applications requiring real-time data updates, without the performance headaches associated with intermittent polling. Java applets and Flash provide a sophisticated environment capable of supporting real-time applications, but we believe a Javascript-based push or streaming technology will be more suitable in the future.

CONCLUSION

It is possible to build real-time applications using service-oriented architectures and Ajax-style user interface technology. However, Ajax technology, due to its inherently synchronous nature, is not ideally suited for applications that require real-time updates. For Ajax technology to be widely adopted for applications involving real-time data updates, a server-side push mechanism is needed.

REFERENCES

Alinone, A. (2005). *Changing the Web paradigm: Moving from traditional Web applications to a new Streaming AJAX style.* Retrieved April 3, 2007, from http://www.lightstreamer.com/Lightstreamer_Paradigm.pdf

Crane, D., Pascarello, E., & James, D. (2005). *Ajax in action.* Manning Publications.

Esri.com. (2007). *ESRI GIS Web Services API.* Retrieved April 3, 2007, from http://arcweb.esri.com/arcwebonline/index.htm

Garrett, J. J. (2005). *Ajax: A new approach to Web applications.* Retrieved April 3, 2007, from http://adaptivepath.com/publications/essays/archives/000385.php

Garrett, J. J. (2005). *Why Ajax matters now.* Retrieved April 3, 2007, from http://www.ok-cancel.com/archives/article/2005/09/why-ajax-matters-now.html

Google.com. (2007). *Google Maps API.* Retrieved April 3, 2007, from http://www.google.com/apis/maps/

Hinchcliffe, D. (2006). *The state of Web 2.0.* Retrieved April 3, 2007, from http://web2.wsj2.com/the_state_of_web_20.htm

Mozilla.org. (2007). *An introduction to AJAX*. Retrieved April 3, 2007, from http://developer. mozilla.org/en/docs/AJAX

O'Reilly, T. (2005). *What is Web 2.0?* Retrieved April 3, 2007, from http://www.oreillynet.com/ pub/a/oreilly/tim/news/2005/09/30/what-is-web-20.html

Wikipedia. (2007). *Comet (programming)*. Retrieved April 3, 2007, from http://en.wikipedia. org/wiki/Comet_(programming)

Wikipedia. (2007). *Rich Internet Application*. Retrieved April 3, 2007, from http://en.wikipedia. org/wiki/Rich_Internet_Application

Xul.fr. (2007). *Ajax tutorial for creating dynamic Web pages, client side*. Retrieved April 3, 2007, *from* http://www.xul.fr/en-xml-ajax.html

Chapter XXVII
Towards Adaptive Security for Ubiquitous Computing Systems:
MOSQUITO and Serenity

Volkmar Lotz
SAP Research, France

Luca Compagna
SAP Research, France

Konrad Wrona
SAP Research, France

ABSTRACT

The flexibility and dynamism of ubiquitous computing systems have a strong impact on the way their security can be achieved, reaching beyond traditional security paradigms like perimeter security and communication channel protection. Constant change of both the system and its environment demand adaptive security architectures, capable of reacting to events, evaluating threat exposure, and taking evolving protection needs into account. We introduce two examples of projects that contribute to meeting the challenges on adaptive security. The first focuses on an architecture that allows for adaptive security in mobile environments based on security services whose adaptation is guided by context information derived from sensor networks. The second addresses engineering aspects of secure ubiquitous computing systems through making security solutions accessible and deployable on demand and following emerging application-level requirements.

INTRODUCTION

A major challenge in securing ubiquitous computing systems is to cope with the increased flexibility and dynamism these systems show: the actual structure and behavior of a system at a particular point of time during its operation is not known in advance and depends on the physical and application context at that time. Consider a service-oriented architecture (cf., the chapter "Ubiquitous Services and Business Processes"), where a business service providing access to a resource—for example, performing a transfer to a bank account—is used in two applications being composed on demand and referring to a different business environment—for example, invoicing in a supply chain management application, and monthly employee payment in a human resources application. Otherwise, in a spontaneous interaction scenario (cf., the section "Ad-Hoc Interaction" of the chapter "Security for Ubiquitous Computing") the number of participants in a communication as well as their roles change over time, with the particular type of interaction depending on the location of an entity, the networking capabilities available, and the particular features of the devices being used.

The flexibility of ubiquitous computing systems has a strong impact on security. The constant change of characteristics of both the system and its environment leads to different protection goals and exposure to threats over the system lifespan. Security thus needs to be adaptive: the security architecture, comprising both policies and mechanisms—as explicated in section "Sample Solutions" of the chapter "Security for Ubiquitous Computing"—needs to react to events, to evaluate the current threat exposure, and to take the actual protection needs into account. For example, the bank transfer service, being used in the human resources application environment, is likely to be subject to privacy regulations and confidentiality requirements protecting the information about an employee's salary, whereas the same service, in a supply chain management environment, is probably required to provide strong traceability of transfers and to enforce the four-eye principle on their approval. The service might only be permitted to run on a mobile device in cases where the transferred amount does not exceed a given threshold, due to the increased vulnerability of wireless communication and the mobile environ-ment to eavesdropping, unless it deploys strong authentication and encryption mechanisms.

The challenge of security solutions adapting to the system's context occurs in development, deployment and operation of ubiquitous computing systems. In a service-oriented architecture, applications are designed on demand in a composite manner through orchestrating services, while taking advantage of the reuse of services in different application contexts. This asks for the application designer to specify the individual protection needs and security policies, and the service ecosystem (cf., the chapter "Ubiquitous Services and Business Processes") and infrastructure to support the selection and the set-up of the appropriate security architecture as well as its configuration, all being accessible to an application designer not assumed to be a security expert. Such an effort needs to take into account that the system as well as its environment and protection needs might change over time; thus, events indicating a security relevant change—for example, change of a physical condition or location—need to be identified, the actions to be taken upon detection of the event—for example, the modification of the access control policy or the strength of encryption—need to be specified, and the monitoring of the events as well as the execution of the appropriate actions need to be enforced.

The remainder of this chapter introduces two examples of projects that contribute to meeting the challenges on adaptive security. The first focuses on an architecture that allows for adaptive security in mobile environments based on security services that—like application services in a service ecosystem—can be composed on demand to meet individual security requirements, and whose adaptation is guided by context information derived from sensor networks. The second addresses engineering aspects of secure ubiquitous computing systems through making security solutions accessible and applicable—in terms of integration and operation—on demand

and following emerging application-level requirements.

MOBILE WORKERS' SECURE BUSINESS APPLICATIONS IN UBIQUITOUS ENVIRONMENTS: THE MOSQUITO PROJECT

Background

The aim of a European research project—MOSQUITO (Mobile Workers' Secure Business Applications in Ubiquitous Environment) (MOSQUITO, 2007; Wrona & Gomez, 2006)—was to provide a secure, trusted and ubiquitous access to business applications. The project developed an easy-to-use and flexible technical infrastructure, required so that mobile workers and their clients can perform daily business processes in a secure and collaborative manner. A particularly important segment of the teleworking market is mobile professionals, such as medical personnel, social workers, insurance agents, technicians, traveling executives, consultants and sales representatives. In today's businesses, sensitivity to the needs of customers, closeness to their demands and tight relations with customers' daily operational business processes is essential for success. This is why marketing, sales and production companies send out their mobile work forces in order to be as close to their customers as possible, if not permanently on their sites. However, this world is still characterized by obstacles such as inadequate communication facilities, incompatibilities between applications, and system boundaries that actually hinder interoperability between clients' and customers' systems more than they support it. This is equally true for security mechanisms that are insufficient, meeting neither the requirements of business users nor those of their clients—for example, when data is being used on systems that do not belong to the owner of the data.

MOSQUITO Architecture

Figure 1 gives an overview of the MOSQUITO architecture. The platform provides basic security functionalities like protecting key material, authenticating a user connected to a device, or ensuring the integrity of the sensitive data. The platform also gives access to local context information through sensors. The heart of the MOSQUITO architecture is a middleware including a set of security services. Finally, applications are either written on top of the middleware or, in case of legacy applications, are adapted to use this middleware. Application-specific policies are defined to configure the middleware.

At a high level, the developer of a MOSQUITO-based system may be confronted with the assembly of a workflow together with some basic initialization of the MOSQUITO components.

Figure 2 depicts the interactions taking place between the various components that implement this workflow behind the scenes and how they have to be set up to properly interoperate with a service-based application. The interface to the

Figure 1. The MOSQUITO architecture

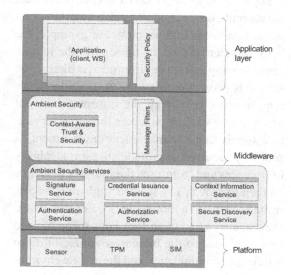

Figure 2. MOSQUITO framework from developer's point of view

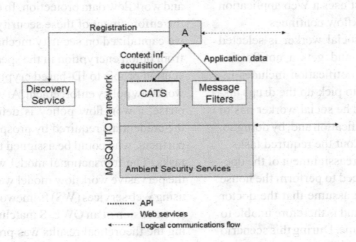

MOSQUITO framework from the application developer's point of view consists of the message filters, Context Information Acquisition and Trust Service (CATS) and the discovery service.

MOSQUITO Scenario

In the following, we describe a typical scenario for how the MOSQUITO framework is used in the healthcare application domain, in particular, elderly care. A patient Bob, who suffers from restricted mobility and stays more or less at home, has subscribed to a monitoring service that ensures assistance in case of illness. Bob's health status is monitored by several sensors, for example, temperature or pulse sensors. A monitoring application analyzes the data and in case of irregularities (high temperature or high pulse rate) a workflow is initiated to schedule a house visit to the patient and provide medication if necessary.

The first step of the triggered workflow is to select physicians who are able to make a house visit. The selection is based on the patient's preferences and needs such as language and location. The first physician gets a notification via mobile

phone about the house visit to make, which he has to accept. If he refuses the next doctor is notified. Once a doctor has accepted the notification, he is responsible for scheduling an appointment with the patient and for making the house call on time.

The physician visits the patient and conducts an examination of the patient. The physician may require access to the patient's medical data. The patient's data are stored on a Medical Information Portal (MIP). The physician uses a Web application on his laptop or his mobile device (PDA) to view the medical data. Access to the medical data is controlled on a context-aware way. In particular, the physician gets access to the patient's data only when he has accepted the house call notification (workflow is in the examination state) and when he is close to the patient. Proximity is evaluated based on the physical distance (GPS-based) between the patient and the physician. Both patient and doctor are equipped with a mobile phone that can provide the GPS location.

The examination may end with the prescription of a drug. The prescription is issued electronically via Web application and is sent automatically to the nearest pharmacy. A pharmacist will take care of the medication and prepare or order the drugs if necessary. As soon as the medication is ready for dispatch, the pharmacist uses a Web application to confirm and the workflow continues.

In the next step, a social worker is selected (based on availability) and gets a notification via mobile phone. The notification includes information about where to pick up the drugs and their delivery address. The social worker has to explicitly accept the notification and, by doing so, he commits to carrying out the required tasks.

A special case is the reassignment of the doctor who has already agreed to perform the house call. In our scenario we assume that the doctor gets an emergency call and is therefore unable to make the house visit in time. During this scenario the issued workflow task is reassigned to the next available doctor.

Pervasive Workflow

The demonstrator that has been developed throughout the MOSQUITO project outlines the collaboration between actors from the healthcare application domain. As part of the MOSQUITO framework, we also developed a workflow management system—so-called pervasive workflow (Montagut & Molva, 2006a; 2006b)—easing the dynamic collaboration of partners across organizational boundaries. The pervasive workflow engine deployed on each site involved in a distributed collaboration is in charge of orchestrating the overall process execution. Compared to usual agent-based solutions, this model lowers the risk of malicious code hidden in messages exchanged during a workflow instance. As opposed to centralized workflow management systems, the distributed execution of workflows raises security constraints due to the lack of dedicated infrastructure assuring the management and control tasks of workflow instances. As a result, basic security features such as compliance of the workflow execution with the predefined plan are no longer assured. We categorize the security requirements we identified for distributed workflow systems into three

main categories: authorization, proof of execution and workflow data protection. In order to achieve the enforcement of these security requirements, we capitalized on security mechanisms ranging from onion encryption in the specification of execution proofs to ID-based cryptography for the workflow policy enforcement. At workflow design phase, a workflow policy is defined to specify the credentials required by prospective business partners, who could be assigned to the workflow tasks. The transactional model we designed for the pervasive workflow model was implemented using Web services (WS) framework. On one hand an extension of an OWL-S matchmaker integrating the theoretical results was proposed. On the other hand, we implemented a proof of concept of the suggested transactional protocol capitalizing on the WS-Coordination specification. Use of contextual information during the workflow execution was demonstrated by including doctor's availability as one of the parameters.

Evaluation

Basic security mechanisms, for example, integrity, confidentiality, and availability, are common grounds for any business scenario. However, healthcare applications introduce specific security requirements such as non-repudiation or accountability. Our work towards the integration of security mechanisms to match these requirements included two aspects. First, our demonstrator makes use of the special security component (CryptoTerminal) in order to assign business partners to workflow tasks and in order to enable signing of relevant workflow documents. This is, for instance, the case for electronic prescriptions that are exchanged throughout the healthcare workflow. This enables, on the one hand, to gather commitments from business partners during the partner discovery procedure as soon as they accept to be involved in a given workflow instance, and, on the other hand, to identify the issuer of critical documents, as those are digitally signed.

Second, we have designed security mechanisms to ensure both runtime and "a posteriori" verification of compliance with the actual plan of execution by means of a policy-based approach. The solutions that we currently provide are basic mechanisms that partially answer the required security mechanisms, which are accountability and non-repudiation. Designing and implementing mobile and secure logs would have been a perfect means to solve the limitations of our current solutions yet this research effort was outside of the MOSQUITO project main focus.

Context-awareness is a key feature in MOSQUITO that comes in several flavors. Context may be used directly by applications that want to adapt to their environment, in which case its accuracy has an impact on the correct operation of an application. However, context may also be used by security mechanisms, in particular at the access control level, in which case accuracy is fundamental to prevent security breaches that may threaten the availability of services or the confidentiality or integrity of their data. This in particular requires the context acquisition process to be able to check how trustworthy the acquired context information is. The integration of context information into MOSQUITO framework relies on two components: the Context Information Acquisition and Trust Service (CATS), and the Context Information Service (CIS). The CATS is used in order to figure out where to acquire the CI among a set of available CIS servers. The CATS may either select an appropriate CIS out of a static list of known and reliable services, or rely on the Secure Discovery Service to locate CI Services based on a dynamic and semantically rich profile. The CATS also provides basic algorithms for evaluating the trustworthiness and reliability of the context information acquired before providing it to interested applications. The prototype implementation of the CATS and the CIS was equipped with two trust evaluation methods: a PKI-based validation of context information, and a voting-based validation of context information, based on the comparison of context acquisition from a set of redundant CI Services.

The MOSQUITO framework supports a wide range of underlying communication technologies and execution platforms, including wireless networks and mobile devices. Nevertheless, implementing a service-oriented architecture, and heavily relying on Web services has twofold consequences: on one hand, it ensures an easy integration with existing service ecosystems and enterprise systems and makes the framework easier to use for developers familiar with standard Web services technology. On the other hand, it puts higher requirements regarding the communications bandwidth and computing power of end-user devices. In particular, it is currently not possible to execute the full MOSQUITO framework on a small mobile device. In our demonstration and experiments we have relied on laptops and tablet PCs, limiting the use of the phone to personal authentication and signature. However, high-end mobile phones and PDAs already support Web services, and we believe that in the near future, the execution of a complete MOSQUITO framework on much smaller devices should be possible. The bandwidth requirements of the MOSQUITO applications are compatible with most of the existing technologies, including GPRS, 3G, and WLAN. The delay induced by the processing and communication is noticeable in our demonstrator, but we believe that it could be significantly reduced by optimizing the implementation and deployment configuration.

The MOSQUITO framework provides a robust and innovative middleware concept for context-aware business applications in mobile environments. Although it does support the dynamic formation and execution of a workflow, the implemented interaction scheme is however not fully spontaneous—that is, although it does permit dynamic utilization of WLAN or mobile networks, currently it does not support fully ad hoc communications. In every ubiquitous environment, a significant amount of implementation work is currently related to the development of an interface between middleware (i.e., CIS) and the physical sensor or sensor network. An easy and seamless integration of sensors and sensor networks with services is still an open issue.

Conclusions

The MOSQUITO project investigated into a middleware supporting secure, collaborative, and ubiquitous access to applications for mobile workers. Key features of MOSQUITO include the support of context-awareness through sensor networks and pervasive workflows that allow distributing workflows across a set of devices without central control. MOSQUITO has been validated by means of a prototype supporting an elderly care scenario, where context information is used to control access to medical data through a mobile device, and a pervasive workflow facilitates the coordination of the actions of the different stakeholders being involved.

SYSTEMS ENGINEERING FOR SECURITY AND DEPENDABILITY: THE SERENITY PROJECT

Background

There is a common understanding that security solutions built into systems after the fact (of design decisions made and system development done) turn out to be ineffective or even inappropriate. Security needs to be designed into a system from the very beginning, leading to a discipline of security engineering supporting all phases of secure system construction from security requirements analysis to security mechanisms design, and stretching out to system deployment and operation. While there is a rich body of design principles, building blocks, and case studies available, for example, Anderson (2001), their integration in

development and deployment environments is still immature. The systems engineer is, thus, required to be security aware, and the assessment of the security contribution of a mechanism and its appropriateness for the requirements at hand are left to the security experts.

The engineering challenge is amplified when considering ubiquitous computing: flexibility and dynamism demand adaptive security architectures, as motivated in the introduction, and new security solutions have to be deployed on the fly. Thus, a designer or developer needs an immediate link between emerging security requirements and implemented solutions to satisfy them. The highly distributed nature of and decentralized control in ubiquitous computing systems demand the consideration of interoperability and the heterogeneity of infrastructures. For instance, in a service ecosystem, a security mechanism protecting a service or a resource needs to interact with other security mechanisms owned by different entities, taking interoperability, consistency of security properties, and potential side effects into account. Still, dynamic behavior does not allow evidence to be provided that a security architecture effective at one point of time will still be appropriate at some future point of time, thus requiring continuous monitoring of the security status of the running system.

The Serenity Approach

Following the above, ubiquitous computing demands the dynamic application of security expertise (Mana et al., 2007). The Serenity project (Serenity, 2006) provides a framework to support this goal through:

- Systematic capture of security expertise in terms of enhanced security and dependability (S&D) patterns and integration schemes, linked to ready-to-integrate implementations of security solutions, for example, in terms of security services.

- Access to expertise through a S&D library integrated into the development and run-time environment.
- A monitoring framework, able to capture context information and triggered by events being specified in the S&D patterns.
- Deployment support for S&D solutions based on S&D patterns and integration schemes, taking information about the system architecture and its context into account.
- An end-user interface, allowing the specification of S&D requirements and their mapping to solutions and implementations through the S&D library, and a system interface allowing retrieval of context and interaction across Serenity-enabled systems.

Figure 3 shows the framework architecture resulting from this approach (Sánchez-Cid et al., 2006). The Serenity framework has to be instantiated each time it has to be applied to a concrete scenario, for example, an application, a device, or a security domain. After specifying the

Figure 3. The Serenity framework

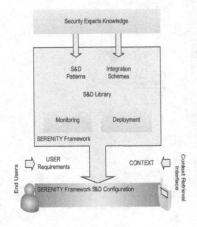

security requirements by the user (i.e., a designer, a developer, an administrator, or an application user), the framework, based on the context information retrieved, suggests appropriate security solutions through S&D patterns and integration schemes, allowing reasoning about alternate options, constraints, and interdependencies. This investigation leads to a final selection of a set of security solutions comprising the system's security architecture and its deployment. Note that the framework is aware of the deployed architecture through a model describing the actual security configuration, allowing exploitation of this information upon monitoring the system at run-time or even exchanging it with other framework instances.

Patterns and Integration Schemes

The notions of S&D patterns and integration schemes are crucial to the approach, since they contain the information about an S&D solution's effects, the link to satisfied requirements and implementations, as well as the specification of potential interferences when combining different solutions.

Patterns were first introduced in software engineering (Beck & Cunningham, 1987; Buschmann et al., 1996). This approach was then adopted to schematically describe security solutions in an informal way, for example, in Fernandez (2000; 2004), Schumacher (2003), and Schumacher et al. (2006). Security patterns describe a security solution in terms of the problem context (an abstract description of assumptions made and not to be confused with the use of the notion of "context" above), a problem statement, a solution description and implementation advice. They explicitly target humans taking the patterns as guidelines or rules-of-thumb in their development activities.

Serenity significantly extends the notion of patterns in several dimensions:

- Serenity patterns refer to properties that are provided upon deployment of the pattern (assuming all specified constraints are met, or enforced by the framework). This allows us to link user requirements to patterns, since they are expressed in terms of properties as well.

- Serenity patterns, in general, refer to an implementation, that is, program code, that is ready to be integrated into a given system implementation through a defined interface.

- Serenity patterns include obligations on the run-time of the system in terms of events to be monitored and controls to be imposed. The obligations are enforced through the framework.

- Serenity patterns are parameterized and can be hierarchical, thus increasing their flexibility and applicability.

- Security solutions in Serenity patterns are verified, preferably through formal methods. This asks for much more precise specification of a solution than the standard pattern approach does.

- A particular type of Serenity patterns, called integration schemes, allow capturing potential interference in case of patterns being combined, as well as imposing constraints with respect to their deployment.

Figure 4 shows the modeling artifacts used in Serenity. In addition to patterns, properties and implementations, the figure introduces classes as an additional abstraction level. This allows consideration of the fact that security requirements are often given in terms of general notions (like confidentiality, integrity, non-repudiation), with these notions then being refined according to individual interpretations.

Evaluation

The Serenity idea is ambitious and likely to change the way secure systems are developed, deployed and operated. The Serenity library of patterns and integration schemes facilitates a systematic approach to accessing security expertise, based

Figure 4. Serenity modeling artifacts: Classes, patterns, and implementation

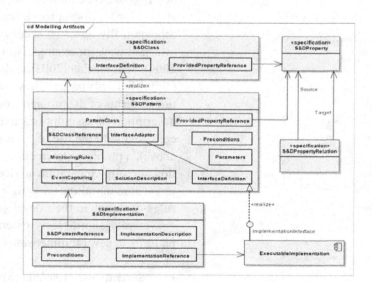

on specifications of security properties covering different layers of abstraction, from business level to network and devices level. The Serenity framework provides means to monitor and reason about a deployed security architecture and to adapt it if necessary. Thus, major requirements on security in ubiquitous computing systems are met: accessibility of security solutions to the non-expert developer, and automated support for adapting security solutions to system evolution.

The key success factors for the Serenity approach include the coverage and quality of the library entries, the integration of the specification means across the abstraction levels, the control of security architectures through the framework, and the interoperability of the security solutions. The latter is particularly challenging in heterogeneous infrastructures that are characteristic to ubiquitous computing. To ensure the feasibility of the approach, Serenity is evaluated through a number of case studies, including such varying domains as e-business, sensor networks, mobile communications, e-government, and air traffic management.

Conclusions

Serenity addresses the problem of security engineering for ubiquitous computing systems through capturing security expertise by means of enhanced patterns and integration schemes as well as providing a framework for components and devices supporting the systematic development, deployment and control of security solutions. Since the framework is aware of the deployed security architecture, feedback from security monitoring can be used to adapt the architecture according to new requirements or system evolution. Serenity's feasibility critically depends on meeting the challenge of interoperability of the solutions made available through the patterns of the Serenity library.

REFERENCES

Anderson, R. (2001). *Security engineering*. Wiley & Sons.

Buschmann, F., Meunier, R., Rohnert, H., & Sommerlad, P. (1996). *A system of patterns. Pattern-oriented software architecture*. Wiley & Sons.

Beck, K., & Cunningham, W. (1987). *Using pattern languages for object-oriented programs* (Technical Report CR-87-43). Apple Computer, Tektronix.

Fernandez, E.B. (2000). *Metadata and authorization patterns* (Technical Report). Florida: Atlantic University.

Fernandez, E.B. (2004). Two patterns for Web services security. In *Proceedings of the International Symposium on Web Services and Applications* (ISWS04), Las Vegas, Nevada.

MOSQUITO. (2007). Retrieved from www.mosquito-project.org

Mana, A., Rudolph, C., Spanoudakis, G., Lotz, V., Massacci, F., Melideo, M., & Lopez-Cobo, J.S. (2007). Security engineering for ambient intelligence: A manifesto. In H. Mouratidis & P. Giorgini (Eds.), *Integrating Security and Software Engineering*. Hershey, PA: IDEA Group Publishing.

Montagut, F., & Molva, R. (2006a). Augmenting Web services composition with transactional requirements. In *Proceedings of the IEEE International Conference on Web Services*. Chicago, USA (pp. 91-98).

Montagut, F., & Molva, R. (2006b). Towards transactional pervasive workflows. In *Proceedings of the 10th IEEE International Enterprise Distributed Object Computing Conference*, Hong-Kong (pp. 141-152).

Schumacher, M. (2003). *Security engineering with patterns: Origins, theoretical models, and new applications* (LNCS 2754). Springer Verlag.

Schumacher, M., Fernadez, E.B., Hybertson, D., Buschmann, F., & Sommerlad, P. (2006). *Security patterns: Integrating security and systems engineering.* Wiley & Sons.

Serenity. (2006). Retrieved from www.serenity-project.org

Sánchez-Cid, F., Munoz, A., Serrano, D., & Gago, M.C. (2006). *Software engineering techniques applied to AmI: Security patterns.* In *Proceedings of the First International Conference on Ambient Intelligence Developments* (AmID'06). Springer Verlag.

Wrona, K., & Gomez, L. (2006). Context-aware security and secure context-awareness in ubiquitous computing environments. In *Annales Universitatis Mariae Curie-Sklodowska, Sectio AI Informatica* (Vol. 4).

Chapter XXVIII
Multimodal Warehouse Project

Samir Raiyani
Dolcera Inc., USA

Matthias Winkler
SAP Research CEC Dresden, Germany

ABSTRACT

In this chapter, we present the Multimodal Warehouse Project, which aimed at applying multimodal interaction to a warehouse picking process. We provide an overview of the warehouse picking procedure as well as the overall architecture of the multimodal picking application and technologies applied to design the application. Furthermore, we describe the execution of user tests of the picking application at a warehouse and present the results of these tests. In this way, the authors hope to provide the reader with a better understanding of how multimodal systems can be built and the opportunities as well as the challenges of applying multimodal technology to real-world application scenarios.

INTRODUCTION

Multimodal interaction is described in the chapter "Multimodal and Federated Interaction" of this book as "… the use of more than one modality in a single interface." In a pilot project, SAP Research applied multimodality to a warehouse picking process, where mobile workers collect goods into deliveries. The goal was to apply mobile technology combined with multimodal interaction in order to improve the user efficiency and accuracy (Raiyani & Kumar, 2006).

In this chapter, we will present the multimodal warehouse application and the pilot project we did at a distribution center for video games. The reader will get an insight into a possible architectural approach for building a mobile multimodal system. She will also see some of the advantages as well as difficulties of applying multimodal user interface (UI) technology in real life.

Figure 1. Warehouse scenario

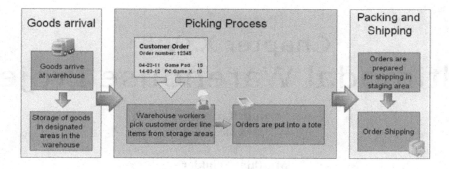

THE PICKING PROCESS

As goods make their way from a manufacturer to a customer, they are "staged" at warehouses along the way. When goods arrive at a warehouse, they are stored in their designated shelves. Thereafter, they are assembled into deliveries based on customer orders. A warehouse worker picks the items from the shelves according to a customer order. The worker reads the printed order form, selects the relevant items, and places them into a tote or a box. Once all the items have been picked, they are packed together and shipped to the customer. The entire process is illustrated in Figure 1.

PROBLEM DESCRIPTION

The picking process is very time consuming and errors, such as picking incorrect items or incorrect quantities, occur frequently. Errors may occur, for example, when a warehouse worker accidentally skips a line or when they may pick the wrong item.

It was the goal of the multimodal warehouse project to improve the accuracy and speed of the picking process by using a mobile device with multiple modalities.

THE MULTIMODAL WAREHOUSE APPLICATION

The warehouse system consists of two main parts: a multimodal user interface running on a handheld device (an Intermec 700 PDA), and a customer order application running on the server. The PDA is connected to the server over a wireless LAN. The setup is depicted in Figure 2. The communication between the multimodal user interface and the customer order application is handled over a wireless connection. The server may access order data from a data source. Both the multimodal user interface, as well as the customer order application, are described below in detail.

The Multimodal User Interface

The multimodal user interface runs inside a multimodal Web browser, which provides standard Web browser functionality such as HTML rendering and JavaScript handling. Besides that, it offers voice recognition and text-to-speech services. These technologies are provided by IBM voice technology (ViaVoice).

The multimodal Web browser also supports the XHTML + VoiceXML (X+V) standard (Axelsson, Cross, Ferrans, McCobb, Raman, & Wilson, 2004), which combines technologies

Figure 2. Warehouse application setup

such as XHTML, VoiceXML, and XML Events. XHTML forms the host language and VoiceXML is used to enhance the GUI interface with speech interaction. XML Events form the glue between these two languages by allowing the designer to integrate event listeners into the markup and defining the corresponding event handlers for events such as shifting focus to a form element or loading a page.

It is possible, for example, to present an HTML form on a screen that corresponds to a speech dialog. When the user shifts focus on the HTML form from one field to another, the speech dialog also shifts to the corresponding section. User input can be given through both modalities. The input information will be synchronized between the modalities through JavaScript code or special elements of the X+V standard. It is thus possible to provide a seamless multimodal user experience. Figure 3 shows a form, which is rendered for graphical user interfaces, and a possible corresponding speech dialog.

The speech recognition system uses grammars, which describe the vocabulary needed for the dialog. This has been described in Chapter XVII ("Mouth and Ear Interaction"). In the above example, grammars would be needed for the possible responses to the name and city questions. The designer can create her own grammars according to her special needs. More information about grammars can be found in the W3C's Speech Recognition Grammar Specifications (Hunt & McGlashan, 2004).

The example voice dialog presented in Figure 4 should give an understanding of the structure of the voice dialog used in the multimodal warehouse application.

The voice engine used for the multimodal Web browser runs fully on the client side of a multimodal application. The advantage of this approach is that no communication between the client and the server is needed in order to recognize and evaluate users' voice inputs. The major

Figure 3. GUI form and corresponding speech dialog

Name: [ ]
City: [ ]
[Submit]

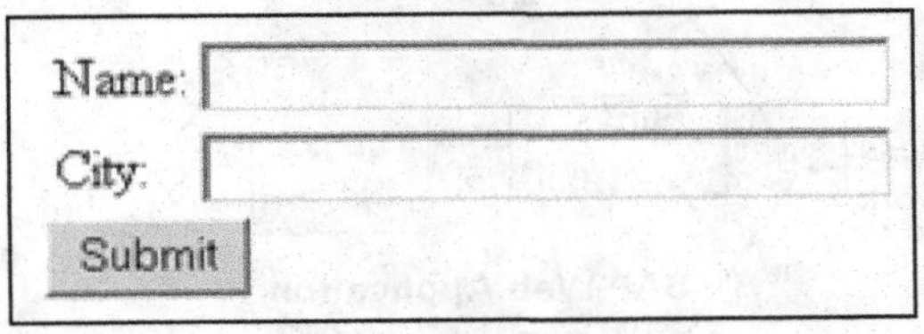

Device: *What is your name?* User response: _____

Device: *What city?* User response: _____

drawback is that voice recognition is a CPU and memory-intensive process. Mobile client devices have limited processing power and memory and are not always suited to executing such a task.

Multimodal interaction is supported by the handheld device, which provides a number of technological features for interacting with applications. The following list presents different modalities that are applied for the warehouse application and the technical features of the PDA supporting these modalities.

- Display of visual information -> small color screen
- Stylus-based interaction -> touch sensitive screen
- Voice-based interaction -> headset
- Reading of barcode information -> bar code scanner
- Keyboard interaction -> small Qwerty keyboard integrated into the device

The Customer Order Application

The customer order application was developed using the Apache Struts framework (The Apache Software Foundation, 2006) and J2EE. The Struts framework enables a separation of concerns according to the MVC paradigm (model-view-

controller) (Sun Microsystems Inc., 2003). While the model and controller were implemented using J2EE, the views were implemented as Java Server Pages (JSP).

Figure 5 presents an overview of the architecture of the multimodal warehouse application presenting the components of the user interface as well as the application server.

THE WAREHOUSE PILOT PROJECT

The warehouse picking application was tested in an actual warehouse environment. The user tests took place in a relatively noisy environment (conveyer belts and forklifts running in the back-

Figure 4. Voice dialog from picking application

System: *Please go to Aisle 30, section 11.*
System: *Level 04, bin 08.*
User: *Ready.*
System: *Pick 10 each.*
User: *Finished.*

Figure 5. Architecture of the warehouse application

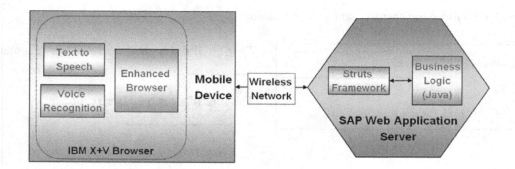

ground). We executed the tests in this real-world setting in order to find answers to some of the following questions:

- How well does a voice-enabled system work in a noisy work environment?
- What is the performance of such a system?
- What voice commands are best suited for the process?
- Does multimodal interaction improve the accuracy of the picking process?
- What modalities do the users prefer for the interaction with the application?

In order to test our application, we executed three different tests. The first test was executed by two experienced male workers whom we gave a five-minute introduction to the system. This test helped us evaluate our first prototype, which led to some changes in the voice dialog as well as to the HTML user interface.

For the second test, we were mainly concerned with the performance of the system. Two female and three male warehouse workers participated in this test. All of them were relatively inexperienced in the picking process. As a result of this test, we found that our system was relatively slow (30-40 seconds per pick) as compared to the standard picking procedure (about 10 seconds per pick). We therefore made a number of changes to the voice dialog, since their rendering was found to be the most time consuming component.

We also found that high-pitched female voices were difficult to recognize by the speech recognition engine. It was not possible for us to find a solution to this problem. Most likely this would have involved changes to the speech recognition engine itself, which is a product of a different software company and is not under our control.

The last test was conducted together with three experienced male warehouse workers to whom we gave a 10-20 minute introduction to the system.

We also had them experiment with the application and made adjustments to their headsets in order to ensure the workers had a basic confidence in interacting with the system.

There are a number of test results that are important to mention, as they provide answers for the questions listed above:

- **Voice recognition:** From our observation the voice recognition works very well, even in as noisy an environment as the warehouse. Nevertheless, there were two limitations: the system does have trouble in recognizing high-pitched voices as well as those with strong accents. For our tests, we had some workers with a Spanish language background. For them, it was considerably harder to pronounce the voice commands well enough for the system to recognize them. In general, it is important for people to get used to the voice-based interaction.
- **Speed of the system:** The system was too slow in comparison to the standard work process. During the testing phase, we were able to decrease the duration of a pick from 30-40 seconds to an average of 24 seconds through restructuring of the voice dialog. The target time was 10 seconds per pick.
- **Voice commands:** When users receive good instructions as to which commands to use, there are fewer problems. Users will eventually use different words with the same meaning: yes, sure, yep... The designer should be aware of this when designing the grammar.
- **Accuracy:** We assume that the accuracy of the picking process increases when it is executed using the multimodal warehouse application. This assumption is based on the fact that we observed a number of mistakes during the standard picking procedure but no mistake while our application was used. Our observation sample, though, was too small to draw a well-founded conclusion.

- **Choice of modality:** We observed that the workers used a certain modality constantly for a certain task. The choice happened very early in the course of the test. Once a certain modality seemed to work better for them, they always used this one. This is in line with research results in Oviatt, DeAngeli, & Kuhn (2003).

CONCLUSION

In general people seemed to enjoy working with the system. Some people found it to be "cool." Nevertheless there were some issues such as the performance of the system. These issues were addressed and the multimodal warehouse application is in use by several customers of the SAP partner Topsystem SystemHaus GmbH. It can thus be said that multimodality can successfully contribute to facilitate user interaction in ubiquitous computing scenarios.

REFERENCES

Axelsson, J., Cross, C., Ferrans, J., McCobb, G., Raman, T.V., & Wilson, L. (2004). *XHTML+Voice Profile 1.2*. Retrieved February 23, 2007, from http://www.voicexml.org/specs/multimodal/x+v/12/spec.html

Hunt, A., & McGlashan, S. (2004, March 16). *Speech Recognition Grammar Specification Version 1.0*. W3C Recommendation. Retrieved February 23, 2007, from http://www.w3.org/TR/speech-grammar/

IBM WebSphere (ViaVoice). (n.d.). Retrieved February 23, 2007, from http://www-306.ibm.com/software/voice/viavoice/dev/

Oviatt, S., DeAngeli, A., & Kuhn, K. (2003). Integration and synchronization of input modes during multimodal human-computer interaction. Retrieved February 23, 2007, from http://www.cse.ogi.edu/CHCC/Publications/Integration_Synchronization_Input_Modes_oviatt.pdf

Raiyani, S., & Kumar, J.M. (2006). Multimodal warehouse application. *In ACM Special Issue: Gadgets '06* (pp. 34-37). New York: ACM Press.

Sun Microsystems Inc. (2003). *Model-View-Controller*. Retrieved February 23, 2007, from http://java.sun.com/blueprints/patterns/MVC.html

The Apache Software Foundation. (2006). *Apache Struts Framework*. Retrieved February 23, 2007, from http://struts.apache.org/1.3.5/

Chapter XXIX
Business Grids:
Grid Computing for Business Applications

Wolfgang Gerteis
SAP Research, UK

ABSTRACT

The following short chapter discusses upcoming opportunities for using research results and developments provided by the grid computing community in a business computing context. In particular, grid-based approaches may offer various opportunities to access compute and storage power as well as expensive organizational settings of business software dynamically, as need arises and grows. The chapter starts with an introduction and motivation, followed by a systematic outline of possible application scenarios. Finally, the relevant state-of-the-art in grid computing is reviewed in the light of the goals outlined before.

BUSINESS GRIDS: MOTIVATION AND OBJECTIVES

The market for business software applications is evolving rapidly, driven by an increasing need to make processes more agile and more effective as business strategies and operating models evolve, and also to reduce the total cost of ownership (TCO) associated with these applications. In fact, the speed and cost of accommodating business level changes within an ICT landscape will increasingly become a competitive advantage for businesses, and therefore ICT concepts and technologies that support this notion of an "adaptive enterprise" will be a competitive advantage for SAP solutions.

At the same time, the complexity of software applications has grown rapidly, to the point where future applications can no longer be built as monolithic silos. In response, many enterprise application providers, including SAP, have migrated to service-oriented architectures to provide greater flexibility and adaptability. This affects at least the application layer. However, this approach also presents greater challenges on providing and managing the supporting ICT infrastructures needed to host, allocate, and execute these new applications. In this context, an infrastructure includes general hardware (CPU, memory and storage), local and wide-area networking infrastructures, and database implementations. The traditional methods of sizing and resource planning that were suitable for very large, but fairly standard and static, application configurations do not scale well to much more flexible applications based on SOA technology. This applies both during the initial deployment of a SOA-based solution and during its operational phase, if forced to "adapt" quickly to new business strategies.

We foresee two related technologies, namely grid computing and adaptive computing, as potential solutions to these infrastructure level challenges. Grid computing is now emerging from the research labs and starting to materialize into concrete technologies and products that provide greater flexibility and adaptability for software hosting and execution environments. Nevertheless, grid computing still primarily targets scientific domains rather than business applications. The Next Generation Grid expert group has developed a European vision for grid research to accelerate the evolution from tools for solving computation and data-intensive problems towards a much more general purpose infrastructure supporting complex business processes and workflows across virtual organizations spanning multiple administrative domains (see NGG, 2006). This vision is consistent with SAP's requirements for more flexible ICT infrastructures. At the same time, hardware vendors are providing a broad range of adaptive computing solutions based on concepts such as virtualization technology. At present these are well suited for a "general purpose" ICT infrastructure but are usually based on proprietary technologies and therefore lack the independency from hardware vendors, which has always been critical for SAP.

We have adopted the term *business grid* (Franke et al., 2007) as a vision for bringing together different aspects of adaptive computing and grid computing to build more effective and more efficient general-purpose infrastructures for hosting service-oriented enterprise applications. In effect, we foresee that business grids will extend the flexibility of service-oriented architectures from the application level to the infrastructure level, delivering a number of significant benefits to SAP, including:

- Being able to more flexibly adapt ICT solutions for businesses will not only strengthen the market position of SAP customers but also the market position of SAP itself, since flexibility of SAP solutions is a core requirement of businesses.
- Flexibility from the application level to the infrastructure level will become a cornerstone for hosting future SAP solutions.
- Reduction in TCO as well as an increased return on investment (ROI) and reliability arising from more flexible and re-configurable infrastructures will help open up the multi-tenancy and SME market for SAP.
- Improving the way SAP deals with non-functional requirements, especially performance and resource consumption, will be an important step towards an industrialized development of software and operation of IT solutions.

In summary, our motivation for business grids research is that it could significantly extend the flexibility of service-oriented architectures from the application level to the infrastructure level. The remainder of this chapter explores various aspects of this vision in more detail. We first explore the concepts of business grids by considering a number of different solution perspectives. Then we present an initial gap analysis that compares the current state-of-the-art in various grid related technologies, relative to the requirements of SAP for an adaptive landscape. Finally we outline some technical challenges for SAP Research and roadmap a research strategy and initial project portfolio toward addressing those challenges.

A VISION FOR BUSINESS GRIDS

Business grids aim to provide SAP infrastructures "as a utility" so that software and hardware resources (such as applications, components, systems, and servers) can be easily operated under frequently changing business conditions (such as changing strategies, models, processes, workload, etc.). This spans across the whole life-cycle of solutions and systems from their first specification up to the final end of operation. The following sections detail the vision of business grids from various solution perspectives.

Solution Perspective: Automation Areas

The goal of business grids is to automate the operation of SAP infrastructures. This may span across the following areas:

- **Engineering:** Software engineering (of applications, components, and middleware) may integrate or even automates the capture of business grids' related requirements.
- **Landscape Design:** Landscape design and, in particular, sizing, consist in determining the amount of hardware needed to host a specific customer solution. Typically, sizing is a joint activity of customers and consultants combining knowledge about the customer business and the relevant software solutions. At the moment, sizing can be supported by some tools that map solution requirements onto hardware demand. Business grids should support such an automated sizing procedure, which relates model information about the customized business solution to respective resource demands.

- **Resource Allocation:** The allocation of hardware resources to host specific software components must be automated. Furthermore, it would be beneficial if the allocated hardware resources are even sized corresponding to the provider's objectives.
- **Deployment:** The deployment of solutions on existing hardware resources is to be automated. This may include the deployment of operating systems, application servers, and business components.
- **Resource Adaptation:** Hardware resources are dynamically re-sized and re-allocated during run-time depending on changes in the demand. This includes the migration of solutions already deployed if necessary.
- **Operation:** The full system operation and administration (e.g., software logistics) are automated as much as possible. Furthermore, the systems have to have a kind of self-adapting capability, such as self-healing or self-adjusting.

Solution Perspective: Environments

Business grids can operate in various contexts, which may influence the focus on specific automation areas and specific research challenges. Following, we list some of the most relevant ones.

Data Centre Automation

This is the traditional setup of large-scale enterprise customers who operate large SAP installations but still lack an overall and consistent picture of their operational management. Business grids will support this scenario by automating the whole range of operational tasks, especially the management of cross-installation issues (e.g., resource sharing between different applications of different users). Specific issues are to learn about conceptual limitations and drawbacks of various approaches.

Mass Hosting

Mass hosting is highly relevant for SAP's recent focus shift onto small and medium-sized enterprises (SMEs). The costs of operating an SAP system are currently prohibitive for such companies. Hosting is the main option that promises to reduce operation costs to an acceptable level.

Business grids should support the maximum level of automation for mass hosting scenarios, especially reducing the need for manual interaction for single customers. Specific issues are isolation between the hosted parties (security, confidentiality), SLA provisioning, and QoS monitoring.

Dynamic Outsourcing

Following the overall SAP strategy to allow customers highly flexible business operations, a specific aspect here is on outsourcing/insourcing. Customers with smaller businesses, who originally started with a hosted solution, might at some point in time decide to insource that solution, for example, to save costs or for security reasons. Other customers operating SAP solutions on their own might decide to outsource some solutions, which are of no strategic importance but just became a general-purpose service.

Business grids will support dynamic in and outsourcing by combining features of the data center and the mass hosting scenario. Additional specific issues are on-demand negotiation of requirements and licensing issues.

Virtual Organizations

A virtual organization comprises a set of (legally) independent organizations that share resources and skills to achieve a common goal.

Business grids will support flexible collaboration within a virtual organization in such a way that different infrastructures, operated by different organizations, can be linked together and share resources in a flexible but nonetheless reliable and secure way.

Service-Oriented Knowledge Utilities

Service-Oriented Knowledge Utilities [SOKU, see NGG (2006)] envisage an upcoming economy where hardware and software solutions are provided as a single service and individual services can be easily combined to achieve higher-level services. Business grids will support the infrastructure underlying a SOKU in a flexible and automated way (following the vision of a utility). The technical challenges are similar to the previously described scenarios with the distinction that the environment is much more dynamic and heterogeneous. Stakeholders may join or leave the SOKU, new services are introduced, and non-functional properties such as security, confidentiality, SLAs or QoS have to be managed in a multi-party context. Furthermore, a high demand for interoperability is observed.

STATE-OF-THE-ART

This section presents the state-of-the-art in grid and adaptive computing. This is followed by an analysis of the state of SAP technology and that of the technology used in other companies. This section then further continues to provide a brief assessment of the application of the previously discussed technologies in real systems. As the vision of business grids is largely based on both grid and adaptive computing, we will first describe the state-of-the-art in these domains.

Grid Computing

Architecturally, business grids are to be built on top of existing grid technologies. Therefore we provide a definition of the grid followed by an overview of the organizations shaping this area. Lastly information regarding grid services and specifically data grids are presented.

Definition

Traditionally grid computing is seen as a model for executing extremely large computational tasks using both unused and dedicated resources, for example, CPU and disk space, which exist in many distributed and heterogeneous computers. These resources are combined as a virtual cluster connected by the Internet. Grid computing differs from traditional computing clusters or distributed computing, since it supports computation across administrative and geographical domains.

In the scientific community, grids have been used in numerous fields, for example, the biological, medical, financial and geosciences domains, to solve large computational problems. This requirement is as a result of the computational demand outgrowing supercomputers' capabilities. The problems are broken down into smaller manageable tasks, which are then distributed across the network and executed in parallel. Commonly, problems in this domain are viewed from a computational perspective, that is, jobs are individually small and highly contained. This is based on a best effort approach rather than meeting the needs of a customer from quality of service (QoS) level.

Relevant Organizations

The grid is a global initiative and as such has numerous organizations and consortiums contributing to it. A brief overview of a selection that demonstrates the range of activities is now provided.

The U.K. e-science program (eScience, see http://www.rcuk.ac.uk/escience/) is a government-industry funded initiative involving the various research councils, Department of Trade & Industry and 8 distributed research centers (one of which is located in Belfast).

The Globus Alliance (see http://www.globus.org/) conducts research and development to define technology, standards, and systems that form the basis for grid computing applications. The Globus Toolkit is the most frequently used means to initially generate grid infrastructures in various application fields. It includes software services and APIs for distributed security, resource management, monitoring and discovery, and data management. Version GT4 includes a set of components for building systems that follow the Open Grid Services Architecture (OGSA, see http://www.globus.org/ogsa/) framework defined by the Global Grid Forum (GGF, see http://www.gridforum.org), of which the Globus Alliance is a leading member. Components and software development tools of GT4 are also often combined with the Web Services Resource Framework (WSRF, see http://www.globus.org/wsrf/), a set of standards in development in OASIS (see http://www.oasis-open.org/home/index.php). The Enterprise Grid Alliance (EGA, see http://www.gridalliance.org/en/index.asp) is a consortium of more than 25 member organizations. The EGA focuses on enterprise users and enabling businesses to realize some benefits of grid computing, such as faster response to changing business needs, better utilization of resources, service level performance, and lower IT operating costs. In essence, it represents the collective understanding from the EGA member organizations of the requirements for enterprise environments running business critical applications and their experience in addressing the associated problems. Recently EGA and GGF merged to form the Open Grid Forum (OGF).

Grid Services

Grid systems are built by logically combining several smaller grid services. Grid services inherit all aspects of Web services and provide the infrastructure for a grid. They have a specific set of capabilities that support grid architectures as defined in examples from the OGSA. This complex distributed system comprises transient grid service instances and defines standard mechanisms for their creation, naming, and discovery. These mechanisms also include conventions for lifecycle management, change management, and notification. Each grid service can inspect its own state and notify a monitoring application or management software either by automatic event notifications over time, or on demand from a specific request. Each service is uniquely identifiable and dynamically deployable, therefore affording (potentially real-time) portability and reliability where a service can be deployed across heterogeneous environments and in a fail-safe manner. Also, security requirements are supported at a low level of the service infrastructure, thereby providing a common mechanism between all communicating services that abstracts them from other security implementation considerations.

Data Grids

Data grids commonly refer to the federation of data sources in a grid computing environment. The complexity of this scenario stems from the need for a controlling client application to require access to large data sets from disparate locations, on different computing platforms, and in different formats, for example, object databases, relational databases, flat files, and so forth.

Adaptive Computing

Adaptive computing is another approach to provide modern businesses with more flexible IT infrastructures. Here, the goal is to transform the IT infrastructure into a more responsive and resilient entity in order to address business-driven needs. A computing infrastructure can

be considered adaptive if it allows the dynamic assignment of hardware resources to serve specific application services. This new paradigm can empower the customer to run any service, anytime, on any server.

Hardware and network partners of SAP have developed their own adaptive system infrastructure schemes, such as *Adaptive Enterprise* for HP and *On Demand* for IBM. These schemes virtualize customers' system landscapes to allocate hardware resources on demand. SAP provides the *Adaptive Computing Controller* to support SAP software running on the virtualized system landscapes.

Besides the adaptive hardware schemes from large companies, virtualization technologies at different levels provide new adaptive environments for business needs. System level virtualizations, such as VMWare and Xen, abstract the entire hardware of a computer system against the view of hosted operating systems. Virtualization of disk storage allows servers to access storage over networks instead of local connection mechanisms. These new virtualization technologies enable new opportunities for adaptive computing.

Virtualization is one of the main issues in developing business grid/adaptive computing solutions. This enables the flexible deployment of services and provides further flexibility during the reallocation of services. Even more importantly, virtualization introduces abstraction from the real hardware and operating system, which is beneficial for SAP solutions.

Several virtual machines can be placed within one physical resource. Each virtual machine then takes a portion of the computational resources of the underlying physical machine. The computational resources of each virtual machine can be specified as needed. VMWare and Xen provide typical software for running such virtual machines on physical machines. Intel VT-x and AMD Pacifica are the latest technologies to support virtualization software at hardware level.

Additionally, we can combine computational resources of multiple physical machines to form one virtual resource. Mosix, Linux Virtual Server, and J2EE Clustering are representative software alternatives in this field. Grid computing is also a virtualization approach to aggregating computational resources. The grid itself can be viewed as a virtual resource for all computational resources in it.

Virtualization also affects data storage. Today data are typically not attached locally but accessed over some networking mechanism. Storage area networks use block level storage device abstractions, usually attached over special purpose storage network fabrics (i.e., FiberChannel). Network attached storage (NAS) uses network file system level interfaces, typically over general-purpose network interfaces (i.e., NFS or CIFS). There is a general trend away from special-purpose network fabrics towards putting everything on top of Ethernet and unifying the transport protocol onto TCP/IP (i.e., iSCSI).

On top of these, modern operating systems offer features such as online resizing and migration, snapshots, transparent backups, and background replication.

Special cluster-aware file systems can extend the notion of a storage array across individual servers, usually with a restricted set of semantics.

PERFORMANCE ENGINEERING

This section summarizes some of the latest public research activities in the area of performance engineering. The software performance engineering (SPE) method has been a research topic for quite some time (Smith, 1990). The foundation for SPE has been widely adopted. A range of performance analysis tools is available, of which the Queuing Network Model (QNM) is frequently used to predict the demand and contention of resources [cf., Balsamo et al. (2002)]. Although the sophistication of quantitative models has reached a fairly high level, the validity of these models needs to be scrutinized in the context of modern IT systems.

More recent work has attempted to apply SPE methods to distributed and component-based systems [see Smith & Williams (2000), Bertolino & Mirandola (2004)]. A new UML profile (RT-UML) that introduces quantitative annotations to UML sequence and activity diagrams model-driven creation of quantitative models has attracted some research activity [cf., Bertolino et al. (2002)]. Component-based or service-based SPE (CB-SPE) is another trend that is attempting to meet the need for a methodology appropriate for SOA. The core idea behind this approach is the separation of the quantitative model for the component itself and the component's composition. Quantitative values are exposed at service interface level and can thus be used for quantitative evaluation at service composition level. The general CB-SPE procedure has been shown to work at least for simple scenarios. This layered approach has certain similarities with more naïve models considered at SAP such as those developed in a project code-named "MORE," which is investigating into modeling non-functional requirements. The latter model stresses the dependence of the performance quantities on the input values and the state of a service. Indeed, in a data intensive application such as the SAP's Business Process Platform (BPP), performance strongly depends on at least the amount of data that is to be processed. This issue appears to have not yet been addressed in the research literature where quantitative values are assumed to be, for the most part, constant. According to the literature, it is sufficient to quote a mean value, lower and upper boundaries (worst case/ best case considerations) rather than introducing complex dependencies in terms of functions. The newly emerging challenge is the complexity that results from these dependencies. Causal and statistical models might provide the

Table 1. Business grids vs. e-science grids

Application and System Properties		Business Grids	Traditional E-Science Grids
Data			
	Working Mode	Online Transaction Processing (OLTP)	Federation
	Movability of Data	some restrictions (e.g., HR or financial data)	no restrictions on data movement
	Structure	highly structured business data, such as sales order details	Simple numeric data
Jobs			
	State of jobs	Stateful	Stateless
	Deployment times	Typically minutes or hours	Usually sub-second
	Execution time	Often long jobs (e.g., hours), potentially never-ending in the context of application server "sessions"	short "jobs" (e.g., seconds, minutes) ???
	Movability of code	Licensing and confidentiality issues may limit movability	Highly mobile executable code, disruption issues (only)
	Encapsulation	Loosely-coupled services hosted on different nodes may need to collaborate, meaning inter-node discovery and communication at the application level	Self-contained on single node, meaning no inter-node communication required.
Main security concerns		Must be able to guarantee and secure data separation between different systems co-hosted in a shared environment.	Access control applied on a per-grid basis. Not necessary to restrict access to specific zones or systems within a single grid.
Size of the grid		Restricted size, typically intranet-based, on a company or hosting partner's LAN with few administrative domains	Typically intranet or more generally accessible world-wide Grid
Robustness		Fault tolerance is a prerequisite	Faults can be worked around by re-executing jobs again
Main benefits		Improve administrative flexibility and hardware utilization; "get it done efficiently" approach to reduce cost and improve QoS	Access to raw compute power; "get it done quicker" otherwise job cannot be executed at all
Quality		Must adhere to pre-defined QoS, SLAs demands	No pre-defined SLAs, just get job done as quickly as possible
Legacy software support		Is a prerequisite	Not important

means to cope with the large number of unknown parameters and correlations.

Performance and quality of service has always been of high relevance for real-time systems. The need for quantitative modeling tools in this area has driven the introduction of a UML profile for scheduling, performance and time, OMG-RT-UML. Primarily meant for real-time systems, this UML profile turns out to be useful for business applications as well. One shortcoming is the dominance of time and the lack of other performance quantities. Still, the RT-UML profile is extensible and might be amended with other measures.

ASSESSMENT

Within this section, possible solution approaches will be compared. To this end, we will discuss the differences between business grids and e-science grids, between the current state of SAP and the state-of-the-art, and we compare the state of SAP with our vision. Finally, we will present the gap between the state-of-the-art and our vision.

Table 1 summarizes the main difference between the requirements and characteristics of business grids as compared to more traditional and e-science oriented grids. It represents the generalized case; there will be exceptions to the general rule in some situations.

The planned developments in the grid computing community that will potentially lead to a global or World Wide Grid are still very much at the conceptual stage. In addition, current products such as the Globus Toolkit or job management systems such as Condor or Sun Grid Engine are either dedicated to specific tasks, for example, batch job management, or only provide partial solutions of the needs of business grid customers. Current grid solutions aim for a fine granularity and large multiplicity with thousands of jobs; on the other hand, current adaptive computing in enterprise environments target a coarse level of granularity and small multiplicity with less than

hundreds of servers. One aim of business grids is to bridge the gap in granularity and multiplicity between grid computing and adaptive computing. The overall vision of business grids will develop very much in tandem with developments, such as automated SLA and QoS provisioning and cross-organizational security, but will extend this to enable adaptive enterprise applications where these applications are much larger than current typical grid applications and a permanent operation is a necessity. Based on the above gap analysis, research on business grids will be focused on the following five research areas.

1. Investigating how to use virtualization technologies efficiently in grid computing and adaptive computing environments.
2. Working on performance engineering for business grids.
3. Working on software engineering for business grids.
4. Investigating database performance in business grids.
5. Investigating automation for operating business grids.

REFERENCES

Balsamo, S., Di Marco, A., Inverardi, P., & Simeoni, M. (2002). *Software performance: State of the art and perspectives.* (Tech. Rep. MIUR SAHARA Project; TR SAH/04). University of Venice.

Bertolino, A., Marchetti, E., & Mirandola, R. (2002). Real-time UML-based performance engineering to aid manager's decisions in multi-project planning. In *Proceedings of the 3rd International Workshop on Software and Performance*, Rome, Italy (pp. 251-261). New York: ACM Press.

Bertolino, A., & Mirandola, R. (2004). CB-SPE Tool: Putting component-based performance engineering into practice. In, *Proceedings of the 7th*

International Symposium on Component-Based Software Engineering (CBSE 2004), Edinburgh, UK, (LNCS 3054, pp. 233-248). Springer.

Franke, C., Theilmann, W., Zhang, Y., & Sterritt, R. (2007). Towards the autonomic business grid. *In Proceedings of the Fourth IEEE International Workshop on Engineering of Autonomic and Autonomous Systems (EASe'07)* (pp. 107-112).

NGG. (2006, January). *The future for European Grids: GRIDs and service oriented knowledge utilities* (Next Generation GRIDs Expert Group Report 3). Retrieved from ftp://ftp.cordis.lu/pub/ist/docs/grids/ngg3_eg_final.pdf.

Smith, C.U. (1990). *Performance engineering of software systems*. Reading, MA: Addison-Wesley.

Smith, C.U., & Williams, L.G. (2000). Performance and scalability of distributed software architectures: An SPE approach, *Parallel and Distributed Computing Practices*, *3*(4).

About the Contributors

Max Mühlhäuser is head of the Telecooperation Division at Technische Universität Darmstadt, Computer Science Department. He has about 25 years of experience in research and teaching in areas related to ubiquitous computing (UC) at the Universities of Kaiserslautern, Karlsruhe, Linz, Darmstadt, Montréal, Sophia Antipolis, and San Diego (UCSD). In 1993, he founded the TeCO Institute (www.teco.edu) in Karlsruhe, Germany that became one of the pacemakers for UC research in Europe. SAP Research is one of his major industrial partners. Max regularly publishes in UC conferences and journals and is an author of chapters about ubiquitous computing in computer science textbooks, readers, and so forth, with a total of more than 200 publications. He is a reviewer for UC conferences, member of editorial boards in journals, and guest editor in journals like *Pervasive Computing*, *ACM Multimedia*, *Pervasive and Mobile Computing*, and so forth.

Iryna Gurevych is head of the Ubiquitous Knowledge Processing Group at the Technische Universität Darmstadt. She has a PhD in natural language processing (NLP) and worked in the Mobile Assistance Systems and Natural Language Processing Groups in basic and applied research at European Media Lab in Heidelberg, Germany. Her expertise is in unstructured information management, knowledge-based methods, and human-computer interaction. Gurevych is principal investigator in several research projects funded by the German Research Foundation in the areas of semantic computing, ontology applications and language based human-computer interaction. She publishes and is a reviewer for international conferences about NLP, dialogue systems and computational semantics.

* * *

Erwin Aitenbichler received an MSc in computer science from Johannes Kepler University in Linz, Austria and a PhD in computer science from Darmstadt University of Technology, Germany. Currently he is a post-doctoral researcher in the Telecooperation Group in the Department of Computer Science at the Technische Universität Darmstadt. His research interests are smart environments and ubiquitous computing. Aitenbichler is a member of the ACM.

Michael Altenhofen studied computer science at the University of Karlsruhe, where he graduated in 1990 with his diploma thesis on tutoring support in NESTOR, a joint research project between the University of Karlsruhe and the CEC Karlsruhe, the European Applied Research Center of Digital Equipment Corporation. After joining Digital at the CEC Karlsruhe, he became technical project leader in various German and European funded research projects working on multi-media collaboration and electronic commerce systems. Within the national L3 Lighthouse Project, he designed and developed various runtime components and coordinated their transfer into SAP product offering, the SAP Learning Solution. In his current role as a development architect within SAP Research, he is working on topics in the areas of software engineering, service-oriented architectures, modelling, and semantics.

Jürgen Anke is research associate and joined SAP Research in early 2005. In the PROMISE Project, he is mainly responsible for the middleware. He studied information systems at Dresden University of Technology and the University of Auckland, New Zealand, and holds a master's degree in that subject. Currently, he is working on his PhD thesis on deployment planning of components in smart item environments.

Emile Aarts holds an MSc and a PhD in physics. For more than 20 years he has been active as a research scientist in computing science. Since 1991 he has held a teaching position at the Eindhoven University of Technology as a part-time professor of computing science. He also serves on numerous scientific and governmental advisory boards. He holds a part-time position of senior consultant with the Center for Quantitative Methods in Eindhoven, The Netherlands. Aarts is the author of 10 books and more than 150 scientific papers on a diversity of subjects including nuclear physics, VLSI design, combinatorial optimization and neural networks. In 1998 he launched the concept of ambient intelligence, and in 2001 he founded Philips' HomeLab. His current research interests include intelligent systems and interaction technology.

Gerhard Austaller received a master's degree in computer science from the Johannes Kepler University Linz in 1999. For another two years he worked there as research assistant and was involved in an industrial project with Siemens, Austria. The focus of his research was distributed object-oriented systems. In 2001 he joined the Telecooperation Group at the Technische Universität Darmstadt led by Dr. Max Mühlhäuser. The focus of his current research is service-oriented architectures in the context of ubiquitous computing. His research interests are the application of SOA to UC. This includes service descriptions for services in UC and feasible application development models.

Alistair Barros is research leader at SAP Research with interests in business process management, software architectures and services sciences. He has a PhD in computer science from the University of Queensland and 21 years experience working at CITEC and the Distributed Systems Technology Centre, before joining SAP in 2004. Barros has around 40 publications in referred journals and international conferences, and his research has contributed to international standards, references (notably patterns in the BPM field), product transfers, patents and consultancies including Boeing, Queensland Government and Australian Defence. At SAP Research, he leads the Internet of Services research field.

Christof Bornhövd is a senior research scientist at the SAP Research Center in Palo Alto focusing on data management, semantics and event-based computing for SAP's next-generation enterprise business applications architecture. Prior to joining SAP Labs, he worked from 2002 to 2004 as a research staff member at the IBM Almaden Research Center on database caching and replication for e-business applications and the integration of DB2 and WebSphere. From 2000 to 2002 he worked at HP Labs on CRM and data warehousing projects. During his time at the Technische Universität Darmstadt, where he received a PhD in computer science in 2000, he was working on semantic data integration and metadata management. His expertise and research interests are in the areas of databases and distributed systems, Web services technology, and RFID and sensor network technology. Dr. Bornhövd has published in highly recognized conferences and journals like *VLDB*, *SIGMOD*, *ICDE*, and *JEIM*, and has filed multiple patent applications in the areas of RFID and sensor technology and database caching.

Luca Compagna is a member of SAP Research Lab in Sophia Antipolis where he is contributing to the security and trust research area and leading the EU research project SERENITY. Compagna received a master's degree in informatic engineering from the University of Genova and a PhD in electronics and computer science engineering from the Universities of Genova and of Edinburgh (joint program). The areas of his professional interests include security engineering (e.g., security patterns), automated reasoning (e.g., model-checking), and their application to the modeling and analysis of Internet security protocols and industrial relevant scenarios. He contributed to various projects on information security, including AVISPA (shortlisted for the EU Descartes Prize for Research in 2006), and he has published various scientific publications in his area of interest.

Jan Gerke studied computer science at the University Karlsruhe (TH), Germany, received his Diplom-Informatiker degree (MS, computer science) in March 2000, and received his doctoral degree at ETH Zürich in June 2006. During his studies he worked as a scientific assistant for the Research Center for Information Technologies, Karlsruhe, and as a software engineer for Albatros Datenservice GmbH, Karlsruhe. From 2000 to 2006, Gerke was employed as a research assistant for the Computer Engineering and Networks Laboratory (TIK) at ETH Zurich, participating in the European Union project "Market Managed Multiservice Internet" (M3I) and "Market Managed Peer-to-Peer Services" (MMAPPS). His research focus is on Internet services, their charging and accounting, quality-of-service mechanisms, and service composition and provision in peer-to-peer environments. Since July 2006 he has been continuing his research as a postdoc in the Communication Systems Group (CSG) of the Department of Informatics (IFI) at University of Zurich.

Wolfgang Gerteis is the director of the SAP Research CEC Belfast (Campus-based Engineering Centre), which he built up starting from 2005. His main research interests are business grids bringing together technologies from adaptive computing and grid computing with enterprise business applications. He is a member of the Next Generation Grid Expert Group consulting the European Union regarding future research in grid computing. In his role as chief European officer his is also responsible for the operative setup of new research locations in Europe, which he did for Belfast, Dresden, Karlsruhe and St. Gallen. Before moving to Belfast, Gerteis was deputy director at the SAP Research CEC Karlsruhe, which is the first research center to be founded of SAP Research. Till 2003 he led the e-Learning Research Program where he made major contributions to the development of the SAP Learning Solution. Prior to joining SAP, Gerteis was project manager at the European Research Organization of Digital Equipment Corporation. He received his doctoral degree in informatics as well as his diploma in informatics from the Technical University of Karlsruhe, Germany.

Iryna Gurevych is head of the Ubiquitous Knowledge Processing Group at the Technische Universität Darmstadt. She has a PhD in natural language processing (NLP) and worked in the Mobile Assistance Systems and Natural Language Processing Groups in basic and applied research at European Media Lab in Heidelberg, Germany. Her expertise is in unstructured information management, knowledge-based methods, and human-computer interaction. Gurevych is principal investigator in several research projects funded by the German Research Foundation in the areas of semantic computing, ontology applications and language-based human-computer interaction. She publishes and is a reviewer for international conferences about NLP, dialogue systems and computational semantics.

Rama Gurram is currently working as a research scientist at SAP Labs, Palo Alto, USA. In his current role at SAP, he is involved in the research of advanced Web technologies for enterprise applications. Prior to joining SAP, Gurram worked as a software architect at Hewlett-Packard, USA. His current interests include Web 2.0, SOA, REST, messaging, mobility, HCI and open source frameworks. Gurram received a master's degree in computer science from Birla Institute of Technology & Science (BITS - Pilani), India.

Gregor Hackenbroich is a senior researcher at SAP Research. He is responsible for several research projects with German or EU funding. He manages the PROMISE project that explores the strategic advantages of smart items in product lifecycle management. Hackenbroich received his habilitation in theoretical physics from Essen University, and his doctoral degree and diploma in physics from the University of Munich.

Do Hong Hai finished his PhD thesis in 2006 on "Schema Matching and Mapping-based Data Integration" in computer science at the University of Leipzig, Germany. Since 2005, he has worked as a senior researcher for SAP AG at the SAP Research CEC Dresden and is currently involved in project activities of smart items and data management and analytics.

Louenas Hamdi received an engineer diploma in computer science from Université de Tizi-Ouzou, Algeria and a master's degree in software engineering from ETS (École de Technologie Supérieure), Montreal, Canada. He joined the SAP Research team in Montreal in January 2004. He is leading a project in Web 2.0 for Mobility and has been involved in different projects related to real world awareness, mobility and the advanced Web technologies. His research interests are: mobile applications/architectures, occasionally dis-/connected architectures, Mobile Web 2.0, mobile search and real world awareness.

Andreas Hartl has been working on adaptive user interfaces since 1999. Born in 1977, he studied computer science at the Johannes Kepler University in Linz, Austria where he worked on user interfaces for cell phone applications as a junior researcher. After finishing his Master of Engineering in 2002, he joined the Telecooperation Group of the Technische Universität Darmstadt in Germany with the goal to couple usability with ubiquitous computing via adaptive user interfaces. At the time of writing, he is about to finish a PhD thesis on the subject and to move back to Austria.

Melanie Hartmann received her diploma degree in 2006 from the Technische Universität Darmstadt. Then she joined the Telecooperation Group at the Technische Universität Darmstadt led by Dr. Max Mühlhäuser. She is working there for the project "AUGUR" and is investigating how context can be used for building proactive user interfaces. Her research interests are context-aware computing, intelligent user interfaces and ubiquitous computing

David Hausheer received his diploma degree in electrical engineering and his doctoral degree in communication systems from ETH Zurich in 2001 and 2006, respectively. During his PhD studies, he was involved in the European Union projects M3I and MMAPPS. Since 2005 Dr. Hausheer is employed as a postdoctoral researcher in the Department of Informatics (IFI) at the University of Zurich, focusing on accounting and charging for grid and P2P services as well as decentralized auctions for bandwidth trading. He is currently involved in several EU projects, such as EMANICS, Akogrimo, and EC-GIN. Furthermore, he served as PC co-chair for the 2006 IEEE International Workshop on Bandwidth on Demand, Tutorial Co-chair for ACM Autonomous Infrastructure, Management and Security (AIMS 2007), and TPC member for AIMS 2007 and ICC 2007. He has written more than 10 peer-reviewed publications and acted as a reviewer for more than 20 conferences and workshops.

Andreas Heinemann received his diploma degree in 1999 from the University of Tübingen, Germany. From 2000 to 2001 he worked as a software developer for a financial institute. From 2002 to 2005, he was a PhD student in the PhD program "Enabling Technologies for Electronic Commerce." The program studies the technical, legal and social aspects of electronic commerce. Since 2005 he has worked as a research assistant at the Telecooperation Group, led by Dr. Max Mühlhäuser at the Technische Universität Darmstadt. His research interests are opportunistic networks, mobile peer-to-peer networks and security for ubiquitous computing.

Marc Hermann received his diploma degree in 2001 from the Ulm University. He then joined the e-learning project "Docs 'n Drugs – The Virtual Polyclinic" at the Ulm University Institute of Media Informatics led by Dr. Michael Weber. He is currently working there as research associate. His research interests are alternative user interfaces, especially tangible interfaces and ambient displays for use in ubiquitous computing.

Frankie James is a senior researcher in human-computer interaction at SAP Research. Dr. James received a PhD in computer science from Stanford University in June 1998 for research on audio HTML interfaces for blind users. While at Stanford, she also worked with the Archimedes Project at the Center for the Study of Language and Information (CSLI). Dr. James joined SAP Research in March 2001 from RIACS (Research Institute for Advanced Computer Science), a NASA contractor, where she studied voice interfaces. She is a member of ACM's Special Interest Groups on Computer-Human Interaction (SIGCHI) and Accessible Computing (SIGACCESS).

Matthias Joest is a senior scientist active in the areas of location-based services, spatial-information theory, human-computing interaction, personalization and context-aware applications. Since 1998 he has been contributing at the European Media Laboratory to a number of third-party funded research projects such as SmartKom and ATTRACT, or projects funded by the Klaus Tschira Foundation, for example Deep Map I & II. He has published various book chapters, journal and conference papers in the above-mentioned areas. Furthermore he is assistant lecturer for geographic information systems and location-based services at the University of Heidelberg. Since 2005 he has been managing the transition of some of EML's research results into a product, namely a wireless pedestrian information portal. This product is currently deployed in Heidelberg and Beijing.

Jussi Kangasharju received an MSc from Helsinki University of Technology in 1998 and a DEA from the University of Nice Sophia Antipolis, also in 1998. He received a PhD from the University of Nice Sophia Antipolis/Institut Eurecom in 2002. Currently he is an assistant professor in the Department of Computer Science at the Technische Universität Darmstadt, heading the research group "Ubiquitous Peer-to-Peer Infrastructures." His research interests are peer-to-peer technologies, Internet content distribution, and ubiquitous computing. He has published over 40 articles in major international journals and conferences. Kangasharju is a member of IEEE and ACM.

Anja Klein is a research associate at SAP Research. She is currently working on the PROMISE project, where her focus lies on management and visualization of product lifecycle data in smart item environments. Furthermore, she participates in the SAP PhD program. Her thesis discusses data quality and non-functional requirements for streaming data and data analytics.

Tobias Limberger studied computer science at the Technische Universität Darmstadt where he also received a doctor's degree from the Department of Computer Science and the Department of Psychology. In his first course of studies, he concentrated on artificial intelligence and neural networks, choosing neurobiology as a minor field of study. His special interest in data bionics influenced his PhD in which he worked on bio-analog data management software and cooperated with the Center of Biotechnical Engineering Darmstadt.

Volkmar Lotz is the research program manager for security and trust at SAP Research. His responsibilities include the definition and implementation of SAP's security research agenda, its strategic alignment to SAP's business needs, and the maintenance of a global research partner network. Before joining SAP, he was heading the Formal Methods in Security Analysis Group at Siemens Corporate Technology, emphasizing on security requirements engineering, evaluation and certification, cryptographic protocol verification, and mobile code security. He has been the main contributor to the LKW model, a formal security model for smartcard processors. His experience includes context-aware mobile systems, legally binding agent transactions, and authorization and delegation in mobile code systems.

Fernando Lyardet obtained an MSc in informatics from the Universidad Nacional de La Plata (UNLP), Argentina, where he then worked as a software developer and subsequently as a research assistant, until August 2002. After that, he joined the Telecooperation group as a PhD candidate at the Technische Universität Darmstadt, Germany. His research interests include smart environments and ubiquitous computing.

Rainer Malaka is a professor of computer science at the University of Bremen and heads the Digital Media Research Group. He has been responsible for a number of research projects related to human-computer interaction, mobile systems and adaptive systems. These projects were done in close collaboration with various national and international institutes and companies. He started working at the University of Bremen in April 2006. Before that, he worked at the European Media Laboratory (EML) where he initiated and led a research group, which worked on projects dealing with mobile assistance systems, language understanding, geographical information systems, and computer vision. Before joining the EML, he did a diploma at the University of Karlsruhe and worked there as a research scientist on neural networks and modeling the learning mechanisms in biological brains.

Cristian Morariu received an MSc from the Technical University of Cluj-Napoca, Romania (June 2004). His major at the Faculty of Automation and Computer Science was performed in computer science. While holding an ERASMUS scholarship he developed his master's thesis at ETH Zürich, Laboratory of Software Technology. Since September 2004 he has been a junior researcher at the University of Zurich, Department of Informatics, Communication Systems Group. His work experience includes—besides being an instructor on laboratory demonstrators and the Cisco Certified Networking Associate (CCNA) Program—managing Unix systems and networks. His areas of research include the theory of operation, design principles, and troubleshooting of protocols, such as TCP/IP, IP routing (BGP, OSPF, RIP), multicast, and data link layer protocols. In detail he knows about ethernet, fast ethernet, PPP, and frame relay. Additionally, he has much practical experience with network management systems, network security, AAA Architectures, and QoS mechanisms.

Jens Müller studied computer science at the University of Tübingen. He is a research associate at SAP Research in Karlsruhe and a PhD student at the Wilhelm-Schickard-Institute for Computer Science, University of Tübingen. He is a member of the ACM.

Mario Neugebauer is a senior researcher at SAP Research. He works in the EU-funded project PROM-ISE and explores the potential of embedded systems for enterprise software. Previously, he worked at the chair for technical information systems at the TU Dresden. Neugebauer received his doctoral degree in computer science in the area of wireless sensor networks from the TU Dresden.

Zoltán Nochta studied computer science at the Budapest University of Technology and Economy in Hungary and at the University of Karlsruhe, Germany. He worked for four years as research assistant at the Institute for Telematics at the University of Karlsruhe and conducted research in the area of secure networking and applied cryptography. He was involved in several industrial projects with Deutsche Telekom. In 2004, he joined the Smart Items research team of SAP Research. Since then he has been contributing to several research projects in this area. He is focusing on the conceptual design of ubiquitous system architectures as well as on their service-oriented integration into enterprise business software systems.

Daniel Oberle received a PhD from the University of Karlsruhe, Germany, Institute AIFB, Professor Studer's Group, in 2005. His thesis discussed the application of Semantic Web technologies (ontologies, reasoning) in current middleware solutions, such as application servers and Web services, to facilitate the daily tasks of developers and administrators. The corresponding book is entitled *Semantic Management of Middleware* (Springer Verlag). Oberle (co-)authored about 40 refereed publications in selected books, conferences, and journals. He has been working at SAP Research since March 2006.

Peter Racz received an MSc in computer science from the Budapest University of Technology and Economics (BME) in 2000. After his studies he joined the Department of Mobile Networks at Siemens AG, Germany, and worked for three years as a researcher, focusing on next generation mobile networks and QoS provisioning in 3G networks. In 2003 he joined the University of Federal Armed Forces Munich (UniBwM) as a research assistant and started his doctoral studies. Since 2005 he has been a research assistant at the Department of Informatics (IFI) at the University of Zurich and is pursuing his doctoral degree. His main research area includes accounting and charging for IP-based services in mobile, multi-domain networks, AAA architectures, and mobility and QoS support in IP networks. He is involved in several research projects such as the European IST projects Akogrimo and EC-GIN and the industry funded DAMMO and DAMMO II projects.

Samir Raiyani is CEO of Dolcera (http://www.dolcera.com). Raiyani has more than a decade of experience in technology innovation. Prior to Dolcera, Raiyani was director at SAP Research in Palo Alto, California. At SAP, Raiyani helped launch several new initiatives in the areas of metro wireless networks, RFID, sensor networking and multimodality. He designed innovative mobile and voice-enabled supply chain applications that are now part of SAP's portfolio. Raiyani co-founded MediSpark (iScribe), a mobile healthcare startup. He designed the iScribe platform. He has a master's degree in computer science from Stanford University and an undergraduate degree from Gujarat University, India.

Sebastian Ries received his diploma degree in 2006 at the Technische Universität Darmstadt. Since October 2005, he has been a PhD student in the PhD program "Enabling Technologies for Electronic Commerce." The program studies the technical, legal and social aspects of electronic commerce. He is closely associated with the Telecooperation Group at the Technische Universität Darmstadt, led by Dr. Max Mühlhäuser. His research interests are computational and representational models of trust, ubiquitous computing and its relation to security relevant issues.

Joachim Schaper received his Diploma (1988) and PhD (1995) from the Technical University of Karlsruhe. Since 1989, he worked for Digital Equipment Corp. in their European Research Center, CEC Karlsruhe. He became the manager of that center, which in turn became part of SAP AG Corporate Research in 1999. In 2001, Schaper took over additional responsibilities as a founding manager of the Corporate Research Groups at SAP Labs France and SAP Africa. From 2003 to 2005, he managed the SAP Research Center in Palo Alto and a research group in Montreal. A vice president of EMEA, Schaper is responsible for all research activities of SAP in Europe, Middle East, and Africa, reporting to the head of corporate research and to the executive board. His research interests comply with the topics investigated in the SAP research groups on e-learning, smart items, mobile computing, and technology for application integration and advanced customer interfaces.

Jochen H. Schiller is head of the working group Computer Systems & Telematics at the Institute of Computer Science, Freie Universitaet Berlin, Germany. Dr. Schiller studied computer science at the University of Karlsruhe (PhD, 1996, summa cum laude). After being a postdoc in Uppsala University, Sweden, and a guest professor at ETS Montreal, Canada, and Kiel University, Germany, Dr. Schiller got his habilitation and published the book *Mobile Communications* that is currently used by over 200 universities as a textbook in five languages. Since April 2001 he has been full professor at the Freie Universität Berlin. From 2003-2007 he was dean of the Department for Mathematics and Computer Science. His research focus is on wireless, mobile, and embedded devices, communication protocols, operating systems for devices with small footprint, and security aspects in communication systems. Up to now, Dr. Schiller has published five books and more than 120 international papers.

Dirk Schnelle received his diploma degree in 1995 from the University of Erlangen-Nürnberg, Germany. From 1996 to 1999 he worked as a software developer in the field of voice application development. From 1999 to 2003 he worked as a developer in the telecommunications industry. From 2003 to 2006, he was a PhD student in the Telecooperation Group at the Technische Universität Darmstadt, led by Dr. Max Mühlhäuser. His research interests are voice user interface design in the ubiquitous computing area. Since 2007 he has worked as a solution architect with a focus on workflow processes.

Patrik Spieß is a research associate at SAP Research's CEC Karlsruhe. Prior to joining SAP Research in 2004, he obtained a Diplom (master's equivalent) from the University of Karlsruhe. He works in the SOCRADES project, which transfers best practices of enterprise software design (like SOA) to automation systems engineering. Collaborating with the Institute of Operating Systems and Computer Networks of the University of Braunschweig, he is pursuing a PhD on the topic of efficient integration of ubiquitous systems with business processes. His research interests include ubiquitous systems, user-friendly software, end-user development, open source research, and social networking research.

Burkhard Stiller received his diploma degree in computer science and his doctoral degree from the University of Karlsruhe in 1990 and 1994, respectively. After being a research assistant at the University of Karlsruhe, and on leave for an EC research fellowship at the University of Cambridge, Computer Laboratory, UK, he joined the Computer Engineering and Networks Laboratory, TIK of ETH Zürich. After his assistant professorship for communication systems at ETH he held a full professorship at the University of Federal Armed Forces Munich (UniBwM). Since September 2004 he has held the communication systems full professorship at the University of Zürich, Department of Informatics, IFI. He participated in or managed several national research projects within Germany, Switzerland, and the UK as well as European IST projects, such as Akogrimo, Daidalos, EMANICS, MMAPPS, MobyDick, CATI, M3I, DAMMO, DaCaPo++, and BioLANCC. His main research interests include charging and accounting for IP-based networks, economics of IP services, grid services, auctions for services, communication protocols in the Internet, biometric access control, quality-of-service aspects, peer-to-peer systems, and network management.

Tobias Straub has been a researcher at the Fraunhofer Institute for Secure Information Technology in Darmstadt since 2005. Currently, he is in charge of the Fraunhofer Competence Center PKI. Tobias Straub received his PhD in computer science from the Technische Universität Darmstadt and a master's degree in mathematics from the University of Tübingen. Since 2001, he has worked as a part-time lecturer at the Information Technology Department of the University of Cooperative Education in Lörrach. His research interests include PKI and its applications as well as usability aspects of cryptography.

Martin Waldburger holds a Master of Science in informatics (MSc), which he received in 2004 from the University of Zurich. In the same year, he joined the Communication Systems Group (CSG) at the University of Zurich in the position of an assistant and doctoral student. He participates in the EU project "Access to Knowledge through the Grid in a Mobile World" (Akogrimo) and the European Union Network of Excellence "Management of Internet Technologies and Complex Services" (EMANICS). His research work is mainly concerned with legal aspects of electronic service provisioning in multi-domain environments, adding business modeling, service level agreements, and various applications of these methods in the aquaculture supported by mobile grid services.

Michael Weber holds a PhD in computer science from the University of Kaiserslautern. After a number of years in industry, working on parallel and multimedia systems, he joined the University of Ulm as a professor for computer science in 1994 and was appointed director of the Institute of Media Informatics in 2000. He has authored and co-authored more than 100 peer reviewed contributions, edited three books and written a textbook. He has led projects funded by the state of Baden-Württemberg, by the German Ministry for Education and Research (BMBF), by the European Commission and by industrial partners. His current research interests include mobile and ubiquitous computing systems and human-computer interaction.

Matthias Winkler received a bachelor's degree in media and computer science from Dresden University of Technology, Germany, and a master's degree in interactive systems engineering from the Royal Institute of Technology (KTH) in Stockholm, Sweden. He joined the SAP Research group in Dresden in 2006. There he is leading the "EMODE" project, which investigates the modelling of multimodal, adaptive applications. His research interests are multimodal user interfaces and UI adaptation, and model-driven development.

Bernhard Wolf is a research associate in SAP Research's PhD program and joined the PROMISE project at the beginning of 2006. His current area of research is the integration of field device information with enterprise software systems. He holds a master's degree in electrical engineering with specialization in automation from the Dresden University of Technology.

Konrad Wrona is currently a principal investigator at SAP Research Lab in Sophia Antipolis, France. He has over 10 years of work experience in an industrial (SAP Research and Ericsson Research) and in an academic (RWTH Aachen University, Media Lab Europe, and Rutgers University) research and development environment. He earned his MEng in telecommunications from Warsaw University of Technology, Poland and a PhD in electrical engineering from RWTH Aachen University, Germany. He is an author and a co-author of over twenty publications, as well as a co-inventor of several patents. The areas of his professional interests include security in communication networks, wireless and mobile applications, distributed systems, applications of sensor networks, and electronic commerce. He was a technical coordinator of the EU FP6 Specific Targeted Research Project: Mobile Workers' Secure Business Applications in Ubiquitous Environments (MOSQUITO).

Index

Symbols

2-D mouse 458
3-D mouse 458

A

absolute positioning 430
abstract user interfaces 509, 520
abstract user interfaces, examples of 522
abstract user interfaces, requirements of 521
account, definition 305
accountability 364, 378
accountability, definition 305
accounting 303
accounting, definition 305
accounting, events 322
accounting, protocols 313
accounting records, definition 305
accumulative systems 380
activity based costing (ABC) 318
ad-hoc network 43
adaptability 230
adaptation, and computing environments 283
adaptation, interaction 284
adaptation, of content 285
adaptation, personalized 286
adaptation, presentation 285
adaptive, computing 597
adaptive, security 575
adaptivity 237
addressing 180, 181
ad hoc, interaction 340
ad hoc, wireless federation 501
advanced hands and eyes interaction 446
affordance 449
Ajax 573
ambient, display 464
ambient, intelligence 2
ambient, learning 531
analytic approach 39, 54
angulation 263
ant colony optimization 40

application service provider 306
artificial intelligence (AI) 3, 4, 6, 7, 8, 545
artificial neural networks (ANN) 417
asset tracking 259
asymmetric, cryptosystems 346
asymmetric, digital subscriber line (ASDL) cable 325
asymmetric, intelligence 543
asynchronous transfer mode (ATM) services 324
attention-awareness 462
attention detection 461
attribute-value-pairs (AVP) 314
audio, output 429
audio, streaming 404
audio, streaming, speech recognizer 404
audio, user interfaces (AUIs) 425
auditing, definition 305
auditory, displays 456
auditory, icons 429
augmented reality 460
automated teller machines (ATMs) 495
automatic, speech recognition (ASR) request 406
automatic vehicle location, (AVL) technology 568, 569
autonomous system (AS) number 309
average systems 380
AVL application architecture 570
AVL mashup application 570

B

back-end enterprise systems 552
background sounds 429
beginning-of-life (BOL) 562
behaviorism 534
billing, definition 305
bio-analogy 50, 54
bionics 38, 39, 54, 55, 38
BitTorrent 174, 175, 176, 177, 186, 187, 189
blocker tags 358
Bluetooth 135, 137, 139, 145, 146, 147, 148, 150